H A M M O N D

Explorer
World
Atlas

Contents

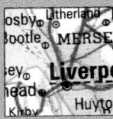
LIBRARY OF CONGRESS
CATALOGING-IN-PUBLICATION
DATA

Hammond World Atlas Corporation.
    Hammond explorer world atlas.
        p. cm.
    Rev. ed. of: Explorer Atlas of the World/Hammond Incorporated.
    Copyright 2000 by Hammond World Atlas Corporation.
    Includes index.
    ISBN 0-8437-1357-7
    1. Atlases.
I Hammond Incorporated. Explorer atlas of the world. II. Title. III. Title: Explorer world atlas.
    G1021. H2457 1999 <G&M>
    912–DC21   99-28550
                        CIP
                        MAPS

Map Projections

Simply stated, the map-maker's challenge is to project the earth's curved surface onto a flat plane. To achieve this elusive goal, cartographers have developed map projections — equations which govern this conversion of geographic data.

This section explores some of the most widely used projections. It also introduces a new projection, the Hammond Optimal Conformal.

GENERAL PRINCIPLES AND TERMS

The earth rotates around its axis once a day. Its end points are the North and South poles; the line circling the earth midway between the poles is the equator. The arc from the equator to either pole is divided into 90 degrees of latitude. The equator represents 0° latitude. Circles of equal latitude, called parallels, are traditionally shown at every fifth or tenth degree.

The equator is divided into 360 degrees. Lines circling the globe from pole to pole through the degree points on the equator are called meridians, or great circles. All meridians are equal in length, but by international agreement the meridian passing through the Greenwich Observatory near London has been chosen as the prime meridian or 0° longitude. The distance in degrees from the prime meridian to any point east or west is its longitude.

While meridians are all equal in length, parallels become shorter as they approach the poles. Whereas one degree of latitude represents approximately 69 miles (112 km.) anywhere on the globe, a degree of longitude varies from 69 miles (112 km.) at the equator to zero at the poles. Each degree of latitude and longitude is divided into 60 minutes. One minute of latitude equals one nautical mile (1.15 land miles or 1.85 km.).

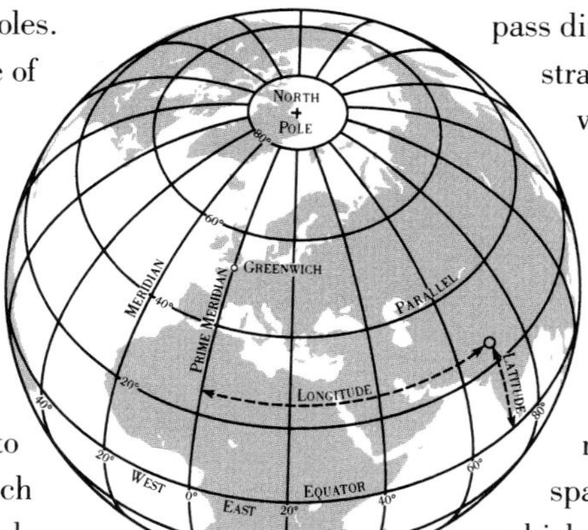

HOW TO FLATTEN A SPHERE: THE ART OF CONTROLLING DISTORTION

There is only one way to represent a sphere with absolute precision: on a globe. All attempts to project our planet's surface onto a plane unevenly stretch or tear the sphere as it flattens, inevitably distorting shapes, distances, area (sizes appear larger or smaller than actual size), angles or direction.

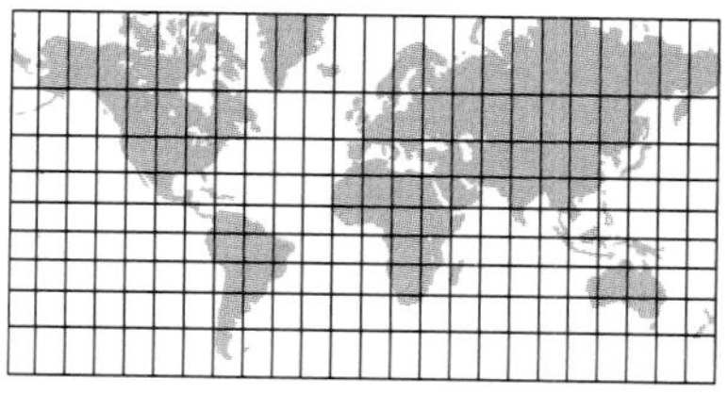

Since representing a sphere on a flat plane always creates distortion, only the parallels or the meridians (or some other set of lines) can maintain the same length as on a globe of corresponding scale. All other lines must be either too long or too short. Accordingly, the scale on a flat map cannot be true everywhere; there will always be different scales in different parts of a map. On world maps or very large areas, variations in scale may be extreme. Most maps seek to preserve either true area relationships (equal area projections) or true angles and shapes (conformal projections); some attempt to achieve overall balance.

PROJECTIONS: SELECTED EXAMPLES

Mercator (Fig. 1): This projection is especially useful because all compass directions appear as straight lines, making it a valuable navigational tool. Moreover, every small region conforms to its shape on a globe — hence the name conformal. But because its meridians are evenly-spaced vertical lines which never converge (unlike the globe), the horizontal parallels must be drawn farther and farther apart at higher latitudes to maintain a correct relationship.

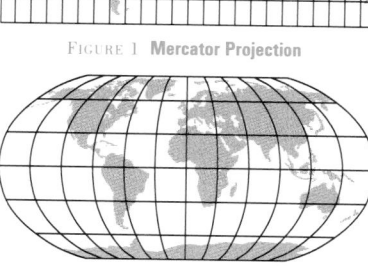

FIGURE 1 Mercator Projection

FIGURE 2 Robinson Projection

Only the equator is true to scale, and the size of areas in the higher latitudes is dramatically distorted.

Robinson (Fig. 2): To create the thematic maps in Global Relationships and the two-page world map in the Maps of the World section, the Robinson projection was used. It combines elements of both conformal and equal area projections to show the whole earth with relatively true shapes and reasonably equal areas.

Conic (Fig. 3): This projection has been used frequently for air navigation charts and to create most of the national and regional maps in this atlas. (See text in margin at left).

HAMMOND OPTIMAL CONFORMAL

As its name implies, this new conformal projection (Fig. 4) presents the optimal view of an area by reducing shifts in scale over an entire region to the minimum degree possible. While conformal maps generally preserve all small shapes, large shapes can become very distorted because of varying scales, causing considerable inaccuracy in distance measurements. The concept underlying the Optimal Conformal is that for any region on the globe, there is an ideal projection for which scale variation can be made as small as possible. Consequently, unlike other projections, the Optimal Conformal does not use one standard formula to construct a map. Each map is a unique projection — the optimal projection for that particular area.

After a cartographer defines the subject area, a sophisticated computer program evaluates the size and shape of the region, projecting the most distortion-free map possible. All of the continent maps in this atlas, except Antarctica, have been drawn using the Optimal projection.

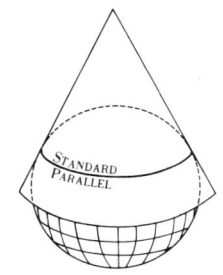

FIGURE 3
Conic Projection
The original idea of a conic projection is to cap the globe with a cone, and then project onto the cone from the planet's center the lines of latitude and longitude (the parallels and meridians). To produce a working map, the cone is simply cut open and laid flat. The conic projection used here is a modification of this idea. A cone can be made tangent to any standard parallel you choose. One popular version of a conic projection, the Lambert Conformal Conic, uses two standard parallels near the top and bottom of the map to further reduce errors of scale.

FIGURE 4
Hammond Optimal Conformal Projection
Like all conformal maps, the Optimal projection preserves angles exactly and minimizes distortion in shapes. This projection is more successful than any previous projection at spreading curvature across the entire map, producing the most distortion-free map possible.

Using This Atlas

How to Locate Information Quickly
Our Maps of the World section is organized by continent. If you're looking for a major region of the world, consult the Contents on page two.

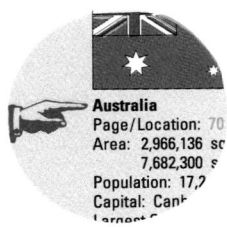

World Reference Guide
This concise guide lists the countries of the world alphabetically. If you're looking for the largest scale map of any country, you'll find a page and alpha-numeric reference at a glance, as well as information about each country, including its flag.

Master Index
When you're looking for a specific place or physical feature, your quickest route is the Master Index. This 6,000-entry alphabetical index lists both the page number and alpha-numeric reference for major places and features in Maps of the World.

This new atlas is created from a unique digital database, and its computer-generated maps represent a new phase in map-making technology.

How Computer-Generated Maps Are Made

To build a digital database capable of generating this world atlas, the latitude and longitude of every significant town, river, coastline, natural and political border, transportation network and peak elevation was researched and digitized. Hundreds of millions of data points describing every important geographic feature are organized into thousands of different map feature codes.

There are no maps in this unique system. Rather, it consists entirely of coded points, lines and polygons. To create a map, cartographers simply determine what specific information they wish to show, based upon considerations of scale, size, density and importance of different features.

New technology developed by mathematical physicist Mitchell Feigenbaum uses fractal geometry to describe and re-configure coastlines, borders and mountain ranges to fit a variety of map scales and projections. Dr. Feigenbaum has also created a computerized type placement program which allows thousands of map labels to be placed accurately in minutes. After these steps have been completed, the computer then draws the final map.

Each section of this atlas has been designed to be both easy and enjoyable to use. Familiarizing yourself with its organization will help you to benefit fully from its use.

World Flags and Reference Guide

This colorful section portrays each nation of the world, its flag, important geographical data, such as size, population and capital, and its location in the Maps of the World section.

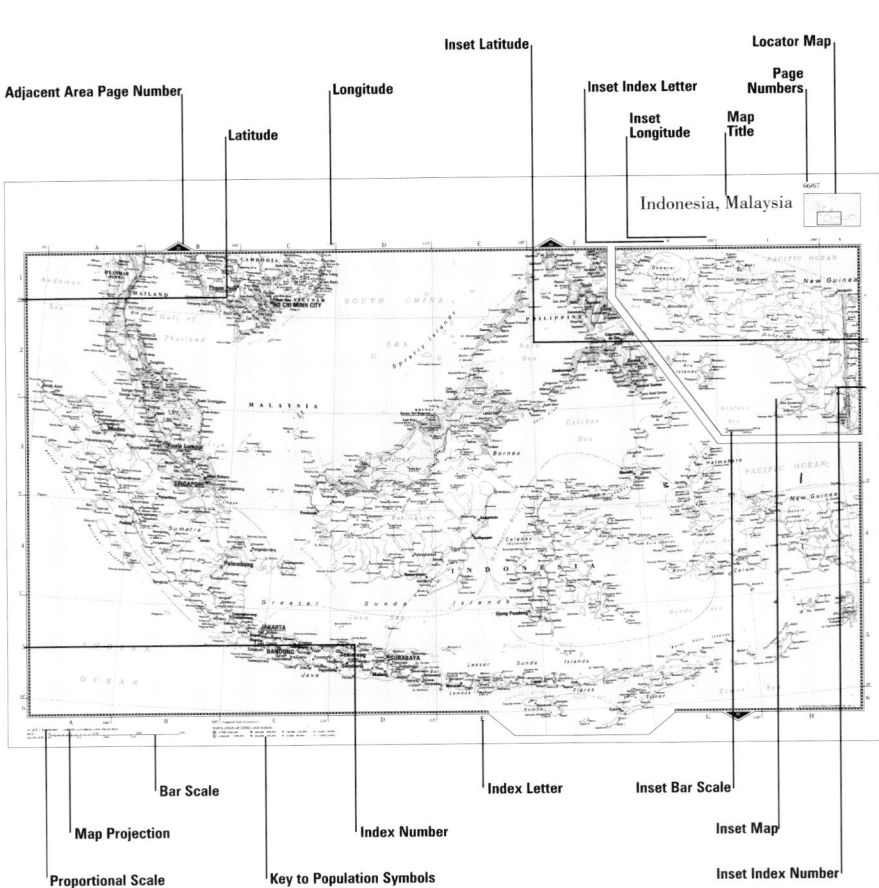

Symbols Used on Maps of the World

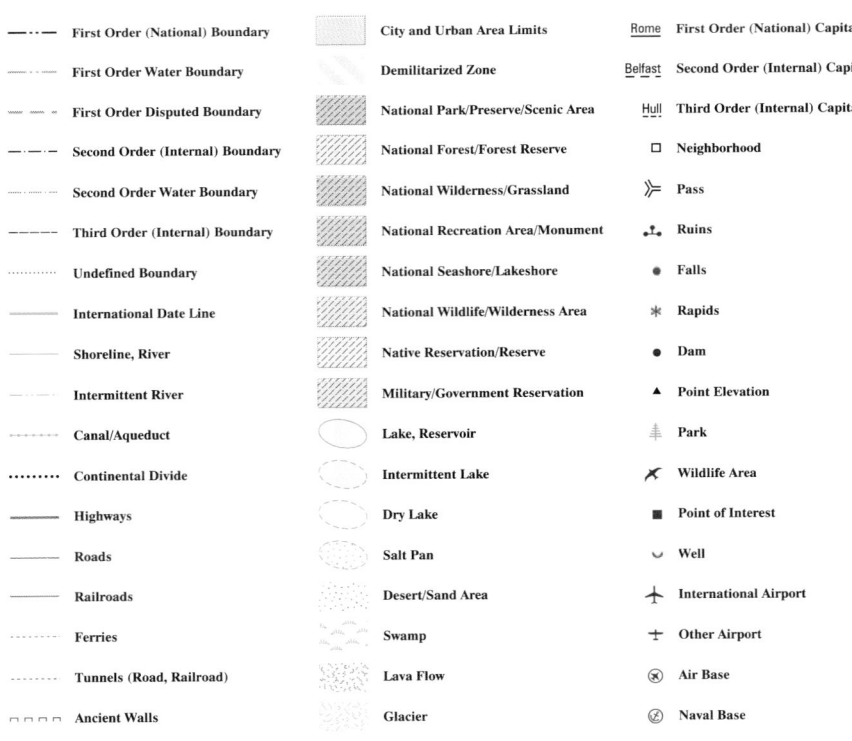

First Order (National) Boundary	City and Urban Area Limits	Rome First Order (National) Capital
First Order Water Boundary	Demilitarized Zone	Belfast Second Order (Internal) Capital
First Order Disputed Boundary	National Park/Preserve/Scenic Area	Hull Third Order (Internal) Capital
Second Order (Internal) Boundary	National Forest/Forest Reserve	Neighborhood
Second Order Water Boundary	National Wilderness/Grassland	Pass
Third Order (Internal) Boundary	National Recreation Area/Monument	Ruins
Undefined Boundary	National Seashore/Lakeshore	Falls
International Date Line	National Wildlife/Wilderness Area	Rapids
Shoreline, River	Native Reservation/Reserve	Dam
Intermittent River	Military/Government Reservation	Point Elevation
Canal/Aqueduct	Lake, Reservoir	Park
Continental Divide	Intermittent Lake	Wildlife Area
Highways	Dry Lake	Point of Interest
Roads	Salt Pan	Well
Railroads	Desert/Sand Area	International Airport
Ferries	Swamp	Other Airport
Tunnels (Road, Railroad)	Lava Flow	Air Base
Ancient Walls	Glacier	Naval Base

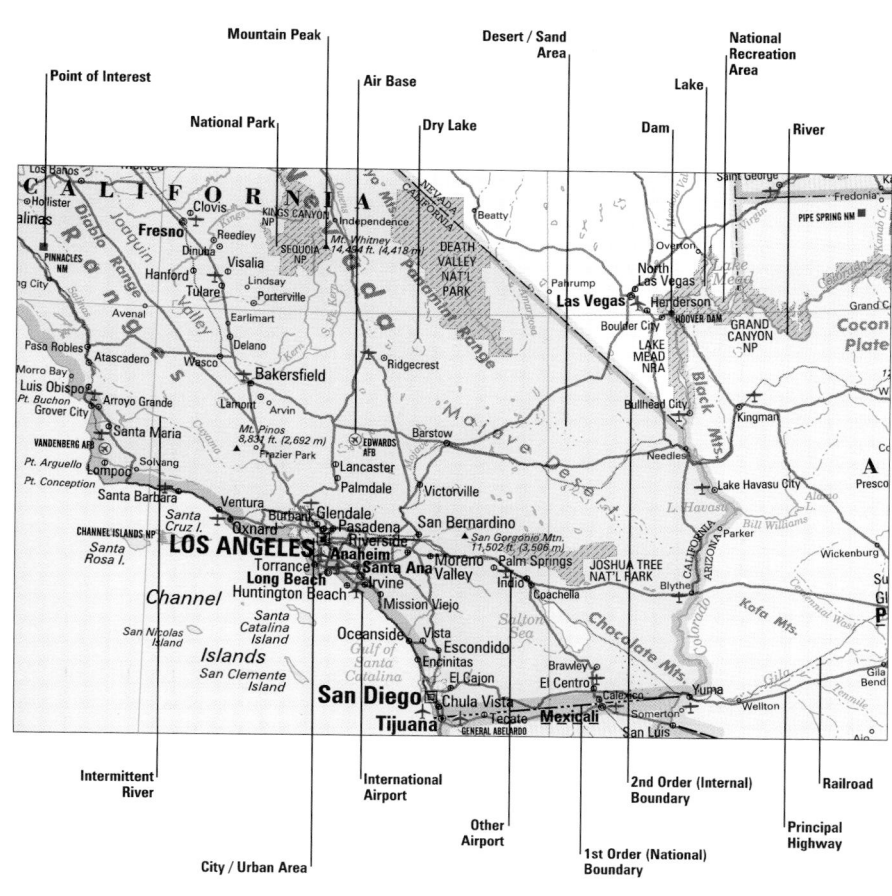

Point of Interest

Mountain Peak

National Park

Air Base

Desert / Sand Area

Dry Lake

Lake

National Recreation Area

Dam

River

Intermittent River

International Airport

Other Airport

City / Urban Area

2nd Order (Internal) Boundary

1st Order (National) Boundary

Railroad

Principal Highway

PRINCIPAL MAP ABBREVIATIONS

ABOR. RSV.	ABORIGINAL RESERVE	IND. RES.	INDIAN RESERVATION	NWR	NATIONAL WILDLIFE RESERVE
ADMIN.	ADMINISTRATION	INT'L	INTERNATIONAL		
AFB	AIR FORCE BASE	IR	INDIAN RESERVATION	OBL.	OBLAST
AMM. DEP.	AMMUNITION DEPOT	ISTH.	ISTHMUS	OCC.	OCCUPIED
ARCH.	ARCHIPELAGO	JCT.	JUNCTION	OKR.	OKRUG
ARPT.	AIRPORT	L.	LAKE	PAR.	PARISH
AUT.	AUTONOMOUS	LAG.	LAGOON	PASSG.	PASSAGE
B.	BAY	LAKESH.	LAKESHORE	PEN.	PENINSULA
BFLD.	BATTLEFIELD	MEM.	MEMORIAL	PK.	PEAK
BK.	BROOK	MIL.	MILITARY	PLAT.	PLATEAU
BOR.	BOROUGH	MISS.	MISSILE	PN	PARK NATIONAL
BR.	BRANCH	MON.	MONUMENT	PREF.	PREFECTURE
C.	CAPE	MT.	MOUNT	PROM.	PROMONTORY
CAN.	CANAL	MTN.	MOUNTAIN	PROV.	PROVINCE
CAP.	CAPITAL	MTS.	MOUNTAINS	PRSV.	PRESERVE
C.G.	COAST GUARD	NAT.	NATURAL	PT.	POINT
CHAN.	CHANNEL	NAT'L	NATIONAL	R.	RIVER
CO.	COUNTY	NAV.	NAVAL	RA	RECREATION AREA
CR.	CREEK	NB	NATIONAL BATTLEFIELD	RA.	RANGE
CTR.	CENTER			REC.	RECREATION(AL)
DEP.	DEPOT	NBP	NATIONAL BATTLEFIELD PARK	REF.	REFUGE
DEPR.	DEPRESSION			REG.	REGION
DEPT.	DEPARTMENT	NBS	NATIONAL BATTLEFIELD SITE	REP.	REPUBLIC
DES.	DESERT			RES.	RESERVOIR, RESERVATION
DIST.	DISTRICT	NHP	NATIONAL HISTORICAL PARK		
DMZ	DEMILITARIZED ZONE			RVWY.	RIVERWAY
DPCY.	DEPENDENCY	NHPP	NATIONAL HISTORICAL PARK AND PRESERVE	SA.	SIERRA
ENG.	ENGINEERING			SD.	SOUND
EST.	ESTUARY	NHS	NATIONAL HISTORIC SITE	SEASH.	SEASHORE
FD.	FIORD, FJORD			SO.	SOUTHERN
FED.	FEDERAL	NL	NATIONAL LAKESHORE	SP	STATE PARK
FK.	FORK	NM	NATIONAL MONUMENT	SPR., SPRS.	SPRING, SPRINGS
FLD.	FIELD	NMEMP	NATIONAL MEMORIAL PARK	ST.	STATE
FOR.	FOREST			STA.	STATION
FT.	FORT	NMILP	NATIONAL MILITARY PARK	STM.	STREAM
G.	GULF			STR.	STRAIT
GOV.	GOVERNOR	NO.	NORTHERN	TERR.	TERRITORY
GOVT.	GOVERNMENT	NP	NATIONAL PARK	TUN.	TUNNEL
GD.	GRAND	NPP	NATIONAL PARK AND PRESERVE	TWP.	TOWNSHIP
GT.	GREAT			VAL.	VALLEY
HAR.	HARBOR	NPRSV	NATIONAL PRESERVE	VILL.	VILLAGE
HD.	HEAD	NRA	NATIONAL RECREATION AREA	VOL.	VOLCANO
HIST.	HISTORIC(AL)			WILD.	WILDLIFE,
HTS.	HEIGHTS	NRSV	NATIONAL RESERVE		WILDERNESS
I., IS.	ISLAND(S)	NS	NATIONAL SEASHORE	WTR.	WATER

WORLD STATISTICS

World Statistics lists the dimensions of the earth's principal mountains, islands, rivers and lakes, along with other useful geographic information.

MAPS OF THE WORLD

These detailed regional maps are arranged by continent, and introduced by a political map of that continent. The continent maps, which utilize Hammond's new Optimal Conformal projection, are distinguished by individual colors for each country to highlight political divisions.

On the regional maps, different colors and textures highlight distinctive features such as parks, forests, deserts and urban areas. These maps also provide considerable information concerning geographic features and political divisions.

MASTER INDEX

This is an A-Z listing of names found on the political maps. It also has its own abbreviation list which, along with other Index keys, appears on page 110.

MAP SCALES

A map's scale is the relationship of any length on the map to an identical length on the earth's surface. A scale of 1:3,000,000 means that one inch on the map represents 3,000,000 inches (47 miles, 76 km.) on the earth's surface. Thus, a 1:1,000,000 scale is larger than 1:3,000,000, just as 1/1 is larger than 1/3.

The most densely populated areas are shown at a scale of 1:1,170,000, while selected metropolitan areas are covered at either 1:587,000 or 1:1,170,000. Other populous areas are presented at 1:3,500,000 and 1:7,000,000, allowing you to accurately compare areas and distances of similar regions. Remaining regions are scaled at 1:10,500,000. The continent maps, as well as the United States, Canada, Russia, Pacific and World have smaller scales.

World Flags and Reference Guide

Afghanistan
Page/Location: 53/H2
Area: 250,775 sq. mi.
649,507 sq. km.
Population: 23,738,085
Capital: Kabul
Largest City: Kabul
Highest Point: Noshaq
Monetary Unit: afghani

Albania
Page/Location: 39/F2
Area: 11,100 sq. mi.
28,749 sq. km.
Population: 3,293,252
Capital: Tiranë
Largest City: Tiranë
Highest Point: Korab
Monetary Unit: lek

Algeria
Page/Location: 76/F2
Area: 919,591 sq. mi.
2,381,740 sq. km.
Population: 29,830,370
Capital: Algiers
Largest City: Algiers
Highest Point: Tahat
Monetary Unit: Algerian dinar

Andorra
Page/Location: 35/F1
Area: 174 sq. mi.
450 sq. km.
Population: 74,839
Capital: Andorra la Vella
Largest City: Andorra la Vella
Highest Point: Coma Pedrosa
Monetary Unit: Fr. franc, Sp. peseta

Angola
Page/Location: 82/C3
Area: 481,351 sq. mi.
1,246,700 sq. km.
Population: 10,623,994
Capital: Luanda
Largest City: Luanda
Highest Point: Morro de Môco
Monetary Unit: new kwanza

Antigua and Barbuda
Page/Location: 104/F3
Area: 171 sq. mi.
443 sq. km.
Population: 66,175
Capital: St. John's
Largest City: St. John's
Highest Point: Boggy Peak
Monetary Unit: East Caribbean dollar

Argentina
Page/Location: 109/C4
Area: 1,068,296 sq. mi.
2,766,890 sq. km.
Population: 35,797,536
Capital: Buenos Aires
Largest City: Buenos Aires
Highest Point: Cerro Aconcagua
Monetary Unit: nuevo peso argentino

Armenia
Page/Location: 45/H5
Area: 11,506 sq. mi.
29,800 sq. km.
Population: 3,465,611
Capital: Yerevan
Largest City: Yerevan
Highest Point: Alagez
Monetary Unit: dram

Australia
Page/Location: 70
Area: 2,966,136 sq. mi.
7,682,300 sq. km.
Population: 18,438,824
Capital: Canberra
Largest City: Sydney
Highest Point: Mt. Kosciusko
Monetary Unit: Australian dollar

Austria
Page/Location: 33/L3
Area: 32,375 sq. mi.
83,851 sq. km.
Population: 8,054,078
Capital: Vienna
Largest City: Vienna
Highest Point: Grossglockner
Monetary Unit: schilling

Azerbaijan
Page/Location: 45/H4
Area: 33,436 sq. mi.
86,600 sq. km.
Population: 7,735,918
Capital: Baku
Largest City: Baku
Highest Point: Bazardyuzyu
Monetary Unit: manat

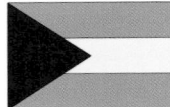

Bahamas
Page/Location: 104/B2
Area: 5,382 sq. mi.
13,939 sq. km.
Population: 262,034
Capital: Nassau
Largest City: Nassau
Highest Point: 207 ft. (63 m)
Monetary Unit: Bahamian dollar

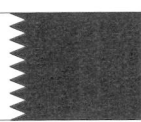

Bahrain
Page/Location: 52/F3
Area: 240 sq. mi.
622 sq. km.
Population: 603,318
Capital: Manama
Largest City: Manama
Highest Point: Jabal Dukhān
Monetary Unit: Bahraini dinar

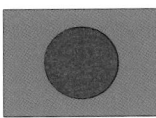

Bangladesh
Page/Location: 60/E3
Area: 55,598 sq. mi.
144,000 sq. km.
Population: 125,340,261
Capital: Dhākā
Largest City: Dhākā
Highest Point: Keokradong
Monetary Unit: taka

Barbados
Page/Location: 104/G4
Area: 166 sq. mi.
430 sq. km.
Population: 257,731
Capital: Bridgetown
Largest City: Bridgetown
Highest Point: Mt. Hillaby
Monetary Unit: Barbadian dollar

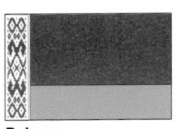

Belarus
Page/Location: 18/F3
Area: 80,154 sq. mi.
207,600 sq. km.
Population: 10,439,916
Capital: Minsk
Largest City: Minsk
Highest Point: Dzerzhinskaya
Monetary Unit: Belarusian ruble

Belgium
Page/Location: 30/C2
Area: 11,781 sq. mi.
30,513 sq. km.
Population: 10,203,683
Capital: Brussels
Largest City: Brussels
Highest Point: Botrange
Monetary Unit: Belgian franc

Belize
Page/Location: 102/D2
Area: 8,867 sq. mi.
22,966 sq. km.
Population: 224,663
Capital: Belmopan
Largest City: Belize City
Highest Point: Victoria Peak
Monetary Unit: Belize dollar

Benin
Page/Location: 79/F4
Area: 43,483 sq. mi.
112,620 sq. km.
Population: 5,342,000
Capital: Porto-Novo
Largest City: Cotonou
Highest Point: Nassoukou
Monetary Unit: CFA franc

Bhutan
Page/Location: 62/E2
Area: 18,147 sq. mi.
47,000 sq. km.
Population: 1,865,191
Capital: Thimphu
Largest City: Thimphu
Highest Point: Kula Kangri
Monetary Unit: ngultrum

Bolivia
Page/Location: 106/F7
Area: 424,163 sq. mi.
1,098,582 sq. km.
Population: 7,669,868
Capital: La Paz; Sucre
Largest City: La Paz
Highest Point: Nevado Ancohuma
Monetary Unit: boliviano

Bosnia and Herzegovina
Page/Location: 40/C3
Area: 19,940 sq. mi.
51,645 sq. km.
Population: 2,607,734
Capital: Sarajevo
Largest City: Sarajevo
Highest Point: Maglič
Monetary Unit: dinar

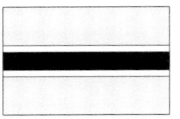

Botswana
Page/Location: 82/D5
Area: 231,803 sq. mi.
600,370 sq. km.
Population: 1,500,765
Capital: Gaborone
Largest City: Gaborone
Highest Point: Tsodilo Hills
Monetary Unit: pula

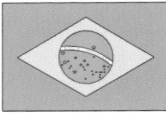

Brazil
Page/Location: 105/D3
Area: 3,286,470 sq. mi.
8,511,965 sq. km.
Population: 164,511,366
Capital: Brasília
Largest City: São Paulo
Highest Point: Pico da Neblina
Monetary Unit: real

Brunei
Page/Location: 66/D2
Area: 2,226 sq. mi.
5,765 sq. km.
Population: 307,616
Capital: Bandar Seri Begawan
Largest City: Bandar Seri Begawan
Highest Point: Bukit Pagon
Monetary Unit: Brunei dollar

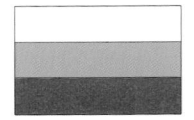

Bulgaria
Page/Location: 41/G4
Area: 42,823 sq. mi.
110,912 sq. km.
Population: 8,652,745
Capital: Sofia
Largest City: Sofia
Highest Point: Musala
Monetary Unit: lev

Burkina Faso
Page/Location: 79/E3
Area: 105,869 sq. mi.
274,200 sq. km.
Population: 10,891,159
Capital: Ouagadougou
Largest City: Ouagadougou
Highest Point: 2,405 ft. (733 m)
Monetary Unit: CFA franc

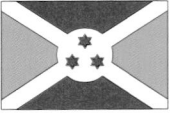

Burundi
Page/Location: 82/E1
Area: 10,747 sq. mi.
27,835 sq. km.
Population: 6,052,614
Capital: Bujumbura
Largest City: Bujumbura
Highest Point: 8,760 ft. (2,670 m)
Monetary Unit: Burundi franc

Cambodia
Page/Location: 65/D3
Area: 69,898 sq. mi.
181,036 sq. km.
Population: 11,163,861
Capital: Phnom Penh
Largest City: Phnom Penh
Highest Point: Phnom Aoral
Monetary Unit: new riel

Cameroon
Page/Location: 76/H7
Area: 183,568 sq. mi.
475,441 sq. km.
Population: 14,677,510
Capital: Yaoundé
Largest City: Douala
Highest Point: Mt. Cameroon
Monetary Unit: CFA franc

Canada
Page/Location: 86
Area: 3,851,787 sq. mi.
9,976,139 sq. km.
Population: 29,123,194
Capital: Ottawa
Largest City: Toronto
Highest Point: Mt. Logan
Monetary Unit: Canadian dollar

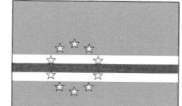

Cape Verde
Page/Location: 74/K9
Area: 1,557 sq. mi.
4,033 sq. km.
Population: 393,843
Capital: Praia
Largest City: Praia
Highest Point: 9,282 ft. (2,829 m)
Monetary Unit: Cape Verde escudo

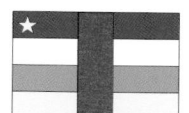

Central African Republic
Page/Location: 77/J6
Area: 240,533 sq. mi.
622,980 sq. km.
Population: 3,342,051
Capital: Bangui
Largest City: Bangui
Highest Point: Mt. Kayagangiri
Monetary Unit: CFA franc

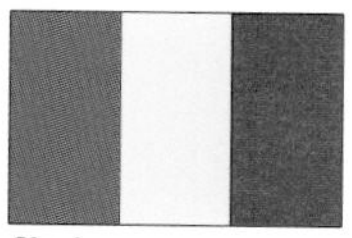

Chad
Page/Location: 77/J4
Area: 495,752 sq. mi.
1,283,998 sq. km.
Population: 7,166,023
Capital: N'Djamena
Largest City: N'Djamena
Highest Point: Emi Koussi
Monetary Unit: CFA franc

Chile
Page/Location: 109/B3
Area: 292,257 sq. mi.
756,946 sq. km.
Population: 14,508,168
Capital: Santiago
Largest City: Santiago
Highest Point: Nevado Ojos del Salado
Monetary Unit: Chilean peso

China
Page/Location: 48/J6
Area: 3,705,386 sq. mi.
9,596,960 sq. km.
Population: 1,221,591,778
Capital: Beijing
Largest City: Shanghai
Highest Point: Mt. Everest
Monetary Unit: yuan

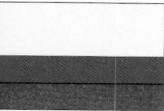

Colombia
Page/Location: 106/D3
Area: 439,513 sq. mi.
1,138,339 sq. km.
Population: 37,418,290
Capital: Bogotá
Largest City: Bogotá
Highest Point: Pico Cristóbal Colón
Monetary Unit: Colombian peso

Comoros
Page/Location: 74/G6
Area: 838 sq. mi.
2,170 sq. km.
Population: 589,797
Capital: Moroni
Largest City: Moroni
Highest Point: Karthala
Monetary Unit: Comorian franc

Congo, Dem. Rep. of the
Page/Location: 74/E5
Area: 905,563 sq. mi.
2,345,410 sq. km.
Population: 47,440,362
Capital: Kinshasa
Largest City: Kinshasa
Highest Point: Margherita Peak
Monetary Unit: zaire

Congo, Rep. of the
Page/Location: 74/D5
Area: 132,046 sq. mi.
342,000 sq. km.
Population: 2,583,198
Capital: Brazzaville
Largest City: Brazzaville
Highest Point: Lékéti Mts.
Monetary Unit: CFA franc

Costa Rica
Page/Location: 103/F4
Area: 19,730 sq. mi.
51,100 sq. km.
Population: 3,534,174
Capital: San José
Largest City: San José
Highest Point: Cerro Chirripó Grande
Monetary Unit: Costa Rican colón

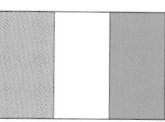

Côte d'Ivoire
Page/Location: 78/D5
Area: 124,504 sq. mi.
322,465 sq. km.
Population: 14,986,218
Capital: Yamoussoukro
Largest City: Abidjan
Highest Point: Mt. Nimba
Monetary Unit: CFA franc

Croatia
Page/Location: 40/C3
Area: 22,050 sq. mi.
57,110 sq. km.
Population: 5,026,995
Capital: Zagreb
Largest City: Zagreb
Highest Point: Veliki Troglav
Monetary Unit: Croatian kuna

Cuba
Page/Location: 103/F1
Area: 42,803 sq. mi.
110,860 sq. km.
Population: 10,999,041
Capital: Havana
Largest City: Havana
Highest Point: Pico Turquino
Monetary Unit: Cuban peso

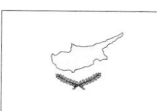

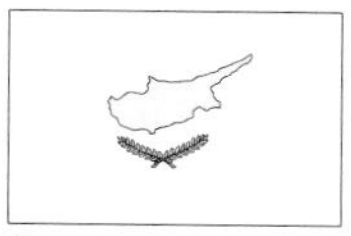

Cyprus
Page/Location: 49/C2
Area: 3,571 sq. mi.
9,250 sq. km.
Population: 752,808
Capital: Nicosia
Largest City: Nicosia
Highest Point: Olympus
Monetary Unit: Cypriot pound

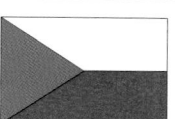

Czech Republic
Page/Location: 27/H4
Area: 30,387 sq. mi.
78,703 sq. km.
Population: 10,318,958
Capital: Prague
Largest City: Prague
Highest Point: Sněžka
Monetary Unit: Czech koruna

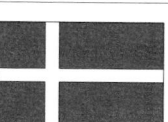

Denmark
Page/Location: 20/C5
Area: 16,629 sq. mi.
43,069 sq. km.
Population: 5,268,775
Capital: Copenhagen
Largest City: Copenhagen
Highest Point: Yding Skovhøj
Monetary Unit: Danish krone

Djibouti
Page/Location: 77/P5
Area: 8,494 sq. mi.
22,000 sq. km.
Population: 434,116
Capital: Djibouti
Largest City: Djibouti
Highest Point: Moussa Ali
Monetary Unit: Djibouti franc

Dominica
Page/Location: 104/F4
Area: 290 sq. mi.
751 sq. km.
Population: 83,226
Capital: Roseau
Largest City: Roseau
Highest Point: Morne Diablotin
Monetary Unit: EC dollar

Dominican Republic
Page/Location: 104/D3
Area: 18,815 sq. mi.
48,730 sq. km.
Population: 8,228,151
Capital: Santo Domingo
Largest City: Santo Domingo
Highest Point: Pico Duarte
Monetary Unit: Dominican peso

Ecuador
Page/Location: 106/C4
Area: 109,483 sq. mi.
283,561 sq. km.
Population: 11,690,535
Capital: Quito
Largest City: Guayaquil
Highest Point: Chimborazo
Monetary Unit: sucre

Egypt
Page/Location: 77/L2
Area: 386,659 sq. mi.
1,001,447 sq. km.
Population: 64,791,891
Capital: Cairo
Largest City: Cairo
Highest Point: Mt. Catherine
Monetary Unit: Egyptian pound

El Salvador
Page/Location: 102/D3
Area: 8,124 sq. mi.
21,040 sq. km.
Population: 5,661,827
Capital: San Salvador
Largest City: San Salvador
Highest Point: Santa Ana
Monetary Unit: Salvadoran colón

Equatorial Guinea
Page/Location: 76/G7
Area: 10,831 sq. mi.
28,052 sq. km.
Population: 442,516
Capital: Malabo
Largest City: Malabo
Highest Point: Pico de Santa Isabel
Monetary Unit: CFA franc

Eritrea
Page/Location: 52/C5
Area: 46,842 sq. mi.
121,320 sq. km.
Population: 3,589,687
Capital: Asmara
Largest City: Asmara
Highest Point: Soira
Monetary Unit: nafka

Estonia
Page/Location: 42/E4
Area: 17,413 sq. mi.
45,100 sq. km.
Population: 1,444,721
Capital: Tallinn
Largest City: Tallinn
Highest Point: Munamägi
Monetary Unit: kroon

Ethiopia
Page/Location: 77/N6
Area: 435,184 sq. mi.
1,127,127 sq. km.
Population: 58,732,577
Capital: Addis Ababa
Largest City: Addis Ababa
Highest Point: Ras Dashen Terara
Monetary Unit: birr

Fiji
Page/Location: 68/G6
Area: 7,055 sq. mi.
18,272 sq. km.
Population: 792,441
Capital: Suva
Largest City: Suva
Highest Point: Tomaniivi
Monetary Unit: Fijian dollar

Finland
Page/Location: 20/H2
Area: 130,128 sq. mi.
337,032 sq. km.
Population: 5,109,148
Capital: Helsinki
Largest City: Helsinki
Highest Point: Kahperusvaara
Monetary Unit: markka

France
Page/Location: 32/D3
Area: 211,208 sq. mi.
547,030 sq. km.
Population: 58,470,421
Capital: Paris
Largest City: Paris
Highest Point: Mont Blanc
Monetary Unit: French franc

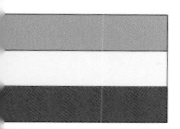

Gabon
Page/Location: 76/H7
Area: 103,346 sq. mi.
267,666 sq. km.
Population: 1,190,159
Capital: Libreville
Largest City: Libreville
Highest Point: Mt. Iboundji
Monetary Unit: CFA franc

Gambia, The
Page/Location: 78/B3
Area: 4,363 sq. mi.
11,300 sq. km.
Population: 1,248,085
Capital: Banjul
Largest City: Banjul
Highest Point: 98 ft. (30 m)
Monetary Unit: dalasi

Georgia
Page/Location: 45/G4
Area: 26,911 sq. mi.
69,700 sq. km.
Population: 5,174,642
Capital: T'bilisi
Largest City: T'bilisi
Highest Point: Kazbek
Monetary Unit: lari

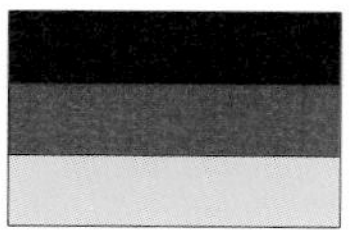

Germany
Page/Location: 26/E3
Area: 137,803 sq. mi.
356,910 sq. km.
Population: 84,068,216
Capital: Berlin
Largest City: Berlin
Highest Point: Zugspitze
Monetary Unit: Deutsche mark

Ghana
Page/Location: 79/E4
Area: 92,099 sq. mi.
238,536 sq. km.
Population: 18,100,703
Capital: Accra
Largest City: Accra
Highest Point: Afadjoto
Monetary Unit: new cedi

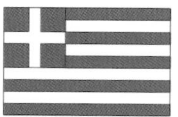

Greece
Page/Location: 39/G3
Area: 50,944 sq. mi.
131,945 sq. km.
Population: 10,583,126
Capital: Athens
Largest City: Athens
Highest Point: Mt. Olympus
Monetary Unit: drachma

World Flags and Reference Guide

Grenada
Page/Location: 104/F5
Area: 133 sq. mi.
344 sq. km.
Population: 95,537
Capital: St. George's
Largest City: St. George's
Highest Point: Mt. St. Catherine
Monetary Unit: East Caribbean dollar

Guatemala
Page/Location: 102/D3
Area: 42,042 sq. mi.
108,889 sq. km.
Population: 11,558,407
Capital: Guatemala
Largest City: Guatemala
Highest Point: Tajumulco
Monetary Unit: quetzal

Guinea
Page/Location: 78/C4
Area: 94,925 sq. mi.
245,856 sq. km.
Population: 7,405,375
Capital: Conakry
Largest City: Conakry
Highest Point: Mt. Nimba
Monetary Unit: Guinea franc

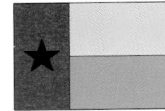

Guinea-Bissau
Page/Location: 78/B3
Area: 13,948 sq. mi.
36,125 sq. km.
Population: 1,178,584
Capital: Bissau
Largest City: Bissau
Highest Point: 689 ft. (210 m)
Monetary Unit: Guinea-Bissau peso

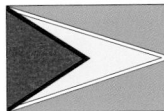

Guyana
Page/Location: 106/G2
Area: 83,000 sq. mi.
214,970 sq. km.
Population: 706,116
Capital: Georgetown
Largest City: Georgetown
Highest Point: Mt. Roraima
Monetary Unit: Guyana dollar

Haiti
Page/Location: 103/H2
Area: 10,694 sq. mi.
27,697 sq. km.
Population: 6,611,407
Capital: Port-au-Prince
Largest City: Port-au-Prince
Highest Point: Pic la Selle
Monetary Unit: gourde

Honduras
Page/Location: 102/E3
Area: 43,277 sq. mi.
112,087 sq. km.
Population: 5,751,384
Capital: Tegucigalpa
Largest City: Tegucigalpa
Highest Point: Cerro de las Minas
Monetary Unit: lempira

Hungary
Page/Location: 40/D2
Area: 35,919 sq. mi.
93,030 sq. km.
Population: 9,935,774
Capital: Budapest
Largest City: Budapest
Highest Point: Kékes
Monetary Unit: forint

Iceland
Page/Location: 20/N7
Area: 39,768 sq. mi.
103,000 sq. km.
Population: 272,550
Capital: Reykjavík
Largest City: Reykjavík
Highest Point: Hvannadalshnúkur
Monetary Unit: króna

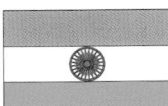

India
Page/Location: 62/C3
Area: 1,269,339 sq. mi.
3,287,588 sq. km.
Population: 967,612,804
Capital: New Delhi
Largest City: Calcutta
Highest Point: Nanda Devi
Monetary Unit: Indian rupee

Indonesia
Page/Location: 67/E4
Area: 741,096 sq. mi.
1,919,440 sq. km.
Population: 209,774,138
Capital: Jakarta
Largest City: Jakarta
Highest Point: Puncak Jaya
Monetary Unit: rupiah

Iran
Page/Location: 51/H3
Area: 636,293 sq. mi.
1,648,000 sq. km.
Population: 67,540,002
Capital: Tehrān
Largest City: Tehrān
Highest Point: Qolleh-ye Damāvand
Monetary Unit: Iranian rial

Iraq
Page/Location: 50/E3
Area: 168,753 sq. mi.
437,072 sq. km.
Population: 22,219,289
Capital: Baghdad
Largest City: Baghdad
Highest Point: Haji Ibrahim
Monetary Unit: Iraqi dinar

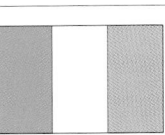

Ireland
Page/Location: 21/A4
Area: 27,136 sq. mi.
70,282 sq. km.
Population: 3,555,500
Capital: Dublin
Largest City: Dublin
Highest Point: Carrantuohill
Monetary Unit: Irish pound

Israel
Page/Location: 49/D3
Area: 8,019 sq. mi.
20,770 sq. km.
Population: 5,534,672
Capital: Jerusalem
Largest City: Tel Aviv-Yafo
Highest Point: Har Meron
Monetary Unit: new Israeli shekel

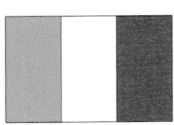

Italy
Page/Location: 18/E4
Area: 116,303 sq. mi.
301,225 sq. km.
Population: 57,534,088
Capital: Rome
Largest City: Rome
Highest Point: Monte Rosa
Monetary Unit: Italian lira

Jamaica
Page/Location: 103/G2
Area: 4,243 sq. mi.
10,990 sq. km.
Population: 2,615,582
Capital: Kingston
Largest City: Kingston
Highest Point: Blue Mountain Pk.
Monetary Unit: Jamaican dollar

Japan
Page/Location: 55/M4
Area: 145,882 sq. mi.
377,835 sq. km.
Population: 125,716,637
Capital: Tokyo
Largest City: Tokyo
Highest Point: Fujiyama
Monetary Unit: yen

Jordan
Page/Location: 49/E4
Area: 34,445 sq. mi.
89,213 sq. km.
Population: 4,324,638
Capital: Ammān
Largest City: Ammān
Highest Point: Jabal Ramm
Monetary Unit: Jordanian dinar

Kazakhstan
Page/Location: 46/G5
Area: 1,049,150 sq. mi.
2,717,300 sq. km.
Population: 16,898,572
Capital: Astana
Largest City: Almaty
Highest Point: Khan-Tengri
Monetary Unit: Kazakstani tenge

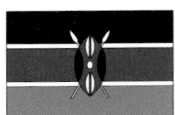

Kenya
Page/Location: 77/M7
Area: 224,960 sq. mi.
582,646 sq. km.
Population: 28,803,085
Capital: Nairobi
Largest City: Nairobi
Highest Point: Mt. Kenya
Monetary Unit: Kenya shilling

Kiribati
Page/Location: 69/H5
Area: 277 sq. mi.
717 sq. km.
Population: 82,449
Capital: Tarawa
Largest City: —
Highest Point: Banaba Island
Monetary Unit: Australian dollar

Korea, North
Page/Location: 58/D2
Area: 46,540 sq. mi.
120,539 sq. km.
Population: 24,317,004
Capital: P'yŏngyang
Largest City: P'yŏngyang
Highest Point: Paektu-san
Monetary Unit: North Korean won

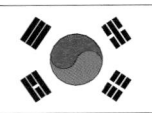

Korea, South
Page/Location: 58/D4
Area: 38,023 sq. mi.
98,480 sq. km.
Population: 45,948,811
Capital: Seoul
Largest City: Seoul
Highest Point: Halla-san
Monetary Unit: South Korean won

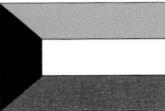

Kuwait
Page/Location: 51/F4
Area: 6,880 sq. mi.
17,820 sq. km.
Population: 2,076,805
Capital: Kuwait
Largest City: Kuwait
Highest Point: 951 ft. (290 m)
Monetary Unit: Kuwaiti dinar

Kyrgyzstan
Page/Location: 46/H5
Area: 76,641 sq. mi.
198,500 sq. km.
Population: 4,540,185
Capital: Bishkek
Largest City: Bishkek
Highest Point: Pik Pobedy
Monetary Unit: som

Laos
Page/Location: 65/C2
Area: 91,428 sq. mi.
236,800 sq. km.
Population: 5,116,959
Capital: Vientiane
Largest City: Vientiane
Highest Point: Phou Bia
Monetary Unit: new kip

Latvia
Page/Location: 42/E4
Area: 24,749 sq. mi.
64,100 sq. km.
Population: 2,437,649
Capital: Riga
Largest City: Riga
Highest Point: Gaizina Kalns
Monetary Unit: Latvian let

Lebanon
Page/Location: 49/D3
Area: 4,015 sq. mi.
10,399 sq. km.
Population: 3,858,736
Capital: Beirut
Largest City: Beirut
Highest Point: Qurnat as Sawdā'
Monetary Unit: Lebanese pound

Lesotho
Page/Location: 80/E3
Area: 11,720 sq. mi.
30,355 sq. km.
Population: 2,007,814
Capital: Maseru
Largest City: Maseru
Highest Point: Thabana-Ntlenyana
Monetary Unit: loti

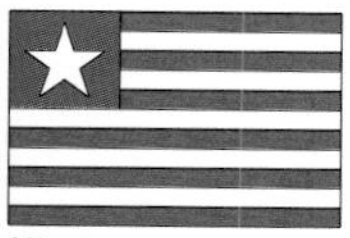

Liberia
Page/Location: 78/C4
Area: 43,000 sq. mi.
111,370 sq. km.
Population: 2,602,068
Capital: Monrovia
Largest City: Monrovia
Highest Point: Mt. Wuteve
Monetary Unit: Liberian dollar

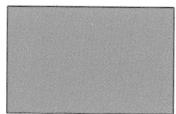

Libya
Page/Location: 77/J2
Area: 679,358 sq. mi.
1,759,537 sq. km.
Population: 5,648,359
Capital: Tripoli
Largest City: Tripoli
Highest Point: Picco Bette
Monetary Unit: Libyan dinar

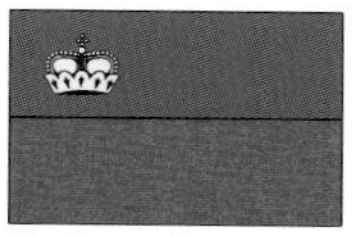

Liechtenstein
Page/Location: 37/F3
Area: 61 sq. mi.
158 sq. km.
Population: 31,461
Capital: Vaduz
Largest City: Vaduz
Highest Point: Grauspitz
Monetary Unit: Swiss franc

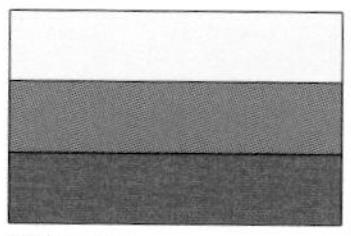

Lithuania
Page/Location: 42/D5
Area: 25,174 sq. mi.
65,200 sq. km.
Population: 3,635,932
Capital: Vilnius
Largest City: Vilnius
Highest Point: Nevaišių
Monetary Unit: litas

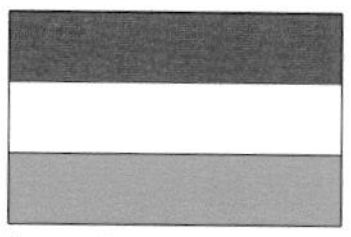

Luxembourg
Page/Location: 31/F4
Area: 999 sq. mi.
2,587 sq. km.
Population: 422,474
Capital: Luxembourg
Largest City: Luxembourg
Highest Point: Ardennes Plateau
Monetary Unit: Luxembourg franc

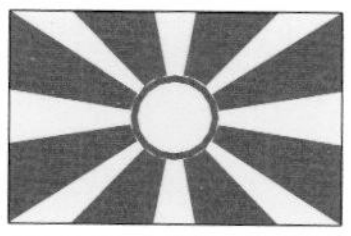

Macedonia (F.Y.R.O.M.)
Page/Location: 39/G2
Area: 9,781 sq. mi.
25,333 sq. km.
Population: 2,113,866
Capital: Skopje
Largest City: Skopje
Highest Point: Korab
Monetary Unit: denar

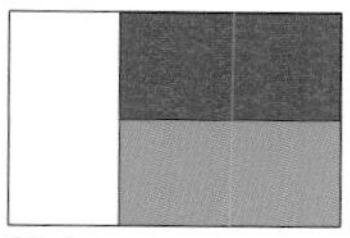

Madagascar
Page/Location: 81/H8
Area: 226,657 sq. mi.
587,041 sq. km.
Population: 14,061,627
Capital: Antananarivo
Largest City: Antananarivo
Highest Point: Maromokotro
Monetary Unit: Malagasy franc

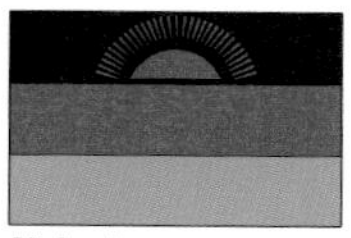

Malawi
Page/Location: 82/F3
Area: 45,747 sq. mi.
118, 485 sq. km.
Population: 9,609,081
Capital: Lilongwe
Largest City: Blantyre
Highest Point: Mulanje Mts.
Monetary Unit: Malawi kwacha

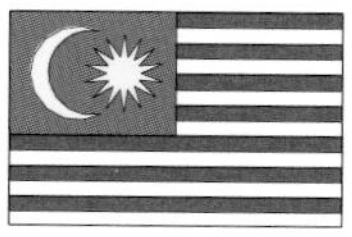

Malaysia
Page/Location: 67/C2
Area: 127,316 sq. mi.
329,750 sq. km.
Population: 20,376,235
Capital: Kuala Lumpur
Largest City: Kuala Lumpur
Highest Point: Gunung Kinabalu
Monetary Unit: ringgit

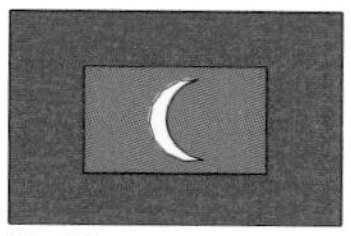

Maldives
Page/Location: 48/G9
Area: 115 sq. mi.
298 sq. km.
Population: 280,391
Capital: Male
Largest City: Male
Highest Point: 20 ft. (6 m)
Monetary Unit: rufiyaa

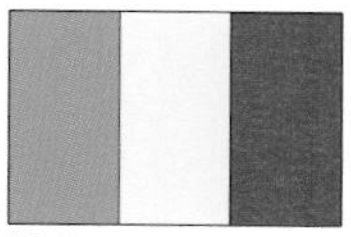

Mali
Page/Location: 76/E4
Area: 478,764 sq. mi.
1,240,000 sq. km.
Population: 9,945,383
Capital: Bamako
Largest City: Bamako
Highest Point: Hombori Tondo
Monetary Unit: CFA franc

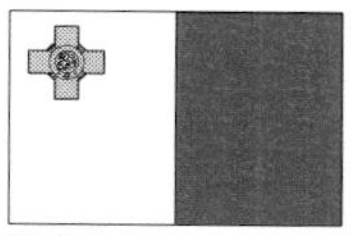

Malta
Page/Location: 38/D5
Area: 122 sq. mi.
316 sq. km.
Population: 379,365
Capital: Valletta
Largest City: Sliema
Highest Point: 830 ft. (253 m)
Monetary Unit: Maltese lira

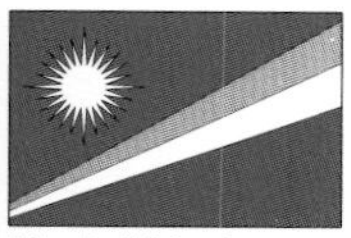

Marshall Islands
Page/Location: 68/G3
Area: 70 sq. mi.
181 sq. km.
Population: 60,652
Capital: Majuro
Largest City: —
Highest Point: 20 ft. (6 m)
Monetary Unit: U.S. dollar

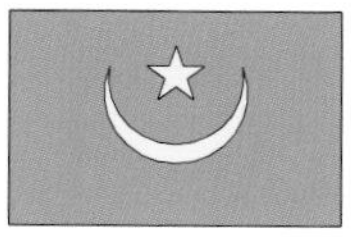

Mauritania
Page/Location: 76/C4
Area: 397,953 sq. mi.
1,030,700 sq. km.
Population: 2,411,317
Capital: Nouakchott
Largest City: Nouakchott
Highest Point: Kediet Ijill
Monetary Unit: ouguiya

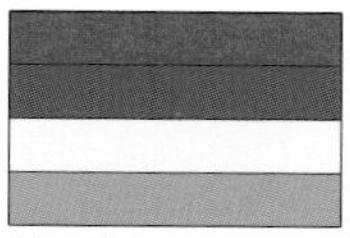

Mauritius
Page/Location: 81/S15
Area: 718 sq. mi.
1,860 sq. km.
Population: 1,154,272
Capital: Port Louis
Largest City: Port Louis
Highest Point: 2,713 ft. (827 m)
Monetary Unit: Mauritian rupee

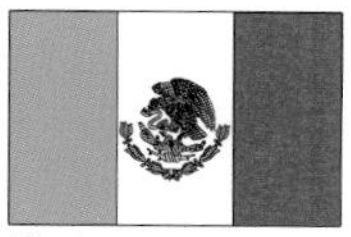

Mexico
Page/Location: 84/G7
Area: 761,601 sq. mi.
1,972,546 sq. km.
Population: 97,563,374
Capital: Mexico
Largest City: Mexico
Highest Point: Citlaltépetl
Monetary Unit: new Mexican peso

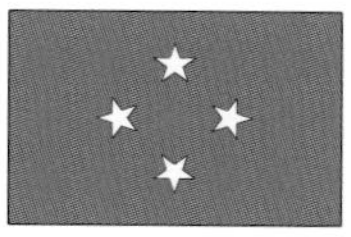

Micronesia
Page/Location: 68/D4
Area: 271 sq. mi.
702 sq. km.
Population: 122,950
Capital: Palikir
Largest City: —
Highest Point: —
Monetary Unit: U.S. dollar

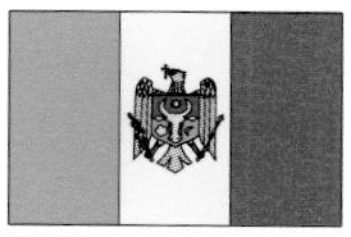

Moldova
Page/Location: 41/J2
Area: 13,012 sq. mi.
33,700 sq. km.
Population: 4,475,232
Capital: Chişinău
Largest City: Chişinău
Highest Point: 1,408 ft. (429 m)
Monetary Unit: leu

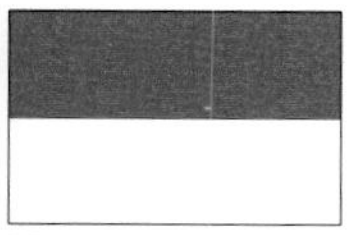

Monaco
Page/Location: 33/G5
Area: 0.7 sq. mi.
1.9 sq. km.
Population: 31,892
Capital: Monaco
Largest City: —
Highest Point: —
Monetary Unit: French franc

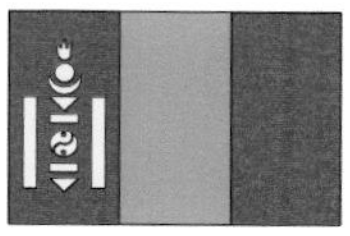

Mongolia
Page/Location: 54/D2
Area: 606,163 sq. mi.
1,569, 962 sq. km.
Population: 2,538,211
Capital: Ulaanbaatar
Largest City: Ulaanbaatar
Highest Point: Tavan Bogd Uul
Monetary Unit: tughrik

Morocco
Page/Location: 76/C1
Area: 172,414 sq. mi.
446,550 sq. km.
Population: 30,391,423
Capital: Rabat
Largest City: Casablanca
Highest Point: Jebel Toubkal
Monetary Unit: Moroccan dirham

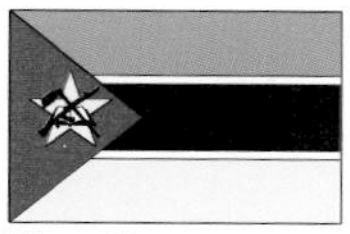

Mozambique
Page/Location: 82/G4
Area: 309,494 sq. mi.
801,590 sq. km.
Population: 18,165,476
Capital: Maputo
Largest City: Maputo
Highest Point: Monte Binga
Monetary Unit: metical

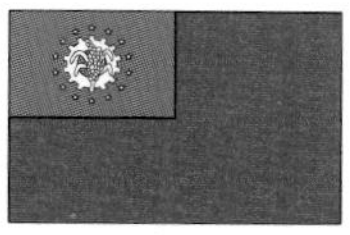

Myanmar (Burma)
Page/Location: 63/G3
Area: 261,969 sq. mi.
678,500 sq. km.
Population: 46,821,943
Capital: Rangoon
Largest City: Rangoon
Highest Point: Hkakabo Razi
Monetary Unit: kyat

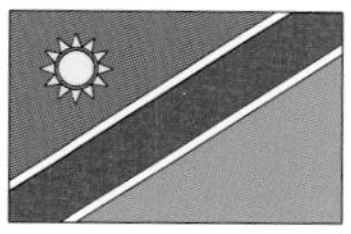

Namibia
Page/Location: 82/C5
Area: 318,694 sq. mi.
825,418 sq. km.
Population: 1,727,183
Capital: Windhoek
Largest City: Windhoek
Highest Point: Brandberg
Monetary Unit: Namibian dollar

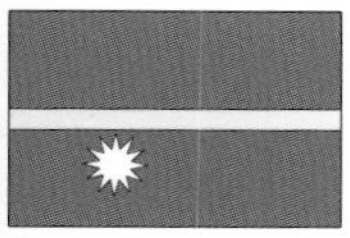

Nauru
Page/Location: 68/F5
Area: 7.7 sq. mi.
20 sq. km.
Population: 10,390
Capital: Yaren (district)
Largest City: —
Highest Point: 230 ft. (70 m)
Monetary Unit: Australian dollar

Nepal
Page/Location: 62/D2
Area: 54,663 sq. mi.
141,577 sq. km.
Population: 22,641,061
Capital: Kāthmāndu
Largest City: Kāthmāndu
Highest Point: Mt. Everest
Monetary Unit: Nepalese rupee

Netherlands
Page/Location: 28/B5
Area: 14,413 sq. mi.
37,330 sq. km.
Population: 15,653,091
Capital: The Hague; Amsterdam
Largest City: Amsterdam
Highest Point: Vaalserberg
Monetary Unit: Netherlands guilder

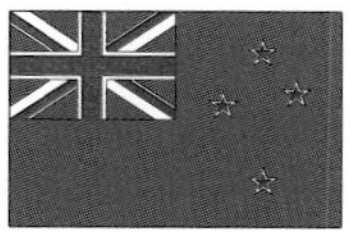

New Zealand
Page/Location: 71/Q10
Area: 103,736 sq. mi.
268,676 sq. km.
Population: 3,587,275
Capital: Wellington
Largest City: Auckland
Highest Point: Mt. Cook
Monetary Unit: New Zealand dollar

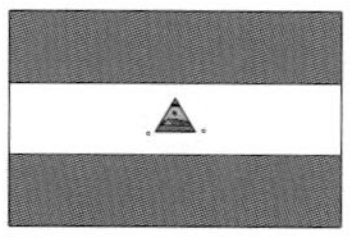

Nicaragua
Page/Location: 103/E3
Area: 49,998 sq. mi.
129,494 sq. km.
Population: 4,386,399
Capital: Managua
Largest City: Managua
Highest Point: Pico Mogotón
Monetary Unit: gold cordoba

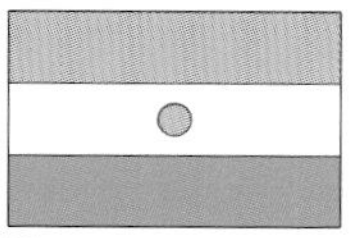

Niger
Page/Location: 76/G4
Area: 489,189 sq. mi.
1,267,000 sq. km.
Population: 9,388,859
Capital: Niamey
Largest City: Niamey
Highest Point: Bagzane
Monetary Unit: CFA franc

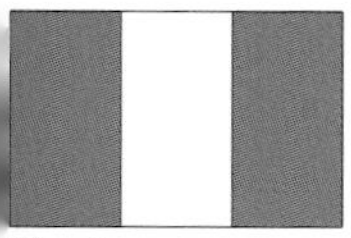

Nigeria
Page/Location: 76/G6
Area: 356,668 sq. mi.
923,770 sq. km.
Population: 107,129,469
Capital: Abuja
Largest City: Lagos
Highest Point: Dimlang
Monetary Unit: naira

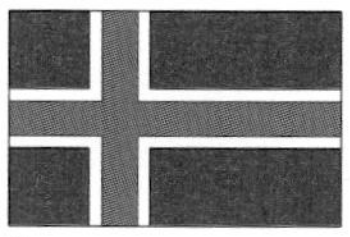

Norway
Page/Location: 20/C3
Area: 125,053 sq. mi.
323,887 sq. km.
Population: 4,404,456
Capital: Oslo
Largest City: Oslo
Highest Point: Glittertjnden
Monetary Unit: Norwegian krone

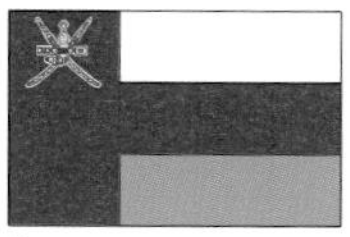

Oman
Page/Location: 53/G4
Area: 82,031 sq. mi.
212,460 sq. km.
Population: 2,264,590
Capital: Muscat
Largest City: Muscat
Highest Point: Jabal ash Shām
Monetary Unit: Omani rial

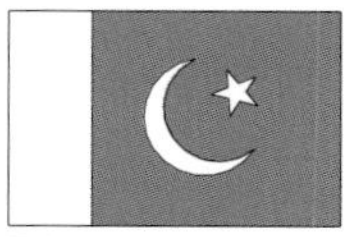

Pakistan
Page/Location: 53/H3
Area: 310,403 sq. mi.
803,944 sq. km.
Population: 132,185,299
Capital: Islāmābād
Largest City: Karāchi
Highest Point: K2 (Godwin Austen)
Monetary Unit: Pakistani rupee

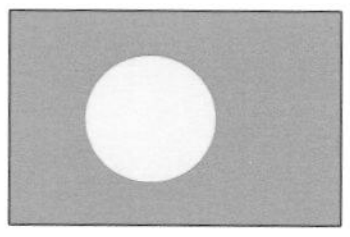

Palau
Page/Location: 68/C4
Area: 177 sq. mi.
458 sq. km.
Population: 17,240
Capital: Koror
Largest City: Koror
Highest Point: 699 ft. (213m)
Monetary Unit: U.S. dollar

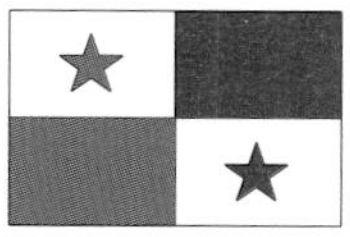

Panama
Page/Location: 103/F4
Area: 30,193 sq. mi.
78,200 sq. km.
Population: 2,693,417
Capital: Panamá
Largest City: Panamá
Highest Point: Barú
Monetary Unit: balboa

World Flags and Reference Guide

Papua New Guinea
Page/Location: 68/D5
Area: 178,259 sq. mi.
461,690 sq. km.
Population: 4,496,221
Capital: Port Moresby
Largest City: Port Moresby
Highest Point: Mt. Wilhelm
Monetary Unit: kina

Paraguay
Page/Location: 105/D5
Area: 157,047 sq. mi.
406,752 sq. km.
Population: 5,651,634;
Capital: Asunción
Largest City: Asunción
Highest Point: Sierra de Amambay
Monetary Unit: guaraní

Peru
Page/Location: 106/C5
Area: 496,222 sq. mi.
1,285,215 sq. km.
Population: 24,949,512
Capital: Lima
Largest City: Lima
Highest Point: Nevado Huascarán
Monetary Unit: nuevo sol

Philippines
Page/Location: 48/M8
Area: 115,830 sq. mi.
300,000 sq. km.
Population: 76,103,564
Capital: Manila
Largest City: Manila
Highest Point: Mt. Apo
Monetary Unit: Philippine peso

Poland
Page/Location: 27/K2
Area: 120,725 sq. mi.
312,678 sq. km.
Population: 38,700,291
Capital: Warsaw
Largest City: Warsaw
Highest Point: Rysy
Monetary Unit: zloty

Portugal
Page/Location: 34/A3
Area: 35,549 sq. mi.
92,072 sq. km.
Population: 9,867,654
Capital: Lisbon
Largest City: Lisbon
Highest Point: Serra da Estrela
Monetary Unit: Portuguese escudo

Qatar
Page/Location: 52/F3
Area: 4,247 sq. mi.
11,000 sq. km.
Population: 665,485
Capital: Doha
Largest City: Doha
Highest Point: Dukhān Heights
Monetary Unit: Qatari riyal

Romania
Page/Location: 41/F3
Area: 91,699 sq. mi.
237,500 sq. km.
Population: 21,399,114
Capital: Bucharest
Largest City: Bucharest
Highest Point: Moldoveanul
Monetary Unit: leu

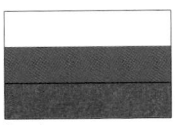

Russia
Page/Location: 46/H3
Area: 6,592,812 sq. mi.
17,075,400 sq. km.
Population: 147,987,101
Capital: Moscow
Largest City: Moscow
Highest Point: El'brus
Monetary Unit: Russian ruble

Rwanda
Page/Location: 82/E1
Area: 10,169 sq. mi.
26,337 sq. km.
Population: 7,737,537
Capital: Kigali
Largest City: Kigali
Highest Point: Karisimbi
Monetary Unit: Rwanda franc

Saint Kitts and Nevis
Page/Location: 104/F3
Area: 104 sq. mi.
269 sq. km.
Population: 41,803
Capital: Basseterre
Largest City: Basseterre
Highest Point: Mt. Misery
Monetary Unit: East Caribbean dollar

Saint Lucia
Page/Location: 104/F4
Area: 238 sq. mi.
616 sq. km.
Population: 159,639
Capital: Castries
Largest City: Castries
Highest Point: Mt. Gimie
Monetary Unit: East Caribbean dollar

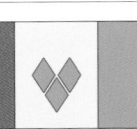

Saint Vincent and the Grenadines
Page/Location: 104/F4
Area: 131 sq. mi.
340 sq. km.
Population: 119,092
Capital: Kingstown
Largest City: Kingstown
Highest Point: Soufrière
Monetary Unit: East Caribbean dollar

Samoa
Page/Location: 69/H6
Area: 1,104 sq. mi.
2,860 sq. km.
Population: 219,509
Capital: Apia
Largest City: Apia
Highest Point: Mt. Silisili
Monetary Unit: tala

San Marino
Page/Location: 33/K5
Area: 23.4 sq. mi.
60.6 sq. km.
Population: 24,714
Capital: San Marino
Largest City: San Marino
Highest Point: Monte Titano
Monetary Unit: Italian lira

São Tomé and Príncipe
Page/Location: 76/G7
Area: 371 sq. mi.
960 sq. km.
Population: 147,865
Capital: São Tomé
Largest City: São Tomé
Highest Point: Pico de São Tomé
Monetary Unit: dobra

Saudi Arabia
Page/Location: 104/F3
Area: 756,981 sq. mi.
1,960,582 sq. km.
Population: 20,087,965
Capital: Riyadh
Largest City: Riyadh
Highest Point: Jabal Sawdā'
Monetary Unit: Saudi riyal

Senegal
Page/Location: 78/B3
Area: 75,954 sq. mi.
196,720 sq. km.
Population: 9,403,546
Capital: Dakar
Largest City: Dakar
Highest Point: Fouta Djallon
Monetary Unit: CFA franc

Seychelles
Page/Location: 74/H5
Area: 176 sq. mi.
455 sq. km.
Population: 78,142
Capital: Victoria
Largest City: Victoria
Highest Point: Morne Seychellois
Monetary Unit: Seychelles rupee

Sierra Leone
Page/Location: 78/B4
Area: 27,699 sq. mi.
71,740 sq. km.
Population: 4,891,546
Capital: Freetown
Largest City: Freetown
Highest Point: Loma Mansa
Monetary Unit: leone

Singapore
Page/Location: 66/B3
Area: 244 sq. mi.
632.6 sq. km.
Population: 3,461,929
Capital: Singapore
Largest City: Singapore
Highest Point: Bukit Timah
Monetary Unit: Singapore dollar

Slovakia
Page/Location: 27/K4
Area: 18,924 sq. mi.
49,013 sq. km.
Population: 5,393,016
Capital: Bratislava
Largest City: Bratislava
Highest Point: Gerlachovský Štít
Monetary Unit: Slovak koruna

Slovenia
Page/Location: 40/B3
Area: 7,898 sq. mi.
20,456 sq. km.
Population: 1,945,998
Capital: Ljubljana
Largest City: Ljubljana
Highest Point: Triglav
Monetary Unit: tolar

Solomon Islands
Page/Location: 68/E6
Area: 11,500 sq. mi.
29,785 sq. km.
Population: 462,855
Capital: Honiara
Largest City: Honiara
Highest Point: Mt. Makarakomburu
Monetary Unit: Solomon Islands dollar

Somalia
Page/Location: 77/Q6
Area: 246,200 sq. mi.
637,658 sq. km.
Population: 9,940,232
Capital: Mogadishu
Largest City: Mogadishu
Highest Point: Shimber Berris
Monetary Unit: Somali shilling

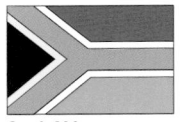

South Africa
Page/Location: 80/C3
Area: 471,008 sq. mi.
1,219,912 sq. km.
Population: 42,327,458
Capital: Cape Town; Pretoria
Largest City: Johannesburg
Highest Point: Injasuti
Monetary Unit: rand

Spain
Page/Location: 34/C2
Area: 194,881 sq. mi.
504,742 sq. km.
Population: 39,244,195
Capital: Madrid
Largest City: Madrid
Highest Point: Pico de Teide
Monetary Unit: peseta

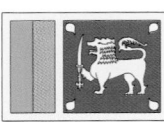

Sri Lanka
Page/Location: 62/D6
Area: 25,332 sq. mi.
65,610 sq. km.
Population: 18,762,075
Capital: Colombo
Largest City: Colombo
Highest Point: Pidurutalagala
Monetary Unit: Sri Lanka rupee

Sudan
Page/Location: 77/L5
Area: 967,494 sq. mi.
2,505,809 sq. km.
Population: 32,594,128
Capital: Khartoum
Largest City: Omdurman
Highest Point: Jabal Marrah
Monetary Unit: Sudanese pound

Suriname
Page/Location: 107/G3
Area: 63,039 sq. mi.
163,270 sq. km.
Population: 443,446
Capital: Paramaribo
Largest City: Paramaribo
Highest Point: Juliana Top
Monetary Unit: Suriname guilder

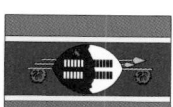

Swaziland
Page/Location: 81/E2
Area: 6,705 sq. mi.
17,366 sq. km.
Population: 1,031,600
Capital: Mbabane; Lobamba
Largest City: Mbabane
Highest Point: Emlembe
Monetary Unit: lilangeni

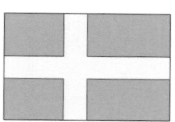

Sweden
Page/Location: 20/E3
Area: 173,665 sq. mi.
449,792 sq. km.
Population: 8,946,193
Capital: Stockholm
Largest City: Stockholm
Highest Point: Kebnekaise
Monetary Unit: krona

Switzerland
Page/Location: 36/D4
Area: 15,943 sq. mi.
41,292 sq. km.
Population: 7,248,984
Capital: Bern
Largest City: Zürich
Highest Point: Dufourspitze
Monetary Unit: Swiss franc

Syria
Page/Location: 50/D3
Area: 71,498 sq. mi.
185,180 sq. km.
Population: 16,137,899
Capital: Damascus
Largest City: Damascus
Highest Point: Jabal ash Shaykh
Monetary Unit: Syrian pound

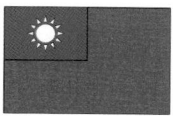

Taiwan
Page/Location: 61/J3
Area: 13,971 sq. mi.
36,185 sq. km.
Population: 21,655,515
Capital: T'aipei
Largest City: T'aipei
Highest Point: Yü Shan
Monetary Unit: new Taiwan dollar

Tajikistan
Page/Location: 46/H6
Area: 55,251 sq. mi.
143,100 sq. km.
Population: 6,013,855
Capital: Dushanbe
Largest City: Dushanbe
Highest Point: Communism Peak
Monetary Unit: Tajikistani ruble

Tanzania
Page/Location: 82/F2
Area: 364,699 sq. mi.
945,090 sq. km.
Population: 29,460,753
Capital: Dar es Salaam
Largest City: Dar es Salaam
Highest Point: Kilimanjaro
Monetary Unit: Tanzanian shilling

Thailand
Page/Location: 65/C3
Area: 198,455 sq. mi.
513,998 sq. km.
Population: 59,450,818
Capital: Bangkok
Largest City: Bangkok
Highest Point: Doi Inthanon
Monetary Unit: baht

Togo
Page/Location: 79/F4
Area: 21,927 sq. mi.
56,790 sq. km.
Population: 4,735,610
Capital: Lomé
Largest City: Lomé
Highest Point: Mt. Agou
Monetary Unit: CFA franc

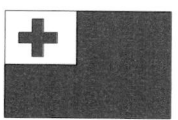

Tonga
Page/Location: 69/H7
Area: 289 sq. mi.
748 sq. km.
Population: 107,335
Capital: Nuku'alofa
Largest City: Nuku'alofa
Highest Point: Kao Island
Monetary Unit: pa'anga

Trinidad and Tobago
Page/Location: 104/F5
Area: 1,980 sq. mi.
5,128 sq. km.
Population: 1,273,141
Capital: Port-of-Spain
Largest City: Port-of-Spain
Highest Point: El Cerro del Aripo
Monetary Unit: Trin. & Tobago dollar

Tunisia
Page/Location: 76/G1
Area: 63,170 sq. mi.
163,610 sq. km.
Population: 9,183,097
Capital: Tūnis
Largest City: Tūnis
Highest Point: Jabal ash Sha'nabī
Monetary Unit: Tunisian dinar

Turkey
Page/Location: 50/C2
Area: 301,382 sq. mi.
780,580 sq. km.
Population: 63,528,225
Capital: Ankara
Largest City: Istanbul
Highest Point: Mt. Ararat
Monetary Unit: Turkish lira

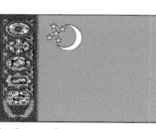

Turkmenistan
Page/Location: 46/F6
Area: 188,455 sq. mi.
488,100 sq. km.
Population: 4,225,351
Capital: Ashgabat
Largest City: Ashgabat
Highest Point: Rize
Monetary Unit: manat

Tuvalu
Page/Location: 68/G5
Area: 9.78 sq. mi.
25.33 sq. km.
Population: 10,297
Capital: Funafuti
Largest City: —
Highest Point: 16 ft. (5 m)
Monetary Unit: Australian dollar

Uganda
Page/Location: 77/M7
Area: 91,076 sq. mi.
235,887 sq. km.
Population: 20,604,874
Capital: Kampala
Largest City: Kampala
Highest Point: Margherita Peak
Monetary Unit: Ugandan shilling

Ukraine
Page/Location: 44/D2
Area: 233,089 sq. mi.
603,700 sq. km.
Population: 50,684,635
Capital: Kiev
Largest City: Kiev
Highest Point: Goverla
Monetary Unit: hryvnia

United Arab Emirates
Page/Location: 52/F4
Area: 29,182 sq. mi.
75,581 sq. km.
Population: 2,262,309
Capital: Abu Dhabi
Largest City: Dubayy
Highest Point: Hajar Mts.
Monetary Unit: Emirian dirham

United Kingdom
Page/Location: 21
Area: 94,399 sq. mi.
244,493 sq. km.
Population: 58,610,182
Capital: London
Largest City: London
Highest Point: Ben Nevis
Monetary Unit: pound sterling

United States
Page/Location: 88
Area: 3,618,765 sq. mi.
9,372,610 sq. km.
Population: 267,954,767
Capital: Washington, D.C.
Largest City: New York
Highest Point: Mt. McKinley
Monetary Unit: U.S. dollar

Uruguay
Page/Location: 109/E3
Area: 68,039 sq. mi.
176,220 sq. km.
Population: 3,261,707
Capital: Montevideo
Largest City: Montevideo
Highest Point: Cerro Catedral
Monetary Unit: Uruguayan peso

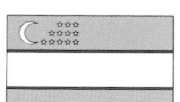

Uzbekistan
Page/Location: 46/G5
Area: 172,741 sq. mi.
447,400 sq. km.
Population: 23,860,452
Capital: Tashkent
Largest City: Tashkent
Highest Point: Khodzha-Pir'yakh
Monetary Unit: som

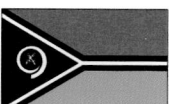

Vanuatu
Page/Location: 68/F6
Area: 5,700 sq. mi.
14,763 sq. km.
Population: 181,358
Capital: Port-Vila
Largest City: Port-Vila
Highest Point: Tabwemasana
Monetary Unit: vatu

Vatican City
Page/Location: 38/C2
Area: 0.17 sq. mi.
0.44 sq. km.
Population: 830
Capital: —
Largest City: —
Highest Point: —
Monetary Unit: Vatican lira

Venezuela
Page/Location: 106/E2
Area: 352,143 sq. mi.
912,050 sq. km.
Population: 22,396,407
Capital: Caracas
Largest City: Caracas
Highest Point: Pico Bolívar
Monetary Unit: bolívar

Vietnam
Page/Location: 65/D2
Area: 127,243 sq. mi.
329,560 sq. km.
Population: 75,123,880
Capital: Hanoi
Largest City: Ho Chi Minh City
Highest Point: Fan Si Pan
Monetary Unit: new dong

Yemen
Page/Location: 52/E5
Area: 203,849 sq. mi.
527,970 sq. km.
Population: 13,972,477
Capital: Sanaa
Largest City: Aden
Highest Point: Nabī Shu'ayb
Monetary Unit: Yemeni rial

Yugoslavia
Page/Location: 40/E3
Area: 39,517 sq. mi.
102,350 sq. km.
Population: 10,655,317
Capital: Belgrade
Largest City: Belgrade
Highest Point: Đaravica
Monetary Unit: Yugoslav new dinar

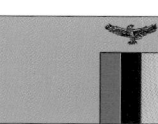

Zambia
Page/Location: 82/E3
Area: 290,586 sq. mi.
752,618 sq. km.
Population: 9,349,975
Capital: Lusaka
Largest City: Lusaka
Highest Point: Sunzu
Monetary Unit: Zambian kwacha

Zimbabwe
Page/Location: 82/E4
Area: 150,803 sq. mi.
390,580 sq. km.
Population: 11,423,175
Capital: Harare
Largest City: Harare
Highest Point: Inyangani
Monetary Unit: Zimbabwe dollar

World Statistics

	Mean Distance from Sun: in Miles	in Kilometers	Period of Revolution around Sun	Period of Rotation on Axis	Equatorial Diameter in Miles	in Kilometers	Surface Gravity (Earth = 1)	Mass (Earth = 1)	Mean Density (Water = 1)	Number of Satellites
Mercury	35,990,000	57,900,000	87.97 days	58.7 days	3,032	4,880	0.38	0.055	5.4	0
Venus	67,240,000	108,200,000	224.70 days	243.7 days†	7,521	12,104	0.91	0.815	5.2	0
Earth	93,000,000	149,700,000	365.26 days	23h 56m	7,926	12,755	1.00	1.00	5.5	1
Mars	141,610,000	227,900,000	686.98 days	24h 37m	4,221	6,794	0.38	0.107	3.9	2
Jupiter	483,675,000	778,400,000	11.86 years	9h 55m	88,846	142,984	2.36	317.8	1.3	16
Saturn	886,572,000	1,426,800,000	29.46 years	10h 30m	74,898	120,536	0.92	95.2	0.7	18
Uranus	1,783,957,000	2,871,000,000	84.01 years	17h 14m†	31,763	51,118	0.89	14.5	1.3	15
Neptune	2,795,114,000	4,498,300,000	164.79 years	16h 6m	30,778	49,532	1.13	17.1	1.6	8
Pluto	3,670,000,000	5,906,400,000	247.70 years	6.4 days†	1,413	2,274	0.07	0.002	2.1	1

† Retrograde motion

Source: NASA, National Space Science Data Center

DIMENSIONS OF THE EARTH

	Area in: Sq. Miles	Sq. Kilometers
Superficial area	196,939,000	510,072,000
Land surface	57,506,000	148,940,000
Water surface	139,433,000	361,132,000

	Distance in: Miles	Kilometers
Equatorial circumference	24,902	40,075
Polar circumference	24,860	40,007
Equatorial diameter	7,926.4	12,756.4
Polar diameter	7,899.8	12,713.6
Equatorial radius	3,963.2	6,378.2
Polar radius	3,949.9	6,356.8

Volume of the Earth	2.6×10^{11} cubic miles	10.84×10^{11} cubic kilometers
Mass or weight	6.6×10^{21} short tons	6.0×10^{21} metric tons
Maximum distance from Sun	94,600,000 miles	152,000,000 kilometers
Minimum distance from Sun	91,300,000 miles	147,000,000 kilometers

OCEANS AND MAJOR SEAS

	Area in: Sq. Miles	Sq. Kms.	Greatest Depth in: Feet	Meters
Pacific Ocean	63,855,000	166,241,000	36,198	11,033
Atlantic Ocean	31,744,000	82,217,000	28,374	8,648
Indian Ocean	28,417,000	73,600,000	25,344	7,725
Arctic Ocean	5,427,000	14,056,000	17,880	5,450
Caribbean Sea	970,000	2,512,300	24,720	7,535
Mediterranean Sea	969,000	2,509,700	16,896	5,150
South China Sea	895,000	2,318,000	15,000	4,600
Bering Sea	875,000	2,266,250	15,800	4,800
Gulf of Mexico	600,000	1,554,000	12,300	3,750
Sea of Okhotsk	590,000	1,528,100	11,070	3,370
East China Sea	482,000	1,248,400	9,500	2,900
Yellow Sea	480,000	1,243,200	350	107
Sea of Japan	389,000	1,007,500	12,280	3,740
Hudson Bay	317,500	822,300	846	258
North Sea	222,000	575,000	2,200	670
Black Sea	185,000	479,150	7,365	2,245
Red Sea	169,000	437,700	7,200	2,195
Baltic Sea	163,000	422,170	1,506	459

THE CONTINENTS

	Area in: Sq. Miles	Sq. Kms.	Percent of World's Land
Asia	17,128,500	44,362,815	29.5
Africa	11,707,000	30,321,130	20.2
North America	9,363,000	24,250,170	16.2
South America	6,879,725	17,818,505	11.9
Antarctica	5,405,000	14,000,000	9.4
Europe	4,057,000	10,507,630	7.0
Australia	2,967,893	7,686,850	5.1

MAJOR SHIP CANALS

	Length in: Miles	Kms.	Minimum Depth in: Feet	Meters
Volga-Baltic, Russia	225	362	–	
Baltic-White Sea, Russia	140	225	16	
Suez, Egypt	100.76	162	42	1
Albert, Belgium	80	129	16.5	5
Moscow-Volga, Russia	80	129	18	
Volga-Don, Russia	62	100	–	
Göta, Sweden	54	87	10	
Kiel (Nord-Ostsee), Germany	53.2	86	38	1
Panama Canal, Panama	50.72	82	41.6	1
Houston Ship, U.S.A.	50	81	36	1

LARGEST ISLANDS

	Area in: Sq. Miles	Sq. Kms.		Area in: Sq. Miles	Sq. Kms.		Area in: Sq. Miles	Sq. Kms.
Greenland	840,000	2,175,600	Hispaniola, Haiti & Dom. Rep.	29,399	76,143	Somerset, Canada	9,570	24,786
New Guinea	305,000	789,950	Banks, Canada	27,038	70,028	Sardinia, Italy	9,301	24,090
Borneo	286,000	740,740	Ceylon,Sri Lanka	25,332	65,610	Shikoku, Japan	6,860	17,761
Madagascar	226,656	587,040	Tasmania, Australia	24,600	63,710	New Caledonia, France	6,530	16,913
Baffin, Canada	195,928	507,454	Svalbard, Norway	23,957	62,049	Nordaustlandet, Norway	6,409	16,599
Sumatra, Indonesia	164,000	424,760	Devon, Canada	21,331	55,247	Samar, Philippines	5,050	13,080
Honshu, Japan	88,000	227,920	Novaya Zemlya (north isl.), Russia	18,600	48,200	Negros, Philippines	4,906	12,704
Great Britain	84,400	218,896	Marajó, Brazil	17,991	46,597	Palawan, Philippines	4,550	11,785
Victoria, Canada	83,896	217,290	Tierra del Fuego, Chile & Argentina	17,900	46,360	Panay, Philippines	4,446	11,515
Ellesmere, Canada	75,767	196,236	Alexander, Antarctica	16,700	43,250	Jamaica	4,232	10,961
Celebes, Indonesia	72,986	189,034	Axel Heiberg, Canada	16,671	43,178	Hawaii, United States	4,038	10,456
South I., New Zealand	58,393	151,238	Melville, Canada	16,274	42,150	Viti Levu, Fiji	4,010	10,388
Java, Indonesia	48,842	126,501	Southhampton, Canada	15,913	41,215	Cape Breton, Canada	3,981	10,311
North I., New Zealand	44,187	114,444	New Britain, Papua New Guinea	14,100	36,519	Mindoro, Philippines	3,759	9,735
Cuba	42,803	110,860	Taiwan, China	13,836	35,835	Kodiak, Alaska, U.S.A.	3,670	9,505
Newfoundland, Canada	42,031	108,860	Kyushu, Japan	13,770	35,664	Cyprus	3,572	9,251
Luzon, Philippines	40,420	104,688	Hainan, China	13,127	33,999	Puerto Rico, U.S.A.	3,435	8,897
Iceland	39,768	103,000	Prince of Wales, Canada	12,872	33,338	Corsica, France	3,352	8,681
Mindanao, Philippines	36,537	94,631	Spitsbergen, Norway	12,355	31,999	New Ireland, Papua New Guinea	3,340	8,651
Ireland	32,589	84,406	Vancouver, Canada	12,079	31,285	Crete, Greece	3,218	8,336
Hokkaidō, Japan	30,436	78,829	Timor, Indonesia	11,527	29,855	Anticosti, Canada	3,066	7,941
Sakhalin, Russia	29,500	76,405	Sicily, Italy	9,926	25,708	Wrangel, Russia	2,819	7,300

PRINCIPAL MOUNTAINS

	Height in: Feet	Meters
Everest, Nepal-China	29,028	8,848
K2 (Godwin Austen), Pakistan-China	28,250	8,611
Kanchenjunga, Nepal-India	28,208	8,598
Lhotse, Nepal-China	27,923	8,511
Makalu, Nepal-China	27,789	8,470
Dhaulagiri, Nepal	26,810	8,172
Nanga Parbat, Pakistan	26,660	8,126
Annapurna, Nepal	26,504	8,078
Nanda Devi, India	25,645	7,817
Rakaposhi, Pakistan	25,550	7,788
Kongur Shan, China	25,325	7,719
Tirich Mir, Pakistan	25,230	7,690
Gongga Shan, China	24,790	7,556
Ismail Samani Peak, Tajikistan	24,590	7,495
Pobedy Peak, Kyrgyzstan	24,406	7,439
Chomo Lhari, Bhutan-China	23,997	7,314
Muztag, China	23,891	7,282
Cerro Aconcagua, Argentina	22,831	6,959
Ojos del Salado, Chile-Argentina	22,572	6,880
Bonete, Chile-Argentina	22,546	6,872
Tupungato, Chile-Argentina	22,310	6,800
Pissis, Argentina	22,241	6,779
Mercedario, Argentina	22,211	6,770
Huascarán, Peru	22,205	6,768
Llullaillaco, Chile-Argentina	22,057	6,723
Nevada Ancohuma, Bolivia	21,489	6,550
Chimborazo, Ecuador	20,561	6,267
McKinley, Alaska	20,320	6,194
Logan, Yukon, Canada	19,524	5,951
Cotopaxi, Ecuador	19,347	5,897
Kilimanjaro, Tanzania	19,340	5,895
El Misti, Peru	19,101	5,822
Pico Cristóbal Colón, Colombia	18,947	5,775
Huila, Colombia	18,865	5,750
Citlaltépetl (Orizaba), Mexico	18,700	5,700
Damavand, Iran	18,605	5,671
El'brus, Russia	18,510	5,642
St. Elias, Alaska, U.S.A.-Yukon, Canada	18,008	5,489
Dykh-tau, Russia	17,070	5,203
Batian (Kenya), Kenya	17,058	5,199
Ararat, Turkey	16,946	5,165
Vinson Massif, Antarctica	16,864	5,140
Margherita (Ruwenzori), Africa	16,795	5,119
Kazbek, Georgia-Russia	16,558	5,047
Puncak Jaya, Indonesia	16,503	5,030
Blanc, France	15,771	4,807
Klyuchevskaya Sopka, Russia	15,584	4,750
Fairweather, Br. Col., Canada	15,300	4,663
Dufourspitze (Mte. Rosa), Italy-Switzerland	15,203	4,634
Ras Dashen, Ethiopia	15,157	4,620
Matterhorn, Switzerland	14,691	4,478
Whitney, California, U.S.A.	14,494	4,418
Elbert, Colorado, U.S.A.	14,433	4,399
Rainier, Washington, U.S.A.	14,410	4,392
Shasta, California, U.S.A.	14,162	4,317
Pikes Peak, Colorado, U.S.A.	14,110	4,301
Finsteraarhorn, Switzerland	14,022	4,274
Mauna Kea, Hawaii, U.S.A.	13,796	4,205
Mauna Loa, Hawaii, U.S.A.	13,677	4,169
Jungfrau, Switzerland	13,642	4,158
Grossglockner, Austria	12,457	3,797
Fujiyama, Japan	12,389	3,776
Cook, New Zealand	12,349	3,764

LONGEST RIVERS

	Length in: Miles	Kms.
Nile, Africa	4,145	6,671
Amazon, S. America	4,007	6,448
Mississippi-Missouri-Red Rock, U.S.A.	3,710	5,971
Chang Jiang (Yangtze), China	3,500	5,633
Ob'-Irtysh, Russia-Kazakhstan	3,362	5,411
Yenisey-Angara, Russia	3,100	4,989
Huang He (Yellow), China	2,950	4,747
Congo (Zaire), Africa	2,780	4,474
Amur-Shilka-Onon, Asia	2,744	4,416
Lena, Russia	2,734	4,400
Mackenzie-Peace-Finlay, Canada	2,635	4,241
Paraná-La Plata, S. America	2,630	4,232
Mekong, Asia	2,610	4,200
Niger, Africa	2,580	4,152
Missouri-Red Rock, U.S.A.	2,564	4,125
Yenisey, Russia	2,500	4,028
Mississippi, U.S.A.	2,348	3,778
Murray-Darling, Australia	2,310	3,718
Volga, Russia	2,290	3,685
Madeira, S. America	2,013	3,240
Purus, S. America	1,995	3,211
Yukon, Alaska-Canada	1,979	3,185
Zambezi, Africa	1,950	3,138
São Francisco, Brazil	1,930	3,106
St. Lawrence, Canada-U.S.A.	1,900	3,058
Rio Grande, Mexico-U.S.A.	1,885	3,034
Syrdar'ya-Naryn, Asia	1,859	2,992
Indus, Asia	1,800	2,897
Danube, Europe	1,775	2,857
Brahmaputra, Asia	1,700	2,736
Tocantins, Brazil	1,677	2,699
Salween, Asia	1,675	2,696
Euphrates, Asia	1,650	2,655
Xi (Si), China	1,650	2,655
Amu Darya, Asia	1,616	2,601
Nelson-Saskatchewan, Canada	1,600	2,575
Orinoco, S. America	1,600	2,575
Paraguay, S. America	1,584	2,549
Kolyma, Russia	1,562	2,514
Ganges, Asia	1,550	2,494
Ural, Russia-Kazakhstan	1,509	2,428
Japurá, S. America	1,500	2,414
Arkansas, U.S.A.	1,450	2,334
Colorado, U.S.A.-Mexico	1,450	2,334
Negro, S. America	1,400	2,253
Dnepr, Russia-Belarus-Ukraine	1,368	2,202
Orange, Africa	1,350	2,173
Irrawaddy, Myanmar	1,325	2,132
Brazos, U.S.A.	1,309	2,107
Ohio-Allegheny, U.S.A.	1,306	2,102
Kama, Russia	1,252	2,031
Don, Russia	1,222	1,967
Red, U.S.A.	1,222	1,966
Columbia, U.S.A.-Canada	1,214	1,953
Tigris, Asia	1,181	1,901
Darling, Australia	1,160	1,867
Angara, Russia	1,135	1,827
Sungari, Asia	1,130	1,819
Pechora, Russia	1,124	1,809
Snake, U.S.A.	1,038	1,670
Churchill, Canada	1,000	1,609
Pilcomayo, S. America	1,000	1,609
Uruguay, S. America	994	1,600
Platte-N. Platte, U.S.A.	990	1,593
Ohio, U.S.A.	981	1,578
Magdalena, Colombia	956	1,538
Pecos, U.S.A.	926	1,490
Oka, Russia	918	1,477
Canadian, U.S.A.	906	1,458
Colorado, Texas, U.S.A.	894	1,439
Dniester, Ukraine-Moldova	876	1,410
Fraser, Canada	850	1,369
Rhine, Europe	820	1,319
Northern Dvina, Russia	809	1,302
Ottawa, Canada	790	1,271

PRINCIPAL NATURAL LAKES

	Area in: Sq. Miles	Sq. Kms.	Max. Depth in: Feet	Meters
Caspian Sea, Asia	143,243	370,999	3,264	995
Lake Superior, U.S.A.-Canada	31,820	82,414	1,329	405
Lake Victoria, Africa	26,628	69,215	270	82
Lake Huron, U.S.A.-Canada	23,010	59,596	748	228
Lake Michigan, U.S.A.	22,400	58,016	923	281
Aral Sea, Kazakhstan-Uzbekistan	15,830	41,000	213	65
Lake Tanganyika, Africa	12,650	32,764	4,700	1,433
Lake Baykal, Russia	12,162	31,500	5,316	1,620
Great Bear Lake, Canada	12,096	31,328	1,356	413
Lake Nyasa (Malawi), Africa	11,555	29,928	2,320	707
Great Slave Lake, Canada	11,031	28,570	2,015	614
Lake Erie, U.S.A.-Canada	9,940	25,745	210	64
Lake Winnipeg, Canada	9,417	24,390	60	18
Lake Ontario, U.S.A.-Canada	7,540	19,529	775	244
Lake Balkhash, Kazakhstan	7,081	18,340	87	27
Lake Ladoga, Russia	6,900	17,871	738	225
Lake Maracaibo, Venezuela	5,120	13,261	100	31
Lake Chad, Africa*	10,000 –	25,900 –		
	4,000	10,360	25	8
Lake Onega, Russia	3,761	9,741	377	115
Lake Eyre, Australia*	3,500-0	9,000-0	–	–
Lake Titicaca, Peru-Bolivia	3,200	8,288	1,000	305
Lake Nicaragua, Nicaragua	3,100	8,029	230	70
Lake Athabasca, Canada	3,064	7,936	400	122
Reindeer Lake, Canada*	2,568	6,651	–	–
Lake Turkana (Rudolf), Africa	2,463	6,379	240	73
Ysyk-Köl, Kyrgyzstan	2,425	6,281	2,303	702
Lake Torrens, Australia*	2,230	5,776	–	–
Vänern, Sweden	2,156	5,584	328	100
Nettilling Lake, Canada*	2,140	5,543	–	–
Lake Winnipegosis, Canada	2,075	5,374	38	12
Lake Mobutu Sese Seko (Albert), Africa	2,075	5,374	160	49
Kariba Lake, Zambia-Zimbabwe	2,050	5,310	295	90
Lake Nipigon, Canada	1,872	4,848	540	165
Lake Mweru, Dem. Rep. of the Congo-Zambia	1,800	4,662	60	18
Lake Manitoba, Canada	1,799	4,659	12	4
Lake Taymyr, Russia	1,737	4,499	85	26
Lake Khanka, China-Russia	1,700	4,403	33	10
Lake Kioga, Uganda	1,700	4,403	25	8
Lake of the Woods, U.S.A.-Canada	1,679	4,349	70	21

* Area and depth figures subject to great seasonal variations.

ARCTIC OCEAN

CANADA
BASIN

Beaufort Sea

Wrangel I.

Pt. Barrow

Banks I.

Victoria I.

Ellesmere I.

QUEEN ELIZABETH
ISLANDS

Devon I.

GREENLAND

Gre

Chukchi
Sea

Baffin
Island

Baffin
Bay

Arctic Circle

Denmark Str.

Iceland

Norwe
Se

Bering Sea

ALEUTIAN
BASIN
ALEUTIAN   ISLANDS

Yukon

Mt. McKinley

Gulf of Alaska

ROCKY

Mackenzie

Great
Bear L.

Peace

Great
Slave L.

Hudson
Bay

LABRADOR
BASIN

IRMINGER BASIN

ICELAND BASIN

Great
Britain

ALEUTIAN   TRENCH

MOUNTAINS

NORTH

A

Great
Bear Penis.

CHARLIE-GIBBS
FRACTURE ZONE

MID-ATLANTIC RIDGE

Ireland

MENDOCINO FRACTURE ZONE

C. Mendocino

E

R

I

C

A

N

Missouri

Great
Lakes

Ohio

Appalachian Mts.

Newfoundland

C. Race

ATLANTIC

Atlas

HAWAIIAN

ISLANDS

MOLOKAI FRACTURE ZONE

Colorado

Lower

California

Rio
Grande

Mississippi

C. Hatteras

Gulf of
Mexico

Cuba

WEST

─26,232 ft.
(─8605 m)

S

e

a

HAWAIIAN RIDGE

Tropic of Cancer

Caribbean
Sea

INDIES

C. Verde

CENTRAL

PACIFIC

BASIN

CLIPPERTON FRACTURE ZONE

PACIFIC

GUATEMALA
BASIN

Orinoco

Negro

Amazon

ROMANCHE FRACTURE ZONE

Equator

PACIFIC

O C E A N

PERU

BASIN

PERU-CHILE TRENCH

Andes

Madeira

SOUTH

San Francisco

AMERICA

BRAZIL

BASIN

OCEA

BASIN

MID-ATLANTIC RIDGE

TONGA
TRENCH

Tropic of Capricorn

NAZCA RIDGE

CHILE

BASIN

─26,457 ft.
(─8064 m)

Cerro
Aconcagua

Paraná

KERMADEC
TRENCH

EAST   PACIFIC   RISE

PERU-CHILE TRENCH

Sur

Plundm

ARGENTINE

BASIN

SOUTHWEST

PACIFIC

BASIN

Falkland Is.

Tierra del Fuego

─27,313 ft.
(─8325 m)

SOUTH
SANDWICH
TRENCH

C. Horn

Drake Passage

PACIFIC-ANTARCTIC RIDGE

AMUNDSEN ABYSSAL PLAIN

Antarctic
Peninsula

WEDDELL

Antarctic Circle

Bellingshausen
Sea

ABYSSAL PLAIN

W e d d e l l

Ross Sea

ANTARCTICA

S e a

World

ARCTIC   O C E A N

-17,881 ft.
(-5450 m)

FRANZ JOSEF LAND

SEVERNAYA
ZEMLYA

NEW SIBERIAN IS.

SVALBARD

NOVAYA
ZEMLYA

Nordkapp

Kara
Sea

Laptev   Sea

Wrangel I.

Barents
Sea

Kjölen

S i b e r i a

Bering
Sea

EGIAN

L. Ladoga

Ob.

Yenisey

Lena

ALEUTIAN
BASIN

Baltic Sea

Volga

Irtysh

Angara

Vitim

Aldan

Kamchatka
Pen.

ALEUTIAN ISLANDS

ALEUTIAN TRENCH

E U R O P E

Dnieper

L. Baykal

Sea
of
Okhotsk

KURIL-KAMCHATKA TRENCH

Danube

Black Sea

Caspian Sea

Aral
Sea

L. Balkhash

A   S   I   A

Amur

Sakhalin

NORTHWEST

Mediterranean Sea

Gobi

Sea of
Japan

Honshu

JAPAN
TRENCH

PACIFIC

Euphrates

Kuntun

Huang

East
China
Sea

BASIN

FR-CA

Nile

Red Sea

Himalayas

Indus

Mt. Everest

Chang

P A C I F I C

Tropic of Cancer

Ganges

Mekong

Salween

Taiwan

MARIANA

RICA

Arabian
Sea

ARABIAN
BASIN

PHILIPPINE

MARIANA IS.

MARSHALL IS.

CENTRAL

Bay
of
Bengal

C. Comorin

Ceylon

Luzon

BASIN

TRENCH

Challenger Deep
-36,198 ft.
(-11,033 m)

PACIFIC

CARLSBERG
RIDGE

South
China
Sea

Mindanao

BASIN

Victoria

CEYLON
PLAIN

CAROLINE IS.

Kilimanjaro

SOMALI
BASIN

CENTRAL

Borneo

Equator

Congo

New Guinea

MELANESIAN
BASIN

INDIAN

Sumatra

Java

Celebes

O C E A N

Zambezi

RIDGE

28,343 ft.
(-7450 m)

JAVA TRENCH

Coral
Sea

Fiji Is.

Madagascar

NINETYEAST RIDGE

Great Barrier Reef

I N D I A N

Tropic of Capricorn

APE

Orange

BROKEN
PLATEAU

A U S T R A L I A

Tasman
Sea

North Cape

ood Hope

C. Leeuwin

North I.

ASIN

SOUTHWEST   INDIAN   RIDGE

O C E A N

S. AUSTRALIA BASIN

Tasmania

South I.

S Ridge

SOUTHEAST   INDIAN   RIDGE

KERGUELEN
PLATEAU

SOUTHEAST   INDIAN   RIDGE

ENDERBY ABYSSAL PLAIN

AUSTRALIAN-ANTARCTIC BASIN

Antarctic Circle

C. Adare

Amery
Ice Shelf

A N T A R C T I C A

Ross Sea

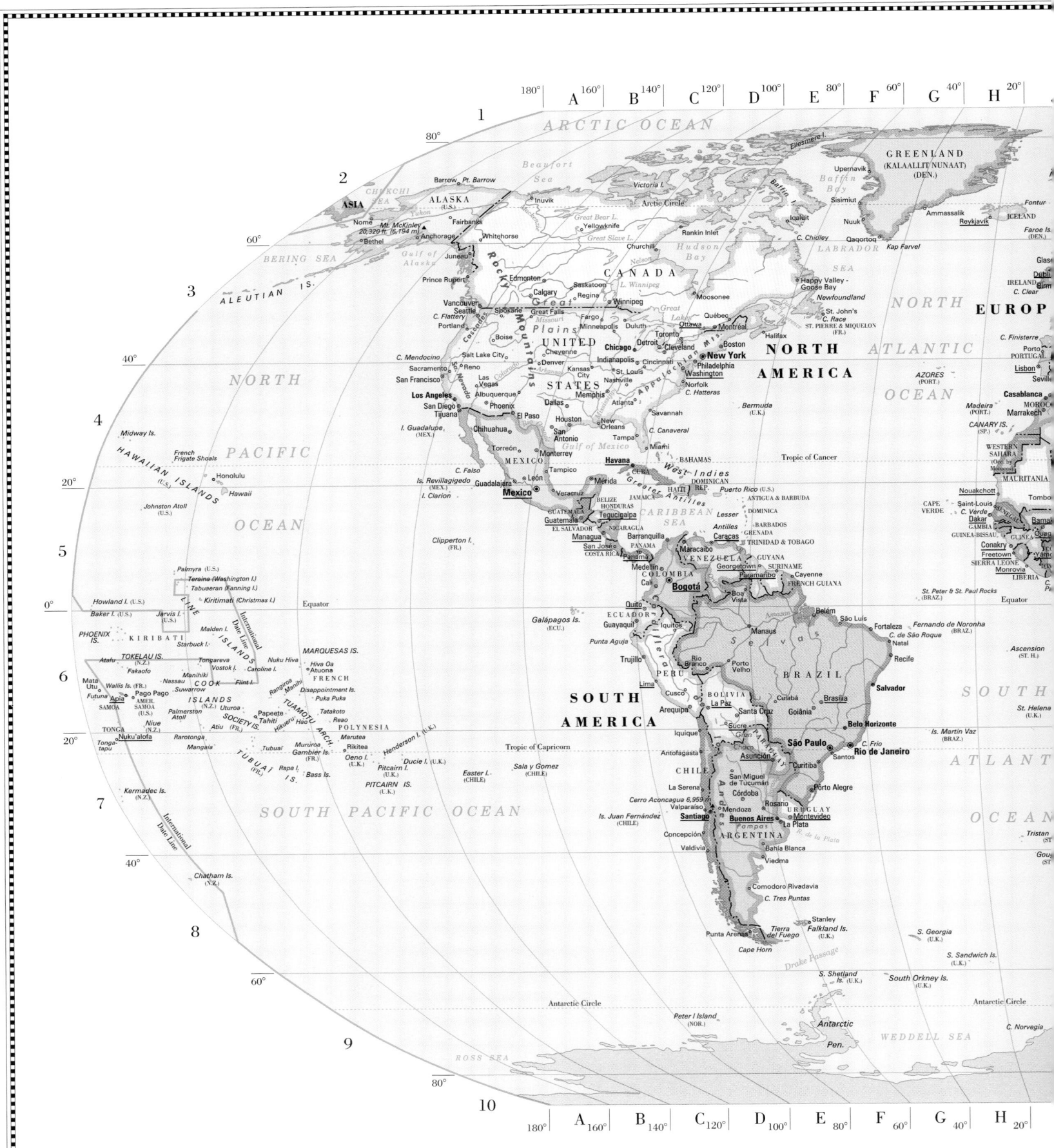

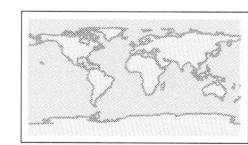

ARCTIC OCEAN

FRANZ JOSEF LAND (RUS.)

Severnaya Zemlya

New Siberian Is.

80°

BARENTS SEA

Novaya Zemlya

Kara Sea

Khatanga

Arctic Circle

Hammerfest
Tromsø
North Cape
Murmansk
Kiruna
Oulu
Archangel'sk
Nar'yan-Mar
Vorkuta
Salekhard
Noril'sk
Verkhoyansk
Anadyr'

FINLAND
Umeå
Tampere
Helsinki
SWEDEN
Göteborg
Oslo
EST.
St. Petersburg
Nizhniy Novgorod
Perm'
Izhevsk
Yekaterinburg
Syktyvkar
Surgut
Nizhnevartovsk
Tomsk
Yakutsk
Magadan

60°

RUSSIA

Siberia

BERING SEA

Kamchatka

Moscow
Yaroslavl'
Kazan'
Nizhniy Tagil
Chelyabinsk
Omsk
Novosibirsk
Krasnoyarsk
Bratsk
Bodaybo
Okhotsk
Petropavlovsk-Kamchatskiy
Mys Lopatka

Berlin
Warsaw
POLAND
Prague
Minsk
BELARUS
Tula
Ryazan'
Voronezh
Saratov
Samara
Ufa
Magnitogorsk
Novokuznetsk
Irkutsk
Ulan-Ude
Chita
Blagoveshchensk
Komsomol'sk-na-Amure
Khabarovsk
Sakhalin
OKHOTSK

UKRAINE
Kiev
Kharkiv
Donets'k
Rostov
Volgograd
Astrakhan'
Atyraū
Qaraghandy
Astana
Barnaul
Ulaanbaatar
Choybalsan
Qiqihar
Harbin
Vladivostok
KURIL IS.

Budapest
ROMANIA
Bucharest
MOL.
Odesa
KAZAKHSTAN
Aral Sea
L. Balkhash
Ili
MONGOLIA
Gobi
Shenyang
Changchun
Jilin
Hokkaido
Sapporo
Sea of Japan
N. KOREA

Belgrade
Sofia
Istanbul
Ankara
GEORGIA
El'brus 5,642 m
Astrakhan'
AZER.
Baku
UZBEKISTAN
Nukus
Aral
Bishkek
KYRGY STAN
Almaty
Yining
Ürümqi
Baotou
Beijing
Tianjin
Pyŏngyang
S. KOREA
Seoul
Pusan
Kyōto
Tōkyō
Yokohama

Rome
GREECE
Athens
İzmir
Adana
TURKEY
ARMENIA
Tabriz
TURKM ISTAN
Ashgabat
Dushanbe
TAJIKISTAN
Takla Makan
Yumen
Yinchuan
Lanzhou
Taiyuan
Jinan
Dalian
Qingdao
Ōsaka
Fukuoka
JAPAN
Kyūshū
Sendai
Honshu

CYPRUS
LEBANON
Damascus
SYRIA
ISRAEL
Amman
Baghdad
IRAQ
Mashhad
Tehrān
AFGHANISTAN
Kabul
Islāmābād
Tibet
CHINA
Xi'an
Chengdu
Lhasa
Kāthmāndu
BHUTAN
Huang
Zhengzhou
Nanjing
Wuhan
Shanghai
EAST CHINA SEA
RYUKYU IS.
Okinawa

Tripoli
Benghāzī
Alexandria
Cairo
Al Başrah
Kuwait
BAHRAIN
QATAR
Shiraz
Eşfahān
IRAN
Lahore
Delhi
New Delhi
Mt. Everest 8,848 m
NEPAL
Kānpur
Chongqing
Changsha
Guiyang
Fuzhou
Kunming
Guangzhou
T'aipei
TAIWAN

LIBYA
Sabhā
EGYPT
Medina
Aswān
SAUDI ARABIA
Riyadh
Mecca
Muscat
OMAN
Karāchi
Hyderābād
PAKISTAN
Ahmadābād
Calcutta
Dhaka
BANGLADESH
MYANMAR
Mandalay
Hanoi
Hainan
HONG KONG
Nanning
BONIN IS. (JAP.)
Iwo Jima
VOLCANO IS. (JAP.)
Minami-Tori-Shima (JAP.)
Tropic of Cancer

NIGER
CHAD
L. Chad
N'Djamena
SUDAN
Khartoum
ERITREA
Asmara
YEMEN
Sanaa
Aden
DJIBOUTI
Socotra (YEMEN)
Mumbai
Pune
Hyderābād
Bangalore
Chennai
BAY OF BENGAL
ANDAMAN AND NICOBAR IS. (INDIA)
Yangon
THAI-LAND
Bangkok
CAMBODIA
Phnom Penh
VIETNAM
Ho Chi Minh City
SOUTH CHINA SEA
Manila
PHILIPPINES
Palawan
Samar
Luzon
C. Engaño
Okino-Tori-Shima (JAP.)
NORTHERN MARIANAS (U.S.)
Pagan
Alamagan
Anathan
Saipan
Hagåtña Guam (U.S.)
Farallon de Pajaros Maug Is.

PACIFIC OCEAN

CENTRAL AFRICAN REP.
Bangui
CAMEROON
Yaoundé
Abuja
NIGERIA
Kano
Zinder
Sarh
Juba
ETHIOPIA
Addis Ababa
KENYA
SOMALIA
Mogadishu
Caseyr
Lakshadweep (INDIA)
Coimbatore
C. Comorin
SRI LANKA
Colombo
Dondra Head
MALDIVES
Male
Medan
Kuala Lumpur
BRUNEI
MALAYSIA
SINGA-PORE
Sumatra
Palembang
Borneo
Banjarmasin
INDONESIA
Sulu Sea
Davao
Mindanao
Babelthuap
Koror
PALAU
Yap Is.
Ulithi
Ngulu
Sonsorol Is.
Halmahera
Celebes
Celebes Sea
Morotai
CAROLINE IS.
FED. STATES OF MICRONESIA
Truk Is.
Elato
Lamotrek
Satawan
Hall Is.
Namonuito
Senyavin Is.
Ponape
Enewetak
Ujelang
RALIK CHAIN
Kwajalein
Ailinglapalap
Namu
MARSHALL IS.
Bikini
Rongelap
Likiep
Maloelap
Majuro
Mili
Jaluit
Butaritari
GILBERT IS.
Tarawa
KIRIBATI
Banaba
NAURU
Tabiteuea
Arorae

GABON
Libreville
CONGO
Brazzaville
Kinshasa
DEM. REP. OF THE CONGO
RWANDA
BURUNDI
Kampala
Nairobi
Kilimanjaro 5,895 m
Kisangani
TANZANIA
Dar es Salaam
Mombasa
Nyasa
SEYCHELLES
Victoria
Mahé
Amirante Is.
Coetivy I.
Agalega Is. (MRTS.)
BRITISH INDIAN OCEAN TERR.
Chagos Arch.
Diego Garcia
Equator
Jayapura
New Guinea
PAPUA NEW GUINEA
Port Moresby
Admiralty Is.
Bismarck Arch.
New Ireland
New Britain
Bougainville
SOLOMON IS.
Sta. Isabel
Guadalcanal
Honiara
Malaita
San Cristobal
Ontong Java
Nanumea
Nukumanu
Rennell I.
TUVALU
Funafuti

INDIAN OCEAN

ANGOLA
Luanda
Benguela
Huambo
ZAMBIA
Lubumbashi
MALAWI
Lusaka
Lilongwe
COMOROS
Mayotte (FR.)
Aldabra
Farquhar Group
Tanjon'i Bobaomby
Antsiranana
Toamasina
Antananarivo
MADAGASCAR
Christmas I. (AUSTL.)
Cocos Is. (AUSTL.)
Java
Bandung
Jakarta
Surabaya
Ujung Pandang
Bali
Sumbawa
Timor
Java Sea
Banda Sea
Sumba
Timor Sea
Arafura Sea
Darwin
Gulf of Carpentaria
Cape York Pen.
Torres Str.
Cairns
Townsville
CORAL SEA
Espiritu Santo
VANUATU
Port-Vila
New Caledonia (FR.)
Nouméa
FIJI
Suva
Rotuma I. (FIJI)
Sta. Cruz Is.

NAMIBIA
Windhoek
BOTSWANA
ZIMBABWE
Harare
MOZAMBIQUE
Beira
Tromelin I. (FR.)
Rodrigues (MRTS.)
MAURITIUS
Réunion (FR.)
Port Louis
Tropic of Capricorn
Port Hedland
North West C.
Great Sandy Desert
Alice Springs
Rockhampton
Brisbane
Norfolk I. (AUSTL.)
Loyalty Is.

Kalahari
Gaborone
Pretoria
Johannesburg
Maputo
SWAZILAND
LESOTHO
Bloemfontein
SOUTH AFRICA
Durban
Toliara
Tanjona Vohimena
AUSTRALIA
Geraldton
Great Victoria Desert
Kalgoorlie
Perth
Whyalla
Broken Hill
Adelaide
Newcastle
Sydney
Mt. Kosciusko 2,228 m
Canberra
Melbourne
Great Australian Bight
C. Leeuwin
Albany
Lord Howe I. (AUSTL.)
North C.

Cape Town
Cape of Good Hope
Port Elizabeth
C. Agulhas
Amsterdam I. (FR.)
St. Paul I. (FR.)
Tasmania
Hobart
South East C.
TASMAN SEA
Wellington
Christchurch
Dunedin
South I.
NEW ZEALAND
North I.
Auckland
40°

Prince Edward Is. (S. AFR.)
Crozet Is. (FR.)
Kerguélen (FR.)
McDonald Is. (AUSTL.)
South C.
Bounty Is. (N.Z.)
Auckland Is. (N.Z.)
Antipodes Is. (N.Z.)
Campbell I. (N.Z.)
Macquarie I. (AUSTL.)

C. Batterbee
Antarctic Circle
80°
C. Adare
ROSS SEA
ANTARCTICA

INT'L DATE LINE
Wake I. (U.S.)

NORTH PACIFIC OCEAN

© HAMMOND WORLD ATLAS CORPORATION CI - 1001 - A A A

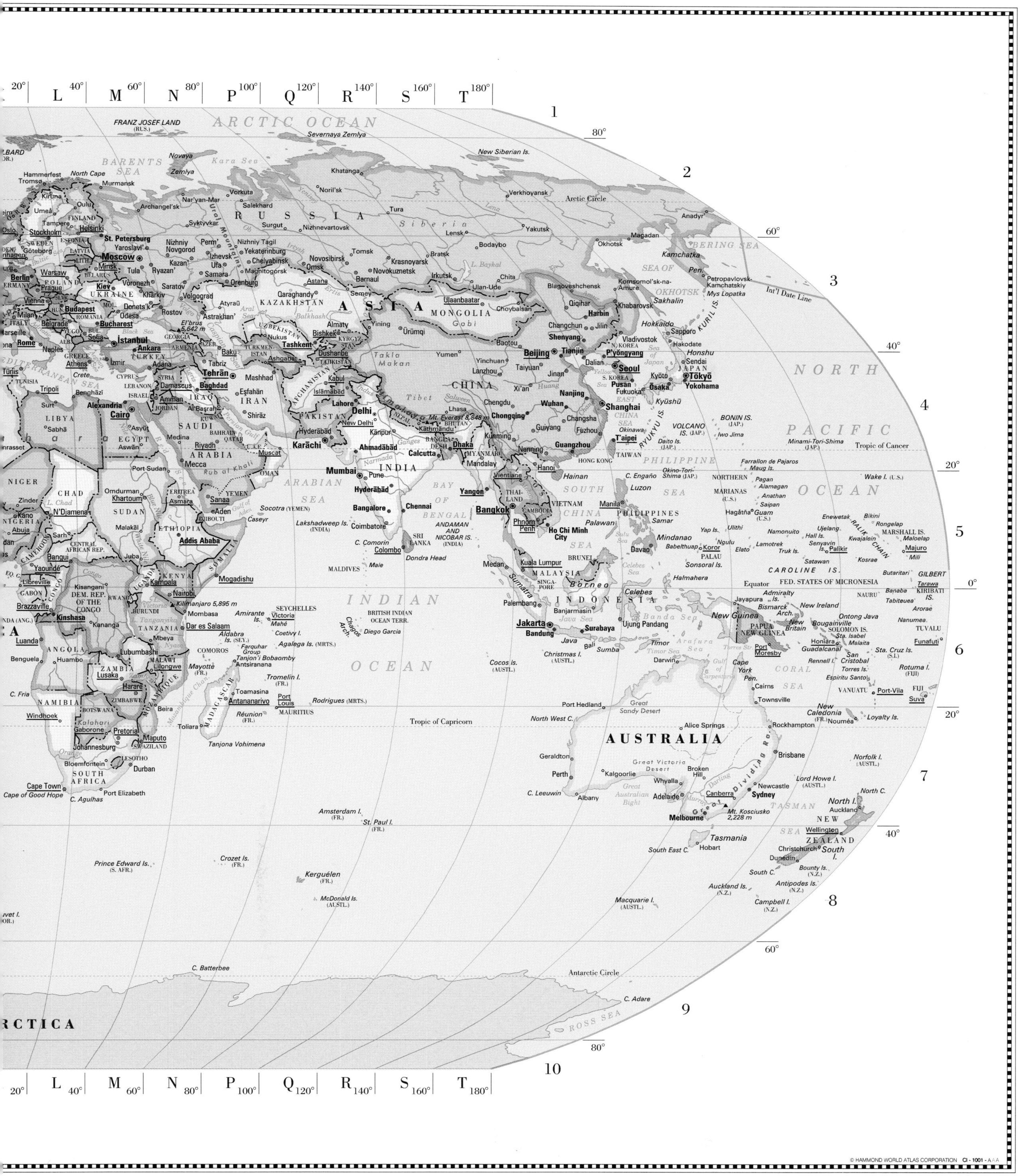

POPULATION OF CITIES AND TOWNS

- ◉ OVER 5,000,000
- ◉ 2,000,000 - 4,999,999
- ● 500,000 - 1,999,999
- ○ UNDER 500,000

SCALE 1:81,700,000   ROBINSON PROJECTION   STANDARD PARALLELS 38°N AND 38°S

MILES 0 — 1000 — 2000 — 3000 — 4000

KILOMETERS 0 — 1000 — 2000 — 3000 — 4000

AREA OF
OPTIMIZATION
The red band which
surrounds this map
defines the "Area of
Optimization." Within
this bounding curve is
the most accurate
conformal map that can
be made of the region.
Outside the optimized
area, distortion increases
rapidly, and tears or
other irregularities in
the grid may occur.

AREA OF OPTIMIZATION

GREENLAND
(KALAALLIT NUNAAT)
(DENMARK)

Arctic Circle

Denmark Strait

Jan Mayen
(NOR.)

BARENTS SEA

Novaya Zemlya

Mys Kanin Nos
Kanin
Pen.

North Cape
Hammerfest
Vadsø

Isafjördhur
Horn

Akureyri

Vesterålen
Harstad
Tromsø
Narvik
Kiruna
Kebnekaise 2,111 m
Gällivare
Murmansk
Monchegorsk
Apatity
Kola
Pen.
Kandalaksha

Reykjavík
Keflavík

ICELAND
Hekla 1,491 m

Fontur

Neskaupstadhur

Mo
Boden
Luleå
Kemi
Oulu
Rovaniemi
Kemijärvi
White Sea
Kem'
Severodvinsk
Onega
Archangel

Vestmannaeyjar

NORWEGIAN SEA

Lofoten

Faroe Is.
(DEN.)
Tórshavn

Namsos
Steinkjer
Glittertinden
2,470 m
Trondheim
Östersund
Sundsvall
Örnsköldsvik
Umeå
Skellefteå

FINLAND
Kokkola
Kajaani
Vaasa
Jyväskylä
Kuopio
Joensuu
Lake
Onega
Medvezh'yegorsk
Petrozavodsk
Vytegra

Shetland
Is.

Lillehammer
Bergen
SWEDEN
Gävle

Tampere
Hämeenlinna
Lahti
Lappeenranta
Mikkeli

C. Wrath
Orkney
Is.
Thurso

Hebrides
Moray Firth
Inverness
Ben Nevis
1,343 m
Aberdeen
Dundee

Haugesund
Stavanger
Drammen
Oslo
Skien
Gjøvik
Moss
Falun
Uppsala
Åland
Pori
Turku
Vyborg
Kotka

St. Petersburg
Tikhvin
Cherepovets

ATLANTIC OCEAN

Rockall
(U.K.)

Kristiansund
Molde
Ålesund

Västerås

ESTONIA
Tallinn
Narva
Pärnu
Tartu

Luga
Novgorod
Borovichi
L. Il'men'
Staraya
Russa
Vyshniy
Volochek

Mos

Glasgow
Edinburgh
Dumfries

Kristiansand
Arendal
Uddevalla
Lindesnes

Stockholm
Norrköping
Linköping
Visby
Gotland

Öland

Riga
LATVIA
Rēzekne
Velikiye
Luki

Rzhev

Londonderry
Errish Head
Sligo
Belfast
Carlisle
Newcastle upon Tyne
Middlesbrough
Great
Britain

NORTH SEA

DENMARK
Århus
Vejle
Esbjerg
Ålborg

Halmstad
Jönköping
Borås
Göteborg
Kalmar
Karlskrona

Lake
Peipus
Pskov

Ostashkov
Vyaz'ma

Smolensk
Roslavl'

IRELAND
Galway
Sligo

UNITED KINGDOM
Bradford
Manchester
Leeds

Copenhagen
Odense
Malmö
Helsingborg

Liepāja
Klaipėda

Šiauliai
Jelgava
Panevėžys
Daugavpils
Polatsk
Vitsyebsk

Limerick
Tralee
Waterford
Dublin
Liverpool
Stoke-on-Trent
Sheffield
Nottingham
Irish
Sea

Helgoland
Flensburg
Kiel
Rostock
Bornholm

Słupsk
Gdynia
Kaliningrad
RUS.
Gdańsk
Elbląg

LITHUANIA
Kaunas
Vilnius
Hrodna
Minsk
Barysaw

BELARUS
Mahilyow
Babruysk
Salihorsk
Homyel'
Klintsy

Zhlobin

C. Clear
Cork

St. George's Chan.

Swansea
Cardiff
Bristol
Exeter
Birmingham
Coventry
Oxford

Norwich

Bremerhaven
Lübeck
Schwerin
Hamburg
Bremen
Hannover

Szczecin
Bydgoszcz
Toruń
Olsztyn
Łomża
Białystok
Mazur

Pinsk
Prypyats
Pruzhany
Chornobyl'

Land's End
Plymouth
London
Reading
Southampton
Portsmouth
Dover
Calais

NETHERLANDS
Amsterdam
The Hague
Rotterdam
Enschede
Utrecht
Osnabrück
Münster
Potsdam
Magdeburg
Braunschweig
Dortmund
Essen
Kassel
Halle
Leipzig

Berlin
Frankfurt
Gorzów Wielkopolski
Poznań
Płock
Brest

POLAND
Łódź
Warsaw
Radom
Lublin
Kovel'

Rivne
Zhytomyr

Kiev
UKRAINE

English Channel
Cherbourg
Le Havre
Lille
Ghent
Antwerp
Brussels
Liège
Düsseldorf
Cologne
Bonn

BELGIUM
Duisburg

Dresden
Görlitz
Chemnitz

Wrocław
Kalisz
Częstochowa
Katowice
Kielce
Tarnów
Kraków
Przemyśl

L'viv
Ternopil'
Vinnytsya
Drohobych
Ivano-Frankivs'k

Cherkasy
Kremenchuk
Dnipro
Kirovohrad

Kam'yanets'-Podil's'kyy

Channel
Is. (U.K.)
Brest
Caen
Rouen
Amiens
Reims

LUX.
Luxembourg
Frankfurt am
Main
Wiesbaden
Mannheim
Würzburg

GERMANY
Halle
Leipzig

Prague
Hradec
Králové
Pardubice
Pilsen

CZECH REP.
Brno
Zlín
Olomouc

Banská
Štiavnica
Bielsko-Biała

SLOVAKIA
Košice
Uzhhorod

MOLDOVA
Chişinău
Tiraspol
Bălţi

Chernivtsi

Quimper
Rennes
Laval
Le Mans
Angers
Chartres
Versailles
Paris
Troyes
Nancy
Metz
Strasbourg
Karlsruhe
Saarbrücken
Stuttgart
Nürnberg
Regensburg
Bayreuth

Passau
Linz

Vienna
Bratislava
Győr
Miskolc
Satu Mare

Saint-Brieuc

Nantes
Tours
Orléans
Dijon
Besançon
Mulhouse
Basel
Zürich
Augsburg
Munich
Salzburg

LIECHT.
Bern

Innsbruck

AUSTRIA
Graz
Klagenfurt

Sopron
Szombathely

HUNGARY
Szeged
Arad
Oradea

Debrecen
Cluj-Napoca

ROMANIA
Tîrgu Mureş
Bacău

FRANCE
Poitiers
Niort
Limoges
Clermont-Ferrand
Mâcon
Lyon
Chambéry
Geneva
Mont Blanc 4,807 m
Grenoble

SWITZERLAND
Como
Bolzano
Trento

Udine
Maribor

SLOVENIA
Ljubljana
Zagreb
Rijeka

Bacău
Sibiu
Braşov
Piatra Neamţ

Odesa

La Rochelle
Angoulême
Périgueux
Saint-Étienne
Le Puy
Valence

Milan
Turin
Genoa
Brescia
Verona
Padua
Venice
Parma
Modena
Bologna
Ferrara

Banja
Luka

Osijek
Novi
Sad
Subotica
Timişoara

Belgrade

Kragujevac

Pitești
Bucharest
Craiova
Giurgiu
Ruse

Bay of
Biscay
Cabo Finisterre
La Coruña
El Ferrol
Gijón
Santander
San
Sebastián
Oviedo
León

Bordeaux
Bayonne
Pau
Tarbes
Toulouse
Montauban
Nîmes
Montpellier
Béziers
Avignon
Aix-en-Provence

Nice
MONACO
Cannes

CROATIA
La Spezia
Livorno
Pisa
Florence
Rimini
Ancona

SAN MARINO
Pescara

BOSNIA AND
HERZEGOVINA
Sarajevo
Mostar
Split
Dubrovnik
Podgorica
Shkodër

YUGOSLAVIA
Niš
Priština
Peterik

Pleven
Plovdiv

BULGARIA
Sofia
Stara Zagora
Sliven
Burgas
Varna

Vigo
Orense
Braga
Porto
Viseu
Santiago de
Compostela

Burgos
Logroño
Pamplona
Vitoria
Bilbao
Valladolid
Huesca
Lleida
Girona
Perpignan
G. of Lions

Toulon
Bastia
Corsica
Ajaccio

Grosseto
Perugia

ITALY
Rome
VATICAN CITY

Foggia
Bari
Potenza
Barletta
Brindisi
Lecce
Taranto

Durrës
Tiranë

F.Y.R.O.M.
Skopje
Bitola
Priština

Khaskovo

TURKEY
Istanbul

PORTUGAL
Coimbra
Santarém
Lisbon
Setúbal
Évora
Beja

SPAIN
Salamanca
Béjar
Cáceres
Madrid
Guadalajara
Toledo
Cuenca
Sabadell
Barcelona
Tarragona
Castellón de
la Plana

Balearic Islands
Minorca
Majorca
Palma
Ibiza

Sardinia
Cagliari
Sassari
Nuoro

Adriatic Sea

Cosenza

Serrai
Kozáni
Thessaloníki
Kaválla

Cabo de São Vicente
Sierra Morena
Santarém
Badajoz
Mérida
Ciudad Real
Albacete
Valencia
Gandia

Capo Teulada

Tyrrhenian
Sea

Ioánnina
Vólos
Lárisa

Aegean Sea

İzmir

Huelva
Córdoba
Linares
Jaén
Murcia
Alicante

Jerez de la Frontera
Seville
Granada
Cerro de Mulhacén
3,478 m
Cádiz
Málaga
Almería
Cartagena
Str. of Gibl.

Messina
Reggio di Calabria
Palermo
Mt. Etna 3,323 m
Catania
Siracusa

Ionian
Is.
Ionian Sea
Pirgos

GREECE
Lamía
Pátrai
Corinth
Athens
Piraiévs
Kalamáta
Ákra Taínaron

Rhode

Tangier
Ceuta (SP.)
Gibraltar (U.K.)
Melilla
(SP.)
Oran

Algiers

MEDITERRANEAN

Trapani
Marsala
Sicily
Ragusa
Capo Passero

MALTA
Valletta

Khaniá
Iráklion
Crete

Casablanca
Rabat

MOROCCO

AFRICA

ALGERIA

TUNISIA
Túnis

Pantelleria
Lampedusa

SEA

© Copyright by HAMMOND WORLD ATLAS CORPORATION   CD - 1002 - A-A-A

SCALE 1:17,500,000   OPTIMAL CONFORMAL PROJECTION

MILES   0   250   500   750
KILOMETERS   0   250   500   750

Longitude West of Greenwich   0°   Longitude East of Greenwich

POPULATION OF CITIES AND TOWNS
▣ OVER 3,000,000   ✦ 500,000 - 999,999   ○ UNDER 100,000
▢ 1,000,000 - 2,999,999   ● 100,000 - 499,999

Europe

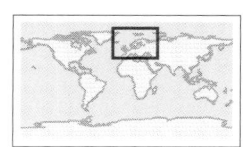

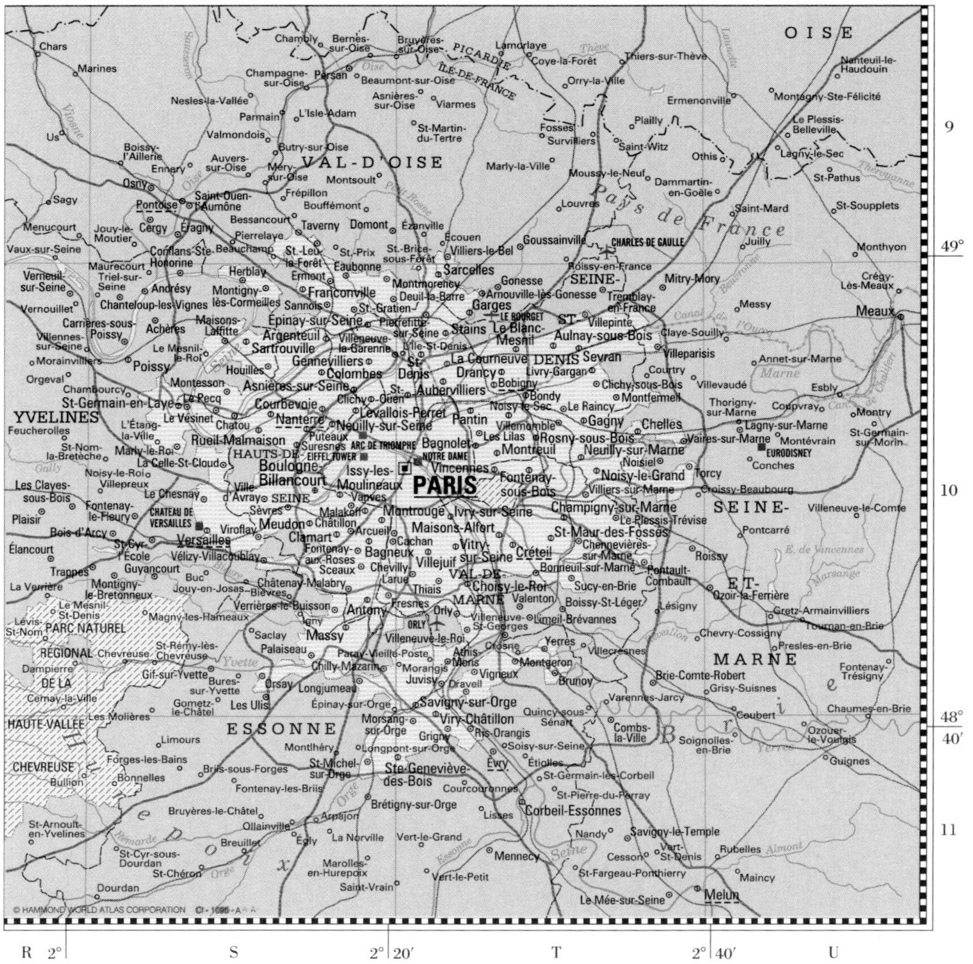

Map 1 (London and Greater London)

LONDON

GREATER LONDON

Regions/Counties: HERTFORDSHIRE, ESSEX, KENT, SURREY, BERKSHIRE, BUCKINGHAMSHIRE

Boroughs and places: Berkhamsted, Vale of St. Albans, Saint Albans, Hatfield, Hoddesdon, Harlow, Moreton, Fyfield, Hemel Hempstead, Welham Green, Wormley, Lower Nazeing, Epping, North Weald Bassett, Chipping Ongar, Bovingdon, Kings Langley, Bedmond, London Colney, Brookmans Park, Hammond Street, Cuffley, Ingatestone, Blackmore, Ashley Green, Colney Heath, Chiswell Green, Cheshunt, Waltham Abbey, Stanford Rivers, Doddinghurst, Latimer, Little Chalfont, Abbots Langley, Bricket Wood, Radlett, Potters Bar, Theydon Bois, Rodine, Pilgrims Hatch, Hutton, Chorleywood, Croxley Green, Watford, Borehamwood, BARNET, King George's Res., Loughton, Abridge, Stapleford Abbotts, Buckhurst Hill, Chigwell, Brentwood, Ingrave, Great Warley, West Horndon, Bulphan, Rickmansworth, South Oxhey, Bushey, EAST BARNET, Finchley, EDMONTON, ENFIELD, Epping Forest, Chalfont Saint Peter, HARROW, HENDON, SOUTHGATE, CHINGFORD, REDBRIDGE, HAVERING, ROMFORD, HORNCHURCH, UPMINSTER, Gerrards Cross, Denham, RUISLIP, Brent Res., HAMPSTEAD, HARINGEY, TOTTENHAM, LEYTON, WANSTEAD, ILFORD, BARKING & DAGENHAM, RAINHAM, Iver Heath, HILLINGDON, UXBRIDGE, WILLESDEN, CAMDEN, HACKNEY, NEWHAM, WEST HAM, Aveley, South Ockenden, Orsett, Slough, Iver, Langley, HAYES, EALING, SOUTHALL, ACTON, PADDINGTON, REGENT'S PARK, BRITISH MUSEUM, TOWER OF LONDON, WOOLWICH, West Thurrock, Grays, Datchet, HEATHROW, CHISWICK, HYDE PARK, W. ABBEY, Buckingham Palace, CHELSEA, DEPTFORD, GREENWICH, BEXLEY, Tilbury, BERKSHIRE, Old Windsor, Stanwell, HOUNSLOW, KEW GARDENS, BATTERSEA, Greenwich Observatory, CRAYFORD, Northfleet, Virginia Water, Egham, Thorpe, FELTHAM, RICHMOND UPON THAMES, RICHMOND PARK, WANDSWORTH, CAMBERWELL, LAM. BETH, LEWISHAM, ELTHAM, Dartford, Swanscombe, Gravesend, Staines, Ashford, East Molesey, WIMBLEDON, STREATHAM, PENGE, BECKENHAM, SIDCUP, Wilmington, Longfield, Sunbury, HAMPTON COURT, KINGSTON UPON THAMES, MERTON, MORDEN, BROMLEY, Horton Kirby, Meopham, Addlestone, Walton-on-Thames, Long Ditton, LONDON, SUTTON, CROYDON, ORPINGTON, Swanley, Farningham, Eynsford, Ash, Ottershaw, Weybridge, Esher, Claygate, Ewell, CROYDON, PURLEY, BROMLEY COMMON, West Kingsdown, Hartley, Byfleet, Chertsey, Cobham, Oxshott, Banstead, COULSDON, BIGGIN HILL, Stansted, Wrotham, Trottiscliffe, Woking, Ripley, Fetcham, Ashstead, Tadworth, Chipstead, Caterham, Warlingham, Titsey, Westerham, Seal, Sevenoaks, Ightham, Mereworth, Leatherhead, East Horsley, Great Bookham, Woldingham, Tatsfield, Limpsfield, Shipbourne, West Clandon, Effingham, Merstham, Oxted, Godstone, West Peckham, Hadlow, Guildford, East Clandon, SURREY, Redhill, Bletchingley, Westerham, KENT, West Horsley, Dorking, Reigate, Leigh, Vale of Kent, Holmesdale, North Downs, Ragstone Range, Edenbridge, Chiddingstone, Tonbridge, Tudeley, Capel, South Holmwood, Horley, Newdigate, Smallfield, Dormans Land, Penshurst, Pembury, Charlwood, GATWICK, Southborough

Boroughs indicated by number:
1 HAMMERSMITH & FULHAM
2 ISLINGTON
3 KENSINGTON & CHELSEA
4 CITY OF LONDON
5 SOUTHWARK
6 TOWER HAMLETS
7 WALTHAM FOREST
8 CITY OF WESTMINSTER

© HAMMOND WORLD ATLAS CORPORATION   CD - 1094 - A - A - A

Map 2 (Russia / Caucasus region)

RUSSIA, **KAZAKHSTAN**, **SIBERIA**, **Ural Mountains**

Vorkuta, Salekhard, Nadym, Nizhnevartovsk, Nar'yan Mar, Pechora, Inta, Ukhta, Surgut, Ob, Syktyvkar, Gora Narodnaya 1894 m, Solikamsk, Berezniki, Nizhniy Tagil, Tyumen, Tobol'sk, Ishim, Kirov, Glazov, Izhevsk, Perm', Yekaterinburg, Kungur, Kamyshlov, Kurgan, Nizhniy Novgorod, Cheboksary, Kazan', Naberezhnyye Chelny, Ufa, Kasli, Chelyabinsk, Petropavlovsk, Ul'yanovsk, Tol'yatti, Samara, Orenburg, Aqtöbe, Penza, Saratov, Engel's, Uralsk, Volgograd, Astrakhan, Atyrau, Aqtau, Rostov, Krasnodar, Stavropol', Groznyy, Makhachkala, CAUCASUS, Gora El'brus 5,642 m, GEORGIA, Tbilisi, ARMENIA, AZERBAIJAN, Baku, Yerevan, CASPIAN SEA, BLACK SEA, SEA OF AZOV, TURKEY, Ankara, SYRIA, Aleppo, Damascus, Beirut, LEBANON, CYPRUS, Nicosia, IRAQ, Baghdad, IRAN, Tabriz, Bakhtaran, JORDAN, SAUDI ARABIA

Map 3 (Paris region)

PARIS, **VAL-D'OISE**, **OISE**, **SEINE-ST-DENIS**, **SEINE-ET-MARNE**, **ESSONNE**, **YVELINES**, **HAUTS-DE-SEINE**, **VAL-DE-MARNE**

Chars, Marines, Chambly, Persan, Beaumont-sur-Oise, Bruyères-sur-Oise, PICARDIE, ÎLE-DE-FRANCE, Lamorlaye, Thiers-sur-Thève, Nanteuil-le-Haudouin, Nesles-la-Vallée, L'Isle-Adam, Viarmes, Orry-la-Ville, Montagny-Ste-Félicité, Us, Boissy-l'Aillerie, Ennery, Frépillon, Montsoult, Fosses, Survilliers, Le Plessis-Belleville, Lagny-le-Sec, VAL-D'OISE, Marly-la-Ville, Moussy-le-Neuf, Othis, St-Pathus, Sagy, Pontoise, Saint-Ouen l'Aumône, Taverne, Domont, Écouen, Louvres, Pays de France, Saint-Mard, St-Soupplets, Menucourt, Cergy, Conflans-Ste-Honorine, St-Leu-la-Forêt, St-Prix, St-Brice-sous-Forêt, Villiers-le-Bel, Goussainville, CHARLES DE GAULLE, Juilly, Monthyon, Vaux-sur-Seine, Jouy-le-Moutier, Herblay, Ermont, Montmorency, Deuil-la-Barre, Sarcelles, Gonesse, Mitry-Mory, Crégy-lès-Meaux, Verneuil-sur-Seine, Maurecourt, Triel-sur-Seine, Andrésy, Montigny-lès-Cormeilles, Franconville, Soisy-sous-Montmorency, Stains, SEINE, Tremblay-en-France, Messy, Meaux, Vernouillet, Chanteloup-les-Vignes, Poissy, Houilles, Argenteuil, Villeneuve-la-Garenne, Pierrefitte-sur-Seine, LE BLANC-MESNIL, LE BOURGET, Aulnay-sous-Bois, Claye-Souilly, Annet-sur-Marne, Villennes-sur-Seine, Morainvilliers, Carrières-sous-Poissy, Sartrouville, Gennevilliers, Colombes, LA COURNEUVE, Drancy, Sevran, Villeparisis, Marne, St-Germain-en-Laye, Le Mesnil-le-Roi, Le Pecq, Montesson, Asnières-sur-Seine, Clichy, ST-DENIS, Aubervilliers, Bobigny, Bondy, Le Raincy, Clichy-sous-Bois, Montfermeil, Thorigny-sur-Marne, Lagny-sur-Marne, Esbly, YVELINES, Feucherolles, L'Étang-la-Ville, Le Vésinet, Chatou, Rueil-Malmaison, Puteaux, Courbevoie, Levallois-Perret, Pantin, Les Lilas, Rosny-sous-Bois, Villemomble, Gagny, Chelles, Vaires-sur-Marne, Coupvray, St-Germain-sur-Morin, St-Nom-la-Bretèche, Marly-le-Roi, HAUTS-DE-SEINE, ARC DE TRIOMPHE, EIFFEL TOWER, Neuilly-sur-Seine, Montreuil, Noisy-le-Sec, Neuilly-sur-Marne, EURODISNEY, Noisy-le-Roi, Noisy-le-Grand, Torcy, Conches, Bois-d'Arcy, Celle-St-Cloud, Boulogne-Billancourt, NOTRE DAME, Bagnolet, Fontenay-sous-Bois, Vincennes, Villiers-sur-Marne, Noisy-Beaubourg, Les Clayes-sous-Bois, Villepreux, Issy-les-Moulineaux, PARIS, Champigny-sur-Marne, Le Plessis-Trévise, SEINE-ET-, Villeneuve-le-Comte, Plaisir, Le Chesnay, Ville d'Avray, Sèvres, Vanves, Malakoff, Montrouge, Ivry-sur-Seine, St-Maur-des-Fossés, Chennevières-sur-Marne, Pontcarré, Élancourt, Vélizy-Villacoublay, Viroflay, Meudon, Clamart, Cachan, Vitry, SEINE CRÉTEIL, Sucy-en-Brie, Boissy-St-Léger, Roissy, La Verrière, Le Mesnil-St-Denis, Guyancourt, Buc, Jouy-en-Josas, Bièvres, Verrières-le-Buisson, Fresnes, VAL-DE-MARNE, Ozoir-la-Ferrière, ET-, Gretz-Armainvilliers, Trappes, CHÂTEAU DE VERSAILLES, Versailles, Bagneux, Chevilly-Larue, Choisy-le-Roi, Bonneuil-sur-Marne, Lésigny, Lévis-St-Nom, Châtenay-Malabry, Sceaux, Antony, Villejuif, L'Haÿ-les-Roses, Valenton, Brie-Comte-Robert, MARNE, Tournan-en-Brie, Magny-les-Hameaux, Saclay, Palaiseau, Massy, Orly, ORLY, Villeneuve-St-Georges, Limeil-Brévannes, Grisy-Suisnes, Fontenay-Trésigny, St-Rémy-lès-Chevreuse, Igny, Chilly-Mazarin, Juvisy, Draveil, Montgeron, Chevry-Cossigny, PARC NATUREL, Gif-sur-Yvette, Morangis, Savigny-sur-Orge, Ablon, Vigneux, Brunoy, Presles-en-Brie, RÉGIONAL, Chevreuse, Orsay, Longjumeau, Épinay-sur-Orge, Montgeron, Yerres, Varennes-Jarcy, Dampierre, Cernay-la-Ville, Les Ulis, Villebon, Ballainvilliers, Viry-Châtillon, Soisy-sur-Seine, MARNE, DE LA, Orsay, Bures-sur-Yvette, Savigny-sur-Orge, Morsang-sur-Orge, Combs-la-Ville, Gometz-le-Châtel, ESSONNE, Montlhéry, Longpont-sur-Orge, Ris-Orangis, Soignolles-en-Brie, HAUTE-VALLÉE, Les Molières, Épinay-sur-Orge, Évry, St-Germain-lès-Corbeil, Coubert, Limours, Forges-les-Bains, Brétigny-sur-Orge, Ste-Geneviève-des-Bois, Nandy, Savigny-le-Temple, CHEVREUSE, Bullion, St-Michel-sur-Orge, Courcouronnes, Corbeil-Essonnes, St-Pierre-du-Perray, Bonnelles, Fontenay-lès-Briis, Bruyères-le-Châtel, St-Vrain, Mennecy, Cesson, Rubelles, St-Cyr-sous-Dourdan, La Norville, Vert-le-Grand, Ollainville, Guignes, St-Fargeau-Ponthierry, St-Chéron, Breuillet, La Norville, Marolles-en-Hurepoix, St-Vrain, Le Mée-sur-Seine, Melun, Dourdan, Saint-Vrain, Vert-le-Petit

© HAMMOND WORLD ATLAS CORPORATION   CI - 1095 - A - A - A

SCALE 1:587,000   LAMBERT CONFORMAL CONIC PROJECTION

MILES   0   10   20
KILOMETERS   0   10   20

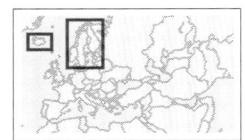

Scandinavia and Finland, Iceland

SCALE 1:3,500,000   LAMBERT CONFORMAL CONIC PROJECTION

© HAMMOND WORLD ATLAS CORPORATION

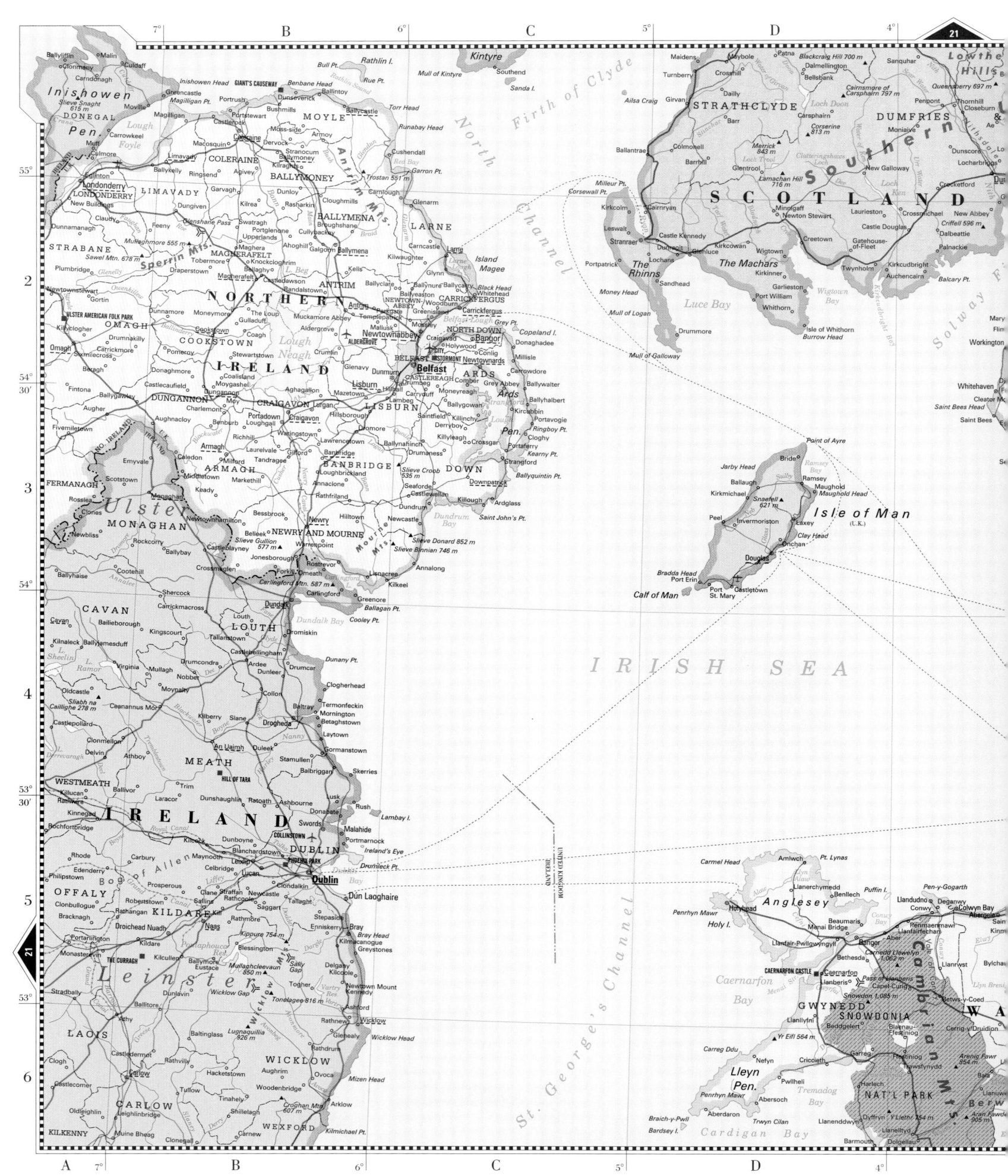

7°   B   6°   C   5°   D   4°

Kintyre

Rathlin I.
Bull Pt.
Benbane Head
Rue Pt.
Mull of Kintyre
Southend
Sanda I.

North Channel

Firth of Clyde

Maidens
Maybole
Patna
Blackcraig Hill 700 m
Sanquhar
Turnberry
Crosshill
Dalmellington
Bellsbank
Dailly
Cairnsmore of Carsphairn 797 m
Penpont
Thornhill
Closeburn

STRATHCLYDE

Ballantrae
Colmonell
Barr
Merrick 843 m
Corserine 813 m
Moniaive

DUMFRIES

Barrhill
Loch Doon
Carsphairn
New Galloway
Dunscore
Locharbriggs

S C O T L A N D

Kirkcolm
Cairnryan
Minigaff
Newton Stewart
Laurieston
Crossmichael
New Abbey
Crocketford

Leswalt
Castle Kennedy
Kirkcowan
Wigtown
Castle Douglas
Dalbeattie

Stranraer
Dunragit
Glenluce
Kirkcudbright
Palnackie

Portpatrick
The Rhinns
Lochans
The Machars
Garlieston
Twynholm
Auchencairn

Sandhead
Port William
Kirkinner
Balcary Pt.

Money Head
Luce Bay
Wigtown Bay

Mull of Logan
Whithorn

Drummore
Isle of Whithorn
Burrow Head

Mull of Galloway

Solway F.

Inishowen
Ballyliffin
Malin
Clonmany
Carndonagh
Culdaff

Lough Foyle

DONEGAL PEN.
Slieve Snaght 615 m
Moville
Magilligan Pt.
Portrush
GIANT'S CAUSEWAY
Dunseverick
Benbane Head
Ballintoy
Torr Head
Runabay Head
Ballycastle
Cushendun

MOYLE

Carrowkeel
Mutt
Greencastle
Bushmills
Moss-side
Armoy
Glendun Mts.

Carndonagh
Quigley's Pt.
Muff
Moville
Macosquin
Dervock
Cushendall

Culmore
Limavady
COLERAINE
Ballymoney
Glenariff
Red Bay
Garron Pt.

Eglinton
Ballykelly
Garvagh
Dunloy
Rasharkin
Trostan 551 m
Glenarm

Londonderry
New Buildings
LIMAVADY
Ringsend
Agivey
Cloughmills
Carnlough

LONDONDERRY
Claudy
Dungiven
Kilrea
Kells
LARNE
Larne

Dunnamanagh
Feeny
Swatragh
Portglenone
Broughshane
Carncastle
Island Magee

STRABANE
Newtownstewart
Gortin
Mullaghmore 555 m
Upperlands
Cullybackey
Kilwaughter
Larne Lough

Plumbridge
Draperstown
MAGHERAFELT
Tobermore
Knockcloughrim
BALLYMENA
Ballymena
Glynn

Gortin
Sawel Mtn. 678 m
Maghera
Castledawson
Ballyclare
Whitehead

Sperrin Mts.
Glenelly
Randalstown
ANTRIM
Ballycarry
Black Head

Killyclogher
The Loup
Moneymore
Muckamore Abbey
NEWTOWN ABBEY
CARRICKFERGUS

OMAGH
Drumnakilly
Cookstown
Coagh
Aldergrove
Templepatrick
Greenisland
Carrickfergus

Omagh
Sixmilecross
Pomeroy
ALDERGROVE
Mossley
Craigavad
Copeland I.

Carrickmore
Stewartstown
Crumlin
Newtownabbey
NORTH DOWN
Bangor
Donaghadee

Beragh
Donaghmore
IRELAND
Glenavy
Dunmurry
STORMONT
Newtownards
Millisle

Fintona
Castlecaulfield
Moygashel
Aghagallon
Lisburn
BELFAST CITY
Comber
Grey Abbey
Ballywalter

Augher
DUNGANNON
Dungannon
Mazetown
BELFAST
CASTLEREAGH
Carryduff
ARDS

Fivemiletown
Moy
CRAIGAVON
Lurgan
Hillsborough
Ballygowan
Saintfield
Killinchy
Portavogie

Aughnacloy
Charlemont
Portadown
Loughgall
Craigavon
LISBURN
Dromore
Derryboy
Ringboy
Cloghy

Caledon
Benburb
Richhill
Watersnatown
Lawrencetown
Ballynahinch
Killyleagh
Portaferry

Emyvale
Laurelvale
Tandragee
Gilford
Banbridge
Drumaness
Crossgar
Kearny Pt.

Monaghan
Middletown
Keady
ARMAGH
Markethill
BANBRIDGE
Loughbrickland
Slieve Croob 535 m
Seaforde
Strangford

FERMANAGH
Scotstown
Armagh
Annaclone
Rathfriland
Castlewellan
Ballyquintin Pt.

Rosslea
Clones
Emyvale
Newtownhamilton
Bessbrook
DOWN
Dundrum
Downpatrick

Ulster
Newbliss
MONAGHAN
Belleek
Hilltown
Clough
Ardglass

Ballyhaise
Rockcorry
Ballybay
Castleblayney
Slieve Gullion 577 m
NEWRY AND MOURNE
Newcastle
Saint John's Pt.

Cootehill
Shercock
Crossmaglen
Forkill
Warrenpoint
Slieve Donard 852 m
Dundrum Bay

CAVAN
Carrickmacross
Louth
Omeath
Rostrevor
Slieve Binnian 746 m
Annalong

Cavan
Bailieborough
Kingscourt
Carlingford Mtn. 587 m
Lisnacree
Kilkeel

Kilnaleck
Ballyjamesduff
Drumcondra
LOUTH
Tallanstown
Carlingford Lough
Greenore

Virginia
Mullagh
Ardee
Dunleer
Carlingford
Baligan Pt.

L. Sheelin
Oldcastle
Nobber
Dunany Pt.

Sliabh na Caillighe 278 m
Moynalty
Collon
Drumcar
Clogherhead

L. Ramor
Ceanannus Mór
Kilberry
Beltray
Termonfeckin

Castlepollard
Kilmainhamwood
Slane
Mornington
Betaghstown

Delvin
Athboy
An Uaimh
Duleek
Laytown

MEATH
Trim
Stamullen
Gormanstown

WESTMEATH
HILL OF TARA
Balbriggan

Killucan
Ballivor
Laracor
Dunshaughlin
Ratoath
Ashbourne
Skerries

Rathwire
Kinnegad
Dunboyne
Swords
Rush

Rochfortbridge
Maynooth
Blanchardstown
Donabate
Lambay I.

Rhode
Edenderry
Carbury
Leixlip
Lucan
Malahide
Portmarnock

Philipstown
Prosperous
Celbridge
DUBLIN
PHOENIX PARK
Ireland's Eye
Drumleck Pt.

OFFALY
Clane
Straffan
Newcastle
Clondalkin
Dublin

Clonbulloge
Robertstown
Saggart
Tallaght
Dublin Bay
Dún Laoghaire

Bracknagh
Rathangan
KILDARE
Rathcoole
Rathmore
Stepaside

Portarlington
Droichead Nuadh
Kildare
Kill
Saggart
Enniskerry
Bray

Monasterevin
Kilcullen
THE CURRAGH
Ballymore Eustace
Kippure 754 m
Delgany
Kilcoole

Stradbally
Athy
Ballitore
Mullaghcleevaun 850 m
Sally Gap
Newtown Mount Kennedy
Greystones

Leinster
IRELAND
Dunlavin
Vartry Res.
Wicklow Gap
Tonelagee 816 m
Ashford

LAOIS
Rathvilly
Baltinglass
Lugnaquillia 926 m
Wicklow Gap
Roundwood
Rathnew
Wicklow

Clogh
Castledermot
Hacketstown
Aughrim
Ovoca
Wicklow Head

Castlecomer
Carlow
Tullow
Tinahely
Woodenbridge
Mizen Head

Leighlinbridge
Shillelagh
Croghan Mtn. 607 m
Arklow

CARLOW
Oldleighlin
Muine Bheag
Tinahely
Clonegal
Carnew

KILKENNY
WEXFORD
Kilmichael Pt.

North Channel

Point of Ayre

Jurby Head
Bride
Ramsey Bay
Ballaugh
Sulby
Ramsey
Maughold Head

Kirkmichael
Maughold
Snaefell 621 m
Isle of Man
(U.K.)

Peel
Invermoriston
Laxey
Clay Head

Bradda Head
Onchan

Port Erin
Douglas
Port St. Mary
Castletown

Calf of Man

I R I S H   S E A

Amlwch
Pt. Lynas
Carmel Head
Llanerchymedd
Benllech
Puffin I.
Pen-y-Gogarth

Anglesey
Llandudno
Deganwy
Colwyn Bay
Abergele

Holyhead
Beaumaris
Penmaenmawr
Llanfairfechan
Conwy

Holy I.
Menai Bridge
Bangor
Aber
Bethesda
Llanrwst

Llanfair-Pwllgwyngyll
Bethesda
Carnedd Llewelyn 1,062 m
Betws-y-Coed

CAERNARFON CASTLE
Caernarfon
Llanberis
Pass of Llanberis
Capel Curig

Caernarfon Bay
Llanllyfni
Snowdon 1,085 m
SNOWDONIA

GWYNEDD
Yr Eifl 564 m
Beddgelert
Blaenau Ffestiniog
W A

Nefyn
Criccieth
Ffestiniog
Arenig Fawr 854 m

Lleyn Pen.
Pwllheli
Cambrian Mts.

Carreg Ddu
Penrhyn Mawr
Abersoch
NAT'L PARK
Harlech

Braich-y-Pwll
Aberdaron
Trwyn Cilan
Tremadog Bay
Dyffryn
Y Llethr 754 m
Barmouth

Bardsey I.
Llanenddwyn
Llanelltyd
Garreg

Cardigan Bay

St. George's Channel

UNITED KINGDOM

IRELAND

A   7°   B   6°   C   5°   D   4°

55°
2
54° 30'
3
54°
4
53° 30'
5
53°
6

Northeastern Ireland, Northern England and Wales

POPULATION OF CITIES AND TOWNS

- ■ OVER 2,000,000
- ◉ 500,000 - 999,999
- ● 100,000 - 249,999
- ◎ 10,000 - 29,999
- ◻ 1,000,000 - 1,999,999
- ◉ 250,000 - 499,999
- ● 30,000 - 99,999
- ○ UNDER 10,000

SCALE 1:1,170,000   LAMBERT CONFORMAL CONIC PROJECTION

MILES 0 10 20 30 40 50

KILOMETERS 0 10 20 30 40 50

Longitude West of Greenwich

© HAMMOND WORLD ATLAS CORPORATION   CD-2005-A-A

Southern England and Wales

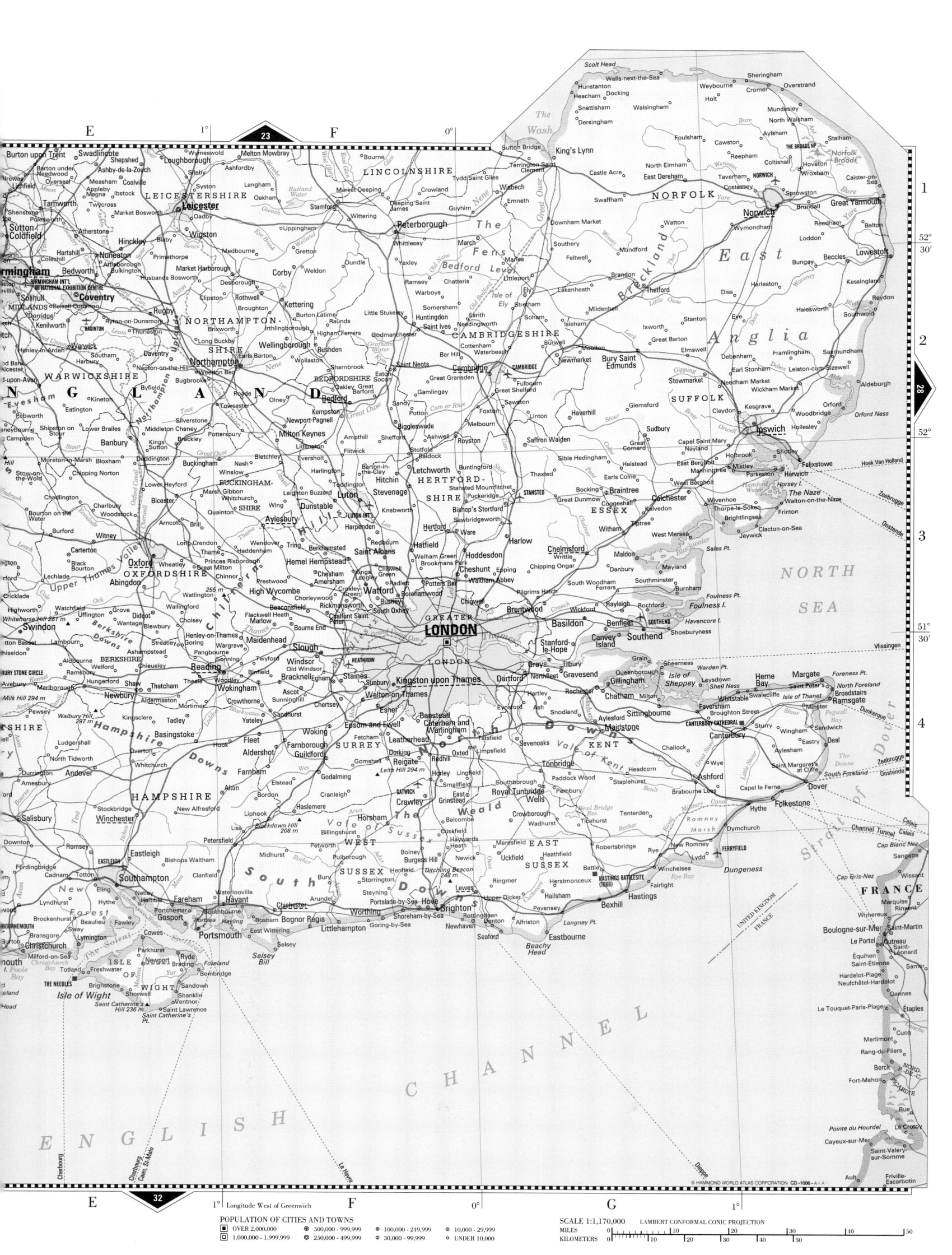

POPULATION OF CITIES AND TOWNS

■ OVER 2,000,000   ● 500,000 - 999,999   ◉ 100,000 - 249,999   ○ 10,000 - 29,999
▣ 1,000,000 - 1,999,999   ● 250,000 - 499,999   ◉ 30,000 - 99,999   · UNDER 10,000

SCALE 1:1,170,000   LAMBERT CONFORMAL CONIC PROJECTION

MILES 0   10   20   30   40   50
KILOMETERS 0   10   20   30   40   50

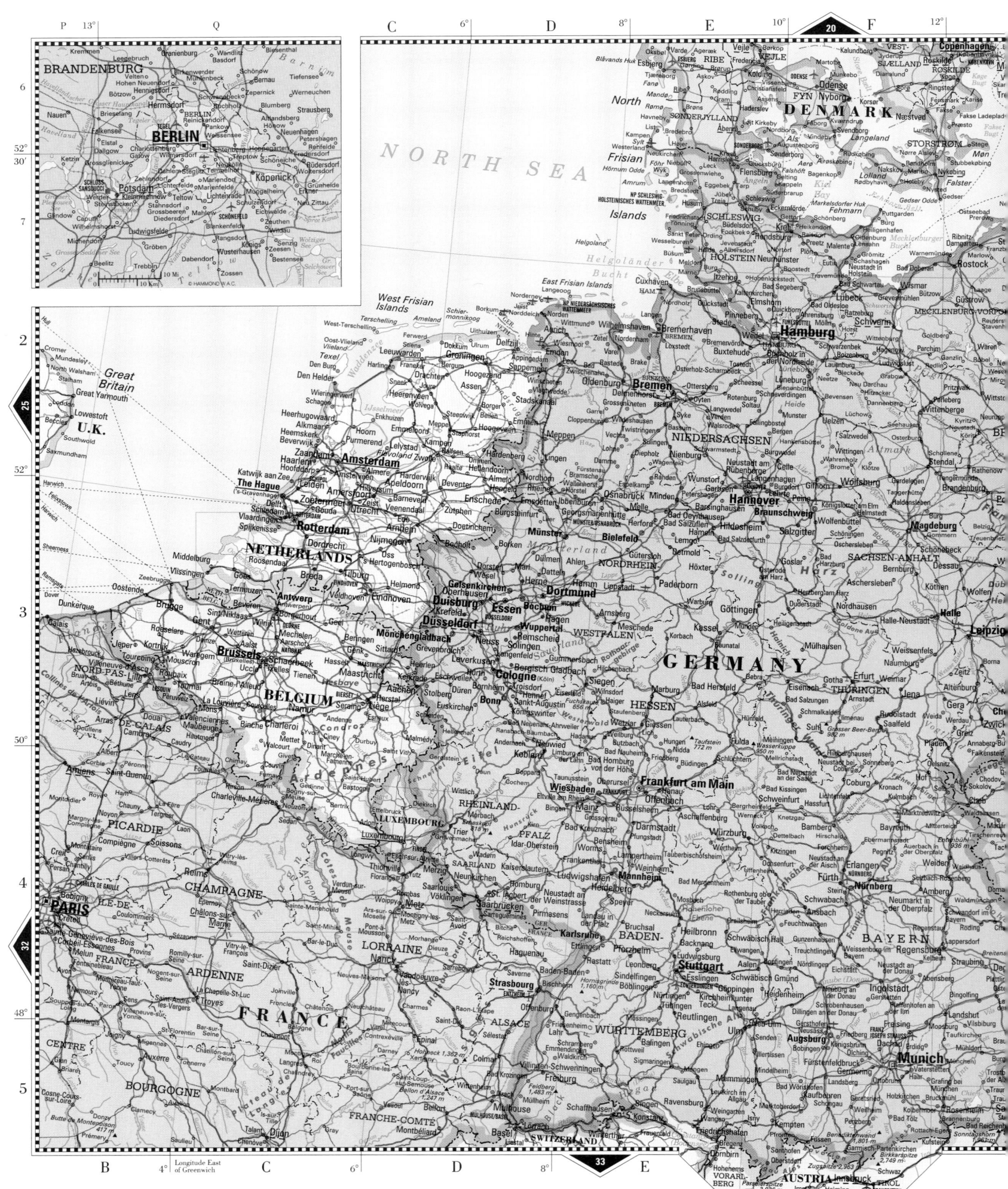

North Central Europe

BALTIC SEA

RUSSIA
KALININGRAD OBLAST
LITHUANIA
BELARUS
POLAND
CZECH REPUBLIC
SLOVAKIA
AUSTRIA
HUNGARY
ROMANIA
UKRAINE
SWEDEN
DENMARK

Carpathian Mountains
Beskids
Sudeten
Małopolska Uplands
Lubelska Uplands
Bohemia

Major cities: Warsaw, Kraków, Gdańsk, Gdynia, Szczecin, Poznań, Wrocław, Łódź, Lublin, Białystok, Kaunas, Vilnius, Kaliningrad, Brest, L'viv, Prague, Brno, Bratislava, Vienna, Budapest, Dresden

POPULATION OF CITIES AND TOWNS
■ OVER 2,000,000
□ 1,000,000 - 1,999,999
◉ 500,000 - 999,999
◎ 250,000 - 499,999
● 100,000 - 249,999
○ 30,000 - 99,999
◦ 10,000 - 29,999
· UNDER 10,000

SCALE 1:3,500,000   LAMBERT CONFORMAL CONIC PROJECTION
MILES   0   50   100   150
KILOMETERS   0   50   100   150

HAMMOND WORLD ATLAS CORPORATION

Netherlands, Northwestern Germany

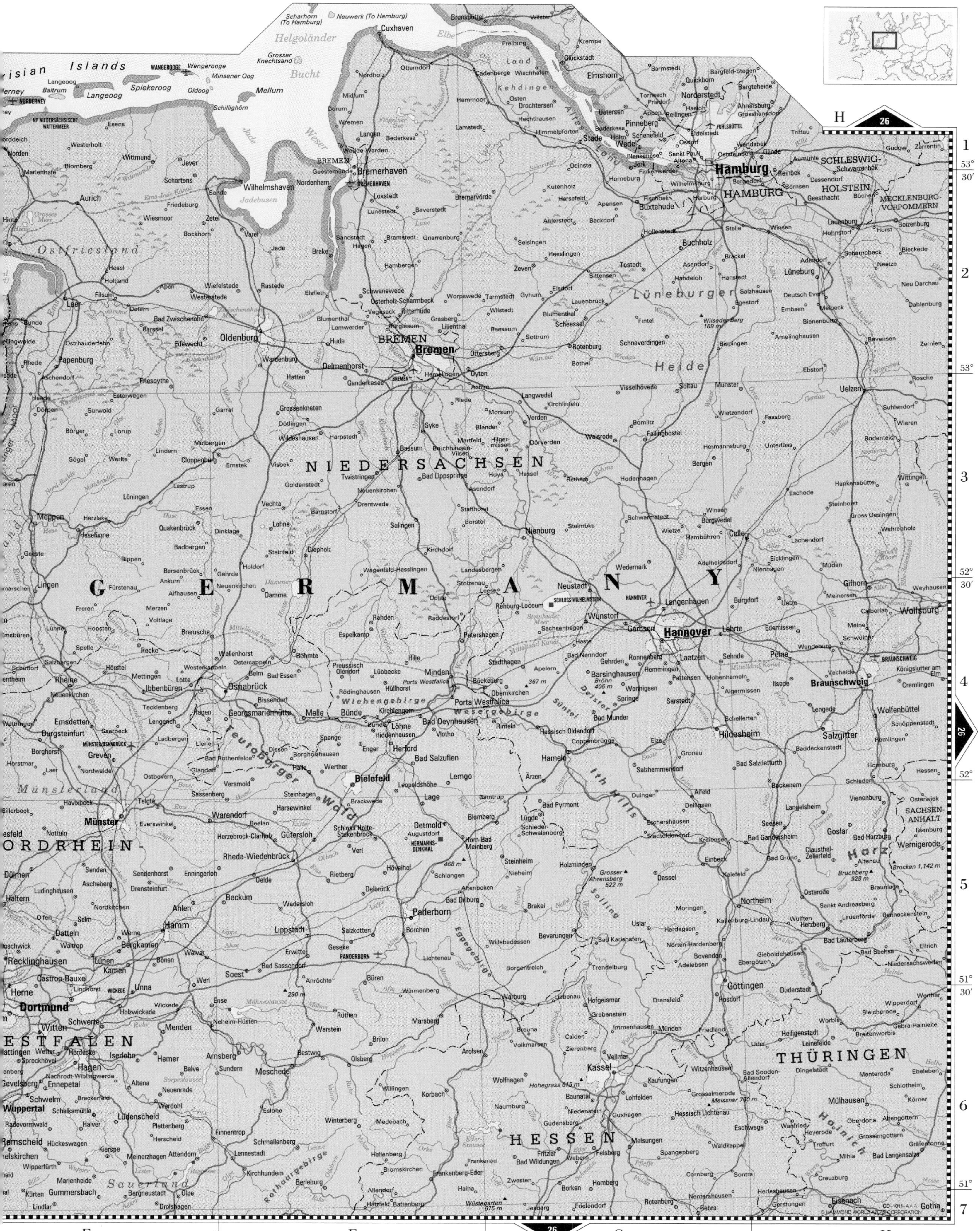

Frisian Islands
Helgoländer Bucht
Neuwerk (To Hamburg)
Scharhorn (To Hamburg)
Cuxhaven
Wangerooge
Spiekeroog
Langeoog
Baltrum
Norderney
Mellum
Minsener Oog
Oldoog
Schillighörn
Grosser Knechtsand
NP NIEDERSÄCHSISCHE WATTENMEER
Jade
Weser
Elbe
Jadebusen
Wilhelmshaven
Jever
Wittmund
Esens
Norden
Aurich
Ostfriesland
Emden
Leer
Papenburg
Oldenburg
Bremerhaven
Bremen
BREMEN
Delmenhorst
Cloppenburg
Vechta
Meppen
Lingen
Nordhorn
Osnabrück
Münster
Münsterland
Teutoburger Wald
Wiehengebirge
Wesergebirge
Bielefeld
Gütersloh
Paderborn
Detmold
Minden
Herford
Hamm
Dortmund
Unna
Soest
Lippstadt
Wuppertal
Hagen
Sauerland
Rothaargebirge
Eggegebirge
Stade
Buxtehude
Hamburg
HAMBURG
SCHLESWIG-HOLSTEIN
MECKLENBURG-VORPOMMERN
Lüneburg
Lüneburger Heide
Uelzen
Celle
Verden
Nienburg
Neustadt
Hannover
Wolfsburg
Braunschweig
Salzgitter
Hildesheim
Hameln
Ith Hills
Süntel
Deister
Solling
Göttingen
Northeim
Goslar
Harz
Brocken 1,142 m
Wilseder Berg 169 m
Steinhuder Meer
Mittelland Kanal
Kassel
Fulda
Eschwege
Mühlhausen
Eisenach
Gotha
Hainich
NIEDERSACHSEN
GERMANY
NORDRHEIN-WESTFALEN
HESSEN
THÜRINGEN
SACHSEN-ANHALT

POPULATION OF CITIES AND TOWNS
- OVER 2,000,000
- 1,000,000 - 1,999,999
- 500,000 - 999,999
- 250,000 - 499,999
- 100,000 - 249,999
- 30,000 - 99,999
- 10,000 - 29,999
- UNDER 10,000

SCALE 1:1,170,000 LAMBERT CONFORMAL CONIC PROJECTION

MILES 0 10 20 30 40 50

KILOMETERS 0 10 20 30 40 50

Belgium, Northern France, Western Germany

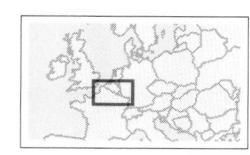

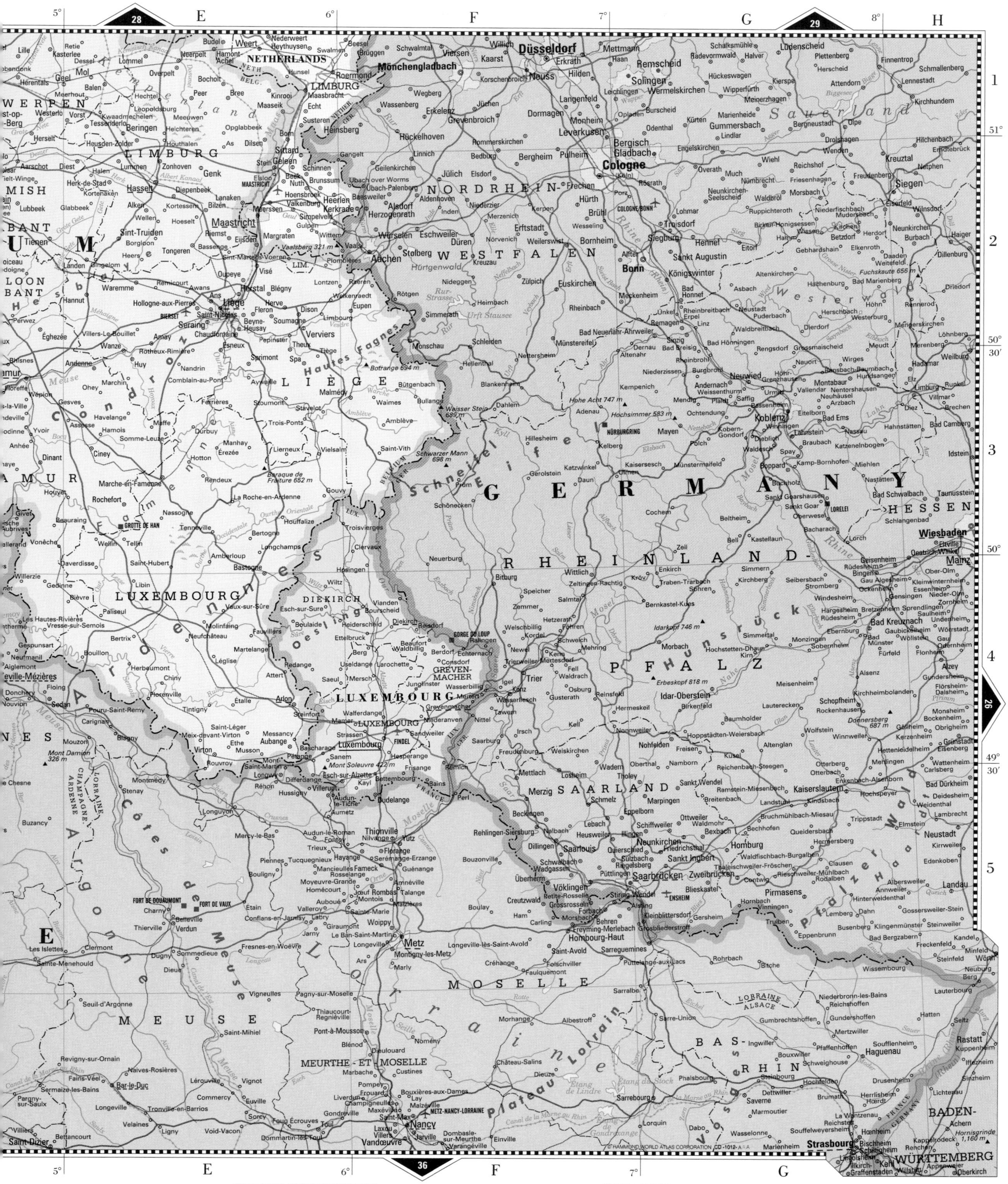

POPULATION OF CITIES AND TOWNS
- ■ OVER 2,000,000
- ◉ 500,000 - 999,999
- ● 100,000 - 249,999
- ○ 10,000 - 29,999
- ▣ 1,000,000 - 1,999,999
- ◉ 250,000 - 499,999
- ● 30,000 - 99,999
- ∘ UNDER 10,000

SCALE 1:1,170,000   LAMBERT CONFORMAL CONIC PROJECTION

MILES 0   10   20   30   40   50

KILOMETERS 0   10   20   30   40   50

West Central Europe

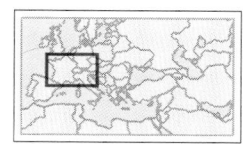

POPULATION OF CITIES AND TOWNS

- ■ OVER 2,000,000
- □ 1,000,000 - 1,999,999
- ● 500,000 - 999,999
- ◉ 250,000 - 499,999
- ● 100,000 - 249,999
- ● 30,000 - 99,999
- ● 10,000 - 29,999
- ∘ UNDER 10,000

SCALE 1:3,500,000   LAMBERT CONFORMAL CONIC PROJECTION

MILES   0   50   100   150

KILOMETERS   0   50   100   150

HAMMOND WORLD ATLAS CORPORATION CI - 1015 - A-A-A

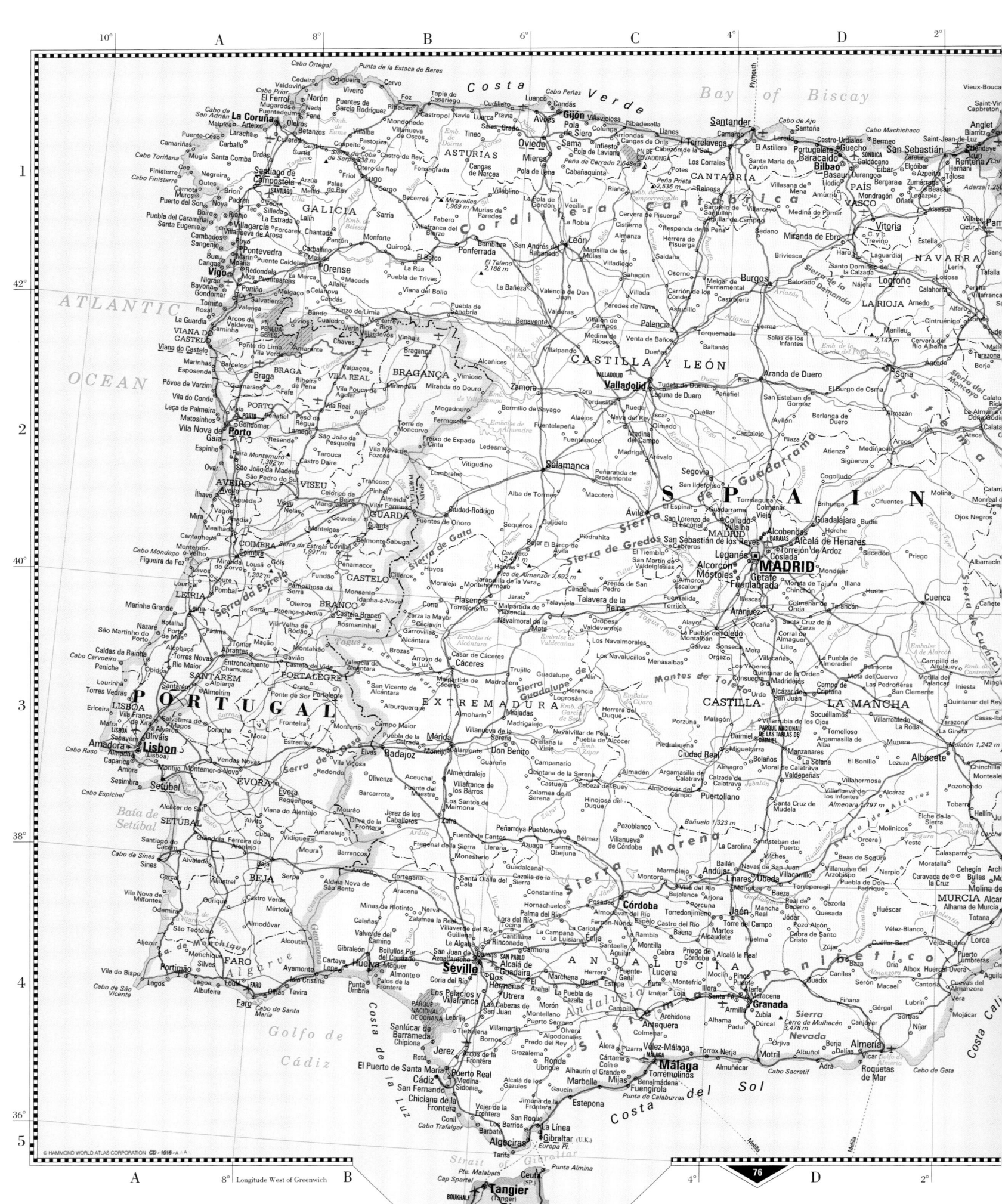

Spain, Portugal

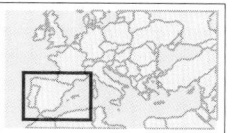

MEDITERRANEAN SEA

ATLANTIC OCEAN

Gulf of Lion

POPULATION OF CITIES AND TOWNS

- ■ OVER 2,000,000
- □ 1,000,000 - 1,999,999
- ● 500,000 - 999,999
- ◉ 250,000 - 499,999
- ● 100,000 - 249,999
- ◉ 30,000 - 99,999
- ⊙ 10,000 - 29,999
- ⊙ UNDER 10,000

SCALE 1:3,500,000 LAMBERT CONFORMAL CONIC PROJECTION

MILES 0   50   100   150

KILOMETERS 0   50   100   150

© HAMMOND WORLD ATLAS CORPORATION

Central Alps Region

POPULATION OF CITIES AND TOWNS

| OVER 2,000,000 | 500,000 - 999,999 | 100,000 - 249,999 | 10,000 - 29,999 |
| 1,000,000 - 1,999,999 | 250,000 - 199,999 | 30,000 - 99,999 | UNDER 10,000 |

SCALE 1:1,170,000   LAMBERT CONFORMAL CONIC PROJECTION
MILES 0 ... 10 ... 20 ... 30 ... 40 ... 50
KILOMETERS 0 ... 10 ... 20 ... 30 ... 40 ... 50

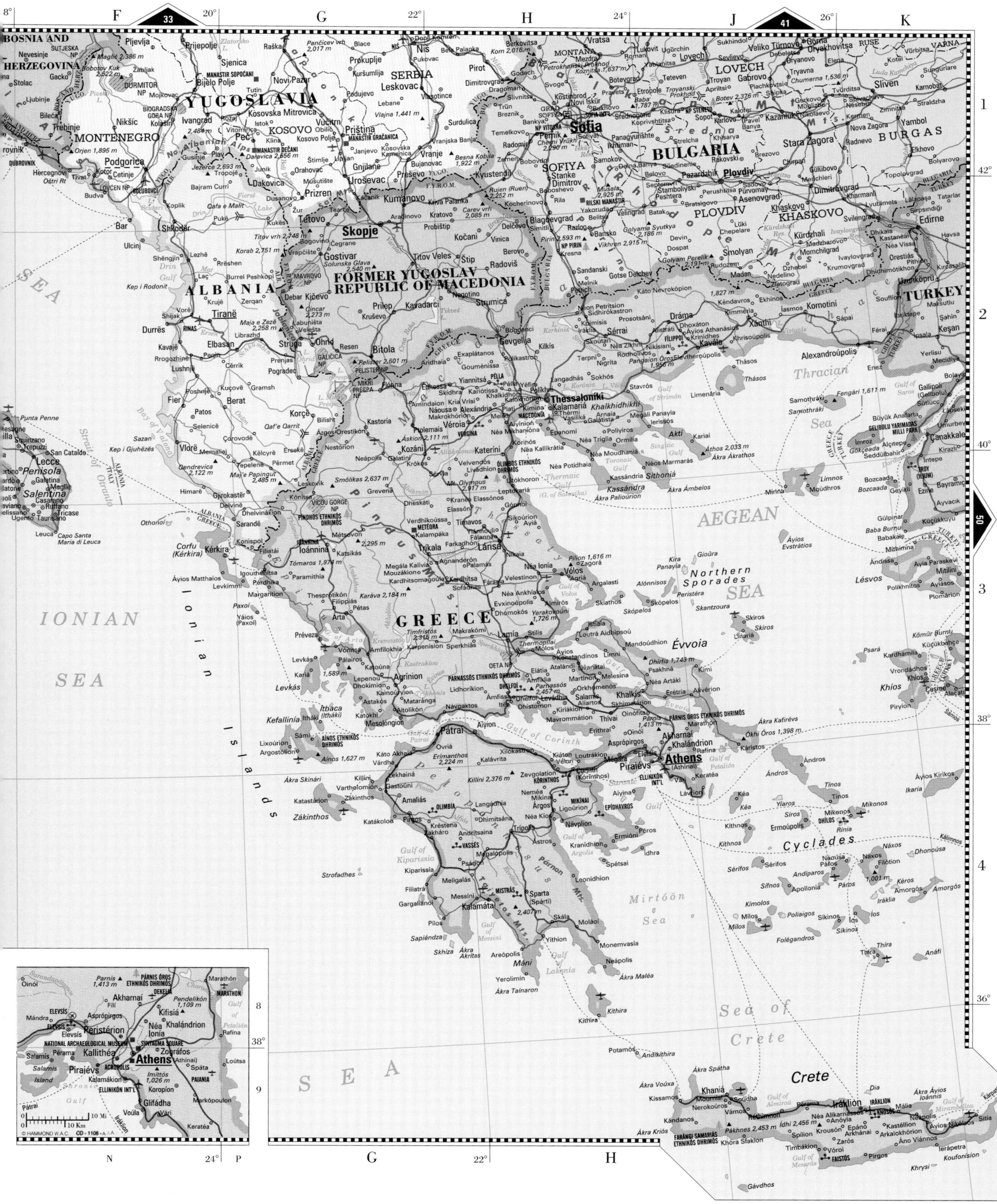

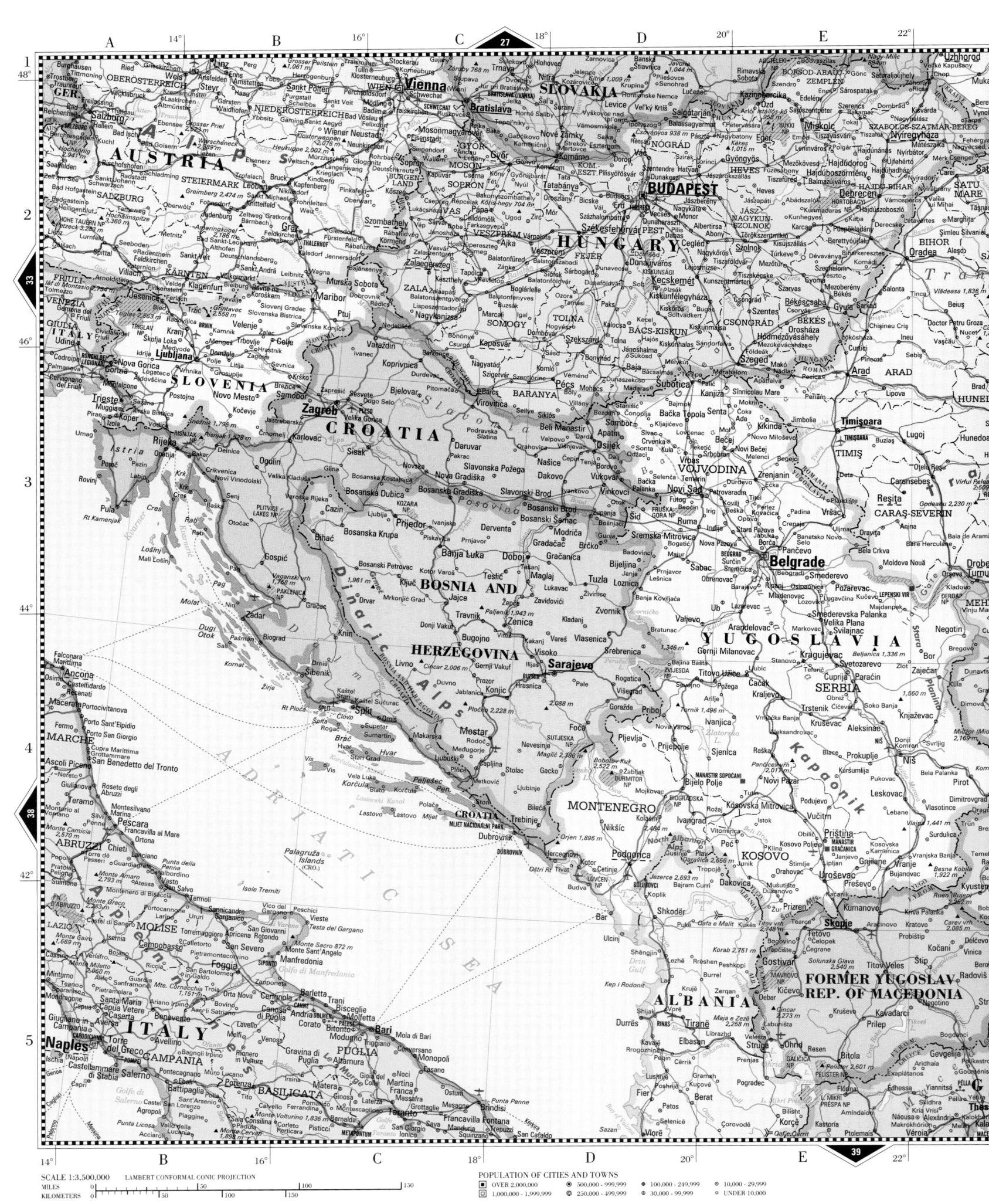

POPULATION OF CITIES AND TOWNS

■ OVER 2,000,000	● 500,000 - 999,999	● 100,000 - 249,999	○ 10,000 - 29,999
▣ 1,000,000 - 1,999,999	● 250,000 - 499,999	● 30,000 - 99,999	○ UNDER 10,000

Hungary and Northern Balkan States

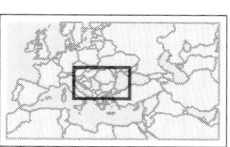

© HAMMOND WORLD ATLAS CORPORATION

Northeastern Europe

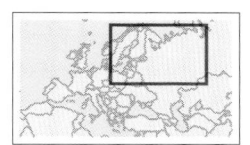

POPULATION OF CITIES AND TOWNS

| ■ OVER 2,000,000 | ● 500,000 - 999,999 | ● 100,000 - 249,999 | ○ 10,000 - 29,999 |
| ☐ 1,000,000 - 1,999,999 | ● 250,000 - 499,999 | ● 30,000 - 99,999 | ○ UNDER 10,000 |

SCALE 1:7,000,000   LAMBERT CONFORMAL CONIC PROJECTION

MILES 0 ⌐ 100 ⌐ 200 ⌐ 300

KILOMETERS 0 ⌐ 100 ⌐ 200 ⌐ 300

© HAMMOND W.A.C.

© HAMMOND WORLD ATLAS CORPORATION   CD · 109A · A A A

POPULATION OF CITIES AND TOWNS

| ■ OVER 2,000,000 | ● 500,000 - 999,999 | ● 100,000 - 249,999 | ○ 10,000 - 29,999 |
| ▣ 1,000,000 - 1,999,999 | ◉ 250,000 - 499,999 | ⊙ 30,000 - 99,999 | ○ UNDER 10,000 |

Southeastern Europe

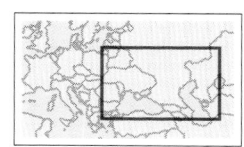

Russia and Neighboring Countries

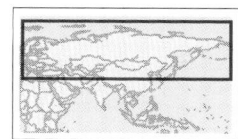

RUSSIA
(Administrative divisions are named only when they differ from their respective capitals.)

1. ADYGEA AUT. REP.
2. KARACHAY-CHERKESSIA AUT. REP.
3. KABARDINO-BALKARIA AUT. REP.
4. NORTH OSSETIA AUT. REP.
5. INGUSHETIA AUT. REP.
6. CHECHNYA AUT. REP.
7. DAGESTAN AUT. REP.
8. MORDOVIA AUT. REP.
9. CHUVASHIA AUT. REP.
10. MARI EL AUT. REP.
11. TATARSTAN AUT. REP.
12. BASHKORTOSTAN AUT. REP.
13. UDMURTIA AUT. REP.
14. PERMYAKIA AUT. OKRUG
15. KHAKASSIA AUT. REP.
16. UST'-ORDA AUT. OKRUG
17. AGA AUT. OKRUG

POPULATION OF CITIES AND TOWNS

- ■ OVER 2,000,000
- ◻ 1,000,000 - 1,999,999
- ● 500,000 - 999,999
- ◉ 100,000 - 499,999
- ⊙ 50,000 - 99,999
- ○ UNDER 50,000

SCALE 1:21,000,000   LAMBERT CONFORMAL CONIC PROJECTION

MILES 0   300   600   900
KILOMETERS 0   300   600   900

Occupied by Russia since 1945, claimed by Japan.

Asia

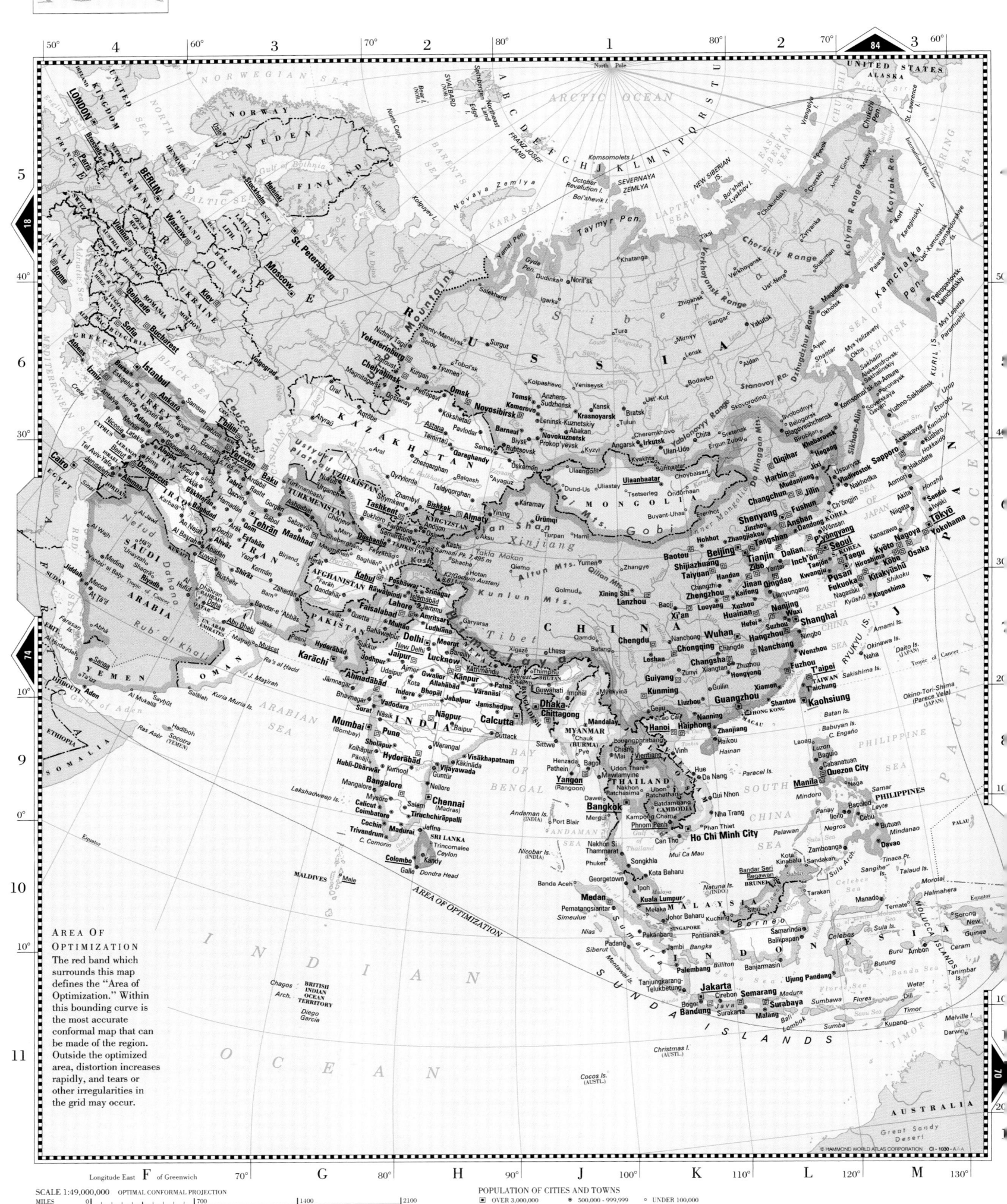

AREA OF
OPTIMIZATION
The red band which
surrounds this map
defines the "Area of
Optimization." Within
this bounding curve is
the most accurate
conformal map that can
be made of the region.
Outside the optimized
area, distortion increases
rapidly, and tears or
other irregularities in
the grid may occur.

SCALE 1:49,000,000   OPTIMAL CONFORMAL PROJECTION
Longitude East F of Greenwich

MILES   0   700   1400   2100
KILOMETERS 0   700   1400   2100

POPULATION OF CITIES AND TOWNS
☒ OVER 3,000,000   ⊛ 500,000 - 999,999   ○ UNDER 100,000
☐ 1,000,000 - 2,999,999   ● 100,000 - 499,999

© HAMMOND WORLD ATLAS CORPORATION   CI - 1030 - A-A

Eastern Mediterranean Region

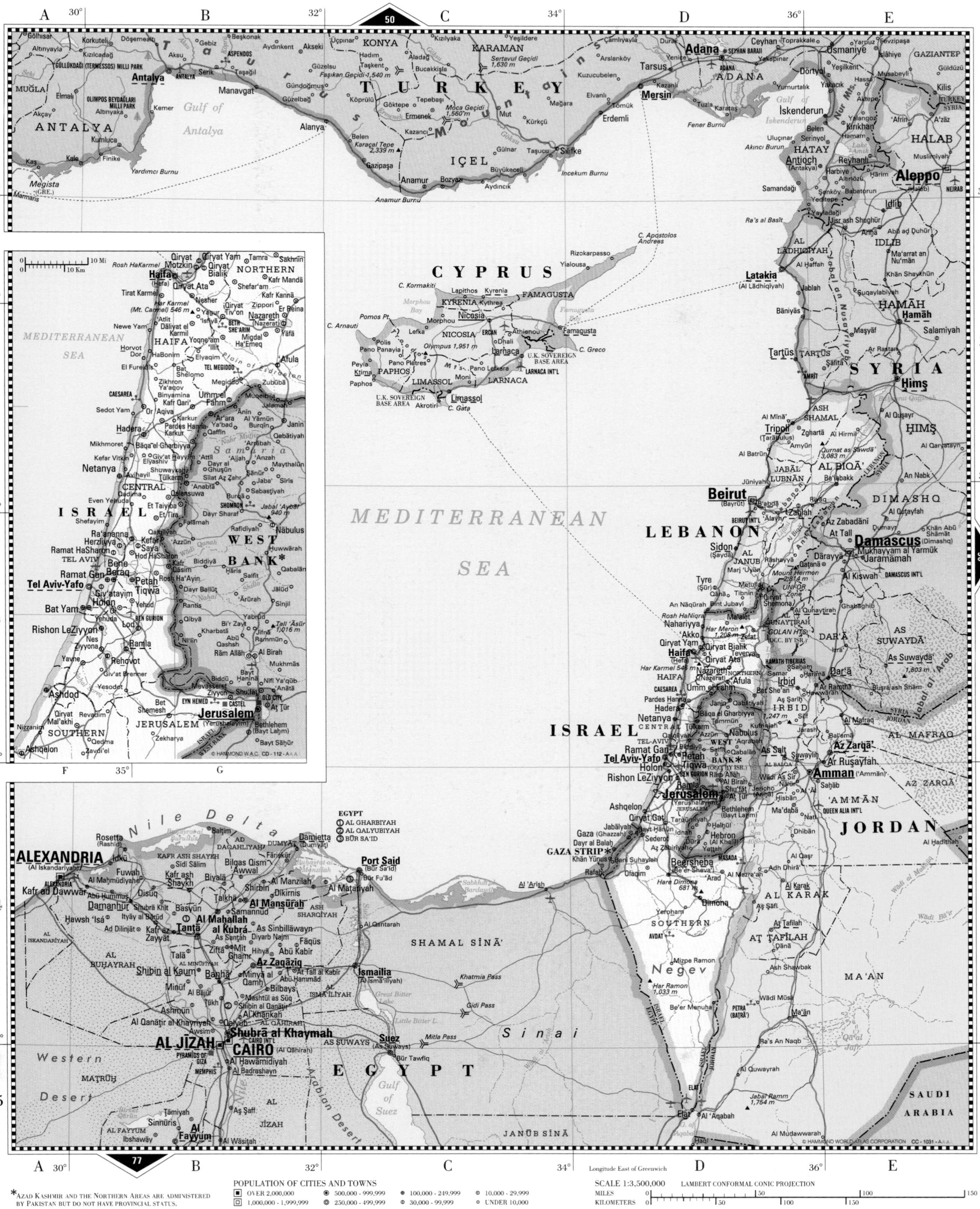

*Azad Kashmir and the Northern Areas are administered by Pakistan but do not have provincial status.

POPULATION OF CITIES AND TOWNS

■ OVER 2,000,000	● 500,000 - 999,999
▣ 1,000,000 - 1,999,999	◉ 250,000 - 499,999
● 100,000 - 249,999	◌ 10,000 - 29,999
◌ 30,000 - 99,999	○ UNDER 10,000

SCALE 1:3,500,000   LAMBERT CONFORMAL CONIC PROJECTION

MILES   0   50   100   150
KILOMETERS   0   50   100   150

Longitude East of Greenwich

© HAMMOND WORLD ATLAS CORPORATION   CC - 1031 - A - A - A

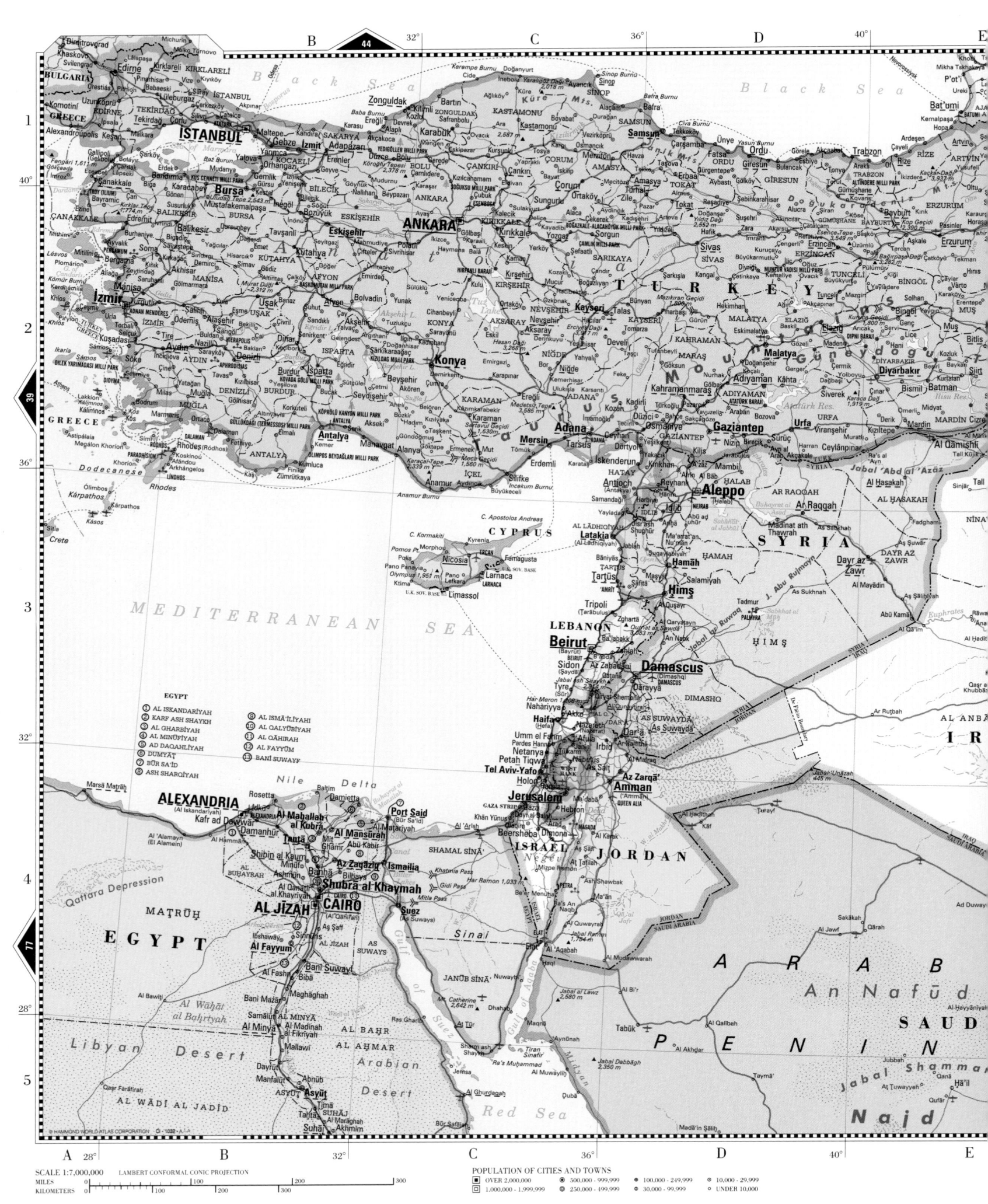

SCALE 1:7,000,000   LAMBERT CONFORMAL CONIC PROJECTION

MILES 0   100   200   300

KILOMETERS 0   100   200   300

POPULATION OF CITIES AND TOWNS

| ■ OVER 2,000,000 | ◉ 500,000 - 999,999 | ● 100,000 - 249,999 | ◎ 10,000 - 29,999 |
| ▣ 1,000,000 - 1,999,999 | ◉ 250,000 - 499,999 | ● 30,000 - 99,999 | ○ UNDER 10,000 |

EGYPT

① AL ISKANDARÏYAH
② KARF ASH SHAYKH
③ AL GHARBÏYAH
④ AL MINÜFÏYAH
⑤ AD DAQAHLÏYAH
⑥ DUMYAT
⑦ BÜR SAÏD
⑧ ASH SHARQÏYAH
⑨ AL ISMÄ'ÏLÏYAH
⑩ AL QALYÜBÏYAH
⑪ AL QÄHIRAH
⑫ AL FAYYÜM
⑬ BANÏ SUWAYF

Northern Middle East

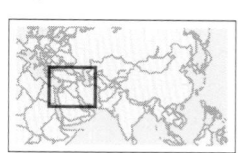

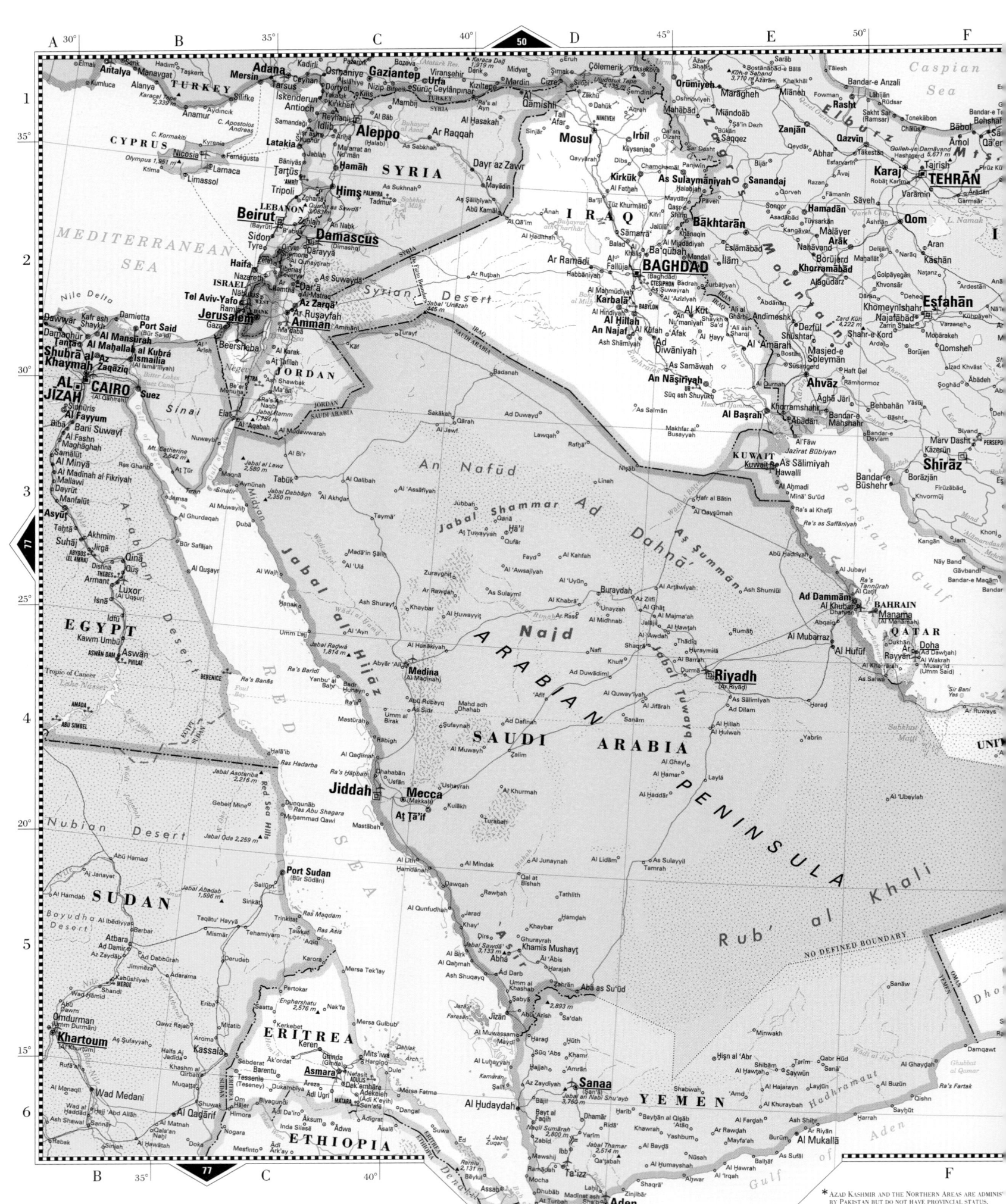

A | 30° | B | 35° | C | 40° | 50 | D | 45° | E | 50° | F

MEDITERRANEAN SEA

TURKEY

Antalya Manavgat Senk
Elmali Kumluca Alanya Anamur Aydıncık Silifke
Hadım Taşkent Kadirli Bozova Siverek Batman Midyat Cizre Şırnak Silopi Uludoruk Tepe Hakkari Çölemerik Yüksekova Çeruh Eruh
Mersin Tarsus Ceyhan Osmaniye Islâhiye Gaziantep Nizip Birecik Urfa Viranşehir Kızıltepe Mardin Dahük Zakhū
Adana Kilis Mambij Ra'ş al 'Ayn Al Qāmishlī NINEVEH 'Aqrah
İskenderun Antioch Reyhanlı Idlib Al Bāb TURKEY Al Ḥasakah Sinjār Tall 'Afar **Mosul** Irbīl Kūysanjaq Mahābād Miāndoab Bandar-e Anzalī

CYPRUS C. Kormakiti Kyrenia Famagusta
Nicosia Larnaca Limassol Ktima Olympus 1,951 m C. Apostolos Andreas

Latakia Jablah
Banıyas Ṭarṭūs 'AMRIT Tripoli

Aleppo (Halab) Ma'arrat an Nu'mān Ar Raqqah Dayr az Zawr Al Mayādīn Qayyārah Dibs Chamchamāl Panjwin Sanandaj **Zanjān** **Qazvīn**

Hamāh PALMYRA Tadmur As Sukhnah Abū Kamāl Ba'ī Kirkūk Al Fatḥah Tūz Khurmātū Kifrī Paveh Qorveh Razan **Hamadān**

Ḥimṣ Qubbat as Sawdā' 3,083 m Sabkhat Maydān Ḫānaqīn Khorri Şonqor Āvej Āshtiān

SYRIA

Beirut (Bayrūt) Zahlah An Nabk **Damascus** (Dimashq) Al Quṣayr Al Qā'im Anah Al Ḥadīthah Ar Ruṭbah **Bākhtarān** Malāyer Arāk Sāveh

LEBANON Sidon Tyre Shtora Ḥermon 2,814 m At Tanf

IRAQ Sāmarrā' Balad Khāliş Ba'qūbah Eslāmābād İlām Borūjerd Golpāyegān **Qom**

Haifa Nazareth Tiberias Dar'ā As Suwaydā' Az Zarqā' Jabal 'Unāzah 1,445 m Turayf **BAGHDAD** CTESIPHON Al Maḥmūdīyah As Suwayrah Zurbāṭīyah Delījān

Nablus **Tel Aviv-Yafo** Ramla WEST BANK **Amman** 'Ammān Ar Ramādī Fallūjah Al Kūt 'Alī al Gharbī Dehlorān Khvonsār

Jerusalem Gaza Bethlehem JORDAN SAUDI ARABIA Karbalā' BABYLON Al Hindīyah An Nu'mānīyah 'Alī ash Sharqī Andimeshk Nāṭanz

ISRAEL Beersheba Negev Al Karak Ma'ān Kāf Ṣakākah Qārah Ad Duwayd An Najaf **An Najaf** Afak Al Ḥayy Al 'Amārah Dezfūl Shūshtar Shahr-e Kord

Esfahān Mobārakeh Ardal

AL JIZAH **CAIRO** (Al Qāhirah) Suez Sinai Al 'Aqabah Al Mudawwarah Lawqah Rafḥā' Ad Qādisīyah As Samāwah Süq ash Shuyūkh Al Qurnah **Ahvāz** Āghā Jārī Rāmhormoz

SAUDI ARABIA

Asyūṭ Tahṭā Suhāj Akhmīm Jirgā Qinā THEBES Luxor Isnā Idfū EGYPT Kawm Umbū ASWĀN DAM Aswān PHILAE

An Nafūd Al Qalībah Al Jawf Taymā' Madā'in Ṣāliḥ Zuraynib **Ḥā'il** Jabal Shammar Qafār Fayd Buraydah

Ad Dahnā' As Summān Linah Ḥafr al Bāṭin Al Qaysūmah Ra's al Khafjī

KUWAIT **Kuwait** As Sālimīyah Ḥawallī Al Aḥmadī Minā' Su'ūd Jabal al Ḥasā

BAHRAIN **Manama** QATAR **Doha** (Ad Dawḥah)

SUDAN

RED SEA

ERITREA

ETHIOPIA

YEMEN

ARABIAN PENINSULA

Najd Riyadh (Ar Riyāḍ)

Rub' al Khali NO DEFINED BOUNDARY

Jiddah Mecca (Makkah) Aṭ Ṭā'if

Medina (Al Madīnah)

SAUDI ARABIA

Sanaa (San'ā')

Aden

*AZAD KASHMIR AND THE NORTHERN AREAS ARE ADMINIS... BY PAKISTAN BUT DO NOT HAVE PROVINCIAL STATUS.

Gulf of Aden

Southwestern Asia

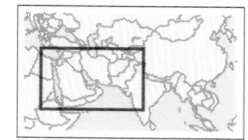

POPULATION OF CITIES AND TOWNS

- ■ OVER 2,000,000
- ◉ 300,000 - 999,999
- ● 100,000 - 249,999
- ○ 10,000 - 29,999
- ▣ 1,000,000 - 1,999,999
- ◎ 250,000 - 499,999
- ◯ 30,000 - 99,999
- ◦ UNDER 10,000

SCALE 1:10,500,000   LAMBERT CONFORMAL CONIC PROJECTION

MILES 0   150   300   450
KILOMETERS 0   150   300   450

© HAMMOND WORLD ATLAS CORPORATION

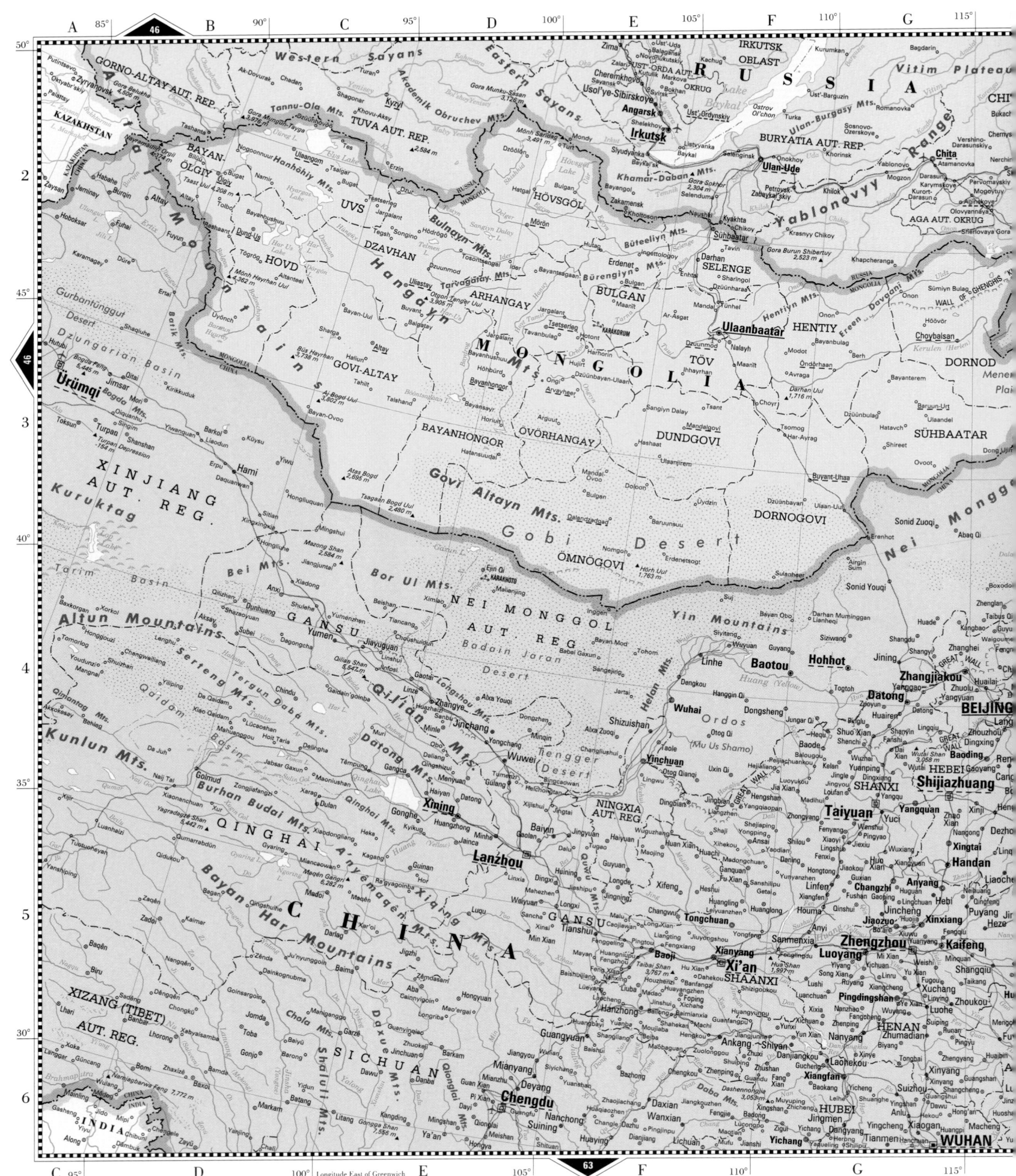

Eastern Asia

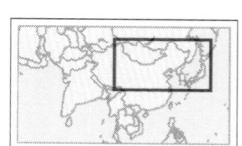

POPULATION OF CITIES AND TOWNS

- ■ OVER 2,000,000
- ▣ 1,000,000 - 1,999,999
- ● 500,000 - 999,999
- ● 250,000 - 499,999
- ● 100,000 - 249,999
- ● 30,000 - 99,999
- ○ 10,000 - 29,999
- ○ UNDER 10,000

SCALE 1:10,500,000 LAMBERT CONFORMAL CONIC PROJECTION

MILES 0 — 150 — 300 — 450
KILOMETERS 0 — 150 — 300 — 450

© HAMMOND WORLD ATLAS CORPORATION CD - 1034 - A A A

Longitude East of Greenwich

38°

SŎRAKSAN NAT'L PARK
Inje
Hongch'ŏn Yangyang
ODAESAN NAT'L PARK
KANGWŎN-DO
Kangnŭng
Paektŏk-san 1,350 m
Nogwak-san 1,321 m
Wŏnju Samch'ŏk
P'yŏngch'ang
Chech'ŏn Yŏng-yang
CH'UNGCH'ŎNG-
BUKTO
KYŎNGSANG-

2

58

Ullŭng I.
(S. KOREA)

SEA   OF   JAPAN

Liancourt Rocks
(Sovereignty Disputed)

Yŏngju
Chŏmch'ŏn
Andong Ch'ŏngsong
Andong Lake
BUKTO CHUWANG-SAN NAT'L PARK
Sangju Ŭisong Yŏngdŏk

SOUTH

KOREA

36°

Kumi
Kimch'ŏn
P'algong-san 1,192 m P'ohang
TAEGU- Sŏngju JIKHALSI TAEGU Yŏngch'ŏn
TAEGU Kyŏngsan Kyŏngju
SILLA TOMBS
Hwayang KYŎNGJU NAT'L PARK
PULGUK-SA
Kyŏngju
Miryang
KYŎNGSANG- Samnangjin Ulsan
NAMDO
Ŭiryŏng
Ch'angwŏn
Masan Chinhae KIMHAE
Kosŏng Kimhae
PUSAN-JIKHALSI
UNITED NATIONS MEMORIAL CEM.
PUSAN
Ch'ungmu Shinhyŏn
HALLYŎ HAESANG Koje Island
NAT'L PARK

OKI
ISLANDS
Dōgo
Saigō
OKI
DAISEN-OKI
Dōzen NAT'L PARK

DAISEN-OKI
NAT'L PARK
Sakaiminato
Jizō-zaki
Hino-misaki Hirata Matsue
Taisha YONAGO Yonago Toyo'oka
Izumo Yasugi Kurayoshi TOTTORI Miyazu
Ōda SHIMANE Shinji DAISEN-OKI Wakasa Tottori Hyō-sen 1,510 m
Dai-sen 1,711 m

SAN'IN KAIGIN
NATIONAL PARK
Iwami Kasumi
Komatsu
Kaga
Mikuni Sakai
Fukui
Sabae
Takefu
Kyōga-misaki Tsuruga Mihama
Obama
Waskasa
Bay
Nagahama
Maihara
Hikone
Biwa
Ōtsu
Kyōto

3

Hamada
Gōtsu Go
Masuda
Mi-shima
Shōbara
Tōjō
Niimi
Tsuyama
Takahashi Ako
OKAYAMA
Fukuchiyama Sonobe KYŌTO
Ayabe CHŪBU
KINKI
Kameoka
Nishiwaki
HYŌGO
Himeji
HIMEJI CASTLE Yokawa
KORAKUEN GARDEN Sanda
Kurashiki Kasai
Okayama Akō Akashi
Kōbe

Kyōto
Ōtsu SHIGA
Moriyama
Yōkaichi
Uji
Yao Nara
Kashihara
ŌSAKA
Takatsuki
Hirakata

34°

Iki IKI
Ko-saki
Kara-saki
Kamitsushima
SOUTH KOREA
JAPAN
Tsu Island
Izuhara
TSUSHIMA

Ai-shima
Kanmuriyama 1,339 m
Nagato Hagi
YAMAGUCHI
Yamaguchi
Shimonoseki
Kitakyūshū
KITAKYŪSHŪ
Fukuoka
FUKUOKA
Nogata Yukuhashi
Iizuka Tagawa
FUKUOKA Amagi Usa
Kurume Nakatsu
Tosu
Saga Okawa
SAGA Kashima Yamaga
Ōmuta Yamaga
Nagasaki Isahaya Ōmura
NAGASAKI PEACE PARK KUMAMOTO
Shimabara
Hondo
Yatsushiro

CHŪGOKU MTS.

Hōfu
Onoda UBE Tokuyama
Ube Kudamatsu
SETO-NAIKAI
NAT'L PARK
Iwakuni Yanai
Ōtake
Hiroshima
HIROSHIMA
PEACE MEMORIAL PARK
Takehara Mihara Onomichi
Kure Tadotsu
SETO-NAIKAI Marugame
NAT'L PARK Zentsuji
Hōjō
Sea of Suō Imabari
Niihama
Matsuyama
MATSUYAMA

Fuchū
Ibara Sōja
Fukuyama
Kasaoka
Fukuyama
Takamatsu
TAKAMATSU Shido
Shōdo
KAGAWA
Sakaide
Ikeda
Kan'onji
Saijō
Tonoshō
Sumoto
Awaji
Harima
Sea
Naruto
Waki
Kamojima
Tokushima

WAKAYAMA
Arida
Kainan
Wakayama
Yamatotakada
Gose
Gojō
YOSHINO-
KUMANO
NAT'L PARK
NARA
Kishiwada
Izumi-Sano
ŌSAKA
Nabari M
Matsusaka
Hakken-san 1,915 m
Ōdaiga

4

GOTŌ
ISLANDS
Nakadōri
KAMIGOTŌ
Hirado
SAIKAI Imari
NAT'L PARK Sasebo
Fukue SAIKAI NAT'L PARK
Fukue
Fukue

SHIMANE Yasugi
HIROSHIMA
Yoshida Ōzu
Yawatahama
EHIME
Uwajima
Nakamura
Kubokawa

Kurume Tosu
SAGA Yamaga
Amagi
FUKUOKA Kurume
Ōmuta
Yanagawa
Yamaga
ASO NAT'L PARK
Kuju-san 1,787 m
Takeda
Mie
Ōita
ŌITA
Beppu
Ōita
Usa
Hiji
ŌITA
Usuki
Saiki

SHIKOKU MTS.
Ishizuchi-san 1,982 m
Ino
Kōchi
KŌCHI
KŌCHI
Nankoku
Tosa
Saijō
TOKUSHIMA
Anan
Tosa Bay
Muroto
Komatsushima
Tsurugi-san 1,955 m
Kii
Channel
Gobō

Tanabe
Shingū
Nachi-Katsuura
Kushimoto
Ō-shima
Shio-no-misaki
Kumano
Owase

Amakusa
Sea
UNZEN-AMAKUSA
NATIONAL PARK
Minamata
Ushibuka
Akune
Izumi

KUMAMOTO
KUMAMOTO
Aso-san 1,592 m
Takamori
Nobeoka
Kunimi-dake 1,739 m
Hyūga
Saito Takanabe
MIYAZAKI
Hitoyoshi
Kirishima-yama
1,700 m
MIYAZAKI
Kobayashi Sadowara
MIYAZAKI
Kyūshū Highlands

Shikoku

PACIFIC

Ashizuri-misaki
Sukumo
Tosashimizu
Okino-
shima

OCEAN

32°

EAST

CHINA

SEA

Kami-
Koshiki I.
Shimo-
Koshiki I.
Sendai Kushikino
Ijūin
Kagoshima
KAGOSHIMA
Miyanojō
Ōkuchi
Miyakonojō
Kokubu
Kyūshū
Miyazaki

Nichinan

5

Nomo-misaki
Makurazaki
KIRISHIMA
Kaseda
Kanoya
Kōyama
Ōsumi Pen.
Satsuma
Osumi Bay
YAKU NAT'L PARK
Kagoshima Bay

Kuro-
shima
Iō-
shima
Nishino'omote
Mage-
shima Tanega
Nakatane
ŌSUMI ISLANDS
Kuchinoerabu
Kamiyaku
Yaku
KIRISHIMA-YAKU NAT'L PARK

Shanghai

Central and Southern Japan

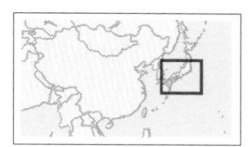

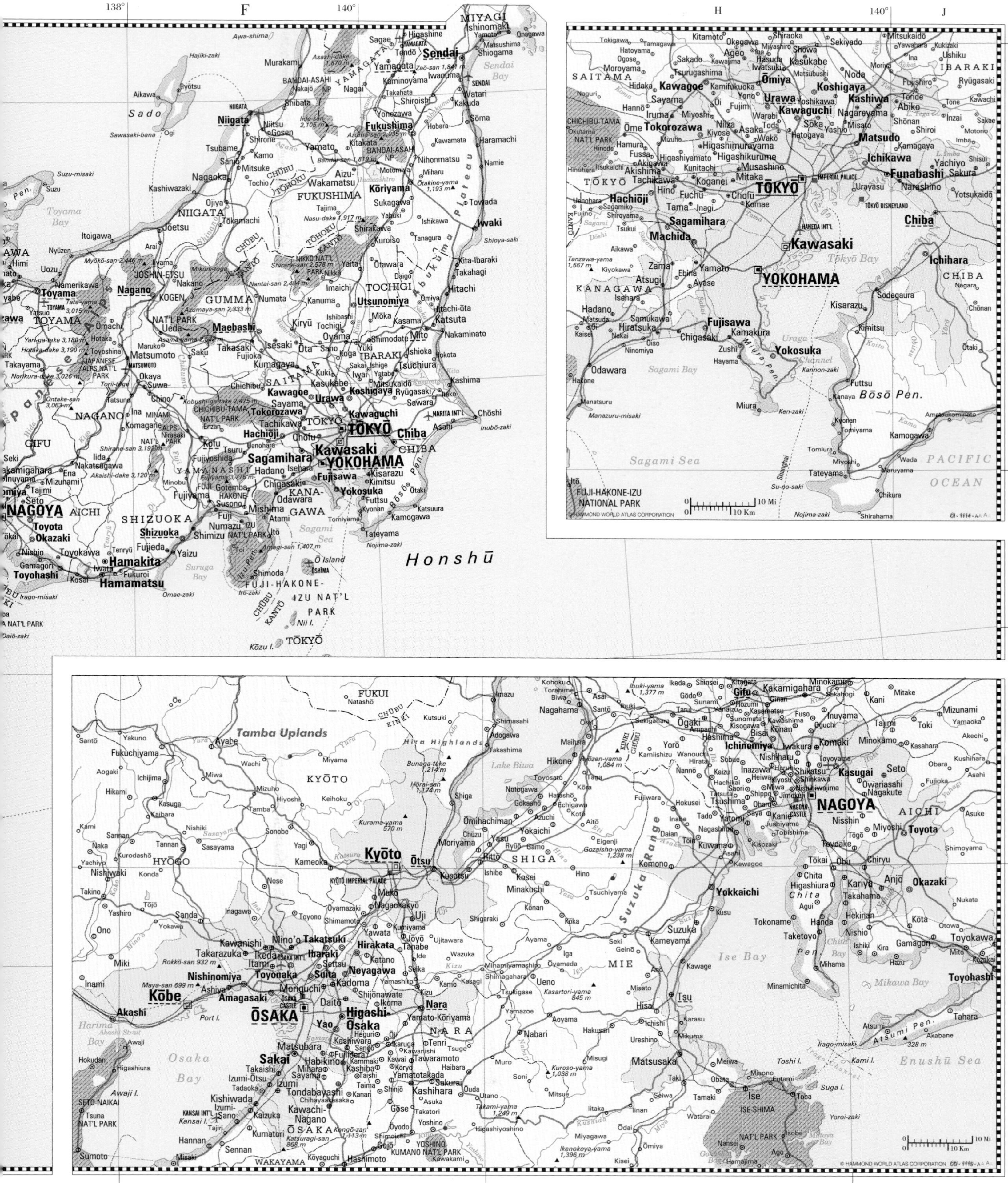

POPULATION OF CITIES AND TOWNS

■ OVER 2,000,000 ● 500,000 - 999,999 ● 100,000 - 249,999 ● 10,000 - 29,999
▣ 1,000,000 - 1,999,999 ● 250,000 - 499,999 ● 30,000 - 99,999 ● UNDER 10,000

SCALE 1:3,500,000   LAMBERT CONFORMAL CONIC PROJECTION

MILES 0   50   100   150
KILOMETERS 0   50   100   150

Honshū

© HAMMOND WORLD ATLAS CORPORATION

Korea

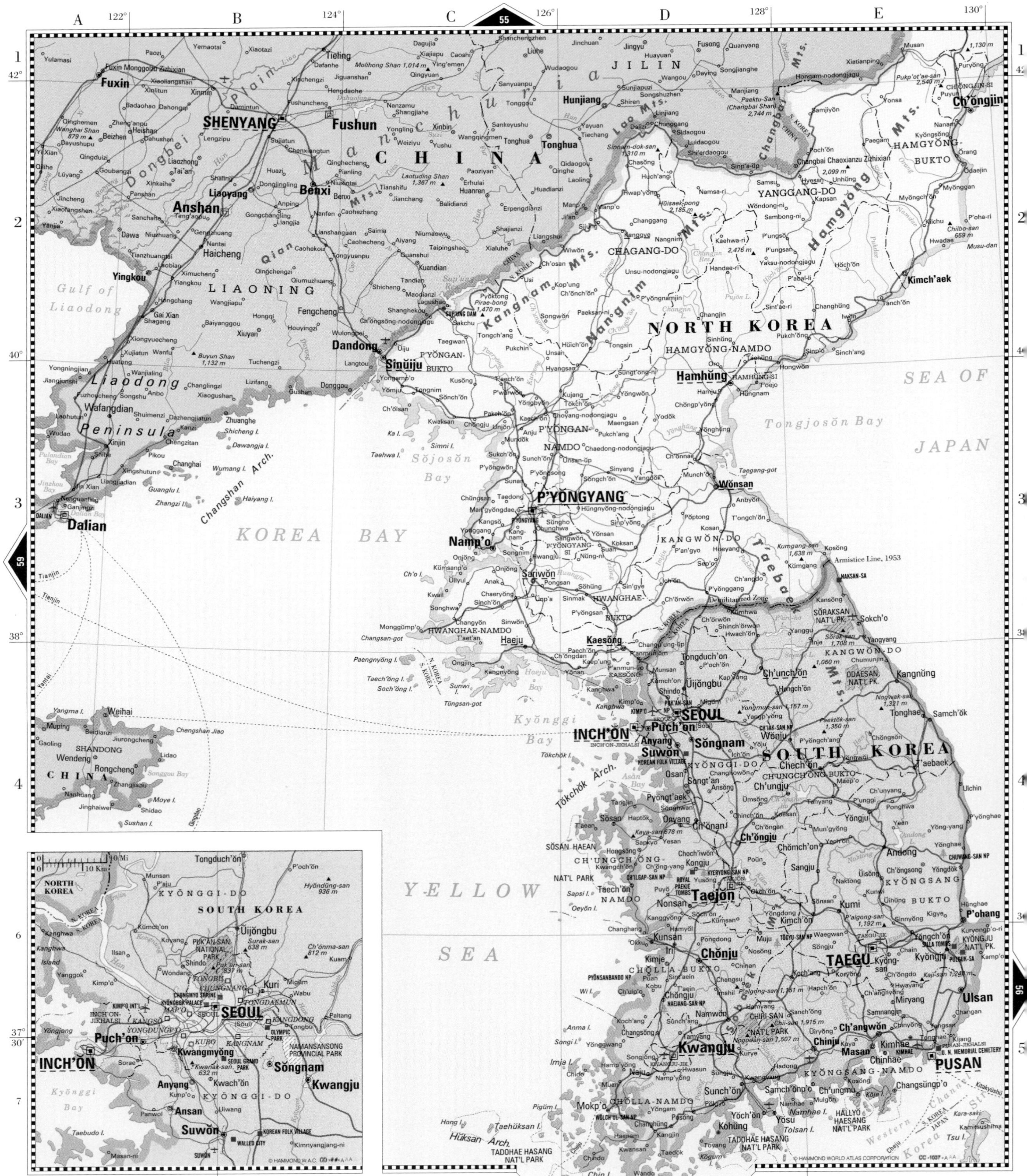

SCALE 1:3,500,000 LAMBERT CONFORMAL CONIC PROJECTION

MILES

KILOMETERS

POPULATION OF CITIES AND TOWNS

- ◼ OVER 2,000,000
- ◻ 1,000,000 - 1,999,999
- ● 500,000 - 999,999
- ◉ 250,000 - 499,999
- ● 100,000 - 249,999
- ● 30,000 - 99,999
- ◦ 10,000 - 29,999
- ◦ UNDER 10,000

Northeastern China

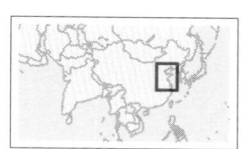

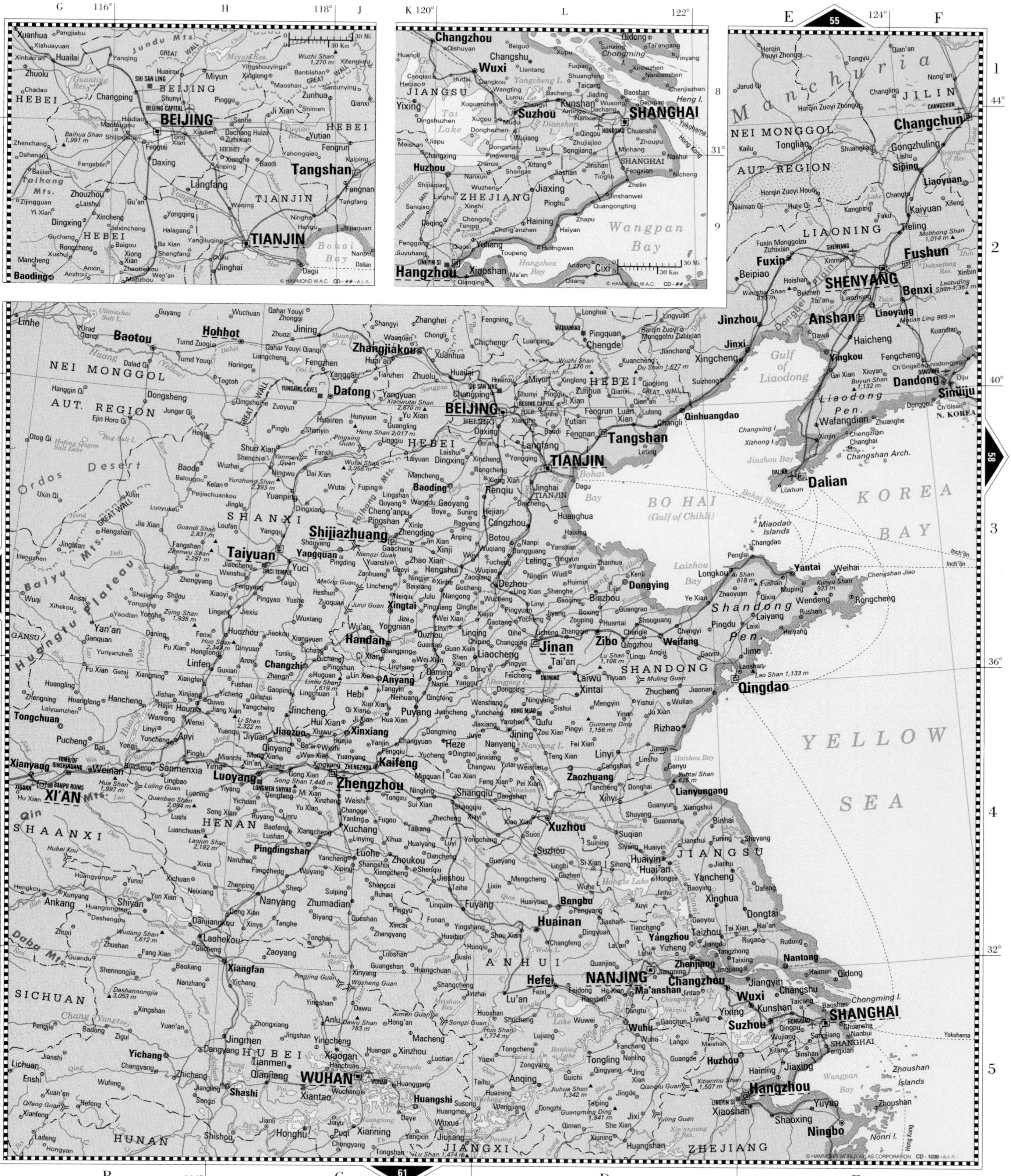

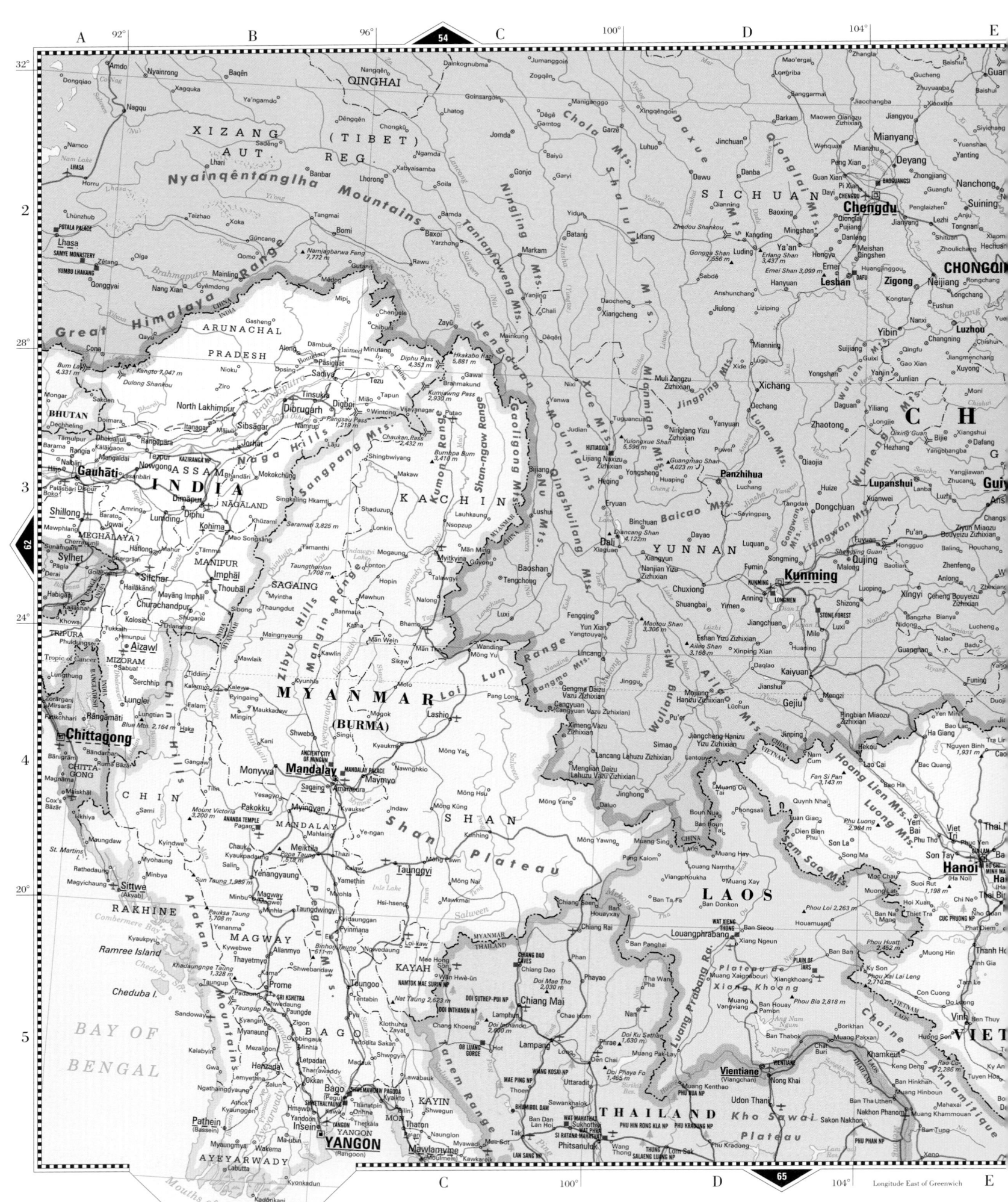

Southeastern China, Northern Indochina

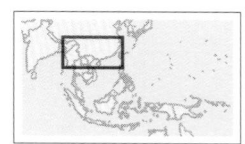

POPULATION OF CITIES AND TOWNS

- ■ OVER 2,000,000
- □ 1,000,000 - 1,999,999
- ● 500,000 - 999,999
- ● 250,000 - 499,999
- ● 100,000 - 249,999
- ● 30,000 - 99,999
- ○ 10,000 - 29,999
- ○ UNDER 10,000

SCALE 1:7,000,000   LAMBERT CONFORMAL CONIC PROJECTION

MILES   0   100   200   300
KILOMETERS   0   100   200   300

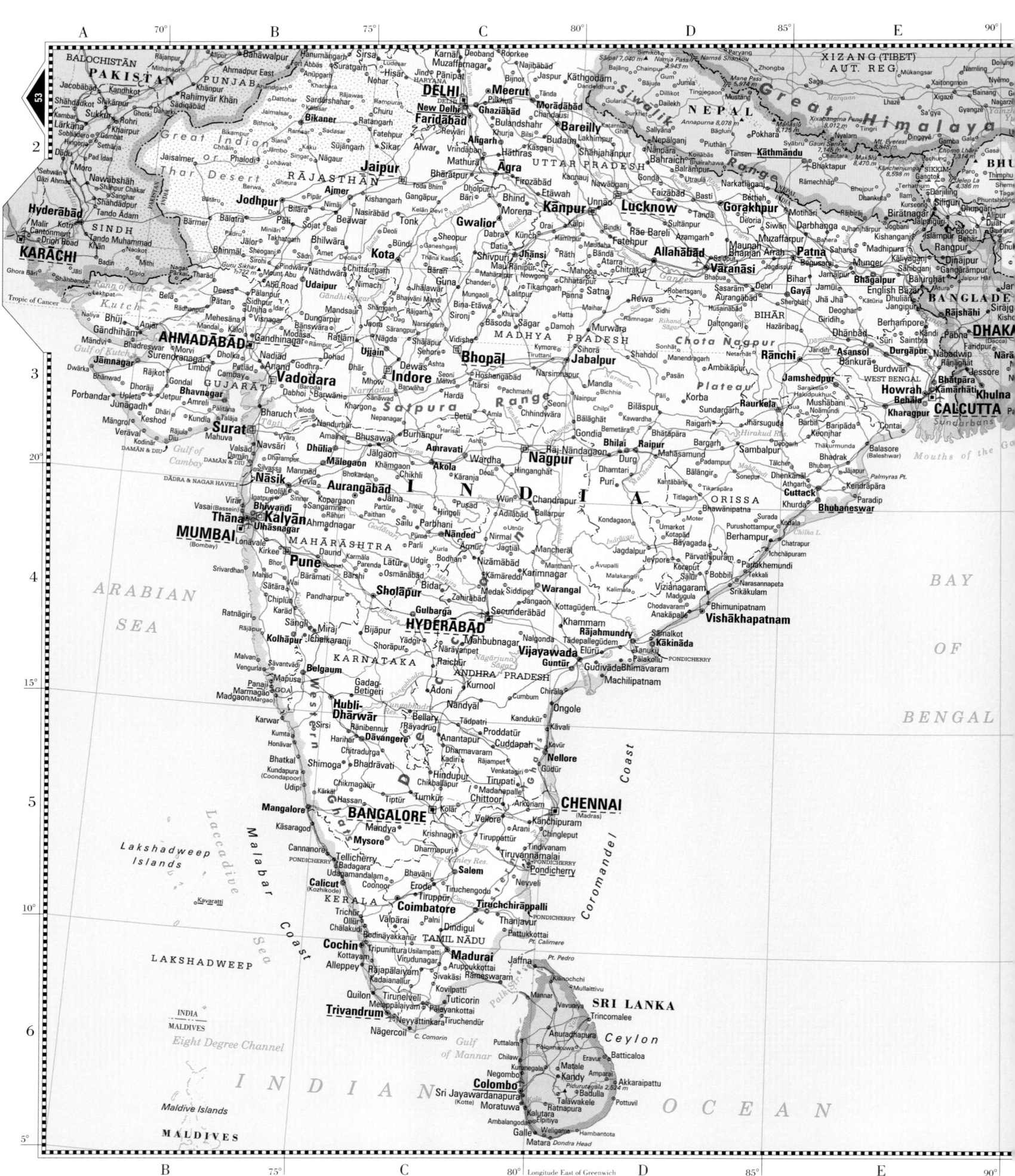

Southern Asia

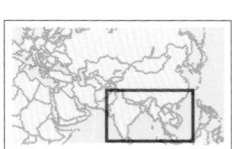

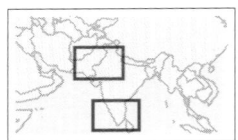

Punjab Plain, Southern India

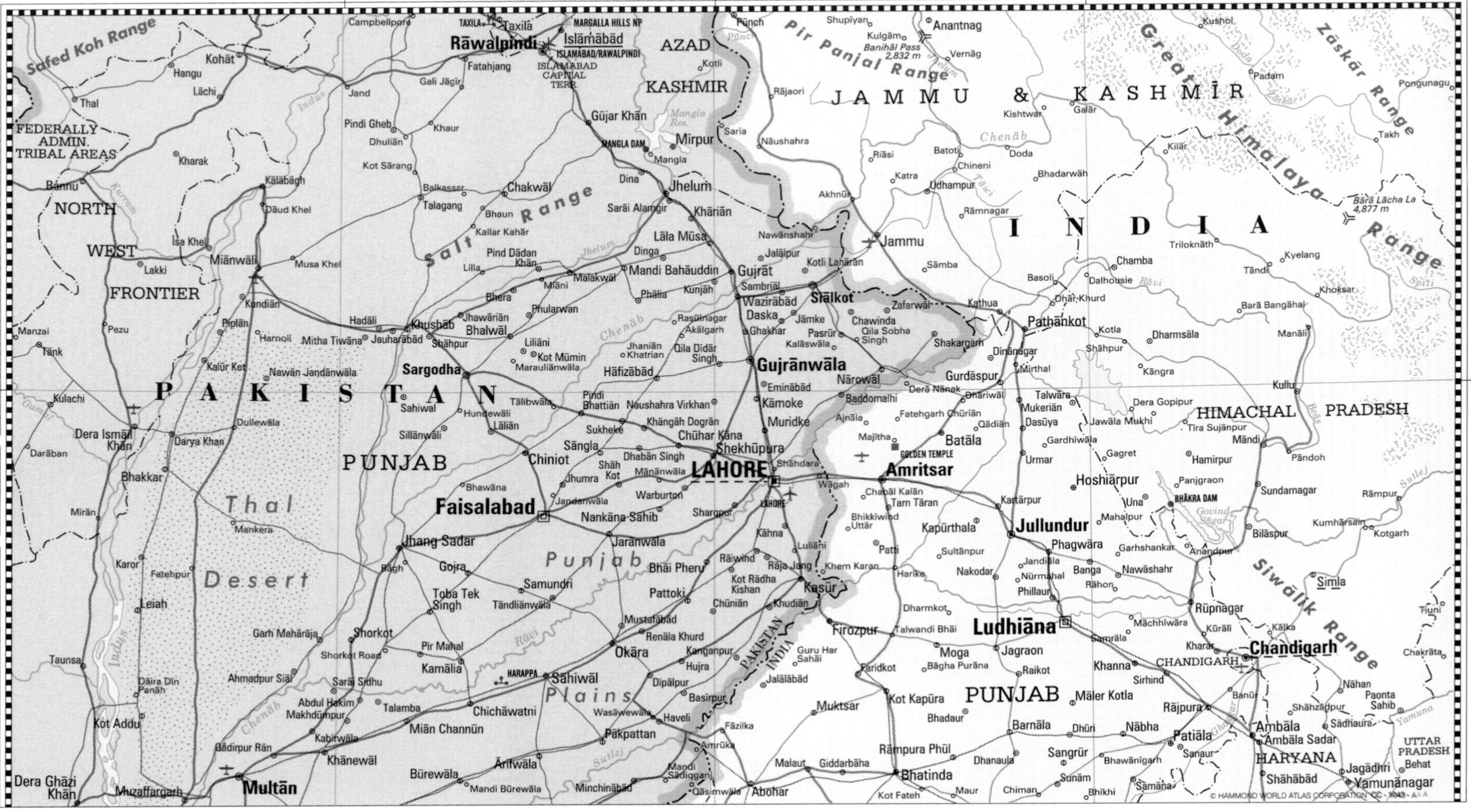

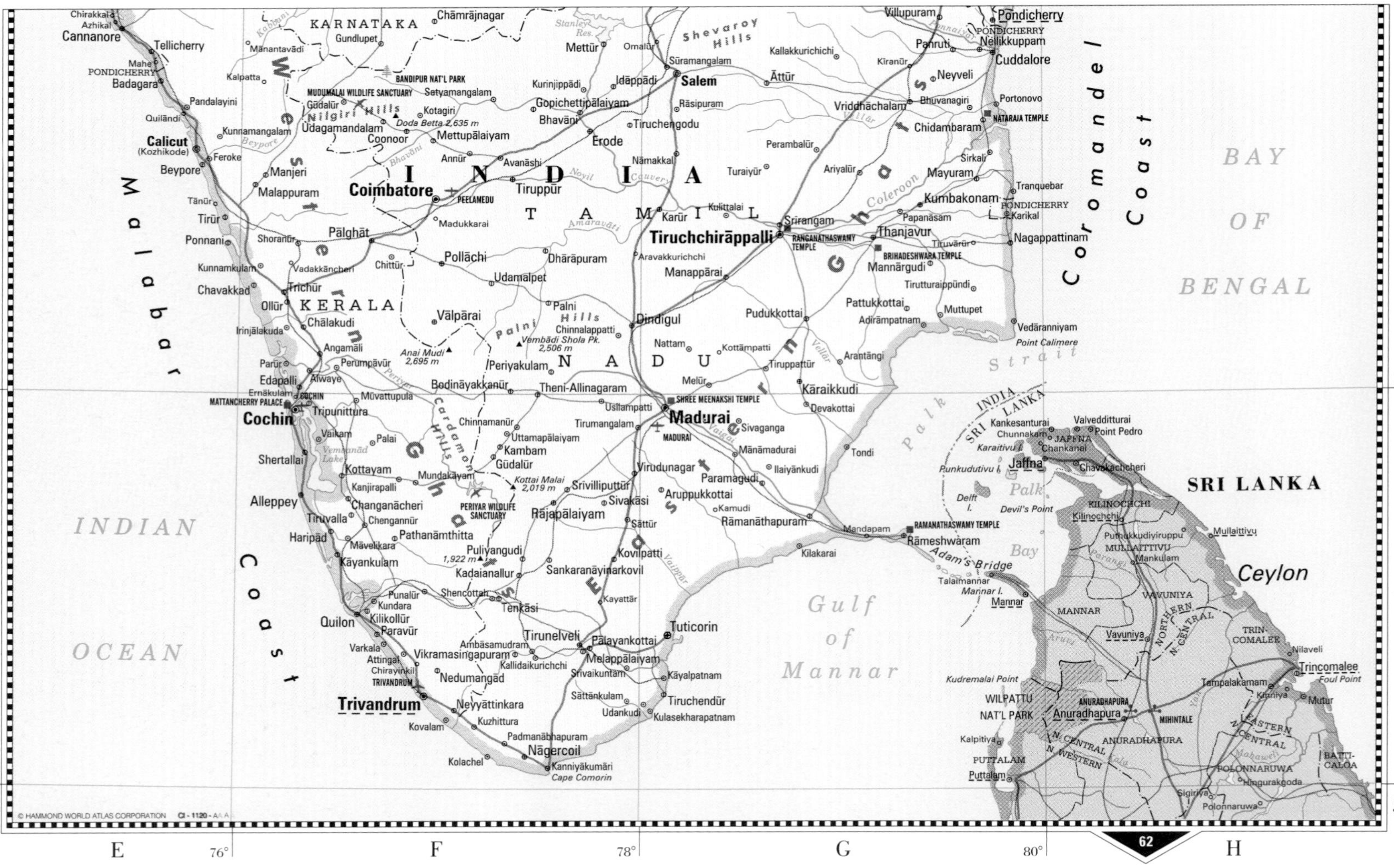

SCALE 1:3,500,000   LAMBERT CONFORMAL CONIC PROJECTION

MILES 0 | 50 | 100 | 150
KILOMETERS 0 | 50 | 100 | 150

POPULATION OF CITIES AND TOWNS

- ■ OVER 2,000,000
- ◉ 500,000 - 999,999
- ● 100,000 - 249,999
- ◉ 10,000 - 29,999
- ▣ 1,000,000 - 1,999,999
- ● 250,000 - 499,999
- ● 30,000 - 99,999
- ○ UNDER 10,000

Indochina

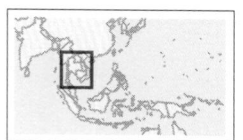

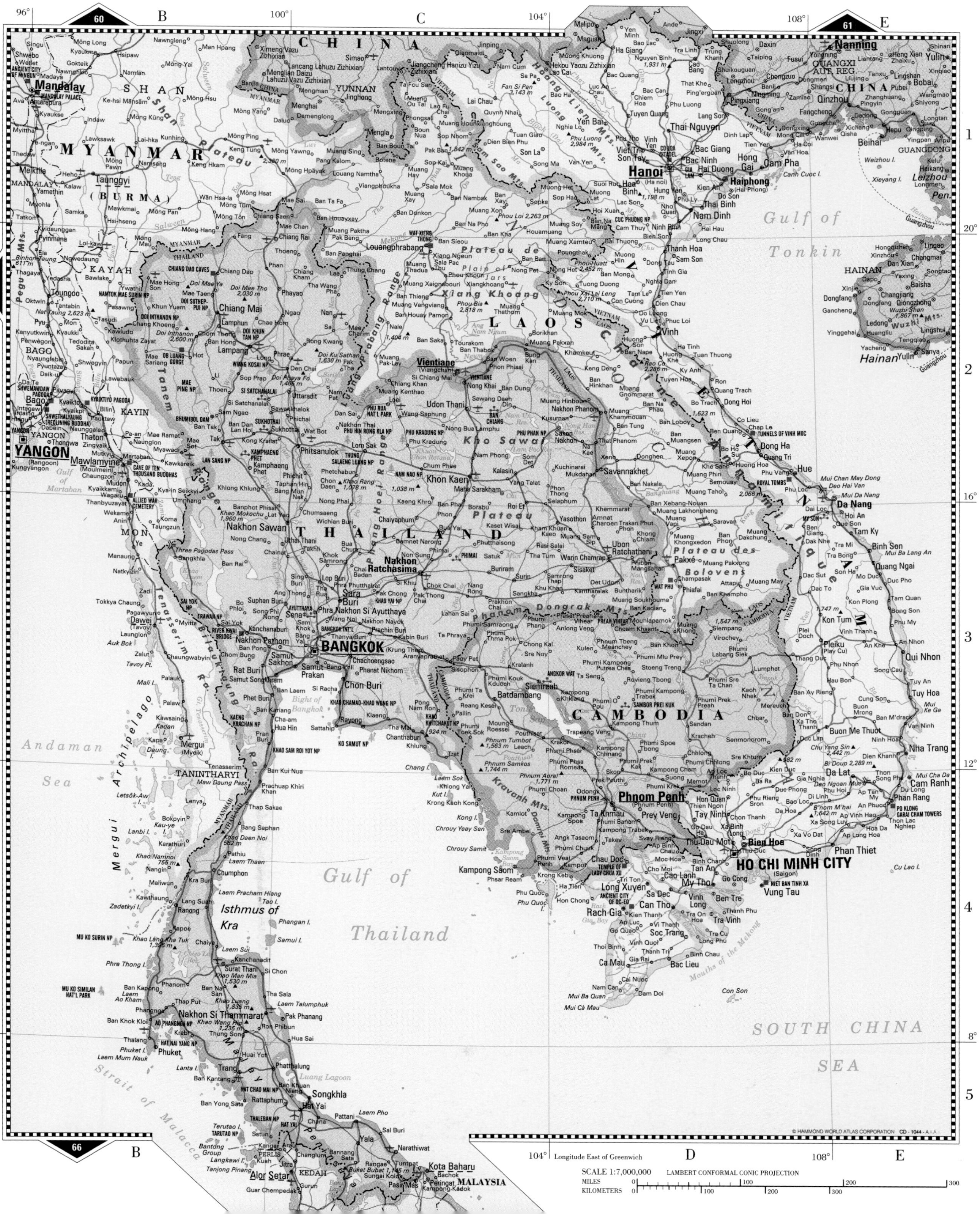
CHINA
MYANMAR
(BURMA)
THAILAND
LAOS
CAMBODIA
VIETNAM
MALAYSIA
YUNNAN
SHAN
KAYAH
KAYIN
MON
TANINTHARYI
HAINAN
GUANGXI AUT. REG.
GUANGDONG
KEDAH
PERLIS
Mandalay
YANGON (Rangoon)
Hanoi
Vientiane
BANGKOK
Phnom Penh
HO CHI MINH CITY (Saigon)
Nanning
Haiphong
Da Nang
Hue
Chiang Mai
Nakhon Ratchasima
Songkhla
Hat Yai
Alor Setar
Kota Baharu
Gulf of Tonkin
Gulf of Thailand
Andaman Sea
SOUTH CHINA SEA
Gulf of Martaban
Strait of Malacca
Isthmus of Kra
Mergui Archipelago
Plateau de Xiang Khoang
Plateau des Bolovens
Kho Sawat Plateau
Dongrak Mts.
Kravanh Mts.
Tenasserim Ra.
Bilauktaung Ra.
Shan Plateau
Phetchabun Range
Luang Prabang Range
Annamitique
Mouths of the Mekong
Longitude East of Greenwich
SCALE 1:7,000,000
LAMBERT CONFORMAL CONIC PROJECTION
MILES 0 100 200 300
KILOMETERS 0 100 200 300
© HAMMOND WORLD ATLAS CORPORATION CD-1044-AAA

Indonesia, Malaysia

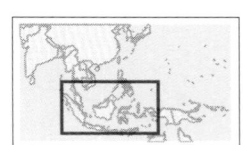

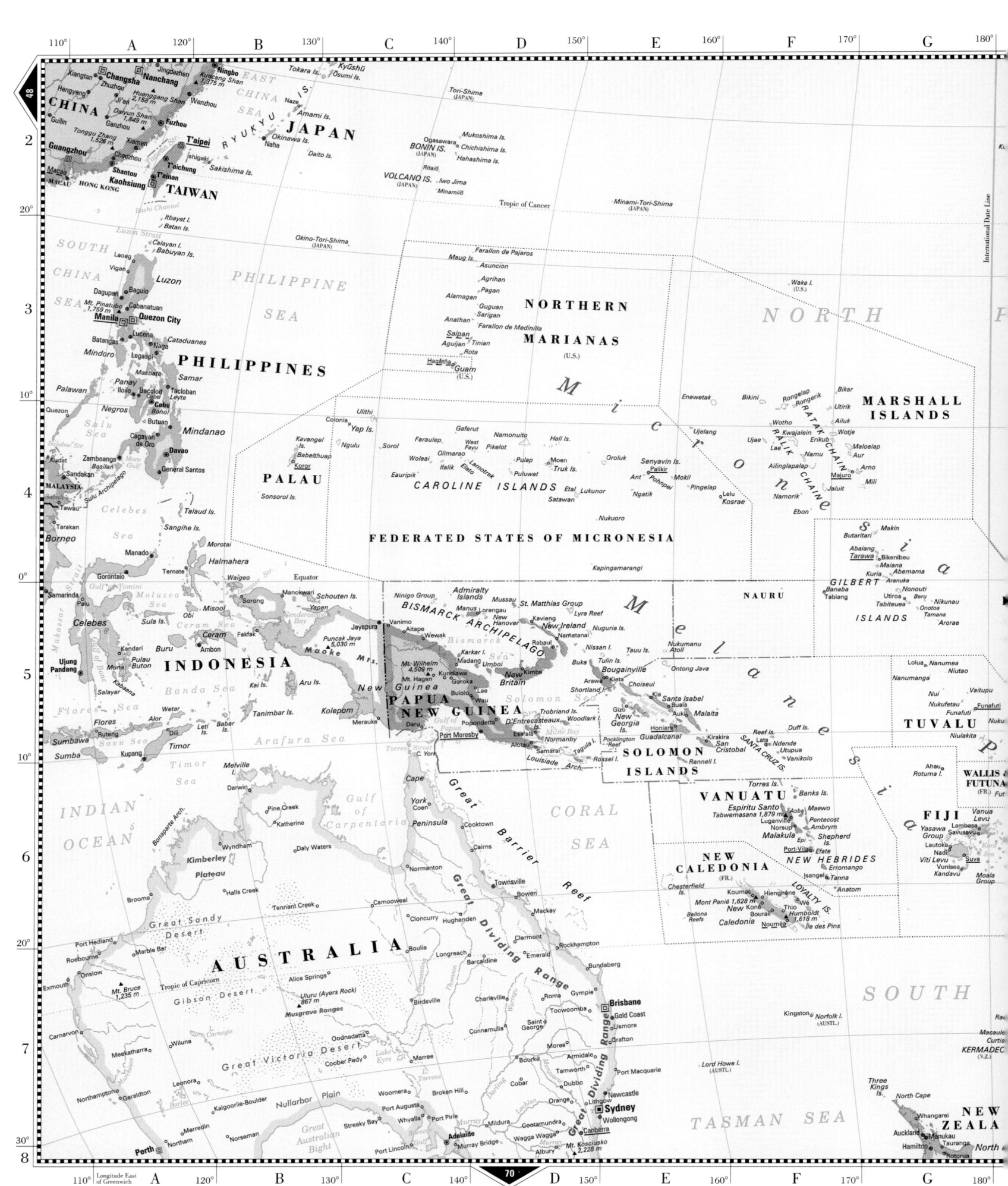

Central Pacific Ocean

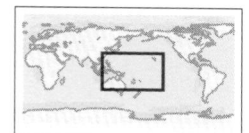

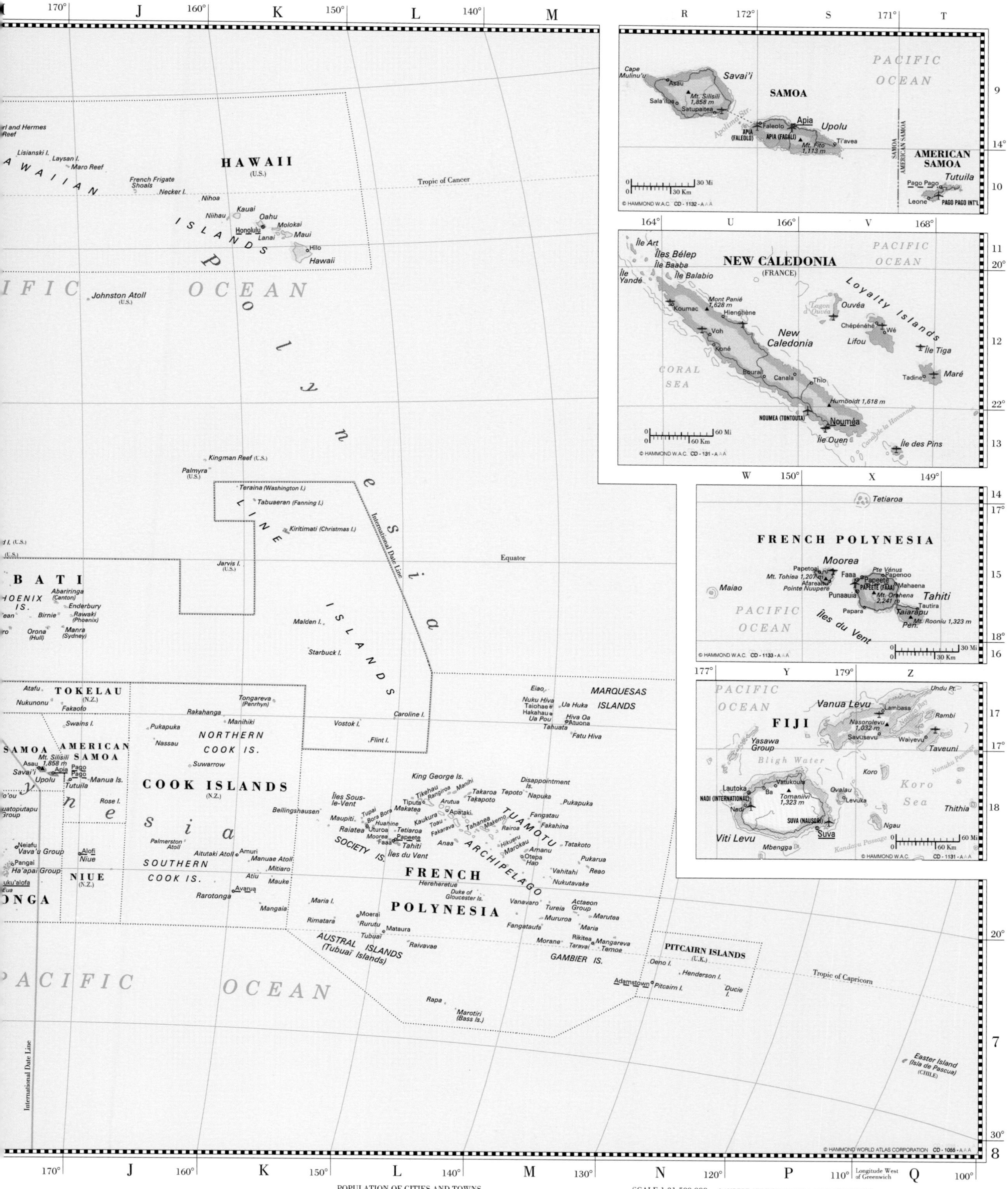

Main map

170° J 160° K 150° L 140° M

HAWAII (U.S.)

Pearl and Hermes Reef
Lisianski I.
Laysan I.
Maro Reef
French Frigate Shoals
Necker I.
Nihoa
Niihau
Kauai
Oahu
Honolulu
Lanai
Molokai
Maui
Hilo
Hawaii

HAWAIIAN ISLANDS

P A C I F I C   O C E A N

Tropic of Cancer

Johnston Atoll (U.S.)

P o l y n e s i a

Kingman Reef (U.S.)
Palmyra (U.S.)
Teraina (Washington I.)
Tabuaeran (Fanning I.)
Kiritimati (Christmas I.)
Jarvis I. (U.S.)

LINE ISLANDS

International Date Line

Equator

Malden I.
Starbuck I.

...I. (U.S.)
...(U.S.)

...BATI
...HOENIX IS.
Abariringa (Canton)
Enderbury
Birnie
Rawaki (Phoenix)
...ean
Orona (Hull)
Manra (Sydney)

TOKELAU (N.Z.)
Atafu
Nukunonu
Fakaofo
Swains I.

SAMOA
AMERICAN SAMOA
Asau
Mt. Silisili 1,858 m
Savai'i
Apia
Pago Pago
Upolu
Tutuila
Manua Is.
Rose I.

...o'o
...uatoputapu
...group
Rakahanga
Pukapuka
Nassau
Manihiki
NORTHERN COOK IS.
Suwarrow
Tongareva (Penrhyn)

COOK ISLANDS (N.Z.)

Îles Sous-le-Vent
Maupiti
Tupai
Bora Bora
Huahine
Raiatea
Uturoa
Tahaa
Maupiti
Tetiaroa
Moorea
Papeete
Faaa
Tahiti
Îles du Vent
SOCIETY IS.
Bellingshausen
Palmerston Atoll
Aitutaki Atoll
Amuri
Manuae Atoll
Mitiaro
Atiu
Mauke
SOUTHERN COOK IS.
Avarua
Rarotonga
Mangaia

NIUE (N.Z.)
Neiafu
Vava'u Group
Alofi
Niue
Pangai
Ha'apai Group
...uku'alofa
Eua

...NGA

...ONGA

Vostok I.
Caroline I.
Flint I.

King George Is.
Tikehau
Rangiroa
Manihi
Tiputa
Takaroa
Takapoto
Arutua
Kaukura
Apataki
Makatea
Toau
Fakarava
Faaa
Anaa
Tahanea
Marokau
Hikueru
Amanu
Otepa
Hao
Vahitahi
Nukutavake
Hereheretue
Duke of Gloucester Is.
Vanavaro
Tureia
Marutea

Disappointment Is.
Napuka
Pukapuka
Tepoto
Fangatau
Fakahina
Takaroa
Tatakoto
Fangataufa
Puka rua
Reao

TUAMOTU ARCHIPELAGO

MARQUESAS ISLANDS
Eiao
Nuku Hiva
Taiohae
Ua Huka
Hakahau
Ua Pou
Hiva Oa
Atuona
Tahuata
Fatu Hiva

FRENCH POLYNESIA

Maria I.
Moerai
Rurutu
Mataura
Maria
Raivavae
Rimatara
Tubuai
AUSTRAL ISLANDS (Tubuai Islands)
Rapa
Marotiri (Bass Is.)

Morane
Actaeon Group
Mururoa
Vanavaro
Rikitea
Mangareva
Taravai
Temoe
GAMBIER IS.

PITCAIRN ISLANDS (U.K.)
Oeno I.
Henderson I.
Adamstown
Pitcairn I.
Ducie I.

Tropic of Capricorn

P A C I F I C   O C E A N

International Date Line

Easter Island (Isla de Pascua) (CHILE)

170° J 160° K 150° L 140° M 130° N 120° P 110° Q 100°

Longitude West of Greenwich

Inset: SAMOA

R 172° S 171° T

PACIFIC OCEAN

Cape Mulinu'u
Asau
Savai'i
Mt. Silisili 1,858 m
Sala'ilua
Satupaitea
SAMOA
Apolima Str.
APIA (FALEOLO)
Faleolo
APIA (FAGALI)
Apia
Upolu
Mt. Fito 1,113 m
Ti'avea

SAMOA / AMERICAN SAMOA

AMERICAN SAMOA
Tutuila
Pago Pago
Leone
PAGO PAGO INT'L

9
14°
10

0 — 30 Mi
0 — 30 Km

© HAMMOND W.A.C.   CD - 1132 - A·A·A

Inset: NEW CALEDONIA

164° U 166° V 168°

Île Art
Îles Bélep
Île Baaba
Île Yandé
Île Balabio
NEW CALEDONIA (FRANCE)
PACIFIC OCEAN
Koumac
Mont Panié 1,628 m
Hienghène
Lagon d'Ouvéa
Ouvéa
Voh
Koné
Chépénéhé
Wé
Loyalty Islands
Lifou
Île Tiga
New Caledonia
Bourail
Canala
Thio
Tadine
Maré
CORAL SEA
Humboldt 1,618 m
Corniche de la Hienneville
NOUMÉA (TONTOUTA)
Nouméa
Île Ouen
Île des Pins

11
20°
12
22°
13

0 — 60 Mi
0 — 60 Km

© HAMMOND W.A.C.   CD - 131 - A·A·A

Inset: FRENCH POLYNESIA (Tahiti)

W 150° X 149°

Tetiaroa
FRENCH POLYNESIA
Moorea
Papetoai
Pte Vénus
Papenoo
Maiao
Mt. Tohiea 1,207 m
Afareaitu
Faaa
Pointe Nuupere
PAPEETE (FAAA)
Papeete
Mahaena
Punaauia
Mt. Orohena 2,241 m
Tahiti
Tautira
PACIFIC OCEAN
Papara
Taiarapu
Pen.
Mt. Rooniu 1,323 m
Îles du Vent

14
17°
15
18°
16

0 — 30 Mi
0 — 30 Km

© HAMMOND W.A.C.   CD - 1133 - A·A·A

Inset: FIJI

177° Y 179° Z

PACIFIC OCEAN
Undu Pt.
Vanua Levu
Lambasa
Nasorolevu 1,032 m
Rambi
FIJI
Yasawa Group
Savusavu
Waiyevu
Taveuni
Nananu Passage
Lautoka
Vatukoula
Koro
Bligh Water
Ba
Koro Sea
NADI (INTERNATIONAL)
Nadi
Tomaniivi 1,323 m
Ovalau
Levuka
Thithia
SUVA (NAUSORI)
Suva
Viti Levu
Mbengga
Ngau
Kandavu Passage

17
17°
18

0 — 60 Mi
0 — 60 Km

© HAMMOND W.A.C.   CD - 1131 - A·A·A

Legend

POPULATION OF CITIES AND TOWNS

- ■ OVER 3,000,000
- ● 500,000 - 999,999
- ○ UNDER 100,000
- ▣ 1,000,000 - 2,999,999
- ◉ 100,000 - 499,999

SCALE 1:31,500,000   LAMBERT AZIMUTHAL EQUAL-AREA PROJECTION

MILES   0 — 400 — 800 — 1200
KILOMETERS   0 — 400 — 800 — 1200

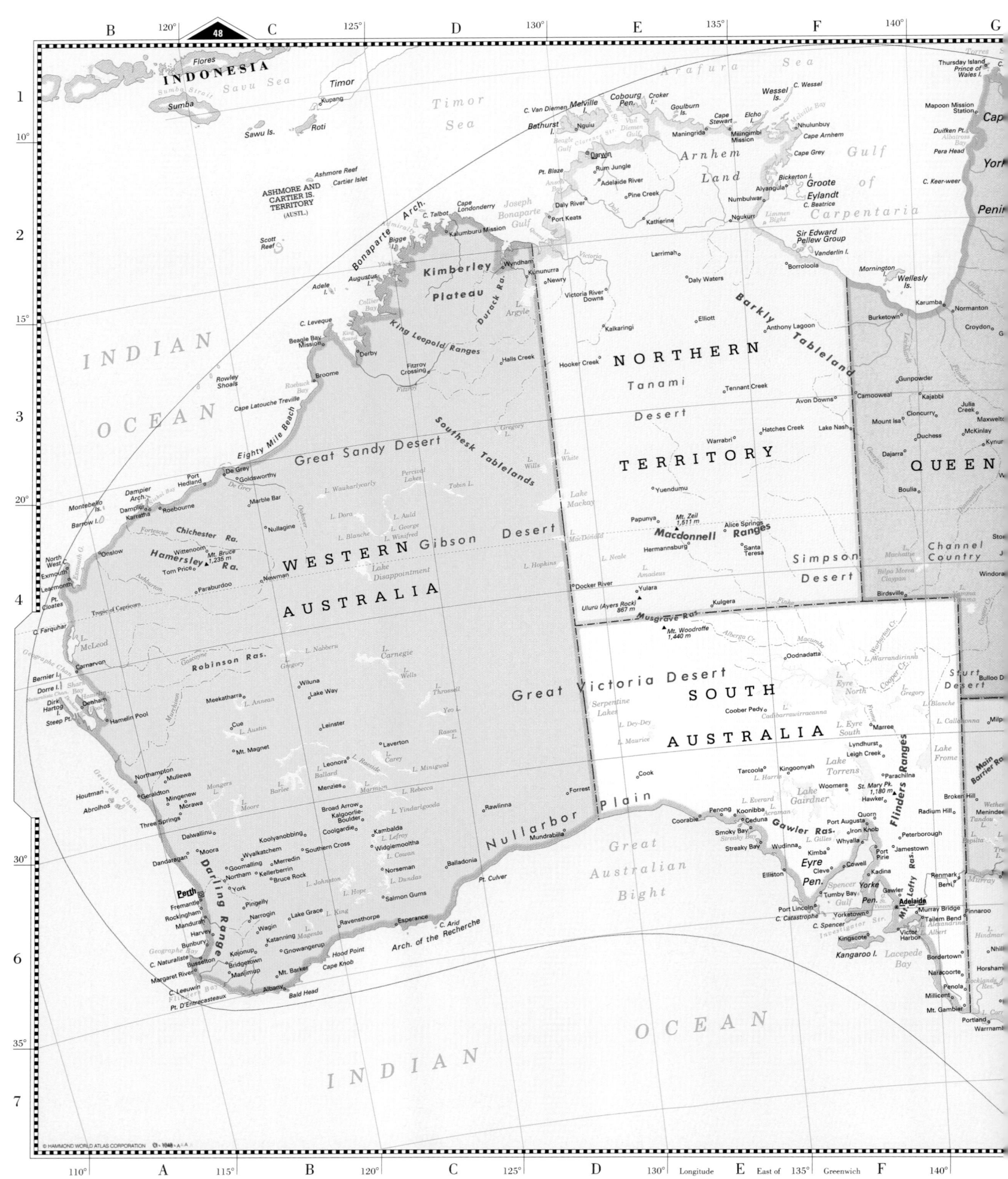

INDONESIA
Flores
Sumba
Sumba Strait
Savu Sea
Sawu Is.
Kupang
Roti
Timor

Arafura Sea

Timor Sea

Torres Strait
Thursday Island
Prince of
Wales I.

C. Van Diemen   Melville
Bathurst   Nguiu
Cobourg   Croker
Pen.   I.
Goulburn
Is.
Cape
Stewart
Elcho
I.
Wessel
Is.
C. Wessel

Mapoon Mission
Station
Duifken Pt.

Cap

Albatross
Bay
York

Pera Head

Peni

Ashmore Reef
Cartier Islet
Ashmore Reef

ASHMORE AND
CARTIER IS.
TERRITORY
(AUSTL.)

Scott
Reef

Maningrida
Milingimbi
Mission

Darwin
Pt. Blaze
Rum Jungle
Adelaide River
Pine Creek

Nhulunbuy
Cape Arnhem

Arnhem

Land

Cape Grey

Bickerton I.
Alyangula

Groote
Eylandt

Numbulwar

Gulf

of

C. Keer-weer

Bonaparte
Arch.
C. Talbot
Admiralty
Gulf
Bigge
Kalumburu Mission

Cape
Londonderry
Joseph
Bonaparte
Gulf

Daly River
Port Keats

Katherine

Ngukurr

Limmen
Bight

Carpentaria

Adele
Augustus
I.
Collier
Bay

Wyndham
Kununurra
Newry

Victoria

Larrimah

Sir Edward
Pellew Group
Vanderlin I.

Beagle Bay
Mission
King
Sound
Derby

Kimberley

Plateau

Durack Ra.
L.
Argyle

Victoria River
Downs

Borroloola

Mornington
I.

Wellesly
Is.

C. Leveque

King Leopold Ranges

Halls Creek

Daly Waters

Barkly Tableland

Karumba
Normanton

Rowley
Shoals
Roebuck
Bay
Broome

Fitzroy
Crossing

Hooker Creek

Kalkaringi

Elliott

Burketown

Croydon

NORTHERN

Anthony Lagoon

Fitzroy

Cape Latouche Treville

Eighty Mile Beach

Southesk Tablelands

Gregory

Tanami

Desert

TERRITORY

Tennant Creek

Avon Downs
Hatches Creek
Lake Nash

Gunpowder

Camooweal
Kajabbi

Julia
Creek

QUEEN

Great Sandy Desert

Port
Hedland
De Grey
Goldsworthy
Marble Bar

De Grey

Oakover

L. Wauharlyearly

Percival
Lakes

L. Wills

L.
White

Warrabri

Mount Isa
Cloncurry

Duchess

McKinlay

Maxwelt

Dajarra

Kynur

Dampier
Arch.
Karratha
Roebourne

Nullagine

Tobin L.

Boulia

Windora

Montebello
Is.
Barrow I.

Chichester Ra.

L. Dora
L. Blanche

L. Auld
L. George
L. Winifred

L.
MacDonald

Papunya

Mt. Zeil
1,511 m

Alice Springs

Yuendumu

Macdonnell Ranges

Santa
Teresa

L.
Mackattie

Channel

Stor

North
West C.
Exmouth
Learmonth

Dampier

Fortescue

Hamersley
Ra.
Wittenoom
Mt. Bruce
1,235 m
Tom Price

Ashburton

Newman
Paraburdoo

WESTERN

Gibson Desert

Lake
Disappointment

L. Hopkins

Lake
Mackay

Hermannsburg

L. Neale

L. Amadeus

Docker River

Yulara

Simpson

Desert

Birdsville

Country

Bilpa Morea
Clayypan

J

P.
Cloates
C. Farquhar

Tropic of Capricorn

L.
McLeod

AUSTRALIA

Uluru (Ayers Rock)
867 m

Kulgera

Mt. Woodroffe
1,440 m

Alberga Cr.

Macumba

Warrandirinna

Sturt
Desert

Geographe Chan.

Carnarvon

Robinson Ras.

Gregory

L. Nabberu

L.
Carnegie

L.
Wells

Great Victoria Desert

SOUTH

Oodnadatta

L. Warrandirinna

Cooper Cr.

Bulloo Di

Bernier I.
Dorre I.
Dirk
Hartog
I.
Steep Pt.

Shark
Bay
Hamelin Pool

Denham

Murchison

Wiluna

Lake Way

Meekatharra

L. Annean
Cue

L. Austin

Leinster

Thrassell

Yeo L.

Raeson

Serpentine
Lakes

Coober Pedy

Cadibarrawirracanna

L. Dey-Dey

L. Eyre
North

AUSTRALIA

L. Eyre
South

Marree

L. Blanche

L. Gregory

L. Callabonna

Milpa

Northampton
Mullewa

Mt. Magnet

Leonora
Leinster
L. Ballard
Menzies

L. Carey
L. Rionside

L. Minigwal

Rawlinna

L. Maurice

Lyndhurst
Leigh Creek

Lake
Frome

Houtman
Abrolhos

Geraldton
Mingenew
Morawa

Mongers

Barlee

L. Rebecca

L. Yindarlgooda

Cook

Tarcoola
Kingoonya

Lake
Torrens

L. Harris

Lake
Gairdner

Woomera

St. Mary Pk.
1,180 m
Hawker

Main
Barrier Ra

Menindee
Tandou

Three Springs

Dalwallinu

Moore

Broad Arrow
Kalgoorlie-
Boulder
Coolgardie

Koolyanobbing

Kambalda

L. Lefroy

L. Cowan

Nullarbor Plain

Mundrabilla

Coorabie

Penong

Koonibba
Ceduna

Smoky Bay

Everard

Kimba

Port Augusta

Gawler Ras.

L. Gilles
Iron Knob

Whyalla

Port
Pirie

Peterborough

Quorn

Radium Hill
Jamestown

Broken Hill

Dandaragan
Moora
Wyalkatchem
Goomalling
Northam
Kellerberrin
Merredin
Southern Cross

Widgiemooltha

Balladonia

Pt. Culver

Streaky Bay

Wudinna

Elliston

Great

Eyre
Pen.

Cleve

Cowell

Kadina

Spencer

Renmark
Berri

Perth
Fremantle
Rockingham
Mandurah

Darling Range

York
Pingelly
Narrogin
Wagin

Bruce Rock

L. Johnston

L. King
L. Hope
L. Dundas

Norseman

Esperance

C. Arid

Arch. of the Recherche

Port Lincoln
C. Catastrophe

Tumby Bay
Spencer
Gulf
C. Spencer

Kingscote

Yorke
Pen.

Gawler

Mt. Lofty Ras.

Adelaide

Murray Bridge

Tailem Bend

Murray

Pinnar

Harvey
Bunbury
Busselton
Margaret River
C. Leeuwin
Pt. D'Entrecasteaux

Kojonup
Bridgetown
Manjimup

Katanning

Gnowangerup

Mt. Barker
Albany

Narrogin
Lake Grace
Ravensthorpe

Salmon Gums

Hood Point
Cape Knob

Bald Head

Great

Australian

Bight

Victor
Harbor

Kangaroo I.

Lacepede
Bay

Bordertown

Naracoorte

Kingscote

Penola

Millicent
Mt. Gambier
Portland

Hindmarsh

Horsham

INDIAN

OCEAN

OCEAN

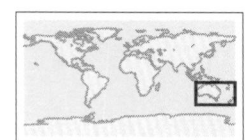

PAPUA NEW GUINEA

Louisiade Arch.
Misima
Tagula I.
Rossel I.
Pocklington Reef

CORAL

SEA

Osprey Reef

Cape Melville
Cape Flattery
Cooktown
Mossman
Cairns
Mareeba
Gordonvale
Atherton
Bartle Frere 1,622 m
Innisfail
avenshoe

Bougainville Reef

Holmes Reefs

Willis Islets
Magdelaine Cays
Coringa Islets

Lihou Reef and Kays

Mellish Reef

ISLANDS

TERRITORY

(AUSTL.)

Marion Reef

Hinchinbrook I.
Ingham
Palm Is.
Halifax Bay
Townsville
S. Bowling Green
Home Hill
Bowen
Charters Towers
henden
Dalrymple Lake
Proserpine
Whitsunday I.
Repulse Bay
Walkerston
Mackay
Sarina

Flinders Reef

Frederick Reef

Kenn Reef

Saumarez Reef

West Islet
Bird Islet
Wreck Reef

SEA

Great

Barrier

Reef

Ogmore
C. Manifold
Yeppoon
Rockhampton
Curtis I.
Gladstone
Biloela
Moura
Monto
Sandy Cape
Bundaberg
Hervey Bay
Maryborough
Fraser I.
Hervey Bay

Percy Isles
Swain Reefs
Capricorn Channel
Broad St. Chan.

Cato I.

D

Dividing

Range

ngreach
Barcaldine
Alpha
Emerald
Blackwater
Clermont

Warrego Ra.
Augathella
Charleville
Mitchell
Cooladdi
Roma
Miles
Chinchilla
Surat
Dalby
Gympie
Tewantin-Noosa
Caloundra

Chesterton Ra.
Maranoa

Darling
Downs
Toowoomba
Ipswich
Brisbane
Beenleigh
N. Stradbroke I.
Moreton I.

Cunnamulla
Bollon
Saint George
Goondiwindi
Warwick
Stanthorpe
Gold Coast
Tweed Heads
Dirranbandi
Boomi
Casino
Lismore

Moree
Tenterfield

Brewarrina
Walgett
Inverell
Glen Innes
Grafton

Bourke
Coonamble
Narrabri

NEW
Cobar
Nyngan
Armidale
Coffs Harbour

SOUTH
Warren
Gilgandra
Tamworth
Kempsey

WALES
Narromine
Dubbo
Gunnedah
Taree
Port Macquarie

Condobolin
Wellington
Singleton
Maitland
Sugarloaf Pt.
Port Stephens

Hillston
Parkes
Forbes
Orange
Bathurst
Lithgow
Katoomba
Newcastle

West Wyalong
Cowra
Mudgee
Blue Mountains

Griffith
Young
Sydney

Hay
Leeton
Temora
Cootamundra
Camden
Wollongong

Narrandera
Tumut
Canberra
Goulburn
Jervis Bay
Bomaderry

Finley
Wagga Wagga
AUSTL. CAP. TERR.
Queanbeyan

Riverina
Albury
AUSTRALIAN
CAPITAL TERR.
Cooma

epparton
Wangaratta
Wodonga
Mt. Kosciusko 2,228 m
Bega

ymour
L. Eildon
Darmouth Res.
Orbost
C. Howe

VICTORIA
Melbourne
Barnsdale
Sale
Bairnsdale

Melton
Moe
Morwell
Traralgon

Wonthaggi
Corner Inlet
Wilsons Promontory
South East Pt.

QS
ing I.
Bass
Furneaux
Group
Flinders I.
Cape Barren I.
George Oyster
Tasman

r I.
Smithton
Wynyard
George Town
Eddystone Pt.
Ulverstone
Devonport
Launceston

Mt. Ossa 1,617 m
TASMANIA
New Norfolk
Gordon
Queenstown
Hobart
arie Har.
Tasman Pen.

South West C.

SCALE 1:14,000,000   OPTIMAL CONFORMAL PROJECTION

MILES 0 | 200 | 400 | 600
KILOMETERS 0 | 200 | 400 | 600

Three Kings Is.
North C.
C. Maria van Diemen
Te Kao
C. Kerikeri
Kaitaia
C. Brett
Kaikohe
Whangarei
Dargaville
Great Barrier I.
Warkworth

TASMAN

SEA

Kaipara Har.
Waitemata
Takapura
Coromandel
Auckland
Manukau
Coromandel Peninsula
Thames
Te Aroha
Mount Maunganui

North
Huntly
Island
Te Awamutu
Hamilton
Cambridge
Tauranga
Whakatane
Te Araroa
East C.

Te Kuiti
Tokoroa
Kawerau
Rotorua
Murupara
Hikurangi 1,754 m

NEW
Taupo
Turangi
Wairoa
Gisborne

ZEALAND
New Plymouth
Waitara
Mt Ngauruhoe 2,291 m

North Taranaki Bight
C. Egmont
Stratford
Mt Egmont 2,518 m
Mt Raupehu 2,797 m
Mahia Pen.

Hawera
Hastings
Napier

South Taranaki Bight
Wanganui
Havelock North

Dannevirke
Ashhurst
Waibukurau

C. Farewell
Collingwood
Palmerston North
Tasman Bay
Motueka
Paraparaumu
Levin
Karamea
Porirua
Masterton

Karamea Bight
Mt Owen 1,875 m
Wellington
Upper Hutt
Nelson
Blenheim
Lower Hutt

Westport
C. Foulwind
Murchison
Ward
C. Palliser

Reefton
Mt Una 2,301 m
Clarence

Greymouth
Lewis Pass
Kaikoura

Hokitika
Otira
Arthur's Pass
Waiau

Fox Glacier
Rangiora
Pegasus Bay

Mt Cook 3,764 m
Darfield
Kaiapoi
Christchurch

Haast
Banks Pen.

Mt Aspiring 3,027 m
Geraldine
Temuka
Ashburton

South
Twizel
Timaru
Island

Wanaka
Waimate

Queenstown
Cromwell
Oamaru

Alexandra
Canterbury Bight

Te Anau
Lumsden
Milton
Palmerston

West C.
Mosgiel
Dunedin

Riverton
Gore
Balclutha

Invercargill
Bluff

Mt Anglem 980 m
Oban

Southern Alps

South C.
Stewart I.

Snares Is.

PACIFIC

OCEAN

SCALE 1:10,500,000   LAMBERT CONFORMAL CONIC PROJECTION

MILES 0 | 150 | 300
KILOMETERS 0 | 150 | 300

© HAMMOND W.A.C. CD - 1200 - A

Norfolk I.
(AUSTL.)
Kingston

PACIFIC

Lord Howe I.
(N.S. WALES)

OCEAN

TASMAN

SEA

Three Kings Is.
North C.

NEW
ZEALAND
Auckland
Great Barrier I.
North
Island

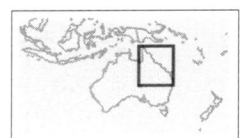

Northeastern Australia

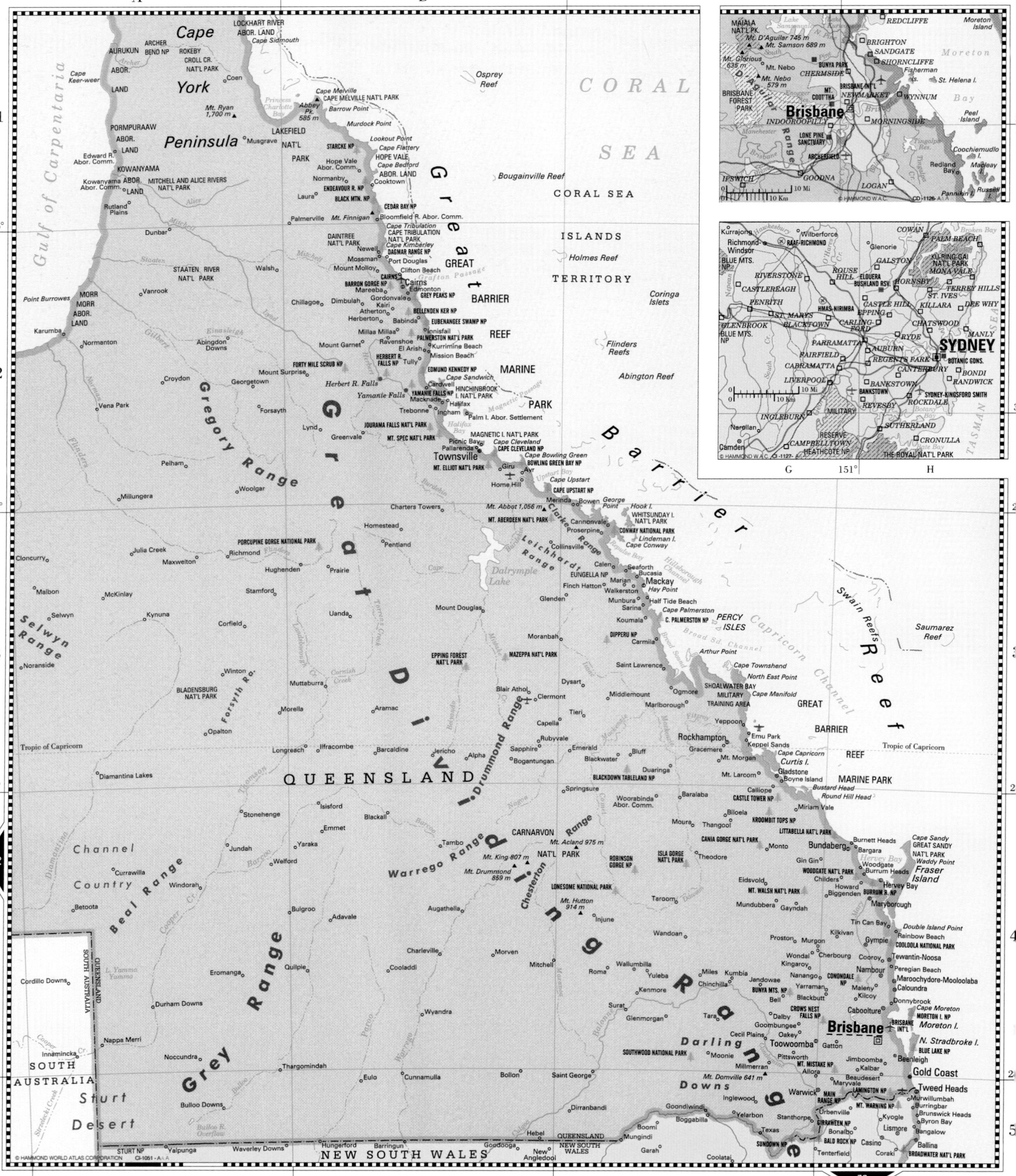

A   144°   B   148°   E   153°   F

Brisbane (inset)

MAIALA NAT'L PK. · Mt. D'Aguilar 746 m · Mt. Samson 689 m · REDCLIFFE · Moreton Island
BRIGHTON · SANDGATE · Moreton · Bay
Mt. Glorious 635 m · Mt. Nebo · BUNYA PARK · SHORNCLIFFE
Mt. Nebo 579 m · CHERMSIDE · Fisherman · St. Helena I.
BRISBANE FOREST PARK · MT. COOT-THA · BRISBANE INT'L · NEWMARKET · WYNNUM · Peel Island
Brisbane · INDOOROOPILLY · LONE PINE SANCTUARY · MORNINGSIDE · Coochiemudlo
IPSWICH · ARCHERFIELD · Redland Bay · Macleay I.
GOODNA · LOGAN · Pannikin I. Russell
SCALE 10 Km

Sydney (inset)

Kurrajong · Wilberforce · COWAN · Broken Bay
Richmond · Windsor · RAAF-RICHMOND · Glenorie · PALM BEACH
BLUE MTS. NP · GALSTON · KU-RING-GAI NAT'L PARK · MONA VALE
RIVERSTONE · ROUSE HILL · ELOUERA BUSHLAND RSV. · HORNSBY · TERREY HILLS
CASTLEREAGH · CASTLE HILL · ST. IVES
PENRITH · ST. MARYS · EPPING · KILLARA · DEE WHY
GLENBROOK · BLACKTOWN · CARLING-FORD · CHATSWOOD
BLUE MTS. NP · HMAS-NIRIMBA · RYDE · MANLY
PARRAMATTA · AUBURN · SYDNEY
FAIRFIELD · REGENT'S PARK · BOTANIC GDNS.
CABRAMATTA · BANKSTOWN · BONDI
LIVERPOOL · BANKSTOWN · CANTERBURY · RANDWICK
MILITARY · REVESBY · SYDNEY-KINGSFORD SMITH · ROCKDALE
INGLEBURN · Botany Bay
Narellan · RESERVE · SUTHERLAND
Camden · CAMPBELLTOWN · CRONULLA
HEATHCOTE NP · THE ROYAL NAT'L PARK
G   151°   H

Main map labels:

Cape York Peninsula · Gulf of Carpentaria · CORAL SEA
LOCKHART RIVER ABOR. LAND · Cape Sidmouth
AURUKUN · ARCHER BEND NP · ROKEBY CROLL CR. NAT'L PARK · Coen
Cape Keer-weer · ABOR. LAND
PORMPURAAW ABOR. LAND · Mt. Ryan 1,700 m · LAKEFIELD NAT'L PARK · Osprey Reef
Edward R. Abor. Comm. · Musgrave · Lookout Point
KOWANYAMA ABOR. LAND · MITCHELL AND ALICE RIVERS NAT'L PARK · STARCKE NP · Cape Flattery · Bougainville Reef
Rutland Plains · HOPE VALE ABOR. COMM. · Cape Bedford · CORAL SEA
Dunbar · Normanby · Cooktown · ISLANDS · Holmes Reef
MORR MORR ABOR. LAND · Laura · ENDEAVOUR R. NP · BLACK MTN. NP · CEDAR BAY NP · TERRITORY
Point Burrowes · Palmerville · Mt. Finnigan · Bloomfield R. Abor. Comm.
Karumba · DAINTREE NAT'L PARK · CAPE TRIBULATION NAT'L PARK · Cape Kimberley · Coringa Islets
Normanton · Vanrook · STAATEN RIVER NAT'L PARK · Walsh · DAGMAR RANGE NP · Mossman · Port Douglas · GREAT
Abingdon Downs · Mount Molloy · Clifton Beach · BARRIER
Croydon · Georgetown · BARRON GORGE NP · Mareeba · CAIRNS · Edmonton · GREY PEAKS NP · REEF
Vena Park · Chillagoe · Dimbulah · Gordonvale · Kairi · Atherton · BELLENDEN KER NP
Forsayth · Herberton · Babinda · EUBENANGEE SWAMP NP · MARINE
Mount Surprise · Millaa Millaa · Innisfail · Flinders Reefs
Pelham · Mount Garnet · Ravenshoe · El Arish · Kurrimine Beach · PARK
Millungera · FORTY MILE SCRUB NP · HERBERT R. FALLS NP · Tully · Mission Beach · Abington Reef
Woolgar · Herbert R. Falls · EDMUND KENNEDY NP · Cape Sandwich
Lynd · Yamanie Falls · Cardwell · YAMANIE FALLS NP · HINCHINBROOK I. NAT'L PARK
Greenvale · Trebonne · Macknade · Halifax
JOURAMA FALLS NAT'L PARK · Ingham · Palm I. Abor. Settlement
MT. SPEC NAT'L PARK · Halifax Bay
Pallarenda · MAGNETIC I. NAT'L PARK · MAGNETIC I. NP · Cape Bowling Green
Townsville · Picnic Bay · CAPE CLEVELAND · CAPE CLEVELAND NP
MT. ELLIOT NAT'L PARK · Giru · Cape Bowling Green · BOWLING GREEN BAY NP
Ayr · Home Hill · Cape Upstart
Charters Towers · Mt. Abbot 1,056 m · CAPE UPSTART NP
Homestead · Bowen · George Point · Hook I.
MT. ABERDEEN NAT'L PARK · Cannonvale · WHITSUNDAY I. NAT'L PARK · Lindeman I.
Pentland · PORCUPINE GORGE NATIONAL PARK · Proserpine · CONWAY NATIONAL PARK · Cape Conway
Cloncurry · Julia Creek · Richmond · Prairie · Collinsville · Calen · Seaforth · Bucasia
Maxwelton · Hughenden · EUNGELLA NP · Marian · Mackay · Hay Point
Malbon · Stamford · Finch Hatton · Walkerston
McKinlay · Uanda · Munbura · Sarina · Half Tide Beach
Selwyn · Corfield · Mount Douglas · Koumala · C. PALMERSTON NP · PERCY ISLES
Kynuna · Glenden · DIPPERU NP · Carmila · Cape Palmerston
Noranside · Winton · Moranbah · Saint Lawrence · Arthur Point · Saumarez Reef
Muttaburra · Aramac · MAZEPPA NAT'L PARK · Dysart · Cape Townshend · GREAT
Bladensburg NAT'L PARK · Morella · EPPING FOREST NAT'L PARK · Clermont · Middlemount · North East Point · BARRIER
Ilfracombe · Jericho · Tieri · Marlborough · Ogmore · SHOALWATER BAY MILITARY TRAINING AREA · Cape Manifold · REEF
Longreach · Barcaldine · Alpha · Capella · Sapphire · Emerald · Yeppoon · Emu Park · Keppel Sands
Diamantina Lakes · Bogantungan · Rubyvale · Blackwater · Bluff · Rockhampton · Mt. Morgan · Curtis I. · MARINE PARK
Tropic of Capricorn · Isisford · Duaringa · Gracemere · Cape Capricorn · REEF
Stonehenge · Blackall · BLACKDOWN TABLELAND NP · Mt. Larcom · Gladstone · Boyne Island
Emmet · Springsure · Woorabinda Abor. Comm. · Baralaba · Bustard Head · Round Hill Head
QUEENSLAND · Jundah · Yaraka · Tambo · CARNARVON RANGE · Mt. Acland 975 m · Biloela · CASTLE TOWER NP · Miriam Vale · Cape Sandy GREAT SANDY NAT'L PARK
Channel Country · Welford · CARNARVON NAT'L PARK · Moura · Thangool · KROOMBIT TOPS NP · Bundaberg · Bargara · Waddy Point
Currawilla · Windorah · Mt. King 807 m · ROBINSON GORGE NP · Monto · LITTABELLA NAT'L PARK · Woodgate · Fraser Island
Betoota · Bulgroo · Adavale · ISLA GORGE NAT'L PARK · CANIA GORGE NAT'L PARK · Gin Gin · WOODGATE NAT'L PARK · Burrum Heads
Mt. Drummond 859 m · Theodore · Eidsvold · MT. WALSH NAT'L PARK · Howard · Biggenden · Childers · BURRUM R. NP
LONESOME NATIONAL PARK · Mt. Hutton 914 m · Taroom · Mundubbera · Gayndah · Hervey Bay · Maryborough
Grey Range · Beal Range · Augathella · Injune · Wandoan · Tin Can Bay · Double Island Point
Windorah · Charleville · Morven · Mitchell · Proston · Murgon · Kilkivan · Gympie · Rainbow Beach
Eromanga · Quilpie · Cooladdi · Roma · Wallumbilla · Miles · Kumbia · Wondai · Cherbourg · Cooroy · COOLOOLA NATIONAL PARK · Tewantin-Noosa
Durham Downs · Yuleba · Jandowae · Chinchilla · Nanango · Kingaroy · Nambour · Peregian Beach
Cordillo Downs · Wyandra · Kenmore · Surat · Dalby · Bell · Blackbutt · Maleny · Kilcoy · Maroochydore-Mooloolaba · Caloundra
Nappa Merri · Glenmorgan · Tara · CROWS NEST NP · BUNYA MTS. NP · CONONDALE · Donnybrook
Innamincka Cr. · Thargomindah · Goombungee · Oakey · Caboolture · Cape Moreton · MORETON I. NP · Moreton I.
SOUTH AUSTRALIA · Eulo · Cunnamulla · Bollon · Saint George · Cecil Plains · Toowoomba · **Brisbane** · BRISBANE INT'L · N. Stradbroke I.
Bulloo Downs · Southwood National Park · Moonie · Millmerran · Pittsworth · Gatton · BLUE LAKE NP
Noccundra · Darling Downs · MT. MISTAKE NP · Allora · Jimboomba · Kalbar · Beenleigh
Sturt Desert · STURT NP · Hungerford · Barringun · Dirranbandi · Boomi · Mt. Domville 641 m · Warwick · MAIN RANGE NP · Beaudesert · Gold Coast
Yalpunga · Waverley Downs · Goodooga · Hebel · Mungindi · Goondiwindi · Inglewood · Stanthorpe · Texas · GIRRAWEEN NP · MT. WARNING NP · Tweed Heads
QUEENSLAND / NEW SOUTH WALES · New Angledool · Garah · Coolatai · BALD ROCK NP · SUNDOWN NP · Tenterfield · CASINO · BROADWATER NAT'L PARK · Murwillumbah · Burringbar · Brunswick Heads · Byron Bay · Kyogle · Lismore · Bangalow · Ballina · Coraki

Gregory Range · Great Dividing Range · Selwyn Range · Drummond Range · Leichhardt Range · Warrego Range · Chesterton Range · Grey Range · Beal Range · Darling Downs · Dalrymple Lake
Flinders R. · Gilbert R. · Mitchell R. · Einasleigh R. · Thomson R. · Barcoo R. · Cooper Cr. · Diamantina R. · Bulloo R. · Barwon R. · Balonne R. · Condamine R. · Warrego R. · Paroo R. · Maranoa R. · Dawson R. · Fitzroy R. · Burdekin R. · Swain Reefs · Great Barrier Reef · Capricorn Channel · Broad Sd. Channel · Shoalwater Bay · Hervey Bay · TASMAN SEA

A   140°   144° Longitude East of Greenwich   B   148°   C   152°   D

SCALE 1:7,000,000   LAMBERT CONFORMAL CONIC PROJECTION
MILES   0   100   200   300
KILOMETERS   0   100   200   300

POPULATION OF CITIES AND TOWNS

Symbol	Population	Symbol	Population
■	OVER 2,000,000	◉	500,000 - 999,999	●	100,000 - 249,999	◎	10,000 - 29,999
□	1,000,000 - 1,999,999	◉	250,000 - 499,999	●	30,000 - 99,999	○	UNDER 10,000

Southeastern Australia

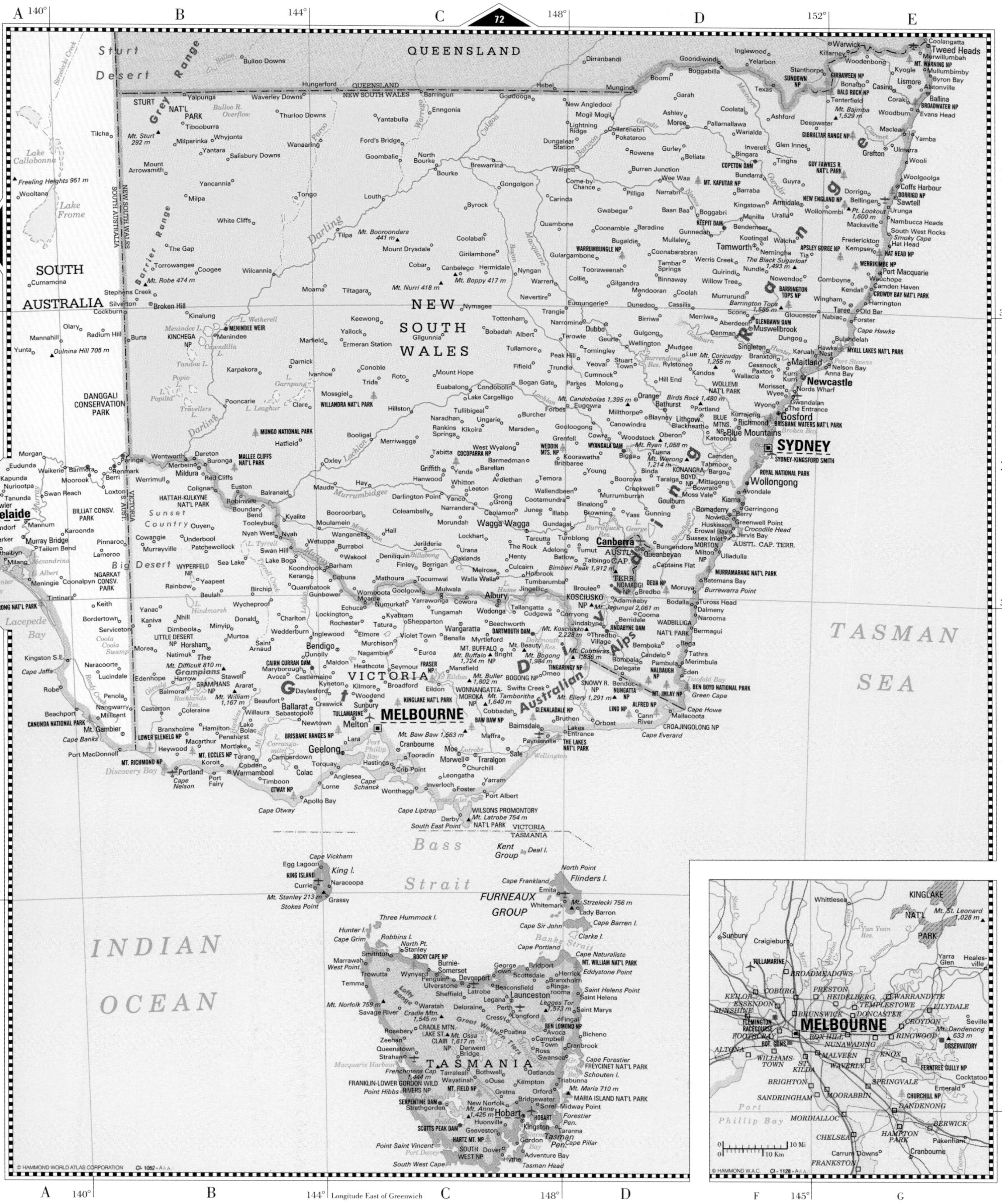

AREA OF
OPTIMIZATION
The red band which
surrounds this map
defines the "Area of
Optimization." Within
this bounding curve is
the most accurate
conformal map that can
be made of the region.
Outside the optimized
area, distortion increases
rapidly, and tears or
other irregularities in
the grid may occur.

SCALE 1:31,500,000   OPTIMAL CONFORMAL PROJECTION
MILES   0   400   800   1200
KILOMETERS 0   400   800   1200

LAMBERT CONFORMAL CONIC PROJECTION   0   60 Mi
                                     0   60 Km

CAPE VERDE

POPULATION OF CITIES AND TOWNS
■ OVER 3,000,000   ● 500,000 - 999,999   ○ UNDER 100,000
▣ 1,000,000 - 2,999,999   ● 100,000 - 499,999

C Longitude 10° East of D Greenwich 20°

Africa

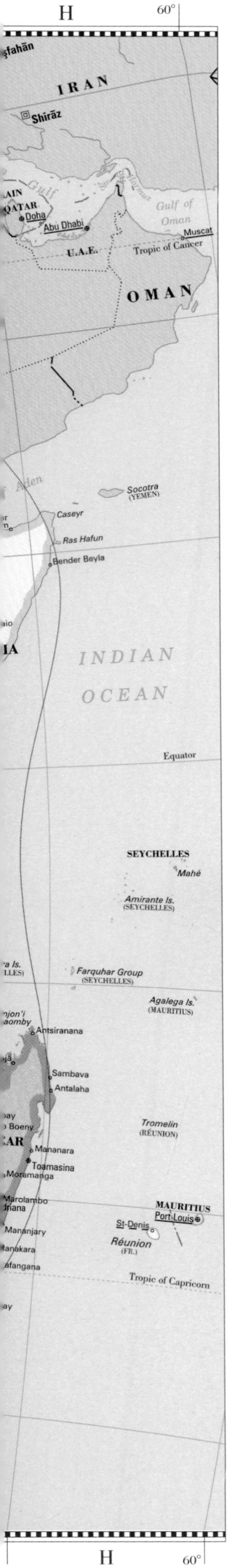

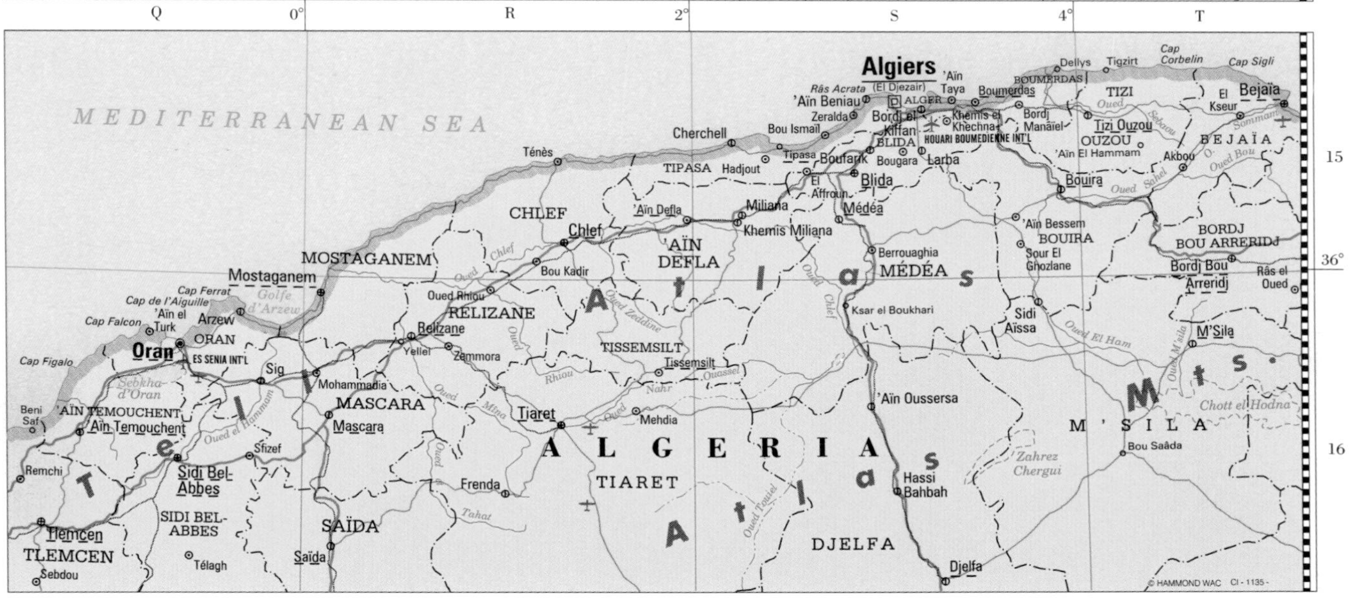

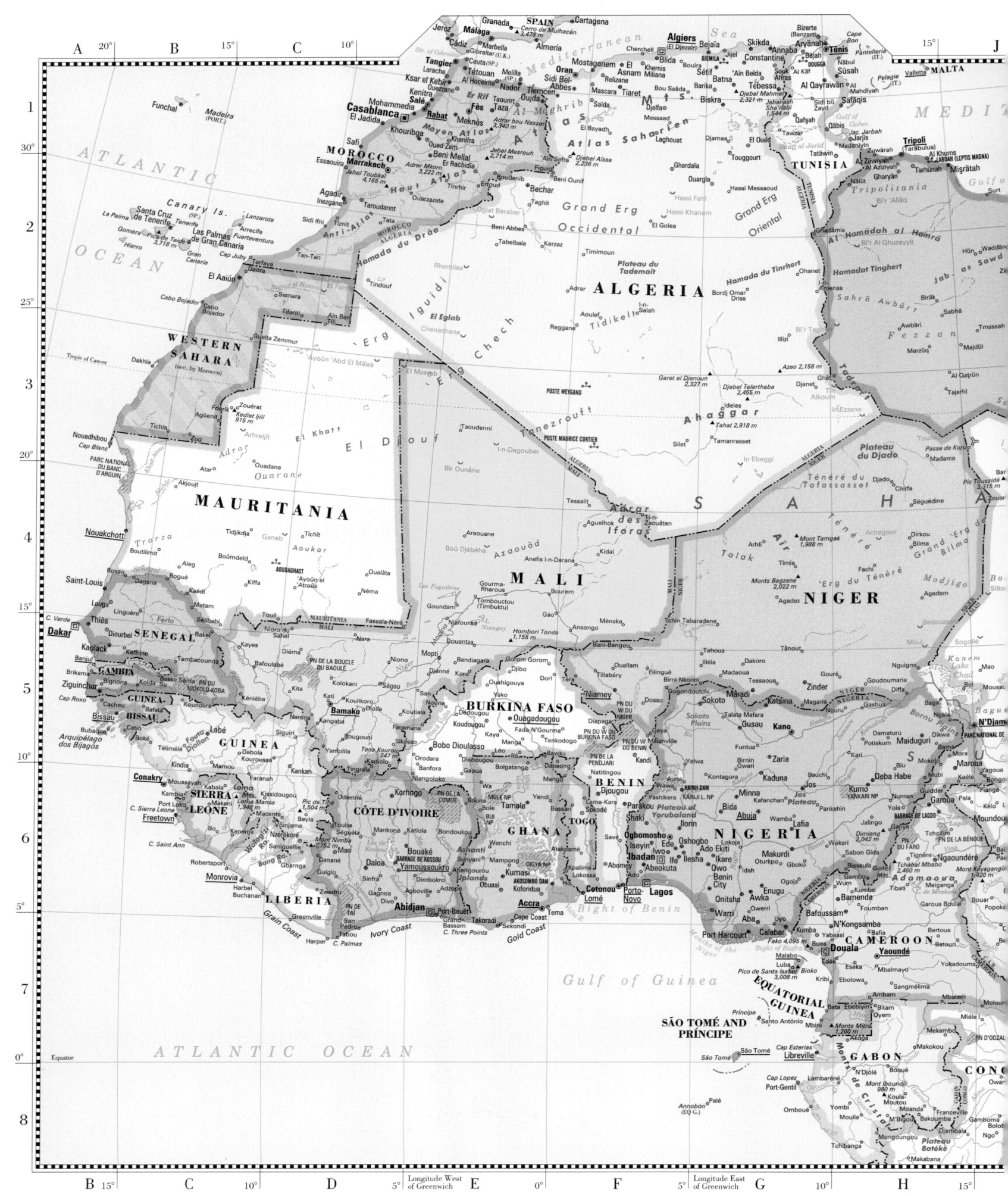

Northern Africa

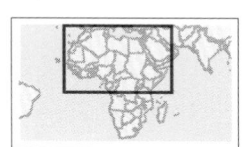

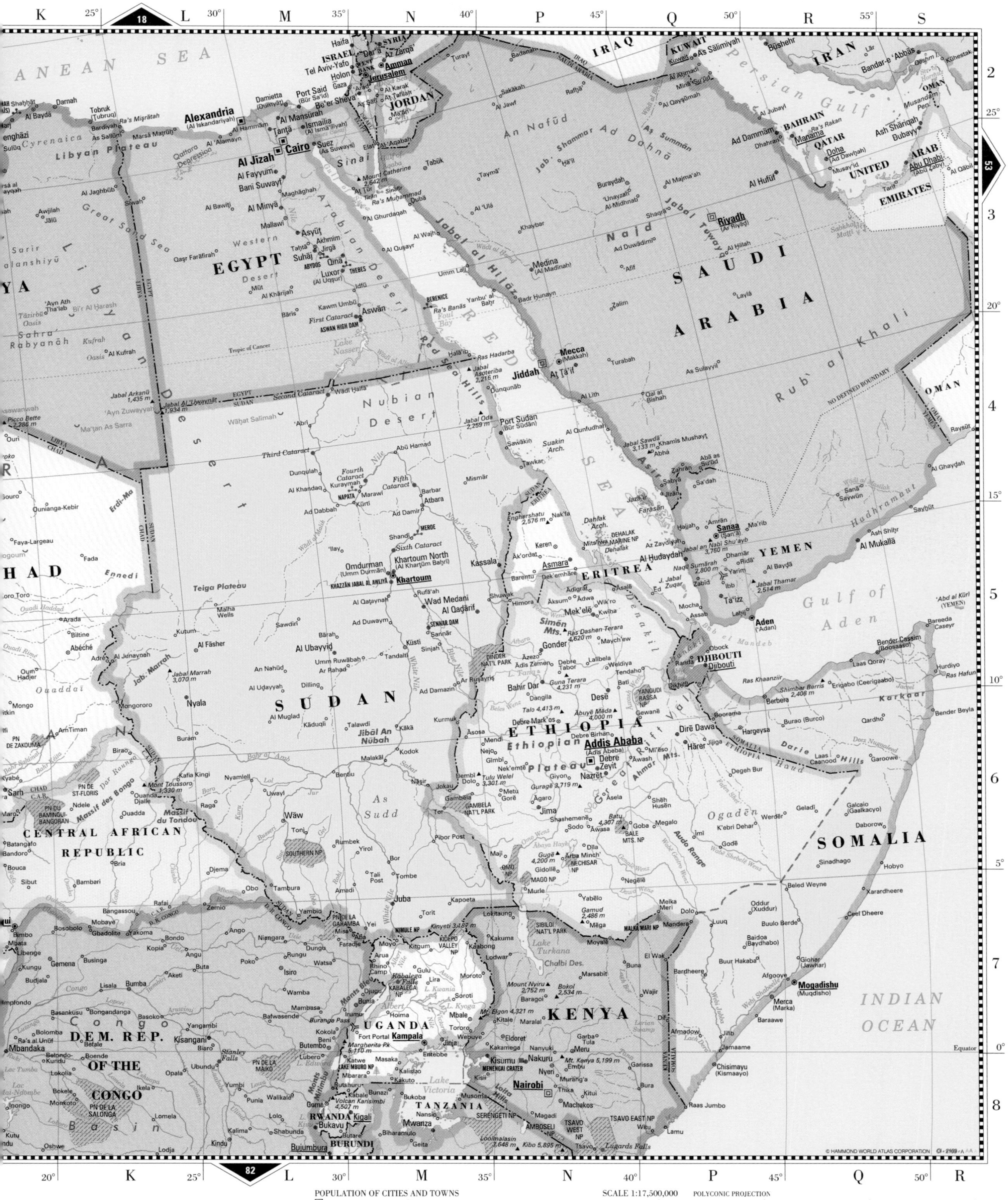

ATLANTIC

OCEAN

© HAMMOND WORLD ATLAS CORPORATION CI - 1058 - A-A-A

SCALE 1:7,000,000   POLYCONIC PROJECTION
MILES
KILOMETERS

Southern West Africa

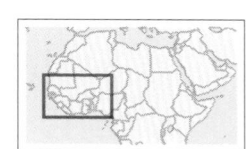

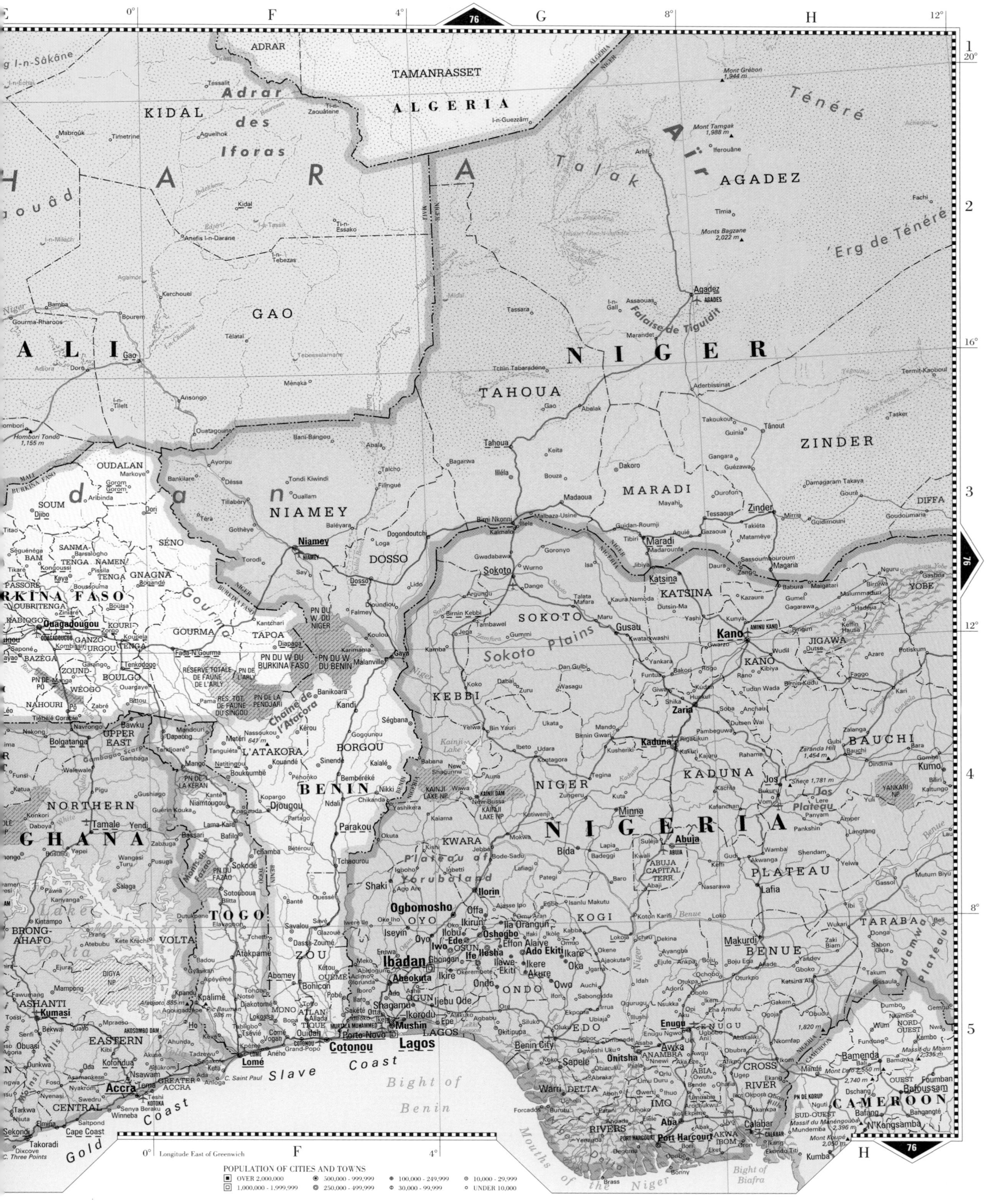

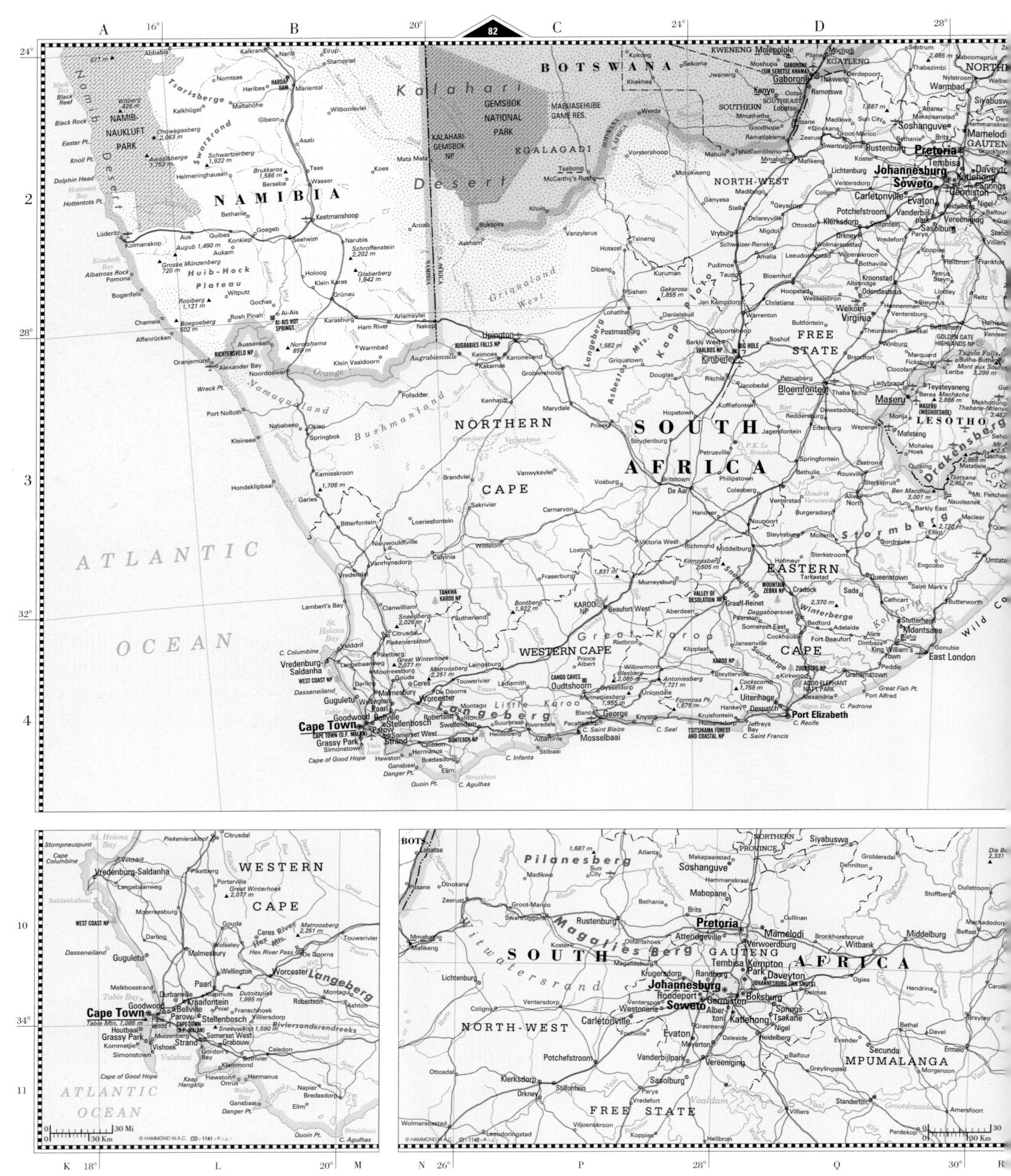

Southern Africa

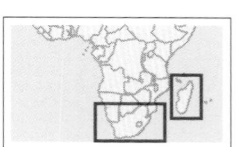

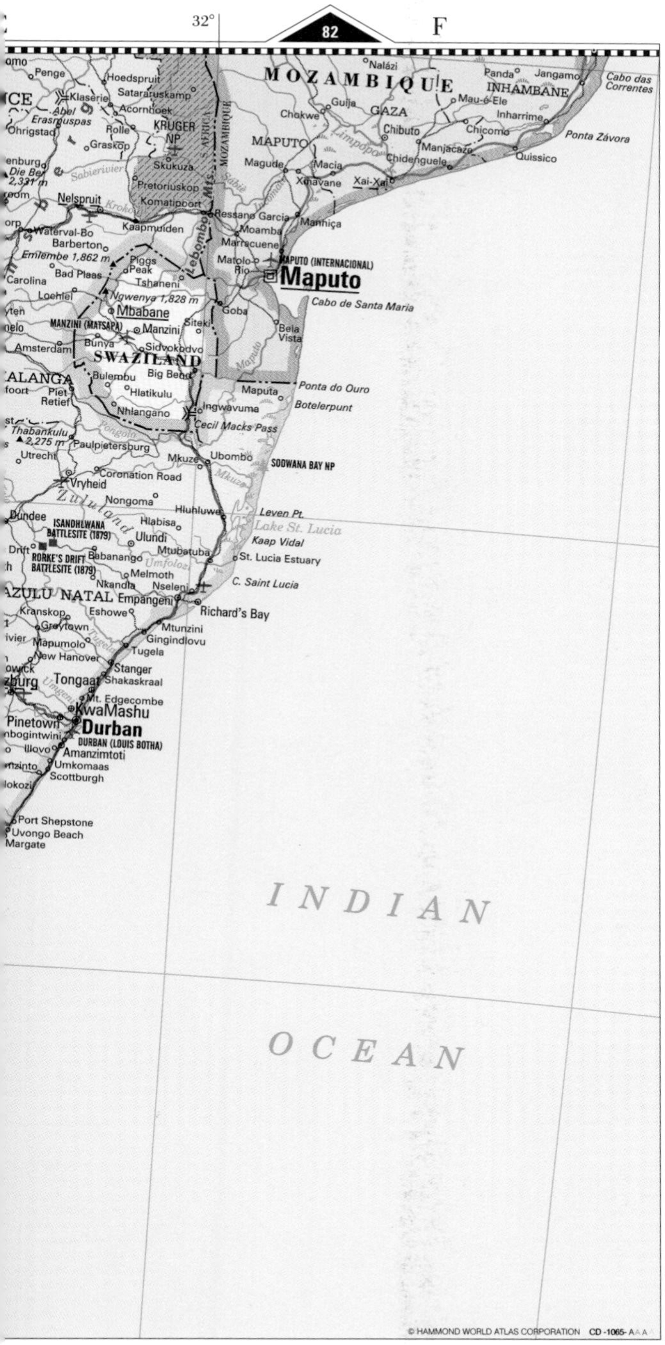

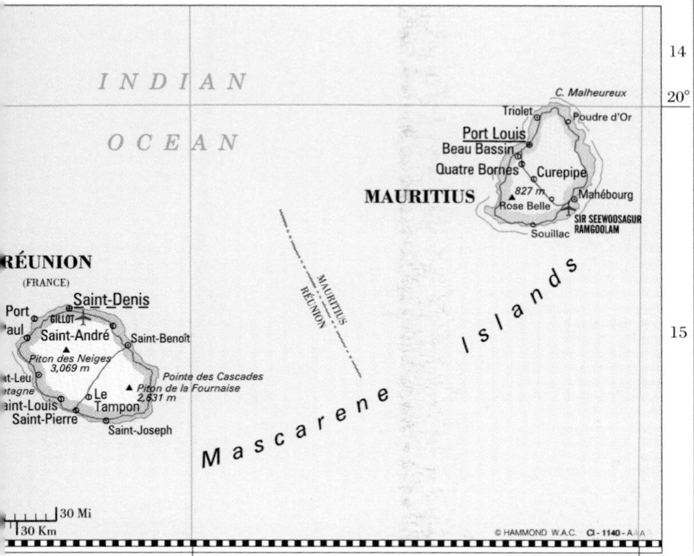

Main map — Madagascar and Mozambique coast

MOZAMBIQUE
GAZA
INHAMBANE
Panda
Jangamo
Cabo das Correntes
Nalázi
Chokwe
Guija
Chibuto
Inharrime
Mau-a-Ele
Chicomo
Ponta Závora
MAPUTO
Magude
Macia
Xai-Xai
Manjacaze
Quissico
Ressano Garcia
Moamba
Marrecuene
Manhiça
Chidenguele
Maputo (Internacional)
Maputo
Matola-Rio
Goba
Bela Vista
Cabo de Santa Maria
Ponta do Ouro
Botelerpunt

KRUGER NP
Skukuza
Komatipoort
Ngwenya 1,828 m
Mbabane
MANZINI (MATSAPA)
Manzini
Sidvokodvo
Siteki
SWAZILAND
Big Bend
Bulembu
Hlatikulu
Nhlangano
Maputo
Ingwavuma
Cecil Macks Pass

Penge
Hoedspruit
Klaserie
Satararuskamp
Acornhoek
Rolle
Ohrigstad
Graskop
Nelspruit
Waterval-Bo
Barberton
Emlembe 1,862 m
Piggs Peak
Tshaneni
Bad Plaas
Carolina
Loehlei
Amsterdam
Bunya
ALANGA
Piet Retief
Paulpietersburg
Thabankulu 2,275 m
Utrecht
Vryheid
Nongoma
Hlabisa
Hluhluwe
Leven Pt.
Lake St. Lucia
Kaap Vidal
Dundee
ISANDHLWANA BATTLESITE (1879)
RORKE'S DRIFT BATTLESITE (1879)
Babanango
Ulundi
Mtubatuba
St. Lucia Estuary
C. Saint Lucia
Coronation Road
Ngome
Nkandla
Nselene
ZULU NATAL
Melmoth
Empangeni
Richard's Bay
Greytown
Eshowe
Mtunzini
Gingindlovu
New Hanover
Tugela
Stanger
Mt. Edgecombe
Shakaskraal
Tongaat
KwaMashu
Pinetown
Durban
DURBAN (LOUIS BOTHA)
Amanzimtoti
Umkomaas
Scottburgh
Port Shepstone
Uvongo Beach
Margate

SODWANA BAY NP
Ubombo
Mkuze

GOBA
Mbabane

Islands (Comoros, Mayotte)

COMOROS
Mitsamiouli
NGAHAYA Grande
Hahaia
Comore
Moroni
Iconi
Foumbouni
Oani
Mohéli
Nioumachoua
Moya
Fomboni
MOHÉLI
OUANI
Sima
Domoni
Mutsamudu
Anjouan
Mamoutzou
Dembeni
DZAOUDZI
Sada
Dzaoudzi
Bandeli
MAYOTTE (FRANCE)

Iles Glorieuses (FRANCE)
Geyser Reef

Madagascar

Tanjon'i Bobaomby
Andranovondronana
Tanjon' Andrantany
Tampon Ambohitra
PN MONTAGNE D'AMBRE
Ambohitra 1,475 m
Antsiranana
Andjoavato
Ampombiantambo
Ampisikinana
Nosy Mitsio
Nosy Be
Ambilobe 1,177 m
Iharana
Dzamandzar
Ambaro Bay
Andoany
Beramanja
ANTSIRANANA
Ambanja
Bemanevika
Marovato
Andrafainkona
Ampanefena
Ambaro Bay
Maromokotro 2,876 m
Bemanevika
Sambava
Befotaka
Analalava
Bealanana
Tsaratanana Massif 2,133 m
Boany
Andapa
Antsambalahy
Antsohihy
Ankerika
Antalaha
Antsirabato
Antonibe
Arahidrano
Antsakabary
Matsoandakana
Maroantsetra
Masoala Pen.
Narinda
Befandriana
Ampanavoana
Mariarano
Port-Berge
Tsarahonenana
Ambinanitelo
Maroantsetra
Tanjon'i Masoala
Mahajanga
Katsepe
Tsinjomitondraka
Marovato
Kalandy
Rantabe
Vinanivao
Mahajanga
Mananara
Mitsinjo
MAHAJANGA
Ankazomborona
Mampikony
Ambohijanang
Mandritsara
Soalala
Marovoay
Manaratsandry
Ambolomoty
Teremandroso
Marotandrano
Sandrakatsy
Antanambe
Madirovalo
Ambato Boeny
Analamaitso Plateau 1,268 m
Miarinarivo
Manompana
Besalampy
Ambalajanakomby
Mahaboboka
Tsaratanana
Andilamena
Nosy Ste. Marie
Mahabe
Maevatanana
Andilamatso
Ambodifototra
Ikahavo Plateau
Mahazoma
Amboasary
Tamboharano
Kandreho
Antsiafabositra
Andriamena
Yohimena
Fenoarivo Atsinanana
Morafenobe
Ambatomaidy
Andriba
Morarano Chrome
Ambohitsilaozana
Maintirano
Bekodoka
Beravina
Kianjara
Manakambahiny 1,565 m
Andilanatoby
Ambodiriana
Betanantanana
Kiranomena
Ankazobe
Ambatomainona
Ivaty
Ambatondrazaka
Nosy Barren (Barren Is.)
Antsalova
Ankavandra
Anjozorobe
Mahitsy
TOAMASINA
Ambinanynony
Imerimandroso
Toamasina
Bongolava
Tsiroanomandidy
Analavory
Miarinarivo
ANTANANARIVO
Ambalarondra
Andjiro Gara
Masoarivo
Bekopaka
Soavinandriana
1,542 m
Antpely
Ambohidratrimo
IVATO
Arivonimamo
Antananarivo
Ampasimanolotra
Iloady
Tsiafajavona 2,643 m
Mandalaza
Moramanga
Andevoranto
Manandaza
Beforona
Lakato
Miandrivazo
Mandoto
Ambatolampy
Beheny
Anosibe an'Ala
Vatomandry
Berevo
Belo-Tsiribihina
Ankazomiriotra
Ambohimandroso
Ampitatafika
Antanambao Manampotsy
Antsirabe
Antanifotsy
Ambohimilanja
Ilaka
Manjakandriana
Belo
Soamanandrariny
Manandona
Mahanoro
Ambodiharina
Marofandila
Marolambo
Ambanindrana
Morafandrana
Ambatolahy
Ambohimahavelona
2,254 m
Malaimbandy
Ilaka
Mahazoarivo
Mesomeloka
Morondava
Mahabo
Ankilizato
Soavina
Sahavato
Soavina
Nosy-Varika
Besafy
Ambatofinandrahana
Itremo
Ivato
Ambositra
Belo
Mandronsonpo
Amborompotsy
Ambovombe
MADAGASCAR
Bekoropaka
Berononô
Mandronarivo
Kalamavony
Vohiposa
Vohipeno
Andranopasy
Mandabe
Marereno
Tsitondroina
Vohiparara
Ambohinihaonana
Kianjavato
Mananjary
Ambahikily
Manja
Berorha
Makay Massif
Fianarantsoa
Ifanadiana
Antsenavolo
Tanandava
Talata Ampano
Mahasoabe
Tolongoina
Sondrôy
Morombe
Ankilizato
Berenty
Mahabo
Ambalavao
Namorona
Ampasimanjeva
Befandriana
Tandrano
FIANARANTSOA
Ankaramena
Faniria
Lokomby
Manakara
Andranolava
Iboby 2,658 m
Zazafotsy
Atambohobe
Ifanirea
Karianga
Andemaka
Antanimieva
Ankazoabo
PN DE L'ISALO
1,304 m
Ranohira
Ivohibe
Ivohibe
Vondrozo
Vaingainony
Manombo
Andranolava
Isalo Ruiniform Massif
Inony
Andriambavontsy
Ranotsara
Jakora
Farafangana
TOLIARA
Ankililoaka
Sakaraha
Bereketa
Andranovory
Betroka
Lavaraty
Vohitrambo
Lopary
Vangaindrano
Tropic of Capricorn
Manombo
Toliara
Ambohimahavelona
Saint-Augustin
Mahaboby
Bezaha
Tongobory
Ianakafy 1,824 m
Andranolaiina
Midongy Atsimo
Matanga
Betroka
Benenitra
Ianapera
Isoanala
Antanimora
Antokonosy Manambondro
Betioky
Soalara
Mahabo
Befotaka
Beheloka
Soamanonga
Bekitra 820 m
Manantenina
Ejeda
Gogogogo
Imanombo
Tsivory
Esira
Bekily
Behara
Beampingaratra
Itampolo
Ampanihy
Tranoroa
Antanimora
Beampingaratra
Androka
Beloha
Amboasary
Toalañaro
Tsiombe
Ambovombe
Antaritarika
Betanty
Tanjona Vohimena

Ocean labels

INDIAN OCEAN
Mozambique Channel

Juan de Nova (FRANCE)
Nosy Chesterfield
Tanjona Vilanandro

Bottom-left inset — Mauritius, Réunion

INDIAN OCEAN

C. Malheureux
Triolet
Poudre d'Or
Port Louis
Beau Bassin
Quatre Bornes
Curepipe
Mahébourg
MAURITIUS 827 m
Rose Belle
SIR SEEWOOSAGUR RAMGOOLAM
Souillac

RÉUNION (FRANCE)
GILLOT
Saint-Denis
Saint-André
Port
Saint-Benoît
Saint-Paul
Piton des Neiges 3,069 m
Pointe des Cascades
Saint-Leu
Le Tampon
Piton de la Fournaise 2,631 m
Saint-Louis
La Montagne
Saint-Pierre
Saint-Joseph

Mascarene Islands
MAURITIUS
RÉUNION

30 Mi
30 Km

Legend

POPULATION OF CITIES AND TOWNS

| ■ OVER 2,000,000 | ● 500,000 - 999,999 | ● 100,000 - 249,999 | ● 10,000 - 29,999 |
| ◻ 1,000,000 - 1,999,999 | ● 250,000 - 499,999 | ● 30,000 - 99,999 | ○ UNDER 10,000 |

SCALE 1:7,000,000 LAMBERT CONFORMAL CONIC PROJECTION
MILES 0 100 200 300
KILOMETERS 0 100 200 300

SAME SCALE AS MAIN MAP

82

Southern Africa

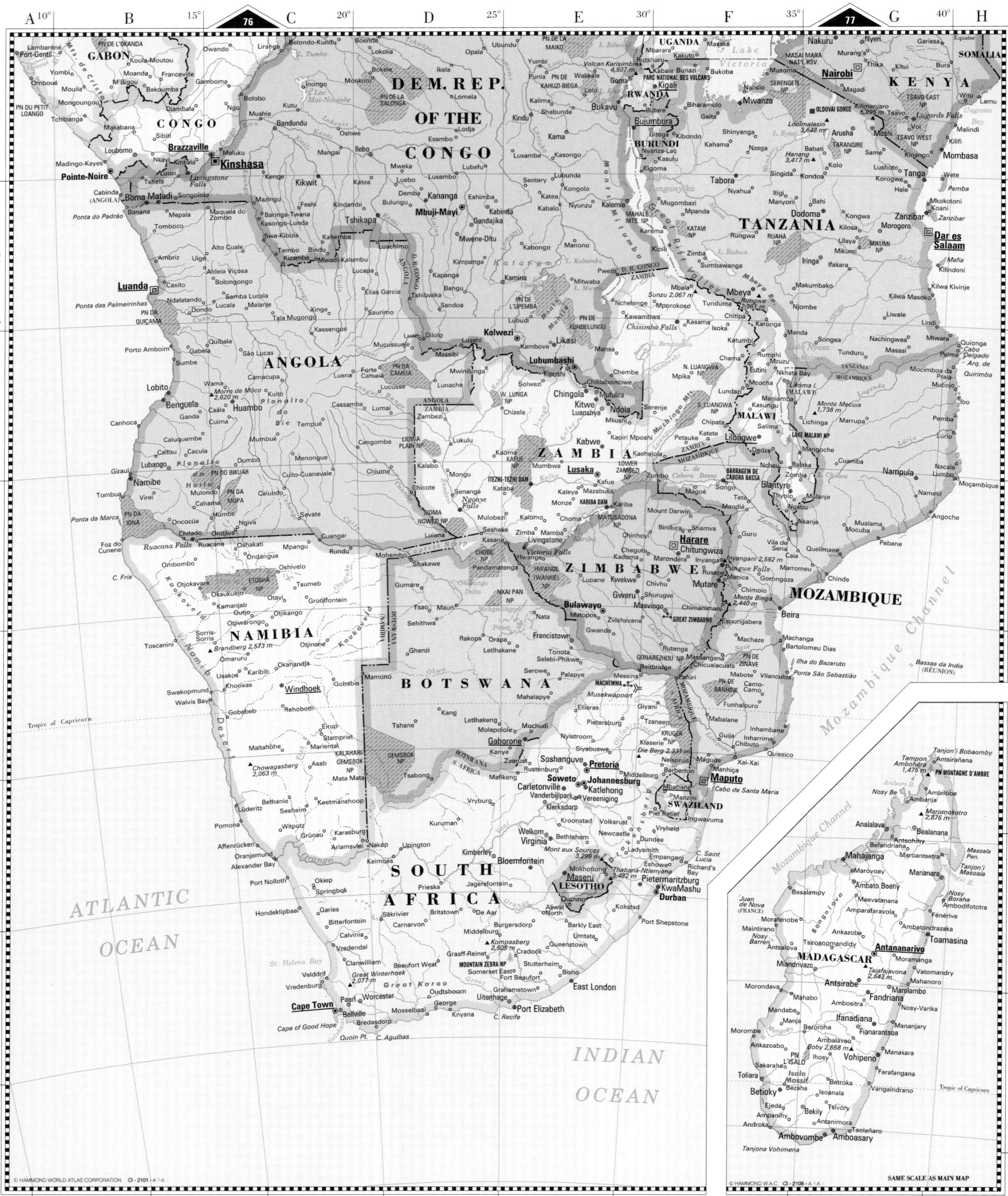

Arctic Regions, Antarctica

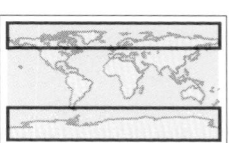

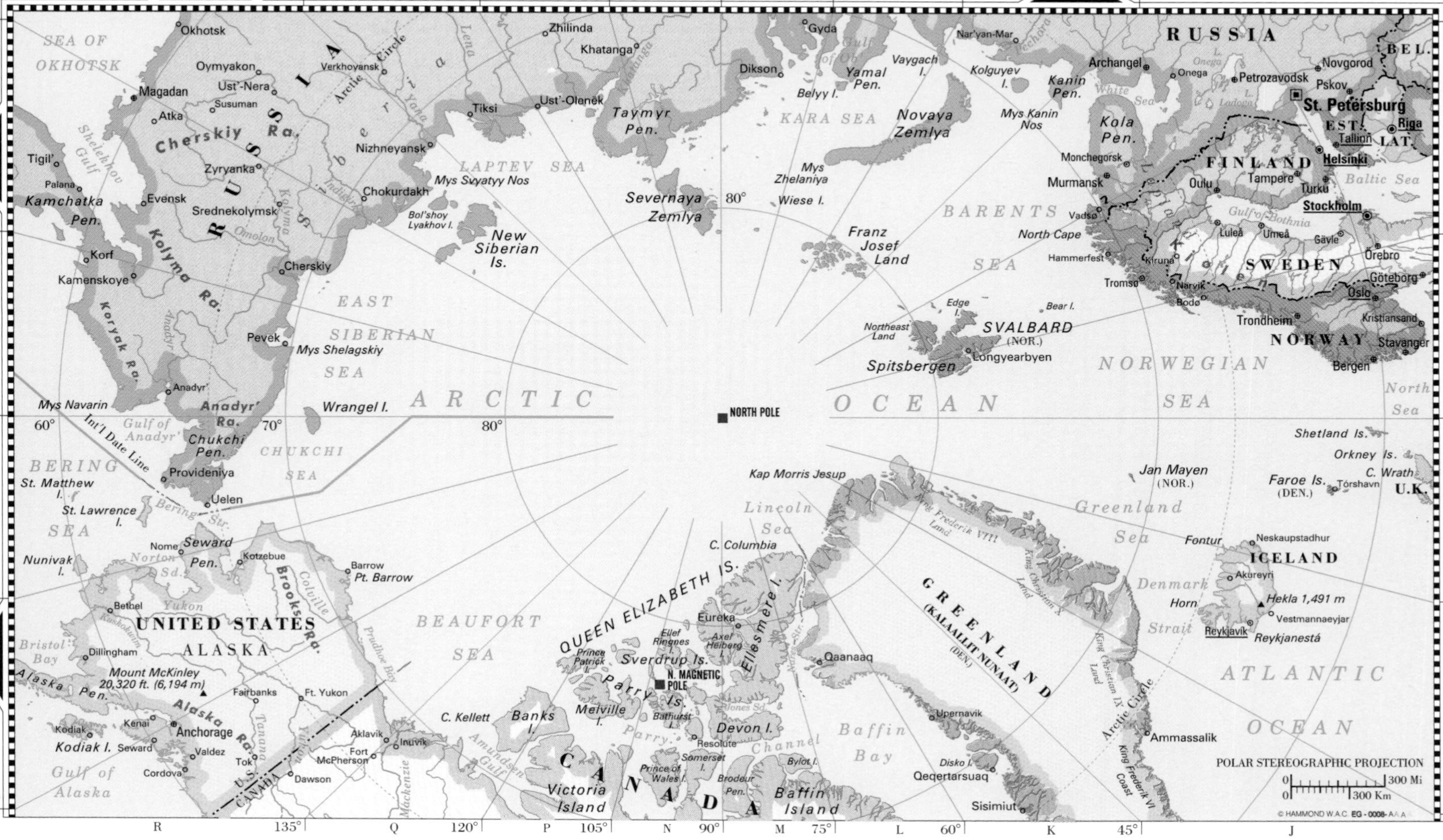

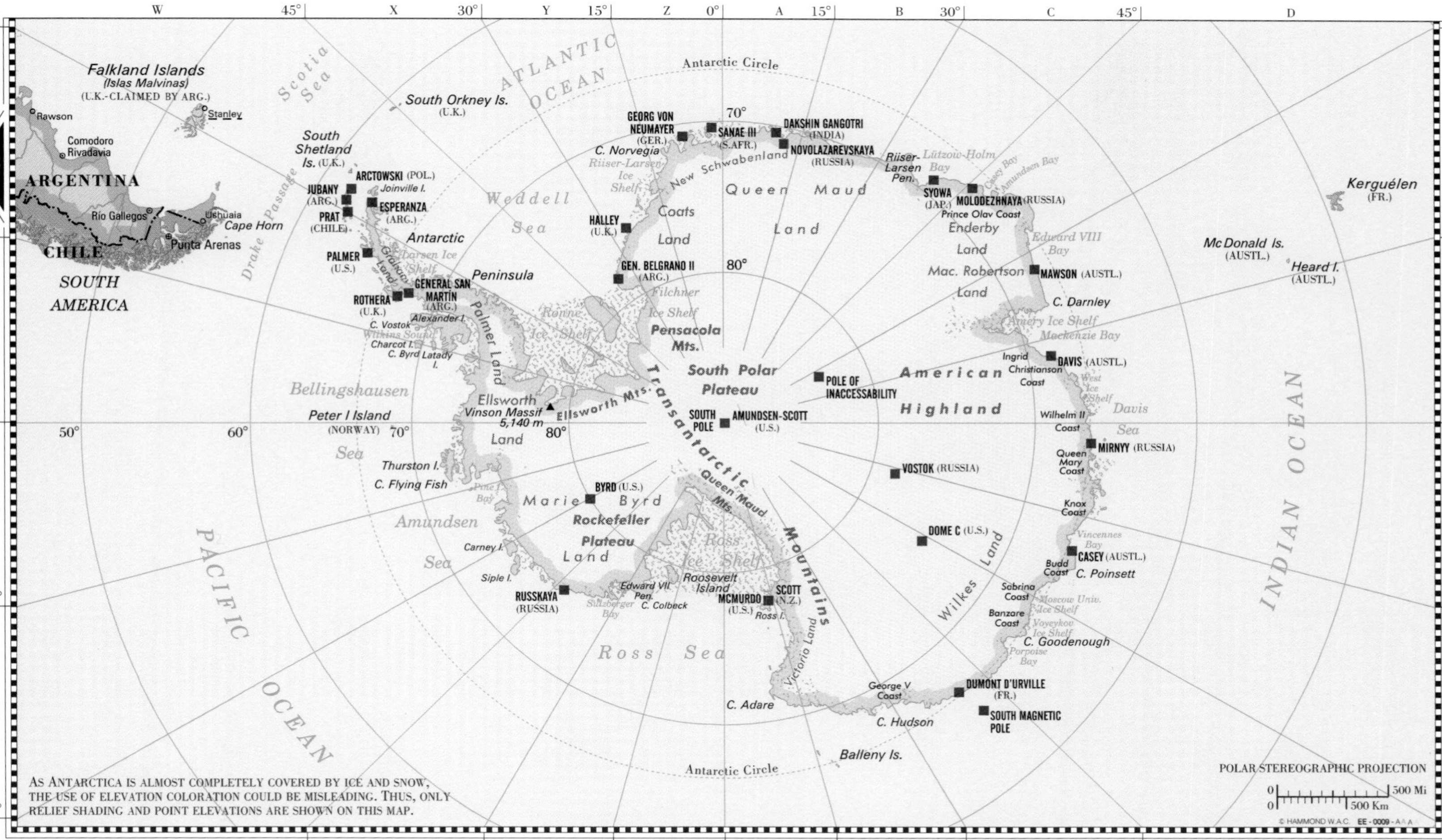

Arctic Regions (top map)

SEA OF OKHOTSK · Okhotsk · Oymyakon · Ust'-Nera · Verkhoyansk · Zhilinda · Khatanga · Gyda · Nar'yan-Mar · Archangel · RUSSIA · BEL. · Novgorod

Magadan · Susuman · Nizhneyansk · Dikson · Yamal Pen. · Vaygach I. · Kolguyev I. · Kanin Pen. · Onega · Petrozavodsk · Pskov

Atka · CHERSKIY RA. · Zyryanka · Taymyr Pen. · KARA SEA · Mys Kanin Nos · White Sea · St. Petersburg · EST. · Riga

Tigil' · Palana · Evensk · Srednekolymsk · Chokurdakh · Mys Svyatyy Nos · Novaya Zemlya · Mys Zhelaniya · Monchegorsk · Kola Pen. · FINLAND · Tallinn · LAT.

Kamchatka Pen. · Korf · RUSSIA · Bol'shoy Lyakhov I. · LAPTEV SEA · Wiese I. · Murmansk · Vadsø · Oulu · Tampere · Helsinki

Kamenskoye · Cherskiy · New Siberian Is. · Severnaya Zemlya · Franz Josef Land · BARENTS SEA · North Cape · Hammerfest · Luleå · Umeå · Gävle · Stockholm · Baltic Sea

Mys Navarin · KORYAK RA. · EAST SIBERIAN SEA · Tromsø · SWEDEN · Örebro · Oslo

Anadyr' Ra. · Gulf of Anadyr · Int'l Date Line · Anadyr · Wrangel I. · ARCTIC OCEAN · NORTH POLE · NORWEGIAN SEA · Narvik · Bodø · NORWAY · Trondheim · Kristiansand

BERING SEA · Chukchi Pen. · Providedeniya · CHUKCHI SEA · Edge I. · Bear I. · SVALBARD (NOR.) · Bergen · Stavanger · North Sea

St. Matthew · Pevek · Mys Shelagskiy · Uelen · Bering Str. · Kap Morris Jesup · Northeast Land · Longyearbyen · Spitsbergen · Shetland Is. · Orkney Is. · C. Wrath

St. Lawrence I. · Nome · Seward Pen. · Barrow · Pt. Barrow · Lincoln Land · Jan Mayen (NOR.) · Faroe Is. (DEN.) · Tórshavn · U.K.

Nunivak I. · Norton Sd. · Kotzebue · C. Columbia · Greenland Sea · Fontur · Neskaupstadhur · ICELAND · Akureyri

Bethel · UNITED STATES · ALASKA · BROOKS RA. · BEAUFORT SEA · QUEEN ELIZABETH IS. · Eureka · Prince Patrick I. · Ellef Ringnes I. · Axel Heiberg I. · Ellesmere I. · Denmark Strait · Horn · Hekla 1,491 m · Vestmannaeyjar · Reykjavík · Reykjanestá

Bristol Bay · Dillingham · Mount McKinley 20,320 ft. (6,194 m) · Fairbanks · Ft. Yukon · Prudhoe Bay · Sverdrup Is. · N. MAGNETIC POLE · Melville I. · Qaanaaq · Upernavik · ATLANTIC OCEAN

Kodiak · Kenai · Anchorage · Valdez · Aklavik · Inuvik · Dawson · C. Kellett · Banks I. · Bathurst I. · GREENLAND (KALAALLIT NUNAAT) (DEN.) · Ammassalik

Kodiak I. · Seward · Gulf of Alaska · Cordova · ALASKA RA. · U.S. CANADA · Fort McPherson · Mackenzie · Amundsen Gulf · Victoria Island · Parry Is. · Devon I. · Baffin Bay · Disko I. · Qeqertarsuaq

Koryak Ra. · CANADA · Somerset I. · Prince of Wales I. · Bylot I. · Baffin Island · Sisimiut

Arctic Circle · 30° · 15° · 0° · POLAR STEREOGRAPHIC PROJECTION · 0 300 Mi · 0 300 Km · © HAMMOND W.A.C. EG-0006-A-A-A

Antarctica (bottom map)

Falkland Islands (Islas Malvinas) (U.K.-CLAIMED BY ARG.) · Rawson · Stanley · Scotia Sea · ATLANTIC OCEAN · Antarctic Circle

Comodoro Rivadavia · South Orkney Is. (U.K.) · GEORG VON NEUMAYER (GER.) · SANAE III (S. AFR.) · DAKSHIN GANGOTRI (INDIA) · Riiser-Larsen Pen. · Lützow-Holm Bay · Amundsen Bay

ARGENTINA · South Shetland Is. (U.K.) · ARCTOWSKI (POL.) · C. Norvegia · NOVOLAZAREVSKAYA (RUSSIA) · Riiser-Larsen Ice Shelf · New Schwabenland · Kerguélen (FR.)

Río Gallegos · JUBANY (ARG.) · Joinville I. · ESPERANZA (ARG.) · Weddell Sea · Queen Maud Land · SYOWA (JAP.) · MOLODEZHNAYA (RUSSIA) · Prince Olav Coast

CHILE · PRAT (CHILE) · Antarctic · Coats Land · Enderby Land · Edward VIII Bay · McDonald Is. (AUSTL.)

SOUTH AMERICA · Ushuaia · Cape Horn · Punta Arenas · Drake Passage · PALMER (U.S.) · Graham Land · HALLEY (U.K.) · Mac. Robertson Land · MAWSON (AUSTL.) · Heard I. (AUSTL.)

ROTHERA (U.K.) · GENERAL SAN MARTIN (ARG.) · Peninsula · GEN. BELGRANO II (ARG.) · Amery Ice Shelf · C. Darnley · Mackenzie Bay

C. Vostok · Alexander I. · Larsen Ice Shelf · Palmer Land · Filchner Ice Shelf · Pensacola Mts. · Ingrid Christianson Coast · DAVIS (AUSTL.)

Charcot I. · C. Byrd · Latady I. · Ronne Ice Shelf · South Polar Plateau · American Highland · West Ice Shelf · Davis Sea

Bellingshausen Sea · Peter I Island (NORWAY) · Ellsworth Land · Vinson Massif 5,140 m · Ellsworth Mts. · Transantarctic · POLE OF INACCESSIBILITY · Wilhelm II Coast

Thurston I. · SOUTH POLE · AMUNDSEN-SCOTT (U.S.) · Queen Mary Coast · MIRNYY (RUSSIA)

C. Flying Fish · Marie Byrd Land · VOSTOK (RUSSIA) · Knox Coast

Amundsen Sea · BYRD (U.S.) · Rockefeller Plateau Land · Queen Maud Mts. · DOME C (U.S.) · CASEY (AUSTL.) · Budd Coast · C. Poinsett

Carney I. · Ross Ice Shelf · Roosevelt Island · Mountains · Sabrina Coast · Banzare Coast · C. Goodenough · Vincennes Bay

Siple I. · RUSSKAYA (RUSSIA) · Edward VII Pen. · C. Colbeck · MCMURDO (U.S.) · SCOTT (N.Z.) · Ross I. · Wilkes Land · Moscow Univ. Ice Shelf · Voyeykov Ice Shelf

PACIFIC OCEAN · Ross Sea · Victoria Land · C. Adare · George V Coast · DUMONT D'URVILLE (FR.) · Porpoise Bay · C. Hudson

SOUTH MAGNETIC POLE · Balleny Is. · Antarctic Circle · INDIAN OCEAN

POLAR STEREOGRAPHIC PROJECTION · 0 500 Mi · 0 500 Km · © HAMMOND W.A.C. EE-0009-A-A-A

AS ANTARCTICA IS ALMOST COMPLETELY COVERED BY ICE AND SNOW, THE USE OF ELEVATION COLORATION COULD BE MISLEADING. THUS, ONLY RELIEF SHADING AND POINT ELEVATIONS ARE SHOWN ON THIS MAP.

POPULATION OF CITIES AND TOWNS
- ■ OVER 2,000,000
- ▣ 1,000,000 - 1,999,999
- ● 500,000 - 999,999
- ◉ 100,000 - 499,999
- ○ 50,000 - 99,999
- ○ UNDER 50,000

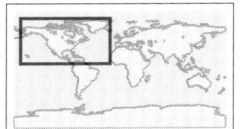

North America

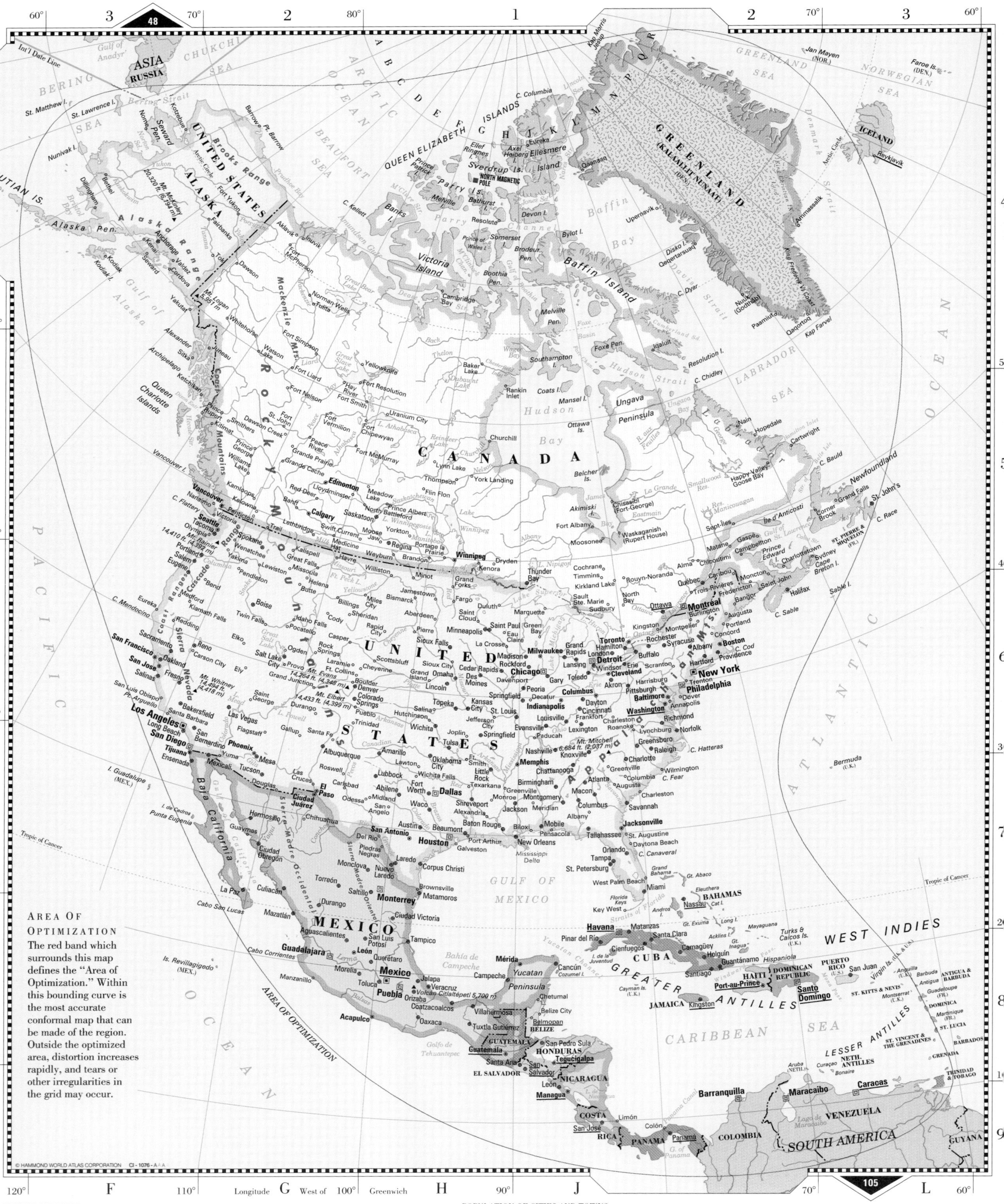

AREA OF OPTIMIZATION

The red band which surrounds this map defines the "Area of Optimization." Within this bounding curve is the most accurate conformal map that can be made of the region. Outside the optimized area, distortion increases rapidly, and tears or other irregularities in the grid may occur.

SCALE 1:35,000,000   OPTIMAL CONFORMAL PROJECTION

MILES

KILOMETERS   0   500   1000   1500

POPULATION OF CITIES AND TOWNS

▣ OVER 3,000,000   ● 500,000 – 999,999   ○ UNDER 100,000
▢ 1,000,000 – 2,999,999   ● 100,000 – 499,999

© HAMMOND WORLD ATLAS CORPORATION   CI - 1076 - A - A - A

Alaska

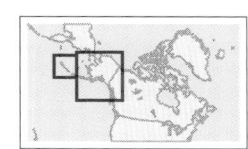

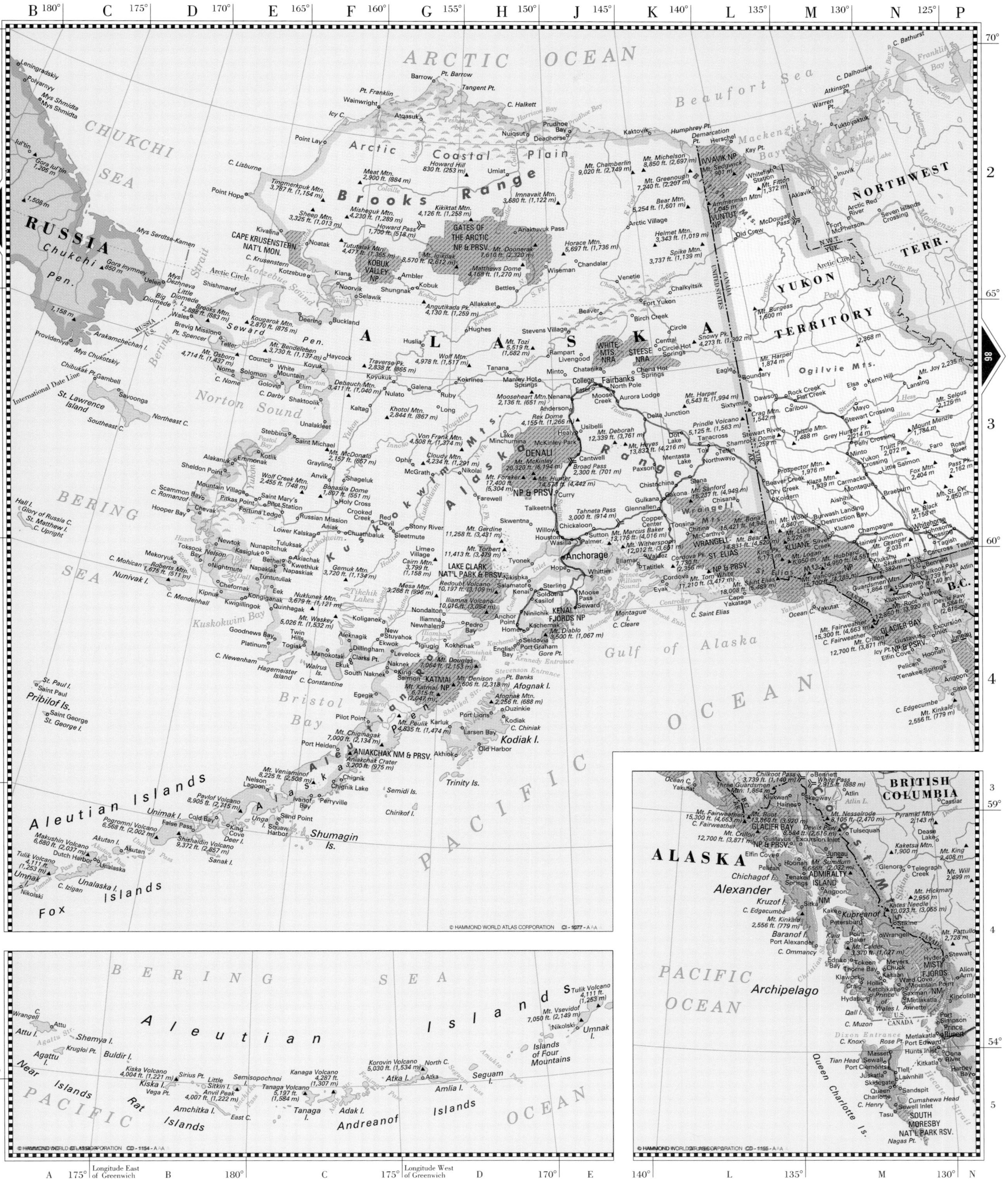

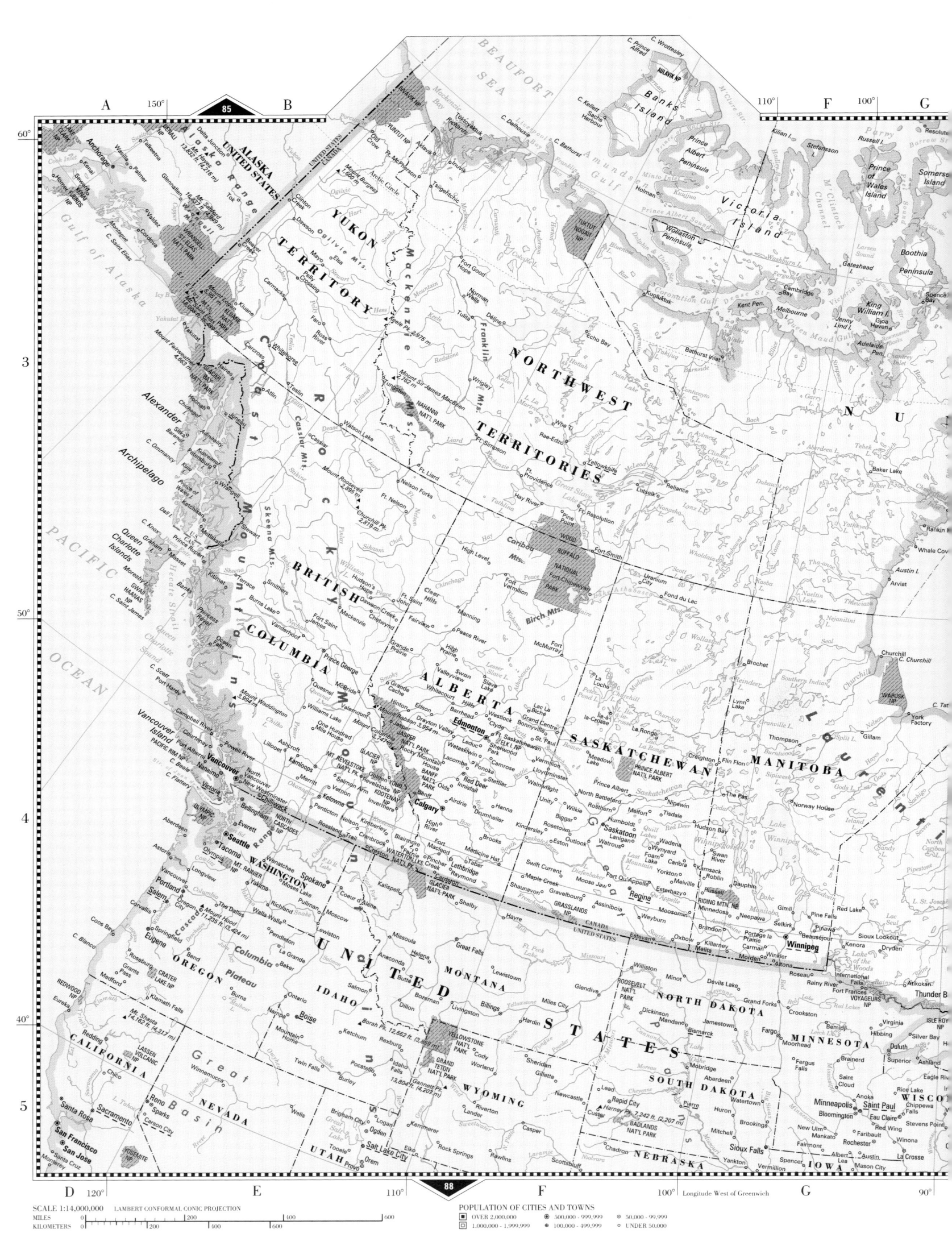

SCALE 1:14,000,000   LAMBERT CONFORMAL CONIC PROJECTION

MILES   0   200   400   600

KILOMETERS   0   200   400   600

POPULATION OF CITIES AND TOWNS

OVER 2,000,000   500,000 - 999,999   50,000 - 99,999

1,000,000 - 1,999,999   100,000 - 499,999   UNDER 50,000

Longitude West of Greenwich

Canada

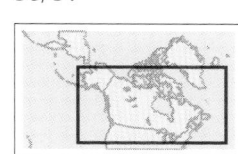

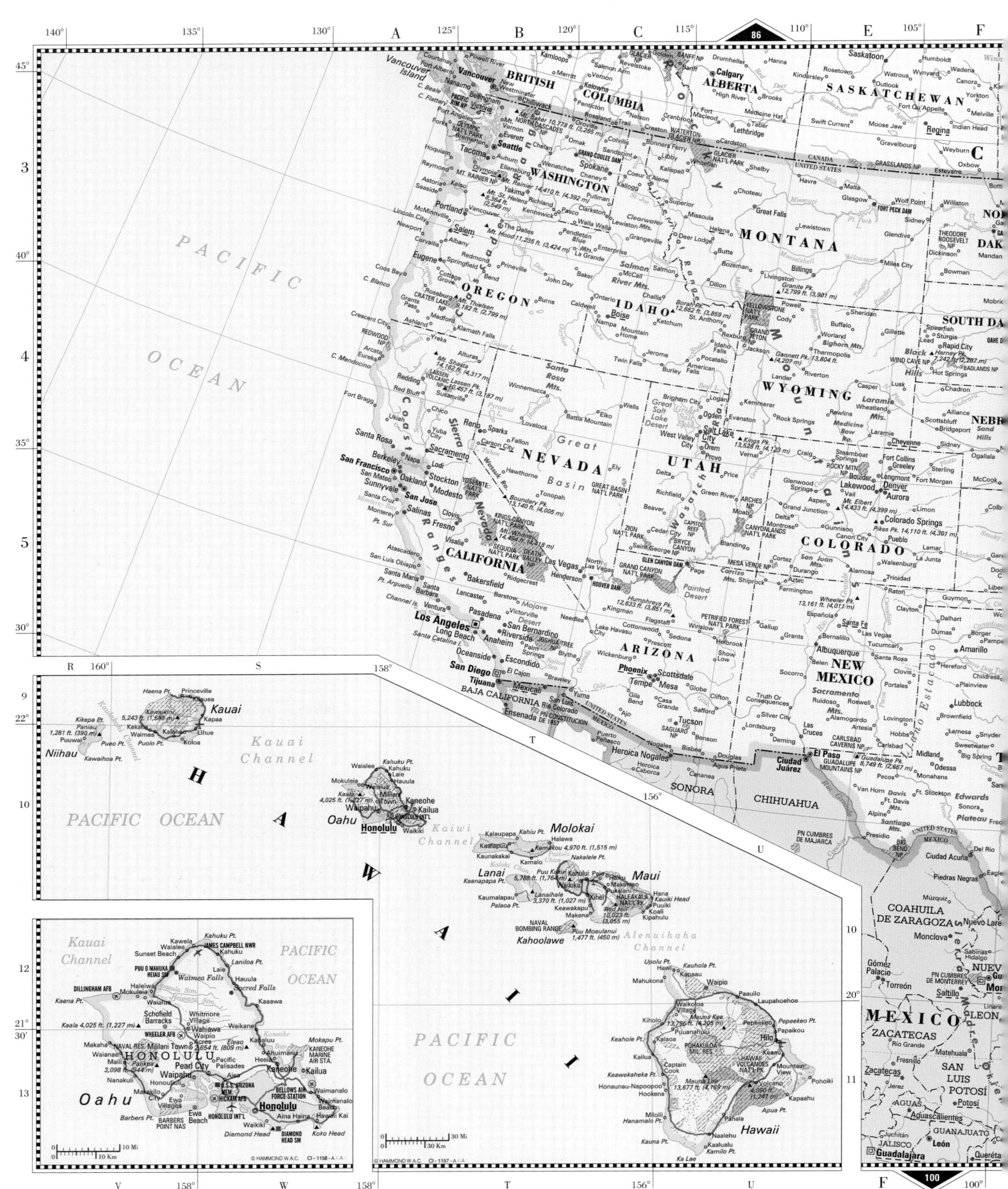

United States

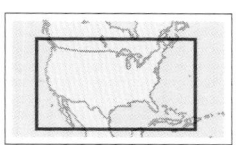

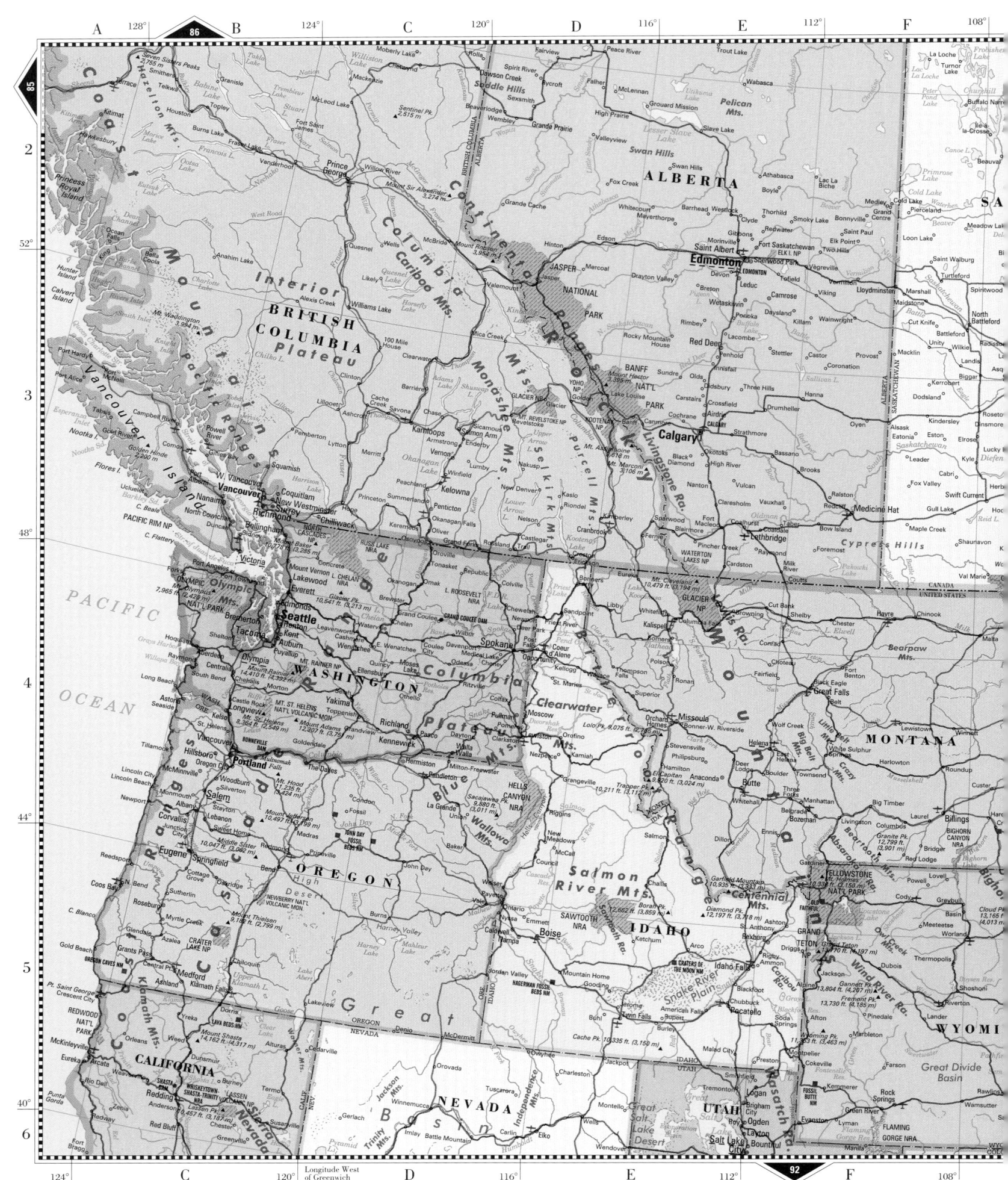

Southwestern Canada, Northwestern United States

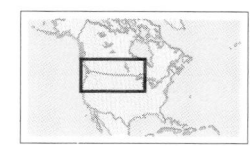

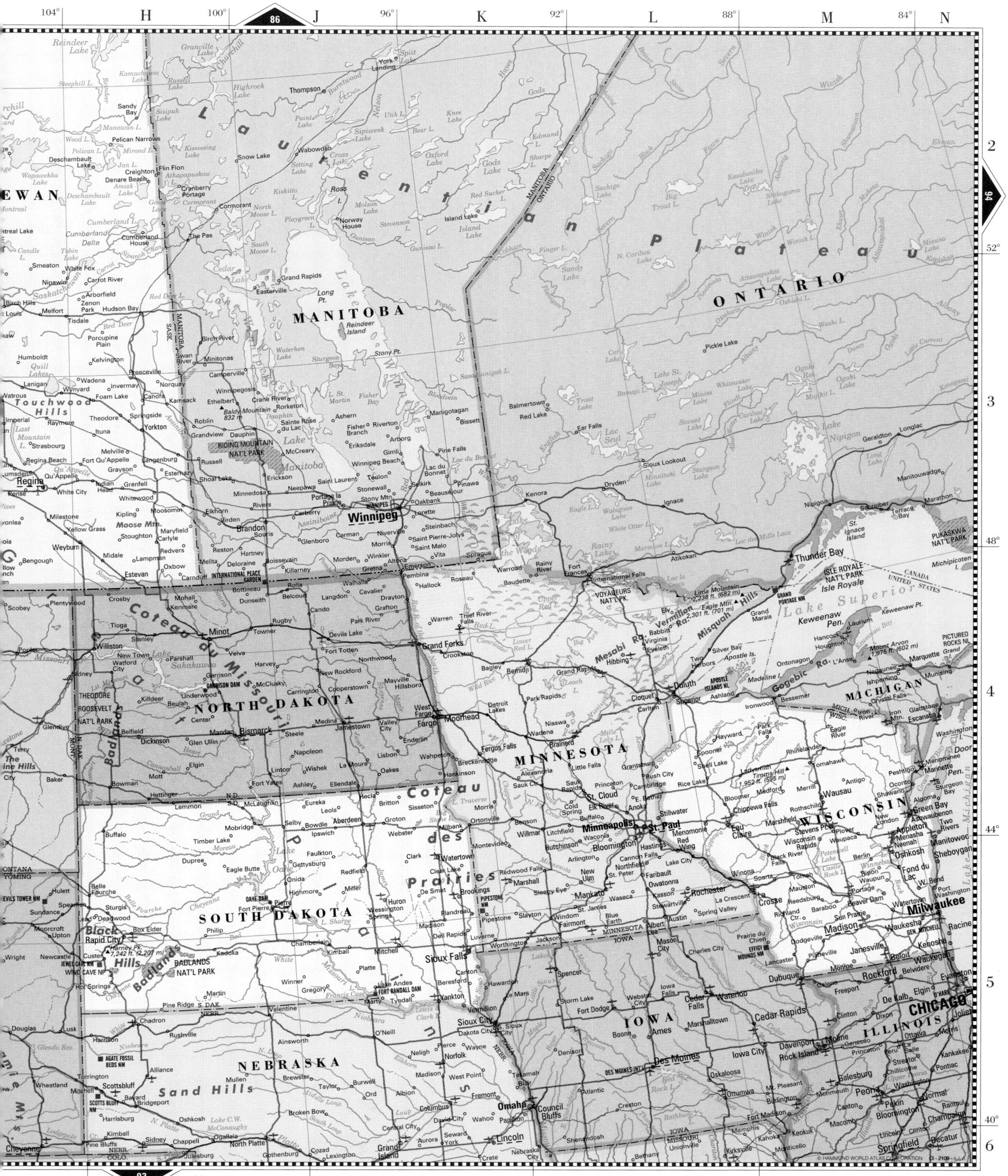

POPULATION OF CITIES AND TOWNS

| ■ OVER 2,000,000 | ● 500,000 - 999,999 | ● 100,000 - 249,999 | ○ 10,000 - 29,999 |
| ◻ 1,000,000 - 1,999,999 | ● 250,000 - 499,999 | ○ 30,000 - 99,999 | ○ UNDER 10,000 |

SCALE 1:7,000,000   LAMBERT CONFORMAL CONIC PROJECTION

MILES 0 · · 100 · · 200 · · 300
KILOMETERS 0 · · 100 · · 200 · · 300

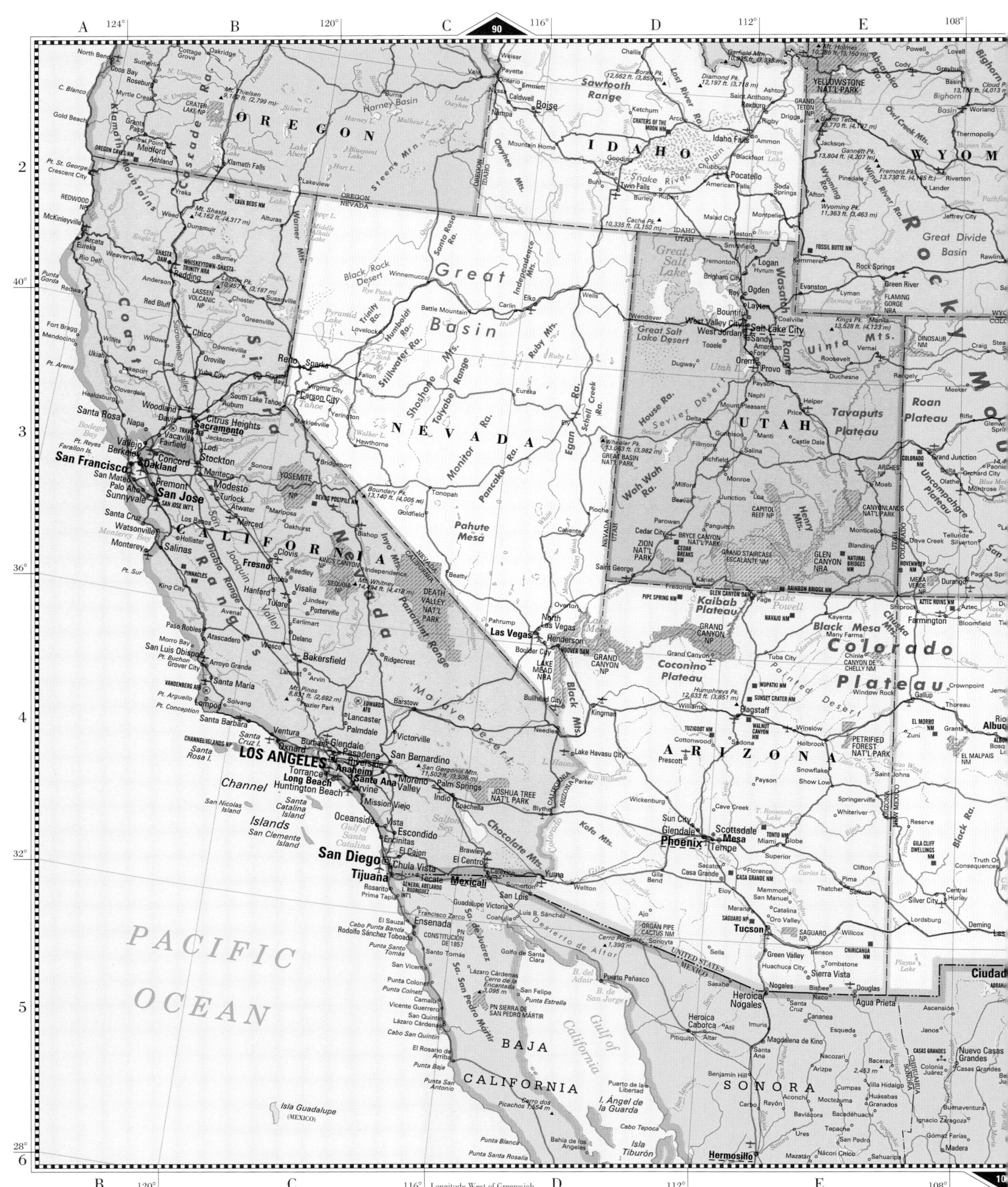

Southwestern United States

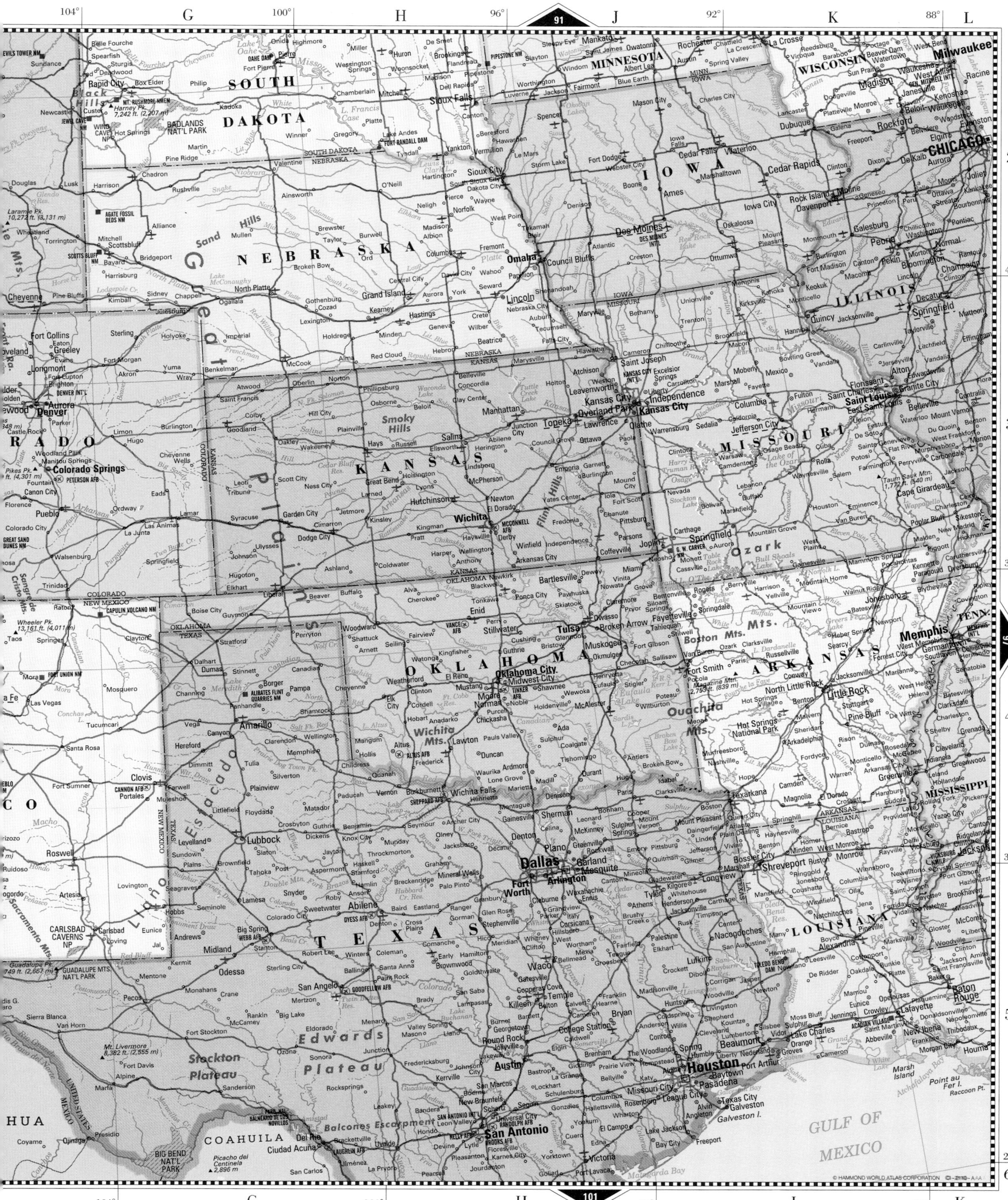

POPULATION OF CITIES AND TOWNS

■ OVER 2,000,000	● 500,000 - 999,999
□ 1,000,000 - 1,999,999	● 250,000 - 499,999

● 100,000 - 249,999   ● 10,000 - 29,999

● 30,000 - 99,999   ○ UNDER 10,000

SCALE 1:7,000,000   LAMBERT CONFORMAL CONIC PROJECTION

MILES 0   100   200   300

KILOMETERS 0   100   200   300

© HAMMOND WORLD ATLAS CORPORATION

Southeastern Canada, Northeastern United States

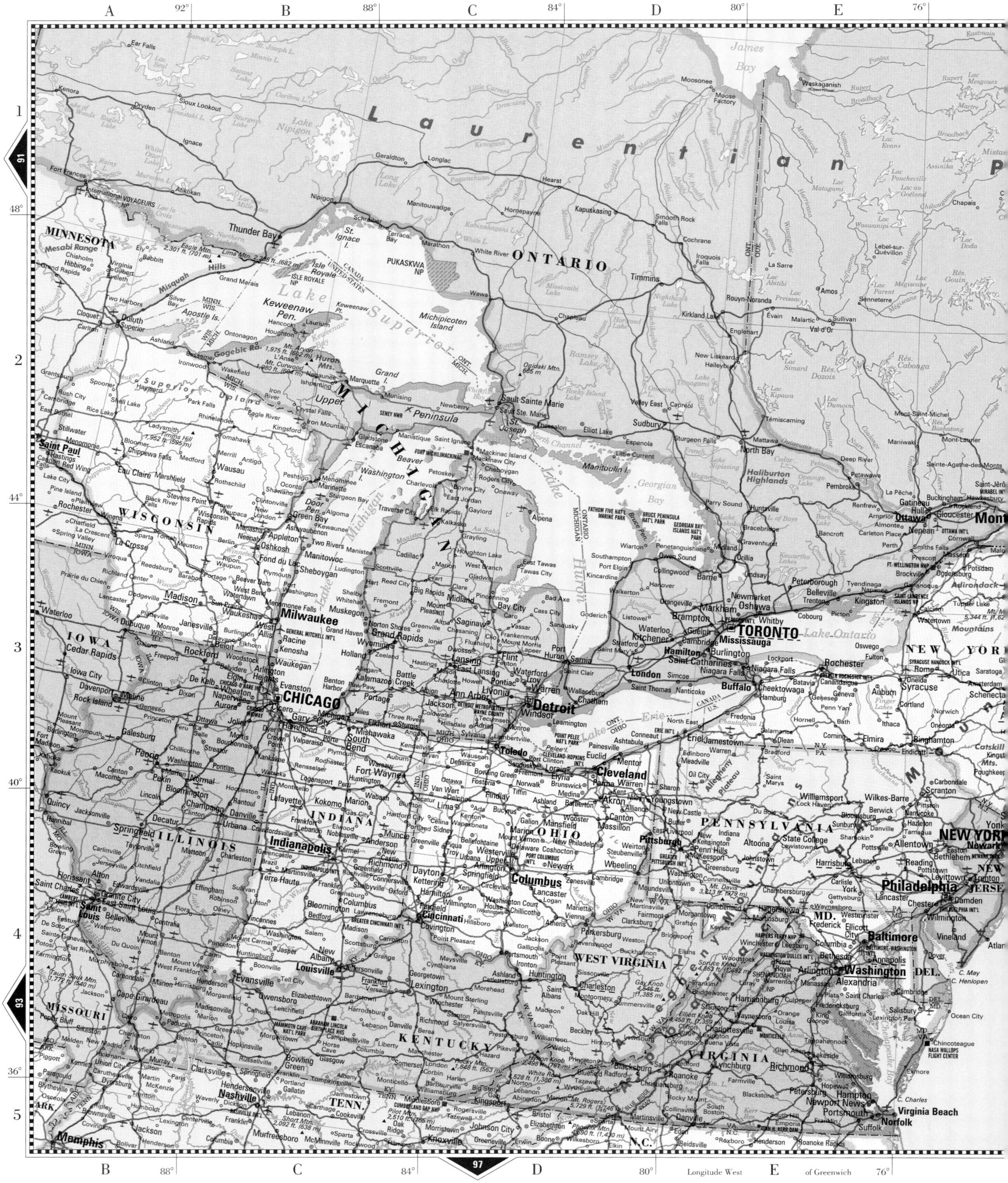

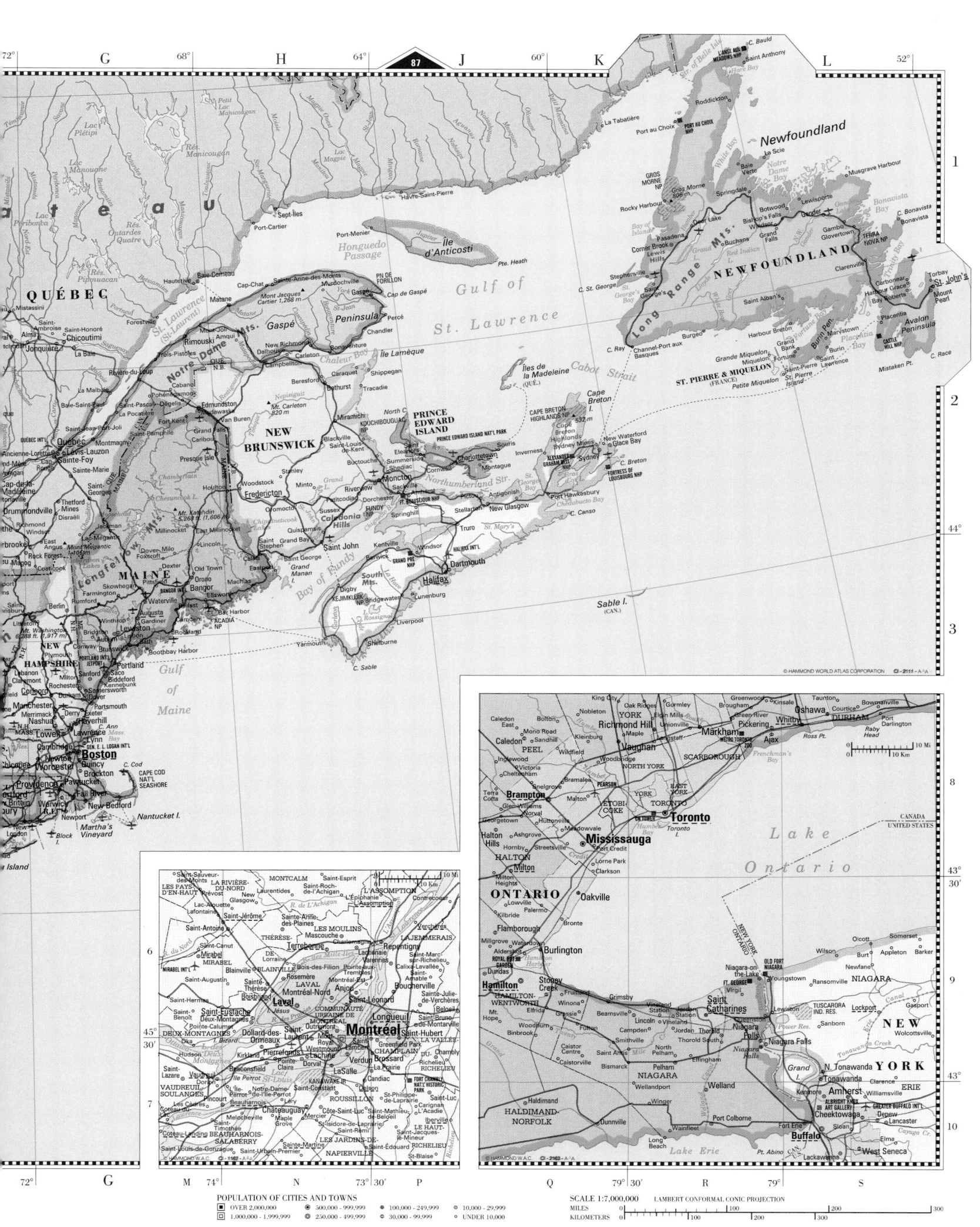

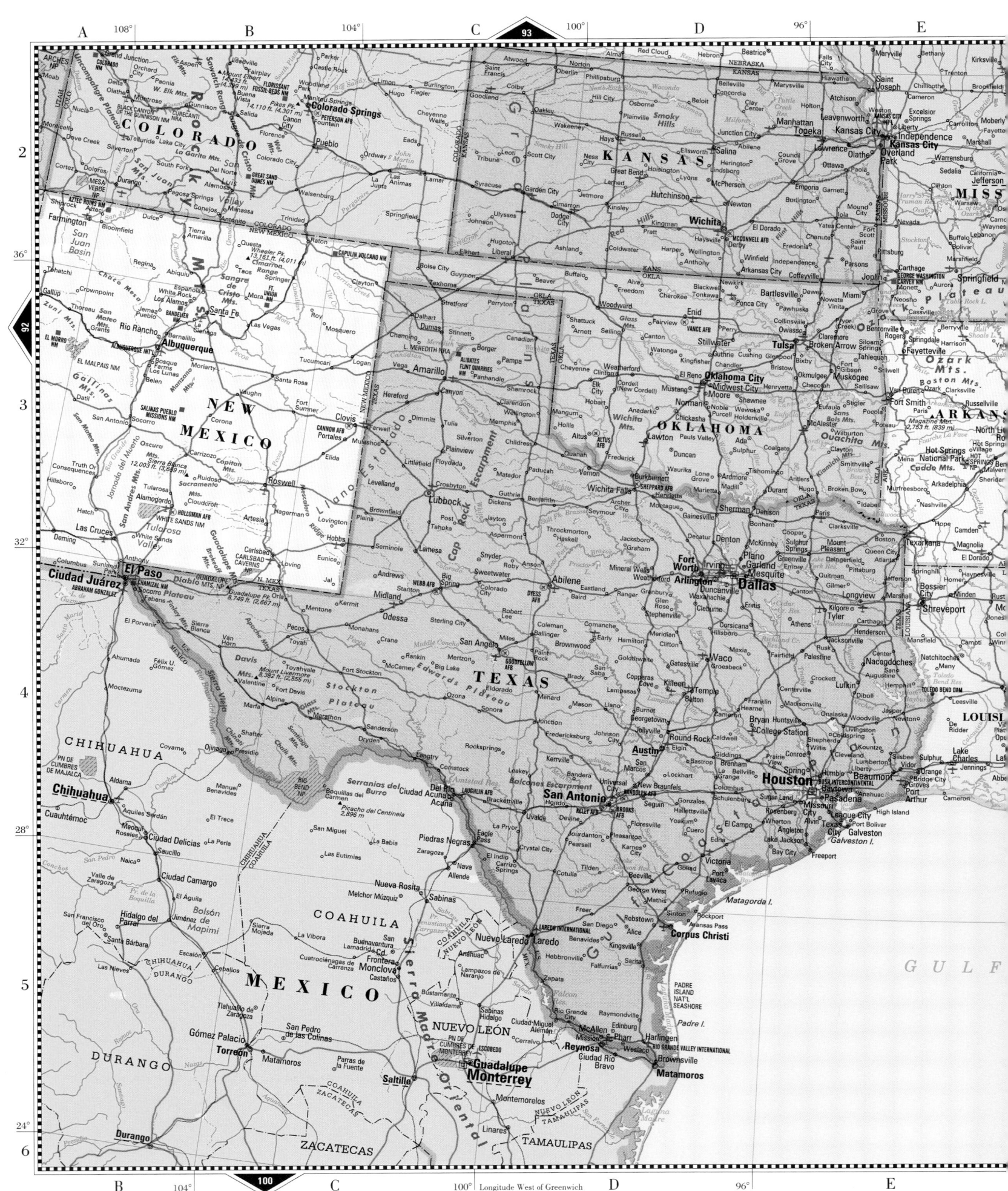

Southeastern United States

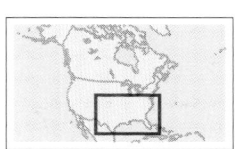

POPULATION OF CITIES AND TOWNS

| ■ OVER 2,000,000 | ● 500,000 - 999,999 | ⊕ 100,000 - 249,999 | ○ 10,000 - 29,999 |
| □ 1,000,000 - 1,999,999 | ● 250,000 - 499,999 | ⊕ 30,000 - 99,999 | ○ UNDER 10,000 |

SCALE 1:7,000,000   LAMBERT CONFORMAL CONIC PROJECTION

MILES 0   100   200   300
KILOMETERS 0   100   200   300

© HAMMOND WORLD ATLAS CORPORATION

Los Angeles, New York, Philadelphia, Washington

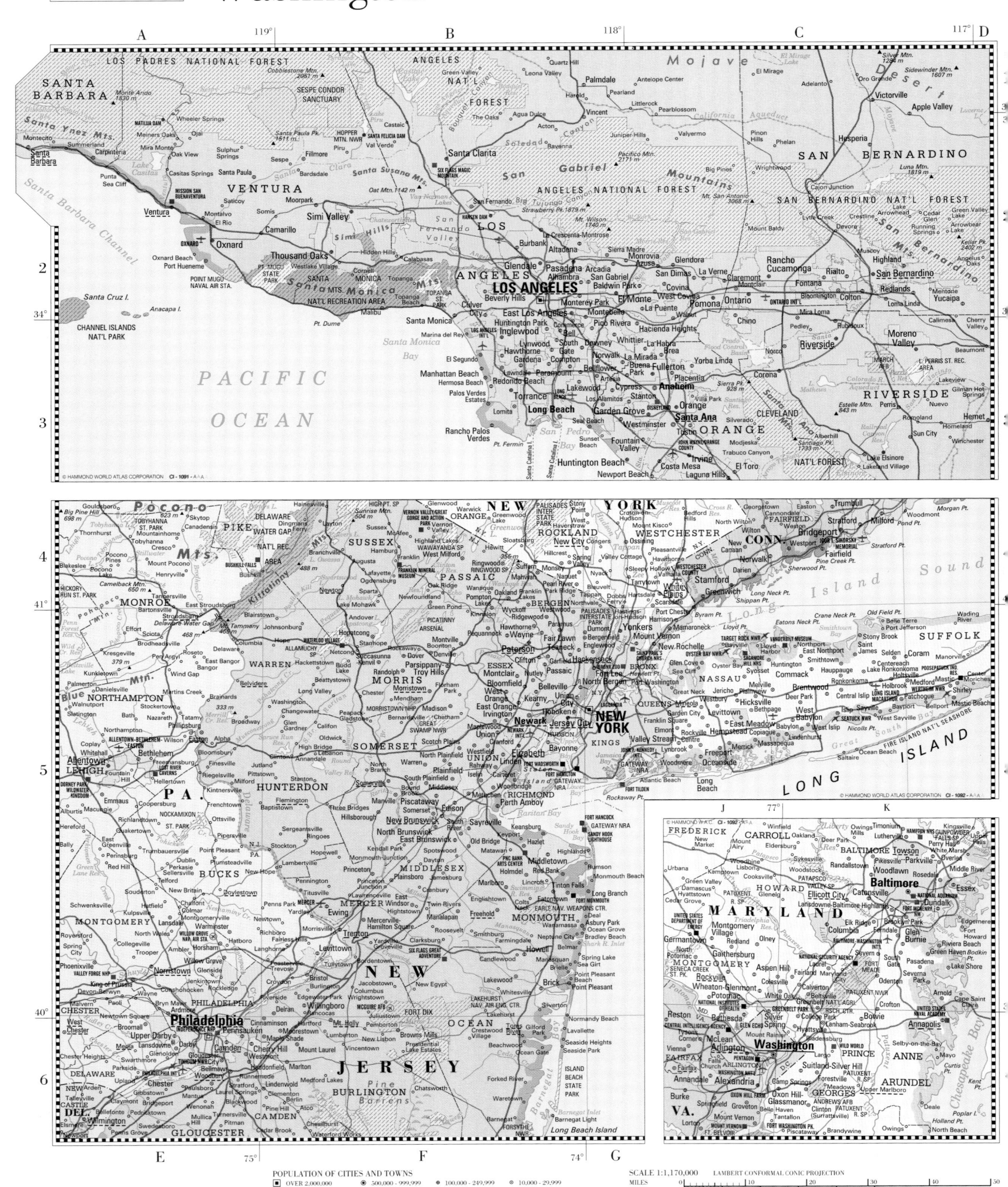

POPULATION OF CITIES AND TOWNS

■ OVER 2,000,000   ■ 500,000 - 999,999   ● 100,000 - 249,999   ○ 10,000 - 29,999
□ 1,000,000 - 1,999,999   □ 250,000 - 499,999   ● 30,000 - 99,999   ○ UNDER 10,000

SCALE 1:1,170,000   LAMBERT CONFORMAL CONIC PROJECTION
MILES
KILOMETERS

Seattle, San Francisco, Detroit, Chicago

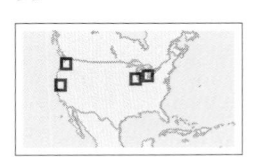

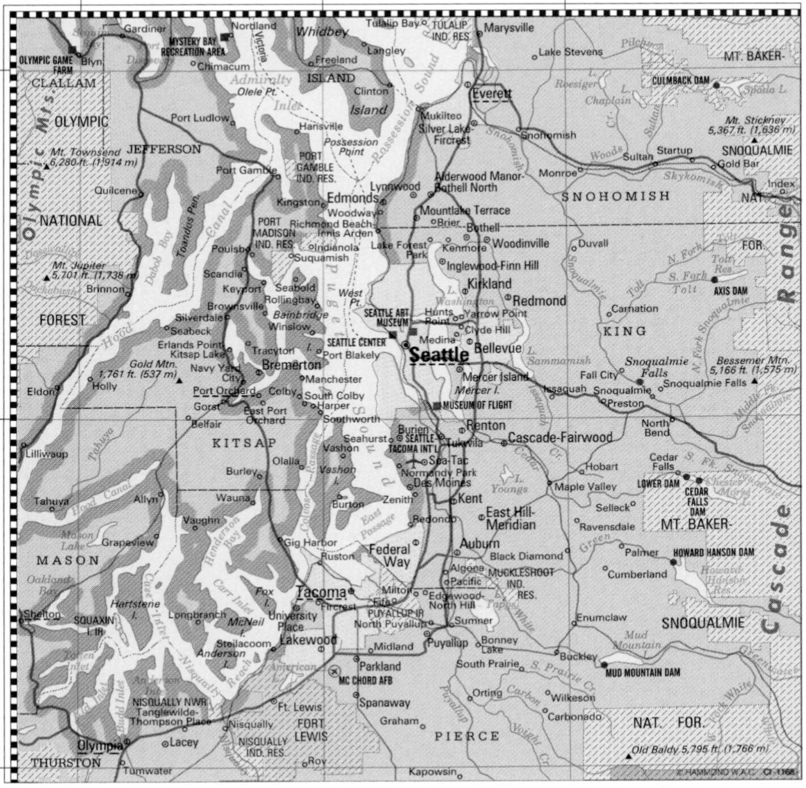

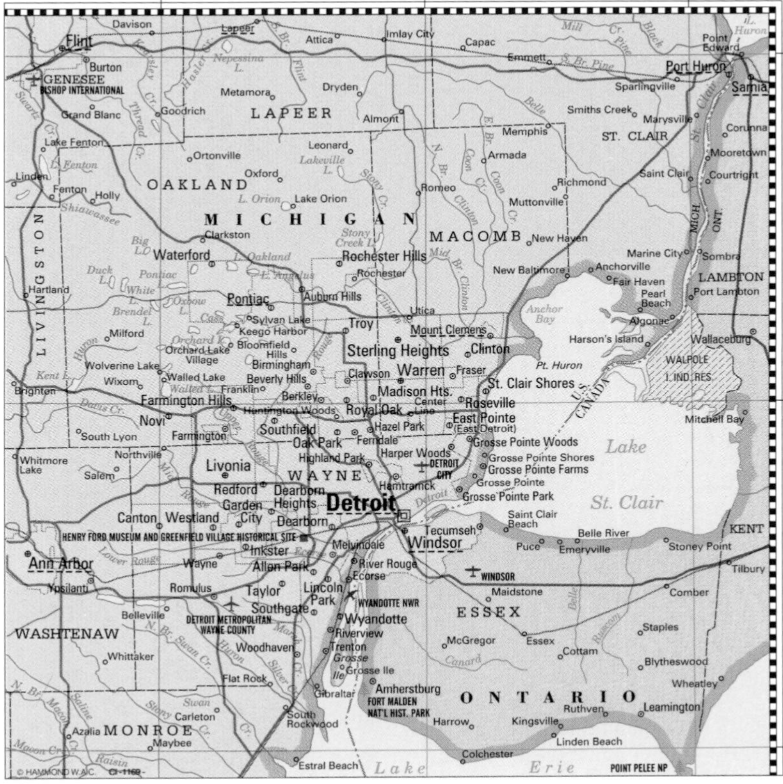

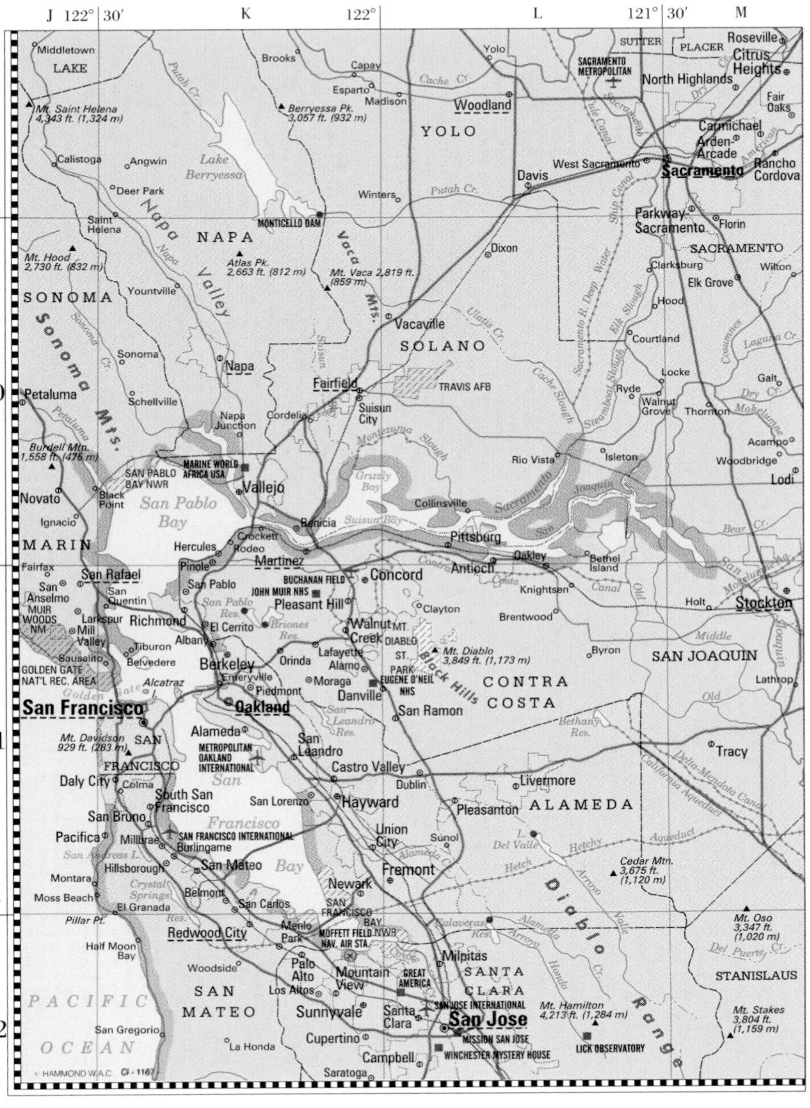

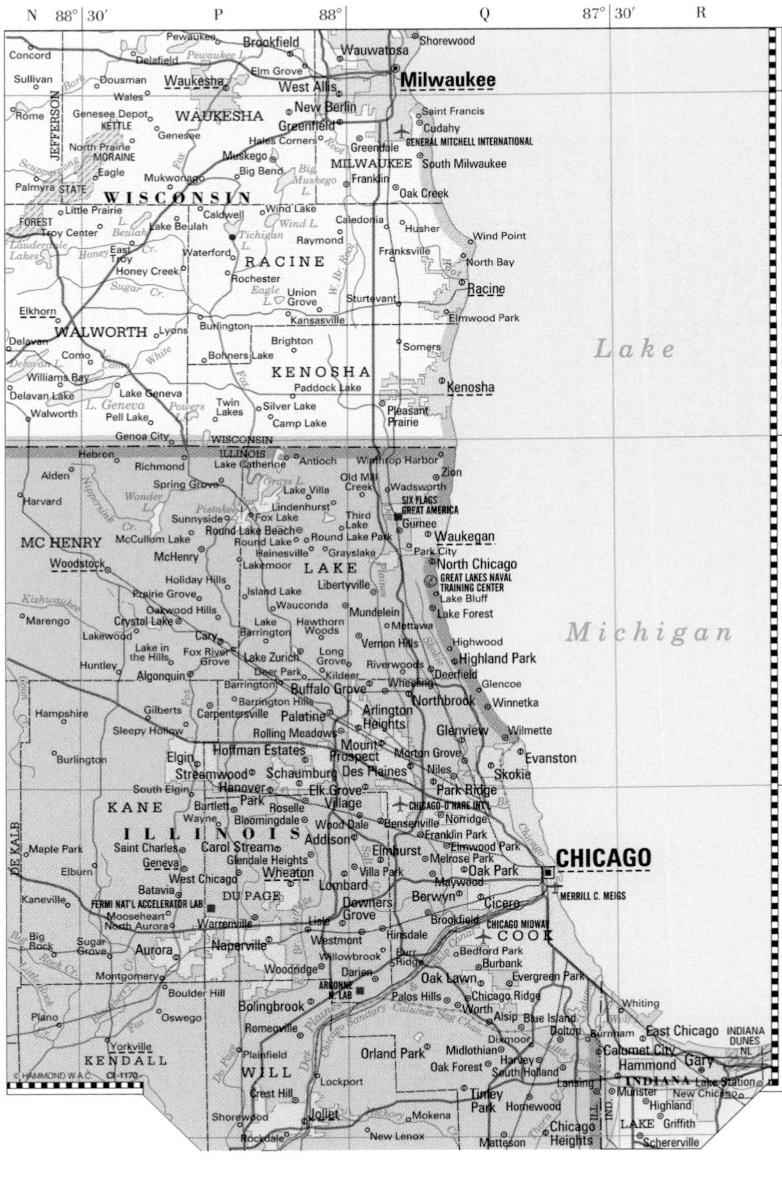

SCALE 1:1,170,000 LAMBERT CONFORMAL CONIC PROJECTION
MILES 0 10 20 30 40 50
KILOMETERS 0 10 20 30 40 50

A 116° **B** 112° **C** 108° **D** 104°

1

32°

2

28°

3

24°

Tropic of Cancer

4

20°

5

PACIFIC

OCEAN

Islas Revillagigedo
(MEXICO)

San Diego
Tijuana
El Cajon
Chula Vista
El Centro
CALIF.
Agua Caliente
Gila Bend
Casa Grande
Florence
Turnbull
Clifton
Pleasanton
Truth Or Consequences
Ruidoso
Whitetail
Roswell
Caprock

Tecate
Mexicali
Yuma
Wellton
Casa Grande Ruins NM
Safford
GILA CLIFF DWELLINGS NM
Tularosa
Elk Silver
Mayhill
Artesia
Lovington

Rosarito
GENERAL ABELARDO L. RODRIGUEZ
Ciudad Morelos
ARIZONA
Catalina
San Manuel
Mt. Graham
Thatcher
Central
Cliff
Santa Rita
San Juan
Garfield
WHITE SANDS NM
Alamogordo
La Luz
NEW MEXICO

Prima Tapia
San Luis Río Colorado
Why
SAGUARO NP
Tucson
SAGUARO NP
Mt. Lemmon 9,157 ft. (2,791 m)
Hurley
University Park
Las Cruces
Chimney Pk.
7,060 ft. (2,152 m)
Carlsbad

Ensenada
Rodolfo Sánchez Toboada
Cabo Punta Banda
Punta Santo Tomás
Francisco Zarco
Luis B. Sánchez
Coahuila
Green Valley
Rincon Pk. 8,482 ft. (2,585 m)
Willcox
Animas
Deming
Anthony
Columbus
Canutillo
White Sands
Wind Mtn. 7,280 ft. (2,219 m)
GUADALUPE MTS. NP
Whites City
Jal
Andrew

PN CONSTITUCIÓN DE 1857
Cerro Pinacate 1,390 m
Benson
Saint David
Tombstone
CHIRICAHUA NM
Chiricahua Pk. 9,796 ft. (2,986 m)
El Paso
Ciudad Juárez
Cerro Diablo
5,749 ft. (2,667 m)

San Tomás
Golfo de Santa Clara
Sonoyta
Sásabe
Sierra Vista
Bisbee
Douglas
Socorro
ABRAHAM GONZÁLEZ
Fabens
Diablo Plateau
Orla
Mentone
Penwell

San Vicente
Punta Colnet
Santo Rosario de la Encantada
San Felipe
Arivaca
TUMACÁCORI NHP
Nogales
Heroica Nogales
Santa Cruz
Naco
Agua Prieta
Ascensión
Praxedis G. Guerrero
El Porvenir
Sierra Blanca
Van Horn
Kent
Pecos
Grandfalls

Vicente Guerrero
Lázaro Cárdenas
PN SIERRA DE SAN PEDRO MÁRTIR
Punta Estrella
Bahía de San Jorge
Cananea
Esqueda
Janos
Buenaventura
Eagle Pk. 7,510 ft. (2,289 m)
Davis Mts.
Sierra Pk.
Black Mtn.
3,100 ft.

San Quintín
Cabo San Quintín
Caborca
Atil
Imuris
Magdalena de Kino
Nacozari
Bacerac
CASAS GRANDES
Nuevo Casas Grandes
Ahumada
FORT DAVIS NHS
Fort Davis
4,600

BAJA
Pitiquito
Altar
Santa Ana
Arizpe
Cumpas
Moctezuma
2,453 m
Colonia Juárez
Casas Grandes
Benito Juárez
Viejo Pk. 6,467 ft. (1,971 m)
Alpine

El Rosario de Arriba
Punta Baja
Punta San Antonio
Benjamín Hill
Querobabi
Aconchi
Rayón
Granados
Huásabas
Ignacio Zaragoza
Cathedral Mtn. 6,869 ft. (2,091 m)
Chinati Pk. 7,730 ft. (2,356 m)
Santiago Pk.
6,521 ft. (1,988 m)

CALIFORNIA
Cerro dos Picachos 1,554 m
I. Ángel de la Guarda
Cabo Tepoca
Baviácora
Tepache
SONORA
Ures
San Pedro
Madera
Gómez Farías
Ojinaga
Presidio
Nine Point Mesa 5,502 ft. (1,677 m)
Shafter

Punta Blanca
Punta Santa Rosalía
Cabo Tepoca
Isla Tiburón
Mazatán
Nácori Chico
Sahuaripa
PARQUE NACIONAL CUMBRES DE MAJALCA
El Sauz
Aldama
Coyame
Terlingua
BIG BEND
Entero Pk. 7,835 ft. (2,398 m)
Boquillas del Carmen

Bahía de los Ángeles
Hermosillo
Arivechi
Bachíniva
SIERRA Madre
Chihuahua
GENERAL VILLALOBOS
Aquiles Serdán

I. Cedros
Isla Sebastián Cedros
L. Playa Noriega
Miguel Alemán
Punta San Gabriel
Yécora
Guerrero
La Junta
Cuauhtémoc
Anáhuac
Meoqui
La Perla
Hércules

Punta Eugenia
Guerrero Negro
Ortiz
Suaqui Grande
PN CASCADA DE BASSASEACHIC
Creel
Rosales
Ciudad Delicias
Saucillo
COAH. DE ZARA

Bahía de Tortugas
Gustavo Díaz Ordaz
Guaymas
Empalme
Rosario
San Juanito
San Pedro
Naica
Ciudad Camargo
Bolsón

Bahía Asunción
San Ignacio
Francisco Javier Mina
Potam
Yaqui
Presa Álvaro Obregón
PN BARRANCA DEL COBRE
Batopilas
Guachochi
Nonoava
Pr. de la Boquilla
Jiménez
Laguna del Rey
de Mapimí

Punta San Hipólito
La Bocana
Cerro Encantado 1,586 m
Santa Rosalía
Marte R. Gómez
Navojoa
San Blas
Choix
San Francisco del Oro
Hidalgo del Parral
Villa López
Escalón
Ceballos

Punta Abreojos
San Bruno
Mulegé
Punta Chivato
Punta Concepción
Villa Juárez
Bacobampo
Etchojoa
Álamos
Masiaca
El Fuerte
Santa Bárbara
Las Nieves

BAJA
CALIFORNIA
Bahía Concepción
Huatabampo
Punta Rosa
Yavaros
Agiabampo
Gustavo Díaz Ordaz
Reforma
Tlahualilo
I. Madero

Punta Santo Domingo
San Juanico
LORETO
Loreto
I. Carmen
Estero de Agiabampo
Higuera de Zaragoza
Ahome
San Blas
Sinaloa
Santa María del Oro
DURANGO
Bermejillo
San Pe

Punta San Juanico
Ciudad Insurgentes
SUR
José Ríos
Los Mochis
Topolobampo
Solano
Guamúchil
Mócorito
Badiraguato
Topia
Nazas
Gómez Palacio
Ciudad Lerdo
Torreón
Matamoros

I. Santa Magdalena
Cabo San Lázaro
Adolfo López Mateos
Ciudad Constitución
San Juanico
I. San José
Layva
Guasave
Angostura
Tepehuanes
Santiago Papasquiaro
Rodeo
Velardeña
Viesca

Puerto Magdalena
Pto. San Carlos
Bahía de Santa María
Costa Rica
Reforma
Pericos
Santa María
Nuevo Ideal
Peñón Blanco
Cuencamé
ZACA

Puerto Cortés
I. Santa Margarita
Puerto Magdalena
San Juan de la Costa
I. Espíritu Santo
Navolato
Villa Juárez
Culiacán
Canatlán
Guadalupe Victoria
Santa Clara
Juan Aldama

La Paz
LEÓN
Punta Arena de la Ventana
I. Cerralvo
El Dorado
Cosalá
El Salto
Durango
SINALOA
Nombre de Dios
Río Grande
Nieves
Sombrerete

Los Planes
San Antonio
La Cruz
San Ignacio
Dimas
Vicente Guerrero
Mezquital
Chalchihuites
Saín Alto

2,164 m
Punta Arena
Todos Santos
Miraflores
San José Viejo
El Quelite
PN DE LA CIUDAD
Concordia
Fresnillo
2,887 m
Víctor Rosales
Zacatecas

Cabo San Lucas
Cabo Falso
San José del Cabo
Cabo San Lucas
BUELNA
Mazatlán
Rosario
Villa Unión
Cacalotán
Valparaíso
CHICOMOSTOC
Jerez
Ojoc

Escuinapa
Huajicori
Concordia
El Nayar
NAYARIT
Colotlán
Rincón de
Pabellón
Arteaga

Teacapán
Rosamorada
Ruiz
Monte Escobedo
Villanueva
Cavillo
Enc
Aquasc

Pericos
Tuxpan
Santiago Ixcuintla
PARQUE NACIONAL ISLA ISABELA
Islas
I. María Madre
San Blas
Villa Hidalgo
Tepic
Jalcocotán
Jalisco
Tlaltenango
Jalpa
Juchipila
Teúl
San Juan de los La

Tres
Marías
I. María Magdalena
I. María Cleófas
Compostela
Ahuacatlán
Ixtlán
Yahualica

San Juan Abajo
Punta de Mita
Amatlán de Cañas
Tequila
Zapopan
Guadala
Lagos
Tlaquepaque

I. San Benedicto
Puerto Vallarta
Mascota
ORDAZ
Ameca
MIGUEL HIDALGO
Cocula
Tequila
Chapala
Ocotlán
Sahuayo

Cabo Corrientes
El Tuito
Talpa de Allende
JALISCO
Zacoalco
Chapala
Jac

I. Roca Partida
Ayutla
Unión de
Sayula
Siguilpan
Los Reyes

El Grullo
Autlán
El Limón
PN NEV. DE COLIMA
Cd. Guzmán
Tamazula de Gordiano
Tuxpan

Casimiro Castillo
Nevado de Colima 4,330 m
Tecalitlán
Pico de Tancítaro 3,860 m
Cuauhtémoc

La Huerta
MANZANILLO
Comala
Tepalcatepec
Apatzing

I. Socorro
Cihuatlán
COLIMA
Colima
Armería
Tecomán
Coalcomán

I. Clarion
Manzanillo
Coahuayana
Pta. San Juan de Lima

Punta San Telmo
Caleta de Campos
Las Guacam
Cá

116° **B** 112° **C** 108° Longitude West of Greenwich **D** 104°

Northern and Central Mexico

GULF OF MEXICO

Bahía de Campeche

Tropic of Cancer

TEXAS

NUEVO LEÓN

TAMAULIPAS

SAN LUIS POTOSÍ

GUANAJUATO

HIDALGO

MORELOS

GUERRERO

OAXACA

VERACRUZ-LLAVE

TABASCO

CHIAPAS

CAMPECHE

QUINTANA ROO

YUCATÁN

Yucatán Peninsula

Isthmus of Tehuantepec

GUATEMALA

BELIZE

Dallas — Fort Worth — Arlington — Austin — San Antonio — Corpus Christi — Laredo — McAllen — Brownsville — Matamoros — Reynosa — Monterrey — Guadalupe — San Nicolás de los Garza — Garza García — Ciudad Victoria — Tampico — Ciudad Madero — Querétaro — Celaya — Morelia — Mérida — Cancún — Cozumel — Campeche — Chetumal — Villahermosa — Coatzacoalcos — Minatitlán — Veracruz — Córdoba — Orizaba — Puebla — Cuernavaca — Toluca — MEXICO (Ciudad de México) — Ecatepec — Nezahualcóyotl — Tlalnepantla — Naucalpan — Acapulco — Jalapa

Inset — HIDALGO / MÉXICO / TLAXCALA / PUEBLA / MORELOS

Pachuca — Tula — Toluca — Metepec — Ecatepec — Naucalpan — Tlalnepantla — MEXICO (Ciudad de México) — Nezahualcóyotl — Cuernavaca — Puebla — Tlaxcala — Jalapa — Veracruz — Córdoba — Orizaba — Papantla — Poza Rica — Volcán Popocatépetl — Volcán Iztaccíhuatl — Pico de Orizaba (Citlaltépetl) 5,700 m — Volcán Cofre de Perote 4,282 m

Inset — DISTRITO FEDERAL

Cuautitlán Izcalli — Coacalco — Tultitlán — López Mateos — Nicolás Romero — Buenavista — MÉXICO — Ecatepec — Tlalnepantla — Naucalpan — Nezahualcóyotl — MEXICO (Ciudad de México) — Chimalhuacán — Los Reyes — Ixtapaluca — Chalco — Toluca — Metepec — XOCHIMILCO — TLALPAN — COYOACÁN — IXTAPALAPA — MILPA ALTA — MORELOS — Volcán Ajusco 3,930 m — Volcán Tláloc 3,690 m — Volcán Pelado 3,340 m

POPULATION OF CITIES AND TOWNS
- ☐ OVER 2,000,000
- ☐ 1,000,000 - 1,999,999
- ● 500,000 - 999,999
- ⊙ 250,000 - 499,999
- ◉ 100,000 - 249,999
- ⊙ 30,000 - 99,999
- ⊙ 10,000 - 29,999
- ○ UNDER 10,000

SCALE 1:7,000,000   LAMBERT CONFORMAL CONIC PROJECTION
MILES 0 100 200 300
KILOMETERS 0 100 200 300

© HAMMOND WORLD ATLAS CORPORATION

GULF OF MEXICO

Bahía de

Campeche

Yucatán

Peninsula

MEXICO

Isthmus of
Tehuantepec

Golfo de
Tehuantepec

GUATEMALA

HONDURAS

BELIZE

EL SALVADOR

Tegucigalpa

San Salvador

P A C I F I C

O C E A N

SCALE 1:7,000,000   LAMBERT CONFORMAL CONIC PROJECTION

MILES   0   100   200   300

KILOMETERS 0   100   200   300

POPULATION OF CITIES AND TOWNS

- ■ OVER 2,000,000
- ◉ 500,000 - 999,999
- ● 100,000 - 249,999
- ◎ 10,000 - 29,999
- ☐ 1,000,000 - 1,999,999
- ◉ 250,000 - 499,999
- ● 30,000 - 99,999
- ○ UNDER 10,000

© HAMMOND WORLD ATLAS CORPORATION

Southern Mexico, Central America, Western Caribbean

Eastern Caribbean, Bahamas

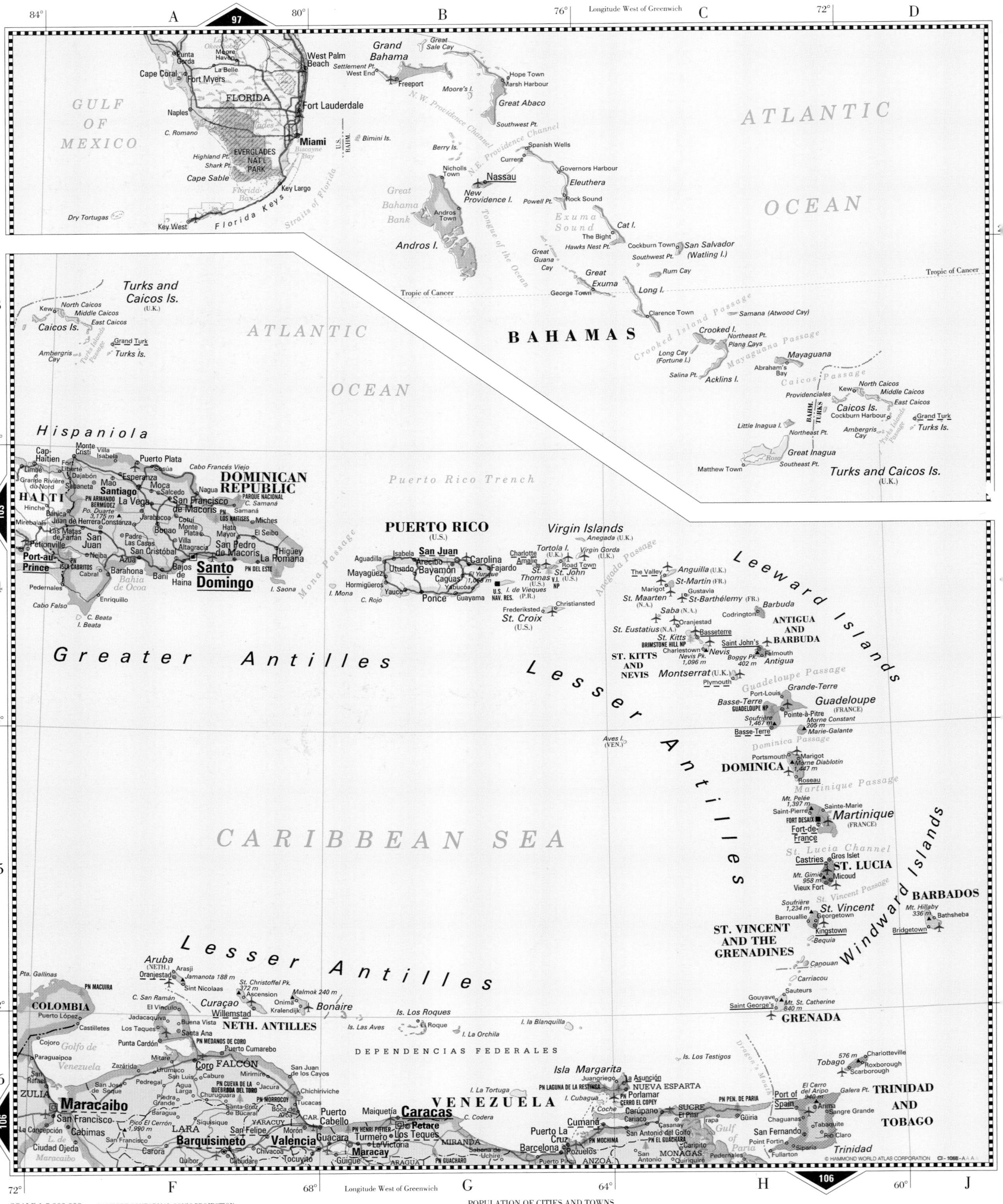

South America

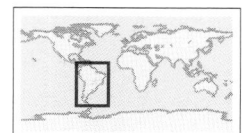

Oceans and Seas
CARIBBEAN SEA
ATLANTIC OCEAN
PACIFIC OCEAN

Countries
COSTA RICA
PANAMA
VENEZUELA
COLOMBIA
ECUADOR
PERU
GUYANA
SURINAME
FRENCH GUIANA
BRAZIL
BOLIVIA
PARAGUAY
CHILE
ARGENTINA
URUGUAY

Selected place names
Panamá, San José, Barranquilla, Cartagena, Santa Marta, Valledupar, Maracaibo, Cabimas, Valencia, Barquisimeto, Caracas, Cumaná, Maracay, Barcelona, Maturín, Coro, Willemstad, Los Teques, Port of Spain, TRINIDAD AND TOBAGO, Mérida, Valera, Barinas, El Tigre, Ciudad Bolívar, Ciudad Guayana, Morawhanna, Delta del Orinoco, Cúcuta, Bucaramanga, Arauca, San Fernando de Apure, Puerto Ayacucho, Georgetown, New Amsterdam, Paramaribo, Saint-Laurent du Maroni, Nieuw Nickerie, Cayenne, Medellín, Bello, Manizales, Pereira, Armenia, Ibagué, Tunja, Bogotá, Villavicencio, Mitú, Caracaraí, Boa Vista, Amapá, Cali, Palmira, Buenaventura, Popayán, Pasto, Florencia, Manaus, Macapá, Belém, Bragança, Tumaco, Esmeraldas, Punta Galera, Quito, Ibarra, Manta, Portoviejo, Ambato, Riobamba, Guayaquil, Milagro, Cuenca, Machala, Loja, Iquitos, Leticia, Benjamin Constant, Tefé, Coari, Codajás, Manacapuru, Novo Aripuanã, Maués, Santarém, Parintins, Óbidos, Alenquer, Ilha de Marajó, São Luís, Parnaíba, Sobral, Fortaleza, Talara, Piura, Sullana, Chiclayo, Moyobamba, Tarapoto, Cruzeiro do Sul, Eirunepé, Humaitá, Manicoré, Porto Velho, Marabá, Imperatriz, Tocantinópolis, Caxias, Teresina, Crateús, Quixadá, Mossoró, Açu, Natal, Trujillo, Cajamarca, Chimbote, Huaraz, Huánuco, Cerro de Pasco, Pucallpa, Rio Branco, Riberalta, Cobija, Guajará-Mirim, Aripuanã, Maloca, Gradaús, Conceição do Araguaia, Balsas, Floriano, Picos, Crato, Juàzeiro do Norte, Campina Grande, João Pessoa, Recife, Olinda, Callao, Lima, Chincha Alta, Pisco, Ica, Nazca, Ayacucho, Cusco, La Paz, Cochabamba, Santa Cruz, Sucre, Oruro, Llallagua, Vallegrande, Roboré, Cáceres, Cuiabá, Rondonópolis, Goiás, Ceres, Iporá, Anápolis, Goiânia, Brasília, Taguatinga, Barreiras, Bom Jesus da Lapa, Xique-Xique, Jacobina, Senhor do Bonfim, Petrolina, Juàzeiro, Paulo Afonso, Aracajú, Maceió, Salvador, Feira de Santana, Estância, Jequié, Itabuna, Ilhéus, Governador Valadares, Montes Claros, Teófilo Otoni, Nanuque, Itapetinga, Arica, Iquique, Tacna, Potosí, Pulacayo, Tupiza, Villazón, Tarija, Villa Montes, Camiri, Fuerte Olimpo, Mariscal Estigarribia, Concepción, Belo Horizonte, Sete Lagoas, Uberaba, Uberlândia, Itumbiara, Jataí, Rio Verde, Mato Grosso, Campo Grande, Aquidauana, Corumbá, Poços de Caldas, Divinópolis, Barbacena, Juiz de Fora, Campos, Vitória, Nova Iguaçu, Niterói, Río de Janeiro, São Paulo, Santos, Campinas, Sorocaba, Piracicaba, Ribeirão Prêto, São José do Rio Prêto, Presidente Prudente, Marília, Bauru, Londrina, Maringá, Dourados, Ponta Grossa, Curitiba, Paranaguá, Joinvile, Blumenau, Itajaí, Florianópolis, Tubarão, Lages, Antofagasta, San Salvador de Jujuy, Salta, San Miguel de Tucumán, Santiago del Estero, Catamarca, La Rioja, Chañaral, Copiapó, La Serena, Coquimbo, Ovalle, San Juan, Mendoza, Viña del Mar, Valparaíso, Santiago, Rancagua, San Luis, San Rafael, Malargüe, Córdoba, Villa María, Río Cuarto, Rosario, San Francisco, Santa Fe, Paraná, Rafaela, Pergamino, Junín, San Nicolás de los Arroyos, Mercedes, Buenos Aires, Lanús, La Plata, Montevideo, San José de Mayo, Punta del Este, Asunción, Villarrica, Encarnación, Ciudad del Este, Foz do Iguaçu, Posadas, Corrientes, Resistencia, Goya, Curuzú Cuatiá, Paso de los Libres, Uruguaiana, Alegrete, Santa Maria, Passo Fundo, Caxias do Sul, Canoas, Porto Alegre, Pelotas, Rio Grande, Bagé, Rivera, Santana do Livramento, Artigas, Salto, Paysandú, Concordia, Concepción del Uruguay, Melo, Rocha, Dolores, Talca, Linares, Chillán, Concepción, Talcahuano, Los Angeles, Temuco, Valdivia, Osorno, Puerto Montt, Ancud, Santa Rosa, General Roca, Neuquén, Zapala, Bahía Blanca, Tres Arroyos, Necochea, Mar del Plata, Tandil, Azul, Olavarría, Pehuajó, Chivilcoy, Viedma, San Antonio Oeste, Puerto Madryn, Rawson, Trelew, Esquel, Sarmiento, Comodoro Rivadavia, Caleta Olivia, Puerto Deseado, San Julián, Santa Cruz, Río Gallegos, Puerto Natales, Punta Arenas, Ushuaia, Río Grande, Tierra del Fuego, Cape Horn, Stanley, Falkland Islands, West Falkland, East Falkland

Physical features
Pico Cristóbal Colón 5,775 m, Pico Bolívar 5,007 m, Alto Ritacuba 5,493 m, Nevado del Huila 5,750 m, Pico de la Neblina 3,014 m, Mt. Roraima 2,772 m, Chimborazo 6,310 m, Nevado Huascarán 6,768 m, Nevado Ancohuma 6,550 m, Volcán Misti 5,822 m, Volcán Llullaillaco 6,723 m, Cerro Ojos del Salado 6,880 m, Cerro Aconcagua 6,959 m, Pico de Bandeira 2,890 m, Cabo de São Tomé, Cabo Frio, Andes Mountains, Serra dos Parecis, Selvas, Guiana Highlands, Mato Grosso, Meseta del, Brazilian Highlands, Caatingas, Altiplano, Gran Chaco, Patagonia, Amazon, Orinoco, Río Negro, Lago Titicaca, Mar Chiquita, Golfo San Jorge, Golfo de San Matías, Estrecho de Magallanes, Tropic of Capricorn, Equator

Islands (Chile)
Isla de Malpelo (COL.), I. de San Félix (CHILE), I. San Ambrosio (CHILE), Is. Juan Fernández (CHILE), I. Robinson Crusoe, I. Alejandro Selkirk, I. Fernando de Noronha (BRAZIL), Isla de Chiloé, Arch. de Los Chonos, Arch. Reina Adelaida, Isla Wellington, Tierra del Fuego

POPULATION OF CITIES AND TOWNS
■ OVER 3,000,000
■ 1,000,000 - 2,999,999
● 500,000 - 999,999
● 100,000 - 499,999
○ UNDER 100,000

SCALE 1:28,000,000   OPTIMAL CONFORMAL PROJECTION

MILES   0   400   800   1200
KILOMETERS   0   400   800   1200

Longitude West of Greenwich

AREA OF OPTIMIZATION
The red band which surrounds this map defines the "Area of Optimization." Within this bounding curve is the most accurate conformal map that can be made of the region. Outside the optimized area, distortion increases rapidly, and tears or other irregularities in the grid may occur.

Northern South America

POPULATION OF CITIES AND TOWNS

- ■ OVER 2,000,000
- ◉ 500,000 - 999,999
- ○ 50,000 - 99,999
- ☐ 1,000,000 - 1,999,999
- ● 100,000 - 499,999
- ○ UNDER 50,000

SCALE 1:15,000,000   LAMBERT CONFORMAL CONIC PROJECTION

MILES	0	200	400	600
KILOMETERS	0	200	400	600

© HAMMOND WORLD ATLAS CORPORATION   CI - 2107 - A.A.A

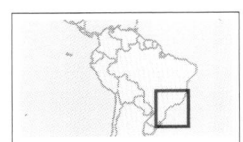

Southeastern Brazil

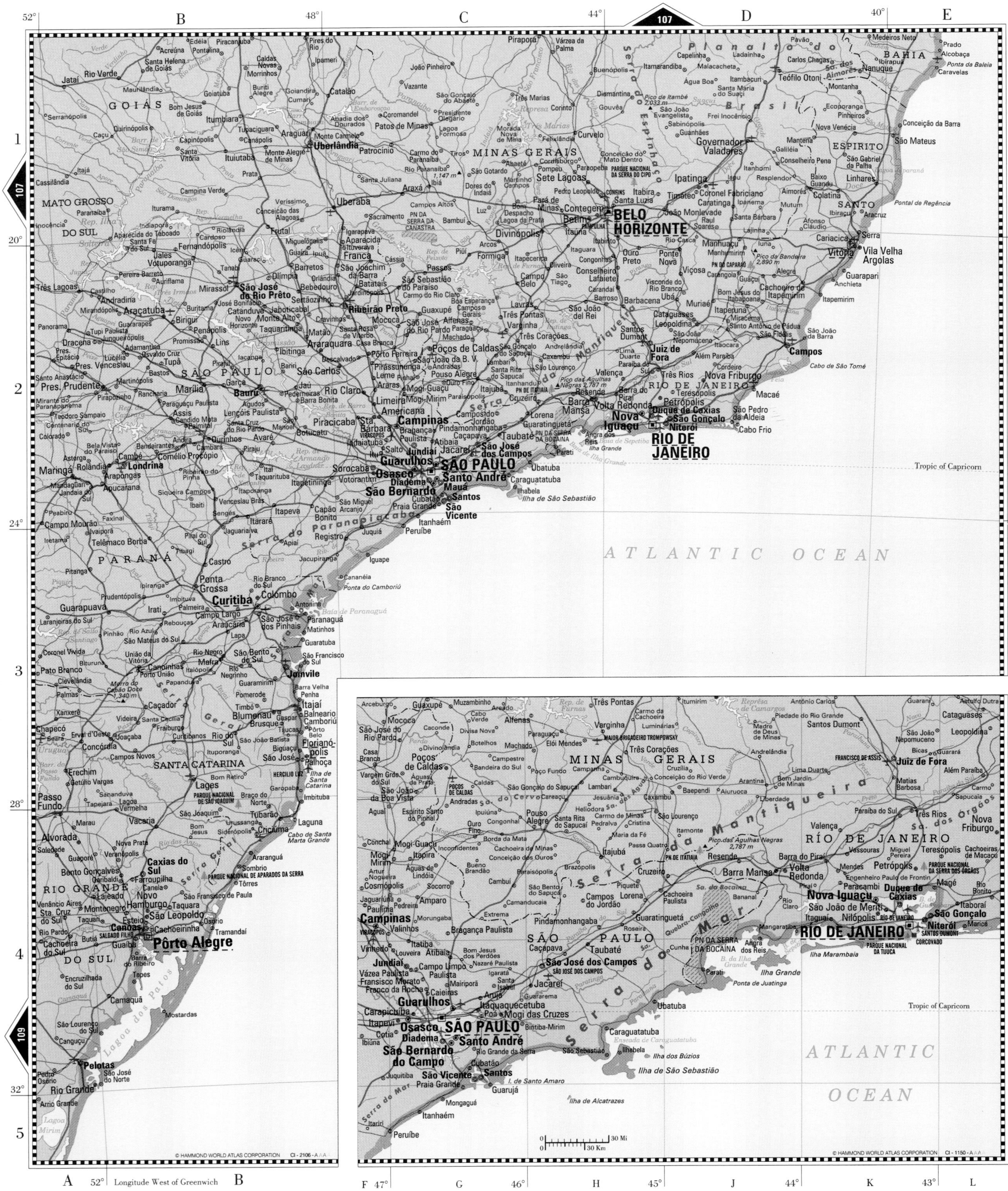

SCALE 1:7,000,000 LAMBERT CONFORMAL CONIC PROJECTION

Longitude West of Greenwich

MILES

KILOMETERS

POPULATION OF CITIES AND TOWNS

| ■ OVER 2,000,000 | ● 500,000 - 999,999 | ○ 100,000 - 249,999 | ◉ 10,000 - 29,999 |
| □ 1,000,000 - 1,999,999 | ● 250,000 - 499,999 | ○ 30,000 - 99,999 | ○ UNDER 10,000 |

© HAMMOND WORLD ATLAS CORPORATION   CI - 2106 - A - A - A

© HAMMOND WORLD ATLAS CORPORATION   CI - 1150 - A - A - A

Southern South America

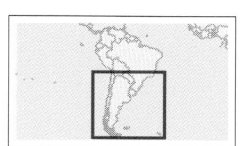

Index of the World

This index lists places and geographic features found in the atlas. Every name is followed by the country or area to which it belongs. Except for cities, towns, countries and cultural areas, all entries include a reference to feature type, such as province, river, island, peak, and so on. The page number and alpha-numeric code appear in blue to the right of each listing. The page number directs you to the largest scale map on which the name can be found. The code refers to the grid squares formed by the horizontal and vertical lines of latitude and longitude on each map. Following the letters from left to right, and the numbers from top to bottom, helps you to locate quickly the square containing the place or feature. Inset maps have their own alpha-numeric codes. Names that are accompanied by a point symbol are indexed to the symbol's location on the map. Other names are indexed to the initial letter of the name. The primary abbreviations used in this index are listed below.

Index Abbreviations

A
Ab,Can	Alberta
Afg.	Afghanistan
Afr.	Africa
Ak,US	Alaska
Al,US	Alabama
Alb.	Albania
Alg.	Algeria
And.	Andorra
Ang.	Angola
Angu.	Anguilla
Ant.	Antarctica
Anti.	Antigua and Barbuda
Ar,US	Arkansas
Arch.	Archipelago
Arg.	Argentina
Arm.	Armenia
Aru.	Aruba
ASam.	American Samoa
Ash.	Ashmore and Cartier Islands
Aus.	Austria
Austl.	Australia
Az,US	Arizona
Azer.	Azerbaijan
Azor.	Azores

B
Bahm.	Bahamas, The
Bahr.	Bahrain
Bang.	Bangladesh
Bar.	Barbados
BC,Can	British Columbia
Bela.	Belarus
Belg.	Belgium
Belz.	Belize
Ben.	Benin
Berm.	Bermuda
Bhu.	Bhutan
Bol.	Bolivia
Bosn.	Bosnia and Herzegovina
Bots.	Botswana
Braz.	Brazil
Bru.	Brunei
Bul.	Bulgaria
Burk.	Burkina Faso
Buru.	Burundi
BVI	British Virgin Islands

C
Ca,US	California
CAfr.	Central African Republic
Camb.	Cambodia
Camr.	Cameroon
Can.	Canada
Can.	Canal
Canl.	Canary Islands
Cap.	Capital

Cap. Terr.	Capital Territory
Cay.	Cayman Islands
C.d'Iv.	Côte d'Ivoire
Chan.	Channel
Chl.	Channel Islands
Co,US	Colorado
Col.	Colombia
Com.	Comoros
Cont.	Continent
CpV.	Cape Verde Islands
CR	Costa Rica
Cr.	Creek
Cro.	Croatia
Ct,US	Connecticut
Cyp.	Cyprus
Czh.	Czech Republic

D
DC,US	District of Columbia
De,US	Delaware
Den.	Denmark
Depr.	Depression
Des.	Desert
Dist.	District
Djib.	Djibouti
Dom.	Dominica
Dpcy.	Dependency
D.R.Congo	Democratic Republic of the Congo
DRep.	Dominican Republic

E
Ecu.	Ecuador
Eng,UK	England
EqG.	Equatorial Guinea
Erit.	Eritrea
ESal.	El Salvador
Est.	Estonia
Eth.	Ethiopia
Eur.	Europe

F
Falk.	Falkland Islands
Far.	Faroe Islands
Fed. Dist.	Federal District
Fin.	Finland
Fl,US	Florida
Fr.	France
FrG.	French Guiana
FrPol.	French Polynesia
FYROM	Former Yugoslav Rep. of Macedonia

G
Ga,US	Georgia
Gam.	Gambia, The
Gaza	Gaza Strip
GBis.	Guinea-Bissau
Geo.	Georgia
Ger.	Germany
Gha.	Ghana
Gib.	Gibraltar

Gre.	Greece
Grld.	Greenland
Gren.	Grenada
Grsld.	Grassland
Guad.	Guadeloupe
Guat.	Guatemala
Gui.	Guinea
Guy.	Guyana

H
Har.	Harbor
Hi,US	Hawaii
Hon.	Honduras
Hts.	Heights
Hun.	Hungary

I
Ia,US	Iowa
Ice.	Iceland
Id,US	Idaho
Il,US	Illinois
IM	Isle of Man
In,US	Indiana
Indo.	Indonesia
Int'l	International
Ire.	Ireland
Isl., Isls.	Island, Islands
Isr.	Israel
Isth.	Isthmus
It.	Italy

J
Jam.	Jamaica
Jor.	Jordan

K
Kaz.	Kazakhstan
Kiri.	Kiribati
Ks,US	Kansas
Kuw.	Kuwait
Ky,US	Kentucky
Kyr.	Kyrgyzstan

L
La,US	Louisiana
Lat.	Latvia
Lcht.	Liechtenstein
Leb.	Lebanon
Les.	Lesotho
Libr.	Liberia
Lith.	Lithuania
Lux.	Luxembourg

M
Ma,US	Massachusetts
Madg.	Madagascar
Madr.	Madeira
Malay.	Malaysia
Mald.	Maldives
Malw.	Malawi
Mart.	Martinique
May.	Mayotte
Mb,Can	Manitoba
Md,US	Maryland

Me,US	Maine
Mex.	Mexico
Mi,US	Michigan
Micr.	Micronesia, Federated States of
Mn,US	Minnesota
Mo,US	Missouri
Mol.	Moldova
Mon.	Monument
Mona.	Monaco
Mong.	Mongolia
Monts.	Montserrat
Mor.	Morocco
Moz.	Mozambique
Mrsh.	Marshall Islands
Mrta.	Mauritania
Mrts.	Mauritius
Ms,US	Mississippi
Mt.	Mount
Mt,US	Montana
Mtn., Mts.	Mountain, Mountains

N
NAm.	North America
Namb.	Namibia
NAnt.	Netherlands Antilles
Nat'l	National
NB,Can	New Brunswick
NC,US	North Carolina
NCal.	New Caledonia
ND,US	North Dakota
Ne,US	Nebraska
Neth.	Netherlands
Nf,Can	Newfoundland
Nga.	Nigeria
NH,US	New Hampshire
NI,UK	Northern Ireland
Nic.	Nicaragua
NJ,US	New Jersey
NKor.	North Korea
NM,US	New Mexico
NMar.	Northern Mariana Islands
Nor.	Norway
NP	National Park
NS,Can	Nova Scotia
Nv,US	Nevada
NW,Can	Northwest Territories
NY,US	New York
NZ	New Zealand

O
Oh,US	Ohio
Ok,US	Oklahoma
On,Can	Ontario
Or,US	Oregon

P
Pa,US	Pennsylvania
PacUS	Pacific Islands, U.S.
Pak.	Pakistan

Pan.	Panama
Par.	Paraguay
PE,Can	Prince Edward Island
Pen.	Peninsula
Phil.	Philippines
Phys. Reg.	Physical Region
Pitc.	Pitcairn Islands
Plat.	Plateau
PNG	Papua New Guinea
Pol.	Poland
Port.	Portugal
PR	Puerto Rico
Prov.	Province
Pt.	Point

Q
Qu,Can	Quebec

R
Rec.	Recreation(al)
Reg.	Region
Rep.	Republic
Res.	Reservoir, Reservation
Reun.	Réunion
RI,US	Rhode Island
Riv.	River
Rom.	Romania
Rsv.	Reserve
Rus.	Russia
Rwa.	Rwanda

S
SAfr.	South Africa
Sam.	Samoa
SAm.	South America
SaoT.	São Tomé and Príncipe
SAr.	Saudi Arabia
Sc,UK	Scotland
SC,US	South Carolina
SD,US	South Dakota
Sen.	Senegal
Sey.	Seychelles
Sing.	Singapore
Sk,Can	Saskatchewan
SKor.	South Korea
SLeo.	Sierra Leone
Slov.	Slovenia
Slvk.	Slovakia
SMar.	San Marino
Sol.	Solomon Islands
Som.	Somalia
Sp.	Spain
Spr., Sprs.	Spring, Springs
SrL.	Sri Lanka
StH.	Saint Helena
Str.	Strait
StK.	Saint Kitts and Nevis
StL.	Saint Lucia
StV.	Saint Vincent and the Grenadines

Sur.	Suriname
Sval.	Svalbard
Swaz.	Swaziland
Swe.	Sweden
Swi.	Switzerland

T
Tah.	Tahiti
Tai.	Taiwan
Taj.	Tajikistan
Tanz.	Tanzania
Terr.	Territory
Thai.	Thailand
Tn,US	Tennessee
Tok.	Tokelau
Trin.	Trinidad and Tobago
Trkm.	Turkmenistan
Trks.	Turks and Caicos Islands
Turk.	Turkey
Tuv.	Tuvalu
Tx,US	Texas

U
UAE	United Arab Emirates
Ugan.	Uganda
UK	United Kingdom
Ukr.	Ukraine
Uru.	Uruguay
US	United States
USVI	U.S. Virgin Islands
Ut,US	Utah
Uzb.	Uzbekistan

V
Va,US	Virginia
Val.	Valley
Van.	Vanuatu
VatC.	Vatican City
Ven.	Venezuela
Viet.	Vietnam
Vol.	Volcano
Vt,US	Vermont

W
Wa,US	Washington
Wal,UK	Wales
Wall.	Wallis and Futuna
WBnk.	West Bank
Wi,US	Wisconsin
WSah.	Western Sahara
WV,US	West Virginia
Wy,US	Wyoming

Y
Yem.	Yemen
Yk,Can	Yukon Territory
Yugo.	Yugoslavia

Z
Zam.	Zambia
Zim.	Zimbabwe

A

Aachen, Ger. 31/F2
Aalen, Ger. 33/J2
Aalsmeer, Neth. 28/B4
Aalst, Belg. 30/D2
Aalten, Neth. 28/D5
Aalter, Belg. 28/A6
Aarau, Swi. 36/E3
Aarschot, Belg. 28/B7
Aba, Nga. 79/G5
Abā as Su'ūd, SAr. 52/D5
Ābādān, Iran 51/G4
Ābādeh, Iran 51/H4
Abaeté, Braz. 108/C1
Abaetetuba, Braz. 107/J4
Abakan, Rus. 46/K4
Abancay, Peru 106/D6
Abashiri, Japan 55/N3
Abasolo, Mex. 101/E4
Abay, Kaz. 46/H5
Abaza, Rus. 46/K4
Abbeville, La, US 93/J5
Abbeville, Fr. 30/A3
Abbottābād, Pak. 53/K2
Abdulino, Rus. 45/K1
Abéché, Chad 77/K5
Abengourou, C.d'Iv. 78/E5
Åbenrå, Den. 26/E1
Abeokuta, Nga. 79/F5
Aberdare, Wal, UK 24/C3
Abhá, SAr. 52/D5
Abhar, Iran 51/G2
Abidjan, C.d'Iv. 78/D5
Abilene, Tx, US 93/H4
Abingdon, Eng, UK 25/E3
Abnūb, Egypt 50/B5
Åbo (Turku), Fin. 42/D3
Abomey, Ben. 79/F5
Abony, Hun. 40/D2
Abu Dhabi (cap.), UAE 53/F4
Abū Ḩammād, Egypt 49/B4
Abū Ḩummuş, Egypt 49/B4
Abū Kabīr, Egypt 49/B4
Abū Kamāl, Syria 50/E3
Abuja (cap.), Nga. 79/G4
Abulog, Phil. 61/J5
Acadia National Park, Me, US 95/G2
Acámbaro, Mex. 101/E4
Acaponeta, Mex. 100/D4
Acapulco de Juárez, Mex. 102/B2
Acarigua, Ven. 106/E2
Acatzingo, Mex. 101/M7
Acayucan, Mex. 102/C2
Accra (cap.), Gha. 79/E5
Accrington, Eng, UK 23/F4
Acheng, China 55/K2
Achern, Ger. 31/H6
Achinsk, Rus. 46/K4
Acireale, It. 38/D4
Aconcagua (peak), Arg.,Chile 109/B3
Acopiara, Braz. 107/L5
Acqui Terme, It. 33/H4
Actopan, Mex. 101/L6
Açu, Braz. 107/L5
Ad Damīr, Sudan 52/B5
Ad Dammām, SAr. 52/F3
Ad Dilinjāt, Egypt 49/B4
Ad Dīwānīyah, Iraq 51/F4
Ad Duwaym, Sudan 77/M5
Ad-Dakhla, Mor. 76/B3
Ada, Ok, US 93/H4
Adamantina, Braz. 108/B2
Adams (mt.), Wa, US 90/C4
Adamstown (cap.), Pitc. 69/M7
'Adan, Yem. 52/D6
Adana, Turk. 49/D1
Adapazarı, Turk. 41/K5
Addis Ababa (cap.), Eth. 77/N6
Addison, Il, US 99/P16
Adekeieh (Ādī K'eyih), Erit. 52/C6
Adelaide, Austl. 73/A2
Aden (gulf) 52/E6
Adilābād, India 62/C4
Adirondack (mts.), NY, US 94/F2
Adıyaman, Turk. 50/D2
Adjud, Rom. 41/H2
Adliswil, Swi. 37/E3
Ado Ekiti, Nga. 79/G5
Ado Odo, Nga. 79/F5
Ādoni, India 62/C4
Adra, Sp. 34/D4
Adrano, It. 38/D4
Adrar, Alg. 76/E2
Adrian, Mi, US 94/C3
Adriatic (sea), It. 40/B4
Ādwa, Eth. 52/C6
Aegean (sea), Gre.,Turk. 39/J3
'Afak, Iraq 51/F3
Afghanistan (ctry.) 53/H2
Afragola, It. 38/D2
Africa (cont.) 74/*
'Afula, Isr. 49/G6
Afyon, Turk. 44/D5
Agadez, Niger 79/G2
Agadir, Mor. 76/D1
Agartala, India 63/F3
Agboville, C.d'Iv. 78/D5
Ağdam, Azer. 45/H5
Agde, Fr. 32/E5
Agen, Fr. 32/D4
Āghā Jārī, Iran 51/G4
Agoo, Phil. 61/J5
Āgra, India 62/C2
Agrigento, It. 38/C4
Agrínion, Gre. 39/G3
Agryz, Rus. 43/M4
Agua Dulce, Mex. 102/C2
Agua Prieta, Mex. 92/E5
Aguachica, Col. 103/H4
Aguadilla, PR 104/E3
Aguaí, Braz. 108/G7
Agualva-Cacém, Port. 35/P10
Aguascalientes, Mex. 100/E4
Agudos, Braz. 108/B2
Aguilares, Arg. 109/C2
Aguilas, Sp. 34/E4
Agüimes, Canl. 35/X17
Agustín Codazzi, Col. 103/H4
Ahar, Iran 45/H5
Ahaus, Ger. 28/E4
Ahlat, Turk. 50/E2
Ahlen, Ger. 29/E5
Ahmadābād, India 62/B3
Ahmadnagar, India 62/B4
Ahmadpur East, Pak. 62/B2
Ahrensburg, Ger. 29/H1
Ahuachapán, ESal. 102/D3
Ahvāz, Iran 51/G4
Aichach, Ger. 37/H1
Aiken, SC, US 97/H3
'Aïn Beïda, Alg. 76/G1
'Aïn Sefra, Alg. 76/E1
Aina Haina, Hi, US 88/W13
Airdrie, Ab, Can. 90/E3
Aiud, Rom. 41/F2
Aix-en-Provence, Fr. 32/F5
Aíyion, Gre. 39/H3
Aīzawl, India 60/B4
Aizu-Wakamatsu, Japan 57/F2
Ajaccio, Fr. 38/A2
Ajalpan, Mex. 101/M8
Ajax, On, Can. 95/U8
Ajdābiyā, Libya 77/K1
Ajka, Hun. 40/C2
Ajmer, India 62/B2
Akashi, Japan 56/D3
Akçaabat, Turk. 44/F4
Akçakale, Turk. 50/D2
Akhalts'ikhe, Geo. 45/G4
Akharnaí, Gre. 39/N8
Akhisar, Turk. 44/C5
Akhmīm, Egypt 50/B5
Akhtubinsk, Rus. 45/H2
Aki, Japan 56/C4
Akita, Japan 55/N4
Akjoujt, Mrta. 78/B2
Akkaraipattu, SrL. 62/D6
'Akko, Isr. 49/D3
Akō, Japan 56/D3
Akola, India 62/C3
Åkrehamn, Nor. 20/C4
Akron, Oh, US 94/D3
Aksaray, Turk. 50/C2
Akşehir, Turk. 50/B2
Aksu, China 46/J5
Akune, Japan 56/B4
Akure, Nga. 79/G5
Akyazı, Turk. 41/K5
Al Aḩmadī, Kuw. 51/G4
Al 'Amārah, Iraq 51/F4
Al 'Aqabah, Jor. 49/D5
Al 'Ayn, UAE 53/G4
Al Azīzīyah, Libya 76/H1
Al Bāb, Syria 50/D2
Al Badrashayn, Egypt 49/B5
Al Bājūr, Egypt 49/B4
Al Başrah, Iraq 51/F4
Al Baydā, Libya 77/K1
Al Fāsher, Sudan 77/L5
Al Fashn, Egypt 50/B4
Al Fatḩah, Iraq 51/E3
Al Fāw, Iraq 51/G4
Al Fayyum, Egypt 49/B5
Al Hammām, Egypt 50/B4
Al Ḩammāmāt, Tun. 38/B4
Al Ḩasakah, Syria 50/E2
Al Ḩawāmidīyah, Egypt 49/B5
Al Ḩayy, Iraq 51/F3
Al Ḩillah, Iraq 51/F3
Al Hindīyah, Iraq 51/F3
Al Hoceima, Mor. 76/E1
Al Ḩudaydah, Yem. 52/D6
Al Hufūf, SAr. 52/E3
Al Iskandarīyah, Egypt 49/A4
Al Ismā'īlīyah, Egypt 49/C4
Al Jamm, Tun. 38/B5
Al Jīzah, Egypt 49/B4
Al Junaynah, Sudan 77/K5
Al Kāf, Tun. 76/G1
Al Karak, Jor. 49/D4
Al Khābūrah, Oman 53/G4
Al Khalīl (Hebron), WBnk. 49/D4
Al Khānkah, Egypt 49/B4
Al Khārijah, Egypt 77/M2
Al Kharţūm Baḩrī (Khartoum North), Sudan 77/M4
Al Khubar, SAr. 52/F3
Al Khums, Libya 76/H1
Al Kiswah, Syria 49/E3
Al Kūfah, Iraq 51/F3
Al Kūt, Iraq 51/F3
Al Lādhiqīyah (Latakia), Syria 49/D2
Al Madīnah, SAr. 52/C4
Al Madīnah al Fikrīyah, Egypt 50/B5
Al Maḩallah al Kubrá, Egypt 49/B4
Al Mahdīyah, Tun. 38/B5
Al Maḩmūdīyah, Egypt 49/B4
Al Mansūrah, Egypt 49/B4
Al Manzilah, Egypt 49/B4
Al Marāghah, Egypt 50/B5
Al Marj, Libya 77/K1
Al Marsá, Tun. 38/B4
Al Maţarīyah, Egypt 49/C4
Al Mawşil (Mosul), Iraq 51/E2
Al Mayādin, Syria 50/E3
Al Minyā, Egypt 50/B4
Al Mubarraz, SAr. 52/E4
Al Mukallā, Yem. 52/E6
Al Muknīn, Tun. 38/B5
Al Munastīr, Tun. 38/B5
Al Musayyib, Iraq 51/F3
Al Qaḑārif, Sudan 52/C6
Al Qāmishlī, Syria 50/E2
Al Qanāţir al Khayrīyah, Egypt 49/B4
Al Qayrawān, Tun. 38/B5
Al Quşayr, Syria 49/E2
Al Ubayyiḑ, Sudan 77/M5
Al Wāsiţah, Egypt 49/B5
Alabama (state), US 97/G3
Alabaster, Al, US 97/G3
Alaca, Turk. 44/E4
Alagir, Rus. 45/H4
Alagoinhas, Braz. 107/L6
Alajuela, CR 103/E4
Alameda, Ca, US 99/K11
Alamo, Mex. 102/B1
Alamo, Ca, US 99/K11
Alamogordo, NM, US 93/F4
Alamosa, Co, US 93/F3
Åland (isl.), Fin. 20/G3
Alanya, Turk. 49/C1
Alaşehir, Turk. 50/B2
Alaska (pen.), US 85/F4
Alaska (gulf), US 85/J4
Alaska (state), US 85/G2
Alaska (range), Ak, US 85/H3
Alatyr', Rus. 45/H1
Alaverdi, Arm. 45/H4
Alba, It. 33/H4
Alba Iulia, Rom. 41/F2
Albacete, Sp. 34/E3
Albania (ctry.), Alb. 39/F2
Albany, Or, US 90/C4
Albany, Ga, US 97/G4
Albany (cap.), NY, US 94/F3
Albany, Ca, US 99/K11
Albemarle, NC, US 97/H3
Albenga, It. 33/H4
Albert (lake), D.R. Congo 77/M7
Albert Lea, Mn, US 91/K5
Alberta (prov.), Can. 86/E3
Alberton, SAfr. 80/Q13
Albertville, Al, US 97/G3
Albertville, Fr. 33/G4
Albi, Fr. 32/E5
Albina, Sur. 107/H2
Albion, Mi, US 94/C3
Alblasserdam, Neth. 28/B5
Ålborg, Den. 20/D4
Albufeira, Port. 34/A4
Albuquerque, NM, US 92/F4
Albury, Austl. 73/C3
Alcabideche, Port. 35/P10
Alcalá de Guadaira, Sp. 34/C4
Alcalá de Henares, Sp. 35/N9
Alcalá la Real, Sp. 34/D4
Alcamo, It. 38/C4
Alcantarilla, Sp. 34/E4
Alcázar de San Juan, Sp. 34/D3
Alcira, Sp. 35/E3
Alcobendas, Sp. 35/N8
Alcora, Sp. 35/E2
Alcorcón, Sp. 35/N9
Alcoy, Sp. 35/E3
Aldan, Rus. 47/N4
Aldershot, Eng, UK 25/F4
Alderwood Manor-Bothell North, Wa, US 99/C2
Aldine, Tx, US 93/J5
Aldridge, Eng, UK 25/E1
Aleg, Mrta. 78/B2
Alegrete, Braz. 109/E2
Aleksandrov, Rus. 42/H4
Aleksandrovsk, Rus. 43/N4
Aleksandrovsk-Sakhalinskiy, Rus. 55/N1
Aleksandrów Łódzki, Pol. 27/K3
Alekseyevka, Rus. 44/F2
Aleksin, Rus. 44/F1
Aleksinac, Yugo. 40/E4
Além Paraíba, Braz. 108/L6
Alençon, Fr. 32/D2
Alenquer, Braz. 107/H4
Alessandria, It. 33/H4
Ålesund, Nor. 20/C3
Aleutian (isls.), Ak, US 85/B5
Alexander (isl.), Ant. 83/V
Alexander (arch.), US 85/L4
Alexander City, Al, US 97/G3
Alexandria, La, US 93/J5
Alexandria, MN, US 91/K4
Alexandria, Rom. 41/G4
Alexandroúpolis, Gre. 41/G5
Aleysk, Rus. 46/J4
Alfeld, Ger. 29/G5
Alfenas, Braz. 108/H6
Alfreton, Eng, UK 23/G5
Alfter, Ger. 31/G2
Algeciras, Sp. 34/C4
Algemesí, Sp. 35/E3
Algeria (ctry.) 76/F2
Alghero, It. 38/A2
Algiers (cap.), Alg. 76/F1
Algonquin, Il, US 99/P14
Algueirão, Port. 35/P10
Algund (Lagundo), It. 37/H4
Alhama de Murcia, Sp. 34/E4
Alhaurín el Grande, Sp. 34/C4
'Alī al Gharbī, Iraq 51/F3
Äli Bayramlı, Azer. 51/G2
Aliağa, Turk. 44/C5
Alibeyköy, Turk. 41/J5
Alicante, Sp. 35/E3
Alice, Tx, US 96/D5
Alice Springs, Austl. 68/C7
Alīgarh, India 62/C2
Alingsås, Swe. 20/E4
Alīpur, Pak. 62/B2
Alīpur Duār, India 62/E2
Alirājpur, India 53/K4
Alkmaar, Neth. 28/B3
Allada, Ben. 79/F5
Allahābād, India 62/D2
Allanmyo, Myan. 60/B5
Allegheny (mts.), US 94/D4
Allen Park, Mi, US 99/F7
Allende, Mex. 101/E3
Allende, Mex. 96/C4
Allentown, Pa, US 94/F3
Alleppey, India 62/C6
Alliance, Ne, US 91/H5
Alliance, Oh, US 94/D3
Allschwil, Swi. 36/D2
Alma, Qu, Can. 95/G1
Alma, Mi, US 94/C3
Almada, Port. 35/P10
Almansa, Sp. 35/E3
Almaty, Kaz. 46/H5
Almazora, Sp. 35/E3
Almelo, Neth. 28/D4
Almenara, Braz. 107/K7
Almendralejo, Sp. 34/B3
Almere, Neth. 28/C4
Almería, Sp. 34/D4
Al'met'yevsk, Rus. 43/M5
Älmhult, Swe. 20/E4
Almonte, Sp. 34/B4
Almuñécar, Sp. 34/D4
Alofi, NZ 69/J6
Alor Setar, Malay. 65/C5
Alotau, PNG 68/E6
Alphen aan de Rijn, Neth. 28/B4
Alps (mts.), It. 33/G4
Alsdorf, Ger. 31/F2
Alsfeld, Ger. 33/H1
Alsip, Il, US 99/Q16
Alta, Nor. 20/G1
Alta Floresta, Braz. 107/G5
Alta Gracia, Arg. 109/D3
Altagracia, Nic. 102/E4
Altamira, Braz. 107/H4
Altamira, Mex. 102/B1
Altamonte Springs, Fl, US 97/H4
Altamura, It. 40/C5
Altay, Mong. 54/D2
Altay, China 54/B2
Altdorf, Swi. 37/E4
Altena, Ger. 29/E6
Altenburg, Ger. 26/G3
Alton, Il, US 93/K3
Alton, Eng, UK 25/F4
Altoona, Pa, US 94/E3
Altos, Braz. 107/K5
Altrincham, Eng, UK 23/F5
Altus, Ok, US 93/H4
Alushta, Ukr. 44/E3
Alvarado, Mex. 101/P8
Alverca, Port. 35/P10
Alvesta, Swe. 20/E4
Alvin, Tx, US 93/J5
Alvorada, Braz. 108/A4
Alytus, Lith. 27/N1
Alzey, Ger. 31/H4
Am Timan, Chad 77/K5
Amadora, Port. 35/P10
Amagasaki, Japan 55/M5
Amagi, Japan 56/B4
Amaliás, Gre. 39/G4
Amalner, India 62/C3
Amambaí, Braz. 109/E1
Amanzimtoti, SAfr. 81/E3
Amarillo, Tx, US 93/G4
Amasya, Turk. 44/E4
Amazon (riv.), Braz. 106/G4
Ambahikily, Madg. 81/G8
Ambajogai, India 53/L5
Ambāla, India 53/L2
Ambalavao, Madg. 81/H8
Ambanja, Madg. 81/J6
Ambato, Ecu. 106/C4
Ambato Boeny, Madg. 81/H7
Ambatofinandrahana, Madg. 81/H8
Ambatolampy, Madg. 81/H7
Ambatondrazaka, Madg. 81/J7
Amberg, Ger. 33/J2
Ambikāpur, India 62/D3
Ambinanindrano, Madg. 81/J8
Ambinanitelo, Madg. 81/J6
Amboasary, Madg. 81/H9
Amboavory, Madg. 81/J7
Ambodiharina, Madg. 81/J8
Ambohimandroso, Madg. 81/H7
Ambon, Indo. 67/G4
Ambositra, Madg. 81/H8
Ambovombe, Madg. 81/H9
Ameca, Mex. 100/D4
Amecameca de Juárez, Mex. 101/R10
American Fork, Ut, US 92/E2
Americana, Braz. 108/C2
Americus, Ga, US 97/G3
Amersfoort, Neth. 28/C4
Amersham, Eng, UK 25/F3
Amet, India 62/B2
Amherst, NY, US 95/V10
Amiens, Fr. 30/B4
Amla, India 62/C3
Amman (cap.), Jor. 49/D4
Āmol, Iran 51/H2
Amozoc, Mex. 101/L7
Ampanefena, Madg. 81/J6
Ampanihy, Madg. 81/H9
Amparafaravola, Madg. 81/J7
Amparai, SrL. 62/D6
Amparo, Braz. 108/G7
Ampitatafika, Madg. 81/H7
Amposta, Sp. 35/F2
Amravati, India 62/C3
Amreli, India 62/B3
Amritsar, India 53/K2
Amstelveen, Neth. 28/B4
Amsterdam, NY, US 94/F3
Amsterdam (cap.), Neth. 28/B4
Amstetten, Aus. 40/B1
Amu Darya (riv.), Trkm. 46/G5
Amursk, Rus. 55/M1
An Nabk, Syria 49/E2
An Nahūd, Sudan 77/L5
An Najaf, Iraq 51/F4
An Nāşirīyah, Iraq 51/F4
Anaco, Ven. 106/F2
Anaheim, Ca, US 92/C4
Anakāpalle, India 62/D4
Analalava, Madg. 81/H6
Analavory, Madg. 81/H7
Anamur, Turk. 49/C1
Anan, Japan 56/D4
Anand, India 62/B3
Anantapur, India 62/C5
Anantnag, India 53/L2
Anapa, Rus. 44/F3
Anápolis, Braz. 107/J7
Añatuya, Arg. 109/D2
Ancaster, On, Can. 95/T9
Anchorage, Ak, US 85/J3
Ancona, It. 40/A4
Ancud, Chile 109/B5
Anda, China 55/K2
Andalusia, Al, US 97/G4
Andaman (sea), Asia 63/F5
Andaman (isls.), India 63/F5
Andenne, Belg. 31/E3
Andernach, Ger. 31/G3
Anderson, In, US 97/G1
Anderson, SC, US 97/H3
Andes, Cordillera de los (mts.), SAm. 106/C4
Andijon, Uzb. 46/H5
Andilamena, Madg. 81/J7
Andilanatoby, Madg. 81/J7
Andīmeshk, Iran 51/G3
Andira, Braz. 108/B2
Andong, SKor. 56/A2
Andorra (ctry.) 35/F1
Andorra la Vella (cap.), And. 35/F1
Andover, Eng, UK 25/E4
Andradas, Braz. 108/G7
Andradina, Braz. 108/B2
Andria, It. 40/C5
Andriba, Madg. 81/H7
Androka, Madg. 81/H9
Andros (isl.), Bah. 97/J5
Andújar, Sp. 34/C3
Anegada Passage (chan.), NAm. 104/E3
Anécho, Togo 79/F5
Angarsk, Rus. 54/E1
Ángel, Salto (falls), Ven. 106/F2
Ängelholm, Swe. 20/E4
Angers, Fr. 32/C3
Angkor (ruin), Camb. 65/C3
Anglesey (isl.), Wal, UK 22/D5
Anglet, Fr. 34/E1
Angleton, Tx, US 93/J5
Angol, Chile 109/B4
Angola, Afr. 82/B2
Angola (ctry.) 82/C3
Angoulême, Fr. 32/D4
Angra dos Reis, Braz. 108/J7
Angren, Uzb. 46/H5
Anjār, India 62/B3
Anjou, Qu, Can. 95/N6
Ankang, China 59/B4
Ankara (cap.), Turk. 44/E5
Ankazoabo, Madg. 81/H8
Anklam, Ger. 27/G2
Anlong, China 63/J2
Anlu, China 61/G2
Ann Arbor, Mi, US 99/E7
Annaba, Alg. 76/G1
Annaberg-Buchholz, Ger. 33/K1
Annapolis (cap.), Md, US 94/E4
Annecy, Fr. 36/C6
Annecy-le-Vieux, Fr. 36/C6
Annemasse, Fr. 36/C5
Anniston, Al, US 97/G3
Annonay, Fr. 32/F4
Anosibe an' Ala, Madg. 81/J7
Ans, Belg. 31/E2
Ansan, SKor. 58/F7
Ansbach, Ger. 33/J2
Ansfelden, Aus. 40/B1
Anshan, China 58/B2
Anshun, China 60/E3
Ansŏng, SKor. 58/D4
Antakya, Turk. 49/E1
Antalaha, Madg. 81/J6
Antalya, Turk. 49/B1
Antananarivo (cap.), Madg. 81/H7
Antanifotsy, Madg. 81/H7
Antarctic (pen.), Ant. 83/W
Antarctic Circle 83/Z
Antarctica (cont.) 83/*
Antequera, Sp. 34/C4
Antibes, Fr. 33/G5
Anticosti, Île d' (isl.), Qu, Can. 95/J1
Antigua and Barbuda (ctry.), Anti. 104/F3
Antigua Guatemala, Guat. 102/D3
Antioch, Ca, US 99/L11
Antofagasta, Chile 109/B1
Antony, Fr. 30/B6
Antrim, NI, UK 22/B2
Antsalova, Madg. 81/H7
Antsirabe, Madg. 81/H7
Antsirañana, Madg. 81/J6
Antwerpen, Belg. 28/B6
Anūpgarh, India 62/B2
Anuradhapura, SrL. 62/D6
Anyang, SKor. 58/F7
Anzhero-Sudzhensk, Rus. 46/J4
Anzio, It. 38/C2
Aomori, Japan 55/N3
Aosta, It. 33/G4
Apan, Mex. 101/L7
Aparecida, Braz. 108/C2
Aparri, Phil. 61/J5
Apartadó, Col. 103/G5
Apatin, Yugo. 40/D3
Apatity, Rus. 42/G2
Apatzingán de la Constitución, Mex. 100/E5
Apeldoorn, Neth. 28/C4
Apennines (mts.), It. 38/C1
Apia (cap.), Sam. 69/S9
Apizaco, Mex. 101/L7
Apóstoles, Arg. 109/E2
Appalachian (mts.), US 94/D4
Appenzell, Swi. 37/F3
Aprilia, It. 38/C2
Apsheronsk, Rus. 44/F3
Apucarana, Braz. 108/B2
Aqtaū, Kaz. 45/J4
Aqtöbe, Kaz. 45/L2
Aquidauana, Braz. 107/G8
Ar Ramādī, Iraq 51/E3
Ar Ramthā, Jor. 49/D3
Ar Rayyān, Qatar 52/F3
Ar Ruşayfah, Jor. 49/E3
Arabian (des.), Egypt 77/M2
Arabian (pen.), SAr. 52/D3
Arabian (sea), Asia 53/H5
Aracaju, Braz. 107/L6

Araca – Beala

Aracati, Braz. 107/L4
Araçatuba, Braz. 108/B2
Aracruz, Braz. 108/D1
Araçuaí, Braz. 107/K7
'Arad, Isr. 49/D4
Arad, Rom. 40/E2
Araguaína, Braz. 107/J5
Araguari, Braz. 108/B1
Arai, Japan 57/F2
Arāk, Iran 51/G3
Aral (sea), Kaz., Uzb. 46/G5
Aral, Kaz. 46/G5
Ārān, Iran 51/G3
Aranda de Duero, Sp. 34/D2
Arandelovac, Yugo. 40/E3
Arani, India 62/C5
Aranjuez, Sp. 34/D2
Arapiraca, Braz. 107/L5
Arapongas, Braz. 108/B2
Araranguá, Braz. 108/B4
Araraquara, Braz. 108/B2
Araras, Braz. 108/C2
Araripina, Braz. 107/K5
Arauca, Col. 106/D2
Araucária, Braz. 108/B3
Arawa, PNG 68/E5
Araxá, Braz. 108/C1
Ārba Minch', Eth. 77/N6
Arcata, Ca, US 90/B5
Archangel (Arkhangel'sk), Rus. 42/J2
Arches National Park, Ut, US 92/E3
Archman, Trkm. 45/L5
Arcos, Braz. 108/C2
Arcos de la Frontera, Sp. 34/C4
Arcoverde, Braz. 107/L5
Arctic (ocean) 84/A2
Arctic Circle 86/C2
Ardabīl, Iran 51/G2
Ardahan, Turk. 45/G4
Ardakān, Iran 51/H3
Arden-Arcade, Ca, US 99/M9
Ardeşen, Turk. 45/G4
Ardmore, Ok, US 93/H4
Arecibo, PR 104/E3
Areia Branca, Braz. 107/L4
Arendal, Nor. 20/D4
Arequipa, Peru 106/D7
Arezzo, It. 33/J5
Argentan, Fr. 32/C2
Argenteuil, Fr. 30/B6
Argentina (ctry.), Arg. 109/C4
Árgos, Gre. 39/H4
Århus, Den. 20/D4
Arica, Chile 106/D7
Arida, Japan 56/D3
Arima, Trin. 104/F5
Ariquemes, Braz. 106/F5
Arivonimamo, Madg. 81/H7
Arizona (state), US 92/D4
Arjona, Col. 103/H4
Arkadelphia, Ar, US 93/J4
Arkansas (state), US 96/E3
Arkansas (riv.), US 88/F3
Arkansas City, Ks, US 93/H3
Arkonam, India 62/C5
Arles, Fr. 32/F5
Arlington, Tx, US 93/H4
Arlington, Va, US 97/J2
Arlington Heights, Il, US 99/P15
Arlon, Belg. 31/E4
Armant, Egypt 52/B3
Armavir, Rus. 45/G3
Armenia, Col. 106/C3
Armenia (ctry.) 45/H5
Armentières, Fr. 30/B2
Armería, Mex. 100/E5
Armidale, Austl. 73/D1
Ārmūr, India 62/C4
Arnavutköy, Turk. 51/M6
Arnhem, Neth. 28/C5
Arnold, Eng, UK 23/G6
Arnsberg, Ger. 29/F6
Arnstadt, Ger. 33/J1
Arolsen, Ger. 29/G6
Arona, Canl. 35/X16
Arqalyq, Kaz. 46/G4
Arrah, India 62/D2
Arraiján, Pan. 103/G4
Arras, Fr. 30/B3
Arrecife, Canl. 35/Y16
Arriaga, Mex. 102/C2
Arroyo Grande, Ca, US 92/B4
Arsen'yev, Rus. 55/L3
Árta, Gre. 39/G3
Arteixo, Sp. 34/A1
Artem, Rus. 55/L3
Artemisa, Cuba 103/F1
Artesia, NM, US 93/F4
Artigas, Uru. 109/E3
Artvin, Turk. 45/G4
Arua, Ugan. 77/M7
Aruba (isl.), Neth. 104/D4
Arucas, Canl. 35/X16
Arujá, Braz. 108/G8
Aruppukkottai, India 62/C6
Arusha, Tanz. 82/G1
Arvayheer, Mong. 54/E2
Arvika, Swe. 20/E4
Arvin, Ca, US 92/C4
Aryānah, Tun. 38/B4
Arys', Kaz. 46/G5
Arzamas, Rus. 45/G1
Aş Şaff, Egypt 49/B5
As Sālimīyah, Kuw. 51/G4
As Salṭ, Jor. 49/D3
As Samāwah, Iraq 51/F4
As Sanṭah, Egypt 49/B4
As Sinbillāwayn, Egypt 49/B4
As Sulaymānīyah, Iraq 51/F3
As Suwaydā', Syria 49/E3
As Suways, Egypt 49/C4
Asahi, Japan 57/G3
Asahikawa, Japan 55/N3
Asansol, India 62/E3
Asbest, Rus. 43/P4
Aschaffenburg, Ger. 33/H2
Aschersleben, Ger. 26/F3
Ascoli Piceno, It. 40/A4
Āsela, Eth. 77/N6
Asenovgrad, Bul. 41/G4
Ash Shāriqah, UAE 53/G3
Ash Shaṭrah, Iraq 51/F4
Ashdod, Isr. 49/F8
Asheboro, NC, US 97/J3
Asheville, NC, US 97/H3
Ashford, Eng, UK 25/G4
Ashgabat (cap.), Trkm. 51/J2
Ashington, Eng, UK 23/G1
Ashland, Or, US 90/C5
Ashland, Ky, US 97/H2
Ashland, Oh, US 94/D3
Ashmūn, Egypt 49/B4
Ashqelon, Isr. 49/F8
Ashta, India 62/C3
Ashtabula, Oh, US 94/D3
Ashton-in-Makerfield, Eng, UK 23/F5
Ashton-under-Lyne, Eng, UK 23/F5
Asia (cont.) 48/*
Asino, Rus. 46/J4
Aşkale, Turk. 45/G5
Asker, Nor. 20/D4
Asmara (cap.), Erit. 52/C5
Asnières-sur-Seine, Fr. 30/B6
Aspe, Sp. 35/E3
Asprópirgos, Gre. 39/N8
Assab, Erit. 52/D6
Asse, Belg. 31/D2
Assemini, It. 38/A3
Assen, Neth. 28/D3
Assiniboine (mt.), BC, Can. 90/E3
Assis, Braz. 108/B2
Astana (cap.), Kaz. 46/H4
Asten, Neth. 28/C6
Asti, It. 33/H4
Astorga, Braz. 108/B2
Astoria, Or, US 90/C4
Astrakhan', Rus. 45/J3
Asunción (cap.), Par. 109/E2
Aswān, Egypt 52/B4
Asyūṭ, Egypt 50/B5
Aṭ Ṭafīlah, Jor. 49/D4
Aṭ Ṭā'if, SAr. 52/D4
At Tall, Syria 49/E3
At Tall al Kabīr, Egypt 49/B4
Atacama (des.), Chile 109/C2
Atakpamé, Togo 79/F5
Atami, Japan 57/F3
Atar, Mrta. 78/B1
Atarra, India 62/D2
Atascadero, Ca, US 92/B4
Atbara, Sudan 77/M4
Atbasar, Kaz. 46/G4
Atchison, Ks, US 93/J3
Atenco, Mex. 101/Q10
Ath, Belg. 30/C2
Athabasca (riv.), Ab, Can. 86/E3
Athabasca (lake), Ab,Sk, Can. 86/E3
Athens, Tx, US 93/J4
Athens, Ga, US 97/H3
Athens, Oh, US 97/H2
Athens, Al, US 97/G3
Athens, Tn, US 97/G3
Athens (cap.), Gre. 39/N9
Atherton, Eng, UK 23/F4
Ati, Chad 76/J5
Atibaia, Braz. 108/G8
Atkarsk, Rus. 45/H2
Atlanta (cap.), Ga, US 97/G3
Atlantic (ocean) 16/G3
Atlantic City, NJ, US 94/F4
Atlixco, Mex. 101/L8
Atoyac, Mex. 101/E5
Attendorn, Ger. 29/E6
Atteridgeville, SAfr. 80/Q12
Attu, Ak, US 85/A5
Atwater, Ca, US 92/B3
Atyraū, Kaz. 45/J3
Auburn, Ca, US 92/B3
Auburn, Al, US 97/G3
Auburn, In, US 94/C3
Auburn, Me, US 95/G2
Auburn, NY, US 94/E3
Auburn, Wa, US 99/C3
Auburn Hills, Mi, US 99/F6
Auch, Fr. 32/D5
Auckland, NZ 71/R10
Auderghem, Belg. 31/D2
Audincourt, Fr. 36/C3
Aue, Ger. 33/K1
Auer (Ora), It. 37/H5
Auerbach, Ger. 33/K1
Augsburg, Ger. 37/G1
Augusta, Ga, US 97/H3
Augusta (cap.), Me, US 95/G2
Augusta, It. 38/D4
Augustów, Pol. 27/M2
Auki, Sol. 68/F5
Aurangābād, India 62/C4
Aurangābād, India 62/D3
Aurich, Ger. 29/E2
Aurillac, Fr. 32/E4
Aurora, Co, US 93/F3
Aurora, Il, US 99/P16
Austin, Mn, US 91/K5
Austin (cap.), Tx, US 93/H5
Australia (cont.) 70/*
Australia (ctry.) 70/*
Austria (ctry.) 33/L3
Autlán de Navarro, Mex. 100/D5
Autun, Fr. 32/F3
Auxerre, Fr. 32/E3
Avaré, Braz. 108/B2
Aveiro, Port. 34/A2
Avellino, It. 40/B5
Avenal, Ca, US 92/B3
Aversa, It. 40/B5
Avesta, Swe. 42/C3
Avezzano, It. 38/C1
Avignon, Fr. 32/F5
Ávila de los Caballeros, Sp. 34/C2
Avilés, Sp. 34/C1
Avion, Fr. 30/B3
Avola, It. 38/D4
Awbārī, Libya 76/H2
Awka, Nga. 79/G5
Awsīm, Egypt 49/B4
Ayabe, Japan 56/D3
Ayacucho, Peru 106/D6
Ayagöz, Kaz. 46/J5
Ayamonte, Sp. 34/B4
Ayapel, Col. 103/H4
Aybastı, Turk. 44/F4
Aydın, Turk. 50/A2
Ayeyarwady (riv.), Myan. 63/G4
Aylesbury, Eng, UK 25/F3
Aylesford, Eng, UK 25/G4
Aytos, Bul. 41/H4
Ayvalık, Turk. 44/C5
Az Zabadānī, Syria 49/E3
Az Zaqāzīq, Egypt 49/B4
Az Zarqā', Jor. 49/E3
Az Zāwiyah, Libya 76/H1
Az Zubayr, Iraq 51/F4
Azamgarh, India 62/D2
A'zāz, Syria 49/E1
Azerbaijan (ctry.) 45/H4
Azogues, Ecu. 106/C4
Azores (dpcy.), Port. 35/R12
Azov, Rus. 44/F3
Azul, Arg. 109/E4
Azur, Côte d' (coast), Fr. 33/G5

B

Baar, Swi. 37/E3
Baarn, Neth. 28/C4
Babaeski, Turk. 41/H5
Babahoyo, Ecu. 106/C4
Bābil (Babylon) (ruin), Iraq 51/F3
Bābol, Iran 51/H2
Babruysk, Bela. 44/D1
Bac Giang, Viet. 65/D1
Bac Lieu, Viet. 65/D4
Bac Ninh, Viet. 65/D1
Bacabal, Braz. 107/K4
Bacarra, Phil. 61/J5
Bacău, Rom. 41/H2
Bačka Palanka, Yugo. 40/D3
Bačka Topola, Yugo. 40/D3
Backnang, Ger. 33/H2
Bacolod, Phil. 67/F1
Bad Driburg, Ger. 29/G5
Bad Dürkheim, Ger. 31/H5
Bad Harzburg, Ger. 29/H5
Bad Hersfeld, Ger. 33/H1
Bad Homburg vor der Höhe, Ger. 33/H1
Bad Honnef, Ger. 31/G2
Bad Kissingen, Ger. 26/F3
Bad Kreuznach, Ger. 31/G4
Bad Langensalza, Ger. 29/H6
Bad Mergentheim, Ger. 33/H2
Bad Munder am Deister, Ger. 29/G4
Bad Nauheim, Ger. 33/H1
Bad Neuenahr-Ahrweiler, Ger. 31/G2
Bad Neustadt an der Saale, Ger. 33/J1
Bad Oeynhausen, Ger. 29/F4
Bad Oldesloe, Ger. 26/F2
Bad Pyrmont, Ger. 29/G5
Bad Reichenhall, Ger. 40/A2
Bad Salzuflen, Ger. 29/F4
Bad Salzungen, Ger. 26/F3
Bad Schwartau, Ger. 26/F2
Bad Segeberg, Ger. 26/F2
Bad Tölz, Ger. 37/H2
Bad Waldsee, Ger. 37/F2
Bad Wildungen, Ger. 29/G6
Bad Zwischenahn, Ger. 29/F2
Badagara, India 62/C5
Badajoz, Sp. 34/B3
Badalona, Sp. 35/L7
Baden, Aus. 40/C1
Baden, Swi. 37/E3
Baden-Baden, Ger. 33/H2
Badīn, Pak. 62/A3
Badlands (plat.), SD, US 91/H5
Badlands National Park, SD, US 91/H5
Bādrāh, Pak. 53/J3
Badulla, SrL. 62/D6
Baena, Sp. 34/C4
Baesweiler, Ger. 31/F2
Baeza, Sp. 34/D4
Bafang, Camr. 79/H5
Baffin (isl.), Can. 87/H1
Bafia, Camr. 76/H7
Bafoussam, Camr. 79/H5
Bafra, Turk. 44/E4
Baganga, Phil. 67/G2
Bagé, Braz. 109/F3
Baghdad (cap.), Iraq 51/F3
Bagheria, It. 38/C3
Baghlān, Afg. 53/J1
Bagnols-sur-Cèze, Fr. 32/F4
Bago (Pegu), Myan. 65/B2
Baguio, Phil. 61/J5
Bahamas (ctry.), Bahm. 103/H1
Bahāwalpur, Pak. 62/B2
Bahçe, Turk. 50/D2
Bahía Blanca, Arg. 109/D4
Bahir Dar, Eth. 77/N5
Bahlah, Oman 53/G4
Bahraich, India 62/D2
Bahrain (ctry.), Bahr. 52/F3
Baia Mare, Rom. 41/F2
Baia Sprie, Rom. 41/F2
Băicoi, Rom. 41/G3
Baie-Comeau, Qu, Can. 95/G1
Baiersbronn, Ger. 37/E1
Baildon, Eng, UK 23/G4
Bailén, Sp. 34/D3
Băileşti, Rom. 41/F3
Bainbridge, Ga, US 97/G4
Baixa da Banheira, Port. 35/P10
Baixo Guandu, Braz. 108/D1
Baiyin, China 54/E4
Baja, Hun. 40/D2
Baja California (pen.), Mex. 92/D5
Bājah, Tun. 38/A4
Bakau, Gam. 78/A3
Baker, La, US 93/K5
Baker (mt.), Wa, US 90/C3
Baker City, Or, US 90/D4
Bakersfield, Ca, US 92/C4
Bakhchysaray, Ukr. 44/E3
Bakhmach, Ukr. 44/E2
Bākhtarān, Iran 51/F3
Baku (cap.), Azer. 45/J4
Balabac, Phil. 67/E2
Ba'labakk, Leb. 49/E2
Bālāghāt, India 62/D3
Balakhna, Rus. 43/J4
Balakovo, Rus. 45/H1
Bālāngir, India 62/D3
Balaoan, Phil. 61/J5
Balashikha, Rus. 43/W9
Balashov, Rus. 45/G2
Balasore (Baleshwar), India 62/E3
Balassagyarmat, Hun. 40/D1
Balcarce, Arg. 109/E4
Balearic (isls.), Sp. 35/G3
Balen, Belg. 28/C6
Baley, Rus. 54/H1
Balıkesir, Turk. 44/C5
Balikpapan, Indo. 67/E4
Balimbing, Phil. 67/E2
Balingen, Ger. 37/E1
Balkan (mts.), Bul. 41/F4
Balkhash (lake), Kaz. 46/H5
Ballarat, Austl. 73/B3
Ballarpur, India 62/C4
Ballina, Austl. 73/E1
Ballymena, NI, UK 22/B2
Balmazújváros, Hun. 40/E2
Balneário Camboriú, Braz. 108/B3
Bālotra, India 62/B2
Balqash, Kaz. 46/H5
Balrāmpur, India 62/D2
Balş, Rom. 41/G3
Balsas, Braz. 107/J5
Bălţi, Mol. 41/H2
Baltic (sea), Eur. 18/E3
Balṭīm, Egypt 49/B4
Baltimore, Md, US 97/J2
Baltiysk, Rus. 27/K1
Bālurghāt, India 62/E2
Balykshi, Kaz. 45/J3
Bam, Iran 51/J4
Bamako (cap.), Mali 78/D3
Bambari, CAfr. 77/K6
Bamberg, Ger. 33/J2
Bambuí, Braz. 108/C2
Bamenda, Camr. 79/H5
Banbury, Eng, UK 25/E2
Bāndā, India 62/D2
Banda Aceh, Indo. 66/A2
Bandar Seri Begawan (cap.), Bru. 66/D3
Bandar-e 'Abbās, Iran 51/J5
Bandar-e Anzalī, Iran 51/G2
Bandar-e Būshehr, Iran 51/G4
Bandar-e Māhshahr, Iran 51/G4
Bandeirantes, Braz. 108/B2
Bandırma, Turk. 41/H5
Bandundu, D.R. Congo 82/C1
Bandung, Indo. 66/C5
Banes, Cuba 103/H1
Banff National Park, Can. 90/E3
Banfora, Burk. 78/D4
Bangalore, India 62/C5
Bangangté, Camr. 79/H5
Bangar, Phil. 61/J5
Bangassou, CAfr. 77/K7
Bangkok (cap.), Thai. 65/C3
Bangkok, Bight of (bay), Thai. 63/H5
Bangladesh (ctry.) 62/E3
Bangor, Me, US 95/G2
Bangor, NI, UK 22/C2
Bangued, Phil. 61/J5
Bangui (cap.), CAfr. 77/J7
Banhā, Egypt 49/B4
Banī Mazār, Egypt 50/B4
Banikoara, Ben. 79/F4
Bāniyās, Syria 49/D2
Banja Luka, Bosn. 40/C3
Banjarmasin, Indo. 66/D4
Banjul (cap.), Gam. 78/A3
Bānkurā, India 62/E3
Bannu, Pak. 53/K2
Banská Bystrica, Slvk. 27/K4
Banstead, Eng, UK 25/F4
Bānswāra, India 62/B3
Banyoles, Sp. 35/G1
Banyuwangi, Indo. 66/D5
Banzart (Bizerte), Tun. 38/A4
Baoding, China 59/H2
Baoji, China 54/F5
Baoshan, China 60/C3
Baotou, China 59/B2
Bāqa el Gharbiyya, Isr. 49/G7
Ba'qūbah, Iraq 51/F3
Bar, Yugo. 40/D4
Bar-le-Duc, Fr. 31/E6
Barabai, Indo. 66/E4
Barabinsk, Rus. 46/H4
Baraboo, Wi, US 91/L5
Baracaldo, Sp. 34/D1
Baracoa, Cuba 103/H1
Baramula, India 53/K2
Bāran, India 62/C2
Baranavichy, Bela. 44/C1
Baranoa, Col. 103/H4
Barão de Cocais, Braz. 108/D1
Barbacena, Braz. 108/D2
Barbados (ctry.), Bar. 104/G4
Barbastro, Sp. 35/F1
Barbate de Franco, Sp. 34/C4
Barberà del Vallès, Sp. 35/L6
Barberton, Oh, US 94/D3
Barbil, India 62/E3
Barcellona Pozzo di Gotto, It. 38/D3
Barcelona, Ven. 106/F1
Barcelona, Sp. 35/L7
Bardejov, Slvk. 27/L4
Bārdoli, India 53/K4
Bareilly, India 62/C2
Barendrecht, Neth. 28/B5
Barentu, Erit. 52/C5
Bargarh, India 62/D3
Bari, It. 40/C5
Barika, Alg. 76/G1
Barillas, Guat. 102/D3
Barinas, Ven. 106/D2
Baripāda, India 62/E3
Bariri, Braz. 108/B2
Barisāl, Bang. 62/F3
Barletta, It. 40/C5
Barmer, India 62/B2
Barnāla, India 53/L2
Barnaul, Rus. 46/J4
Barneveld, Neth. 28/C4
Barnsley, Eng, UK 23/G4
Barnstaple, Eng, UK 24/B4
Barpeta, India 62/F2
Barquisimeto, Ven. 106/E1
Barra, Braz. 107/K6
Barra Bonita, Braz. 108/B2
Barra Del Colorado, CR 103/F4
Barra do Corda, Braz. 107/J5
Barra do Garças, Braz. 107/H7
Barra do Piraí, Braz. 108/K7
Barra Mansa, Braz. 108/J7
Barranca, Peru 106/C6
Barrancabermeja, Col. 106/D2
Barranquilla, Col. 103/H4
Barreiras, Braz. 107/K6
Barretos, Braz. 108/B2
Barrie, On, Can. 94/E2
Barrington, Il, US 99/P15
Barroso, Braz. 108/D2
Barrow (pt.), Ak, US 85/G1
Barrow, Ak, US 85/G1
Barrow-in-Furness, Eng, UK 23/E3
Barry, Wal, UK 24/C4
Bārshi, India 62/C4
Barsinghausen, Ger. 29/G4
Barstow, Ca, US 92/C4
Bartica, Guy. 106/G2
Bartın, Turk. 41/L5
Bartlesville, Ok, US 93/J3
Bartlett, Il, US 99/P16
Bartolomé Masó, Cuba 103/G1
Bartoszyce, Pol. 27/L1
Bartow, Fl, US 97/H5
Barus, Indo. 66/A3
Baruun-Urt, Mong. 54/G2
Barwāha, India 62/C3
Barwāni, India 62/B3
Barysaw, Bela. 42/F5
Barysh, Rus. 45/H1
Basauri, Sp. 34/D1
Basel, Swi. 36/D2
Basildon, Eng, UK 25/G3
Basingstoke, Eng, UK 25/E4
Başkale, Turk. 51/F2
Bāsoda, India 62/C3
Bassano del Grappa, It. 33/J4
Bassari, Togo 79/F4
Basse-Terre, Fr. 104/F4
Bassein (Vasai), India 53/K5
Basseterre (cap.), StK. 104/F3
Bastī, India 62/D2
Bastia, Fr. 38/A1
Bastos, Braz. 108/B2
Basyūn, Egypt 49/B4
Bat Yam, Isr. 49/F7
Bata, EqG. 76/G7
Batac, Phil. 61/J5
Batāla, India 53/L2
Batangas, Phil. 68/B3
Batatais, Braz. 108/C2
Batavia, NY, US 94/E3
Batavia, Il, US 99/P16
Bataysk, Rus. 44/F3
Bătdambang, Camb. 65/C3
Bath, Me, US 95/G3
Bath, Eng, UK 24/D4
Bathurst, Austl. 73/D2
Batley, Eng, UK 23/G4
Batman, Turk. 50/E2
Batna, Alg. 76/G1
Baton Rouge (cap.), La, US 93/K5
Batouri, Camr. 76/H7
Batticaloa, SrL. 62/D6
Battipaglia, It. 40/B5
Battle Creek, Mi, US 94/C3
Batu Pahat, Malay. 66/B3
Bat'umi, Geo. 45/G4
Baturaja, Indo. 66/B4
Baturité, Braz. 107/L4
Batys Qazaqstan, Kaz. 46/E5
Baunatal, Ger. 29/G6
Baurú, Braz. 108/B2
Bautzen, Ger. 27/H3
Bawku, Gha. 79/E4
Bay City, Tx, US 93/J5
Bayamo, Cuba 103/G1
Bayamón, PR 104/E3
Bayanhongor, Mong. 54/E2
Bayawan, Phil. 67/F2
Bayburt, Turk. 44/G4
Baydhabo (Baidoa), Som. 77/P7
Bayeux, Braz. 107/M5
Bayeux, Fr. 32/C2
Baykal (lake), Rus. 46/L4
Bayombong, Phil. 61/J5
Bayonet Point, Fl, US 97/H4
Bayonne, Fr. 34/E1
Bayramaly, Trkm. 53/H1
Bayreuth, Ger. 33/J2
Baytown, Tx, US 93/J5
Baza, Sp. 34/D4
Beaconsfield, Qu, Can. 95/N7
Bealanana, Madg. 81/J6

113

Beatr – Bruss

Beatrice, Ne, US 93/H2
Beau Bassin, Mrts. 81/T15
Beaufort, SC, US 97/H3
Beaufort West, SAfr. 80/C4
Beaume, Fr. 32/F3
Beaumont, Tx, US 93/J5
Beauvais, Fr. 30/B5
Beāwar, India 62/B2
Bebedouro, Braz. 108/B2
Bebington, Eng, UK 23/E5
Bebra, Ger. 29/G7
Bečej, Yugo. 40/E3
Béchar, Alg. 76/E1
Beckingen, Ger. 31/F5
Beckley, WV, US 97/H2
Beckum, Ger. 29/F5
Bedburg, Ger. 28/D6
Bedford, In, US 97/G2
Bedford, Eng, UK 25/F2
Bedlington, Eng, UK 23/G1
Bedworth, Eng, UK 25/E2
Beek, Neth. 31/E2
Beenleigh, Austl. 72/D4
Be'er Sheva', Isr. 49/D4
Beerzel, Belg. 28/B6
Beeville, Tx, US 96/D4
Begusarai, India 62/E2
Behbahān, Iran 51/G4
Behshahr, Iran 51/H2
Bei'an, China 55/K2
Beihai, China 65/E1
Beijing (cap.), China 59/H7
Beipiao, China 59/E2
Beira, Moz. 82/F4
Beirut (cap.), Leb. 49/D3
Beja, Port. 34/B3
Bejaïa, Alg. 76/G1
Béjar, Sp. 34/C2
Bekasi, Indo. 66/C5
Békés, Hun. 40/E2
Békéscsaba, Hun. 40/E2
Bekily, Madg. 81/H9
Belā, India 62/D2
Bela Crkva, Yugo. 40/E3
Bela Vista, Braz. 107/G8
Belarus (ctry.) 18/F3
Belas, Port. 35/P10
Bełchatów, Pol. 27/K3
Belebey, Rus. 43/M5
Belém, Braz. 107/J4
Belen, Turk. 49/E1
Belev, Rus. 44/F1
Belfast (cap.), NI, UK 22/C2
Belfort, Fr. 36/C2
Belgaum, India 62/B4
Belgium (ctry.) 26/C3
Belgorod, Rus. 44/F2
Belgrade (cap.), Yugo. 40/E4
Beli Manastir, Cro. 40/D3
Belize (ctry.), Belz. 102/D2
Belize City, Belz. 102/D2
Bell Ville, Arg. 109/D3
Bella Vista, Arg. 109/E2
Bellary, India 62/C4
Belle Glade, Fl, US 97/H5
Bellefontaine, Oh, US 94/D3
Belleville, On, Can. 94/E2
Bellevue, Wa, US 99/C2
Bellingham, Wa, US 90/C3
Bellinzona, Swi. 37/F5
Bello, Col. 106/C2
Belluno, It. 33/K3
Bellville, SAfr. 80/L10
Belmont, Ca, US 99/K11
Belmopan (cap.), Belz. 102/D2
Belo Horizonte, Braz. 108/D1
Belo Jardim, Braz. 107/L5
Belo-Tsiribihina, Madg. 81/H7
Beloeil, Qu, Can. 95/P6
Belogorsk, Rus. 55/K1
Beloha, Madg. 81/H9
Beloit, Wi, US 91/L5
Belomorsk, Rus. 42/G2
Belorechensk, Rus. 44/F3
Beloretsk, Rus. 43/N5
Belovo, Rus. 46/J4
Belper, Eng, UK 23/G5
Belton, Tx, US 93/H5
Belvidere, Il, US 91/L5
Bembèrèkè, Ben. 79/F4
Bemetāra, India 62/D3
Bemmel, Neth. 28/C5
Ben Tre, Viet. 65/D4
Benalmádena, Sp. 34/C4
Benavente, Sp. 34/C1
Bend, Or, US 90/C4
Bendigo, Austl. 73/C3
Bene Beraq, Isr. 49/F7
Benešov, Czh. 33/L2
Benevento, It. 40/B5
Bengal, Bay of (gulf), Asia 62/E4
Benghāzī, Libya 76/K1
Bengkayang, Indo. 66/C3
Bengkulu, Indo. 66/B4
Benguela, Ang. 82/B3
Beni, D.R. Congo 77/L7
Beni Mellal, Mor. 76/D1
Benicarló, Sp. 35/F2
Benicia, Ca, US 99/K10
Benidorm, Sp. 35/E3
Benin (ctry.) 79/F4
Benin City, Nga. 79/G5
Benin, Bight of (bay), Afr. 76/F6
Bennettsville, SC, US 97/J3
Bennington, Vt, US 94/F3
Bensenville, Il, US 99/Q16
Bensheim, Ger. 33/H2
Bentley, Eng, UK 23/G4
Bento Gonçalves, Braz. 108/B4
Benton, Ar, US 93/J4
Benton Harbor, Mi, US 94/C3
Bentong, Malay. 66/B3
Benxi, China 58/B2
Beppu, Japan 56/B4
Beraketa, Madg. 81/H8
Berat, Alb. 40/D5
Berbera, Som. 77/Q5
Berbérati, CAfr. 76/J7
Berchem, Belg. 28/B6
Berck, Fr. 25/H6
Berdsk, Rus. 46/J4
Berdyans'k, Ukr. 44/F3
Berdychiv, Ukr. 44/D2
Berea, Ky, US 97/G2
Berehove, Ukr. 40/F1
Berekum, Gha. 79/E5
Berettyóújfalu, Hun. 40/E2
Berezniki, Rus. 43/N4
Bergama, Turk. 44/C5
Bergamo, It. 33/H4
Bergara, Sp. 34/D1
Bergen, Nor. 20/C3
Bergen, Ger. 27/G1
Bergen op Zoom, Neth. 28/B5
Bergerac, Fr. 32/D4
Bergheim, Ger. 31/F2
Bergisch Gladbach, Ger. 31/G2
Bergkamen, Ger. 29/E5
Bergneustadt, Ger. 29/E6
Bergum, Neth. 28/D2
Berhampore, India 62/E3
Berhampur, India 62/D4
Bering (sea), Asia, NAm. 47/U4
Bering (str.), Rus., US 85/E3
Beringen, Belg. 28/C6
Berkel, Neth. 28/B5
Berkeley, Ca, US 99/K11
Berkhamsted, Eng, UK 25/F3
Berkley, Mi, US 99/F6
Berkovitsa, Bul. 41/F4
Berleburg, Ger. 29/F6
Berlin, NH, US 95/G2
Berlin (cap.), Ger. 27/G2
Bermejo, Bol. 109/D1
Bermeo, Sp. 34/D1
Bern (cap.), Swi. 36/D4
Bernal, Peru 106/B5
Bernburg, Ger. 26/F3
Beroun, Czh. 33/L2
Berovo, FYROM 40/F5
Bertoua, Camr. 76/H7
Berwick, Pa, US 94/E3
Berwyn, Il, US 99/Q16
Besançon, Fr. 36/C3
Beslan, Rus. 45/H4
Bessacarr, Eng, UK 23/G5
Bessemer, Al, US 97/G3
Best, Neth. 28/C5
Bet She'an, Isr. 49/D3
Bet Shemesh, Isr. 49/F8
Bethesda, Md, US 97/J2
Bethlehem, Pa, US 94/F3
Béthune, Fr. 30/B2
Betim, Braz. 108/C1
Betioky, Madg. 81/H8
Bettiah, India 62/D2
Betūl, India 62/C3
Beuningen, Neth. 28/C5
Beveren, Belg. 28/B6
Beverley, Eng, UK 23/H4
Beverly Hills, Mi, US 99/F6
Beverungen, Ger. 29/G5
Beverwijk, Neth. 28/B4
Bexbach, Ger. 31/G5
Bexhill, Eng, UK 25/G5
Beypazarı, Turk. 41/K5
Beyşehir, Turk. 50/B2
Bezhetsk, Rus. 42/H4
Béziers, Fr. 32/E5
Bhabua, India 62/D2
Bhadrak, India 62/E3
Bhadreswar, India 62/A3
Bhāgalpur, India 62/E2
Bhakkar, Pak. 53/K2
Bhaktapur, Nepal 62/E2
Bhānwad, India 62/A3
Bhārātpur, India 62/C2
Bhātāpāra, India 62/D3
Bhatinda, India 53/K2
Bhatkal, India 62/B5
Bhātpāra, India 62/E3
Bhavāni, India 62/C5
Bhavnagar, India 62/B3
Bhawāni Mandi, India 62/C3
Bhawānipatna, India 62/D4
Bhilai, India 62/D3
Bhīlwāra, India 62/B2
Bhīmavaram, India 62/D4
Bhimunipatnam, India 62/D4
Bhind, India 62/C2
Bhiwandi, India 62/B4
Bhopāl, India 62/C3
Bhor, India 62/B4
Bhuban, India 62/E3
Bhubaneswar, India 62/E3
Bhusawal, India 62/C3
Bhutan (ctry.) 62/E2
Biafra, Bight of (bay), Camr. 76/G7
Biała Podlaska, Pol. 27/M2
Białogard, Pol. 27/J2
Białystok, Pol. 27/M2
Biancavilla, It. 38/D4
Biarritz, Fr. 34/E1
Bibā, Egypt 50/B4
Biberach an der Riss, Ger. 37/F1
Bicester, Eng, UK 25/E3
Bida, Nga. 79/G4
Bīdar, India 62/C4
Biddeford, Me, US 95/G3
Biddulph, Eng, UK 23/F5
Biel, Swi. 36/D3
Bielawa, Pol. 27/J3
Bielefeld, Ger. 29/F4
Biella, It. 33/H4
Bielsk Podlaski, Pol. 27/M2
Bielsko-Biała, Pol. 27/K4
Bien Hoa, Viet. 65/D4
Big Rapids, Mi, US 94/C3
Big Spring, Tx, US 93/G4
Biga, Turk. 41/H5
Bignona, Sen. 78/A3
Biguaçu, Braz. 108/B3
Bihać, Bosn. 40/B3
Bīhar, India 62/E2
Bijeljina, Bosn. 40/D3
Bijelo Polje, Yugo. 40/D4
Bijnor, India 62/C2
Bīkaner, India 62/B2
Bikin, Rus. 55/L2
Bila Tserkva, Ukr. 44/D2
Bilāra, India 62/B2
Bilāspur, India 62/D3
Bilbao, Sp. 34/D1
Bilbays, Egypt 49/B4
Bilecik, Turk. 44/D4
Biłgoraj, Pol. 27/M3
Bilhorod-Dnistrovs'kyy, Ukr. 41/K2
Billingham, Eng, UK 23/G2
Billings, Mt, US 90/F4
Biloxi, Ms, US 97/F4
Bilqas Qism Awwal, Egypt 49/B4
Bilsi, India 62/C2
Bilzen, Belg. 31/E2
Bima, Indo. 67/E5
Bimbo, CAfr. 77/J7
Bin 'Arūs, Tun. 38/B4
Bina-Etāwa, India 62/C3
Binche, Belg. 31/D3
Bindki, India 62/D2
Bindura, Zim. 82/F4
Bingen, Ger. 31/G4
Bingerville, C.d'Iv. 78/E5
Binghamton, NY, US 94/F3
Bingley, Eng, UK 23/G4
Bingöl, Turk. 50/E2
Binh Son, Viet. 65/E3
Binjai, Indo. 66/A3
Biograd, Cro. 40/B4
Bīr, India 53/L5
Birāk, Libya 76/H2
Birao, CAfr. 77/K5
Birātnagar, Nepal 62/E2
Birecik, Turk. 50/D2
Birigui, Braz. 108/B2
Biritiba-Mirim, Braz. 108/G8
Bīrjand, Iran 53/G2
Birkenhead, Eng, UK 23/E5
Bîrlad, Rom. 41/H2
Birmingham, Al, US 97/G3
Birmingham, Eng, UK 25/E2
Birmingham, Mi, US 99/F6
Birni Nkonni, Niger 79/G3
Birobjian, Rus. 55/L2
Birsk, Rus. 43/M5
Biscay (bay), Fr.,Sp. 34/C1
Bisceglie, It. 40/C5
Bischheim, Fr. 31/G6
Bishkek (cap.), Kyr. 46/H5
Bishop Auckland, Eng, UK 23/G2
Bishop's Stortford, Eng, UK 25/G3
Biskra, Alg. 76/G1
Bislig, Phil. 67/G2
Bismarck (arch.), PNG 68/D5
Bismarck (cap.), ND, US 91/H4
Bismil, Turk. 50/E2
Bissau (cap.), GBis. 78/B4
Bistrita, Rom. 41/G2
Bitlis, Turk. 50/E2
Bitola, FYROM 40/E5
Bitonto, It. 40/C5
Bitung, Indo. 67/G3
Bixby, Ok, US 96/E3
Biyalā, Egypt 49/B4
Biysk, Rus. 46/J4
Bjelovar, Cro. 40/C3
Black (sea), Eur.,Asia 41/J4
Blackburn, Eng, UK 23/F4
Blackfoot, Id, US 90/E5
Blackpool, Eng, UK 23/E4
Blagnac, Fr. 32/D5
Blagoevgrad, Bul. 41/F4
Blagoveshchensk, Rus. 55/K1
Blainville, Qu, Can. 95/N6
Blaj, Rom. 41/F2
Blanc (peak), Fr. 36/C6
Blanca, Costa (coast), Sp. 35/E4
Blanes, Sp. 35/G2
Blankenberge, Belg. 30/C1
Blansko, Czh. 33/M2
Blantyre, Malw. 82/G4
Blenheim, NZ 71/R11
Blida, Alg. 76/F1
Blieskastel, Ger. 31/G5
Bloemendaal, Neth. 28/B4
Bloemfontein, SAfr. 80/D3
Blois, Fr. 32/D3
Blomberg, Ger. 29/G5
Bloomingdale, Il, US 99/P16
Bloomington, Il, US 91/L5
Bloomington, In, US 97/G2
Bloomsburg, Pa, US 94/E3
Blora, Indo. 66/D5
Blue Island, Il, US 99/Q16
Blue Mountains, Austl. 73/D2
Blue Ridge (mts.), US 97/H3
Bluefield, WV, US 97/H2
Bluefields, Nic. 103/F4
Bluffton, In, US 94/C3
Blumenau, Braz. 108/B3
Blyth, Eng, UK 23/G1
Blytheville, Ar, US 93/K4
Bo, SLeo. 78/C5
Boa Esperança, Braz. 108/C2
Boa Vista, Braz. 106/F3
Boaco, Nic. 102/E3
Boadilla del Monte, Sp. 35/N9
Bobbili, India 62/D4
Bobigny, Fr. 30/B6
Bobingen, Ger. 37/G1
Böblingen, Ger. 33/H2
Bobo Dioulasso, Burk. 78/D4
Bobrov, Rus. 44/G2
Boca Raton, Fl, US 97/H5
Bocaiúva, Braz. 107/K7
Bocas del Toro, Pan. 103/F4
Bochnia, Pol. 27/L4
Bocholt, Ger. 28/D5
Bochum, Ger. 29/E6
Bodaybo, Rus. 47/M4
Bodegraven, Neth. 28/B4
Boden, Swe. 42/D2
Bodensee (Constance) (lake), Swi 37/F2
Bodhan, India 62/C4
Bodināyakkanūr, India 62/C5
Bodø, Nor. 20/E2
Bodrum, Turk. 50/A2
Bogalusa, La, US 97/F4
Bogandé, Burk. 79/E3
Bogatynia, Pol. 27/H3
Boğazlıyan, Turk. 44/E5
Bognor Regis, Eng, UK 25/F5
Bogor, Indo. 66/C5
Bogotá (cap.), Col. 106/D3
Bohicon, Ben. 79/F5
Boiro, Sp. 34/A1
Boisbriand, Qu, Can. 95/N6
Boise (cap.), Id, US 90/D5
Bojnūrd, Iran 51/J2
Boksburg, SAfr. 80/Q13
Bol, Chad 76/H5
Bolesławiec, Pol. 27/H3
Bolgatanga, Gha. 79/E4
Bolinao, Phil. 61/H5
Bolingbrook, Il, US 99/P16
Bolívar, Arg. 109/D4
Bolívar (peak), Ven. 106/D2
Bolivia (ctry.), Bol. 106/F7
Bologna, It. 33/J4
Bologoye, Rus. 42/G4
Bolton, Eng, UK 23/F4
Bolu, Turk. 41/K5
Bolvadin, Turk. 50/B2
Bolzano, It. 37/H5
Bom Despacho, Braz. 108/C1
Bom Jesus da Lapa, Braz. 107/K6
Bom Jesus do Itabapoana, Braz. 108/D2
Boma, D.R. Congo 82/B2
Bomaderry, Austl. 73/D2
Bon (cape), Tun. 38/B4
Bondoukou, C.d'Iv. 78/E4
Bondowoso, Indo. 66/D5
Bönen, Ger. 29/E5
Bongabong, Phil. 67/F1
Bongao, Phil. 67/E3
Bongor, Chad 76/J5
Bonita Springs, Fl, US 97/H5
Bonn, Ger. 31/G2
Bonthain, Indo. 67/E5
Bontoc, Phil. 61/J5
Bonyhád, Hun. 40/D2
Boone, Ia, US 91/K5
Boosaaso (Bender Cassim), Som. 77/Q5
Bootle, Eng, UK 23/E5
Boppard, Ger. 31/G3
Bor, Rus. 43/K4
Bor, Turk. 50/C2
Bor, Yugo. 40/F3
Borås, Swe. 20/E4
Borāzjān, Iran 51/G4
Borča, Yugo. 40/E3
Bordeaux, Fr. 32/C4
Borehamwood, Eng, UK 25/F3
Borger, Tx, US 93/G4
Borgerhout, Belg. 28/B6
Borghorst, Ger. 29/E4
Borisoglebsk, Rus. 45/G2
Borken, Ger. 28/D5
Borlänge, Swe. 20/E3
Borna, Ger. 26/G3
Borne, Neth. 28/D4
Bornem, Belg. 28/B6
Borneo (isl.), Asia 67/E3
Bornheim, Ger. 31/G2
Borovichi, Rus. 42/G4
Borşa, Rom. 41/F2
Borssele, Neth. 28/A6
Borūjerd, Iran 51/F3
Boryslav, Ukr. 27/M4
Borzya, Rus. 54/H1
Bosanska Dubica, Bosn. 40/C3
Bosanska Gradiška, Bosn. 40/C3
Bosanska Krupa, Bosn. 40/C3
Bosanski Brod, Bosn. 40/D3
Bosanski Petrovac, Bosn. 40/C3
Bosanski Šamac, Bosn. 40/D3
Bose, China 61/E4
Boskoop, Neth. 28/B4
Bosnia and Herzegovina (ctry.) 40/C3
Bosporus (str.), Turk. 44/D4
Bosporus (riv.), Turk. 51/N6
Bossangoa, CAfr. 76/J6
Bossier City, La, US 93/J4
Boston, Eng, UK 23/H6
Boston (cap.), Ma, US 95/G3
Botād, India 53/K4
Botevgrad, Bul. 41/F4
Bothell, Wa, US 99/C2
Bothnia (gulf), Swe., Fin 20/F3
Botoşani, Rom. 41/H2
Botou, China 59/D3
Botswana (ctry.) 82/D5
Bottrop, Ger. 28/D5
Botucatu, Braz. 108/B2
Bouaflé, C.d'Iv. 78/D5
Bouaké, C.d'Iv. 78/D5
Bouar, CAfr. 76/J6
Boucherville, Qu, Can. 95/P6
Bouguenais, Fr. 32/C3
Bouira, Alg. 76/F1
Boukoumbé, Ben. 79/F4
Boulder, Co, US 93/F2
Boulder City, Nv, US 92/D4
Boulogne-Billancourt, Fr. 30/B6
Boulogne-sur-Mer, Fr. 25/H5
Bourg-en-Bresse, Fr. 36/B5
Bourg-lès-Valence, Fr. 32/F4
Bourges, Fr. 32/E3
Bourgoin-Jallieu, Fr. 32/F4
Bournemouth, Eng, UK 25/E5
Bowling Green, Ky, US 97/G2
Bowling Green, Oh, US 94/D3
Boxmeer, Neth. 28/C5
Boxtel, Neth. 28/C5
Boyabat, Turk. 44/E4
Boynton Beach, Fl, US 97/H5
Bozoum, CAfr. 76/J6
Bozova, Turk. 50/D2
Bozüyük, Turk. 44/D5
Bozyazı, Turk. 49/C1
Bra, It. 33/G4
Bracknell, Eng, UK 25/F4
Brad, Rom. 41/F2
Bradenton, Fl, US 97/H5
Bradford, Pa, US 94/E3
Bradford, Eng, UK 23/G4
Braga, Port. 34/A2
Bragado, Arg. 109/D4
Bragança, Braz. 107/J4
Bragança, Port. 34/B2
Bragança Paulista, Braz. 108/G7
Brahmaputra (riv.), India 63/F2
Brăila, Rom. 41/H3
Braine-l'Alleud, Belg. 31/D2
Braine-le-Comte, Belg. 31/D2
Braintree, Eng, UK 25/G3
Brake, Ger. 29/F2
Brakel, Ger. 29/G5
Brampton, On, Can. 95/T8
Bramsche, Ger. 29/F4
Brandenburg, Ger. 26/G2
Brandon, Fl, US 97/H5
Brandon, Ms, US 97/F3
Braniewo, Pol. 27/K1
Brantford, On, Can. 95/S9
Branzoll (Bronzolo), It. 37/H4
Brasília (cap.), Braz. 107/J7
Braşov, Rom. 41/G3
Brasschaat, Belg. 28/B6
Bratislava (cap.), Slvk. 40/C1
Bratsk, Rus. 47/L4
Brattleboro, Vt, US 95/F3
Braulio Carrillo, CR 103/F4
Braunau am Inn, Aus. 33/K2
Braunschweig, Ger. 29/H4
Brava, Costa (coast), Sp. 35/G2
Brawley, Ca, US 92/D4
Bray, Ire. 22/B5
Brazil (ctry.), Braz. 105/D3
Brazzaville (cap.), Congo 82/C1
Brčko, Bosn. 40/D3
Breaza, Rom. 41/G3
Brecht, Belg. 28/B6
Břeclav, Czh. 33/M2
Breda, Neth. 28/B5
Bregenz, Aus. 37/F3
Bremen, Ger. 29/F2
Bremerhaven, Ger. 29/F1
Bremerton, Wa, US 99/B2
Bremervörde, Ger. 29/G2
Brenham, Tx, US 93/H5
Brentwood, Eng, UK 25/G3
Brescia, It. 33/J4
Bressuire, Fr. 32/C3
Brest, Bela. 27/M2
Brest, Fr. 32/A2
Breves, Braz. 107/H4
Brewer, Me, US 95/G2
Brežice, Slov. 40/B3
Bria, CAfr. 77/K6
Bridgend, Wal, UK 24/C3
Bridgeport, Ct, US 94/F3
Bridgetown (cap.), Bar. 104/G4
Bridgwater, Eng, UK 24/D4
Bridlington, Eng, UK 23/H3
Brieg Brzeg, Pol. 27/J3
Brielle, Neth. 28/B5
Brigham City, Ut, US 90/E5
Brighouse, Eng, UK 23/G4
Brighton, Co, US 93/F3
Brighton, Eng, UK 25/F5
Brikama, Gam. 78/A3
Brilon, Ger. 29/F6
Brindisi, It. 40/C5
Brisbane, Austl. 72/F6
Bristol, Tn, US 97/H2
Bristol, Eng, UK 24/D4
Bristol (chan.), Eng,Wal, UK 24/B4
British Columbia (prov.), Can. 86/D3
Brive-la-Gaillarde, Fr. 32/D4
Brno, Czh. 33/M2
Broadstairs, Eng, UK 25/H4
Brockton, Ma, US 95/G3
Brodnica, Pol. 27/K2
Broken Arrow, Ok, US 93/J3
Broken Hill, Austl. 73/B1
Bromsgrove, Eng, UK 24/D2
Bron, Fr. 36/A6
Bronte, It. 38/D4
Brooke's Point, Phil. 67/E2
Brookfield, Il, US 99/Q16
Brookfield, Wi, US 99/P13
Brookhaven, Ms, US 93/K5
Brooks (range), US 85/F2
Brossard, Qu, Can. 95/P7
Brownfield, Tx, US 93/G4
Brownhills, Eng, UK 25/E1
Brownsville, Tn, US 97/F3
Brownsville, Tx, US 96/D5
Bruay-la-Buissière, Fr. 30/B3
Bruchsal, Ger. 33/H2
Brugge, Belg. 30/C1
Brühl, Ger. 31/F2
Brumado, Braz. 107/K6
Brummen, Neth. 28/D4
Brumunddal, Nor. 20/D3
Brunei (ctry.) 66/D2
Brunssum, Neth. 31/E2
Brunswick, Oh, US 94/D3
Brunswick, Me, US 95/G3
Brunswick, Ga, US 97/H4
Brusque, Braz. 108/B3
Brussels (cap.), Belg. 31/D2

114

Bryan – Chicl

Bryan, Tx, US 93/H5
Bryansk, Rus. 44/E1
Bryce Canyon National Park, Ut, US 92/D3
Brynmawr, Wal, UK 24/C3
Brzesko, Pol. 27/L4
Buala, Sol. 68/E5
Bucak, Turk. 50/B2
Bucaramanga, Col. 106/D2
Buchanan, Libr. 78/C5
Bucharest (cap.), Rom. 41/H4
Buchholz in der Nordheide, Ger. 29/G2
Bückeburg, Ger. 29/G4
Buckley, Wal, UK 23/E5
Bucyrus, Oh, US 94/D3
Budaörs, Hun. 40/D2
Budapest (cap.), Hun. 40/D2
Budaun, India 62/C2
Büdingen, Ger. 33/H1
Buea, Camr. 76/G7
Buenaventura, Col. 106/C3
Buenavista, Mex. 101/Q9
Buenos Aires (cap.), Arg. 109/E3
Buffalo, NY, US 95/V10
Buffalo Grove, Il, US 99/Q15
Buftea, Rom. 41/G3
Buga, Col. 106/C3
Bugaba, Pan. 103/F4
Bugojno, Bosn. 40/C3
Bugul'ma, Rus. 43/M5
Buguruslan, Rus. 45/K1
Bühl, Ger. 37/E2
Buhuşi, Rom. 41/H2
Bujumbura (cap.), Buru. 82/E1
Bukavu, D.R. Congo 82/E1
Bukhoro, Uzb. 46/G6
Bukittinggi, Indo. 66/B4
Bukoba, Tanz. 82/F1
Bulan, Phil. 67/F1
Bulancak, Turk. 44/F4
Bulandshahr, India 62/C2
Bulawayo, Zim. 82/E5
Bulgaria (ctry.) 41/G4
Bullhead City, Az, US 92/D4
Bulukumba, Indo. 67/F5
Bumba, D.R. Congo 77/K7
Bundaberg, Austl. 72/D4
Bünde, Ger. 29/F4
Būndi, India 62/C2
Bunia, D.R. Congo 77/M7
Bunschoten, Neth. 28/C4
Bunya Park, Austl. 72/E6
Buon Me Thuot, Viet. 65/E3
Būr Saʽīd (Port Said), Egypt 49/C4
Būr Sūdān, Sudan 52/C5
Buraydah, SAr. 52/D3
Burbank, Ca, US 92/C4
Burbank, Il, US 99/Q16
Burdur, Turk. 50/B2
Burdwān, India 62/E3
Büren, Ger. 29/F5
Būrewāla, Pak. 53/K2
Burg, Ger. 26/F2
Burgdorf, Ger. 29/H4
Burgess Hill, Eng, UK 25/F5
Burghausen, Ger. 40/A1
Burgos, Sp. 34/D1
Burgstall (Postal), It. 37/H4
Burgsteinfurt, Ger. 29/E4
Burgwedel, Ger. 29/G3
Burhaniye, Turk. 44/C5
Burhānpur, India 62/C3
Burien, Wa, US 99/C3
Buriram, Thai. 65/C3
Burjasot, Sp. 35/E3
Burkburnett, Tx, US 93/H4
Burkina Faso (ctry.) 79/E3
Burlingame, Ca, US 99/K11
Burlington, Ia, US 91/L5
Burlington, NC, US 97/J2
Burlington, On, Can. 95/T9
Burnham-on-Sea, Eng, UK 24/D4
Burnie-Somerset, Austl. 73/C4
Burnley, Eng, UK 23/F4
Burntwood, Eng, UK 25/E1
Burrel, Alb. 40/D5
Burriana, Sp. 35/E3
Bursa, Turk. 44/D4
Burscheid, Ger. 29/E6
Burton, Mi, US 99/E6
Burton upon Trent, Eng, UK 23/G6
Burundi (ctry.) 82/E1
Bury, Eng, UK 23/F4
Bury Saint Edmunds, Eng, UK 25/G2
Bushey, Eng, UK 25/F3
Busko-Zdrój, Pol. 27/L3
Bussum, Neth. 28/C4
Busto Arsizio, It. 33/H4
Butare, Rwa. 82/E1
Butembo, D.R. Congo 77/L7
Butiá, Braz. 108/B4
Butler, Pa, US 94/E3
Butte-Silver Bow County, Mt, US 90/E4
Butterworth, Malay. 66/B2
Butuan, Phil. 67/G2
Buturlinovka, Rus. 45/G2
Butzbach, Ger. 33/H1
Buxtehude, Ger. 29/G2
Buxton, Eng, UK 23/G5
Buy, Rus. 42/J4
Buyant-Uhaa, Mong. 54/G3
Buynaksk, Rus. 45/H4
Büyükçekmece, Turk. 51/M6
Buzău, Rom. 41/H3
Buzuluk, Rus. 45/K1
Bydgoszcz, Pol. 27/J2
Bykhov, Bela. 44/D1
Bytom, Pol. 27/K3
Bytów, Pol. 27/J1

C

Ca Mau, Viet. 65/D4
Caazapá, Par. 109/E2
Cabaiguán, Cuba 103/G1
Cabañaquinta, Sp. 34/C1
Cabanatuan, Phil. 68/B3
Cabimas, Ven. 106/D1
Cabinda, Ang. 82/B2
Cabo Frio, Braz. 108/D2
Cabo San Lucas, Mex. 100/C4
Cabo San Lucas (cape), Mex. 100/C4
Cabot (str.), NS,NF, Can. 87/K4
Cabra, Sp. 34/C4
Cabugao, Phil. 61/J5
Caçador, Braz. 108/B3
Čačak, Yugo. 40/E4
Caçapava, Braz. 108/H8
Cáceres, Braz. 106/G7
Cáceres, Sp. 34/B3
Cacheu, GBis. 78/A3
Cachoeira do Sul, Braz. 108/A4
Cachoeira Paulista, Braz. 108/H7
Cachoeirinha, Braz. 108/B4
Cachoeiro de Itapemirim, Braz. 108/D2
Čadca, Slvk. 27/K4
Cadillac, Mi, US 94/C2
Cadiz, Phil. 67/F1
Cádiz, Sp. 34/B4
Cádiz, Golfo de (gulf), Port.,Sp. 34/B4
Caen, Fr. 32/C2
Caerphilly, Wal, UK 24/C3
Cagliari, It. 38/A3
Cagnes-sur-Mer, Fr. 33/G5
Caguas, PR 104/E3
Cahors, Fr. 32/D4
Cahul, Mol. 41/J3
Caibarién, Cuba 103/G1
Caicó, Braz. 107/L5
Caieiras, Braz. 108/G8
Cairns, Austl. 72/B2
Cairo, Ga, US 97/G4
Cairo (cap.), Egypt 49/B5
Cajamarca, Peru 106/C5
Calabar, Nga. 79/H5
Calabozo, Ven. 106/E2
Calafat, Rom. 40/F4
Calahorra, Sp. 34/E1
Calais, Fr. 30/A2
Calama, Chile 109/C1
Călăraşi, Rom. 41/H3
Calatayud, Sp. 34/E2
Calbayog, Phil. 67/F1
Calcutta, India 62/E3
Caldas da Rainha, Port. 34/A3
Caldas Novas, Braz. 108/B1
Caledon, On, Can. 95/T8
Caleta Olivia, Arg. 109/C6
Calexico, Ca, US 92/D4
Calgary, Ab, Can. 90/E3
Cali, Col. 106/C3
Calicut (Kozhikode), India 62/C5
California (state), US 92/B3
California (gulf), Mex. 92/D5
Callao, Peru 106/C6
Callaway, Fl, US 97/G4
Callosa de Segura, Sp. 35/E3
Caloundra, Austl. 72/D4
Calpulálpan, Mex. 101/L7
Caltagirone, It. 38/D4
Caltanissetta, It. 38/D4
Caluire-et-Cuire, Fr. 36/A6
Calumet City, Il, US 99/Q16
Calviá, Sp. 35/G3
Calvillo, Mex. 100/E4
Cam Pha, Viet. 65/D1
Cam Ranh, Viet. 65/E4
Camaçari, Braz. 107/L6
Camagüey, Cuba 103/G1
Camaiore, It. 33/J5
Camajuani, Cuba 103/G1
Camaquã, Braz. 108/B4
Camargo, Sp. 34/D1
Camas, Sp. 34/B4
Cambará, Braz. 108/B2
Cambé, Braz. 108/B2
Cambodia (ctry.) 65/D3
Cambrai, Fr. 30/C3
Cambridge, Oh, US 94/D3
Cambridge, Md, US 97/J2
Cambridge, Ma, US 95/G3
Cambridge, On, Can. 95/S9
Cambridge, Eng, UK 25/G2
Cambrils, Sp. 35/F2
Camden, NJ, US 94/F4
Cameroon (ctry.), Camr. 76/H7
Cametá, Braz. 107/J4
Camiri, Bol. 106/F8
Camoapa, Nic. 102/E3
Camocim, Braz. 107/K4
Campbell, Ca, US 99/L12
Campbell River, BC, Can. 90/B3
Campbellsville, Ky, US 97/G2
Campeche, Mex. 102/D2
Campeche (bay), Mex. 101/G5
Campina Grande, Braz. 107/L5
Campinas, Braz. 108/F7
Campo Belo, Braz. 108/C2
Campo de la Cruz, Col. 103/H4
Campo Formoso, Braz. 107/K6
Campo Grande, Braz. 107/H8
Campo Largo, Braz. 108/B3
Campo Limpo Paulista, Braz. 108/G8
Campo Maior, Braz. 107/K4
Campo Mourão, Braz. 108/A3
Campoalegre, Col. 106/C3
Campobasso, It. 40/B5
Campos do Jordão, Braz. 108/H7
Campos dos Goytacazes, Braz. 108/D2
Campos Novos, Braz. 108/B3
Çan, Turk. 41/H5
Can Tho, Viet. 65/D4
Canada (ctry.) 86/*
Cañada de Gómez, Arg. 109/D3
Çanakkale, Turk. 41/H5
Canandaigua, NY, US 94/E3
Cananea, Mex. 92/E5
Canary (isls.) 76/B2
Cañas, CR 102/E4
Canaveral (cape), Fl, US 97/H4
Canavieiras, Braz. 107/L7
Canberra (cap.), Austr. 73/D2
Cancún, Mex. 102/E1
Candeias, Braz. 107/L6
Cândido Mota, Braz. 108/B2
Candon, Phil. 61/J5
Canela, Braz. 108/B4
Cangas, Sp. 34/A1
Cangas de Narcea, Sp. 34/B1
Cangzhou, China 59/D3
Canicattì, It. 38/C4
Canindé, Braz. 107/L4
Çankırı, Turk. 44/E4
Cannanore, India 62/C5
Cannes, Fr. 33/G5
Cannock, Eng, UK 24/D1
Canoas, Braz. 108/B4
Canoinhas, Braz. 108/B3
Canosa di Puglia, It. 40/C5
Cantaura, Ven. 106/F2
Canterbury, Eng, UK 25/H4
Canton, Il, US 91/L5
Canton, Ms, US 93/K4
Canton, Oh, US 94/D3
Canton, Mi, US 99/E7
Cantù, It. 33/H4
Canvey Island, Eng, UK 25/G3
Canyon, Tx, US 93/G4
Canyonlands National Park, Ut, US 92/E3
Cao Bang, Viet. 65/D1
Cao Lanh, Viet. 65/D4
Cap-de-la-Madeleine, Qu, Can. 95/F2
Cap-Haïtien, Haiti 103/H2
Capanema, Braz. 107/J4
Capannori, It. 33/J5
Capão Bonito, Braz. 108/B3
Caparica, Port. 35/P10
Cape Breton (isl.), Can. 95/J2
Cape Coast, Gha. 79/E5
Cape Cod Nat'l Seashore, Ma, US 95/G3
Cape Coral, Fl, US 97/H5
Cape Girardeau, Mo, US 93/K3
Cape Hatteras Nat'l Seashore, NC, US 97/K3
Cape Town (cap.), SAfr. 80/L10
Cape Verde (ctry.) 74/J9
Cape York (pen.), Austl. 70/G2
Capelinha, Braz. 108/D1
Capitão Poço, Braz. 107/J4
Čapljina, Bosn. 40/C4
Capua, It. 40/B5
Caracal, Rom. 41/G3
Caracas (cap.), Ven. 106/E1
Caraguatatuba, Braz. 108/H8
Carangola, Braz. 108/D2
Caransebeş, Rom. 40/F3
Carapicuíba, Braz. 108/G8
Caratinga, Braz. 108/D1
Caravaca de la Cruz, Sp. 34/E3
Carazinho, Braz. 109/F2
Carballo, Sp. 34/A1
Carbondale, Pa, US 94/F3
Carbonia, It. 38/A3
Carcagente, Sp. 35/E3
Carcassonne, Fr. 32/E5
Cárdenas, Mex. 102/C2
Cárdenas, Mex. 102/B1
Cárdenas, Cuba 103/F1
Cardiff (cap.), Wal, UK 24/C4
Carei, Rom. 40/F2
Cariacica, Braz. 108/D2
Cariaco, Ven. 104/F5
Cariamanga, Ecu. 106/C4
Caribbean (sea) 84/J8
Caribou, Me, US 95/G2
Caripito, Ven. 104/F5
Carletonville, SAfr. 80/P13
Carlisle, Pa, US 94/E3
Carlisle, Eng, UK 23/F2
Carlos M. De Cespedes, Cuba 103/G1
Carlsbad, NM, US 93/F4
Carlton, Eng, UK 23/G6
Carmagnola, It. 33/G4
Carmichael, Ca, US 99/M9
Carmo do Paranaíba, Braz. 108/C1
Carmona, Sp. 34/C4
Carnaxide, Port. 35/P10
Carnot, CAfr. 76/J7
Carol Stream, Il, US 99/P16
Carolina, PR 104/E3
Caroline (isls), Micr. 68/D4
Carouge, Swi. 36/C5
Carpathian (mts.), Eur. 27/J4
Carpentaria (gulf), Austl. 70/F2
Carpentersville, Il, US 99/P15
Carpentras, Fr. 32/F4
Carpi, It. 33/J4
Carrara, It. 33/J4
Carrickfergus, NI, UK 22/C2
Carrollton, Ga, US 97/G3
Çarşamba, Turk. 44/F4
Carson City (cap.), Nv, US 92/C3
Cartagena, Col. 103/H4
Cartagena, Sp. 35/E4
Cartago, Col. 106/C3
Cartago, CR 103/F4
Cartersville, Ga, US 97/G3
Carthage, Mo, US 93/J3
Carthage (Qarṭājannah) (ruin), Tun. 38/B4
Caruaru, Braz. 107/L5
Carúpano, Ven. 106/F1
Carvin, Fr. 30/B3
Cary, NC, US 97/J3
Cary, Il, US 99/P15
Casa Branca, Braz. 108/F6
Casa Grande, Az, US 92/E4
Casablanca, Mor. 76/D1
Casal di Principe, It. 38/D2
Casale Monferrato, It. 33/H4
Casarano, It. 39/F2
Cascade (range), Wa, US 90/C5
Cascade-Fairwood, Or, US 99/C3
Cascais, Port. 35/P10
Cascavel, Braz. 107/L4
Cascavel, Braz. 109/F1
Cascina, It. 33/J5
Caserta, It. 40/B5
Casilda, Arg. 109/D3
Casper, Wy, US 91/G5
Caspian (sea), Asia 46/E5
Cassilândia, Braz. 108/B1
Cassino, It. 40/A5
Castanhal, Braz. 107/J4
Castaños, Mex. 96/C5
Castel del Piano, It. 38/C1
Castellammare di Stabia, It. 40/B5
Castellar del Vallès, Sp. 35/G2
Castelldefels, Sp. 35/K7
Castellón de la Plana, Sp. 35/E3
Castelo Branco, Port. 34/B3
Castelvetrano, It. 38/C4
Castilla, Peru 106/B5
Castleford, Eng, UK 23/G4
Castres, Fr. 32/E5
Castricum, Neth. 28/B3
Castries (cap.), StL. 104/F4
Castro, Chile 109/B5
Castro, Braz. 108/B3
Castro Valley, Ca, US 99/K11
Castrop-Rauxel, Ger. 29/E5
Castrovillari, It. 38/E3
Catacamas, Hon. 102/E3
Cataguases, Braz. 108/L6
Cataingan, Phil. 67/F1
Catalão, Braz. 108/C1
Catamarca, Arg. 109/C2
Catanduva, Braz. 108/B2
Catania, It. 38/D4
Catanzaro, It. 38/E3
Catarman, Phil. 67/F1
Catemaco, Mex. 102/C2
Caterham and Warlingham, Eng, UK 25/F4
Cativá, Pan. 103/G4
Caucaia, Braz. 107/L4
Caucasia, Col. 103/H5
Caucasus (mts.), Geo. 45/G4
Cauquenes, Chile 109/B4
Cavaillon, Fr. 32/F5
Caxambu, Braz. 108/J6
Caxias, Braz. 107/K4
Caxias do Sul, Braz. 108/B4
Cayce, SC, US 97/H3
Çayeli, Turk. 45/G4
Cayenne (cap.), FrG. 107/H3
Cayman (isls.), UK 103/F2
Cazin, Bosn. 40/B3
Ceará-Mirim, Braz. 107/L5
Cebu, Phil. 67/F1
Ceccano, It. 38/C2
Cecina, It. 33/J5
Cedar City, Ut, US 92/D3
Cegléd, Hun. 40/D2
Celaya, Mex. 101/E4
Celebes (isl.), Indo. 67/E4
Celebes (sea), Asia 67/F3
Celina, Oh, US 94/C3
Celle, Ger. 29/H3
Centenario, Arg. 109/C4
Center Point, Al, US 97/G3
Cento, It. 33/J4
Central African Republic (ctry.) 77/J6
Central Siberian (plat.), Rus. 47/L3
Centralia, Il, US 93/K3
Centralia, Wa, US 90/C4
Cerdanyola del Vallès, Sp. 35/L7
Ceres, Braz. 107/J7
Ceres, SAfr. 80/L10
Cereté, Col. 103/H4
Cergy, Fr. 30/B5
Cerignola, It. 40/B5
Çerkezköy, Turk. 41/J5
Çermik, Turk. 50/D2
Cernavodă, Rom. 41/J3
Cerro Azul, Mex. 102/B1
Cerro de Pasco, Peru 106/C6
Cervia, It. 33/K4
Cesena, It. 33/K4
Cesenatico, It. 33/K4
Cēsis, Lat. 42/E4
České Budějovice, Czh. 33/L2
Çeşme, Turk. 39/K3
Cetinje, Yugo. 40/D4
Ceuta, Sp. 34/C5
Ceyhan, Turk. 49/D1
Ceylânpınar, Turk. 50/E2
Ceylon (isl.), SrL. 62/D6
Chachapoyas, Peru 106/C5
Chachoengsao, Thai. 65/C3
Chad (lake), Afr. 76/H5
Chad (ctry.) 77/J4
Chālakudi, India 62/C5
Chalatenango, ESal. 102/D3
Chalco, Mex. 101/R10
Chalfont Saint Peter, Eng, UK 25/F3
Challans, Fr. 32/C3
Chalon-sur-Saône, Fr. 36/A4
Châlons-sur-Marne, Fr. 31/D6
Chālūs, Iran 51/G2
Cham, Ger. 33/K2
Chaman, Pak. 53/J2
Chamba, India 53/L2
Chambas, Cuba 103/G1
Chambersburg, Pa, US 94/E4
Chambéry, Fr. 32/F4
Chambly, Qu, Can. 95/P7
Champaign, Il, US 91/L5
Champlain (lake), Can.,US 94/F2
Champotón, Mex. 102/D2
Champs-sur-Marne, Fr. 30/B6
Chandausi, India 62/C2
Chanderi, India 62/C3
Chandīgarh, India 53/L2
Chandrapur, India 62/C4
Changchun, China 59/F2
Changde, China 61/F2
Changhua, Tai. 61/J3
Changhŭng, SKor. 58/D5
Changsha, China 61/G2
Changshu, China 59/L8
Changshun, China 61/E3
Changsŏng, SKor. 58/D5
Changsŭngp'o, SKor. 58/E5
Ch'angwŏn, SKor. 56/A3
Changzhi, China 59/C3
Changzhou, China 59/K8
Chanthaburi, Thai. 65/C3
Chanute, Ks, US 93/J3
Chapala, Mex. 100/E4
Chapayevsk, Rus. 45/J1
Chapecó, Braz. 108/A3
Chapel Hill, NC, US 97/J3
Chapeltown, Eng, UK 23/G5
Charata, Arg. 109/D2
Chārīkār, Afg. 53/J1
Chärjew, Trkm. 46/G6
Charleroi, Belg. 31/D3
Charleston, Il, US 97/F2
Charleston, SC, US 97/J3
Charleston (cap.), WV, US 94/D4
Charleville-Mézières, Fr. 31/D4
Charlotte, NC, US 97/H3
Charlotte Amalie, USVI 104/E3
Charlottetown (cap.), PE, Can. 95/J2
Chartres, Fr. 32/D2
Chascomús, Arg. 109/E4
Château-Thierry, Fr. 30/C5
Châteaudun, Fr. 32/D2
Châteauguay, Qu, Can. 95/N7
Châteauroux, Fr. 32/D3
Châtelet, Belg. 31/D3
Châtellerault, Fr. 32/D3
Chatham, NB, Can. 95/H2
Chatham, On, Can. 94/D3
Chatham, Eng, UK 25/G4
Chattarpur, India 62/E4
Chattanooga, Tn, US 97/G3
Chau Doc, Viet. 65/D4
Chaudfontaine, Belg. 31/E2
Chauk, Myan. 60/B4
Chaumont, Fr. 36/B1
Chaykovskiy, Rus. 43/M4
Cheb, Czh. 33/K1
Cheboksary, Rus. 43/K4
Chech'ŏn, SKor. 56/A2
Cheektowaga, NY, US 95/V10
Chegdomyn, Rus. 55/L1
Chegutu, Zim. 82/F4
Cheju, SKor. 55/K5
Chełm, Pol. 27/M3
Chełmno, Pol. 27/K2
Chelmsford, Eng, UK 25/G3
Chełmża, Pol. 27/K2
Cheltenham, Eng, UK 24/D3
Chelyabinsk, Rus. 43/P5
Chemnitz, Ger. 26/G3
Chennai (Madras), India 62/D5
Chenôve, Fr. 36/A3
Chenzhou, China 61/G3
Cherbourg, Fr. 32/C2
Cherchell, Alg. 76/F1
Cheremkhovo, Rus. 54/E1
Cherepovets, Rus. 42/H4
Cherkasy, Ukr. 44/E2
Cherkessk, Rus. 45/G3
Chernihiv, Ukr. 44/D2
Chernivtsi, Ukr. 41/G1
Chernushka, Rus. 43/N4
Cherven Bryag, Bul. 41/G4
Chervonohrad, Ukr. 27/N3
Chesapeake (bay), US 89/L4
Chesham, Eng, UK 25/F3
Cheshunt, Eng, UK 25/F3
Chester, Pa, US 94/F4
Chester, Eng, UK 23/F5
Chester-le-Street, Eng, UK 23/G2
Chesterfield, Eng, UK 23/G5
Chetumal, Mex. 102/D2
Cheyenne (cap.), Wy, US 91/G5
Chhatarpur, India 62/C3
Chhindwāra, India 62/C3
Chiai, Tai. 61/J4
Chiang Mai, Thai. 65/B2
Chiapa de Corzo, Mex. 102/C2
Chiat'ura, Geo. 45/G4
Chiautempan, Mex. 101/L7
Chiavari, It. 33/H4
Chiba, Japan 57/G3
Chibuto, Moz. 81/F2
Chicago, Il, US 99/Q16
Chicago Heights, Il, US 99/Q16
Chicago Ridge, Il, US 99/Q16
Chīchāwatni, Pak. 53/K2
Chichester, Eng, UK 25/F5
Chichibu, Japan 57/F3
Chichicastenango, Guat. 102/D3
Chichigalpa, Nic. 102/E3
Chickasha, Ok, US 93/H4
Chiclana de la Frontera, Sp. 34/B4

115
Chicl – Dayrū
Chiclayo, Peru 106/C5
Chico, Ca, US 92/B3
Chicoloapan, Mex. 101/R10
Chicopee, Ma, US 95/F3
Chieti, It. 40/B4
Chigasaki, Japan 57/F3
Chigorodó, Col. 103/G5
Chihuahua, Mex. 96/B4
Chikballāpur, India 62/C5
Chikhli, India 62/C3
Chikmagalūr, India 62/C5
Chilapa de Álvarez, Mex. 102/B2
Chilaw, SrL. 62/C6
Chile (ctry.), Chile 105/B6
Chilecito, Arg. 109/C2
Chililabombwe, Zam. 82/E3
Chillán, Chile 109/B4
Chilliwack, BC, Can. 90/C3
Chilpancingo de los Bravos, Mex. 102/B2
Chimalhuacán, Mex. 101/R10
Chimaltenango, Guat. 102/D3
Chimbay, Uzb. 46/F5
Chimbote, Peru 106/C5
Chimichaqua, Col. 103/H4
Chimoio, Moz. 82/F4
China (ctry.) 48/J6
Chinandega, Nic. 102/E3
Chincha Alta, Peru 106/C6
Chingleput, India 62/C5
Chingola, Zam. 82/E3
Chinhae, SKor. 56/A3
Chinhoyi, Zim. 82/F4
Chiniot, Pak. 53/K2
Chinju, SKor. 58/E5
Chino, Japan 57/F3
Chioggia, It. 33/K4
Chipata, Zam. 82/F3
Chipiona, Sp. 34/B4
Chiplūn, India 62/B4
Chippenham, Eng, UK 24/D4
Chiquimula, Guat. 102/D3
Chiquimulilla, Guat. 102/D3
Chiquinquirá, Col. 106/D2
Chīrāla, India 62/D4
Chirchiq, Uzb. 46/G5
Chirripó, CR 103/F4
Chishtiān Mandi, Pak. 53/K3
Chişinău (cap.), Mol. 41/J2
Chistopol', Rus. 43/L5
Chita, Rus. 54/G1
Chitose, Japan 55/N3
Chitradurga, India 62/C5
Chitrakut, India 62/D2
Chitré, Pan. 103/F5
Chittagong, Bang. 60/A4
Chittoor, India 62/C5
Chitungwiza, Zim. 82/F4
Chivasso, It. 33/G4
Chivilcoy, Arg. 109/D3
Chlef, Alg. 76/F1
Choch'iwŏn, SKor. 58/D4
Chodavaram, India 62/D4
Chodov, Czh. 33/K1
Chodzież, Pol. 27/J2
Chōfu, Japan 57/F3
Choisy-le-Roi, Fr. 30/B6
Chojnice, Pol. 27/J2
Cholet, Fr. 32/C3
Cholula de Rivadabia, Mex. 101/L7
Choluteca, Hon. 102/E3
Choma, Zam. 82/E4
Chŏmch'on, SKor. 56/A2
Chomutov, Czh. 33/K1
Chon Buri, Thai. 65/C3
Ch'ŏnan, SKor. 58/D4
Chone, Ecu. 106/B4
Ch'ŏngjin, NKor. 58/E2
Chŏngju, SKor. 58/D5
Ch'ŏngju, SKor. 58/D4
Chongqing, China 61/E2
Ch'ŏngsong, SKor. 56/A2
Chŏnju, SKor. 58/D5
Chorley, Eng, UK 23/F4
Chortkiv, Ukr. 44/C2
Chorzów, Pol. 27/K3
Chōshi, Japan 57/G3
Choszczno, Pol. 27/H2
Chota Nagpur (plat.), India 62/D3
Choybalsan, Mong. 54/G2
Christchurch, Eng, UK 25/E5
Christchurch, NZ 71/R11
Chrudim, Czh. 33/L2
Chrzanów, Pol. 27/K3
Chukchi (pen.), Rus. 47/T3
Chula Vista, Ca, US 92/C4
Chulucanas, Peru 106/B5
Ch'unch'ŏn, SKor. 58/D4
Ch'ungju, SKor. 58/D4
Ch'ungmu, SKor. 56/A3
Chuquicamata, Chile 109/C1
Chur, Swi. 37/F4
Churachandpur, India 60/B3
Churu, India 62/B2
Chusovoy, Rus. 43/N4
Chuxiong, China 60/D3
Chuzhou, China 61/H1
Ciadîr-Lunga, Mol. 41/J2
Ciamis, Indo. 66/C5
Ciampino, It. 38/C2
Cianjur, Indo. 66/C5
Cicero, Il, US 99/Q16
Ciechanów, Pol. 27/L2
Ciego de Ávila, Cuba 103/G1
Ciénaga, Col. 103/H4
Ciénaga de Oro, Col. 103/H4
Cienfuegos, Cuba 103/F1
Cieplice Śląskie Zdrój, Pol. 27/H3
Cieszyn, Pol. 27/K4
Cieza, Sp. 34/E3
Cifuentes, Cuba 103/F1
Cihanbeyli, Turk. 50/C2
Cijulang, Indo. 66/C5
Cilacap, Indo. 66/C5
Cîmpia Turzii, Rom. 41/F2
Cîmpina, Rom. 41/G3
Cîmpulung, Rom. 41/G3
Cîmpulung Moldovenesc, Rom. 41/G2
Cincinnati, Oh, US 97/G2
Çine, Turk. 50/B2
Cintalapa de Figueroa, Mex. 102/C2
Cipolletti, Arg. 109/C4
Cirebon, Indo. 66/C5
Cirencester, Eng, UK 24/E3
Cisnădie, Rom. 41/G3
Cisterna di Latina, It. 38/C2
Citlaltépetl (vol.), Mex. 101/M7
Citrus Heights, Ca, US 99/M9
Città di Castello, It. 33/K5
Ciudad Acuña, Mex. 93/G5
Ciudad Altamirano, Mex. 101/E5
Ciudad Bolívar, Ven. 106/F2
Ciudad Camargo, Mex. 96/B5
Ciudad Constitución, Mex. 100/C3
Ciudad de Dolores Hidalgo, Mex. 101/E4
Ciudad de Río Grande, Mex. 100/E4
Ciudad del Carmen, Mex. 102/D2
Ciudad Delicias, Mex. 96/B4
Ciudad Fernández, Mex. 102/B1
Ciudad Frontera, Mex. 96/C5
Ciudad Guayana, Ven. 106/F2
Ciudad Guzmán, Mex. 100/E5
Ciudad Hidalgo, Mex. 101/E5
Ciudad Ixtepec, Mex. 102/C2
Ciudad Juárez, Mex. 92/F5
Ciudad Lerdo, Mex. 100/E3
Ciudad Madero, Mex. 102/B1
Ciudad Mante, Mex. 102/B1
Ciudad Mendoza, Mex. 101/M8
Ciudad Miguel Alemán, Mex. 96/D5
Ciudad Obregón, Mex. 100/C3
Ciudad Ojeda, Ven. 106/D1
Ciudad Real, Sp. 34/D3
Ciudad Rodrigo, Sp. 34/B2
Ciudad Serdán, Mex. 101/M8
Ciudad Valles, Mex. 102/B1
Ciudad Victoria, Mex. 101/F4
Ciutadella de Menorca, Sp. 35/G3
Civitavecchia, It. 38/B1
Cixi, China 59/L9
Cizre, Turk. 50/E2
Claremont, NH, US 95/F3
Claremore, Ok, US 93/J3
Clarksburg, WV, US 97/H2
Clarksdale, Ms, US 93/K4
Clarksville, Tn, US 97/G2
Clausthal-Zellerfeld, Ger. 29/H5
Claveria, Phil. 61/J5
Clawson, Mi, US 99/F6
Clay Cross-North Wingfield, Eng, UK 23/G5
Clearwater, Fl, US 97/H5
Cleburne, Tx, US 93/H4
Cleethorpes, Eng, UK 23/H4
Clemson, SC, US 97/H3
Clermont-Ferrand, Fr. 32/E4
Clevedon, Eng, UK 24/D4
Cleveland, Ms, US 93/K4
Cleveland, Oh, US 94/D3
Cleveland, Tn, US 97/G3
Clichy, Fr. 30/B6
Clinton, Ms, US 93/K4
Clinton, Ok, US 93/H4
Clinton, Ia, US 91/L5
Clinton, Mi, US 99/G6
Clonmel, Ire. 21/B10
Cloppenburg, Ger. 29/F3
Clorinda, Arg. 109/E2
Clovis, Ca, US 92/C3
Clovis, NM, US 93/G4
Cluj-Napoca, Rom. 41/F2
Cluses, Fr. 36/C5
Clyde, Firth of (inlet), Sc, UK 22/C1
Coacalco, Mex. 101/Q9
Coachella, Ca, US 92/C4
Coalville, Eng, UK 23/G6
Coari, Braz. 106/F4
Coast (mts.), Can.,US 90/A2
Coast Ranges (range), Ca, US 88/B4
Coatepec, Mex. 101/N7
Coatzacoalcos, Mex. 102/C2
Cobán, Guat. 102/D3
Cobija, Bol. 106/E6
Cobourg, On, Can. 94/E3
Coburg, Ger. 33/J1
Cochabamba, Bol. 106/E7
Cochin, India 62/C6
Cocoa, Fl, US 97/H4
Codlea, Rom. 41/G3
Codó, Braz. 107/K4
Coelho Neto, Braz. 107/K4
Coesfeld, Ger. 29/E5
Coffeyville, Ks, US 93/J3
Coffs Harbour, Austl. 73/E1
Cognac, Fr. 32/C4
Coihaique, Chile 109/B6
Coimbatore, India 62/C5
Coimbra, Port. 34/A2
Coin, Sp. 34/C4
Cojutepeque, ESal. 102/D3
Colatina, Braz. 108/D1
Colchester, Eng, UK 25/G3
Coldwater, Mi, US 94/C3
Çölemerik, Turk. 51/E2
Coleraine, NI, UK 22/B1
Colima, Mex. 100/E5
Collado-Villalba, Sp. 35/N8
College, Ak, US 85/J3
College Station, Tx, US 93/H5
Collegno, It. 33/G4
Collierville, Tn, US 93/K4
Collingwood, On, Can. 94/D2
Colmar, Fr. 36/D1
Colmenar Viejo, Sp. 35/N8
Colne, Eng, UK 23/F4
Cologne (Köln), Ger. 31/F2
Colombia (ctry.), Col. 106/D3
Colombo, Braz. 108/B3
Colombo (cap.), SrL. 62/C6
Colomiers, Fr. 32/D5
Colón, Cuba 103/F1
Colón, Pan. 103/G4
Colorado (riv.), Tx, US 96/C3
Colorado (riv.), Arg. 109/C4
Colorado (state), US 92/F3
Colorado (riv.), US 88/D5
Colorado Springs, Co, US 93/F3
Colquiri, Bol. 106/E7
Columbia, Mo, US 93/J3
Columbia, Md, US 97/J2
Columbia, Tn, US 97/G3
Columbia (plat.), US 90/C2
Columbia (cap.), SC, US 97/H3
Columbia (riv.), Or,Wa, US 90/C4
Columbus, Ne, US 91/J5
Columbus, Ga, US 97/G3
Columbus, Ms, US 97/F3
Columbus, In, US 97/G2
Columbus (cap.), Oh, US 94/D4
Colwyn Bay, Wal, UK 22/E5
Comalcalco, Mex. 102/C2
Comănești, Rom. 41/H2
Comayagua, Hon. 102/E3
Combs-la-Ville, Fr. 30/B6
Comé, Ben. 79/F5
Comendador, DRep. 103/J2
Comilla, Bang. 63/F3
Comines, Belg. 30/B2
Comitán de Domínguez, Mex. 102/C2
Como, It. 37/F6
Comodoro Rivadavia, Arg. 109/C6
Comoros (ctry.) 81/G5
Compiègne, Fr. 30/B5
Compostela, Mex. 100/D4
Comrat, Mol. 41/J2
Conakry (cap.), Gui. 78/B4
Concarneau, Fr. 32/B3
Conceição do Araguaia, Braz. 107/J5
Concepción, Chile 109/B4
Concepción, Arg. 109/C2
Concepción, Par. 109/E1
Concepción del Uruguay, Arg. 109/E3
Conchal, Braz. 108/F7
Concord, NC, US 97/H3
Concord, Ca, US 99/K11
Concord (cap.), NH, US 95/G3
Concordia, Arg. 109/E3
Concórdia, Braz. 108/A3
Condado, Cuba 103/G1
Conegliano, It. 33/K4
Congleton, Eng, UK 23/F5
Congo (basin), D.R. Congo 77/K7
Congo (riv.), D.R. Congo 82/C1
Congo, Democratic Republic of the (ctry.) 74/E5
Congo, Republic of (ctry.) 74/D5
Congonhas, Braz. 108/D2
Conisbrough, Eng, UK 23/G5
Conneaut, Oh, US 94/D3
Connecticut (state), US 95/F3
Connellsville, Pa, US 94/E3
Connersville, In, US 97/G2
Conroe, Tx, US 93/J5
Conselheiro Lafaiete, Braz. 108/D2
Consett, Eng, UK 23/G2
Consolación del Sur, Cuba 103/F1
Constance (Bodensee) (lake), Ger.,Swi. 37/F2
Constanța, Rom. 41/J3
Constantine, Alg. 76/G1
Constitución, Chile 109/B4
Contai, India 62/E3
Contegem, Braz. 108/C1
Contramaestre, Cuba 103/G1
Conversano, It. 40/C5
Conway, Ar, US 93/J4
Conway, SC, US 97/J3
Conway, NH, US 95/G3
Cooch Behār, India 62/E2
Cook (mt.), NZ 71/R11
Cookeville, Tn, US 97/G2
Coonoor, India 62/C5
Coos Bay, Or, US 90/B5
Copenhagen (cap.), Den. 26/G1
Copertino, It. 39/F2
Copiapó, Chile 109/B2
Copperas Cove, Tx, US 93/H5
Coquimbo, Chile 109/B2
Coquitlam, BC, Can. 90/C3
Corabia, Rom. 41/G4
Coral (sea) 68/E6
Coral Gables, Fl, US 97/H5
Coral Sea Islands Territory (dpcy.), Austl. 72/B1
Coral Springs, Fl, US 97/H5
Corato, It. 40/C5
Corbeil-Essonnes, Fr. 32/E2
Corby, Eng, UK 25/F2
Corcovado, CR 103/E4
Cordeiro, Braz. 108/D2
Cordele, Ga, US 97/H4
Córdoba, Arg. 109/D3
Córdoba, Mex. 101/N8
Córdoba, Sp. 34/C4
Coria del Río, Sp. 34/B4
Corinth, Ms, US 97/F3
Corinth (Kórinthos) (ruin), Gre. 39/H4
Corinto, Nic. 102/E3
Corinto, Braz. 108/C1
Cork, Ire. 21/A11
Çorlu, Turk. 41/H5
Cornélio Procópio, Braz. 108/B2
Cornella, Sp. 35/L7
Corner Brook, Nf, Can. 95/K1
Corning, NY, US 94/E3
Cornwall, On, Can. 94/F2
Coro, Ven. 106/E1
Coroatá, Braz. 107/K4
Coromandel, Braz. 108/C1
Coromandel (coast), India 62/D5
Coron, Phil. 67/F1
Coronel, Chile 109/B4
Coronel Fabriciano, Braz. 108/D1
Coronel Oviedo, Par. 109/E2
Coronel Pringles, Arg. 109/D4
Coronel Suárez, Arg. 109/D4
Corozal, Col. 103/H4
Corozal, Belz. 102/D2
Corpus Christi, Tx, US 96/D5
Corralillo, Cuba 103/F1
Corrientes, Arg. 109/E2
Corsica (isl.), Fr. 38/A1
Corsicana, Tx, US 93/H4
Cortez, Co, US 92/E3
Cortland, NY, US 94/E3
Çorum, Turk. 44/E4
Corumbá, Braz. 106/G7
Corvallis, Or, US 90/C4
Cosamaloapan, Mex. 101/P8
Cosenza, It. 38/E3
Coshocton, Oh, US 94/D3
Coslada, Sp. 35/N9
Cosmópolis, Braz. 108/F7
Cosquín, Arg. 109/D3
Cossato, It. 33/H4
Costa Rica (ctry.), CR 103/F4
Cotabato, Phil. 67/F2
Côte D'Ivoire (ctry.) 78/D5
Côte-Saint-Luc, Qu, Can. 95/N7
Cotia, Braz. 108/G8
Cotonou, Ben. 79/F5
Cottbus, Ger. 27/H3
Coudekerque-Branche, Fr. 30/B1
Courcelles, Belg. 31/D3
Cournon-D'Auvergne, Fr. 32/E4
Courtenay, BC, Can. 86/D4
Coventry, Eng, UK 25/E2
Covilhã, Port. 34/B2
Covington, Ga, US 97/H3
Covington, Ky, US 97/G2
Cowes, Eng, UK 25/E5
Coxim, Braz. 107/H7
Coyotepec, Mex. 101/K7
Cozumel, Mex. 102/E1
Crailsheim, Ger. 33/J2
Craiova, Rom. 41/F3
Cramlington, Eng, UK 23/G1
Cran-Gevrier, Fr. 36/C6
Cranbourne, Austl. 73/G6
Cranbrook, BC, Can. 90/E3
Crater (lake), Or, US 92/B2
Crater Lake National Park, Or, US 92/B2
Crateús, Braz. 107/K5
Crato, Braz. 107/L5
Cravinhos, Braz. 108/C2
Crawfordsville, In, US 97/G1
Crawley, Eng, UK 25/F4
Creil, Fr. 30/B5
Crema, It. 33/H4
Cremona, It. 33/J4
Crest Hill, Il, US 99/P16
Crestview, Fl, US 97/G4
Crete (isl.), Gre. 39/J5
Créteil, Fr. 30/B6
Creutzwald-la-Croix, Fr. 31/F5
Crevillente, Sp. 35/E3
Crewe, Eng, UK 23/F5
Criciúma, Braz. 108/B4
Crimean (pen.), Ukr. 44/E3
Cristalina, Braz. 107/J7
Croatia (ctry.) 40/C3
Crosby, Eng, UK 23/E5
Crotone, It. 39/E3
Crowborough, Eng, UK 25/G4
Crowley, La, US 93/J5
Crown Point, In, US 94/C3
Crowthorne, Eng, UK 25/F4
Cruz Alta, Braz. 109/F2
Cruz das Almas, Braz. 107/L6
Cruz del Eje, Arg. 109/D3
Cruzeiro, Braz. 108/J7
Cruzeiro do Sul, Braz. 106/D5
Crystal Lake, Il, US 99/P15
Csongrád, Hun. 40/E2
Cuart de Poblet, Sp. 35/E3
Cuauhtémoc, Mex. 96/B4
Cuautitlán, Mex. 101/Q9
Cuautitlán Izcalli, Mex. 101/Q9
Cuautla, Mex. 101/L8
Cuba (ctry.), Cuba 103/F1
Cubatão, Braz. 108/G8
Çubuk, Turk. 44/E4
Cúcuta, Col. 103/H5
Cudahy, Wi, US 99/Q14
Cuddapah, India 62/C5
Cuenca, Ecu. 106/C4
Cuenca, Sp. 34/D2
Cuernavaca, Mex. 101/K8
Cueto, Cuba 103/H1
Cugir, Rom. 41/F3
Cuiabá, Braz. 107/G7
Cuijk, Neth. 28/C5
Cuilapa, Guat. 102/D3
Culemborg, Neth. 28/C5
Culiacán Rosales, Mex. 100/D3
Cullera, Sp. 35/E3
Culleredo, Sp. 34/A1
Cullman, Al, US 97/G3
Cumaná, Ven. 106/F1
Cumberland, Md, US 97/J2
Çumra, Turk. 50/C2
Cuneo, It. 33/G4
Cupertino, Ca, US 99/K12
Cuprija, Yugo. 40/E4
Ćuprija, Yugo. 40/E4
Curanilahue, Chile 109/B4
Curepipe, Mrts. 81/T15
Curicó, Chile 109/B3
Curitiba, Braz. 108/B3
Curitibanos, Braz. 108/B3
Currais Novos, Braz. 107/L5
Curtea de Argeș, Rom. 41/G3
Curup, Indo. 66/B4
Cururupu, Braz. 107/K4
Curuzú Cuatiá, Arg. 109/E2
Curvelo, Braz. 108/C1
Cusco, Peru 106/D6
Cutral-Có, Arg. 109/C4
Cuttack, India 62/E3
Cuxhaven, Ger. 29/F1
Cuyo, Phil. 67/F1
Cwmbran, Wal, UK 24/C3
Cyprus (ctry.) 49/C2
Czech Republic (ctry.) 27/H4
Częstochowa, Pol. 27/K3
Człuchów, Pol. 27/J2

D

Da Hinggan (mts.), China 55/J2
Da Lat, Viet. 65/E4
Da Nang, Viet. 65/E2
Da Xian, China 61/E2
Da'an, China 55/J2
Dabas, Hun. 40/D2
Dabou, C.d'Iv. 78/D5
Dabra, India 62/C2
Dąbrowa Górnicza, Pol. 27/K3
Dachau, Ger. 37/H1
Dādu, Pak. 62/A2
Dafang, China 60/E3
Dagana, Sen. 78/B2
Dagupan, Phil. 68/B3
Daharki, Pak. 62/A2
Dahūk, Iraq 51/E2
Daigo, Japan 57/G2
Daimiel, Sp. 34/D3
Dajabón, DRep. 103/J2
Dakar (cap.), Sen. 78/A3
Dakoro, Niger 79/G3
Dakovica, Yugo. 40/E4
Dakovo, Cro. 40/D3
Dalaman, Turk. 50/B2
Dalandzadgad, Mong. 54/E3
Dalfsen, Neth. 28/D3
Dali, China 60/D3
Dalian, China 58/A3
Dallas, Tx, US 93/H4
Dal'negorsk, Rus. 55/M3
Dal'nerechensk, Rus. 55/L2
Daloa, C.d'Iv. 78/D5
Dalton, Ga, US 97/G3
Daltonganj, India 62/D3
Daly City, Ca, US 99/J11
Damān, India 62/B3
Damanhūr, Egypt 49/B4
Damascus (cap.), Syria 49/E3
Damietta (Dumyāţ), Egypt 49/B4
Damoh, India 62/C3
Danané, C.d'Iv. 78/C5
Dandong, China 58/C2
Dangriga, Belz. 102/D2
Dangyang, China 61/F2
Danilov, Rus. 42/J4
Dankov, Rus. 44/F1
Danlí, Hon. 102/E3
Danube (riv.), Eur. 18/F4
Danube (delta), Rom. 41/J3
Danube, Mouths of the (delta), Rom.,Ukr. 41/J3
Danville, Ky, US 97/G2
Danville, Il, US 97/G1
Danville, Ca, US 99/K11
Dapaong, Togo 79/F4
Daphne, Al, US 97/G4
Daqing, China 55/K2
Dar es Salaam (cap.), Tanz. 82/G2
Dar'ā, Syria 49/E3
Daraga, Phil. 67/F1
Dārayyā, Syria 49/E3
Darbhanga, India 62/E2
Dardanelles (str.), Turk. 44/C4
Darhan, Mong. 54/F2
Darien, Il, US 99/P16
Darjiling, India 62/E2
Darling (riv.), Austl. 71/G6
Darlington, Eng, UK 23/G2
Darłowo, Pol. 27/J1
Darmstadt, Ger. 33/H2
Darnah, Libya 77/K1
Dartford, Eng, UK 25/G4
Dartmouth, NS, Can. 95/J2
Daru, PNG 68/D5
Daruvar, Cro. 40/C3
Darwen, Eng, UK 23/F4
Darwin, Austl. 68/C6
Dashhowuz, Trkm. 46/F5
Dassa-Zoumé, Ben. 79/F5
Datia, India 62/C2
Datong, China 59/C2
Datteln, Ger. 29/E5
Daugavpils, Lat. 42/E5
Daund, India 62/B4
Dāvangere, India 62/C5
Davao, Phil. 67/G2
Davenport, Ia, US 91/L5
Daventry, Eng, UK 25/E2
Daveyton, SAfr. 80/Q13
David, Pan. 103/F4
Davis, Ca, US 99/L9
Davlekanovo, Rus. 43/M5
Dawei (Tavoy), Myan. 65/B3
Dax, Fr. 32/C5
Dayong, China 61/F2
Dayrūt, Egypt 50/B5

116

Dayto – Evans

Daytona Beach, Fl, US 97/H4
De Aar, SAfr. 80/D3
De Bilt, Neth. 28/C4
De Kalb, Il, US 91/L5
De Land, Fl, US 97/H4
De Ridder, La, US 93/J5
Dead (sea), Isr.,Jor. 49/D4
Deal, Eng, UK 25/H4
Deán Funes, Arg. 109/D3
Dearborn, Mi, US 99/F7
Dearborn Heights, Mi, US 99/F7
Death Valley National Park, US 92/C3
Debar, FYROM 40/E5
Dębica, Pol. 27/L3
Dęblin, Pol. 27/L3
Debre Birhan, Eth. 77/N6
Debre Mark'os, Eth. 77/N5
Debre Tabor, Eth. 77/N5
Debre Zeyit, Eth. 77/N6
Debrecen, Hun. 40/E2
Decatur, Il, US 91/L6
Decatur, Al, US 97/G3
Decatur, Ga, US 97/G3
Děčín, Czh. 27/H3
Décines-Charpieu, Fr. 36/A6
Dédougou, Burk. 78/E3
Dedza, Malw. 82/F3
Deerfield, Il, US 99/P15
Defiance, Oh, US 94/C3
Deggendorf, Ger. 33/K2
Dehra Dūn, India 53/L2
Dehri, India 62/D3
Deinze, Belg. 28/A7
Dej, Rom. 41/F2
Dekemhare (Dek'emhāre), Erit. 52/C5
Del Rio, Tx, US 93/G5
Delano, Ca, US 92/C4
Delaware, Oh, US 94/D3
Delaware (bay), NJ, US 94/F4
Delaware (state), US 94/F4
Delaware (riv.), US 94/F3
Delbrück, Ger. 29/F5
Delčevo, FYROM 40/F5
Delémont, Swi. 36/D3
Delft, Neth. 28/B4
Delfzijl, Neth. 28/D2
Delhi, India 62/C2
Delmenhorst, Ger. 29/F2
Delphi (Dhelfoí) (ruin), Gre. 39/H3
Delray Beach, Fl, US 97/H5
Deltona, Fl, US 97/H4
Deming, NM, US 100/D1
Demirci, Turk. 44/D5
Demmin, Ger. 26/G2
Demopolis, Al, US 97/G3
Den Helder, Neth. 28/B3
Denain, Fr. 30/C3
Denali National Park and Preserve, Ak, US 85/H3
Denderleeuw, Belg. 31/D2
Dendermonde, Belg. 28/B6
Denia, Sp. 35/F3
Denison, Tx, US 93/H4
Denizli, Turk. 50/B2
Denmark (ctry.) 20/C5
Denpasar, Indo. 66/E5
Denton, Tx, US 93/H4
Denton, Tx, US 96/D3
Denton, Eng, UK 23/F5
Denver (cap.), Co, US 93/F3
Deoband, India 62/C2
Deogarh, India 62/D3
Deoghar, India 62/E3
Deolāli, India 62/B4
Deoria, India 62/D2
Depew, NY, US 95/V10
Depok, Indo. 66/C5
Dera Ghāzi Khān, Pak. 53/K2
Dera Ismā'īl Khān, Pak. 53/K2
Derbent, Rus. 45/J4
Derby, Ks, US 93/H3
Derby, Eng, UK 23/G6
Derry, NH, US 95/G3
Derventa, Bosn. 40/C3
Des Moines (cap.), Ia, US 93/J2
Des Moines, Wa, US 99/C3
Des Plaines, Il, US 99/Q15
Descalvado, Braz. 108/C2
Desē, Eth. 77/N5
Desoto, Tx, US 101/F1
Despatch, SAfr. 80/D4
Dessau, Ger. 26/G3
Destelbergen, Belg. 28/A6
Detmold, Ger. 29/F5
Detroit, Mi, US 99/F7
Deurne, Belg. 28/B6
Deurne, Neth. 28/C6
Deux-Montagnes, Qu, Can. 95/N6
Deva, Rom. 40/F3
Develi, Turk. 50/C2
Deventer, Neth. 28/D4
Devils Lake, ND, US 91/J3
Devonport, Austl. 73/C4
Devrek, Turk. 41/K5
Dewās, India 62/C3
Dewsbury, Eng, UK 23/G4
Deyang, China 60/E2
Dezfūl, Iran 51/G3
Dezhou, China 59/D3
Dhaka (cap.), Bang. 62/F3
Dhamtari, India 62/D3
Dhānbād, India 62/E3
Dhankutā, Nepal 62/E2
Dhār, India 62/C3
Dharampur, India 62/B3
Dhāri, India 62/B3
Dharmapuri, India 62/C5
Dharmavaram, India 62/C5
Dhekialjuli, India 60/B3
Dhenkānāl, India 62/E3
Dholka, India 62/B3
Dholpur, India 62/C2
Dhorāji, India 62/B3
Dhubri, India 62/F2
Dhūlia, India 62/B3
Dhuliān, India 62/E3
Dhupgāri, India 62/E2
Diadema, Braz. 108/G8
Diamantina, Braz. 108/D1
Diapaga, Burk. 79/F3
Didam, Neth. 28/D5
Didcot, Eng, UK 25/E3
Dīdwāna, India 53/K3
Diébougou, Burk. 78/E4
Diekirch, Lux. 31/F4
Diemen, Neth. 28/B4
Diepenbeek, Belg. 31/E2
Diepholz, Ger. 29/F3
Dieppe, Fr. 30/A4
Diest, Belg. 28/C7
Dietikon, Swi. 37/E3
Diffa, Niger 76/H5
Digboi, India 60/B3
Digne-les-Bains, Fr. 33/G4
Digos, Phil. 67/G2
Dijon, Fr. 36/A3
Dikirnis, Egypt 49/B4
Diksmuide, Belg. 30/B1
Dilbeek, Belg. 31/D2
Dili, Indo. 67/G5
Dillenburg, Ger. 31/H2
Dillingen, Ger. 31/F5
Dillingen an der Donau, Ger. 26/F4
Dilsen, Belg. 28/C6
Dimāpur, India 60/B3
Dimbokro, C.d'Iv. 78/D5
Dimitrovgrad, Rus. 45/J1
Dimitrovgrad, Yugo. 41/F4
Dimitrovgrad, Bul. 41/G4
Dimona, Isr. 49/D4
Dinājpur, Bang. 62/E2
Dinar, Turk. 50/B2
Dindigul, India 62/C5
Dingolfing, Ger. 33/K2
Dingras, Phil. 61/J5
Dinslaken, Ger. 28/D5
Dinuba, Ca, US 92/C3
Diourbel, Sen. 78/A3
Diphu, India 60/B3
Dipolog, Phil. 67/F2
Dirē Dawa, Eth. 77/P6
Diriamba, Nic. 102/E4
Dishnā, Egypt 52/B3
Dispur, India 60/A3
Distrito Federal (fed. dist.), Mex. 101/K7
Disūq, Egypt 49/B4
Diu, India 62/B3
Divinópolis, Braz. 108/C2
Divo, C.d'Iv. 78/D5
Divriği, Turk. 44/F5
Dixon, Il, US 91/L5
Dixon, Ca, US 99/L10
Diyarb Najm, Egypt 49/B4
Diyarbakır, Turk. 50/E2
Djamaa, Alg. 76/G1
Djelfa, Alg. 76/F1
Djibo, Burk. 79/E3
Djibouti (cap.), Djib. 77/P5
Djibouti (ctry.) 77/P5
Djougou, Ben. 79/F4
Dnipro (riv.), Ukr. 44/E3
Dniprodzerzhyns'k, Ukr. 44/E2
Dnipropetrovs'k, Ukr. 44/E2
Dnister (riv.), Eur. 44/D3
Do Gonbadān, Iran 51/G4
Do Son, Viet. 65/D1
Döbeln, Ger. 26/G3
Doboj, Bosn. 40/D3
Dobrich, Bul. 41/H4
Dobrush, Bela. 44/D1
Dobryanka, Rus. 43/N4
Dodge City, Ks, US 93/G3
Dodoma, Tanz. 82/G2
Doetinchem, Neth. 28/D5
Dogondoutchi, Niger 79/G3
Doğubayazıt, Turk. 45/H5
Doha (cap.), Qatar 52/F3
Dohad, India 62/B3
Dole, Fr. 36/B3
Dolgoprudnyy, Rus. 43/W9
Dollard-des-Ormeaux, Qu, Can. 95/N7
Dolores, Arg. 109/E4
Dolores, Guat. 102/D2
Dolton, Il, US 99/Q16
Dom Pedrito, Braz. 109/F3
Dombóvár, Hun. 40/D2
Dominica (ctry.), Dom. 104/F4
Dominican Republic (ctry.) 104/D3
Domodossola, It. 37/E5
Don Benito, Sp. 34/C3
Donaueschingen, Ger. 37/E2
Doncaster, Eng, UK 23/G4
Donets'k, Ukr. 44/F2
Dong Ha, Viet. 65/D2
Dong Hoi, Viet. 65/D2
Dongchuan, China 60/D3
Dongen, Neth. 28/B5
Dongguan, China 61/G4
Dongsheng, China 59/B3
Dongtai, China 59/E4
Dongying, China 59/D3
Donji Vakuf, Bosn. 40/C3
Dorchester, Eng, UK 24/D5
Dordrecht, Neth. 28/B5
Dori, Burk. 79/E3
Dorking, Eng, UK 25/F4
Dormagen, Ger. 28/D6
Dornbirn, Aus. 37/F3
Dorohoi, Rom. 41/H2
Dorsten, Ger. 28/D5
Dortmund, Ger. 29/E5
Dörtyol, Turk. 49/E1
Dorval, Qu, Can. 95/N7
Dos Hermanas, Sp. 34/C4
Dosso, Niger 79/F3
Dothan, Al, US 97/G4
Douai, Fr. 30/C3
Douala, Camr. 76/G7
Douarnenez, Fr. 32/A2
Douchy-les-Mines, Fr. 30/C3
Douglas, Az, US 100/C2
Douglas, Ga, US 97/H4
Douglas (cap.), IM, UK 22/D3
Dour, Belg. 30/C3
Dourados, Braz. 107/H8
Dover, Eng, UK 25/H4
Dover (cap.), De, US 94/F4
Dover (str.), Fr.,UK 32/D1
Downers Grove, Il, US 99/P16
Dracena, Braz. 108/B2
Drachten, Neth. 28/D2
Drăgăşani, Rom. 41/G3
Draguignan, Fr. 33/G5
Drake (passage) 109/C8
Dráma, Gre. 41/G5
Drammen, Nor. 20/D4
Draveil, Fr. 30/B6
Dresden, Ger. 27/G3
Dreux, Fr. 30/A6
Driebergen, Neth. 28/C4
Drigh Road, Pak. 62/A3
Drobeta-Turnu Severin, Rom. 40/F3
Drogheda, Ire. 22/B4
Drohobych, Ukr. 27/M4
Droitwich, Eng, UK 24/D2
Dronfield, Eng, UK 23/G5
Dronten, Neth. 28/C3
Drummondville, Qu, Can. 95/F2
Drunen, Neth. 28/C5
Druten, Neth. 28/C5
Drvar, Bosn. 40/C3
Dschang, Camr. 79/H5
Dubayy, UAE 53/G3
Dubbo, Austl. 73/D2
Dübendorf, Swi. 37/E3
Dublin, Ga, US 97/H3
Dublin (cap.), Ire. 22/B5
Dublin, Ca, US 99/L11
Dubna, Rus. 42/H4
Dubnica nad Váhom, Slvk. 27/K4
Dubno, Ukr. 44/C2
Dubrovnik, Cro. 40/D4
Dubuque, Ia, US 91/L5
Dudelange, Lux. 31/F5
Duderstadt, Ger. 29/H5
Dudinka, Rus. 46/J3
Dudley, Eng, UK 24/D1
Duffel, Belg. 28/B6
Duisburg, Ger. 28/D6
Duitama, Col. 106/D2
Duiven, Neth. 28/D5
Dülmen, Ger. 29/E5
Dumaguete, Phil. 67/F2
Dumas, Tx, US 93/G4
Dumfries, Sc, UK 22/E1
Dún Laoghaire, Ire. 22/B5
Dunaharaszti, Hun. 40/D2
Dunakeszi, Hun. 40/D2
Dunaújváros, Hun. 40/D2
Duncan, Ok, US 93/H4
Duncanville, Tx, US 96/D3
Dund-Us, Mong. 54/C2
Dundalk, Ire. 22/B4
Dundas, On, Can. 95/T9
Dunedin, Fl, US 97/H4
Dunedin, NZ 71/R12
Dungarpur, India 62/B3
Dunhua, China 55/K3
Dunhuang, China 54/C3
Dunkirk (Dunkerque), Fr. 30/B1
Dunkwa, Gha. 79/E5
Dunmurry, NI, UK 22/B2
Dunstable, Eng, UK 25/F3
Duque de Caxias, Braz. 108/K7
Durango, Co, US 92/F3
Durango, Mex. 96/B5
Durango, Sp. 34/D1
Durant, Ok, US 93/H4
Durazno, Uru. 109/E3
Durban, SAfr. 81/E3
Durbanville, SAfr. 80/L10
Düren, Ger. 31/F2
Durg, India 62/D3
Durgāpur, India 62/E3
Durham, NC, US 97/J3
Durham, NH, US 95/G3
Durham, Eng, UK 23/G2
Durrës, Alb. 40/D5
Dushanbe (cap.), Taj. 46/G6
Düsseldorf, Ger. 28/D6
Duyun, China 60/E3
Düzce, Turk. 41/K5
Düzici, Turk. 50/D2
Dwārka, India 62/A3
Dyat'kovo, Rus. 44/E1
Dyer, In, US 94/C3
Dzaoudzi (cap.), May. 81/H6
Dzerzhinsk, Rus. 42/J4
Dzhankoy, Ukr. 44/E3
Działdowo, Pol. 27/L2
Dzierżoniów, Pol. 27/J3
Dzuunmod, Mong. 54/F2

E

Eagle Pass, Tx, US 96/C4
Easley, SC, US 97/H3
East Chicago, In, US 99/R16
East China (sea), Asia 68/B2
East Detroit (East Pointe), Mi, US 99/G7
East Grinstead, Eng, UK 25/F4
East Hill-Meridian, Wa, US 99/C3
East Lansing, Mi, US 94/C3
East Liverpool, Oh, US 94/D3
East London, SAfr. 80/D4
East Point, Ga, US 97/G3
East Pointe (East Detroit), Mi, US 99/G7
East Retford, Eng, UK 23/H5
East Saint Louis, Il, US 93/K3
East Siberian (sea), Rus. 47/S2
Eastbourne, Eng, UK 25/G5
Eastern Ghats (mts.), India 62/C5
Eastleigh, Eng, UK 25/E5
Easton, Pa, US 94/F3
Eastwood, Eng, UK 23/G6
Eau Claire, Wi, US 91/L4
Ebano, Mex. 102/B1
Ebbw Vale, Wal, UK 24/C3
Eberswalde-Finow, Ger. 27/G2
Ebetsu, Japan 55/N3
Eboli, It. 40/B5
Ebolowa, Camr. 76/H7
Ecatepec, Mex. 101/Q9
Eccles, Eng, UK 23/F5
Échirolles, Fr. 32/F4
Echt, Neth. 28/C6
Écija, Sp. 34/C4
Eckernförde, Ger. 26/E1
Ecorse, Mi, US 99/F7
Ecuador (ctry.), Ecu. 106/C4
Ede, Nga. 79/G5
Ede, Neth. 28/C4
Edéa, Camr. 76/H7
Edegem, Belg. 28/B6
Eden, NC, US 97/J2
Edendale, SAfr. 81/E3
Edewecht, Ger. 29/E2
Edgewood-North Hill, Wa, US 99/C3
Édhessa, Gre. 40/F5
Edinburg, Tx, US 96/D5
Edirne, Turk. 41/H5
Edmonds, Wa, US 99/C2
Edmonton (cap.), Ab, Can. 90/E2
Edremit, Turk. 44/C5
Edwardsville, Il, US 93/K3
Eeklo, Belg. 28/A6
Effingham, Il, US 93/K3
Effon Alaiye, Nga. 79/G5
Eger, Hun. 40/E2
Egglescliffe, Eng, UK 23/G3
Egham, Eng, UK 25/F4
Eğridir, Turk. 50/B2
Egypt (ctry.) 77/L2
Ehingen, Ger. 37/F1
Eibar, Sp. 34/D1
Eibergen, Neth. 28/D4
Eidsvoll, Nor. 20/D3
Einbeck, Ger. 29/G5
Eindhoven, Neth. 28/C6
Eisenach, Ger. 29/H7
Eisenhüttenstadt, Ger. 27/H2
Eisenstadt, Aus. 40/C2
Eiserfeld, Ger. 31/G2
Eitorf, Ger. 31/G2
Ejea de los Caballeros, Sp. 35/E1
Ejeda, Madg. 81/H9
Ekeren, Belg. 28/B6
Ekibastuz, Kaz. 46/H4
Eksjö, Swe. 20/E4
El Aaiún, Mor. 76/C2
El Arahal, Sp. 34/C4
El Bagre, Col. 103/H5
El Banco, Col. 103/H4
El Bayadh, Alg. 76/F1
El Campo, Tx, US 93/H5
El Carmen de Bolívar, Col. 103/H4
El Centro, Ca, US 92/D4
El Cerrito, Ca, US 99/K11
El Dorado, Ar, US 93/J4
El Dorado, Ks, US 93/H3
El Ferrol, Sp. 34/A1
El Golea, Alg. 76/F1
El Grullo, Mex. 100/D5
El Jadida, Mor. 76/D1
El Nevado (peak), Arg. 109/C4
El Oued, Alg. 76/G1
El Paso, Tx, US 92/F5
El Pilar, Ven. 104/F5
El Prat de Llobregat, Sp. 35/L7
El Progreso, Hon. 102/E3
El Progreso, Guat. 102/D3
El Puerto de Santa María, Sp. 34/B4
El Rama, Nic. 103/E3
El Reno, Ok, US 93/H4
El Salto, Mex. 100/D4
El Salvador, Cuba 103/H1
El Salvador (ctry.), ESal. 102/D3
El Tigre, Ven. 106/F2
El Viejo, Nic. 102/E3
El'brus (peak), Rus. 45/G4
Élancourt, Fr. 30/A6
Elat, Isr. 49/D5
Elazığ, Turk. 50/D2
Elbasan, Alb. 40/E5
Elbe (riv.), Ger. 26/E2
Elbeuf, Fr. 32/D2
Elbląg, Pol. 27/K1
Elburg, Neth. 28/C4
Elche, Sp. 35/E3
Elda, Sp. 35/E3
Eldorado, Arg. 109/F2
Eldoret, Kenya 77/N7
Elefsís, Gre. 39/N8
Elektrostal', Rus. 43/X9
Elgin, Il, US 99/P15
Elgon (peak), Ugan. 77/M7
Elista, Rus. 45/H3
Elizabeth City, NC, US 97/J2
Elizabethton, Tn, US 97/H2
Elizabethtown, Ky, US 97/G2
Ełk, Pol. 27/M2
Elk City, Ok, US 93/H4
Elk Grove, Ca, US 99/M10
Elk Grove Village, Il, US 99/P16
Elk River, Mn, US 91/K4
Elk Silver, NM, US 100/D1
Elkhart, In, US 94/C3
Elko, Nv, US 90/E5
Ellensburg, Wa, US 90/C4
Ellesmere Port, Eng, UK 23/F5
Ellicott City, Md, US 94/E4
Ellwangen, Ger. 33/J2
Elmadağ, Turk. 44/E5
Elmhurst, Il, US 99/Q16
Elmina, Gha. 79/E5
Elmira, NY, US 94/E3
Elmshorn, Ger. 29/G1
Elmwood Park, Il, US 99/Q16
Elsdorf, Ger. 31/F2
Elst, Neth. 28/C5
Eltville am Rhein, Ger. 31/H3
Elūrū, India 62/D4
Elverum, Nor. 20/D3
Elwood, In, US 94/C3
Elyria, Oh, US 94/D3
Emāmshahr, Iran 51/H2
Embi, Kaz. 45/L2
Embu, Kenya 77/N8
Emden, Ger. 29/E2
Emeishan, China 60/D2
Emiliano Zapata, Mex. 102/D2
Emirdağ, Turk. 44/D5
Emmeloord, Neth. 28/C3
Emmen, Neth. 28/D3
Emmendingen, Ger. 36/D1
Emmerich, Ger. 28/D5
Empalme, Mex. 100/C3
Empangeni, SAfr. 81/E3
Emporia, Ks, US 93/H3
Emsdetten, Ger. 29/E4
Ena, Japan 57/E3
Encarnación, Par. 109/E2
Encarnación de Díaz, Mex. 100/E4
Encinitas, Ca, US 92/C4
Ende, Indo. 67/F5
Endicott, NY, US 94/E3
Engel's, Rus. 45/H2
Engelskirchen, Ger. 31/G2
Enger, Ger. 29/F4
England, UK 24/D2
English (chan.), UK, Fr. 32/B2
English Bāzār, India 62/E2
Enid, Ok, US 93/H3
Enkhuizen, Neth. 28/C3
Enköping, Swe. 42/C4
Enna, It. 38/D4
Ennepetal, Ger. 29/E6
Enningerloh, Ger. 29/F5
Ennis, Tx, US 93/H4
Enschede, Neth. 28/D4
Ensenada, Mex. 92/C5
Enshi, China 61/F2
Entebbe, Ugan. 77/M7
Enterprise, Al, US 97/G4
Enugu, Nga. 79/G5
Enzan, Japan 57/F3
Epe, Nga. 79/F5
Epe, Neth. 28/C4
Épernay, Fr. 30/C5
Epinal, Fr. 36/C1
Eppelborn, Ger. 31/F5
Epsom and Ewell, Eng, UK 25/F4
Equatorial Guinea (ctry.), EqG. 76/G7
Er Rachidia, Mor. 76/E1
Eravur, SrL. 62/D6
Erba, It. 33/H4
Erbaa, Turk. 44/F4
Erciş, Turk. 51/E2
Érd, Hun. 40/D2
Erdemli, Turk. 49/D1
Erdenet, Mong. 54/E2
Erding, Ger. 33/J2
Erechim, Braz. 108/A3
Ereğli, Turk. 41/K5
Ereğli, Turk. 50/C2
Erenler, Turk. 41/K5
Ereymentaū, Kaz. 46/H4
Erfoud, Mor. 76/E1
Erftstadt, Ger. 31/F2
Erfurt, Ger. 26/F3
Erie (lake), Can.,US 94/D3
Eritrea (ctry.) 77/N5
Erkelenz, Ger. 28/D6
Erkrath, Ger. 28/D6
Erlangen, Ger. 33/J2
Ermelo, SAfr. 80/Q13
Ermelo, Neth. 28/C4
Erode, India 62/C5
Eruwa, Nga. 79/F5
Erzincan, Turk. 44/F5
Erzurum, Turk. 45/G5
Esbjerg, Den. 26/E1
Esbo (Espoo), Fin. 42/E3
Esch-sur-Alzette, Lux. 31/E4
Eschwege, Ger. 29/H6
Eschweiler, Ger. 31/F2
Escondido, Ca, US 92/C4
Escuinapa de Hidalgo, Mex. 100/D4
Escuintla, Guat. 102/D3
Eséka, Camr. 76/H7
Eşfahān, Iran 51/G3
Esher, Eng, UK 25/F4
Esil, Kaz. 46/G4
Eskil, Turk. 50/C2
Eskilstuna, Swe. 42/C4
Eskimalatya, Turk. 50/D2
Eskişehir, Turk. 44/D5
Eslāmābād, Iran 51/F3
Esmeralda, Cuba 103/G1
Esmeraldas, Ecu. 106/C3
Espelkamp, Ger. 29/F4
Esperanza, Mex. 100/C3
Espinal, Col. 106/D3
Esplanada, Braz. 107/L6
Espluges, Sp. 35/L7
Esquel, Arg. 109/B5
Essaouira, Mor. 76/D1
Essen, Belg. 28/B6
Essen, Ger. 28/E6
Esslingen, Ger. 33/H2
Eşţahbān, Iran 51/H4
Estância, Braz. 107/L6
Este, It. 33/J4
Esteio, Braz. 108/B4
Estelí, Nic. 102/E3
Estepona, Sp. 34/C4
Eston and South Bank, Eng, UK 23/G2
Estonia (ctry.), Est. 20/H4
Estoril, Port. 35/P10
Esztergom, Hun. 40/D2
Et Taiyiba, Isr. 49/G7
Etāwah, India 62/C2
Ethiopia (ctry.) 77/N5
Etna (peak), It. 38/D4
Etten-Leur, Neth. 28/B5
Etterbeek, Belg. 31/D2
Ettlingen, Ger. 33/H2
Euclid, Oh, US 94/D3
Eufaula, Al, US 97/G4
Eugene, Or, US 90/C4
Eunice, La, US 93/J5
Eupen, Belg. 31/F2
Euphrates (riv.), Asia 51/F4
Eureka, Ca, US 90/B5
Eurodisney, Fr. 30/B6
Europe (cont.) 18/*
Euskirchen, Ger. 31/F2
Eustis, Fl, US 97/H4
Eutin, Ger. 26/F1
Eutini, Malw. 82/F3
Evans (mt.), Co, US 93/F3
Evanston, Wy, US 90/F5
Evanston, Il, US 99/Q15
Evansville, In, US 97/G2

117
Evato – Grača

Evaton, SAfr. 80/P13
Everest (peak), China, Nep 62/E2
Everett, Wa, US 99/B2
Evergem, Belg. 28/A6
Everglades National Park, Fl, US 97/H5
Evergreen Park, Il, US 99/Q16
Evesham, Eng, UK 25/E2
Évora, Port. 34/B3
Évreux, Fr. 30/A5
Évry, Fr. 30/B6
Évvoia (isl.), Gre. 39/H3
Ewa Beach, Hi, US 88/V13
Excelsior Springs, Mo, US 93/J3
Exeter, NH, US 95/G3
Eyre (lake), Austl. 70/F5
Ezhou, China 61/G2

F

Faaa, FrPol. 69/L6
Faaa, FrPol. 69/X15
Fabriano, It. 38/C1
Facatativá, Col. 106/D3
Faches-Thumesnil, Fr. 30/C2
Fada-N'Gourma, Burk. 79/F3
Faenza, It. 33/J4
Făgăraş, Rom. 41/G3
Failsworth, Eng, UK 23/F4
Fair Oaks, Ca, US 99/M9
Fairbanks, Ak, US 85/J3
Fairfield, Ca, US 99/K10
Fairmont, Mn, US 91/K5
Fairmont, WV, US 97/H2
Faisalābād, Pak. 53/K2
Faizābād, India 62/D2
Fajardo, PR 104/E3
Falconara Marittima, It. 40/A4
Falkenberg, Swe. 20/E4
Falkland (Malvinas) (isls.), UK 109/D7
Falköping, Swe. 20/E4
Fall River, Ma, US 95/G3
Falmouth, Eng, UK 24/A6
Fălticeni, Rom. 41/H2
Falun, Swe. 20/E3
Famagusta, Cyp. 49/C2
Fandriana, Madg. 81/H8
Fano, It. 33/K5
Fāqūs, Egypt 49/B4
Farafangana, Madg. 81/H8
Farāh, Afg. 46/G6
Fareham, Eng, UK 25/E5
Farghona, Uzb. 46/H5
Fargo, ND, US 91/J4
Farīdābād, India 62/C2
Farīdpur, Bang. 62/E3
Fāriskūr, Egypt 49/B4
Farmington, Mo, US 93/K3
Farmington, NM, US 92/E3
Farmington, Mi, US 99/F7
Farmington Hills, Mi, US 99/E6
Farnborough, Eng, UK 25/F4
Farnham, Eng, UK 25/F4
Farnworth, Eng, UK 23/F4
Faro, Port. 34/B4
Faroe (isls.), Den. 18/C2
Farroupilha, Braz. 108/B4
Fasā, Iran 51/H4
Fasano, It. 40/C5
Fastiv, Ukr. 44/D2
Fatehpur, India 62/D2
Fatehpur, India 62/B2
Fatick, Sen. 78/A3
Fatsa, Turk. 44/F4
Favara, It. 38/C4
Faversham, Eng, UK 25/G4
Faya-Largeau, Chad 77/J4
Fayetteville, NC, US 97/J3
Fdérik, Mrta. 76/C3
Fear (cape), NC, US 97/J3
Fécamp, Fr. 32/D2
Federal Way, Wa, US 99/C3
Feira de Santana, Braz. 107/L6
Feldkirch, Aus. 37/F3
Felixstowe, Eng, UK 25/H3
Felling, Eng, UK 23/G2
Fene, Sp. 34/A1
Fengcheng, China 58/C2
Fengyüan, Tai. 61/J3
Feodosiya, Ukr. 44/E3
Fergus Falls, Mn, US 91/J4
Ferkéssédougou, C.d'Iv. 78/D4
Fermo, It. 40/A4
Fernandópolis, Braz. 108/B2
Ferndale, Mi, US 99/F7
Ferrara, It. 33/J4
Fès, Mor. 76/E1
Feteşti, Rom. 41/H3
Fethiye, Turk. 50/B2
Feyẕābād, Afg. 53/K1
Fianarantsoa, Madg. 81/H8
Fidenza, It. 33/J4
Fier, Alb. 40/D5
Figueres, Sp. 35/G1
Fiji (ctry.) 69/Y17
Filchner Ice Shelf, Ant. 83/Y
Filiaşi, Rom. 41/F3
Findlay, Oh, US 94/D3
Finger (lakes), NY, US 94/A1
Finland (ctry.) 20/H2
Finland (gulf), Fin. 42/E4
Finnentrop, Ger. 29/E6
Finspång, Swe. 20/E4
Firenze (Florence), It. 33/J5
Firminy, Fr. 32/F4
Firozābād, India 62/C2
Firozpur, India 53/K2
Fiumicino, It. 38/C2
Fjell, Nor. 20/C3
Flagstaff, Az, US 92/E4
Flamborough, On, Can. 95/T9
Fleet, Eng, UK 25/F4
Fleetwood, Eng, UK 23/E4
Flensburg, Ger. 26/E1
Fleron, Belg. 31/E2
Flers, Fr. 32/C2
Fleurus, Belg. 31/D3
Fleury-les-Aubrais, Fr. 32/D3
Flint, Mi, US 99/E5
Florence, SC, US 97/J3
Florence, Al, US 97/G3
Florence (Firenze), It. 33/J5
Florencia, Col. 106/C3
Flores, Guat. 102/D2
Floriano, Braz. 107/K5
Florianópolis, Braz. 108/B3
Florida, Cuba 103/G1
Florida, Uru. 109/E3
Florida (state), US 97/H4
Floridia, It. 38/D4
Florin, Ca, US 99/M10
Florissant, Mo, US 93/K3
Foča, Bosn. 40/D4
Focşani, Rom. 41/H3
Foggia, It. 40/B5
Foligno, It. 38/C1
Folkestone, Eng, UK 25/H4
Fond du Lac, Wi, US 91/L5
Fondi, It. 38/C2
Fonseca, Col. 103/H4
Fontaine, Fr. 32/F4
Fontaine-L'Evêque, Belg. 31/D3
Fontainebleau, Fr. 32/E2
Fontenay-le-Comte, Fr. 32/C3
Forbach, Fr. 31/F5
Forchheim, Ger. 33/J2
Forlì, It. 33/K4
Formby, Eng, UK 23/E4
Formia, It. 38/C2
Formiga, Braz. 108/C2
Formosa, Braz. 107/J7
Formosa, Arg. 109/E2
Fornacelle, It. 33/J5
Forrest City, Ar, US 93/K4
Forssa, Fin. 42/D3
Fort Abbās, Pak. 62/B2
Fort Collins, Co, US 93/F2
Fort Dodge, Ia, US 91/K5
Fort Erie, On, Can. 95/V10
Fort Lauderdale, Fl, US 97/H5
Fort Lewis, Wa, US 99/B3
Fort Lewis, Wa, US 99/B3
Fort Liberté, Haiti 103/J2
Fort Madison, Ia, US 91/L5
Fort McMurray, Ab, Can. 86/E3
Fort Morgan, Co, US 93/G2
Fort Myers, Fl, US 97/H5
Fort Payne, Al, US 97/G3
Fort Pierce, Fl, US 97/H5
Fort Portal, Ugan. 77/M7
Fort Saint John, BC, Can. 86/D3
Fort Smith, Ar, US 93/J4
Fort Walton Beach, Fl, US 97/G4
Fort Wayne, In, US 94/C3
Fort-de-France, Fr. 104/F4
Fortaleza, Braz. 107/L4
Fortín, Mex. 101/N8
Fortuna Ledge, Ak, US 85/F3
Foshan, China 61/G4
Fossano, It. 33/G4
Fostoria, Oh, US 94/D3
Fougères, Fr. 32/C2
Foumban, Camr. 79/H5
Fountain, Co, US 93/F3
Fourmies, Fr. 30/D4
Foz do Iguaçu, Braz. 109/F2
Fraiburgo, Braz. 108/B3
Frameries, Belg. 30/C3
Franca, Braz. 108/C2
Francavilla Fontana, It. 40/C5
France (ctry.) 32/D3
Franceville, Gabon 82/B1
Francisco Escárcega, Mex. 102/D2
Francisco I. Madero, Mex. 100/E3
Francistown, Bots. 82/E5
Franco da Rocha, Braz. 108/G8
Franconville, Fr. 30/B6
Franeker, Neth. 28/C2
Frankenberg-Eder, Ger. 29/F6
Frankenthal, Ger. 26/E4
Frankfort, In, US 97/G1
Frankfort (cap.), Ky, US 94/C4
Frankfurt, Ger. 27/H2
Frankfurt am Main, Ger. 33/H1
Franklin, La, US 93/K5
Franklin, In, US 97/G2
Franklin, Tn, US 97/G3
Franklin, Wi, US 99/Q14
Franklin Park, Il, US 99/Q16
Fransisco Beltrão, Braz. 109/F2
Fransisco Morato, Braz. 108/G8
Fraser (riv.), BC, Can. 90/C2
Fraser, Mi, US 99/G6
Frauenfeld, Swi. 37/E2
Frechen, Ger. 31/F2
Fredericia, Den. 26/E1
Frederick, Md, US 97/J2
Fredericksburg, Va, US 97/J2
Fredericton (cap.), NB, Can. 95/H2
Frederikshavn, Den. 20/D4
Fredonia, NY, US 94/E3
Fredrikstad, Nor. 20/D4
Freeport, Tx, US 93/J5
Freeport, Il, US 91/L5
Freetown (cap.), SLeo. 78/B4
Freiberg, Ger. 27/G3
Freiburg, Ger. 36/D2
Freising, Ger. 33/J2
Freital, Ger. 27/G3
Fréjus, Fr. 33/G5
Fremont, Ne, US 91/J5
Fremont, Oh, US 94/D3
Fremont, Ca, US 99/L11
French Guiana (dpcy.), Fr. 107/H3
Fresnillo, Mex. 100/E4
Fresno, Ca, US 92/C3
Freudenberg, Ger. 31/G2
Freudenstadt, Ger. 37/E1
Freyming-Merlebach, Fr. 31/F5
Frías, Arg. 109/C2
Fribourg, Swi. 36/D4
Friedberg, Ger. 37/G1
Friedberg, Ger. 33/H1
Friedrichsdorf, Ger. 33/H1
Friedrichshafen, Ger. 37/F2
Friesoythe, Ger. 29/E2
Frolovo, Rus. 45/G2
Frome, Eng, UK 24/D4
Front Royal, Va, US 97/J2
Frontera, Mex. 102/C2
Frontignan, Fr. 32/E5
Frosinone, It. 38/C2
Frutal, Braz. 108/B1
Fryazino, Rus. 43/X9
Frýdek-Místek, Czh. 27/K4
Fu'an, China 61/H3
Fuchū, Japan 56/C3
Fuengirola, Sp. 34/C4
Fuenlabrada, Sp. 35/N9
Fuerte Olimpo, Par. 106/G8
Fuji, Japan 57/F3
Fuji-san (peak), Japan 57/F3
Fujieda, Japan 57/F3
Fujioka, Japan 57/F2
Fujisawa, Japan 57/F3
Fujiyoshida, Japan 57/F3
Fukuchiyama, Japan 56/D3
Fukue, Japan 56/A4
Fukui, Japan 56/E2
Fukuoka, Japan 56/B4
Fukuroi, Japan 57/E3
Fukushima, Japan 57/G2
Fukuyama, Japan 56/C3
Fulda, Ger. 33/H1
Fuling, China 61/E2
Fulton, Mo, US 93/K3
Fulton, NY, US 94/E3
Funafuti (cap.), Tuv. 68/G5
Funchal, Madr. 35/V15
Fundación, Col. 103/H4
Fundy (bay), US,Can. 95/H2
Funhalouro, Moz. 82/F5
Furmanov, Rus. 42/J4
Fürstenfeldbruck, Ger. 37/H1
Fürstenwalde, Ger. 27/H2
Fürth, Ger. 33/J2
Furukawa, Japan 55/N4
Fushun, China 58/B2
Futog, Yugo. 40/D3
Futtsu, Japan 57/F3
Fuwah, Egypt 49/B4
Fuxin, China 58/A1
Fuyu, China 55/J2
Fuzhou, China 61/H3

G

Gaast, Neth. 28/C2
Gabon (ctry.), Gabon 76/H7
Gaborone (cap.), Bots. 80/D2
Gabriel Leyva Solano, Mex. 100/C3
Gabrovo, Bul. 41/G4
Gadsden, Al, US 97/G3
Găeşti, Rom. 41/G3
Gaeta, It. 38/C2
Gaffney, SC, US 97/H3
Gagarin, Rus. 42/G5
Gagnoa, C.d'Iv. 78/D5
Gagny, Fr. 30/B6
Gagra, Geo. 44/G4
Gainesville, Tx, US 93/H4
Gainesville, Ga, US 97/H3
Gainesville, Fl, US 97/H4
Gainsborough, Eng, UK 23/H5
Galaţi, Rom. 41/J3
Galatina, It. 39/F2
Galatone, It. 39/F2
Galdácano, Sp. 34/D1
Gáldar, Canl. 35/X16
Galesburg, Il, US 91/L5
Galich, Rus. 42/J4
Galion, Oh, US 94/D3
Gallatin, Tn, US 97/G2
Galle, SrL. 62/D6
Gallipoli, It. 39/E2
Gällivare, Swe. 42/D2
Gallup, NM, US 92/E4
Galveston, Tx, US 93/J5
Galveston (bay), Tx, US 93/J5
Galway, Ire. 21/A10
Gamagōri, Japan 57/E3
Gambat, Pak. 62/A2
Gambia (ctry.) 78/B3
Gäncä, Azer. 45/H4
Gandajika, D.R. Congo 82/D2
Ganderkesee, Ger. 29/F2
Gāndhīdhām, India 62/B3
Gandhinagar, India 62/B3
Gandía, Sp. 35/E3
Gangāpur, India 62/C2
Gangārāmpur, India 62/E2
Ganges (riv.), India 62/D2
Ganges, Mouths of the (delta), Bang.,Ind 62/E3
Gangtok, India 62/E2
Ganzhou, China 61/G3
Gao, Mali 79/E2
Gaocheng, China 59/C3
Gaoua, Burk. 78/E4
Gap, Fr. 33/G4
Garanhuns, Braz. 107/L5
Garbsen, Ger. 29/G4
Garça, Braz. 108/B2
Garden City, Ks, US 93/G3
Garden City, Mi, US 99/F7
Gardēz, Afg. 53/J2
Garforth, Eng, UK 23/G4
Garibaldi, Braz. 108/B4
Garissa, Kenya 82/G1
Garland, Tx, US 93/H4
Garmisch-Partenkirchen, Ger. 37/H3
Garoua, Camr. 76/H6
Garut, Indo. 66/C5
Garwolin, Pol. 27/L3
Gary, In, US 99/R16
Garza García, Mex. 101/E3
Garzón, Col. 106/C3
Gaspar, Braz. 108/B3
Gaspé, Qu, Can. 95/H1
Gaspé (pen.), Can. 95/H1
Gastonia, NC, US 97/H3
Gatchina, Rus. 42/F4
Gateshead, Eng, UK 23/G2
Gatesville, Tx, US 96/D4
Gatineau, Qu, Can. 94/F2
Gauripur, India 62/E2
Gauting, Ger. 37/H1
Gavà, Sp. 35/L7
Gävle, Swe. 42/C3
Gay, Rus. 45/L2
Gayā, India 62/E3
Gaya, Niger 79/F4
Gaza Strip (ctry.), Isr. 49/C4
Gaziantep, Turk. 50/D2
Gbadolite, D.R. Congo 77/K7
Gbarnga, Libr. 78/C5
Gbongan, Nga. 79/G5
Gdańsk, Pol. 27/K1
Gdynia, Pol. 27/K1
Gebze, Turk. 41/J5
Geel, Belg. 28/B6
Geelong, Austl. 73/C3
Geesthacht, Ger. 29/H2
Geilenkirchen, Ger. 31/F2
Geislingen an der Steige, Ger. 33/H2
Gejiu, China 60/D4
Gela, It. 38/D4
Geldermalsen, Neth. 28/C5
Geldern, Ger. 28/D5
Geldrop, Neth. 28/C6
Geleen, Neth. 31/E2
Gelendzhik, Rus. 44/F3
Gelibolu, Turk. 41/H5
Gelligaer, Wal, UK 24/C3
Gelsenkirchen, Ger. 28/E5
Gembloux, Belg. 31/D2
Gemena, D.R. Congo 77/J7
Gemert, Neth. 28/C5
Gemlik, Turk. 41/J5
Gendringen, Neth. 28/D5
General Alvear, Arg. 109/C3
General Juan José Ríos, Mex. 100/C3
General Juan Madariaga, Arg. 109/E4
General Martín Miguel de Güemes, Arg. 109/C1
General Pico, Arg. 109/D4
General Roca, Arg. 109/C4
Geneva, NY, US 94/E3
Geneva (lake), Fr.,Swi 36/C5
Geneva, Il, US 99/P16
Geneva (Genève), Swi. 33/G3
Genève, Swi. 36/C5
Genk, Belg. 31/E2
Gennep, Neth. 28/C5
Genova (Genoa), It. 33/H4
Gent, Belg. 28/A6
Genteng, Indo. 66/D5
George, SAfr. 80/C4
George Town, Malay. 66/B2
George Town (cap.), UK 103/F2
Georgetown, Tx, US 93/H5
Georgetown, Ky, US 97/G2
Georgetown, SC, US 97/J3
Georgetown (cap.), Guy. 106/G2
Georgia (ctry.) 45/G4
Georgia (state), US 97/G3
Georgian (bay), Can. 94/D2
Georgsmarienhütte, Ger. 29/F4
Gera, Ger. 26/G3
Geraardsbergen, Belg. 30/C2
Geraldton, Austl. 68/A7
Gerede, Turk. 41/L5
Geretsried, Ger. 37/H2
Germantown, Tn, US 93/K4
Germany (ctry.) 26/E3
Germering, Ger. 37/H1
Germiston, SAfr. 80/Q13
Gersthofen, Ger. 37/G1
Gescher, Ger. 28/E5
Geseke, Ger. 29/F5
Getafe, Sp. 35/N9
Gevelsberg, Ger. 29/E6
Gevgelija, FYROM 40/F5
Ghana (ctry.) 79/E4
Ghanzi, Bots. 82/D5
Ghardaïa, Alg. 76/F1
Gharyān, Libya 76/H1
Ghaznī, Afg. 53/J2
Gheorghe Gheorghiu-Dej, Rom. 41/H2
Gheorgheni, Rom. 41/G2
Gherla, Rom. 41/F2
Ghinda (Gīnda), Erit. 52/C5
Ghotki, Pak. 62/A2
Giarre, It. 38/D4
Gibraltar (cap.), Gib. 34/C4
Gibraltar (str.), Eur.,Afr. 34/C5
Gien, Fr. 32/E3
Giengen an der Brenz, Ger. 33/J2
Giessen, Ger. 33/H1
Giessendam, Neth. 28/B5
Gif-sur-Yvette, Fr. 30/B6
Gifhorn, Ger. 29/H4
Gifu, Japan 57/E3
Gijón, Sp. 34/C1
Gillette, Wy, US 91/G4
Gillingham, Eng, UK 25/G4
Gilze, Neth. 28/B5
Gīmbī, Eth. 77/N6
Gingoog, Phil. 67/G2
Ginosa, It. 40/C5
Gioia del Colle, It. 40/C5
Gioia Tauro, It. 38/D3
Girardot, Col. 106/D3
Giresun, Turk. 44/F4
Gīrīdīh, India 62/E3
Girona, Sp. 35/G2
Gisborne, NZ 71/S10
Gitega, Buru. 82/E1
Giugliano in Campania, It. 40/B5
Giulianova, It. 40/A4
Giurgiu, Rom. 41/G4
Giv'atayim, Isr. 49/F7
Givors, Fr. 32/F4
Giyani, SAfr. 82/F5
Gizo, Sol. 68/E5
Giżycko, Pol. 27/L1
Gjirokastër, Alb. 39/G2
Gjøvik, Nor. 20/D3
Glace Bay, NS, Can. 95/K2
Glacier Bay National Park and Preserve, Ak, US 85/L4
Glacier National Park, BC, Can. 86/E3
Glacier National Park, Can. 90/D3
Gladbeck, Ger. 28/D5
Gladstone, Austl. 72/C3
Glan, Phil. 67/G2
Glarus, Swi. 37/F3
Glasgow, Ky, US 97/G2
Glazov, Rus. 43/M4
Glen Canyon Nat'l Rec. Area, US 92/E3
Glendale, Ca, US 92/C4
Glendale, Az, US 92/D4
Glendale Heights, Il, US 99/P16
Glenview, Il, US 99/Q15
Glifádha, Gre. 39/N9
Glinde, Ger. 29/H1
Gliwice, Pol. 27/K3
Głogów, Pol. 27/J3
Glossop, Eng, UK 23/G5
Gloucester, On, Can. 94/F2
Gloucester, Eng, UK 24/D3
Głowno, Pol. 27/K3
Głuchołazy, Pol. 27/J3
Gniezno, Pol. 27/J2
Gnjilane, Yugo. 40/E4
Go Cong, Viet. 65/D4
Goālpāra, India 62/F2
Goba, Eth. 77/N6
Gobi (des.), Mong. 47/L5
Gobō, Japan 56/D4
Goch, Ger. 28/D5
Godalming, Eng, UK 25/F4
Gödöllő, Hun. 27/K5
Godoy Cruz, Arg. 109/C3
Goes, Neth. 28/A5
Goiana, Braz. 107/M5
Goiânia, Braz. 107/J7
Goiás, Braz. 107/H7
Goiatuba, Braz. 108/B1
Goirle, Neth. 28/C5
Gojō, Japan 56/D3
Göksun, Turk. 50/D2
Gölbaşı, Turk. 50/D2
Gölbaşı, Turk. 44/E5
Golborne, Eng, UK 23/F5
Gölcük, Turk. 41/J5
Gold (coast), Gha. 79/E5
Gold Coast, Austl. 72/D5
Golden, Co, US 93/F3
Goldsboro, NC, US 97/J3
Goleniów, Pol. 27/H2
Gölköy, Turk. 44/F4
Golmud, China 54/C4
Golpāyegān, Iran 51/G3
Goma, D.R. Congo 82/E1
Gómez Palacio, Mex. 96/C5
Gonaïves, Haiti 103/H2
Gonbad-e Qābūs, Iran 51/H2
Gondā, India 62/D2
Gonder, Eth. 77/N5
Gondia, India 62/D3
Gondomar, Port. 34/A2
Gönen, Turk. 41/H5
Gonesse, Fr. 30/B6
Gongzhuling, China 59/F2
Good Hope, Cape of (cape), SAfr. 80/L11
Goodwood, SAfr. 80/L10
Goole, Eng, UK 23/H4
Göppingen, Ger. 33/H2
Gorakhpur, India 62/D2
Gorē, Eth. 77/N6
Görele, Turk. 44/F4
Gorgān, Iran 51/H2
Gori, Geo. 45/H4
Gorinchem, Neth. 28/B5
Gorizia, It. 40/A3
Gorki, Bela. 42/F5
Gorlice, Pol. 27/L4
Görlitz, Ger. 27/H3
Gorna Oryakhovitsa, Bul. 41/G4
Gornji Milanovac, Yugo. 40/E3
Gornji Vakuf, Bosn. 40/C4
Gorno-Altaysk, Rus. 46/J4
Gornyak, Rus. 46/J4
Gorodets, Rus. 43/J4
Goroka, PNG 68/D5
Gorontalo, Indo. 67/F3
Gorzów Wielkopolski, Pol. 27/H2
Gōse, Japan 56/D3
Gosen, Japan 57/F2
Gosford, Austl. 73/D2
Gosforth, Eng, UK 23/G2
Goshogawara, Japan 55/N3
Goslar, Ger. 29/H5
Gospić, Cro. 40/B3
Gosport, Eng, UK 25/E5
Gossau, Swi. 37/F3
Gossensass (Colle Isarco), It. 37/H4
Gostivar, FYROM 40/E5
Gostyń, Pol. 27/J3
Gostynin, Pol. 27/K2
Göteborg, Swe. 20/D4
Gotemba, Japan 57/F3
Gotha, Ger. 29/H7
Gotse Delchev, Bul. 41/F5
Gotsu, Japan 56/C3
Göttingen, Ger. 29/G5
Gouda, Neth. 28/B4
Goulburn, Austl. 73/D2
Governador Valadares, Braz. 108/D1
Goya, Arg. 109/E2
Graaff-Reinet, SAfr. 80/D4
Gračanica, Bosn. 40/D3

118

Graci – Hrodn

Gracias, Hon. 102/D3
Gradačac, Bosn. 40/D3
Grafton, Austl. 73/E1
Grahamstown, SAfr. 80/D4
Grajaú, Braz. 107/J5
Grajewo, Pol. 27/M2
Gran Chaco (plain), Arg.,Par. 109/D2
Granada, Col. 106/D3
Granada, Nic. 102/E4
Granada, Sp. 34/D4
Granadilla de Abona, Canl. 35/X16
Grand Canyon National Park, Az, US 92/D3
Grand Cayman (isl.), Cay. 103/F2
Grand Forks, ND, US 91/J4
Grand Haven, Mi, US 94/C3
Grand Portage Nat'l Mon., Mn, US 91/L4
Grand Rapids, Mi, US 94/C3
Grand Rapids, Mn, US 91/K4
Grand Staircase-Escalante Nat'l Mon., Ut, US 92/E3
Grand Teton National Park, Wy, US 92/E2
Grand Turk (cap.), UK 103/J1
Grand-Bassam, C.d'Iv. 78/E5
Grande Prairie, Ab, Can. 90/D2
Grande-Synthe, Fr. 30/B1
Granite City, Il, US 93/K3
Granollers, Sp. 35/L6
Grantham, Eng, UK 23/H6
Grants Pass, Or, US 90/C5
Grasse, Fr. 33/G5
Grassy Park, SAfr. 80/L11
Gravesend, Eng, UK 25/G4
Gravina di Puglia, It. 40/C5
Grays, Eng, UK 25/G4
Graz, Aus. 40/B2
Great (basin), Nv, US 88/C4
Great Bear (lake), NW, Can. 86/D2
Great Bend, Ks, US 93/H3
Great Divide (basin), Wy, US 90/F5
Great Dividing (range), Austl. 73/B3
Great Himalaya (range), China 62/D2
Great Plains (plain), Can.,US 86/F3
Great Salt (lake), Ut, US 92/D2
Great Sandy (des.), Austl. 70/C4
Great Slave (lake), NW, Can. 86/E2
Great Smoky Mountains National Park, US 97/H3
Great Victoria (des.), Austl. 70/D5
Great Wall, China 54/F4
Great Yarmouth, Eng, UK 25/H1
Greater Antilles (isls.), Jam. 103/F1
Greece (ctry.), Gre. 39/G3
Greeley, Co, US 93/F2
Green River, Wy, US 90/F5
Green Valley, Az, US 92/E5
Greendale, Wi, US 99/Q14
Greeneville, Tn, US 97/H2
Greenfield, Ma, US 95/F3
Greenfield, In, US 97/G2
Greenfield, Wi, US 99/P14
Greenfield Park, Qu, Can. 95/P7
Greenland (dpcy.), Den. 87/L1
Greensboro, NC, US 97/J2
Greensburg, In, US 94/C4
Greensburg, Pa, US 94/E3
Greenville, Tx, US 93/H4
Greenville, Ms, US 93/K4
Greenville, Libr. 78/C5
Greenville, NC, US 97/J3
Greenville, SC, US 97/H3
Greenville, Oh, US 97/G1
Greenwood, Ms, US 93/K4
Greenwood, SC, US 97/H3
Greifswald, Ger. 27/G1
Greiz, Ger. 33/K1
Gremyachinsk, Rus. 43/N4
Grenada, Ms, US 93/K4
Grenada (ctry.), Gren. 104/F5
Grenchen, Swi. 36/D3
Grenoble, Fr. 32/F4
Gretna, La, US 97/F4
Greven, Ger. 29/E4
Grevenbroich, Ger. 28/D6
Grevenmacher, Lux. 31/F4
Greymouth, NZ 71/R11
Griffin, Ga, US 97/G3
Griffith, In, US 99/R16
Grigny, Fr. 30/B6
Grimbergen, Belg. 31/D2
Grimsby, Eng, UK 23/H4
Grimsby, On, Can. 95/T9
Grimstad, Nor. 20/D4
Gröbenzell, Ger. 37/H1
Groesbeek, Neth. 28/C5
Gronau, Ger. 28/E4
Groningen, Neth. 28/D2
Grosse Ile, Mi, US 99/F7
Grosse Pointe Farms, Mi, US 99/G7
Grosse Pointe Park, Mi, US 99/G7
Grosse Pointe Woods, Mi, US 99/G7
Grosseto, It. 38/B1
Grossgerau, Ger. 33/H2
Grottaglie, It. 40/C5
Grovdageaidnu-Kautokeino, Nor. 42/D1
Grover City, Ca, US 92/B4
Groves, Tx, US 93/J5
Groznyy, Rus. 45/H4
Grudziądz, Pol. 27/K2
Gryazi, Rus. 44/F1
Gryfice, Pol. 27/H2
Gryfino, Pol. 27/H2
Guaçuí, Braz. 108/D2
Guadalajara, Mex. 100/E4
Guadalajara, Sp. 34/D2
Guadalupe, Pan. 103/G4
Guadalupe, Mex. 100/E4
Guadalupe, Mex. 96/C5
Guadeloupe (dpcy.), Fr. 104/F3
Guadeloupe Passage (chan.), NAm. 104/F3
Guadix, Sp. 34/D4
Guaíba, Braz. 108/B4
Guáimaro, Cuba 103/G1
Guaira, Braz. 109/F1
Guaira, Braz. 108/B2
Guajará-Mirim, Braz. 106/E6
Gualán, Guat. 102/D3
Gualeguaychú, Arg. 109/E3
Guam (isl.), Pac.,US 68/D3
Guamúchil, Mex. 100/C3
Guanabacoa, Cuba 103/F1
Guanajay, Cuba 103/F1
Guanajuato, Mex. 101/E4
Guanambi, Braz. 107/K6
Guanare, Ven. 106/E2
Guangyuan, China 60/E1
Guangzhou, China 61/G4
Guanhães, Braz. 108/D1
Guantánamo, Cuba 103/H1
Guarabira, Braz. 107/L5
Guaranda, Ecu. 106/C4
Guarapari, Braz. 108/D2
Guarapuava, Braz. 108/B3
Guararapes, Braz. 108/B2
Guaratinguetá, Braz. 108/H7
Guarda, Port. 34/B2
Guarujá, Braz. 108/G9
Guarulhos, Braz. 108/G8
Guasave, Mex. 100/C3
Guatemala (cap.), Guat. 102/D3
Guatemala (ctry.), Guat. 102/D3
Guaxupé, Braz. 108/G6
Guayama, PR 104/E3
Guayaquil, Ecu. 106/C4
Guayaramerín, Bol. 106/E6
Guaymas, Mex. 100/C3
Gubakha, Rus. 43/N4
Guben, Ger. 27/H3
Gubin, Pol. 27/H3
Gubkin, Rus. 44/F2
Gudermes, Rus. 45/H4
Gudivāda, India 62/D4
Gūdūr, India 62/C5
Guecho, Sp. 34/D1
Guelph, On, Can. 95/S8
Guéret, Fr. 32/D3
Guguletu, SAfr. 80/L10
Guidder, Camr. 76/H6
Guihulngan, Phil. 67/F1
Guildford, Eng, UK 25/F4
Guilin, China 61/F3
Guinea (ctry.) 78/C4
Guinea (gulf), Gui. 76/G7
Guinea-Bissau (ctry.) 78/B3
Guisborough, Eng, UK 23/G2
Gūjar Khān, Pak. 53/K2
Gujrānwāla, Pak. 53/K2
Gujrāt, Pak. 53/K2
Gukovo, Rus. 44/F2
Gulbarga, India 62/C4
Gulf (coast. pl.), Tx, US 96/D5
Gulf Coastal (plain), US 96/D5
Gulfport, Ms, US 97/F4
Guliston, Uzb. 46/G5
Gulu, Ugan. 77/M7
Gummersbach, Ger. 29/E6
Gümüşhane, Turk. 44/F4
Guntūr, India 62/D4
Günzburg, Ger. 37/G1
Gunzenhausen, Ger. 33/J2
Gura Humorului, Rom. 41/G2
Gurdāspur, India 53/L2
Gürgentepe, Turk. 44/F4
Gurnee, Il, US 99/Q15
Gurupi, Braz. 107/J6
Gus'-Khrustal'nyy, Rus. 42/J5
Gusau, Nga. 79/G3
Güstrow, Ger. 26/G2
Gütersloh, Ger. 29/F5
Guthrie, Ok, US 93/H4
Guyana (ctry.), Guy. 106/G2
Guyancourt, Fr. 30/B6
Guymon, Ok, US 93/G3
Gwādar, Pak. 53/H3
Gwalior, India 62/C2
Gwanda, Zim. 82/E5
Gweru, Zim. 82/E4
Győr, Hun. 40/C2
Gyumri, Arm. 45/G4
Gyzylarbat, Trkm. 45/L5

H

Haaksbergen, Neth. 28/D4
Haaltert, Belg. 30/D2
Haan, Ger. 28/E6
Haar, Ger. 33/J2
Haarlem, Neth. 28/B4
Habiganj, Bang. 60/A3
Hachinohe, Japan 47/Q5
Hachiōji, Japan 57/F3
Hacılar, Turk. 50/C2
Hadano, Japan 57/F3
Ḩadera, Isr. 49/F7
Haderslev, Den. 26/E1
Haeju, NKor. 58/C3
Hāfizābād, Pak. 53/K2
Hagåtña (cap.), Guam 68/D3
Hagen, Ger. 29/E6
Hagerstown, Md, US 94/E4
Hagi, Japan 56/B3
Hague, The (cap.), Neth. 28/B4
Haguenau, Fr. 31/G6
Hai Duong, Viet. 65/D1
Hai Phong, Viet. 65/D1
Haicheng, China 58/B2
Haiger, Ger. 31/H2
Haikou, China 61/F4
Ḩā'il, SAr. 50/E5
Hailākāndi, India 60/B3
Hailar, China 55/H2
Hailsham, Eng, UK 25/G5
Hailun, China 55/K2
Haines City, Fl, US 97/H4
Haining, China 59/L9
Haiti (ctry.), Haiti 102/H3
Hajdúboszormény, Hun. 40/E2
Hajdúdorog, Hun. 40/E2
Hajdúnánás, Hun. 40/E2
Hajdúszoboszló, Hun. 40/E2
Hajnówka, Pol. 27/M2
Hakodate, Japan 55/N3
Hakui, Japan 57/E2
Hāla, Pak. 53/J3
Ḩalab (Aleppo), Syria 49/E1
Halawa, Hi, US 88/T10
Halden, Nor. 20/D4
Haldensleben, Ger. 26/F2
Haldimand, On, Can. 95/T10
Hale, Eng, UK 23/F5
Halesowen, Eng, UK 24/D2
Halifax, Eng, UK 23/G4
Halifax (cap.), NS, Can. 95/J2
Halle, Ger. 29/F4
Halle, Ger. 26/F3
Halle, Belg. 31/D2
Halle-Neustadt, Ger. 26/F3
Hallein, Aus. 40/A2
Hallsberg, Swe. 20/E4
Halluin, Fr. 30/C2
Halmstad, Swe. 20/E4
Ḩalq al Wādī, Tun. 38/B4
Helsingborg, Swe. 20/E4
Haltern, Ger. 29/E5
Halton Hills, On, Can. 95/T8
Halver, Ger. 29/E6
Hamada, Japan 56/C3
Hamadān, Iran 51/G3
Hamakita, Japan 57/E3
Hamamatsu, Japan 57/E3
Hamar, Nor. 20/D3
Hamburg, NY, US 94/E3
Hamburg, Ger. 29/G1
Hämeenlinna, Fin. 42/E3
Hameln, Ger. 29/G4
Hamhŭng, NKor. 58/D3
Hamilton, On, Can. 95/T9
Hamilton, NZ 71/S10
Hamīrpur, India 62/D2
Hamm, Ger. 29/E5
Ḩammām Al Anf, Tun. 38/B4
Hamme, Belg. 28/B6
Hamminkeln, Ger. 28/D5
Hammond, La, US 97/F4
Hammond, In, US 99/R16
Hampton, Va, US 97/J2
Hamtramck, Mi, US 99/F7
Hanamaki, Japan 55/N4
Hanau, Ger. 26/E3
Hanford, Ca, US 92/C3
Haninge, Swe. 42/C4
Hannibal, Mo, US 93/K3
Hannover, Ger. 29/G4
Hanoi (cap.), Viet. 65/D1
Hanover, NH, US 95/F3
Hanover Park, Il, US 99/P16
Hānsi, India 53/L3
Hanumāngarh, India 62/B2
Hanzhong, China 54/F5
Haramachi, Japan 57/G2
Harare (cap.), Zim. 82/F4
Harbiye, Turk. 49/E1
Hardā, India 62/C3
Hardenberg, Neth. 28/D3
Harderwijk, Neth. 28/C4
Hardwār, India 53/L3
Harelbeke, Belg. 30/C2
Haren, Neth. 28/D2
Haren, Ger. 29/E3
Härer, Eth. 77/P6
Hargeysa, Som. 77/P6
Harihar, India 62/C5
Harlingen, Tx, US 96/D5
Harlingen, Neth. 28/C2
Harlow, Eng, UK 25/G3
Härnösand, Swe. 42/C3
Harpenden, Eng, UK 25/F3
Harper, Libr. 78/D5
Harper Woods, Mi, US 99/F7
Harrisburg, Il, US 97/F2
Harrisburg (cap.), Pa, US 94/E3
Harrison, Ar, US 93/J3
Harrisonburg, Va, US 97/J2
Harrogate, Eng, UK 23/G4
Harsewinkel, Ger. 29/F5
Harson's Island, Mi, US 99/G6
Harstad, Nor. 20/F1
Hartford (cap.), Ct, US 95/F3
Hartlepool, Eng, UK 23/G2
Hartselle, Al, US 97/G3
Hārūnābād, Pak. 53/K3
Harvey, Il, US 99/Q16
Harwich, Eng, UK 25/H3
Hashimoto, Japan 56/D3
Hāsilpur, Pak. 53/K3
Haslingden, Eng, UK 23/F4
Hassan, India 62/C5
Hasselt, Belg. 31/E2
Hässleholm, Swe. 20/E4
Hastings, Ne, US 93/H2
Hastings, NZ 71/S10
Hastings, Eng, UK 25/G5
Hat Yai, Thai. 65/C5
Hatfield, Eng, UK 25/F3
Hāthras, India 62/C2
Hatta, India 62/C3
Hattiesburg, Ms, US 97/F4
Hattingen, Ger. 29/E6
Hatvan, Hun. 40/D2
Haugesund, Nor. 20/C4
Hautmont, Fr. 30/C3
Havana (cap.), Cuba 103/F1
Havant, Eng, UK 25/F5
Havelock, NC, US 97/J3
Haverhill, Ma, US 95/G3
Haverhill, Eng, UK 25/G2
Havířov, Czh. 27/K4
Havlíčkuv Brod, Czh. 33/L2
Havza, Turk. 44/E4
Hawaii (isl.), US 88/U11
Hawaii (state), US 88/S10
Hawaii Kai, Hi, US 88/W13
Hawaiian (isls.), US 69/H2
Ḩawallī, Kuw. 51/G4
Hawarden, Wal, UK 23/E5
Ḩawsh 'Isá, Egypt 49/B4
Hayange, Fr. 31/F5
Haydock, Eng, UK 23/F5
Haylaastay, Mong. 47/M5
Hayrabolu, Turk. 41/H5
Hays, Ks, US 93/H3
Haysyn, Ukr. 44/D2
Hayward, Ca, US 99/K11
Hazāribag, India 62/E3
Hazebrouck, Fr. 30/B2
Hazel Park, Mi, US 99/F7
Hazleton, Pa, US 94/F3
Healdsburg, Ca, US 92/B3
Heanor, Eng, UK 23/G6
Hechi, China 61/F3
Hechingen, Ger. 37/E1
Hedemora, Swe. 20/E3
Heemskerk, Neth. 28/B3
Heemstede, Neth. 28/B4
Heerde, Neth. 28/D4
Heerenveen, Neth. 28/C3
Heerhugowaard, Neth. 28/B3
Heerlen, Neth. 31/E2
Ḩefa (Haifa), Isr. 49/F6
Hefei, China 61/H2
Hegang, China 55/L2
Heide, Ger. 26/E1
Heidelberg, Ger. 33/H2
Heidenheim, Ger. 33/J2
Heilbronn, Ger. 33/H2
Heiligenhaus, Ger. 28/D6
Heiligenstadt, Ger. 29/H6
Heiloo, Neth. 28/B3
Heinola, Fin. 42/E3
Heinsberg, Ger. 28/D6
Heist-op-den-Berg, Belg. 31/D1
Helden, Neth. 28/D6
Helena (cap.), Mt, US 90/E4
Hellendoorn, Neth. 28/D4
Hellevoetsluis, Neth. 28/B5
Hellín, Sp. 34/E3
Helmond, Neth. 28/C6
Helmstedt, Ger. 26/F2
Helsingfors (Helsinki), Fin. 42/E3
Helsingør, Den. 20/E4
Hemel Hempstead, Eng, UK 25/F3
Hemer, Ger. 29/E6
Hemmingen, Ger. 29/G4
Hendek, Turk. 41/K5
Henderson, Nv, US 92/D3
Henderson, Tx, US 93/J4
Henderson, Ky, US 97/G2
Henderson, NC, US 97/J2
Hendersonville, Tn, US 97/G2
Hendrik-Ido-Ambacht, Neth. 28/B5
Hengelo, Neth. 28/D4
Hengshui, China 59/C3
Hengyang, China 61/G3
Heniches'k, Ukr. 44/E3
Hénin-Beaumont, Fr. 30/B3
Hennef, Ger. 31/G2
Henzada, Myan. 60/B5
Herāt, Afg. 53/H2
Herblay, Fr. 30/B6
Hercegnovi, Yugo. 40/D4
Hercules, Ca, US 99/K10
Herdecke, Ger. 29/E6
Heredia, CR 103/E4
Hereford, Tx, US 93/G4
Hereford, Eng, UK 24/D2
Herentals, Belg. 28/B6
Herford, Ger. 29/F4
Herisau, Swi. 37/F3
Hermansverk, Nor. 20/C3
Hermiston, Or, US 90/D4
Hermosillo, Mex. 92/E5
Hernani, Sp. 34/E1
Herne, Ger. 29/E5
Herne Bay, Eng, UK 25/H4
Herning, Den. 20/D4
Heroica Caborca, Mex. 92/D5
Heroica Matamoros, Mex. 96/D5
Heroica Nogales, Mex. 92/E5
Hérouville-Saint-Clair, Fr. 32/C2
Herstal, Belg. 31/E2
Herten, Ger. 29/E5
Hertford, Eng, UK 25/F3
Herve, Belg. 31/E2
Hervey Bay, Austl. 72/D4
Herzberg am Harz, Ger. 29/H5
Herzele, Belg. 30/C2
Herzliyya, Isr. 49/F7
Herzogenaurach, Ger. 33/J2
Herzogenrath, Ger. 31/F2
Heshan, China 61/F4
Hessisch Oldendorf, Ger. 29/G4
Heusden-Zolder, Belg. 28/C6
Heusweiler, Ger. 31/F5
Heywood, Eng, UK 23/F4
Heze, China 59/C4
Hialeah, Fl, US 97/H5
Hibbing, Mn, US 91/K4
Hickory, NC, US 97/H3
Hidalgo del Parral, Mex. 96/B5
Hiddenhausen, Ger. 29/F4
Higashine, Japan 57/G1
High Point, NC, US 97/H3
High Wycombe, Eng, UK 25/F3
Highland, In, US 99/R16
Highland Park, Il, US 99/Q15
Highland Park, Mi, US 99/F7
Hihyā, Egypt 49/B4
Hiji, Japan 56/B4
Hikone, Japan 56/E3
Hilchenbach, Ger. 31/H2
Hilden, Ger. 28/D6
Hildesheim, Ger. 29/G4
Hille, Ger. 29/F4
Hillegom, Neth. 28/B4
Hillerød, Den. 20/E4
Hillsboro, Or, US 90/C4
Hillsborough, Ca, US 99/K11
Hilo, Hi, US 88/U11
Hilton Head Island, SC, US 97/H3
Hilversum, Neth. 28/C4
Himeji, Japan 56/D3
Himi, Japan 57/E2
Ḩimş, Syria 49/E2
Hinche, Haiti 103/H2
Hinckley, Eng, UK 25/E1
Hindley, Eng, UK 23/F4
Hindupur, India 62/C5
Hinesville, Ga, US 97/H4
Hinganghāt, India 62/C3
Hingoli, India 62/C4
Hingorja, Pak. 62/A2
Hınıs, Turk. 45/G5
Hinsdale, Il, US 99/Q16
Hirado, Japan 56/A4
Hirakata, Japan 56/D3
Hirata, Japan 56/C3
Hirosaki, Japan 55/N3
Hiroshima, Japan 56/C3
Hisai, Japan 56/E3
Hisār, India 62/C2
Hispaniola (isl.), Haiti 103/H1
Hitachi, Japan 57/G2
Hitachi-ōta, Japan 57/G2
Hitchin, Eng, UK 25/F3
Hitoyoshi, Japan 56/B4
Hjørring, Den. 20/D4
Hlohovec, Slvk. 40/C1
Hlukhiv, Ukr. 44/E2
Hmawbi, Myan. 60/C5
Ho, Gha. 79/F5
Hoa Binh, Viet. 65/D1
Hobara, Japan 57/G2
Hobart, Austl. 73/C4
Hobbs, NM, US 93/G4
Hoboken, Belg. 28/B6
Hod Hasharon, Isr. 49/F7
Hoddesdon, Eng, UK 25/F3
Hódmezővásárhely, Hun. 40/E2
Hodonín, Czh. 27/J4
Hoensbroek, Neth. 31/E2
Hof, Ger. 33/J1
Hoffman Estates, Il, US 99/P15
Hofgeismar, Ger. 29/G6
Hōfu, Japan 56/B3
Hohhot, China 54/G3
Hoi An, Viet. 65/E3
Hōjō, Japan 56/C4
Hokkaidō (isl.), Japan 55/N3
Hokota, Japan 57/G2
Holguín, Cuba 103/G1
Holland, Mi, US 94/C3
Hollister, Ca, US 92/B3
Hollogne-aux-Pierres, Belg. 31/E2
Hollola, Fin. 42/E3
Hollywood, Fl, US 97/H5
Holmfirth, Eng, UK 23/G4
Ḩolon, Isr. 49/F7
Holstebro, Den. 20/D4
Holyoke, Ma, US 95/F3
Holzminden, Ger. 29/G5
Holzwickede, Ger. 29/E5
Homberg, Ger. 28/D6
Hombourg-Haut, Fr. 31/F5
Homburg, Ger. 31/G5
Homestead, Fl, US 97/H5
Homewood, Al, US 97/G3
Homewood, Il, US 99/Q16
Homyel', Bela. 44/D1
Hon Quan, Viet. 65/D4
Honāvar, India 62/B5
Hondo, Japan 56/B4
Honduras (ctry.), Hon. 102/D3
Hong Gai, Viet. 65/D1
Hong Kong (reg.), China 61/G4
Hongch'ŏn, SKor. 56/A2
Honghu, China 61/G2
Hongjiang, China 61/F3
Hongsŏng, SKor. 58/D4
Honiara (cap.), Sol. 68/E5
Honolulu (cap.), Hi, US 88/T10
Hood (mt.), Or, US 90/C4
Hoofddorp, Neth. 28/B4
Hoogeveen, Neth. 28/D3
Hoogezand, Neth. 28/D2
Hoogstraten, Belg. 28/B6
Hoorn, Neth. 28/C3
Hopewell, Va, US 97/J2
Hopkinsville, Ky, US 97/G2
Horb am Neckar, Ger. 37/E1
Horgen, Swi. 37/E3
Horley, Eng, UK 25/F4
Horlivka, Ukr. 44/F2
Horn (cape), Chile 109/C8
Horn-Bad Meinberg, Ger. 29/F5
Hornell, NY, US 94/E3
Horsens, Den. 20/D5
Horsforth, Eng, UK 23/G4
Horsham, Eng, UK 25/F4
Horst, Neth. 28/D6
Hörstel, Ger. 29/E4
Horwich, Eng, UK 23/F4
Hoshangābād, India 62/C3
Hotaka, Japan 57/E2
Hot'Kovo, Rus. 43/X9
Houghton-le-Spring, Eng, UK 23/G2
Houma, China 59/B4
Houston, Tx, US 93/J5
Houten, Neth. 28/C4
Hove, Eng, UK 25/F5
Howrah, India 62/E3
Höxter, Ger. 29/G5
Hoyerswerda, Ger. 27/H3
Hoylake, Eng, UK 23/E5
Hoyland Nether, Eng, UK 23/G4
Hradec Králové, Czh. 33/L1
Hrazdan, Arm. 45/H4
Hrodna, Bela. 27/M2

120

Kakho – Kryvy

Kakhovka, Ukr. 41/L2
Kākināda, India 62/D4
Kakuda, Japan 57/G2
Kalaa Kebira, Tun. 38/B5
Kalach, Rus. 45/G2
Kalach-na-Donu, Rus. 45/G2
Kalachinsk, Rus. 46/H4
Kalahari (des.), Afr. 80/B2
Kalamákion, Gre. 39/N8
Kalamariá, Gre. 40/F5
Kalamáta, Gre. 39/H4
Kalamazoo, Mi, US 94/C3
Kalasin, Thai. 65/C2
Kalemie, D.R. Congo 82/E2
Kaltern (Caldaro), It. 37/H4
Kalgoorlie-Boulder, Austl. 68/B8
Kalianda, Indo. 66/C5
Kalibo, Phil. 67/F1
Kaliningrad, Rus. 43/W9
Kaliningrad, Rus. 27/L1
Kalininsk, Rus. 45/H2
Kalinkavichy, Bela. 44/D1
Kalisz, Pol. 27/K3
Kalix, Swe. 42/D2
Kāliyāganj, India 62/E2
Kallithéa, Gre. 39/N9
Kalmar, Swe. 20/F4
Kalmthout, Belg. 28/B6
Kalocsa, Hun. 40/D2
Kālol, India 62/B3
Kālpi, India 62/C2
Kaluga, Rus. 44/F1
Kalundborg, Den. 26/F1
Kalush, Ukr. 44/C2
Kalutara, SrL. 62/C6
Kalyān, India 62/B4
Kamaishi, Japan 55/N4
Kaman, Turk. 44/E5
Kāmāreddi, India 62/C4
Kāmārhāti, India 62/E3
Kambar, Pak. 62/A2
Kamchatka (pen.), Rus. 47/R4
Kamen, Ger. 29/E5
Kamen'-na-Obi, Rus. 46/J4
Kamenka, Rus. 45/H1
Kamensk-Shakhtinskiy, Rus. 44/G2
Kamensk-Ural'skiy, Rus. 43/P4
Kameoka, Japan 56/D3
Kamiisco, Japan 55/N3
Kamina, D.R. Congo 82/E2
Kaminoyama, Japan 57/G1
Kamloops, BC, Can. 90/C3
Kamo, Japan 57/F2
Kamogawa, Japan 57/G3
Kamojima, Japan 56/D3
Kamp-Lintfort, Ger. 28/D5
Kampala (cap.), Ugan. 77/M7
Kampar, Malay. 66/B3
Kampen, Neth. 28/C3
Kampóng Saom, Camb. 65/C4
Kam'yanets'-Podil's'kyy, Ukr. 44/C2
Kamyshin, Rus. 45/H2
Kananga, D.R. Congo 82/D2
Kanash, Rus. 43/K5
Kanasin, Mex. 102/D1
Kanazawa, Japan 57/E2
Kanchanaburi, Thai. 65/B3
Kānchīpuram, India 62/C5
Kandalaksha, Rus. 42/G2
Kandhkot, Pak. 62/A2
Kāndi, India 62/E3
Kandi, Ben. 79/F4
Kandukūr, India 62/C4
Kandy, SrL. 62/D6
Kaneohe, Hi, US 88/W13
Kangar, Malay. 65/C5
Kangasala, Fin. 20/H3
Kangnŭng, SKor. 56/A2
Kanjiža, Yugo. 40/E2
Kankan, Gui. 78/C4
Kannapolis, NC, US 97/H3
Kannauj, India 62/C2
Kano, Nga. 79/H4
Kan'onji, Japan 56/C3
Kanoya, Japan 56/B5
Kānpur, India 62/D2
Kansas (state), US 93/H3
Kansas City, Ks, US 93/J3
Kansas City, Mo, US 93/J3
Kansk, Rus. 46/K4
Kantābānji, India 62/D3
Kanuma, Japan 57/F2
Kanye, Bots. 80/D2
Kaohsiung, Tai. 61/J4
Kaolack, Sen. 78/A3
Kapan, Arm. 45/H5
Kapellen, Belg. 28/B6
Kapfenberg, Aus. 40/B2
Kaposvár, Hun. 40/C2
Kara, Togo 79/F4
Karabük, Turk. 44/E4
Karacabey, Turk. 44/D4
Karachev, Rus. 44/E1
Karāchi, Pak. 62/A3
Karād, India 62/B4
Karaj, Iran 51/G3
Karakol, Kyr. 46/H5
Karaköse, Turk. 45/G5
Karaman, Turk. 50/C2
Karamay, China 46/J5
Karamürsel, Turk. 41/J5
Karangasem, Indo. 67/E5
Kāranja, India 62/C3
Karapınar, Turk. 50/C2
Karasu, Turk. 41/K5
Karasuk, Rus. 46/H4
Karatsu, Japan 56/A4
Karawang, Indo. 66/C5
Karazhal, Kaz. 46/H5
Karbalā', Iraq 51/F3
Karcag, Hun. 27/L5
Kardhítsa, Gre. 39/G3
Karhula, Fin. 20/H3
Karīmnagar, India 62/C4
Kārkāl, India 62/B5
Karleby (Kokkola), Fin. 42/D3
Karlovac, Cro. 40/B3
Karlovo, Bul. 41/G4
Karlovy Vary, Czh. 33/K1
Karlsfeld, Ger. 37/H1
Karlshamn, Swe. 20/E4
Karlskoga, Swe. 20/E4
Karlskrona, Swe. 20/E4
Karlsruhe, Ger. 33/H2
Karlstad, Swe. 20/E4
Karmāla, India 62/C4
Karnāl, India 62/C2
Karnobat, Bul. 41/H4
Karonga, Malw. 82/F2
Kars, Turk. 45/G4
Kartaly, Rus. 45/M1
Kartuzy, Pol. 27/K1
Karviná, Czh. 27/K4
Karwar, India 62/B5
Kasai, Japan 56/D3
Kasama, Japan 57/G2
Kasama, Zam. 82/F3
Kasane, Bots. 82/E4
Kasaoka, Japan 56/C3
Kāsaragod, India 62/C5
Kaseda, Japan 56/B5
Kāsganj, India 62/C2
Kāshān, Iran 51/G3
Kashi, China 46/H6
Kashihara, Japan 56/D3
Kashima, Japan 57/G3
Kashima, Japan 56/B4
Kashin, Rus. 42/H4
Kashiwazaki, Japan 57/F2
Kāshmar, Iran 51/J3
Kasimov, Rus. 45/G1
Kaspiysk, Rus. 45/H4
Kassala, Sudan 52/C5
Kassel, Ger. 29/G6
Kastamonu, Turk. 44/E4
Kasterlee, Belg. 28/B6
Kastoría, Gre. 40/E5
Kasukabe, Japan 57/F3
Kasūr, Pak. 53/K2
Katahdin (mt.), Me, US 95/G2
Kateríni, Gre. 39/H2
Kāthgodām, India 62/C2
Kāthmāndu (cap.), Nepal 62/E2
Kathua, India 53/L2
Kati, Mali 78/C3
Katiola, C.d'Iv. 78/D4
Katlehong, SAfr. 80/Q13
Katowice, Pol. 27/K3
Katsina, Nga. 79/G3
Katsuragi, Japan 56/D3
Katsuta, Japan 57/G2
Katsuura, Japan 57/G3
Katsuyama, Japan 56/E2
Katwijk aan Zee, Neth. 28/B4
Kauai (isl.), US 88/S9
Kaufbeuren, Ger. 37/G2
Kauhajoki, Fin. 42/D3
Kaumalapau, Hi, US 88/T10
Kaunas, Lith. 27/M1
Kavadarci, FYROM 40/F5
Kavajë, Alb. 40/D5
Kavála, Gre. 41/G5
Kavalerovo, Rus. 55/M3
Kāvali, India 62/C5
Kavaratti, India 62/B5
Kavieng, PNG 68/E5
Kawagoe, Japan 57/F3
Kawaguchi, Japan 57/F3
Kawamata, Japan 57/G2
Kawardha, India 62/D3
Kawasaki, Japan 57/F3
Kayes, Mali 78/C3
Kayseri, Turk. 50/C2
Kayuagung, Indo. 66/B4
Kazakhstan (ctry.) 46/G5
Kazan', Rus. 43/L5
Kazanlŭk, Bul. 41/G4
Kāzerūn, Iran 51/G4
Kazincbarcika, Hun. 27/L4
Kazuno, Japan 55/N3
Kearney, Ne, US 93/H2
Keawakapu, Hi, US 88/T10
Kebumen, Indo. 66/C5
Kecskemét, Hun. 40/D2
Kėdainiai, Lith. 27/M1
Kediri, Indo. 66/D5
Kędzierzyn-Koźle, Pol. 27/K3
Keelung (Chilung), Tai. 61/J3
Keene, NH, US 95/F3
Kefar Sava, Isr. 49/F7
Kehl, Ger. 31/G6
Keighley, Eng, UK 23/G4
Kelang, Malay. 66/B3
Kelheim, Ger. 33/J2
Kélo, Chad 76/J6
Kelowna, BC, Can. 90/D3
Kelso, Wa, US 90/C4
Keluang, Malay. 66/B3
Kem', Rus. 42/G2
Kemerovo, Rus. 46/J4
Kemi, Fin. 20/H2
Kempen, Ger. 28/D6
Kempston, Eng, UK 25/F2
Kempten, Ger. 37/G2
Kempton Park, SAfr. 80/Q13
Kendal, Eng, UK 23/F3
Kendall, Fl, US 97/H5
Kendari, Indo. 67/F4
Kendrāpāra, India 62/E3
Kenema, SLeo. 78/C5
Kenilworth, Eng, UK 25/E2
Kénitra, Mor. 76/D1
Kenmore, NY, US 95/V10
Kenner, La, US 97/F4
Kennett, Mo, US 93/K3
Kennewick, Wa, US 90/D4
Kenosha, Wi, US 99/Q14
Kent, Oh, US 94/D3
Kent, Wa, US 99/C3
Kentaū, Kaz. 46/G5
Kentucky (state), US 94/C4
Kenya (peak), Kenya 77/N8
Kenya (ctry.) 74/F4
Keonjhar, India 62/E3
Kerava, Fin. 20/H3
Kerch, Ukr. 44/F3
Keren, Erit. 52/C5
Kérkira, Gre. 39/F3
Kerkrade, Neth. 31/F2
Kermān, Iran 51/J4
Kérou, Ben. 79/F4
Kerrville, Tx, US 93/H5
Keşan, Turk. 41/H5
Kesen'numa, Japan 55/N4
Keshod, India 62/B3
Keskin, Turk. 44/E5
Kestel, Turk. 44/D4
Keszthely, Hun. 40/C2
Ketchikan, Ak, US 85/M4
Kétou, Ben. 79/F5
Kętrzyn, Pol. 27/L1
Kettering, Eng, UK 25/F2
Kevelaer, Ger. 28/D5
Key Largo, Fl, US 97/H5
Key West, Fl, US 97/H5
Kežmarok, Slvk. 27/L4
Khabarovsk, Rus. 55/M2
Khabarovsk Kray, Rus. 47/P4
Khairpur, Pak. 62/A2
Khalándrion, Gre. 39/N8
Khalkís, Gre. 39/H3
Khambhāliya, India 53/J4
Khambhat, India 62/B3
Khāmgaon, India 62/C3
Khamīs Mushayţ, SAr. 52/D5
Khammam, India 62/D4
Khān Yūnus, Gaza 49/D4
Khānābād, Afg. 53/J1
Khānaqīn, Iraq 51/F3
Khandwa, India 53/L4
Khānewāl, Pak. 53/K2
Khaniá, Gre. 39/J5
Khānpur, Pak. 62/B2
Khanty-Mansiysk, Rus. 46/G3
Kharagpur, India 62/E3
Kharkiv, Ukr. 44/F2
Kharmanli, Bul. 41/G5
Khartoum (cap.), Sudan 52/B5
Khasavyurt, Rus. 45/H4
Khashuri, Geo. 45/G4
Khemis Miliana, Alg. 76/F1
Khénifra, Mor. 76/D1
Kherson, Ukr. 41/L2
Khilok, Rus. 54/G1
Khimki, Rus. 43/W9
Khíos, Gre. 39/K3
Khiva, Uzb. 46/G5
Khmel'nytskyy, Ukr. 44/C2
Kholm, Afg. 53/J1
Kholmsk, Rus. 55/N2
Khomeynīshahr, Iran 51/G3
Khon Kaen, Thai. 65/C2
Khorramābād, Iran 51/G3
Khorramshahr, Iran 51/G4
Khouribga, Mor. 76/D1
Khujand, Taj. 46/G5
Khulna, Bang. 62/E3
Khurda, India 62/E3
Khust, Ukr. 27/M4
Khuzdār, Pak. 53/J3
Khvalynka, Rus. 55/L3
Khvoy, Iran 45/H5
Kičevo, FYROM 40/E5
Kidal, Mali 79/F2
Kidapawan, Phil. 67/G2
Kidderminster, Eng, UK 24/D2
Kidsgrove, Eng, UK 23/F5
Kiel, Ger. 26/F1
Kielce, Pol. 27/L3
Kien An, Viet. 65/D1
Kierspe, Ger. 29/E6
Kiev (cap.), Ukr. 44/D2
Kiffa, Mrta. 78/C2
Kifisiá, Gre. 39/N8
Kigali (cap.), Rwa. 77/M8
Kihei, Hi, US 88/T10
Kikinda, Yugo. 40/E3
Kikwit, D.R. Congo 82/C2
Kilgore, Tx, US 93/J4
Kilimanjaro (peak), Tanz. 82/G1
Kilimli, Turk. 41/K5
Kilis, Turk. 49/E1
Kiliya, Ukr. 41/J3
Killeen, Tx, US 93/H5
Kimbe, PNG 68/E5
Kimberley, SAfr. 80/D3
Kimch'aek, NKor. 58/E2
Kimch'ŏn, SKor. 56/A2
Kimhae, SKor. 56/A3
Kimitsu, Japan 57/F3
Kimje, SKor. 58/D5
Kimovsk, Rus. 44/F1
Kimry, Rus. 42/H4
Kindia, Gui. 78/B4
Kindu, D.R. Congo 82/E1
Kinel', Rus. 45/J1
Kineshma, Rus. 42/J4
King William's Town, SAfr. 80/D4
Kingman, Az, US 92/D4
Kings Canyon National Park, Ca, US 92/C3
King's Lynn, Eng, UK 25/G1
Kingsport, Tn, US 97/H2
Kingston, On, Can. 94/E2
Kingston, NY, US 94/F3
Kingston (cap.), Jam. 103/G2
Kingston upon Hull, Eng, UK 23/H4
Kingston upon Thames, Eng, UK 25/F4
Kingstown (cap.), StV. 104/F4
Kingsville, Tx, US 96/D5
Kingswood, Eng, UK 24/D4
Kınık, Turk. 44/C5
Kinshasa (cap.), D.R. Congo 82/C1
Kinston, NC, US 97/J3
Kipushi, D.R. Congo 82/E3
Kiranomena, Madg. 81/H7
Kirchheim unter Teck, Ger. 26/E4
Kirchlengern, Ger. 29/F4
Kiribati (ctry.) 68/H5
Kırıkhan, Turk. 49/E1
Kırıkkale, Turk. 44/E5
Kirishi, Rus. 42/G4
Kırkağaç, Turk. 44/C5
Kirkby, Eng, UK 23/F5
Kirkby in Ashfield, Eng, UK 23/G5
Kirkee, India 62/B4
Kirkland, Qu, Can. 95/N7
Kirkland, Wa, US 99/C2
Kırklareli, Turk. 41/H5
Kirksville, Mo, US 91/K5
Kirkūk, Iraq 51/F3
Kirov, Rus. 43/L4
Kirov, Rus. 44/E1
Kirovo-Chepetsk, Rus. 43/L4
Kirovohrad, Ukr. 44/E2
Kirovsk, Rus. 42/G2
Kirsanov, Rus. 45/G1
Kırşehir, Turk. 44/E5
Kiruna, Swe. 42/D2
Kiryū, Japan 57/F2
Kisangani, D.R. Congo 77/L7
Kisarazu, Japan 57/F3
Kiselevsk, Rus. 46/J4
Kishanganj, India 62/E2
Kishangarh, India 62/B2
Kishiwada, Japan 56/D3
Kishorganj, Bang. 62/F3
Kiskőrös, Hun. 40/D2
Kiskunfélegyháza, Hun. 40/D2
Kiskunhalas, Hun. 40/D2
Kislovodsk, Rus. 45/G4
Kismaayo (Chisimayu), Som. 77/P8
Kissimmee, Fl, US 97/H4
Kisumu, Kenya 77/M8
Kisvárda, Hun. 27/M4
Kita, Mali 78/C3
Kita-Ibaraki, Japan 57/G2
Kitakata, Japan 57/F2
Kitakyūshū, Japan 56/B4
Kitami, Japan 55/N3
Kitchener, On, Can. 94/D3
Kittery, Me, US 95/G3
Kitwe, Zam. 82/E3
Kitzingen, Ger. 33/J2
Kizel, Rus. 43/N4
Kızılhisar, Turk. 50/B2
Kızıltepe, Turk. 50/E2
Kizlyar, Rus. 45/H4
Kladanj, Bosn. 40/D3
Kladno, Czh. 33/L1
Klagenfurt, Aus. 40/B2
Klaipėda, Lith. 42/D5
Klamath Falls, Or, US 90/C5
Klangenan, Indo. 66/C5
Klatovy, Czh. 33/K2
Klausen (Chiusa), It. 37/H4
Kleppestø, Nor. 20/C3
Klerksdorp, SAfr. 80/P13
Kleve, Ger. 28/D5
Klintsy, Rus. 44/E1
Ključ, Bosn. 40/C3
Kłodzko, Pol. 27/J3
Klosterneuburg, Aus. 40/C1
Kloten, Swi. 37/E3
Kluczbork, Pol. 27/K3
Knin, Cro. 40/C3
Knjaževac, Yugo. 40/F4
Knottingley, Eng, UK 23/G4
Knysna, SAfr. 80/C4
Koani, Tanz. 82/G2
Kobayashi, Japan 56/B5
Kōbe, Japan 56/D3
Koblenz, Ger. 31/G3
Kobrin, Bela. 27/N2
Kočani, FYROM 40/F5
Kočevje, Slov. 40/B3
Koch'ang, SKor. 58/D5
Kōchi, Japan 56/C4
Kodiak, Ak, US 85/H4
Kodiak (isl.), US 85/H4
Kodinār, India 62/B3
Koforidua, Gha. 79/E5
Kōfu, Japan 57/F3
Koga, Japan 57/F2
Køge, Den. 26/G1
Kogi, Nga. 79/G4
Kohāt, Pak. 53/K2
Kohīma, India 60/B3
Kohtla-Järve, Est. 42/E4
Kohŭng, SKor. 58/D5
Kokkola (Karleby), Fin. 42/D3
Kokomo, In, US 94/C3
Kokrajhar, India 62/F2
Kökshetaū, Kaz. 46/G4
Koksijde, Belg. 30/B1
Kokubu, Japan 56/B5
Kolār, India 62/C5
Kolbermoor, Ger. 33/K3
Kolda, Sen. 78/B3
Kolding, Den. 26/E1
Kolhāpur, India 62/B4
Kolín, Czh. 33/L1
Koło, Pol. 44/A1
Kołobrzeg, Pol. 27/H1
Kolomna, Rus. 44/F1
Kolomyya, Ukr. 41/G1
Kolpashevo, Rus. 46/J4
Kolpino, Rus. 43/T7
Kolwezi, D.R. Congo 82/E3
Komagane, Japan 57/E3
Komárno, Slvk. 27/K5
Komárom, Hun. 27/K5
Komatsu, Japan 56/E2
Komatsushima, Japan 56/D3
Komló, Hun. 40/D2
Komono, Japan 56/E3
Komotiní, Gre. 41/G5
Komsomol'sk-na-Amure, Rus. 55/M1
Komsomol'skiy, Rus. 43/P2
Kon Tum, Viet. 65/D3
Konakovo, Rus. 42/H4
Kondopoga, Rus. 42/G3
Kondūz, Afg. 46/G6
Kongju, SKor. 58/D4
Kongsberg, Nor. 20/D4
Kongsvinger, Nor. 20/E3
Königs Wusterhausen, Ger. 27/G2
Königsbrunn, Ger. 37/G1
Königslutter am Elm, Ger. 29/H4
Königswinter, Ger. 31/G2
Konin, Pol. 27/K2
Köniz, Swi. 36/D4
Konjic, Bosn. 40/C4
Konotop, Ukr. 44/E2
Końskie, Pol. 27/L3
Konstancin-Jeziorna, Pol. 27/L2
Konstantynów Łódzki, Pol. 27/K3
Konstanz, Ger. 37/F2
Kontich, Belg. 28/B6
Konya, Turk. 50/C2
Konz, Ger. 31/F4
Kopargaon, India 62/B4
Kópavogur, Ice. 20/N7
Köpenick, Ger. 27/G2
Koper, Slov. 40/A3
Kopeysk, Rus. 43/P5
Köping, Swe. 42/C4
Koprivnica, Cro. 40/C2
Koraput, India 62/D4
Korba, India 62/D3
Korbach, Ger. 29/F6
Korçë, Alb. 40/E5
Korea (bay), China, N. 55/J4
Korenovsk, Rus. 44/F3
Korhogo, C.d'Iv. 78/D4
Kórinthos (Corinth), Gre. 39/H4
Kōriyama, Japan 57/G2
Koronadal, Phil. 67/F2
Koror (cap.), Palau 68/C4
Korosten', Ukr. 44/D2
Korostyshiv, Ukr. 44/D2
Korsakov, Rus. 55/N2
Korschenbroich, Ger. 28/D6
Korsør, Den. 26/F1
Kortenberg, Belg. 31/D2
Kortrijk, Belg. 30/C2
Koryazhma, Rus. 43/K3
Kosai, Japan 57/E3
Kościan, Pol. 27/J2
Kościerzyna, Pol. 27/J1
Kosciusko (mt.), Austl. 73/D3
Koshigaya, Japan 57/F3
Košice, Slvk. 27/L4
Kosovo (reg.), Yugo. 39/G1
Kosovska Mitrovica, Yugo. 40/E4
Kostopil', Ukr. 44/C2
Kostroma, Rus. 42/J4
Kostrzyn, Pol. 27/H2
Kostyantynivka, Ukr. 44/F2
Koszalin, Pol. 27/J1
Kot Addu, Pak. 53/K2
Kot Kapūra, India 53/K2
Kota, India 62/C2
Kota Baharu, Malay. 65/C5
Kota Kinabalu, Malay. 67/E2
Kotaagung, Indo. 66/B5
Kotabaru, Indo. 67/E4
Kotabumi, Indo. 66/B4
Kotel'nich, Rus. 43/L4
Kotel'nikovo, Rus. 45/G3
Kothagūdem, India 62/D4
Köthen, Ger. 26/F3
Kotka, Fin. 42/E3
Kotlas, Rus. 43/K3
Kotor, Yugo. 40/D4
Kotovo, Rus. 45/H2
Kotovsk, Rus. 45/G1
Kotri, Pak. 62/A2
Kottayam, India 62/C6
Koudougou, Burk. 79/E3
Koulikoro, Mali 78/D3
Koumra, Chad 76/J6
Koupela, Burk. 79/E3
Koutiala, Mali 78/D3
Kouvola, Fin. 42/E3
Kovel', Ukr. 44/C2
Kovilpatti, India 62/C6
Kovrov, Rus. 42/J4
Kovūr, India 62/C5
Kovylkino, Rus. 45/G1
Kowloon, China 61/G4
Kōyama, Japan 56/B5
Kozan, Turk. 50/C2
Kozáni, Gre. 39/G2
Kozienice, Pol. 27/L3
Kozlu, Turk. 41/K5
Kozluk, Turk. 50/E2
Kozyatyn, Ukr. 44/D2
Kpalimé, Togo 79/F5
Kpandu, Gha. 79/F5
Kraaifontein, SAfr. 80/L10
Kragujevac, Yugo. 40/E3
Kraków, Pol. 27/K3
Kraljevo, Yugo. 40/E4
Kralupy nad Vltavou, Czh. 33/L1
Kramators'k, Ukr. 44/F2
Kramfors, Swe. 42/C3
Kranj, Slov. 40/B2
Krapkowice, Pol. 27/J3
Kraśnik, Pol. 27/M3
Kraśnik Fabryczny, Pol. 27/M3
Krasnoarmeysk, Rus. 45/H2
Krasnodar, Rus. 44/F3
Krasnodar Kray, Rus. 46/D5
Krasnogorsk, Rus. 43/W9
Krasnohrad, Ukr. 44/E2
Krasnokamensk, Rus. 55/H1
Krasnokamsk, Rus. 43/M4
Krasnoslobodsk, Rus. 45/H2
Krasnotur'insk, Rus. 46/G4
Krasnoural'sk, Rus. 43/P4
Krasnoyarsk, Rus. 46/K4
Krasnystaw, Pol. 27/M3
Krasnyy Kut, Rus. 45/H2
Krasnyy Luch, Ukr. 44/F2
Krasnyy Sulin, Rus. 44/G3
Krefeld, Ger. 28/D6
Kremenchuk, Ukr. 44/E2
Krems an der Donau, Aus. 33/L2
Kreuzau, Ger. 31/F2
Kreuzlingen, Swi. 37/F2
Kreuztal, Ger. 31/G2
Kribi, Camr. 76/G7
Krichev, Bela. 44/D1
Kriens, Swi. 37/E3
Krimpen aan de IJssel, Neth. 28/B5
Krishnagiri, India 62/C5
Kristiansand, Nor. 20/C4
Kristianstad, Swe. 20/E4
Kristiansund, Nor. 20/C3
Kristinehamn, Swe. 20/E4
Kriva Palanka, FYROM 40/F4
Krnov, Czh. 27/J3
Krolevets', Ukr. 44/E2
Kroměříž, Czh. 27/J4
Kronach, Ger. 33/J1
Kronshtadt, Rus. 43/S6
Kroonstad, SAfr. 80/D2
Kropotkin, Rus. 45/G3
Krosno, Pol. 27/L4
Krotoszyn, Pol. 27/J3
Krško, Slov. 40/B3
Krugersdorp, SAfr. 80/P13
Krujë, Alb. 40/D5
Kruševac, Yugo. 40/E4
Krymsk, Rus. 44/F3
Kryvyy Rih, Ukr. 41/L2

121

Krzyż – Lough

Krzyż, Pol. 27/J2
Kuala Belait, Bru. 66/D3
Kuala Dungun, Malay. 66/B3
Kuala Lumpur (cap.), Malay. 66/B3
Kuala Terengganu, Malay. 66/B2
Kuantan, Malay. 66/B3
Kubokawa, Japan 56/C4
Kuching, Malay. 66/D3
Kudamatsu, Japan 56/B3
Kudat, Malay. 67/E2
Kudus, Indo. 66/D5
Kudymkar, Rus. 43/M4
Kuji, Japan 55/N3
Kuki, Japan 57/F2
Kula, Yugo. 40/D3
Kula, Turk. 44/D5
Kulai, Malay. 66/B3
Kulebaki, Rus. 45/G1
Kullu, India 53/L2
Kulmbach, Ger. 33/J1
Kŭlob, Taj. 53/J1
Kul'sary, Kaz. 45/K3
Kulu, Turk. 44/E5
Kulunda, Rus. 46/H4
Kumagaya, Japan 57/F2
Kumamoto, Japan 56/B4
Kumano, Japan 56/E4
Kumanovo, FYROM 40/E4
Kumasi, Gha. 79/E5
Kumba, Camr. 79/H5
Kumbo, Camr. 79/H5
Kumertau, Rus. 45/K1
Kumi, SKor. 56/A2
Kumla, Swe. 20/E4
Kumluca, Turk. 49/B1
Kumo, Nga. 79/H4
Kumta, India 62/B5
Kūnch, India 62/C2
Kundapura, India 62/B5
Kundiān, Pak. 53/K2
Kundiawa, PNG 68/D5
Kundla, India 62/B3
Kungälv, Swe. 20/D4
Kungsbacka, Swe. 20/E4
Kungur, Rus. 43/N4
Kuningan, Indo. 66/C5
Kunming, China 60/D3
Kunsan, SKor. 58/D5
Kunshan, China 59/L8
Kuopio, Fin. 42/E3
Kupang, Indo. 67/F6
Kupino, Rus. 46/H4
Kup'yans'k, Ukr. 44/F2
Kurashiki, Japan 56/C3
Kurayoshi, Japan 56/C3
Kŭrdzhali, Bul. 41/G5
Kure, Japan 56/C3
Kurgan, Rus. 43/Q5
Kuri, SKor. 58/G6
Kuril (isls.), Rus. 47/Q5
Kurnool, India 62/C4
Kuroiso, Japan 57/G2
Kurseong, India 62/E2
Kursk, Rus. 44/F2
Kurtalan, Turk. 50/E2
Kürten, Ger. 29/E6
Kurume, Japan 56/B4
Kurunegala, SrL. 62/D6
Kuşadası, Turk. 50/A2
Kushikino, Japan 56/B5
Kushima, Japan 56/B5
Kushimoto, Japan 56/D4
Kushiro, Japan 55/N3
Kūstī, Sudan 77/M5
Kütahya, Turk. 44/D5
K'ut'aisi, Geo. 45/G4
Kutná Hora, Czh. 33/L2
Kutno, Pol. 27/K2
Kuusamo, Fin. 20/J2
Kuusankoski, Fin. 42/E3
Kuvandyk, Rus. 45/L2
Kuwait (ctry.) 51/F4
Kuwait (cap.), Kuw. 51/F4
Kuwana, Japan 57/E3
Kuznetsk, Rus. 45/H1
Kwach'ŏn, SKor. 58/F7
Kwamashu, SAfr. 81/E3
Kwangju, SKor. 58/D5
Kwangju, SKor. 58/G7
Kwangmyŏng, SKor. 58/F7
Kwekwe, Zim. 82/E4
Kwidzyn, Pol. 27/K2
Kyakhta, Rus. 54/F1
Kymore, India 62/C3
Kyŏngju, SKor. 56/A3
Kyŏngsan, SKor. 56/A3
Kyōto, Japan 56/D3
Kyrenia, Cyp. 49/C2
Kyrgyzstan (ctry.) 46/H5
Kyustendil, Bul. 40/F4
Kyzyl, Rus. 54/C1

L

La Asunción, Ven. 104/F5
La Baie, Qu, Can. 95/G1
La Banda, Arg. 109/D2
La Baule-Escoublac, Fr. 32/B3
La Carolina, Sp. 34/D3
La Ceiba, Hon. 102/E3
La Chapelle-Saint-Luc, Fr. 32/F2
La Chaux-de-Fonds, Swi. 36/C3
La Chorrera, Pan. 103/G4
La Ciotat, Fr. 32/F5
La Concepción, Nic. 102/E4
La Coruña, Sp. 34/A1
La Crosse, Wi, US 91/L5
La Dorada, Col. 106/D2
La Esperanza, Hon. 102/D3
La Estrada, Sp. 34/A1
La Flèche, Fr. 32/C3
La Grande, Or, US 90/D4
La Grange, Ga, US 97/G3
La Laguna, Canl. 35/X16
La Libertad, Ecu. 106/B4
La Libertad, Guat. 102/D2
La Línea de la Concepción, Sp. 34/C4
La Louvière, Belg. 31/D3
La Madeleine, Fr. 30/C2
La Oroya, Peru 106/C6
La Paz, Arg. 109/E3
La Paz, Mex. 100/C3
La Paz, Hon. 102/E3
La Paz (cap.), Bol. 106/E7
La Piedad Cavadas, Mex. 100/E4
La Porte, In, US 94/C3
La Prairie, Qu, Can. 95/P7
La Rinconada, Sp. 34/C4
La Rioja, Arg. 109/C2
La Roche-sur-Yon, Fr. 32/C3
La Rochelle, Fr. 32/C3
La Salle, Il, US 91/L5
La Serena, Chile 109/B2
La Seyne-sur-Mer, Fr. 32/F5
La Solana, Sp. 34/D3
La Spezia, It. 33/H4
La Teste, Fr. 32/C4
La Trinidad, Phil. 61/J5
La Unión, ESal. 102/E3
La Unión, Chile 109/B5
La Victoria, Ven. 106/E1
Laas (Lasa), It. 37/G4
Laatzen, Ger. 29/G4
Labé, Gui. 78/B4
Labinsk, Rus. 45/G3
Laboulaye, Arg. 109/D3
Lábrea, Braz. 106/F5
Laces (Latsch), It. 37/G4
Lacey, Wa, US 99/B3
Lachenaie, Qu, Can. 95/N6
Lachine, Qu, Can. 95/N7
Lackawanna, NY, US 95/V10
Laconia, NH, US 95/G3
Ladysmith, SAfr. 81/E3
Lafayette, In, US 94/C3
Lafayette, La, US 93/J5
Lafayette, Ca, US 99/K11
Lafia, Nga. 79/H4
Lagarto, Braz. 107/L6
Lagawe, Phil. 61/J5
Lage, Ger. 29/F5
Lages, Braz. 108/B3
Laghouat, Alg. 76/F1
Lagny-sur-Marne, Fr. 30/B6
Lagoa da Prata, Braz. 108/C2
Lagoa Vermelha, Braz. 108/B4
Lagos, Nga. 79/F5
Lagos, Port. 34/A4
Lagos de Moreno, Mex. 100/E4
Laguna, Braz. 108/B4
Lahad Datu, Malay. 67/E2
Lahat, Indo. 66/B4
Lāhījān, Iran 51/G2
Lahnstein, Ger. 31/G3
Laholm, Swe. 20/E4
Lahore, Pak. 53/K2
Lahr, Ger. 36/D1
Lahti, Fin. 42/E3
Laï, Chad 76/J6
Lai Chau, Viet. 65/C1
Laiwu, China 59/D3
Lajatico, It. 33/J5
Lajeado, Braz. 108/B4
Lake Charles, La, US 93/J5
Lake City, Fl, US 97/H3
Lake Forest, Il, US 99/Q15
Lake Havasu City, Az, US 92/D4
Lake Jackson, Tx, US 93/J5
Lake of the Woods (lake), Can.,US 94/A1
Lake Station, In, US 99/R16
Lake Wales, Fl, US 97/H5
Lake Worth, Fl, US 97/H5
Lake Zurich, Il, US 99/P15
Lakeland, Fl, US 97/H4
Lakewood, Co, US 93/F3
Lakewood, Wa, US 99/B3
Lakhīmpur, India 62/D2
Lakki, Pak. 53/K2
Lakshadweep (isls.), India 62/B5
Lāla Mūsa, Pak. 53/K2
Lalín, Sp. 34/A1
Lalitpur, India 62/C3
Lambaré, Par. 109/E2
Lambaréné, Gabon 82/B1
Lambayeque, Peru 106/C5
Lamesa, Tx, US 93/G4
Lamía, Gre. 39/H3
Lamitan, Phil. 67/F2
Lamont, Ca, US 92/C4
Lampang, Thai. 65/B2
Lampertheim, Ger. 33/H2
Lanaken, Belg. 31/E2
Lancaster, Pa, US 94/E3
Lancaster, Ca, US 92/C4
Lancaster, NY, US 95/V10
Lancaster, Eng, UK 23/F3
Lanciano, It. 40/B4
L'Ancienne-Lorette, Qu, Can. 95/G2
Łańcut, Pol. 27/M3
Lancy, Swi. 36/C5
Land's End (pt.), Eng, UK 24/A6
Landau in der Pfalz, Ger. 31/H5
Landerneau, Fr. 32/A2
Landsberg, Ger. 37/G1
Landshut, Ger. 33/K2
Lanester, Fr. 32/B3
Lang Son, Viet. 65/D1
Langen, Ger. 29/F1
Langenfeld, Ger. 28/D6
Langenhagen, Ger. 29/G4
Langenthal, Swi. 36/D3
Langfang, China 59/H7
Langsa, Indo. 66/A3
Länkäran, Azer. 51/G2
Lannion, Fr. 32/B2
Lansing (cap.), Mi, US 94/C3
Lansing, Il, US 99/Q16
Lanxi, China 61/H2
Lanzhou, China 54/E4
Lanzo d'Intelvi, It. 37/F6
Lao Cai, Viet. 65/C1
Laohekou, China 61/F1
Laon, Fr. 30/C4
Laos (ctry.) 65/C2
Lapa, Braz. 108/B3
Lapland (reg.), Swe. 20/F1
Lappeenranta, Fin. 42/F3
Lapua, Fin. 42/D3
Łapy, Pol. 27/M2
L'Aquila, It. 38/C1
Lār, Iran 51/H5
Larache, Mor. 76/D1
Laramie, Wy, US 93/F2
Laranjeiras do Sul, Braz. 108/A3
Laredo, Tx, US 96/D5
Largo, Fl, US 97/H5
Lárisa, Gre. 39/H3
Lārkāna, Pak. 62/A2
Larkspur, Ca, US 99/J11
Larnaca, Cyp. 49/C2
Larne, NI, UK 22/C2
Larreynaga, Nic. 102/E3
Larsen Ice Shelf, Ant. 83/V
Las Cabezas de San Juan, Sp. 34/C4
Las Choapas, Mex. 101/G5
Las Cruces, NM, US 92/F4
Las Flores, Arg. 109/E4
Las Guacamayas, Mex. 100/E5
Las Matas de Farfán, DRep. 103/J2
Las Palmas, Pan. 103/F4
Las Palmas de Gran Canaria, Canl. 35/X16
Las Rozas de Madrid, Sp. 35/N9
Las Tablas, Pan. 103/F5
Las Vegas, NM, US 93/F4
Las Vegas, Nv, US 92/D3
Lasa (Laas), It. 37/G4
Lasalle, Qu, Can. 95/N7
Lashio, Myan. 60/C4
Lashkar Gāh, Afg. 53/H2
Latacunga, Ecu. 106/C4
Latina, It. 38/C2
Latsch (Laces), It. 37/G4
Lātūr, India 62/C4
Latvia (ctry.) 20/H4
Lauf, Ger. 33/J2
Laukaa, Fin. 42/E3
Launceston, Austl. 73/C4
Laupheim, Ger. 37/F1
Laurel, Ms, US 97/F4
Laurens, SC, US 97/H3
Laurinburg, NC, US 97/J3
Lausanne, Swi. 36/C4
Lauterbach, Ger. 33/H1
Lautoka, Fiji 69/Y18
Laval, Qu, Can. 95/N6
Laval, Fr. 32/C2
Lavras, Braz. 108/C2
Lawrence, Ma, US 95/G3
Lawrence, Ks, US 93/J3
Lawrenceburg, Tn, US 97/G3
Lawrenceville, Ga, US 97/H3
Laxou, Fr. 31/F6
Lázaro Cárdenas, Mex. 100/E5
Le Blanc-Mesnil, Fr. 30/B6
Le Cannet, Fr. 33/G5
Le Creusot, Fr. 32/F3
Le Havre, Fr. 32/D2
Le Mans, Fr. 32/D2
Le Port, Reun. 81/S15
Le Puy-en-Velay, Fr. 32/E4
Le Tampon, Reun. 81/S15
League City, Tx, US 93/J5
Leamington, On, Can. 99/G7
Leatherhead, Eng, UK 25/F4
Leavenworth, Ks, US 93/J3
Lebach, Ger. 31/F5
Lebanon, Or, US 90/C4
Lebanon, Tn, US 97/G2
Lebanon, Mo, US 93/J3
Lebanon, NH, US 95/F3
Lebanon, Pa, US 94/E3
Lebanon, In, US 97/G1
Lebanon (ctry.) 49/D3
Lebbeke, Belg. 28/B6
Lebedyn, Ukr. 44/E2
Lębork, Pol. 27/J1
Lebowakgomo, SAfr. 81/E2
Lebrija, Sp. 34/B4
Lebu, Chile 109/B4
Lecce, It. 39/F2
Lecco, It. 33/H4
Łęczna, Pol. 27/M3
Lede, Belg. 28/A7
Leeds, Eng, UK 23/G4
Leek, Eng, UK 23/F5
Leek, Neth. 28/D2
Leer, Ger. 29/E2
Leerdam, Neth. 28/C5
Leesburg, Fl, US 97/H4
Leeuwarden, Neth. 28/C2
Leganés, Sp. 35/N9
Legaspi, Phil. 68/B3
Legionowo, Pol. 27/L2
Legnago, It. 33/J4
Legnano, It. 33/H4
Legnica, Pol. 27/J3
Lehigh Acres, Fl, US 97/H5
Lehrte, Ger. 29/G4
Leiah, Pak. 53/K2
Leicester, Eng, UK 25/E1
Leichlingen, Ger. 28/E6
Leiden, Neth. 28/B4
Leiderdorp, Neth. 28/B4
Leidschendam, Neth. 28/B4
Leifers (Laives), It. 37/H5
Leigh, Eng, UK 23/F5
Leinefelde, Ger. 29/H6
Leipzig, Ger. 26/G3
Leiria, Port. 34/A3
Leksands-Noret, Swe. 20/E3
Lelystad, Neth. 28/C3
Leme, Braz. 108/C2
Lemgo, Ger. 29/F4
Lempäälä, Fin. 20/G3
Lençóis Paulista, Braz. 108/B2
Lengerich, Ger. 29/E4
Lengshuitan, China 61/F3
Leninogor, Kaz. 46/J4
Leninogorsk, Rus. 43/M5
Leninsk-Kuznetskiy, Rus. 46/J4
Leninváros, Hun. 27/L5
Lennestadt, Ger. 29/F6
Lenoir, NC, US 97/H3
Lens, Fr. 30/B3
Lensk, Rus. 47/M3
Lentini, It. 38/D4
Léo, Burk. 79/E4
Leoben, Aus. 40/B2
León, Mex. 101/E4
León, Nic. 102/E3
León, Sp. 34/C1
Leon Valley, Tx, US 93/H5
Leonberg, Ger. 26/E4
Leonding, Aus. 33/L2
Leonforte, It. 38/D4
Leopoldina, Braz. 108/L6
Lepe, Sp. 34/B4
Lerdo de Tejada, Mex. 101/P8
Les Cayes, Haiti 103/H2
Les Mureaux, Fr. 30/A6
Les Sables-d'Olonne, Fr. 32/C3
Les Ulis, Fr. 30/B6
Leshan, China 60/D2
Leskovac, Yugo. 40/E4
Lesotho (ctry.) 80/D3
Lesozavodsk, Rus. 55/L2
Lesser Antilles (isls.), Neth. 104/E3
Lessines, Belg. 30/C2
Leszno, Pol. 27/J3
Letchworth, Eng, UK 25/F3
Lethbridge, Ab, Can. 90/E3
Leticia, Col. 106/E4
Letpadan, Myan. 60/B5
Leuca, It. 39/F3
Leusden-Zuid, Neth. 28/C4
Leutkirch im Allgäu, Ger. 37/G2
Levádhia, Gre. 39/H3
Levanger, Nor. 20/D3
Levelland, Tx, US 93/G4
Leventina (Prato), Swi. 37/E5
Leverkusen, Ger. 28/D6
Levice, Slvk. 40/D1
Levin, NZ 71/S11
Lévis, Qu, Can. 95/G2
Levittown, Pa, US 94/F3
Lewes, Eng, UK 25/G5
Lewisburg, Tn, US 97/G3
Lewiston, Id, US 90/D4
Lewiston, Me, US 95/G2
Lewistown, Pa, US 94/E3
Lexington, NC, US 97/H3
Lexington, Ky, US 97/G2
Lexington Park, Md, US 97/J2
Leyland, Eng, UK 23/F4
Lezhë, Alb. 40/D5
L'gov, Rus. 44/E2
Lhasa, China 60/A2
L'Hospitalet de Llobregat, Sp. 35/L7
Lianyungang, China 59/D4
Liaocheng, China 59/C3
Liaoyang, China 58/B2
Liaoyuan, China 59/F2
Liāquatpur, Pak. 53/K3
Liberal, Ks, US 93/G3
Liberec, Czh. 27/H3
Liberia, CR 102/E4
Liberia (ctry.) 78/C5
Libertador General San Martín, Arg. 109/D1
Liberty, Mo, US 93/J3
Libertyville, Il, US 99/P15
Libreville (cap.), Gabon 76/G7
Libya (ctry.) 77/J2
Libyan (des.), Afr. 77/K2
Libyan (plat.), Libya 77/K1
Licata, It. 38/C4
Lichfield, Eng, UK 25/E1
Lichinga, Moz. 82/G3
Lichtenfels, Ger. 33/J1
Lichtenvoorde, Neth. 28/D5
Lichuan, China 61/F2
Lida, Bela. 42/E5
Lidköping, Swe. 20/E4
Lido, It. 33/K4
Lido di Ostia, It. 38/C2
Lidzbark Warmiński, Pol. 27/L1
Liechtenstein (ctry.) 37/F3
Liège, Belg. 31/E2
Lieksa, Fin. 42/F3
Liepāja, Lat. 42/D4
Lier, Belg. 28/B6
Liestal, Swi. 36/D3
Liévin, Fr. 30/B3
Ligao, Phil. 67/F1
Likasi, D.R. Congo 82/E3
Lilienthal, Ger. 29/F2
Liling, China 63/K2
Lille, Fr. 30/C2
Lillehammer, Nor. 20/D3
Lillestrøm, Nor. 20/D4
Lilongwe (cap.), Malw. 82/F3
Lima, Oh, US 94/C3
Lima (cap.), Peru 106/C6
Limassol, Cyp. 49/C2
Limbdi, India 62/B3
Limburg an der Lahn, Ger. 31/H3
Limeira, Braz. 108/C2
Limerick, Ire. 21/A10
Limoges, Fr. 32/D4
Limón, CR 103/F4
Linares, Chile 109/B4
Linares, Mex. 96/D5
Linares, Sp. 34/D3
Linchuan, China 61/H3
Lincoln, Il, US 93/K2
Lincoln, Eng, UK 23/H5
Lincoln, On, Can. 95/U9
Lincoln (cap.), Ne, US 91/J5
Lincoln Park, Mi, US 99/F7
Lindau, Ger. 37/F2
Linden, Guy. 106/G2
Lindesberg, Swe. 20/E4
Lindi, Tanz. 82/G3
Lindlar, Ger. 29/E6
Lindsay, On, Can. 94/E2
Linfen, China 59/B3
Lingen, Ger. 29/E3
Lingolsheim, Fr. 31/G6
Linhai, China 61/J2
Linhai, China 55/J1
Linhares, Braz. 108/D1
Linhe, China 59/A2
Linköping, Swe. 20/E4
Linosa, It. 38/C5
Linqing, China 59/C3
Lins, Braz. 108/B2
Linyi, China 59/D4
Linz, Aus. 40/B1
Lion (gulf), Fr.,Sp. 32/D5
Lipetsk, Rus. 44/F1
Lippstadt, Ger. 29/F5
Liptovský Svätý Mikuláš, Slvk. 27/K4
Lira, Ugan. 77/M7
Liria, Sp. 35/E3
Lisbon, Me, US 95/G2
Lisbon (cap.), Port. 35/P10
Lisburn, NI, UK 22/B2
Lishui, China 61/H2
Lisieux, Fr. 32/D2
Liski, Rus. 44/F2
Lisle, Il, US 99/P16
L'Isle-sur-la-Sorgue, Fr. 32/F5
Lismore, Austl. 73/E1
Lisse, Neth. 28/B4
Litherland, Eng, UK 23/F5
Lithuania (ctry.) 42/D5
Littau, Swi. 37/E3
Little Rock (cap.), Ar, US 93/J4
Littlehampton, Eng, UK 25/F5
Liuzhou, China 61/F3
Livermore, Ca, US 99/L11
Liverpool, Eng, UK 23/F5
Livingston, Guat. 102/D3
Livingstone, Zam. 82/E4
Livingstone (falls), Congo 82/B2
Livno, Bosn. 40/C4
Livny, Rus. 44/F1
Livonia, Mi, US 99/F7
Livorno, It. 33/J5
Livry-Gargan, Fr. 30/B6
Ljubljana (cap.), Slov. 40/B2
Ljubuški, Bosn. 40/C4
Ljungby, Swe. 20/E4
Ljusdal, Swe. 42/C3
Llallagua, Bol. 106/E7
Llandudno, Wal, UK 22/E5
Llanes, Sp. 34/C1
Lleida, Sp. 35/F2
Llodio, Sp. 34/D1
Lloret de Mar, Sp. 35/G2
Lloydminster, Sk, Can. 90/F2
Lluchmayor, Sp. 35/G3
Llullaillaco (vol.), Arg.,Chile 109/C1
Lobatse, Bots. 80/N12
Lobito, Ang. 82/B3
Lobos, Arg. 109/E4
Locarno, Swi. 37/E5
Lochem, Neth. 28/D4
Lochristi, Belg. 28/A6
Lock Haven, Pa, US 94/E3
Lockport, NY, US 95/V9
Lockport, Il, US 99/P16
Lod, Isr. 49/F8
Lodeynoye Pole, Rus. 42/G3
Lodi, Ca, US 99/M10
Lodi, It. 33/H4
Łódź, Pol. 27/K3
Logan, Ut, US 92/E2
Logan (mt.), Can. 85/K3
Logansport, In, US 94/C3
Logroño, Sp. 34/D1
Lohja, Fin. 42/E3
Lohmar, Ger. 31/G2
Lohne, Ger. 29/F3
Löhne, Ger. 29/F4
Lohr, Ger. 26/E4
Loja, Ecu. 106/C4
Loja, Sp. 34/C4
Lokeren, Belg. 28/A6
Lokossa, Ben. 79/F5
Lom, Nor. 20/D3
Loma Bonita, Mex. 102/C2
Lomas de Zamora, Arg. 109/E3
Lombard, Il, US 99/P16
Lomé (cap.), Togo 79/F5
Lomme, Fr. 30/B2
Lommel, Belg. 28/C6
Lomonosov, Rus. 43/S7
Lompoc, Ca, US 92/B4
Łomża, Pol. 27/M2
Lonāvale, India 62/B4
Londerzeel, Belg. 28/B6
London, On, Can. 94/D3
London (cap.), Eng, UK 25/F3
Londonderry, NI, UK 22/A2
Londrina, Braz. 108/B2
Long (isl.), NY, US 95/F3
Long Beach, Ca, US 92/C4
Long Branch, NJ, US 94/F3
Long Eaton, Eng, UK 23/G6
Long Xuyen, Viet. 65/D4
Longjumeau, Fr. 30/B6
Longkou, China 59/E3
Longmont, Co, US 93/F2
Longueuil, Qu, Can. 95/P6
Longview, Wa, US 90/C4
Longview, Tx, US 93/J4
Longwy, Fr. 31/E4
Longyan, China 61/H3
Lons-le-Saunier, Fr. 36/B4
Loon op Zand, Neth. 28/C5
Loos, Fr. 30/C2
Lop Buri, Thai. 65/C3
López Mateos, Mex. 101/Q9
Lora del Río, Sp. 34/C4
Lorain, Oh, US 94/D3
Lorca, Sp. 34/E4
Lorena, Braz. 108/H7
Lorengau, PNG 68/D5
Loreto, Mex. 100/E4
Lorica, Col. 103/H4
Lorient, Fr. 32/B3
Lörrach, Ger. 36/D2
Los Alamos, NM, US 93/F4
Los Altos, Ca, US 99/K12
Los Amates, Guat. 102/D3
Los Andes, Chile 109/B3
Los Ángeles, Chile 109/B4
Los Angeles, Ca, US 92/C4
Los Banos, Ca, US 92/B3
Los Barrios, Sp. 34/C4
Los Llanos de Aridane, Canl. 35/X16
Los Mochis, Mex. 100/C3
Los Palacios y Villafranca, Sp. 34/C4
Los Reyes, Mex. 101/R10
Los Reyes de Salgado, Mex. 100/E5
Los Teques, Ven. 106/E1
Losheim, Ger. 31/F4
Losser, Neth. 28/E4
Lota, Chile 109/B4
Louangphrabang, Laos 65/C2
Loubomo, Congo 82/B1
Loudi, China 61/F3
Louga, Sen. 78/A3
Loughborough, Eng, UK 23/G6

123

Meran – Narra

Merano, It. 37/H4
Merauke, Indo. 67/K5
Merced, Ca, US 92/B3
Mercedes, Arg. 109/C3
Mercedes, Uru. 109/E3
Mercedes, Arg. 109/E2
Mercer Island, Wa, US 99/C2
Merefa, Ukr. 44/F2
Merelbeke, Belg. 28/A6
Mergui (Myeik), Myan. 65/B3
Mérida, Ven. 106/D2
Mérida, Mex. 102/D1
Mérida, Sp. 34/B3
Meridian, Ms, US 97/F3
Mérignac, Fr. 32/C4
Merksem, Belg. 28/B6
Merlo, Arg. 109/E3
Merrimack, NH, US 95/G3
Merritt Island, Fl, US 97/H4
Mersin, Turk. 49/D1
Merthyr Tydfil, Wal, UK 24/C3
Meru, Kenya 77/N7
Merzifon, Turk. 44/E4
Merzig, Ger. 31/F5
Mesa, Az, US 92/E4
Mesa Verde National Park, Co, US 92/E3
Mesagne, It. 40/C5
Meschede, Ger. 29/F6
Mesomeloka, Madg. 81/J8
Mesquite, Tx, US 93/H4
Messaad, Alg. 76/F1
Messina, It. 38/D3
Mestre, It. 33/K4
Metairie, La, US 97/F4
Metán, Arg. 109/D2
Metepec, Mex. 101/Q10
Mettmann, Ger. 28/D6
Metz, Fr. 31/F5
Metzingen, Ger. 37/F1
Mevasseret Ziyyon, Isr. 49/G8
Mexborough, Eng, UK 23/G5
Mexicali, Mex. 92/D4
Mexico, Mo, US 93/K3
Mexico (gulf), NAm. 89/H6
Mexico (ctry.), Mex. 84/G7
Mexico (cap.), Mex. 101/Q10
Meybod, Iran 51/H3
Meyerton, SAfr. 80/Q13
Meyrin, Swi. 36/C5
Meyzieu, Fr. 36/A6
Mezhdurechensk, Rus. 46/J4
Mezőkövesd, Hun. 27/L5
Mezőtúr, Hun. 40/E2
Mhamdia Fūshānah, Tun. 38/B4
Mhow, India 62/C3
Miami, Ok, US 93/J3
Miami, Fl, US 97/H5
Miami Beach, Fl, US 97/H5
Mīāndoāb, Iran 51/F2
Miandrivazo, Madg. 81/H7
Mīāneh, Iran 51/F2
Miānwāli, Pak. 53/K2
Mianyang, China 60/E2
Miass, Rus. 43/P5
Michalovce, Slvk. 27/L4
Michigan (lake), US 94/C2
Michigan (state), US 94/C2
Michigan City, In, US 94/C3
Michurinsk, Rus. 45/G1
Micronesia, Federated States of (ctry.) 68/D4
Middelburg, SAfr. 80/Q12
Middelburg, Neth. 28/A5
Middelharnis, Neth. 28/B5
Middelkerke, Belg. 30/B1
Middlesboro, Ky, US 97/H2
Middlesbrough, Eng, UK 23/G2
Middleton, Eng, UK 23/F4
Midland, On, Can. 94/E2
Midland, Mi, US 94/C3
Midland, Tx, US 93/G5
Midlothian, Il, US 99/Q16
Midyat, Turk. 50/E2
Mie, Japan 56/B4
Międzyrzec Podlaski, Pol. 27/M3
Międzyrzecz, Pol. 27/H2
Mielec, Pol. 27/L3
Miercurea Ciuc, Rom. 41/G2
Mieres, Sp. 34/C1
Migdal Ha'emeq, Isr. 49/G6
Miguelópolis, Braz. 108/B2
Mihara, Japan 56/C3
Miharu, Japan 57/G2
Mihrābpur, Pak. 53/J3
Mijas, Sp. 34/C4
Mikhaylovka, Rus. 45/G2
Mikkeli, Fin. 42/E3
Mikuni, Japan 56/E2
Milagro, Ecu. 106/C4
Milan (Milano), It. 33/H4
Milano (Milan), It. 33/H4
Milas, Turk. 50/A2
Milazzo, It. 38/D3
Mildura, Austl. 73/B2
Mililani Town, Hi, US 88/V13
Mill Valley, Ca, US 99/J11
Millau, Fr. 32/E4
Millbrae, Ca, US 99/K11
Milledgeville, Ga, US 97/H3
Millerovo, Rus. 45/G2
Milpitas, Ca, US 99/L12
Milton, On, Can. 95/T8
Milton Keynes, Eng, UK 25/F2
Milwaukee, Wi, US 99/Q13
Mīnā' Su'ūd, Kuw. 51/G4
Minamata, Japan 56/B4
Minas, Cuba 103/G1
Minas, Uru. 109/E3
Minas de Matahambre, Cuba 103/F1
Minatitlán, Mex. 102/C2
Minden, La, US 93/J4
Minden, Ger. 29/F4
Mineiros, Braz. 107/H7
Mineral Wells, Tx, US 93/H4
Mineral'nye Vody, Rus. 45/G3
Mingäçevir, Azer. 45/H4
Mingāora, Pak. 53/K2
Minna, Nga. 79/G4
Minnesota (state), US 91/K4
Mino, Japan 57/E3
Minorca (isl.), Sp. 35/H2
Minsk (cap.), Bela. 42/E5
Mińsk Mazowiecki, Pol. 27/L2
Minturno, It. 40/A5
Minūf, Egypt 49/B4
Minusinsk, Rus. 46/K4
Minyā al Qamḩ, Egypt 49/B4
Mirabel, Qu, Can. 95/M6
Miracema, Braz. 108/D2
Miracema do Norte, Braz. 107/J5
Miraj, India 62/B4
Miramar, Arg. 109/E4
Miranda de Ebro, Sp. 34/D1
Mirandola, It. 33/J4
Mirandópolis, Braz. 108/B2
Mirassol, Braz. 108/B2
Mirfield, Eng, UK 23/G4
Miri, Malay. 66/D3
Mirnyy, Rus. 47/M3
Miryang, SKor. 56/A3
Misaki, Japan 56/D3
Misantla, Mex. 101/N7
Mishawaka, In, US 94/C3
Mishima, Japan 57/F3
Misilmeri, It. 38/C3
Miskolc, Hun. 27/L4
Mişrātah, Libya 76/J1
Mission, Tx, US 96/D5
Mission Viejo, Ca, US 92/C4
Mississauga, On, Can. 95/T8
Mississippi (riv.), US 89/H5
Mississippi (state), US 97/F3
Missouri (state), US 93/J3
Missouri (riv.), US 88/G3
Missouri City, Tx, US 93/J5
Mitchell, SD, US 93/H2
Mitilíni, Gre. 39/K3
Mito, Japan 57/G2
Mitry-Mory, Fr. 30/B6
Mitsinjo, Madg. 81/H7
Mits'iwa, Erit. 77/N4
Mitsukaidō, Japan 57/F2
Mitsuke, Japan 57/F2
Mittweida, Ger. 26/G3
Mitú, Col. 106/D3
Mixquiahuala, Mex. 101/K6
Miyako, Japan 55/N4
Miyakonojō, Japan 56/B5
Miyanojō, Japan 56/B5
Miyazaki, Japan 56/B5
Miyazu, Japan 56/D3
Miyoshi, Japan 56/C3
Mizunami, Japan 57/E3
Mjölby, Swe. 20/E4
Mkokotoni, Tanz. 82/G2
Mladá Boleslav, Czh. 33/L1
Mladenovac, Yugo. 40/E3
Mława, Pol. 27/L2
Moa, Cuba 103/H1
Moaña, Sp. 34/A1
Moanda, Gabon 82/B1
Mobaye, CAfr. 77/K7
Moberly, Mo, US 93/J3
Mobile, Al, US 97/F4
Mochudi, Bots. 80/D2
Mocoa, Col. 106/C3
Mococa, Braz. 108/F6
Modāsa, India 62/B3
Modena, It. 33/J4
Modesto, Ca, US 92/B3
Modica, It. 38/D4
Mödling, Aus. 40/C1
Modriča, Bosn. 40/D3
Modugno, It. 40/C5
Moe, Austl. 73/C3
Moers, Ger. 28/D6
Moga, India 53/L2
Mogadishu (cap.), Som. 77/Q7
Mogi das Cruzes, Braz. 108/G8
Mogi-Guaçu, Braz. 108/G7
Mogi-Mirim, Braz. 108/G7
Mogocha, Rus. 55/H1
Mohács, Hun. 40/D3
Mohammedia, Mor. 76/D1
Mohyliv-Podil's'kyy, Ukr. 41/H1
Moineşti, Rom. 41/H2
Moita, Port. 35/Q10
Mojave (des.), Ca, US 88/C5
Mōka, Japan 57/F2
Mokokchūng, India 60/B3
Mokp'o, SKor. 58/D5
Mol, Belg. 28/C6
Mola di Bari, It. 40/C5
Molde, Nor. 20/C3
Moldova (ctry.) 41/H2
Moldova Nouă, Rom. 40/E3
Molepolole, Bots. 80/D2
Molfetta, It. 40/C5
Molina de Segura, Sp. 34/E3
Moline, Il, US 93/K2
Molins de Rei, Sp. 35/L7
Mollendo, Peru 106/D7
Mollet del Vallès, Sp. 35/L6
Mölln, Ger. 26/F2
Moluccas (arch.), Indo. 67/G3
Mombasa, Kenya 82/G1
Mombetsu, Japan 55/N3
Mona Passage (chan.), NAm. 104/D3
Monaco (cap.), Mona. 33/G5
Monaco (ctry.) 33/G5
Moncada, Sp. 35/E3
Moncalieri, It. 33/G4
Monchegorsk, Rus. 42/G2
Mönchengladbach, Ger. 28/D6
Monclova, Mex. 96/C5
Moncton, NB, Can. 95/H2
Mondovì, It. 33/G4
Mondragón, Sp. 34/D1
Mondragone, It. 40/A5
Monfalcone, It. 40/A3
Monforte, Sp. 34/B1
Mongaguá, Braz. 108/G9
Mongo, Chad 77/J5
Mongolia (ctry.) 54/D2
Mongu, Zam. 82/D4
Monheim, Ger. 28/D6
Monmouth, Il, US 93/K2
Monopoli, It. 40/C5
Monor, Hun. 40/D2
Monreale, It. 38/C3
Monroe, Ga, US 97/H3
Monroe, La, US 93/J4
Monroe, NC, US 97/H3
Monroe, Wi, US 93/K2
Monroe, Mi, US 94/D3
Monrovia (cap.), Libr. 78/C5
Mons, Belg. 30/C3
Monster, Neth. 28/B4
Mont-de-Marsan, Fr. 32/C5
Mont-Royal, Qu, Can. 95/N6
Montana (state), US 90/F4
Montana, Bul. 41/F4
Montargis, Fr. 32/E2
Montauban, Fr. 32/D4
Montbéliard, Fr. 36/C2
Montcada i Reixac, Sp. 35/L7
Montceau-les-Mines, Fr. 32/F3
Monte Alegre, Braz. 107/H4
Monte Alto, Braz. 108/B2
Monte Carmelo, Braz. 108/C1
Monte Caseros, Arg. 109/E3
Monte Sant'Angelo, It. 40/B5
Montego Bay, Jam. 103/G2
Montélimar, Fr. 32/F4
Montemorelos, Mex. 96/D5
Montenegro, Braz. 108/B4
Montereau-Faut-Yonne, Fr. 32/E2
Monterey, Ca, US 92/B3
Montería, Col. 103/H4
Montero, Bol. 106/F7
Monteros, Arg. 109/C2
Monterotondo, It. 38/C1
Monterrey, Mex. 96/C5
Montes Claros, Braz. 107/K7
Montesilvano Marina, It. 40/B4
Montevideo (cap.), Uru. 109/E3
Montgeron, Fr. 30/B6
Montgomery (cap.), Al, US 97/G3
Montigny-le-Bretonneux, Fr. 30/B6
Montigny-lès-Metz, Fr. 31/F5
Montijo, Port. 35/Q10
Montijo, Sp. 34/B3
Montilla, Sp. 34/C4
Montivilliers, Fr. 32/D2
Montluçon, Fr. 32/E3
Montpelier (cap.), Vt, US 95/F2
Montpellier, Fr. 32/E5
Montréal, Qu, Can. 95/N6
Montréal-Nord, Qu, Can. 95/N6
Montreux, Swi. 36/C5
Montserrat (dpcy.), Fr. 104/F3
Monywa, Myan. 60/B4
Monza, It. 33/H4
Monzón, Sp. 35/F2
Moore, Ok, US 93/H4
Mooresville, NC, US 97/H3
Moosburg, Ger. 33/J2
Moose Jaw, Sk, Can. 91/G3
Mopti, Mali 78/D3
Moquegua, Peru 106/D7
Mór, Hun. 40/D2
Mora, NM, US 93/F4
Mora, Swe. 20/E3
Morada Nova, Braz. 107/L5
Morādābād, India 62/C2
Morafenobe, Madg. 81/H7
Moraga, Ca, US 99/K11
Morales, Guat. 102/D3
Moramanga, Madg. 81/J7
Morarano Chrome, Madg. 81/J7
Moratuwa, SrL. 62/C6
Morelia, Mex. 101/E5
Morena, India 62/C2
Moreni, Rom. 41/G3
Moreno Valley, Ca, US 92/C4
Morgan City, La, US 93/K5
Morganton, NC, US 97/H3
Morioka, Japan 55/N4
Moriyama, Japan 56/D3
Morlaix, Fr. 32/B2
Morlanwelz, Belg. 31/D3
Morley, Eng, UK 23/G4
Moro, Pak. 62/A2
Morocco (ctry.) 76/C1
Morogoro, Tanz. 82/G2
Morombe, Madg. 81/G8
Morón, Cuba 103/G1
Morón, Arg. 109/E3
Mörön, Mong. 54/E2
Morón de la Frontera, Sp. 34/C4
Morondava, Madg. 81/H8
Moroni (cap.), Com. 81/G5
Moroto, Ugan. 77/M7
Morrinhos, Braz. 108/B1
Morris, Il, US 93/K2
Morristown, Tn, US 97/H2
Morro Bay, Ca, US 92/B4
Morshansk, Rus. 45/G1
Morton, Il, US 93/K2
Morton Grove, Il, US 99/Q15
Mortsel, Belg. 28/B6
Morvi, India 62/B3
Morwell, Austl. 73/C3
Mosbach, Ger. 33/H2
Moscow (cap.), Rus. 43/W9
Moscow Univ. Ice Shelf, Ant. 83/J
Moses Lake, Wa, US 90/D4
Moshi, Tanz. 82/G1
Mosonmagyaróvár, Hun. 40/C2
Moss, Nor. 20/D4
Moss Point, Ms, US 97/F4
Mosselbaai, SAfr. 80/C4
Mössingen, Ger. 37/F1
Mossoró, Braz. 107/L5
Most, Czh. 33/K1
Mostaganem, Alg. 76/F1
Mostar, Bosn. 40/C4
Móstoles, Sp. 35/N9
Mosul (Al Mawşil), Syria 51/E2
Motala, Swe. 20/E4
Motīhāri, India 62/D2
Motomiya, Japan 57/G2
Motril, Sp. 34/D4
Motul de Carrillo Puerto, Mex. 102/D1
Mouila, Gabon 82/B1
Moulins, Fr. 32/E3
Moultrie, Ga, US 97/H4
Moundou, Chad 76/J6
Moundsville, WV, US 97/H2
Mount Abu, India 62/B3
Mount Baker-Snoqualmie, Wa, US 99/D1
Mount Clemens, Mi, US 99/G6
Mount Gambier, Austl. 73/B3
Mount Hagen, PNG 68/D5
Mount Pearl, Nf, Can. 95/L2
Mount Pleasant, Tx, US 93/J4
Mount Pleasant, Mi, US 94/C3
Mount Prospect, Il, US 99/P15
Mount Rainier National Park, Wa, US 90/C4
Mount Vernon, Wa, US 90/C3
Mount Vernon, Il, US 93/K3
Mount Vernon, Oh, US 94/D3
Mountain Ash, Wal, UK 24/C3
Mountain View, Ca, US 99/K12
Mountlake Terrace, Wa, US 99/C2
Mouscron, Belg. 30/C2
Mouths of the Niger, Nga. 76/G6
Moyuta, Guat. 102/D3
Mozambique (ctry.) 82/G4
Mozambique (chan.), Afr. 82/J10
Mozhaysk, Rus. 42/H5
Mozhga, Rus. 43/M4
Mpika, Zam. 82/F3
Mrągowo, Pol. 27/L2
Mtsensk, Rus. 44/F1
Mualama, Moz. 82/G4
Muar, Malay. 66/B3
Muarabungo, Indo. 66/B4
Mucojo, Moz. 82/H3
Mudanjiang, China 55/K3
Mudanya, Turk. 41/J5
Mudon, Myan. 65/B2
Mufulira, Zam. 82/E3
Muğla, Turk. 50/B2
Mühldorf, Ger. 33/K2
Muju, SKor. 58/D4
Mukacheve, Ukr. 27/M4
Mukhayyam al Yarmūk, Syria 49/E3
Muktsar, India 53/K2
Mülhausen, Ger. 29/H6
Mülheim an der Ruhr, Ger. 28/D6
Mulhouse, Fr. 36/D2
Müllheim, Ger. 36/D2
Multān, Pak. 53/K2
Mumbai (Bombay), India 62/B4
Muncar, Indo. 66/D5
München, Ger. 37/H1
Muncie, In, US 97/G1
Mundelein, Il, US 99/Q15
Münden, Ger. 29/G6
Mundo Novo, Braz. 109/F1
Mungaolī, India 62/C3
Munger, India 62/E2
Münster, Ger. 29/E5
Munster, Ger. 29/H3
Munster, In, US 99/R16
Münstereifel, Ger. 31/F2
Muntok, Indo. 66/C4
Murakami, Japan 57/F1
Murcia, Sp. 35/E4
Muret, Fr. 32/D5
Murfreesboro, Tn, US 97/G3
Muriaé, Braz. 108/D2
Murmansk, Rus. 42/G1
Murom, Rus. 42/J5
Muroran, Japan 55/N3
Muroto, Japan 56/D4
Murphysboro, Il, US 93/K3
Murray, Ky, US 97/F2
Murray (riv.), Austl. 73/A2
Murwāra, India 62/D3
Muş, Turk. 50/E2
Muscat (cap.), Oman 53/G4
Mushābani, India 62/E3
Mushin, Nga. 79/F5
Muskego, Wi, US 99/P14
Musoma, Tanz. 82/F1
Mustafakemalpaşa, Turk. 44/D4
Mustang, Ok, US 93/H4
Mut, Turk. 49/C1
Mutare, Zim. 82/F4
Mutsamudu, Com. 81/H6
Mutsu, Japan 55/N3
Muttenz, Swi. 36/D2
Muzaffargarh, Pak. 53/K2
Muzaffarnagar, India 62/C2
Muzaffarpur, India 62/E2
Mwanza, Tanz. 82/F1
Mwene-Ditu, D.R. Congo 82/D2
My Tho, Viet. 65/D4
Myanmar (Burma) (ctry.) 63/G3
Myaungmya, Myan. 60/B5
Myingyan, Myan. 60/B4
Myitkyinā, Myan. 60/C3
Mykolayiv, Ukr. 41/L2
Myrhorod, Ukr. 44/E2
Myrtle Beach, SC, US 97/J3
Myślenice, Pol. 27/K4
Mysore, India 62/C5
Myszków, Pol. 27/K3
Mytishchi, Rus. 43/W9
Mzuzu, Malw. 82/F3

N

N'Djamena (cap.), Chad 76/J5
Naaldwijk, Neth. 28/B4
Naarden, Neth. 28/C4
Nabadwīp, India 62/E3
Nabari, Japan 56/E3
Naberezhnye Chelny, Rus. 43/M5
Nābul, Tun. 38/B4
Nacaome, Hon. 102/E3
Nachi-Katsuura, Japan 56/D4
Náchod, Czh. 33/M1
Nacogdoches, Tx, US 93/J5
Nadiād, India 62/B3
Nador, Mor. 76/E1
Naga, Phil. 68/B3
Nagahama, Japan 56/E3
Nagai, Japan 57/G1
Nagano, Japan 57/F2
Nagaoka, Japan 57/F2
Nagaokakyō, Japan 56/D3
Nagaon (Nowgong), India 60/B3
Nagasaki, Japan 56/A4
Nagato, Japan 56/B3
Nāgaur, India 62/B2
Nāgda, India 62/C3
Nāgercoil, India 62/C6
Nagold, Ger. 37/E1
Nagoya, Japan 57/E3
Nāgpur, India 62/C3
Nagykanizsa, Hun. 40/C2
Nagykőrös, Hun. 40/D2
Naha, Japan 68/B2
Nahariyya, Isr. 49/D3
Nahāvand, Iran 51/G3
Nainpur, India 62/D3
Nairobi (cap.), Kenya 77/N8
Najafābād, Iran 51/G3
Najībābād, India 62/C2
Naju, SKor. 58/D5
Nakajō, Japan 57/F1
Nakaminato, Japan 57/G2
Nakamura, Japan 56/C4
Nakano, Japan 57/F2
Nakatsu, Japan 56/B4
Nakatsugawa, Japan 57/E3
Nakhodka, Rus. 55/L3
Nakhon Pathom, Thai. 65/C3
Nakhon Phanom, Thai. 65/D2
Nakhon Ratchasima, Thai. 65/C3
Nakhon Sawan, Thai. 65/C3
Nakhon Si Thammarat, Thai. 65/B4
Nakło nad Notecią, Pol. 27/J2
Nakskov, Den. 26/F1
Nakuru, Kenya 82/G1
Nal'chik, Rus. 45/G4
Nalgonda, India 62/C4
Nālūt, Libya 76/H1
Nam Dinh, Viet. 65/D1
Namangan, Uzb. 46/H5
Namerikawa, Japan 57/E2
Namibe, Ang. 82/B4
Namibia (ctry.) 82/C5
Namie, Japan 57/G2
Namp'o, NKor. 58/C3
Nampula, Moz. 82/G4
Nāmrup, India 60/B3
Namur, Belg. 31/D3
Namwŏn, SKor. 58/D5
Namysłów, Pol. 27/J3
Nan, Thai. 65/C2
Nanaimo, BC, Can. 90/C3
Nanakuli, Hi, US 88/V13
Nanao, Japan 57/E2
Nanchang, China 61/G2
Nanchong, China 60/E2
Nancy, Fr. 31/F6
Nānded, India 62/C4
Nandurbār, India 62/B3
Nandyāl, India 62/C4
Nangapinoh, Indo. 66/D4
Nangong, China 59/C3
Nanjing, China 61/H1
Nankoku, Japan 56/C4
Nanning, China 65/E1
Nānpāra, India 62/D2
Nanping, China 61/H3
Nanterre, Fr. 30/B6
Nantes, Fr. 32/C3
Nanticoke, Pa, US 94/E3
Nanticoke, On, Can. 95/R10
Nantong, China 61/J1
Nanuque, Braz. 108/D1
Nanyang, China 59/C4
Náousa, Gre. 40/F5
Napa, Ca, US 99/K10
Naperville, Il, US 99/P16
Napier, NZ 71/S10
Naples, Fl, US 97/H5
Napoli, It. 40/B5
Nara, Japan 56/D3
Naranjos, Mex. 102/B1
Narasannapeta, India 62/D4
Narathiwat, Thai. 65/C5
Nārāyanganj, Bang. 62/F3
Nārāyanpet, India 62/C4
Narbonne, Fr. 32/E5
Nardò, It. 39/F2
Narkatiāganj, India 62/D2
Narón, Sp. 34/A1
Nārowāl, Pak. 53/K2
Närpiö (Närpes), Fin. 42/D3
Narra, Phil. 67/E2

124

Narsi – Ophir

Narsimhapur, India 62/C3
Narsingarh, India 62/C3
Naruto, Japan 56/D3
Narva, Est. 42/F4
Narvacan, Phil. 61/J5
Narvik, Nor. 42/C1
Nar'yan-Mar, Rus. 43/M2
Naryn, Kyr. 46/H5
Nashua, NH, US 87/J4
Nashua, NH, US 95/G3
Nashville (cap.), Tn, US 94/C4
Našice, Cro. 40/D3
Nāsik, India 62/B4
Nasīrābād, India 62/B2
Nassau (cap.), Bahm. 97/J5
Nasser (lake), Egypt 77/M3
Nässjö, Swe. 20/E4
Næstved, Den. 26/F1
Natal, Braz. 107/L5
Natchez, Ms, US 93/K5
Natchitoches, La, US 93/J5
Nāthdwāra, India 62/B3
Naturns (Naturno), It. 37/G4
Naucalpan, Mex. 101/Q10
Naumburg, Ger. 26/F3
Nauru (ctry.) 68/F5
Navalmoral de la Mata, Sp. 34/C3
Navapolatsk, Bela. 42/F5
Navirai, Braz. 109/F1
Năvodari, Rom. 41/J3
Navojoa, Mex. 100/C3
Navolato, Mex. 100/D3
Navsāri, India 62/B3
Nawābganj, India 62/D2
Nawābshāh, Pak. 62/A2
Nawoiy, Uzb. 46/G5
Naxçıvan, Azer. 45/H5
Nazaré, Braz. 107/L6
Nazca, Peru 106/D6
Naze, Japan 68/B2
Nazerat (Nazareth), Isr. 49/G6
Nazilli, Turk. 50/B2
Nazrēt, Eth. 77/N6
Nazyvayevsk, Rus. 46/H4
Ndalatando, Ang. 82/B2
Ndele, CAfr. 77/K6
Ndola, Zam. 82/E3
Néa Ionía, Gre. 39/N8
Néa Ionía, Gre. 39/H3
Neath, Wal, UK 24/C3
Nebitdag, Trkm. 51/H2
Nebraska (state), US 93/G2
Neckarsulm, Ger. 33/H2
Necochea, Arg. 109/E4
Nederland, Tx, US 93/J5
Nederweert, Neth. 28/C6
Neftekamsk, Rus. 43/M4
Negombo, SrL. 62/C6
Negotin, Yugo. 40/F3
Negotino, FYROM 40/F5
Negro (riv.), Arg. 109/D5
Negro (riv.), Uru. 109/E3
Neijiang, China 60/E2
Neiva, Col. 106/C3
Nek'emtē, Eth. 77/N6
Nelidovo, Rus. 42/G4
Nellore, India 62/C5
Nelson, Eng, UK 23/F4
Nelson, NZ 71/R11
Nelson (riv.), Mb, Can. 86/G3
Nelspruit, SAfr. 81/E2
Néma, Mrta. 78/D2
Nemuro, Japan 55/P3
Neosho, Mo, US 93/J3
Nepal (ctry.) 62/D2
Nepālganj, Nepal 62/D2
Nepanagar, India 62/C3
Nepean, On, Can. 94/F2
Nerekhta, Rus. 42/J4
Nerja, Sp. 34/D4
Nes Ziyyona, Isr. 49/F8
Nesher, Isr. 49/G6
Neston, Eng, UK 23/E5
Netanya, Isr. 49/F7
Netherlands (ctry.) 28/B5
Netherlands Antilles (dpcy.), Neth. 106/E1
Netphen, Ger. 31/H2
Nettetal, Ger. 28/D6
Nettuno, It. 38/C2
Neu-Ulm, Ger. 37/G1
Neubrandenburg, Ger. 27/G2
Neuburg an der Donau, Ger. 26/F4
Neuchâtel, Swi. 36/C4
Neufahrn bei Freising, Ger. 37/H1
Neuilly-sur-Seine, Fr. 30/B6
Neumarkt (Enga), It. 37/H5
Neumarkt in der Oberpfalz, Ger. 33/J2
Neumünster, Ger. 26/E1
Neunkirchen, Ger. 31/G5
Neunkirchen-Seelscheid, Ger. 31/G2
Neuquén, Arg. 109/C4
Neuruppin, Ger. 26/G2
Neusäss, Ger. 37/G1
Neuss, Ger. 28/D6
Neustadt am Rübenberge, Ger. 29/G3
Neustadt an der Weinstrasse, Ger. 31/H5
Neustadt bei Coburg, Ger. 33/J1
Neustadt in Holstein, Ger. 26/F1
Neustrelitz, Ger. 26/G2
Neuwied, Ger. 31/G3
Nevada (state), US 92/C3
Nevel', Rus. 42/F4
Nevel'sk, Rus. 55/N2
Nevers, Fr. 32/E3
Nevesinje, Bosn. 40/D4
Nevinnomyssk, Rus. 45/G3
Nevşehir, Turk. 50/C2
New Albany, In, US 97/G2
New Amsterdam, Guy. 106/G2
New Bedford, Ma, US 95/G3
New Berlin, Wi, US 99/P14
New Bern, NC, US 97/J3
New Braunfels, Tx, US 93/H5
New Britain, Ct, US 95/F3
New Brunswick (prov.), Can. 95/H2
New Caledonia (isl.), NCal. 69/U12
New Caledonia (dpcy.), Fr. 69/U11
New Castle, Pa, US 94/D3
New Castle, In, US 97/G2
New Delhi (cap.), India 62/C2
New Guinea (isl.), Indo.,PNG 68/C5
New Hampshire (state), US 95/G3
New Haven, Ct, US 95/F3
New Iberia, La, US 93/K5
New Jersey (state), US 94/F3
New Kensington, Pa, US 94/E3
New Lenox, Il, US 99/Q16
New London, Ct, US 95/F3
New Mexico (state), US 92/F4
New Orleans, La, US 97/F4
New Philadelphia, Oh, US 94/D3
New Plymouth, NZ 71/R10
New Port Richey, Fl, US 97/H4
New Smyrna Beach, Fl, US 97/H4
New South Wales, Austl. 73/D1
New Westminster, BC, Can. 90/C3
New York, NY, US 94/F3
New York (state), US 94/F3
New Zealand (ctry.) 71/Q10
Newark, Oh, US 97/H1
Newark, NJ, US 94/F3
Newark, Ca, US 99/K11
Newark-on-Trent, Eng, UK 23/H5
Newberry, SC, US 97/H3
Newburn, Eng, UK 23/G2
Newbury, Eng, UK 25/E4
Newcastle, SAfr. 81/E2
Newcastle, Austl. 73/D2
Newcastle upon Tyne, Eng, UK 23/G2
Newcastle-under-Lyme, Eng, UK 23/F6
Newfoundland (prov.), Can. 95/K1
Newfoundland (isl.), Can. 95/L1
Newmarket, On, Can. 94/E2
Newmarket, Eng, UK 25/G2
Newnan, Ga, US 97/G3
Newport, Ky, US 97/G2
Newport, RI, US 95/G3
Newport, Eng, UK 25/E5
Newport, Wal, UK 24/D3
Newquay, Eng, UK 24/A6
Newry, NI, UK 22/B3
Newton, Ks, US 93/H3
Newton, Ma, US 95/G3
Newton Abbot, Eng, UK 24/C5
Newton-le-Willows, Eng, UK 23/F5
Newtownabbey, NI, UK 22/C2
Newtownards, NI, UK 22/C2
Neyrīz, Iran 51/H4
Neyshābūr, Iran 51/J2
Neyveli, India 62/C5
Neyyāttinkara, India 62/C6
Nezahualcóyotl, Mex. 101/Q10
Ngabang, Indo. 66/C3
Ngaoundéré, Camr. 76/H6
Nha Trang, Viet. 65/E3
Niagara (falls), Can., US 95/U9
Niagara Falls, On, Can. 95/U9
Niagara Falls, NY, US 95/U9
Niamey (cap.), Niger 79/F3
Nicaragua (ctry.), Nic. 103/E3
Nicaragua (lake), Nic. 103/E4
Nicastro-Sambiase, It. 38/E3
Nice, Fr. 33/G5
Niceville, Fl, US 97/G4
Nichinan, Japan 56/B5
Nicolás Romero, Mex. 101/Q9
Nicosia (cap.), Cyp. 49/C2
Nidda, Ger. 33/H1
Nienburg, Ger. 29/G3
Nieuw-Amsterdam, Sur. 107/G2
Nieuw-Nickerie, Sur. 107/G2
Nieuwegein, Neth. 28/C4
Nieuwerkerk aan de IJssel, Neth. 28/B5
Niğde, Turk. 50/C2
Nigel, SAfr. 80/Q13
Niger (ctry.) 76/G4
Niger (riv.) 76/F5
Nigeria (ctry.) 76/G6
Nigrán, Sp. 34/A1
Nihonmatsu, Japan 57/G2
Niigata, Japan 57/F2
Niihama, Japan 56/C4
Niimi, Japan 56/C3
Niitsu, Japan 57/F2
Nijkerk, Neth. 28/C4
Nijlen, Belg. 28/B6
Nijmegen, Neth. 28/C5
Nikel', Rus. 42/F1
Nikki, Ben. 79/F4
Nikkō, Japan 57/F2
Nikolayevsk-na-Amure, Rus. 47/Q4
Nikol'sk, Rus. 45/H1
Nikopol', Ukr. 44/E3
Niksar, Turk. 44/F4
Nikšic, Yugo. 40/D4
Nile (delta), Egypt 49/B4
Nile (riv.), Afr. 77/M3
Niles, Oh, US 94/D3
Niles, Mi, US 94/C3
Niles, Il, US 99/Q15
Nilópolis, Braz. 108/K7
Nīmāj, India 62/B2
Nîmes, Fr. 32/F5
Ningbo, China 61/J2
Ninh Binh, Viet. 65/D1
Ninove, Belg. 30/D2
Niort, Fr. 32/C3
Nipigon (lake), Can. 94/B1
Nirasaki, Japan 57/F3
Nirmal, India 62/C4
Niš, Yugo. 40/E4
Niscemi, It. 38/D4
Nishino'omote, Japan 56/B5
Nishio, Japan 57/E3
Nishiwaki, Japan 56/D3
Niterói, Braz. 108/K7
Nitra, Slvk. 40/D1
Nivelles, Belg. 31/D2
Nizāmābād, India 62/C4
Nizhnekamsk, Rus. 43/L5
Nizhneudinsk, Rus. 47/K4
Nizhnevartovsk, Rus. 46/H3
Nizhniy Lomov, Rus. 45/G1
Nizhniy Novgorod, Rus. 43/K4
Nizhniy Tagil, Rus. 43/N4
Nizhyn, Ukr. 44/D2
Nizip, Turk. 50/D2
Nkayi, Congo 82/B1
N'kongsamba, Camr. 79/H5
Noākhāli, Bang. 62/F3
Noāmundi, India 62/E3
Nobeoka, Japan 56/B4
Noboribetsu, Japan 55/N3
Nogales, Az, US 92/E5
Nogales, Mex. 101/M8
Nogata, Japan 56/B4
Nogent-sur-Oise, Fr. 30/B5
Noginsk, Rus. 43/X9
Nogoyá, Arg. 109/E3
Nohar, India 62/B2
Noisiel, Fr. 30/B6
Nokia, Fin. 42/D3
Nola, CAfr. 76/J7
Nome, Ak, US 85/E3
Nong Khai, Thai. 65/C2
Nonsan, SKor. 58/D4
Noordwijk aan Zee, Neth. 28/B4
Noordwijkerhout, Neth. 28/B4
Norala, Phil. 67/F2
Norden, Ger. 29/E1
Nordenham, Ger. 29/F1
Norderstedt, Ger. 29/G1
Nordhausen, Ger. 26/F3
Nordhorn, Ger. 29/E4
Nordkapp (cape), Nor. 20/H1
Nördlingen, Ger. 26/F4
Norfolk, Va, US 97/J2
Norfolk, Ne, US 93/H2
Noril'sk, Rus. 46/J3
Normal, Il, US 93/K2
Norman, Ok, US 93/H4
Norridge, Il, US 99/Q16
Norristown, Pa, US 94/F3
Norrköping, Swe. 42/C4
Norrtälje, Swe. 42/C4
North (sea), Eur. 18/D3
North (chan.), UK 22/C1
North (cape), NZ 71/R9
North (isl.), NZ 71/R10
North America (cont.) 84/*
North Bay, On, Can. 94/E2
North Bend, Or, US 92/A2
North Carolina (state), US 97/H3
North Cascades National Park, Wa, US 90/C3
North Charleston, SC, US 97/J3
North Chicago, Il, US 99/Q15
North Cowichan, BC, Can. 90/C3
North Dakota (state), US 91/H4
North Fort Myers, Fl, US 97/H5
North Highlands, Ca, US 99/L9
North Korea (ctry.) 58/D2
North Lakhimpur, India 60/B3
North Las Vegas, Nv, US 92/D3
North Little Rock, Ar, US 93/J4
North Magnetic Pole 83/N
North Platte, Ne, US 93/G2
North Saskatchewan (riv.), Ab,Sk, Can. 86/E3
North Shields, Eng, UK 23/G2
North Tonawanda, NY, US 95/V9
North Vancouver, BC, Can. 86/D4
Northampton, Ma, US 95/F3
Northampton, Eng, UK 25/F2
Northbrook, Il, US 99/Q15
Northeim, Ger. 29/G5
Northern Dvina (riv.), Rus. 43/J3
Northern Ireland, NI, UK 22/B2
Northern Marianas (dpcy.), Pac.,US 68/D3
Northfield, Mn, US 91/K4
Northfleet, Eng, UK 25/G4
Northport, Al, US 97/G3
Northwest Territories (terr.), Can. 86/E2
Northwich, Eng, UK 23/F5
Norton Shores, Mi, US 94/C3
Norwalk, Oh, US 94/D3
Norwalk, Ct, US 94/F3
Norway (ctry.) 20/C3
Norwich, Eng, UK 25/H1
Noshiro, Japan 55/N3
Nosivka, Ukr. 44/D2
Noşratābād, Iran 53/G3
Nosy-Varika, Madg. 81/J8
Noto, It. 38/D4
Nøtterøy, Nor. 20/D4
Nottingham, Eng, UK 23/G6
Nottuln, Ger. 29/E5
Nouâdhibou, Mrta. 76/B3
Nouakchott (cap.), Mrta. 78/B2
Nouméa (cap.), NCal. 69/V13
Nova Andradina, Braz. 107/H8
Nova Cruz, Braz. 107/L5
Nova Friburgo, Braz. 108/L7
Nova Gorica, Slov. 40/A3
Nova Gradiška, Cro. 40/C3
Nova Iguaçu, Braz. 108/K7
Nova Kakhovka, Ukr. 41/L2
Nova Pazova, Yugo. 40/E3
Nova Scotia (prov.), Can. 95/J2
Nova Venécia, Braz. 108/D1
Nova Zagora, Bul. 41/H4
Novara, It. 33/H4
Novato, Ca, US 99/J10
Nové Město nad Váhom, Slvk. 27/J4
Nové Zámky, Slvk. 27/K5
Novelda, Sp. 35/E3
Novgorod, Rus. 42/F4
Novi, Mi, US 99/E7
Novi Bečej, Yugo. 40/E3
Novi Ligure, It. 33/H4
Novi Pazar, Bul. 41/H4
Novi Pazar, Yugo. 40/E4
Novi Sad, Yugo. 40/D3
Novo Hamburgo, Braz. 108/B4
Novo Horizonte, Braz. 108/B2
Novoanninskiy, Rus. 45/G2
Novocheboksarsk, Rus. 43/K4
Novocherkassk, Rus. 44/G3
Novogrudok, Bela. 42/E5
Novohrad-Volyns'kyy, Ukr. 44/C2
Novokuybyshevsk, Rus. 45/J1
Novokuznetsk, Rus. 46/J4
Novomoskovsk, Rus. 44/F1
Novorossiysk, Rus. 44/F3
Novoshakhtinsk, Rus. 44/F3
Novosibirsk, Rus. 46/J4
Novotroitsk, Rus. 45/L2
Novoukrayinka, Ukr. 44/D2
Novovolyns'k, Ukr. 27/N3
Novovyatsk, Rus. 43/L4
Novozybkov, Rus. 44/D1
Novska, Cro. 40/C3
Nový Jičín, Czh. 27/K4
Nowa Ruda, Pol. 27/J3
Nowa Sól, Pol. 27/H3
Nowgong, India 62/C2
Nowogard, Pol. 27/H2
Nowshera, Pak. 53/K2
Nowy Sącz, Pol. 27/L4
Nowy Targ, Pol. 27/L4
Noya, Sp. 34/A1
Noyon, Fr. 30/C4
Nsawam, Gha. 79/E5
Nuenen, Neth. 28/C6
Nueva Concepción, Guat. 102/D3
Nueva Gerona, Cuba 103/F1
Nueva Italia de Ruiz, Mex. 100/E5
Nueva Loja, Ecu. 106/C3
Nueva Ocotepéque, Hon. 102/D3
Nueva Rosita, Mex. 96/C5
Nueve de Julio, Arg. 109/D4
Nuevitas, Cuba 103/G1
Nuevo Casas Grandes, Mex. 92/F5
Nuevo Laredo, Mex. 96/D5
Nuku'alofa (cap.), Tonga 69/H7
Nukus, Uzb. 46/F5
Numata, Japan 57/F2
Numazu, Japan 57/F3
Nunavut (terr.), Can. 87/G2
Nuneaton, Eng, UK 25/E1
Nunspeet, Neth. 28/C4
Nuoro, It. 38/A2
Nurmijärvi, Fin. 20/H3
Nürnberg, Ger. 33/J2
Nürtingen, Ger. 33/H2
Nuth, Neth. 31/E2
Nyala, Sudan 77/K5
Nyandoma, Rus. 42/J3
Nyasa (lake), Afr. 82/F3
Nyborg, Den. 26/F1
Nybro, Swe. 20/E4
Nyeri, Kenya 82/G1
Nyíregyháza, Hun. 27/L5
Nykøbing, Den. 26/F1
Nyköping, Swe. 42/C4
Nynäshamn, Swe. 42/C4
Nyon, Swi. 36/C5
Nysa, Pol. 27/J3
Nyūzen, Japan 57/E2
Nzérékoré, Gui. 78/C5

O

Oahu (isl.), US 88/S10
Oak Creek, Wi, US 99/Q14
Oak Forest, Il, US 99/Q16
Oak Lawn, Il, US 99/Q16
Oak Park, Mi, US 99/F7
Oak Park, Il, US 99/Q16
Oak Ridge, Tn, US 97/G2
Oakland, Ca, US 99/K11
Oakley, Ca, US 99/L10
Oaxaca de Juárez, Mex. 102/B2
Ob' (riv.), Rus. 46/G3
Obama, Japan 56/D3
Oberá, Arg. 109/E2
Oberhausen, Ger. 28/D6
Oberkirch, Ger. 31/H6
Oberursel, Ger. 33/H1
Óbidos, Braz. 107/G4
Obihiro, Japan 55/N3
Obluch'ye, Rus. 55/L2
Obninsk, Rus. 44/F1
Obo, CAfr. 77/L6
Oborniki, Pol. 27/J2
Obrenovac, Yugo. 40/E3
Obuasi, Gha. 79/E5
Ocala, Fl, US 97/H4
Occidental, Cordillera (mts.), Ecu. 106/C3
Oceanside, Ca, US 92/C4
Och'amch'ire, Geo. 45/G4
Ochtrup, Ger. 29/E4
Ocna Mureş, Rom. 41/F2
Ocotal, Nic. 102/E3
Ocotlán, Mex. 100/E4
Ocoyoacac, Mex. 101/Q10
Ocozocoautla de Espinosa, Mex. 102/C2
Octeville, Fr. 32/C2
Oda, Gha. 79/E5
Oda, Japan 56/C3
Ōdate, Japan 55/N3
Odawara, Japan 57/F3
Ödemiş, Turk. 50/A2
Odense, Den. 26/F1
Odesa, Ukr. 41/K2
Odessa, Tx, US 93/G5
Odintsovo, Rus. 43/W9
Odivelas, Port. 35/P10
Oegstgeest, Neth. 28/B4
Oeiras, Braz. 107/K5
Oelde, Ger. 29/F5
Oelsnitz, Ger. 33/K1
Oer-Erkenschwick, Ger. 29/E5
Of, Turk. 44/G4
Ofaqim, Isr. 49/D4
Offa, Nga. 79/G4
Offenbach, Ger. 33/H1
Offenburg, Ger. 36/D1
Oga, Japan 55/M4
Ōgaki, Japan 56/E3
Ogbomosho, Nga. 79/G4
Ogden, Ut, US 92/E2
Ogre, Lat. 42/E4
Ogulin, Cro. 40/B3
Ohio (state), US 94/D3
Ohrid, FYROM 40/E5
Oieras, Port. 35/P10
Oil City, Pa, US 94/E3
Oisterwijk, Neth. 28/C5
Ōita, Japan 56/B4
Ojinaga, Mex. 93/F5
Ojiya, Japan 57/F2
Ojo de Agua, Mex. 101/Q9
Oka, Nga. 79/G5
Okāra, Pak. 53/K2
Ōkawa, Japan 56/B4
Okaya, Japan 57/F2
Okayama, Japan 56/C3
Okazaki, Japan 57/E3
Okeechobee (lake), Fl, US 97/H5
Okha, Rus. 47/Q4
Okhtyrka, Ukr. 44/E2
Oklahoma (state), US 93/H4
Oklahoma City (cap.), Ok, US 93/H4
Okmulgee, Ok, US 93/J4
Oktyabr'sk, Rus. 45/J1
Oktyabr'skiy, Rus. 43/M5
Ōkuchi, Japan 56/B4
Okulovka, Rus. 42/G4
Olathe, Ks, US 93/J3
Olavarría, Arg. 109/D4
Oława, Pol. 27/J3
Olbia, It. 38/A2
Olching, Ger. 37/H1
Oldebroek, Neth. 28/C4
Oldenburg, Ger. 29/F2
Oldenzaal, Neth. 28/D4
Oldham, Eng, UK 23/F4
Olean, NY, US 94/E3
Oleiros, Sp. 34/A1
Oleksandriya, Ukr. 44/E2
Olenegorsk, Rus. 42/G1
Olesa de Montserrat, Sp. 35/K6
Oleśnica, Pol. 27/J3
Ölgiy, Mong. 54/B2
Olhão, Port. 34/B4
Olímpia, Braz. 108/B2
Olinda, Braz. 107/M5
Oliva, Sp. 35/E3
Olivais, Port. 34/A3
Oliveira, Braz. 108/C2
Olivet, Fr. 32/D3
Ollūr, India 62/C5
Olmaliq, Uzb. 46/G5
Olofström, Swe. 20/E4
Olomouc, Czh. 27/J4
Olot, Sp. 35/G1
Olpe, Ger. 29/E6
Olsberg, Ger. 29/F6
Olsztyn, Pol. 27/L2
Olten, Swi. 36/D3
Oltu, Turk. 45/G4
Olympia (cap.), Wa, US 99/B3
Olympic National Park, Wa, US 90/B4
Olympos (Mount Olympus) (peak), Gre. 39/H2
Ōmachi, Japan 57/E2
Omagh, NI, UK 22/A2
Omaha, Ne, US 93/J2
Oman (ctry.) 53/G4
Oman (gulf), Oman 52/G4
Omegna, It. 33/H4
Omiš, Cro. 40/C4
Ōmiya, Japan 57/G2
Ōmiya, Japan 55/M4
Ommen, Neth. 28/D3
Omsk, Rus. 46/H4
Ōmura, Japan 56/A4
Ōmuta, Japan 56/B4
Omutninsk, Rus. 43/M4
Onagawa, Japan 57/G1
Onda, Sp. 35/E3
Ondo, Nga. 79/G5
Ondörhaan, Mong. 54/G2
Onega, Rus. 42/H3
Oneida, NY, US 94/F3
Oneonta, NY, US 94/F3
Onex, Swi. 36/C5
Ongole, India 62/D4
Ongtüstik Qazaqstan, Kaz. 46/G5
Onitsha, Nga. 79/G5
Ono, Japan 56/D3
Ōno, Japan 56/E3
Onoda, Japan 56/B4
Onomichi, Japan 56/C3
Ontario, Or, US 92/C1
Ontario (prov.), Can. 86/H3
Ontario (lake), Can.,US 94/E3
Onteniente, Sp. 35/E3
Onyang, SKor. 58/D4
Oostburg, Neth. 28/A6
Oosterhout, Neth. 28/B5
Oostkamp, Belg. 30/C1
Opatija, Cro. 40/B3
Opava, Czh. 27/J4
Opelika, Al, US 97/G3
Opelousas, La, US 93/J5
Ophir, Ak, US 85/G3

Opoczno, Pol. 27/L3
Opole, Pol. 27/J3
Opportunity, Wa, US 90/D4
Or 'Aqiva, Isr. 49/F6
Or Yehuda, Isr. 49/F7
Orai, India 62/C2
Oral, Kaz. 45/J2
Oran, Alg. 76/E1
Orange, Austl. 73/D2
Orange, Tx, US 93/J5
Orange (riv.), Nam,SAfr. 80/B3
Orange, Fr. 32/F4
Orange Park, Fl, US 97/H4
Orange Walk, Belz. 102/D2
Orangeburg, SC, US 97/H3
Orangeville, On, Can. 95/S8
Oranienburg, Ger. 27/G2
Oranjestad, Aru.. 106/D1
Orăştie, Rom. 41/F3
Oraviţa, Rom. 40/E3
Orchard Homes, Mt, US 90/E4
Ordu, Turk. 44/F4
Örebro, Swe. 20/E4
Oregon (state), US 90/C4
Oregon City, Or, US 90/C4
Orekhovo-Zuyevo, Rus. 42/H5
Orël, Rus. 44/F1
Orenburg, Rus. 45/K2
Orense, Sp. 34/B1
Orhangazi, Turk. 41/J5
Orhei, Mol. 41/J2
Oria, Sp. 34/D4
Oriental, Cordillera (mts.), Col.,Ecu. 106/C5
Orihuela, Sp. 35/E3
Orillia, On, Can. 94/E2
Orinda, Ca, US 99/J11
Oristano, It. 38/A3
Oriximiná, Braz. 107/G4
Orizaba, Mex. 101/M8
Orkney, SAfr. 80/P13
Orland Park, Il, US 99/Q16
Orlândia, Braz. 108/C2
Orlando, Fl, US 97/H4
Orléans, Fr. 32/D3
Orlová, Czh. 27/K4
Ormoc, Phil. 67/F1
Ormond Beach, Fl, US 97/H4
Ormskirk, Eng, UK 23/F4
Örnsköldsvik, Swe. 42/C3
Orodara, Burk. 78/D4
Orono, Me, US 95/G2
Oroquieta, Phil. 67/F2
Orosháza, Hun. 40/E2
Oroszlány, Hun. 40/D2
Oroville, Ca, US 92/B3
Orsay, Fr. 30/B6
Orsha, Bela. 42/F5
Orsk, Rus. 45/L2
Orşova, Rom. 40/F3
Ortaköy, Turk. 50/C2
Ortaköy, Turk. 44/E4
Orūmīyeh, Iran 51/F2
Oruro, Bol. 106/E7
Osa, Rus. 43/M4
Ōsaka, Japan 56/D3
Osan, SKor. 58/D4
Osasco, Braz. 108/G8
Oschersleben, Ger. 26/F2
Osh, Kyr. 46/H5
Oshawa, On, Can. 95/V8
Oshogbo, Nga. 79/G5
Osijek, Cro. 40/D3
Osipovichi, Bela. 44/D1
Oskarshamn, Swe. 20/F4
Öskemen, Kaz. 46/J5
Oslo (cap.), Nor. 20/D4
Osmānābād, India 62/C4
Osmancık, Turk. 44/E4
Osmaniye, Turk. 49/E1
Osnabrück, Ger. 29/F4
Osório, Braz. 108/B4
Osorno, Chile 109/B5
Oss, Neth. 28/C5
Ossett, Eng, UK 23/G4
Ostashkov, Rus. 42/G4
Osten (Oostende), Belg. 30/B1
Osterholz-Scharmbeck, Ger. 29/F2
Osterode am Harz, Ger. 29/H5
Östersund, Swe. 20/E3
Östhammar, Swe. 42/C3
Ostrava, Czh. 27/K4
Ostróda, Pol. 27/K2
Ostrogozhsk, Rus. 44/F2
Ostrołęka, Pol. 27/L2
Ostrov, Rus. 42/F4
Ostrov, Czh. 33/K1
Ostrów Mazowiecka, Pol. 27/L2
Ostrów Wielkopolski, Pol. 27/J3
Ostrowiec Świętokrzyski, Pol. 27/L3
Ostuni, It. 40/C5
Osuna, Sp. 34/C4
Osvaldo Cruz, Braz. 108/B2
Oswego, NY, US 94/E3
Oswestry, Eng, UK 23/E6
Oświęcim (Auschwitz), Pol. 27/K3
Ōta, Japan 57/F2
Ōtake, Japan 56/C3
Otaru, Japan 47/Q5
Ōtawara, Japan 57/G2
Otradnyy, Rus. 45/J1
Otrokovice, Czh. 27/J4
Ōtsu, Japan 56/D3
Ottawa, Ks, US 93/J3
Ottawa (riv.), Can. 94/E2
Ottawa (cap.), On, Can. 94/F2
Ottignies-Louvain-la-Neuve, Belg. 31/D2
Ottobrunn, Ger. 33/J2
Ottumwa, Ia, US 93/J2
Ottweiler, Ger. 31/G5
Otwock, Pol. 27/L2
Ouagadougou (cap.), Burk. 79/E3
Ouargla, Alg. 76/G1
Ouarzazate, Mor. 76/D1
Oud-Beijerland, Neth. 28/B5
Oudenaarde, Belg. 30/C2
Oudtshoorn, SAfr. 80/C4
Oued Zem, Mor. 76/D1
Ouesso, Congo 76/J7
Ouezzane, Mor. 76/D1
Ouidah, Ben. 79/F5
Oujda, Mor. 76/E1
Oullins, Fr. 36/A6
Oulu, Fin. 42/E2
Oupeye, Belg. 31/E2
Ouricuri, Braz. 107/K5
Ourinhos, Braz. 108/B2
Ouro Fino, Braz. 108/G7
Ouro Preto, Braz. 108/D2
Outreau, Fr. 25/H5
Outremont, Qu, Can. 95/N6
Ovalle, Chile 109/B3
Overath, Ger. 31/G2
Overijse, Belg. 31/D2
Overland Park, Ks, US 93/J3
Oviedo, Sp. 34/C1
Owase, Japan 56/E3
Owasso, Ok, US 93/J3
Owen Sound, On, Can. 94/D2
Owensboro, Ky, US 97/G2
Owo, Nga. 79/G5
Owosso, Mi, US 94/C3
Oxford, Ms, US 97/F3
Oxford, Eng, UK 25/E3
Oxkutzcab, Mex. 102/D1
Oxnard, Ca, US 92/C4
Oyabe, Japan 57/E2
Oyama, Japan 57/F2
Oyem, Gabon 76/H7
Oyo, Nga. 79/F5
Oyonnax, Fr. 36/B5
Ozark, Al, US 97/G4
Ozark (mts.), Ar,Mo, US 96/E3
Ózd, Hun. 40/E1
Ozoir-la-Ferrière, Fr. 30/B6
Ozorków, Pol. 27/K3
Ōzu, Japan 56/C4

P

P'yŏngyang (cap.), NKor. 58/C3
Pa-an, Myan. 65/B2
Paarl, SAfr. 80/L10
Pabellón de Arteaga, Mex. 100/E4
Pabianice, Pol. 27/K3
Pābna, Bang. 62/E3
Pacasmayo, Peru 106/C5
Pachino, It. 38/D4
Pachuca, Mex. 101/L6
Pacific (ocean) 16/B4
Pacific Palisades, Hi, US 88/W13
Pacifica, Ca, US 99/K11
Pacitan, Indo. 66/D5
Paço de Arcos, Port. 35/P10
Padang, Indo. 66/B4
Padangpanjang, Indo. 66/B4
Padangsidempuan, Indo. 66/A3
Paderborn, Ger. 29/F5
Padova, It. 33/J4
Paducah, Ky, US 97/F2
Pagadian, Phil. 67/F2
Pago Pago (cap.), ASam. 69/T10
Paignton, Eng, UK 24/C6
Painesville, Oh, US 94/D3
Paithan, India 62/C4
Pakanbaru, Indo. 66/B3
Pakistan (ctry.) 53/H3
Pakokku, Myan. 60/B4
Pākpattan, Pak. 53/K2
Paks, Hun. 40/D2
Pakxe, Laos 65/D3
Palafrugell, Sp. 35/G2
Palagonia, It. 38/D4
Pālakollu, India 62/D4
Palangkaraya, Indo. 66/D4
Pālanpur, India 62/B3
Palapye, Bots. 82/E5
Palatine, Il, US 99/P15
Palatka, Fl, US 97/H4
Palau, Mex. 101/E3
Palau (ctry.) 68/C4
Pālayankottai, India 62/C6
Palembang, Indo. 66/B4
Palencia, Sp. 34/C1
Palenque, Mex. 102/D2
Palermo, It. 38/C3
Pālghar, India 53/K5
Palhoça, Braz. 108/B3
Pāli, India 62/B2
Pālitāna, India 62/B3
Palm Bay, Fl, US 97/H4
Palm Harbor, Fl, US 97/H4
Palm Springs, Ca, US 92/C4
Palma, Sp. 35/G3
Palma del Río, Sp. 34/C4
Palma di Montechiaro, It. 38/C4
Palma Soriano, Cuba 103/H1
Palmares, Braz. 107/L5
Palmas, Braz. 108/A3
Palmdale, Ca, US 92/C4
Palmeira, Braz. 108/B3
Palmeira dos Índios, Braz. 107/L5
Palmerston North, NZ 71/S11
Palmetto, Fl, US 97/H5
Palmi, It. 38/D3
Palmira, Col. 106/C3
Palni, India 62/C5
Palo Alto, Ca, US 99/K12
Palo Verde, CR 102/E4
Palos Hills, Il, US 99/Q16
Palpalá, Arg. 109/C1
Palu, Indo. 67/E4
Pamangkat, Indo. 66/C3
Pamiers, Fr. 32/D5
Pampa, Tx, US 93/G4
Pampas (plain), Arg. 109/D4
Pamplona, Col. 103/H5
Pamplona, Sp. 34/E1
Panagyurishte, Bul. 41/G4
Panaji, India 62/B4
Panama (canal), Pan. 106/B2
Panamá (cap.), Pan. 103/G4
Panama (ctry.), Pan. 103/F2
Panama City, Fl, US 97/G4
Panamá, Golfo de (gulf), Pan. 103/G4
Panama, Isthmus of (isth.), Pan. 103/F4
Pančevo, Yugo. 40/E3
Pandharpur, India 62/C4
Panevėžys, Lith. 42/E5
Panfilov, Kaz. 46/J5
Pangkalanberandan, Indo. 66/A3
Pangkalpinang, Indo. 66/C4
Pangutaran, Phil. 67/F2
Pānīpat, India 62/C2
Panna, India 62/D3
Pánuco, Mex. 102/B1
Panzhihua, China 60/D3
Panzós, Guat. 102/D3
Pápa, Hun. 40/C2
Papantla, Mex. 101/M6
Papeete (cap.), FrPol. 69/X15
Papeete, FrPol. 69/X15
Papenburg, Ger. 29/E2
Papendrecht, Neth. 28/B5
Papillion, Ne, US 93/H2
Papua New Guinea (ctry.) 68/D5
Pará de Minas, Braz. 108/C1
Paracambi, Braz. 108/K7
Paracatu, Braz. 107/J7
Paraćin, Yugo. 40/E4
Paradip, India 62/E3
Paragominas, Braz. 107/J4
Paraguaçu Paulista, Braz. 108/B2
Paraguarí, Par. 109/E2
Paraguay (riv.), Par. 109/E1
Paraguay (ctry.) 105/C5
Paraíba do Sul, Braz. 108/K7
Paraíso, Mex. 102/C2
Paraíso do Norte de Goiás, Braz. 107/J6
Parakou, Ben. 79/F4
Paramaribo (cap.), Sur. 107/G2
Paraná, Arg. 109/D3
Paraná (riv.), Arg.,Braz. 109/E3
Paranaguá, Braz. 108/B3
Paranaíba, Braz. 108/B1
Paranavaí, Braz. 109/F1
Parang, Phil. 67/F2
Parbhani, India 62/C4
Parchim, Ger. 26/F2
Pardes Hanna-Karkur, Isr. 49/F7
Pardubice, Czh. 33/L1
Pare, Indo. 66/D5
Parede, Port. 35/P10
Parepare, Indo. 67/E4
Pariaman, Indo. 66/B4
Parintins, Braz. 107/G4
Paris, Tx, US 93/J4
Paris (cap.), Fr. 30/B6
Park Ridge, Il, US 99/Q16
Parkersburg, WV, US 97/H2
Parkland, Wa, US 99/C3
Parkway-Sacramento, Ca, US 99/L9
Parla, Sp. 35/N9
Parlakhemundi, India 62/D4
Parli, India 62/C4
Parma, Oh, US 94/D3
Parma, It. 33/J4
Parnaíba, Braz. 107/K4
Parnamirim, Braz. 107/L5
Pärnu, Est. 42/E4
Parow, SAfr. 80/L10
Parral, Chile 109/B4
Parras de la Fuente, Mex. 96/C5
Parsons, Ks, US 93/J3
Partinico, It. 38/C3
Partizansk, Rus. 55/L3
Partizánske, Slvk. 27/K4
Partūr, India 62/C4
Pārvathīpuram, India 62/D4
Pasadena, Ca, US 92/C4
Pasadena, Tx, US 93/J5
Pasaje, Ecu. 106/C4
Pasān, India 62/D3
Pascagoula, Ms, US 97/F4
Paşcani, Rom. 41/H2
Pasco, Wa, US 90/D4
Pāsighāt, India 60/B2
Pasinler, Turk. 45/G5
Pasni, Pak. 53/H3
Paso de los Libres, Arg. 109/E2
Paso Robles (El Paso de Robles), Ca, US 92/B4
Passau, Ger. 33/K2
Passo Fundo, Braz. 108/A4
Passos, Braz. 108/C2
Pastavy, Bela. 42/E5
Pasto, Col. 106/C3
Pasuruan, Indo. 66/D5
Patagonia (phys. reg.), Arg. 109/B6
Pātan, India 62/B3
Paterna, Sp. 35/E3
Paternò, It. 38/D4
Paterson, NJ, US 94/F3
Pathānkot, India 53/L2
Pathein (Bassein), Myan. 60/B5
Pati, Indo. 66/D5
Patía, Col. 106/C3
Patiāla, India 53/L2
Patikul, Phil. 67/F2
Patna, India 62/E2
Patnongon, Phil. 67/F1
Patnos, Turk. 51/E2
Pato Branco, Braz. 108/A3
Patos, Braz. 107/L5
Patos de Minas, Braz. 108/C1
Pátrai, Gre. 39/G3
Patrocínio, Braz. 108/C1
Pattani, Thai. 65/C5
Pattukkottai, India 62/C5
Patuākhāli, Bang. 62/F3
Pátzcuaro, Mex. 101/E5
Pau, Fr. 32/C5
Paulínia, Braz. 108/F7
Paulo Afonso, Braz. 107/L5
Paungde, Myan. 60/B5
Pavia, It. 33/H4
Pavlodar, Kaz. 46/H4
Pavlohrad, Ukr. 44/E2
Pavlovo, Rus. 42/J5
Pawtucket, RI, US 95/G3
Payakumbuh, Indo. 66/B4
Paysandú, Uru. 109/E3
Payson, Ut, US 92/E2
Pazarcık, Turk. 50/D2
Pazardzhik, Bul. 41/G4
Peace (riv.), BC, Can. 86/D3
Peachtree City, Ga, US 97/G3
Pearl, Ms, US 97/F3
Pearl (har.), US 88/W13
Pearl City, Hi, US 88/W13
Pechora, Rus. 43/N2
Pecos, Tx, US 96/C4
Pecos (riv.), NM,Tx, US 93/G5
Pécs, Hun. 40/D2
Pedernales, DRep. 103/J2
Pederneiras, Braz. 108/B2
Pedra Azul, Braz. 107/K7
Pedreira, Braz. 108/G7
Pedreiras, Braz. 107/K4
Pedro Betancourt, Cuba 103/F1
Pedro Juan Caballero, Par. 109/E1
Pedro Leopoldo, Braz. 108/C1
Pehuajó, Arg. 109/D4
Peine, Ger. 29/H4
Pekalongan, Indo. 66/C5
Pekin, Il, US 93/K2
Pelham, Al, US 97/G3
Pelhřimov, Czh. 33/L2
Pelotas, Braz. 108/A4
Pematangsiantar, Indo. 66/A3
Pemba, Moz. 82/H3
Penápolis, Braz. 108/B2
Penarth, Wal, UK 24/C4
Pendleton, Or, US 90/D4
Penedo, Braz. 107/L6
Peniche, Port. 34/A3
Penn Hills, Pa, US 94/E3
Pennsylvania (state), US 94/E3
Penonomé, Pan. 103/F4
Pensacola, Fl, US 97/G4
Penticton, BC, Can. 90/D3
Penza, Rus. 45/H1
Penzance, Eng, UK 24/A6
Perabumulih, Indo. 66/B4
Pérama, Gre. 39/N9
Pereira, Col. 106/C3
Pereira Barreto, Braz. 108/B2
Pergamino, Arg. 109/D3
Perico, Cuba 103/F1
Périgueux, Fr. 32/D4
Peringat, Malay. 65/C5
Peristéri, Gre. 39/N8
Perm', Rus. 43/N4
Pernik, Bul. 40/F4
Perote, Mex. 101/M7
Perpignan, Fr. 32/E5
Perry, Ga, US 97/H3
Persian (gulf), Asia 52/E3
Perth, Austl. 68/A8
Pertuis, Fr. 32/F5
Peru, In, US 94/C3
Peru, Il, US 93/K2
Peru (ctry.), Peru 106/C5
Perugia, It. 38/C1
Peruíbe, Braz. 108/G9
Péruwelz, Belg. 30/C2
Pervomaysk, Rus. 45/G1
Pervomays'k, Ukr. 41/K1
Pervoural'sk, Rus. 43/N4
Pesaro, It. 33/K5
Pescara, It. 40/B4
Peshāwar, Pak. 53/K2
Peshtera, Bul. 41/G4
Pessac, Fr. 32/C4
Pestovo, Rus. 42/G4
Petah Tiqwa, Isr. 49/F7
Petaluma, Ca, US 99/J10
Petare, Ven. 106/E1
Petatlán, Mex. 101/E5
Peterborough, On, Can. 94/E2
Peterborough, Eng, UK 25/F1
Peterlee, Eng, UK 23/G2
Petersburg, Va, US 97/J2
Petershagen, Ger. 29/F4
Pétionville, Haiti 103/H2
Petlād, India 62/B3
Petrel, Sp. 35/E3
Petrich, Bul. 41/F5
Petrila, Rom. 41/F3
Petrodvorets, Rus. 43/S7
Petrolina, Braz. 107/K5
Petropavl, Kaz. 46/G4
Petropavlovsk-Kamchatskiy, Rus. 47/R4
Petrópolis, Braz. 108/K7
Petrovsk, Rus. 45/H1
Petrovsk-Zabaykal'skiy, Rus. 54/F1
Petrozavodsk, Rus. 42/G3
Pfaffenhofen an der Ilm, Ger. 33/J2
Pforzheim, Ger. 33/H2
Pfungstadt, Ger. 33/H2
Phalodi, India 62/B2
Phan Rang-Thap Cham, Viet. 65/E4
Phan Thiet, Viet. 65/E4
Pharr, Tx, US 96/D5
Phayao, Thai. 65/B2
Phenix City, Al, US 97/G3
Phet Buri, Thai. 65/B3
Philadelphia, Pa, US 94/F4
Philippine (sea), Asia 68/B3
Philippines (ctry.) 68/B3
Phitsanulok, Thai. 65/C2
Phnom Penh (cap.), Camb. 65/D4
Phoenix (cap.), Az, US 92/D4
Phra Nakhon Si Ayutthaya, Thai. 65/C3
Phrae, Thai. 65/C2
Phu Tho, Viet. 65/D1
Phuket, Thai. 65/B5
Piacenza, It. 33/H4
Piaseczno, Pol. 27/L2
Piazza Armerina, It. 38/D4
Picayune, Ms, US 97/F4
Pickering, On, Can. 95/U8
Picos, Braz. 107/K5
Piedade, Port. 35/P10
Piedmont, Ca, US 99/K11
Piedras Negras, Mex. 96/C4
Piekary Śląskie, Pol. 27/K3
Pierre (cap.), SD, US 91/H4
Pierrefonds, Qu, Can. 95/N7
Piešťany, Slvk. 27/J4
Pietarsdart (Jakobstad), Fin. 42/D3
Pietermaritzburg, SAfr. 81/E3
Pietersburg, SAfr. 82/E5
Pijnacker, Neth. 28/B4
Piła, Pol. 27/J2
Pilar, Par. 109/E2
Pilar, Phil. 67/F1
Pilcomayo (riv.), SAm. 109/D1
Pilkhua, India 62/C2
Pimpri-Chinchwad, India 53/K5
Pinamalayan, Phil. 67/F1
Pinar del Río, Cuba 103/F1
Pinatubo (mt.), Phil. 68/B3
Pindamonhangaba, Braz. 108/H7
Pindaré-Mirim, Braz. 107/J4
Pindi Gheb, Pak. 53/K2
Pindwāra, India 62/B3
Pine Bluff, Ar, US 93/J4
Pinerolo, It. 33/G4
Pinetown, SAfr. 81/E3
Pineville, La, US 93/J5
Pingdingshan, China 59/C4
Pingdu, China 59/D3
P'ingtung, Tai. 61/J4
Pingxiang, China 61/G3
Pingxiang, China 65/D1
Pinhal, Braz. 108/G7
Pinhal Novo, Port. 35/Q10
Pinheiro, Braz. 107/J4
Pinneberg, Ger. 29/G1
Pinole, Ca, US 99/K10
Pinsk, Bela. 44/C1
Pinto, Sp. 35/N9
Piombino, It. 38/B1
Pionki, Pol. 27/L3
Piotrków Trybunalski, Pol. 27/K3
Piplān, Pak. 53/K2
Piqua, Oh, US 94/C3
Piracicaba, Braz. 108/C2
Piraiévs, Gre. 39/N9
Piraju, Braz. 108/B2
Pirapora, Braz. 108/C1
Pirapòzinho, Braz. 108/B2
Pirássununga, Braz. 108/C2
Pires do Rio, Braz. 108/B1
Pírgos, Gre. 39/G4
Piripiri, Braz. 107/K4
Pirmasens, Ger. 31/G5
Pirna, Ger. 27/G3
Pirot, Yugo. 40/F4
Pisa, It. 33/J5
Pisco, Peru 106/C6
Písek, Czh. 33/L2
Pishīn, Pak. 53/J2
Pistoia, It. 33/J5
Pisz, Pol. 27/L2
Pitalito, Col. 106/C3
Pitcairn Islands (dpcy.), UK 69/N7
Piteå, Swe. 42/D2
Piteşti, Rom. 41/G3
Pittsburg, Ks, US 93/J3
Pittsburg, Ca, US 99/L10
Pittsburgh, Pa, US 94/E3
Pittsfield, Ma, US 94/F3
Pittston, Pa, US 94/F3
Piuí, Braz. 108/C2
Piura, Peru 106/B5
Pivdennyy Buh (riv.), Ukr. 44/D2
Pivijay, Col. 103/H4
Placetas, Cuba 103/G1
Plainview, Tx, US 93/G4
Plaisir, Fr. 30/A6
Planeta Rica, Col. 103/H4
Plant City, Fl, US 97/H4
Plantation, Fl, US 97/H5
Plasencia, Sp. 34/B2
Plata, Río de la (estu.), SAm. 109/E4
Plato, Col. 103/H4
Platte (riv.), Ne, US 93/H2
Plattsburgh, NY, US 94/F2
Plauen, Ger. 33/K1
Plav, Yugo. 40/D4
Playas, Ecu. 106/B4
Pleasant Hill, Ca, US 99/K11
Pleasant Prairie, Wi, US 99/Q14
Pleasanton, Ca, US 99/L11
Pleiku, Viet. 65/D3
Pleszew, Pol. 27/J3
Plettenberg, Ger. 29/E6
Pljevlja, Yugo. 40/D4
Płock, Pol. 27/K2
Ploemeur, Fr. 32/B3
Ploieşti, Rom. 41/H3
Płońsk, Pol. 27/L2
Plymouth, Eng, UK 24/B6
Plymouth (cap.), Monts. 104/F3
Plzeň, Czh. 33/K2
Pô, Burk. 79/E4
Po (riv.), It. 33/G4
Poá, Braz. 108/G8
Pobé, Ben. 79/F5
Pocatello, Id, US 92/D2
Pochep, Rus. 44/E1
Poconé, Braz. 107/G7
Poços de Caldas, Braz. 108/G6
Podgorica, Yugo. 40/D4
Podol'sk, Rus. 43/W9
Podporozh'ye, Rus. 42/G3
Podujevo, Yugo. 40/E4
Poggibonsi, It. 33/J5
Pogradec, Alb. 40/E5
P'ohang, SKor. 56/A2
Pohoiki, Hi, US 88/U11
Pointe-à-Pitre, Fr. 104/F3
Pointe-Claire, Qu, Can. 95/N7
Pointe-Noire, Congo 82/B1
Poitiers, Fr. 32/D3
Pokaran, India 53/K3
Pokharā, Nepal 62/D2
Pokhvistnevo, Rus. 45/K1
Pol-e Khomrī, Afg. 53/J1
Pola de Laviana, Sp. 34/C1
Pola de Lena, Sp. 34/C1
Pola de Siero, Sp. 34/C1

126

Polan – Rio d

Poland (ctry.) 27/K2
Polatlı, Turk. 44/E5
Polatsk, Bela. 42/F5
Police, Pol. 27/H2
Polikhni, Gre. 39/H2
Polkowice, Pol. 27/J3
Polomolok, Phil. 67/G2
Polonne, Ukr. 44/C2
Poltava, Ukr. 44/E2
Polyarnyy, Rus. 42/G1
Pombal, Braz. 107/L5
Pompano Beach, Fl, US 97/H5
Pompei (ruin), It. 40/B5
Pompeu, Braz. 108/C1
Ponce, PR 104/E3
Pondicherry, India 62/C5
Ponferrada, Sp. 34/B1
Pont-à-Celles, Belg. 31/D3
Pont-à-Mousson, Fr. 31/F6
Ponta Delgada, Azor., Port. 35/T13
Ponta Grossa, Braz. 108/B3
Ponta Porã, Braz. 109/E1
Pontarlier, Fr. 36/C4
Pontault-Combault, Fr. 30/B6
Pontchartrain (lake), La, US 97/F4
Ponte Nova, Braz. 108/D2
Pontefract, Eng, UK 23/G4
Pontes e Lacerda, Braz. 106/G7
Pontevedra, Sp. 34/A1
Pontiac, Il, US 93/K2
Pontiac, Mi, US 99/F6
Pontianak, Indo. 66/C4
Pontivy, Fr. 32/B2
Pontoise, Fr. 30/B5
Pontypool, Wal, UK 24/C3
Poole, Eng, UK 24/E5
Poortugaal, Neth. 28/B5
Popayán, Col. 106/C3
Poperinge, Belg. 30/B2
Poplar Bluff, Mo, US 93/K3
Popocatépetl (vol.), Mex. 101/L7
Popondetta, PNG 68/D5
Popovo, Bul. 41/H4
Poprad, Slvk. 27/L4
Porangatu, Braz. 107/J6
Porbandar, India 62/A3
Pordenone, It. 33/K4
Poreč, Cro. 40/A3
Pori, Fin. 42/D3
Porirua, NZ 71/R11
Porlamar, Ven. 104/F5
Poronaysk, Rus. 55/N2
Porriño, Sp. 34/A1
Porsgrunn, Nor. 20/D4
Port Alberni, BC, Can. 90/B3
Port Angeles, Wa, US 90/C3
Port Arthur, Tx, US 93/J5
Port Augusta, Austl. 68/C8
Port Blair, India 63/F5
Port Charlotte, Fl, US 97/H5
Port Colborne, On, Can. 95/U10
Port Dickson, Malay. 66/B3
Port Elizabeth, SAfr. 80/D4
Port Huron, Mi, US 99/G6
Port Lavaca, Tx, US 93/H5
Port Louis (cap.), Mrts. 81/T15
Port Macquarie, Austl. 73/E1
Port Moresby (cap.), PNG 68/D5
Port Orange, Fl, US 97/H4
Port Saint Lucie, Fl, US 97/H5
Port-au-Prince (cap.), Haiti 103/H2
Port-de-Paix, Haiti 103/H2
Port-Gentil, Gabon 82/A1
Port-of-Spain (cap.), Trin. 104/F5
Port-Vila (cap.), Van. 68/F6
Porta Westfalica, Ger. 29/F4
Portadown, NI, UK 22/B3
Portage, Mi, US 94/C3
Portalegre, Port. 34/B3
Portales, NM, US 93/G4
Porterville, Ca, US 92/C3
Portimão, Port. 34/A4
Portishead, Eng, UK 24/D4
Portland, Or, US 90/C4
Portland, Tx, US 101/F3
Portland, Me, US 95/G3
Portmore, Jam. 103/G2
Porto, Port. 34/A2
Porto Alegre, Braz. 108/B4
Porto Empedocle, It. 38/C4
Porto Ferreira, Braz. 108/C2
Porto Nacional, Braz. 107/J6
Porto Sant'Elpidio, It. 40/A4
Porto Torres, It. 38/A2
Porto União, Braz. 108/B3
Porto Velho, Braz. 106/F5
Porto-Novo (cap.), Ben. 79/F5
Portocivitanova, It. 40/A4
Portogruaro, It. 33/K4
Portoviejo, Ecu. 106/B4
Portslade-by-Sea, Eng, UK 25/F5
Portsmouth, NH, US 87/J4
Portsmouth, NH, US 95/G3
Portsmouth, Va, US 97/J2
Portsmouth, Oh, US 97/H2
Portsmouth, Eng, UK 25/E5
Portugal (ctry.) 34/A3
Portugalete, Sp. 34/D1
Posadas, Arg. 109/E2
Posŏng, SKor. 58/D5
Postojna, Slov. 40/B3
Potchefstroom, SAfr. 80/P13
Potenza, It. 40/B5
P'ot'i, Geo. 45/G4
Potomac (riv.), US 94/E4
Potosí, Bol. 106/E7
Potsdam, NY, US 94/F2
Potsdam, Ger. 26/G2
Potters Bar, Eng, UK 25/F3
Pottstown, Pa, US 94/F3
Pottsville, Pa, US 94/E3
Poughkeepsie, NY, US 94/F3
Poulton-le-Fylde, Eng, UK 23/F4
Pouso Alegre, Braz. 108/H7
Považská Bystrica, Slvk. 27/K4
Póvoa de Varzim, Port. 34/A2
Povorino, Rus. 45/G2
Poynton, Eng, UK 23/F5
Poza Rica, Mex. 101/M6
Požarevac, Yugo. 40/E3
Poznań, Pol. 27/J2
Pozoblanco, Sp. 34/C3
Pozuelo de Alarcón, Sp. 35/N9
Pozzallo, It. 38/D4
Prad am Stilfserjoch (Prato allo Stelvio), It. 37/G4
Prague (cap.), Czh. 33/L1
Praia (cap.), CpV. 74/K11
Praia Grande, Braz. 108/G9
Prato, It. 33/J5
Pratteln, Swi. 36/D2
Prattville, Al, US 97/G3
Praya, Indo. 67/E5
Preetz, Ger. 26/F1
Premià de Mar, Sp. 35/L7
Prenzlau, Ger. 27/G2
Přerov, Czh. 27/J4
Prescot, Eng, UK 23/F5
Prescott, Az, US 92/D4
Preševo, Yugo. 40/E4
Presidencia Roque Sáenz Peña, Arg. 109/D2
Presidente Dutra, Braz. 107/K5
Presidente Epitácio, Braz. 108/A2
Presidente Prudente, Braz. 108/B2
Presidente Venceslau, Braz. 108/B2
Prešov, Slvk. 27/L4
Presque Isle, Me, US 95/G2
Prestatyn, Wal, UK 23/E5
Prestea, Gha. 79/E5
Preston, Eng, UK 23/F4
Prestwich, Eng, UK 23/F4
Pretoria (cap.), SAfr. 80/Q12
Prey Veng, Camb. 65/D4
Priboj, Yugo. 40/D4
Příbram, Czh. 33/L2
Prichard, Al, US 97/F4
Priego de Córdoba, Sp. 34/C4
Prievidza, Slvk. 27/K4
Prijedor, Bosn. 40/C3
Prijepolje, Yugo. 40/D4
Prikumsk, Rus. 45/H3
Prilep, FYROM 40/E5
Primorskiy Kray, Rus. 47/P5
Primorsko-Akhtarsk, Rus. 44/F3
Prince Albert, Sk, Can. 91/G2
Prince Edward Island (prov.), Can. 95/J2
Prince George, BC, Can. 90/C2
Prince Rupert, BC, Can. 85/M4
Pringsewu, Indo. 66/B5
Priozersk, Rus. 42/F3
Priština, Yugo. 40/E4
Privolzhskiy, Rus. 45/H2
Priyutovo, Rus. 45/K1
Prizren, Yugo. 40/E4
Probištip, FYROM 40/F4
Probolinggo, Indo. 66/D5
Proddatūr, India 62/C5
Progreso, Mex. 102/D1
Prokhladnyy, Rus. 45/G4
Prokop'yevsk, Rus. 46/J4
Prokuplje, Yugo. 40/E4
Promissão, Braz. 108/B2
Propriá, Braz. 107/L6
Prostějov, Czh. 27/J4
Provadiya, Bul. 41/H4
Provence-Alpes-Côte-d'Azur, Fr. 33/G4
Providence (cap.), RI, US 95/G3
Prozor, Bosn. 40/C4
Prudnik, Pol. 27/J3
Pruszcz Gdański, Pol. 27/K1
Pruszków, Pol. 27/L2
Pryluky, Ukr. 44/E2
Pryor, Ok, US 93/J3
Prypyats' (riv.), Bela. 44/D2
Przasnysz, Pol. 27/L2
Przemyśl, Pol. 27/M4
Przeworsk, Pol. 27/M3
Pskov, Rus. 42/F4
Pszczyna, Pol. 27/K4
Ptolemaís, Gre. 40/E5
Ptuj, Slov. 40/B2
Pucallpa, Peru 106/D5
Pucheng, China 59/B4
Puchheim, Ger. 37/H1
Puch'on, SKor. 58/F7
Pucioasa, Rom. 41/G3
Pudsey, Eng, UK 23/G4
Puebla, Mex. 101/L7
Pueblo, Co, US 93/F3
Pueblo Nuevo, Nic. 102/E3
Puente Alto, Chile 109/B3
Puente de Ixtla, Mex. 101/K8
Puente-Genil, Sp. 34/C4
Puenteareas, Sp. 34/A1
Puerto Aisén, Chile 109/B6
Puerto Asís, Col. 106/C3
Puerto Ayacucho, Ven. 106/E2
Puerto Barrios, Guat. 102/D3
Puerto Cabello, Ven. 106/E1
Puerto Cabezas, Nic. 103/F3
Puerto Carreño, Col. 106/E2
Puerto Cortés, Hon. 102/E3
Puerto de la Cruz, Canl. 35/X16
Puerto del Rosario, Canl. 35/Y16
Puerto Iguazú, Arg. 109/F2
Puerto Inírida, Col. 106/E3
Puerto La Cruz, Ven. 106/F1
Puerto Lempira, Hon. 103/F3
Puerto Madryn, Arg. 109/C5
Puerto Maldonado, Peru 106/E6
Puerto Montt, Chile 109/B5
Puerto Natales, Chile 109/B7
Puerto Padre, Cuba 103/G1
Puerto Peñasco, Mex. 92/D5
Puerto Princesa, Phil. 67/E2
Puerto Real, Sp. 34/B4
Puerto Rico (dpcy.), PR 104/E3
Puerto Vallarta, Mex. 100/D4
Puerto Varas, Chile 109/B5
Puertollano, Sp. 34/C3
Pugachev, Rus. 45/J1
Puget (sound), Wa, US 90/C4
Pula, Cro. 40/A3
Pulaski, Va, US 94/D4
Puławy, Pol. 27/L3
Pulheim, Ger. 28/D6
Pullman, Wa, US 90/D4
Pully, Swi. 36/C5
Pułtusk, Pol. 27/L2
Punaauia, FrPol. 69/X15
Poona (Pune), India 62/B4
Punjab (plain), Pak. 53/K2
Puno, Peru 106/D7
Punta Alta, Arg. 109/D4
Punta Arenas, Chile 109/B7
Punta Gorda, Belz. 102/D2
Punta Gorda, Fl, US 97/H5
Puntarenas, CR 103/E4
Puqi, China 61/G2
Puri, India 62/D3
Purmerend, Neth. 28/B3
Pūrna, India 62/C4
Pŭrvomay, Bul. 41/G4
Purwokerto, Indo. 66/C5
Pusad, India 62/C4
Pusan, SKor. 56/A3
Pushkin, Rus. 43/T7
Pushkino, Rus. 43/W8
Püspökladány, Hun. 27/L5
Puttalam, SrL. 62/C6
Putte, Belg. 28/B6
Putten, Neth. 28/C4
Püttlingen, Ger. 31/F5
Putumayo (riv.), Col. 106/D4
Puurs, Belg. 28/B6
Puyallup, Wa, US 99/C3
Puyang, China 59/C4
Pyapon, Myan. 63/G4
Pyatigorsk, Rus. 45/G3
Pyinmana, Myan. 65/B2
Pyŏngt'aek, SKor. 58/D4
Pyryatyn, Ukr. 44/E2

Q

Qaanaaq, Grld. 87/T7
Qābis, Tun. 76/H1
Qā'emshahr, Iran 51/H2
Qafşah, Tun. 76/G1
Qalyūb, Egypt 49/B4
Qandahār, Afg. 53/J2
Qaraghandy, Kaz. 46/H5
Qarataū, Kaz. 46/H5
Qarshi, Uzb. 46/G6
Qaşr Hallāl, Tun. 38/B5
Qaşr-e-Shīrīn, Iran 51/F3
Qatar (ctry.) 52/F3
Qazvīn, Iran 51/G2
Qeqertarsuaq, Grld. 87/L2
Qianjiang, China 61/G2
Qidong, China 59/L8
Qilian (mts.), China 54/D4
Qingdao, China 59/E3
Qingyuan, China 63/K3
Qingzhou, China 59/D3
Qinhuangdao, China 59/D3
Qinyang, China 59/C4
Qinzhou, China 65/E1
Qiqihar, China 55/J2
Qiryat Ata, Isr. 49/G6
Qiryat Bialik, Isr. 49/G6
Qiryat Gat, Isr. 49/D4
Qiryat Mal'akhi, Isr. 49/F8
Qiryat Motzkin, Isr. 49/G6
Qiryat Shemona, Isr. 49/D3
Qiryat Yam, Isr. 49/G6
Qitaihe, China 55/L2
Qom, Iran 51/G3
Qomsheh, Iran 51/G3
Qostanay, Kaz. 43/P6
Qostanay, Kaz. 43/P5
Quang Ngai, Viet. 65/E3
Quang Tri, Viet. 65/D2
Quanzhou, China 61/H3
Quanzhou, China 61/F3
Quaregnon, Belg. 30/C3
Quartu Sant'Elena, It. 38/A3
Quatre Bornes, Mrts. 81/T15
Quba, Azer. 45/J4
Qūchān, Iran 51/J2
Queanbeyan, Austl. 73/D2
Québec (prov.), Can. 87/J3
Québec (cap.), Qu, Can. 95/G2
Queen Charlotte (isls.), BC, Can. 86/C3
Queensland, Austl. 73/B1
Queenstown, SAfr. 80/D3
Quelimane, Moz. 82/G4
Queluz, Port. 35/P10
Querétaro, Mex. 102/A1
Quetta, Pak. 53/J2
Quevedo, Ecu. 106/C4
Quezaltenango, Guat. 102/D3
Quezon, Phil. 67/E2
Quezon City, Phil. 68/B3
Qufu, China 59/D4
Qui Nhon, Viet. 65/E3
Quibdó, Col. 106/C2
Quickborn, Ger. 29/G1
Quierschied, Ger. 31/G5
Quill Lakes, Sk, Can. 86/F3
Quillabamba, Peru 106/D6
Quillacollo, Bol. 106/E7
Quilon, India 62/C6
Quimper, Fr. 32/A2
Quincy, Ma, US 95/G3
Quincy, Il, US 93/K3
Quirinópolis, Braz. 108/B1
Quitilipi, Arg. 109/D2
Quito (cap.), Ecu. 106/C4
Quixadá, Braz. 107/L4
Quixeramobim, Braz. 107/L5
Qujing, China 60/D3
Qulaybīyah, Tun. 38/B4
Quranbālīyah, Tun. 38/B4
Qurbah, Tun. 38/B4
Qŭrghonteppa, Taj. 53/J1
Qūş, Egypt 52/B3
Quşūr As Sāf, Tun. 38/B5
Quzhou, China 61/H2
Qyzylorda, Kaz. 46/G5

R

Raahe, Fin. 42/E2
Raalte, Neth. 28/D4
Ra'anana, Isr. 49/F7
Rabat (cap.), Mor. 76/D1
Rabinal, Guat. 102/D3
Rabkavi-Banhatti, India 53/L5
Race (cape), Nf, Can. 87/L4
Rach Gia, Viet. 65/D4
Racibórz, Pol. 27/K3
Racine, Wi, US 99/Q14
Rădăuţi, Rom. 41/G2
Radcliffe, Eng, UK 23/F4
Radevormwald, Ger. 29/E6
Radford, Va, US 97/H2
Radolfzell, Ger. 37/E2
Radom, Pol. 27/L3
Radomir, Bul. 40/F4
Radomsko, Pol. 27/K3
Radoviš, FYROM 40/F5
Radviliškis, Lith. 42/D5
Radzyń Podlaski, Pol. 27/M3
Rāe Bareli, India 62/D2
Rafaela, Arg. 109/D3
Rafsanjān, Iran 51/J4
Ragusa, It. 38/D4
Rahīmyār Khān, Pak. 62/B2
Rāhuri, India 62/B4
Raichūr, India 62/C4
Raigarh, India 62/D3
Rainier (mt.), Wa, US 90/C4
Raipur, India 62/D3
Raisio, Fin. 20/G3
Rāj-Nāndagaon, India 62/D3
Rājahmundry, India 62/D4
Rājampet, India 62/C5
Rājanpur, Pak. 62/B2
Rājapālaiyam, India 62/C6
Rājbirāj, Nepal 62/E2
Rājgarh, India 62/C3
Rājkot, India 62/B3
Rājpura, India 53/L2
Rājshāhi, Bang. 62/E3
Rājula, India 62/B3
Rakovski, Bul. 41/G4
Rakvere, Est. 42/E4
Raleigh (cap.), NC, US 97/J3
Ramat Gan, Isr. 49/F7
Ramat Hasharon, Isr. 49/F7
Rambouillet, Fr. 30/A6
Ramenskoye, Rus. 43/X9
Rāmeswaram, India 62/C6
Ramla, Isr. 49/F8
Ramotswa, Bots. 80/D2
Ramsbottom, Eng, UK 23/F4
Ramsgate, Eng, UK 25/H4
Rana, Nor. 20/E2
Rānāghāt, India 62/E3
Rancagua, Chile 109/B3
Rancharia, Braz. 108/B2
Rānchī, India 62/E3
Rancho Cordova, Ca, US 99/M9
Randburg, SAfr. 80/P13
Randers, Den. 20/D4
Rāngāmāti, Bang. 60/B4
Rangāpāra, India 60/B3
Rangia, India 60/A3
Rangpur, Bang. 62/E2
Rānībennur, India 62/C5
Ranst, Belg. 28/B6
Rantabe, Madg. 81/J6
Rantoul, Il, US 93/K2
Rapid City, SD, US 93/G1
Ra's Al Jabal, Tun. 38/B4
Ra's al Khaymah, UAE 51/H5
Rashīd, Egypt 49/B4
Rasht, Iran 51/G2
Raška, Yugo. 40/E4
Rasskazovo, Rus. 45/G1
Rastatt, Ger. 31/H6
Rastede, Ger. 29/F2
Rat Buri, Thai. 65/B3
Ratangarh, India 62/B2
Rāth, India 62/C2
Rathenow, Ger. 26/G2
Rathmore, Ire. 21/A10
Ratingen, Ger. 28/D6
Ratlām, India 62/C3
Ratnāgiri, India 62/B4
Ratnapura, SrL. 62/D6
Raton, NM, US 93/F3
Raub, Malay. 66/B3
Raurkela, India 62/D3
Ravanusa, It. 38/C4
Ravenna, It. 33/K4
Ravensburg, Ger. 37/F2
Ravne na Koroškem, Slov. 40/B2
Rawa Mazowiecka, Pol. 27/L3
Rāwalpindi, Pak. 53/K2
Rawicz, Pol. 27/J3
Rawlins, Wy, US 92/F2
Rawmarsh, Eng, UK 23/G5
Rawson, Arg. 109/C5
Rawtenstall, Eng, UK 23/F4
Rāyadrug, India 62/C5
Rāyagada, India 62/D4
Raychikhinsk, Rus. 55/K2
Rayleigh, Eng, UK 25/G3
Rayong, Thai. 65/C3
Razgrad, Bul. 41/H4
Reading, Pa, US 94/F3
Reading, Eng, UK 25/F4
Rechytsa, Bela. 44/D1
Recife, Braz. 107/M5
Recklinghausen, Ger. 29/E5
Reconquista, Arg. 109/E2
Red (riv.), Ok, US 93/H4
Red (sea) 52/C4
Red (riv.), Mn, US 86/G4
Red (riv.), Can. 91/J3
Red Bluff, Ca, US 92/B2
Red Deer, Ab, Can. 90/E2
Red River of the North (riv.), Can.,US 91/J3
Red Wing, Mn, US 91/K4
Redcar, Eng, UK 23/G2
Redding, Ca, US 92/B2
Redditch, Eng, UK 25/E2
Redford, Mi, US 99/F7
Redmond, Wa, US 99/C2
Redondela, Sp. 34/A1
Redwood City, Ca, US 99/K12
Reedley, Ca, US 92/C3
Rees, Ger. 28/D5
Reforma, Mex. 102/C2
Regensburg, Ger. 33/K2
Reggio di Calabria, It. 38/D3
Reggio nell'Emilia, It. 33/J4
Reghin, Rom. 41/G2
Regina (cap.), Sk, Can. 91/G3
Registro, Braz. 108/C3
Rehlingen-Siersburg, Ger. 31/F5
Rehoboth, Namb. 82/C5
Rehovot, Isr. 49/F8
Reichshof, Ger. 31/G2
Reigate, Eng, UK 25/F4
Reims, Fr. 30/D5
Reinach, Swi. 36/D2
Reinbek, Ger. 29/H1
Relizane, Alg. 76/F1
Remagen, Ger. 31/G2
Remanso, Braz. 107/K5
Rembang, Indo. 66/D5
Remscheid, Ger. 29/E6
Rendsburg, Ger. 26/E1
Renens, Swi. 36/C4
Rengat, Indo. 66/B4
Reni, Ukr. 41/J3
Renkum, Neth. 28/C5
Rennes, Fr. 32/C2
Reno, Nv, US 92/C3
Renqiu, China 59/D3
Rentería, Sp. 34/E1
Renton, Wa, US 99/C3
Repentigny, Qu, Can. 95/P6
Requena, Sp. 35/E3
Resen, FYROM 40/E5
Resende, Braz. 108/J7
Resistencia, Arg. 109/E2
Reşiţa, Rom. 40/E3
Retalhuleu, Guat. 102/D3
Réthimnon, Gre. 39/J5
Réunion (dpcy.), Fr. 81/S15
Reus, Sp. 35/F2
Reutlingen, Ger. 37/F1
Reutov, Rus. 43/W9
Rewa, India 62/D3
Rexburg, Id, US 92/E2
Reyhanlı, Turk. 49/E1
Reykjavík (cap.), Ice. 20/N7
Reynosa, Mex. 96/D5
Rezé, Fr. 32/C3
Rēzekne, Lat. 42/E4
Rheda-Wiedenbrück, Ger. 29/F5
Rhede, Ger. 28/D5
Rheden, Neth. 28/D4
Rheinbach, Ger. 31/F2
Rheinberg, Ger. 28/D5
Rheine, Ger. 29/E4
Rheinfelden, Ger. 36/D2
Rhenen, Neth. 28/C5
Rhine (Rhein) (riv.), Eur. 26/D3
Rhode Island (state), US 95/G3
Rhondda, Wal, UK 24/C3
Rhyl, Wal, UK 22/E5
Ribe, Den. 26/E1
Ribeira do Pombal, Braz. 107/L6
Ribeirão Preto, Braz. 108/C2
Ribera, It. 38/C4
Riberalta, Bol. 106/E6
Rîbniţa, Mol. 41/J2
Ribnitz-Damgarten, Ger. 26/G1
Riccione, It. 33/K5
Richard Toll, Sen. 78/B2
Richard's Bay, SAfr. 81/F3
Richland, Wa, US 90/D4
Richmond, BC, Can. 90/C3
Richmond, Ky, US 97/G2
Richmond, Ca, US 99/K11
Richmond (cap.), Va, US 94/E4
Richmond Hill, On, Can. 95/U8
Richmond-Windsor, Austl. 72/G8
Ridderkerk, Neth. 28/B5
Ridgecrest, Ca, US 92/C4
Ridgeland, Ms, US 93/K4
Riehen, Swi. 36/D2
Riemst, Belg. 31/E2
Riesa, Ger. 27/G3
Rietberg, Ger. 29/F5
Rieti, It. 38/C1
Riga (cap.), Lat. 42/E4
Riga (Rīga), Lat. 42/E4
Riga (gulf), Eur. 42/D4
Riihimäki, Fin. 42/E3
Riiser-Larsen Ice Shelf, Ant. 83/Y
Rijeka, Cro. 40/B3
Rijssen, Neth. 28/D4
Rijswijk, Neth. 28/B4
Rillieux-la-Pape, Fr. 36/A6
Rimavská Sobota, Slvk. 27/L4
Rimini, It. 33/K4
Rîmnicu Sărat, Rom. 41/H3
Rîmnicu Vîlcea, Rom. 41/G3
Rimouski, Qu, Can. 95/G1
Rincón De La Vieja, CR 102/E4
Rincón de Romos, Mex. 100/E4
Ringkøbing, Den. 20/D4
Ringsted, Den. 26/F1
Rinteln, Ger. 29/G4
Río Blanco, Mex. 101/M8
Rio Bonito, Braz. 108/L7
Rio Branco, Braz. 106/E5
Rio Branco do Sul, Braz. 108/B3
Río Bravo, Mex. 96/D5
Río Cauto, Cuba 103/G1
Rio Claro, Braz. 108/G8
Río Cuarto, Arg. 109/D3
Rio de Janeiro, Braz. 108/K7

Rio do Sul, Braz. 108/B3
Río Gallegos, Arg. 109/C7
Rio Grande, Arg. 109/C7
Rio Grande, Braz. 108/A5
Rio Grande (riv.), Mex.,US 96/C4
Rio Grande City, Tx, US 96/D5
Rio Grande da Serra, Braz. 108/G8
Rio Largo, Braz. 107/L5
Rio Negrinho, Braz. 108/B3
Río Negro, Braz. 108/B3
Rio Pardo, Braz. 108/A4
Rio Rancho, NM, US 92/F4
Río Tercero, Arg. 109/D3
Rio Verde, Braz. 108/B1
Río Verde, Mex. 102/B1
Riobamba, Ecu. 106/C4
Ríohacha, Col. 103/H4
Riom, Fr. 32/E4
Ripley, Eng, UK 23/G5
Ripollet, Sp. 35/L6
Rishon Leẕiyyon, Isr. 49/F8
Rîşnov, Rom. 41/G3
Rivadavia, Arg. 109/C3
Rivas, Nic. 102/E4
Rive-de-Gier, Fr. 32/F4
River Rouge, Mi, US 99/F7
Rivera, Uru. 109/E3
Riverside, Ca, US 92/C4
Riverton, Wy, US 92/E2
Riverview, NB, Can. 95/H2
Riverview, Mi, US 99/F7
Riviera Beach, Fl, US 97/H5
Rivière-du-Loup, Qu, Can. 95/G2
Rivne, Ukr. 44/C2
Rivoli, It. 33/G4
Rixensart, Belg. 31/D2
Riyadh (cap.), SAr. 52/E4
Rize, Turk. 45/G4
Road Town (cap.), BVI, UK 104/E3
Roanne, Fr. 32/F3
Robertsganj, India 62/D3
Robertsport, Libr. 78/C5
Robstown, Tx, US 96/D5
Rocha, Uru. 109/F3
Rochdale, Eng, UK 23/F4
Rochefort, Fr. 32/C4
Rochester, Mn, US 93/J1
Rochester, NY, US 94/E3
Rochester, NH, US 95/G3
Rochester, Eng, UK 25/G4
Rochester Hills, Mi, US 99/F6
Rock Forest, Qu, Can. 95/G2
Rock Hill, SC, US 97/H3
Rock Island, Il, US 93/K2
Rock Springs, Wy, US 92/E2
Rockford, Il, US 93/K2
Rockhampton, Austl. 72/C3
Rockingham, NC, US 97/J3
Rockledge, Fl, US 97/H4
Rockville, Md, US 97/J2
Rockwall, Tx, US 93/H4
Rocky (mts.), Can.,US 88/C1
Rocky Mount, NC, US 97/J3
Rocky Mountain National Park, Co, US 92/F2
Rodez, Fr. 32/E4
Ródhos (Rhodes), Gre. 50/B2
Roermond, Neth. 28/C6
Roeselare, Belg. 30/C2
Rogachev, Bela. 44/D1
Rogatica, Bosn. 40/D4
Rogers, Ar, US 93/J3
Rohri, Pak. 62/A2
Roi Et, Thai. 65/C2
Rolândia, Braz. 108/B2
Rolla, Mo, US 93/K3
Rolling Meadows, Il, US 99/P15
Roman, Rom. 41/H2
Romania (ctry.) 41/F3
Romans-sur-Isère, Fr. 32/F4
Romblon, Phil. 67/F1
Rome, NY, US 94/F3
Rome, Ga, US 97/G3
Rome (cap.), It. 38/C2
Romeoville, Il, US 99/P16
Romilly-sur-Seine, Fr. 32/E2
Romny, Ukr. 44/E2
Romorantin-Lanthenay, Fr. 32/D3
Romsey, Eng, UK 25/E5
Romulus, Mi, US 99/F7
Ronda, Sp. 34/C4
Rondonópolis, Braz. 107/H7
Rongcheng, China 58/B4
Rønne, Den. 27/H1
Ronne Ice Shelf, Ant. 83/V
Ronneby, Swe. 20/E4
Ronnenberg, Ger. 29/G4
Ronse, Belg. 30/C2
Roodeport, SAfr. 80/P13
Roorkee, India 62/C2
Roosendaal, Neth. 28/B5
Roquetas de Mar, Sp. 34/D4
Rosa Zárate, Ecu. 106/C3
Rosario, Arg. 109/D3
Rosário, Braz. 107/K4
Rosario de la Frontera, Arg. 109/D2
Rosário do Sul, Braz. 109/F3
Rosarito, Mex. 92/C4
Roseau (cap.), Dom. 104/F4
Roseburg, Or, US 92/B2
Roselle, Il, US 99/P16
Rosenberg, Tx, US 93/J5
Rosenheim, Ger. 33/K3
Roseville, Ca, US 99/M9
Roseville, Mi, US 99/G6
Rosh Ha'ayin, Isr. 49/F7
Roşiori de Vede, Rom. 41/G3
Roskilde, Den. 26/G1
Roslavl', Rus. 44/E1
Rosmalen, Neth. 28/C5
Rosolini, It. 38/D4
Rösrath, Ger. 31/G2
Ross Ice Shelf, Ant. 83/N
Rossano Stazione, It. 38/E3
Rosso, Mrta. 78/B2
Rossosh', Rus. 44/F2
Rostock, Ger. 26/G1
Rostov, Rus. 42/H4
Rostov, Rus. 44/F3
Roswell, NM, US 93/F4
Rota, Sp. 34/B4
Rotenburg, Ger. 29/G2
Rotherham, Eng, UK 23/G5
Rothwell, Eng, UK 23/G4
Rothwell, Eng, UK 25/F2
Rotorua, NZ 71/S10
Rottenburg am Neckar, Ger. 37/E1
Rotterdam, Neth. 28/B5
Rottweil, Ger. 37/E1
Roubaix, Fr. 30/C2
Rouen, Fr. 32/D2
Round Lake Beach, Il, US 99/P15
Round Rock, Tx, US 93/H5
Rouyn-Noranda, Qu, Can. 94/E1
Rovaniemi, Fin. 42/E2
Rovereto, It. 37/H6
Rovigo, It. 33/J4
Rovinj, Cro. 40/A3
Roxas, Phil. 67/E1
Roxas, Phil. 67/F1
Roxas, Phil. 61/J5
Roy, Ut, US 92/D2
Royal Oak, Mi, US 99/F7
Royal Tunbridge Wells, Eng, UK 25/G4
Royan, Fr. 32/C4
Royston, Eng, UK 25/F2
Royton, Eng, UK 23/F4
Rožňava, Slvk. 27/L4
Rtishchevo, Rus. 45/G1
Rubí, Sp. 35/L7
Rubizhne, Ukr. 44/F2
Rubtsovsk, Rus. 46/J4
Rucphen, Neth. 28/B5
Rūdnyy, Kaz. 43/P5
Rudolstadt, Ger. 33/J1
Rufino, Arg. 109/D3
Rufisque, Sen. 78/A3
Rugby, Eng, UK 25/E2
Rugeley, Eng, UK 23/G6
Ruma, Yugo. 40/D3
Rumbek, Sudan 77/L6
Rumia, Pol. 27/K1
Rumoi, Japan 55/N3
Runcorn, Eng, UK 23/F5
Rundu, Namb. 82/C4
Ruse, Bul. 41/G4
Rushden, Eng, UK 25/F2
Russas, Braz. 107/L4
Russellville, Ar, US 93/J4
Russellville, Ar, US 97/G3
Rüsselsheim, Ger. 33/H2
Russia (ctry.) 46/H3
Rust'avi, Geo. 45/H4
Rustenburg, SAfr. 80/P12
Ruston, La, US 93/J4
Ruvo di Puglia, It. 38/E2
Ruzayevka, Rus. 45/H1
Ružomberok, Slvk. 27/K4
Rwanda (ctry.) 82/E1
Ryazan', Rus. 44/F1
Ryazhsk, Rus. 44/G1
Rybinsk, Rus. 42/H4
Rybnik, Pol. 27/K3
Ryde, Eng, UK 25/E5
Ryōtsu, Japan 57/F1
Rypin, Pol. 27/K2
Ryton, Eng, UK 23/G2
Ryūgasaki, Japan 57/G3
Ryukyu (isls.), Japan 68/B2
Rzeszów, Pol. 27/M3
Rzhev, Rus. 42/G4

S

's Heerenberg, Neth. 28/D5
's Hertogenbosch, Neth. 28/C5
Sa Dec, Viet. 65/D4
Saalfeld, Ger. 33/J1
Saarbrücken, Ger. 31/F5
Saarlouis, Ger. 31/F5
Šabac, Yugo. 40/D3
Sabadell, Sp. 35/L6
Sabae, Japan 56/E3
Sabanalarga, Col. 103/H4
Sabhā, Libya 76/H2
Sabinas, Mex. 96/C5
Sabinas Hidalgo, Mex. 96/C5
Sablayan, Phil. 67/F1
Sabzevār, Iran 51/J2
Sacavém, Port. 35/P10
Săcele, Rom. 41/G3
Saco, Me, US 95/G3
Sacramento (cap.), Ca, US 99/M9
Sādiqābād, Pak. 62/B2
Sadowara, Japan 56/B4
Sādri, India 62/B2
Safāqis, Tun. 76/H1
Säffle, Swe. 20/E4
Safford, Az, US 92/E4
Safi, Mor. 76/D1
Safonovo, Rus. 42/G5
Safranbolu, Turk. 44/E4
Saga, Japan 56/B4
Sagae, Japan 57/G1
Sagaing, Myan. 60/B4
Sagamihara, Japan 57/F3
Sāgar, India 62/C3
Sagay, Phil. 67/F1
Sagua de Tánamo, Cuba 103/H1
Sagua la Grande, Cuba 103/F1
Sagunto, Sp. 35/E3
Sahagún, Col. 103/H4
Sahagún, Mex. 101/L7
Sahara (des.), Afr. 76/G3
Sahāranpur, India 53/L3
Saharsa, India 62/E2
Sahavato, Madg. 81/J8
Sāhibganj, India 62/E2
Sāhīwāl, Pak. 53/K2
Sahuayo de Morelos, Mex. 100/E4
Saïda, Alg. 76/F1
Saidpur, India 62/D2
Saigō, Japan 56/C2
Saigon, Viet. 65/D4
Saijō, Japan 56/C4
Saiki, Japan 56/B4
Sailu, India 62/C4
Saint Albans, WV, US 97/H2
Saint Albans, Eng, UK 25/F3
Saint Albert, Ab, Can. 90/E2
Saint Augustine, Fl, US 97/H4
Saint Austell, Eng, UK 24/B6
Saint Catharines, On, Can. 95/U9
Saint Charles, Md, US 97/J2
Saint Charles, Mo, US 93/K3
Saint Charles, Il, US 99/P16
Saint Clair Shores, Mi, US 99/G6
Saint Francis, Wi, US 99/Q14
Saint George, Ut, US 92/D3
Saint George's (cap.), Gren. 104/F4
Saint Helens (mt.), Wa, US 90/C4
Saint Helens, Eng, UK 23/F5
Saint Helier (cap.), Chl, UK 32/B2
Saint Ives, Eng, UK 25/F2
Saint John, NB, Can. 95/H2
Saint John's (cap.), Anti. 104/F3
Saint John's (cap.), Nf, Can. 95/L2
Saint Johnsbury, Vt, US 95/F2
Saint Joseph, Mo, US 93/J3
Saint Kitts and Nevis (ctry.), StK. 104/F3
Saint Lawrence (gulf), Can. 95/J1
Saint Lawrence (riv.), Can.,US 94/F2
Saint Louis, Mo, US 93/K3
Saint Lucia (ctry.), StL. 104/F4
Saint Paul (cap.), Mn, US 94/A2
Saint Peter, Mn, US 91/K4
Saint Peter Port (cap.), Chl, UK 32/B2
Saint Petersburg, Fl, US 97/H5
Saint Petersburg, Rus. 43/T7
Saint Pierre and Miquelon (dpcy.), Can. 95/K2
Saint Simons Island, Ga, US 97/H4
Saint Thomas, On, Can. 94/D3
Saint Vincent and the Grenadines (ctry.), StV. 104/F4
Saint-Amand-les-Eaux, Fr. 30/C3
Saint-André, Reun. 81/S15
Saint-Avold, Fr. 31/F5
Saint-Benoît, Reun. 81/S15
Saint-Brieuc, Fr. 32/B2
Saint-Bruno-de-Montarville, Qu, Can. 95/P6
Saint-Chamond, Fr. 32/F4
Saint-Constant, Qu, Can. 95/N7
Saint-Cyr-l'École, Fr. 30/B6
Saint-Denis, Fr. 30/B6
Saint-Denis, Reun. 81/S15
Saint-Dié, Fr. 36/C1
Saint-Dizier, Fr. 31/D6
Saint-Étienne, Fr. 32/F4
Saint-Étienne-du-Rouvray, Fr. 32/D2
Saint-Eustache, Qu, Can. 95/N6
Saint-Georges, Qu, Can. 95/G2
Saint-Germain-en-Laye, Fr. 30/B6
Saint-Ghislain, Belg. 30/C3
Saint-Herblain, Fr. 32/C3
Saint-Hubert, Qu, Can. 95/P6
Saint-Hyacinthe, Qu, Can. 94/F2
Saint-Jean-de-la-Ruelle, Fr. 32/D3
Saint-Jean-sur-Richelieu, Qu, Can. 94/F2
Saint-Jérôme, Qu, Can. 95/N6
Saint-Joseph, Reun. 81/S15
Saint-Lambert, Qu, Can. 95/P6
Saint-Laurent, Qu, Can. 95/N6
Saint-Léonard, Qu, Can. 95/N6
Saint-Leu, Reun. 81/S15
Saint-Lô, Fr. 32/C2
Saint-Louis, Sen. 78/A2
Saint-Louis, Reun. 81/S15
Saint-Louis, Fr. 36/D2
Saint-Luc, Qu, Can. 95/P7
Saint-Malo, Fr. 32/B2
Saint-Marc, Haiti 103/H2
Saint-Martin-d'Hères, Fr. 32/F4
Saint-Maur-des-Fossés, Fr. 30/B6
Saint-Michel-sur-Orge, Fr. 30/B6
Saint-Nazaire, Fr. 32/B3
Saint-Nicolas, Belg. 31/E2
Saint-Omer, Fr. 30/B2
Saint-Paul, Reun. 81/S15
Saint-Pierre, Reun. 81/S15
Saint Pierre-des-Corps, Fr. 32/D3
Saint-Pol-sur-Mer, Fr. 30/B1
Saint-Quentin, Fr. 30/C4
Saint-Raphaël, Fr. 33/G5
Sainte-Foy, Qu, Can. 95/G2
Sainte-Foy-lès-Lyon, Fr. 36/A6
Sainte-Geneviève-des-Bois, Fr. 30/B6
Sainte-Julie, Qu, Can. 95/P6
Sainte-Marie, Fr. 104/F4
Sainte-Thérèse, Qu, Can. 95/N6
Saintes, Fr. 32/C4
Sainthia, India 62/E3
Saito, Japan 56/B4
Sakai, Japan 57/F2
Sakaide, Japan 56/C3
Sakaiminato, Japan 56/C3
Sakata, Japan 55/M4
Sakawa, Japan 56/C4
Sakété, Ben. 79/F5
Sakhalin (isl.), Rus. 47/Q4
Sakhnīn, Isr. 49/G6
Şäki, Azer. 45/H4
Sakon Nakhon, Thai. 65/D2
Sakrand, Pak. 53/J3
Saku, Japan 57/F2
Saky, Ukr. 44/E3
Sala, Swe. 42/C4
Šal'a, Slvk. 40/C1
Salado (riv.), Arg. 109/E4
Salamá, Guat. 102/D3
Salamanca, Mex. 101/E4
Salamanca, Sp. 34/C2
Salamís, Gre. 39/N9
Salamīyah, Syria 49/E2
Salavat, Rus. 45/K1
Salé, Mor. 76/D1
Sale, Eng, UK 23/F5
Salekhard, Rus. 46/G3
Salem, India 62/C5
Salem, NH, US 95/G3
Salem (cap.), Or, US 90/C4
Salerno, It. 40/B5
Salford, Eng, UK 23/F5
Salgótarján, Hun. 40/D1
Salgueiro, Braz. 107/L5
Salihli, Turk. 50/B2
Salina, Ks, US 93/H3
Salina Cruz, Mex. 102/C2
Salinas, Ecu. 107/K7
Salinas, Ca, US 92/B3
Salinópolis, Braz. 107/J4
Salisbury, Md, US 97/K2
Salisbury, NC, US 97/H3
Salisbury, Eng, UK 25/E4
Salmās, Iran 51/F2
Salmon Arm, BC, Can. 90/D3
Salo, Fin. 42/D3
Salon-de-Provence, Fr. 32/F5
Salonta, Rom. 40/E2
Sal'sk, Rus. 45/G3
Salt Lake City (cap.), Ut, US 90/F5
Salta, Arg. 109/C1
Saltillo, Mex. 96/C5
Salto, Braz. 108/C2
Salto, Uru. 109/E3
Salto del Guairá, Par. 109/F1
Sālūr, India 62/D4
Salurn (Salorno), It. 37/H5
Salvador, Braz. 107/L6
Salvatierra, Mex. 101/E4
Salyan, Azer. 51/G2
Salzburg, Aus. 40/A2
Salzgitter, Ger. 29/H4
Salzkotten, Ger. 29/F5
Salzwedel, Ger. 26/F2
Sam Son, Viet. 65/D2
Sama, Sp. 34/C1
Sāmalkot, India 62/D4
Samālūt, Egypt 50/B4
Samandağı, Turk. 49/D1
Samandira, Turk. 51/N7
Samannūd, Egypt 49/B4
Samara, Rus. 45/J1
Samarinda, Indo. 67/E4
Samarqand, Uzb. 46/G6
Sāmarrā', Iraq 51/E3
Samasata, Pak. 53/K3
Şamaxi, Azer. 45/J4
Sambalpur, India 62/D3
Sambas, Indo. 66/C3
Sambava, Madg. 81/J6
Sambir, Ukr. 27/M4
Samch'ŏk, SKor. 56/A2
Samch'ŏnp'o, SKor. 58/E5
Samnangjin, SKor. 56/A3
Samoa (ctry.) 69/R9
Samobor, Cro. 40/B3
Samokov, Bul. 41/F4
Samsun, Turk. 44/F4
Samut Prakan, Thai. 65/C3
Samut Sakhon, Thai. 65/C3
Samut Songkhram, Thai. 65/B3
San, Mali 78/D3
San Andrés, Col. 103/F3
San Andrés del Rabanedo, Sp. 34/C1
San Andrés Tuxtla, Mex. 102/C2
San Angelo, Tx, US 96/C4
San Anselmo, Ca, US 99/J11
San Antonio, Chile 109/B3
San Antonio Abad, Sp. 35/F3
San Antonio del Táchira, Ven. 103/H5
San Benedetto del Tronto, It. 40/A4
San Bernardino, Ca, US 92/C4
San Bernardo, Chile 109/B3
San Bruno, Ca, US 99/K11
San Buenaventura, Mex. 96/C5
San Carlos, Nic. 103/E4
San Carlos, Ven. 106/E2
San Carlos, Chile 109/B4
San Carlos, Uru. 109/F3
San Carlos, Ca, US 99/K11
San Carlos de Bariloche, Arg. 109/B5
San Carlos del Zulia, Ven. 103/J4
San Cataldo, It. 40/D5
San Cristóbal, Ven. 103/H5
San Cristóbal, Cuba 103/F1
San Cristóbal de las Casas, Mex. 102/C2
San Diego, Ca, US 92/C4
San Felipe, Ven. 106/E1
San Felipe, Chile 109/B3
San Felipe Torres Mochas, Mex. 101/E4
San Fernando, Chile 109/B3
San Fernando, Trin. 104/F5
San Fernando, Phil. 61/J5
San Fernando, Sp. 34/B4
San Fernando de Apure, Ven. 106/E2
San Fernando de Henares, Sp. 35/N9
San Fernando de Monte Cristi, DRep. 103/J2
San Fernando de Presas, Mex. 101/F3
San Francisco, Arg. 109/D3
San Francisco, ESal. 102/D3
San Francisco, Ca, US 99/J11
San Francisco del Rincón, Mex. 101/E4
San Gil, Col. 106/D2
San Giovanni in Fiore, It. 38/E3
San Giovanni Rotondo, It. 40/B5
San Ignacio, Belz. 102/D2
San Isidro, CR 103/F4
San Jacinto, Col. 103/H4
San Javier, Sp. 35/E4
San Jose, Phil. 67/F1
San Jose, Ca, US 99/L12
San José (cap.), CR 103/E4
San José de los Remates, Nic. 102/E3
San José de Mayo, Uru. 109/E3
San José del Cabo, Mex. 100/C4
San José del Guaviare, Col. 106/D3
San Juan, Arg. 109/C3
San Juan, PR 104/E3
San Juan Bautista, Par. 109/E2
San Juan Bautista Tuxtepec, Mex. 102/B2
San Juan de Alicante, Sp. 35/E3
San Juan de Aznalfarache, Sp. 34/B4
San Juan de La Maguana, DRep. 103/J2
San Juan de los Lagos, Mex. 100/E4
San Juan de los Morros, Ven. 106/E2
San Juan del Río, Mex. 102/B1
San Juan Nepomuceno, Col. 103/H4
San Justo, Arg. 109/D3
San Leandro, Ca, US 99/K11
San Lorenzo, Hon. 102/E3
San Lorenzo, Nic. 102/E3
San Lorenzo, Ca, US 99/K11
San Luis, Cuba 103/H1
San Luis, Arg. 109/C3
San Luis, Guat. 102/D2
San Luis de la Paz, Mex. 102/A1
San Luis Obispo, Ca, US 92/B4
San Luis Potosí, Mex. 101/E4
San Luis Río Colorado, Mex. 92/D4
San Marcos, Col. 103/H4
San Marcos, Guat. 102/D3
San Marcos, Tx, US 93/H5
San Marino (cap.), SMar. 33/K5
San Marino (ctry.) 33/K5
San Martín, Arg. 109/C3
San Martín de los Andes, Arg. 109/B5
San Mateo, Ca, US 99/K11
San Miguel, ESal. 102/D3
San Miguel de Allende, Mex. 101/E4
San Miguel de Tucumán, Arg. 109/C2
San Nicolás de los Arroyos, Arg. 109/D3
San Nicolás de los Garza, Mex. 101/E3
San Onofre, Col. 103/H4
San Pablo, Ca, US 99/K11
San Pablo de las Salinas, Mex. 101/Q9
San Pédro, C.d'Iv. 78/D5
San Pedro, Arg. 109/E3
San Pedro, Arg. 109/D1
San Pedro, Par. 109/E1
San Pedro Carchá, Guat. 102/D3
San Pedro de las Colonias, Mex. 96/C5
San Pedro Sula, Hon. 102/D3
San Rafael, Arg. 109/C3
San Rafael, Ca, US 99/J11
San Ramon, Ca, US 99/L11
San Ramón de la Nueva Orán, Arg. 109/D1
San Remo, It. 33/G5
San Roque, Sp. 34/C4
San Salvador (cap.), ESal. 102/D3
San Salvador de Jujuy, Arg. 109/C1
San Sebastián, Sp. 34/E1
San Sebastián de los Reyes, Sp. 35/N8
San Sebastián de Yalí, Nic. 102/E3
San Sebastiano, It. 33/J4
San Severo, It. 40/B5
San Vicente, ESal. 102/D3
San Vicente de Cañete, Peru 106/C6
San Vicente del Raspeig, Sp. 35/E3
Sanaa (cap.), Yem. 52/D5
Sanandaj, Iran 51/F3
Sānāwad, India 62/C3
Sancti Spíritus, Cuba 103/G1
Sanda, Japan 56/D3
Sandakan, Malay. 67/E2
Sandanski, Bul. 41/F5
Sandbach, Eng, UK 23/F5
Sandefjord, Nor. 20/D4
Sandhurst, Eng, UK 25/F4
Sandıklı, Turk. 50/B2

Sandn – Siófo

Sion, Swi. 36/D5
Sioux City, Ia, US 93/H2
Siping, China 59/F2
Siracusa (Syracuse), It. 38/D4
Sirājganj, Bang. 62/E3
Sīrjān, Iran 51/H4
Şırnak, Turk. 50/E2
Sironj, India 62/C3
Sirsa, India 62/C2
Sirsi, India 62/B5
Sisak, Cro. 40/C3
Sisimiut, Grld. 87/L2
Sītākunda, Bang. 63/F3
Sitges, Sp. 35/K7
Sitka, Ak, US 85/L4
Sittard, Neth. 28/C7
Sittingbourne, Eng, UK 25/G4
Sittwe (Akyab), Myan. 60/B4
Sivakāsi, India 62/C6
Sivas, Turk. 44/F5
Siverek, Turk. 50/D2
Siwān, India 62/D2
Siyabuswa, SAfr. 80/Q12
Sjenica, Yugo. 40/D4
Skalica, Slvk. 27/J4
Skara, Swe. 20/E4
Skarżysko-Kamienna, Pol. 27/L3
Skawina, Pol. 27/K4
Skegness, Eng, UK 23/J5
Skellefteå, Swe. 42/D2
Skelmersdale, Eng, UK 23/F4
Ski, Nor. 20/D4
Skien, Nor. 20/D4
Skierniewice, Pol. 27/L3
Skikda, Alg. 76/G1
Skive, Den. 20/D4
Skokie, Il, US 99/Q15
Skopin, Rus. 44/F1
Skopje (cap.), FYROM 40/E4
Skövde, Swe. 20/E4
Slagelse, Den. 20/D5
Slantsy, Rus. 42/F4
Slatina, Rom. 41/G3
Slave (coast), Afr. 79/F5
Slavgorod, Rus. 46/H4
Slavonska Požega, Cro. 40/C3
Slavonski Brod, Cro. 40/D3
Slavuta, Ukr. 44/C2
Slavyansk-na-Kubani, Rus. 44/F3
Slidell, La, US 97/F4
Sliedrecht, Neth. 28/B5
Sliema, Malta 38/D5
Sliven, Bul. 41/H4
Slobodskoy, Rus. 43/L4
Slobozia, Rom. 41/H3
Slonim, Bela. 42/E5
Slough, Eng, UK 25/F4
Slovakia (ctry.) 27/K4
Slovenia (ctry.) 40/B3
Slov'yans'k, Ukr. 44/F2
Słubice, Pol. 27/H2
Słupsk, Pol. 27/J1
Slutsk, Bela. 44/C1
Slyudyanka, Rus. 54/E1
Smederevo, Yugo. 40/E3
Smederevska Palanka, Yugo. 40/E3
Smila, Ukr. 44/D2
Smolensk, Rus. 42/G5
Smolyan, Bul. 41/G5
Smyrna, Ga, US 97/G3
Snake (riv.), US 90/D4
Sneek, Neth. 28/C2
Soanierana-Ivongo, Madg. 81/J7
Soanindrariny, Madg. 81/H7
Soavina, Madg. 81/J8
Sobral, Braz. 107/K4
Soc Trang, Viet. 65/D4
Sochaczew, Pol. 27/L2
Sochi, Rus. 44/F4
Socorro, Tx, US 93/F5
Socorro, Braz. 108/G7
Söderhamn, Swe. 42/C3
Södertälje, Swe. 42/C4
Soest, Ger. 29/F5
Soest, Neth. 28/C4
Sofia (cap.), Bul. 41/F5
Sogamoso, Col. 106/D2
Sŏgwip'o, SKor. 55/K5
Soignies, Belg. 31/D2
Soissons, Fr. 30/C5
Sōja, Japan 56/C3
Sojat, India 62/B2
Sokch'o, SKor. 58/E3
Söke, Turk. 50/A2
Sokhumi, Geo. 45/G4
Sokodé, Togo 79/F4
Sokol, Rus. 42/J4
Sokółka, Pol. 27/M2
Sokolov, Czh. 33/K1
Sokołów Podlaski, Pol. 27/M2
Sokoto, Nga. 79/G3
Sol, Costa del (coast), Sp. 34/C4
Sol'-Iletsk, Rus. 45/K2
Sola, Nor. 20/C4
Soledad, Col. 103/H4
Soledad de Graciano, Mex. 101/E4
Soledade, Braz. 108/A4
Soligorsk, Bela. 44/C1
Solihull, Eng, UK 25/E2
Solikamsk, Rus. 43/N4
Solingen, Ger. 28/E6
Sollefteå, Swe. 42/C3
Sollentuna, Swe. 20/F4
Solntsevo, Rus. 43/W9
Solok, Indo. 66/B4
Sololá, Guat. 102/D3
Solomon Islands (ctry.) 68/E6
Solothurn, Swi. 36/D3
Soltau, Ger. 29/G3
Sölvesborg, Swe. 20/E4
Solwezi, Zam. 82/E3
Sōma, Japan 57/G2
Soma, Turk. 44/C5
Somalia (ctry.) 77/Q6
Sombor, Yugo. 40/D3
Sombrerete, Mex. 100/E4
Someren, Neth. 28/C6
Somerset, Ky, US 97/G2
Somerset West, SAfr. 80/L11
Somersworth, NH, US 95/G3
Somoto, Nic. 102/E3
Son La, Viet. 65/C1
Son Tay, Viet. 65/D1
Sønderborg, Den. 26/E1
Sondrio, It. 37/F5
Songea, Tanz. 82/G3
Songkhla, Thai. 65/C5
Songling, China 55/J2
Sŏngnam, SKor. 58/G7
Songt'an, SKor. 58/D4
Sonneberg, Ger. 33/J1
Sonobe, Japan 56/D3
Sonsonate, ESal. 102/D3
Sonthofen, Ger. 37/G2
Sopot, Pol. 27/K1
Sopron, Hun. 40/C2
Sør-Varanger, Nor. 42/E1
Sora, It. 38/C2
Sorel, Qu, Can. 94/F2
Sorgues, Fr. 32/F5
Sorgun, Turk. 44/E5
Soria, Sp. 34/D2
Sorø, Den. 26/F1
Soroca, Mol. 41/J1
Sorocaba, Braz. 108/C2
Sorochinsk, Rus. 45/K1
Sorong, Indo. 67/H4
Soroti, Ugan. 77/M7
Sorrento, It. 38/D2
Sortavala, Rus. 42/F3
Sŏsan, SKor. 58/D4
Soshanguve, SAfr. 80/Q12
Sosnogorsk, Rus. 43/M3
Sosnovka, Rus. 43/L4
Sosnowiec, Pol. 27/K3
Souk Ahras, Alg. 76/G1
Sousa, Braz. 107/L5
South (isl.), NZ 71/R11
South (cape), NZ 71/Q12
South Africa (ctry.) 82/D6
South America (cont.) 105/*
South Augusta, Ga, US 97/H3
South Australia, Austl. 73/B1
South Bend, In, US 94/C3
South Benfleet, Eng, UK 25/G3
South Burlington, Vt, US 94/F2
South Carolina (state), US 97/H3
South China (sea), Asia 48/L8
South Dakota (state), US 91/H4
South Holland, Il, US 99/Q16
South Korea (ctry.) 58/D4
South Lake Tahoe, Ca, US 92/C3
South Milwaukee, Wi, US 99/Q14
South Oxhey, Eng, UK 25/F3
South San Francisco, Ca, US 99/K11
South Saskatchewan (riv.), Sk, Can. 86/E3
South Shields, Eng, UK 23/G2
South Sioux City, Ne, US 93/H2
South Ubian, Phil. 67/F2
Southampton, Eng, UK 25/E5
Southaven, Ms, US 93/K4
Southend-on-Sea, Eng, UK 25/G3
Southern Pines, NC, US 97/J3
Southfield, Mi, US 99/F7
Southgate, Mi, US 99/F7
Southland, Tx, US 101/E1
Southport, Eng, UK 23/E4
Sovetsk, Rus. 27/L1
Sovetskaya Gavan', Rus. 55/N2
Soweto, SAfr. 80/P13
Spain (ctry.) 34/C2
Spalding, Eng, UK 23/H6
Spanaway, Wa, US 99/C3
Spanish Town, Jam. 103/G2
Sparks, Nv, US 92/C3
Sparta, Wi, US 91/L5
Spartanburg, SC, US 97/H3
Spassk-Dal'niy, Rus. 55/L3
Spencer, Ia, US 93/J2
Spennymoor, Eng, UK 23/G2
Speyer, Ger. 33/H2
Spijkenisse, Neth. 28/B5
Spišská Nová Ves, Slvk. 27/L4
Spitsbergen (isl.), Sval. 46/B2
Spittal an der Drau, Aus. 40/A2
Split, Cro. 40/C4
Spokane, Wa, US 90/D4
Spoleto, It. 38/C1
Spring, Tx, US 93/J5
Springdale, Ar, US 93/J3
Springe, Ger. 29/G4
Springfield, Or, US 90/C4
Springfield, Vt, US 95/F3
Springfield, Ma, US 95/F3
Springfield, Mo, US 93/J3
Springfield, Oh, US 97/H2
Springfield, Tn, US 97/G2
Springfield (cap.), Il, US 94/B4
Springs, SAfr. 80/Q13
Sprockhövel, Ger. 29/E6
Squaw Harbor, Ak, US 85/F4
Squinzano, It. 40/D5
Srebrenica, Bosn. 40/D3
Srednogorie, Bul. 41/G4
Śrem, Pol. 27/J2
Sremska Mitrovica, Yugo. 40/D3
Sretensk, Rus. 55/H1
Sri Dungargarh, India 53/K3
Sri Gangānagar, India 53/K3
Sri Jayawardanapura (Kotte), SrL. 62/C6
Sri Lanka (ctry.) 62/D6
Srikākulam, India 62/D4
Srīnagar, India 53/K2
Srīvardhan, India 62/B4
Środa Wielkopolska, Pol. 27/J2
Stabroek, Belg. 28/B6
Stade, Ger. 29/G1
Stadskanaal, Neth. 28/D3
Stadthagen, Ger. 29/G4
Stadtlohn, Ger. 28/D5
Staffanstorp, Swe. 27/G1
Stafford, Eng, UK 23/F6
Staines, Eng, UK 25/F4
Stakhanov, Ukr. 44/F2
Stalowa Wola, Pol. 27/M3
Stalybridge, Eng, UK 23/F5
Stamford, Ct, US 94/F3
Stamford, Eng, UK 25/F1
Standerton, SAfr. 80/Q13
Stanford-le-Hope, Eng, UK 25/G3
Stange, Nor. 20/D3
Stanger, SAfr. 81/E3
Stanley, Eng, UK 23/G2
Stanley (falls), D.R. Congo 77/L8
Stanley (cap.), Falk. 109/E7
Stans, Swi. 37/E4
Stara Pazova, Yugo. 40/E3
Stara Zagora, Bul. 41/G4
Starachowice, Pol. 27/L3
Staraya Russa, Rus. 42/F4
Stargard Szczeciński, Pol. 27/H2
Starkville, Ms, US 97/F3
Starodub, Rus. 44/E1
Starogard Gdański, Pol. 27/K2
Staryy Oskol', Rus. 44/F2
Staszów, Pol. 27/L3
State College, Pa, US 94/E3
Statesboro, Ga, US 97/H3
Statesville, NC, US 97/H3
Staunton, Va, US 97/J2
Stavanger, Nor. 20/C4
Staveley, Eng, UK 23/G5
Stavropol', Rus. 45/G3
Stavropol' Kray, Rus. 46/E5
Steenwijk, Neth. 28/D3
Stein, Neth. 31/E2
Steinhagen, Ger. 29/F4
Steinkjer, Nor. 20/D2
Stekene, Belg. 28/B6
Stellenbosch, SAfr. 80/L10
Stendal, Ger. 26/F2
Stenungsund, Swe. 20/D4
Stephenville, Tx, US 93/H4
Sterling, Co, US 93/G2
Sterling Heights, Mi, US 99/F6
Sterlitamak, Rus. 45/K1
Sterzing (Vipiteno), It. 37/H4
Steubenville, Oh, US 94/D3
Stevenage, Eng, UK 25/F3
Steyr, Aus. 40/B1
Stilfontein, SAfr. 80/P13
Stillwater, Ok, US 93/H3
Štip, FYROM 40/F5
Stjørdal, Nor. 20/D3
Stockholm (cap.), Swe. 42/C4
Stockport, Eng, UK 23/F5
Stockton, Ca, US 99/M11
Stockton-on-Tees, Eng, UK 23/G2
Stoke-on-Trent, Eng, UK 23/F6
Stolac, Bosn. 40/C4
Stolberg, Ger. 31/F2
Stoney Creek, On, Can. 95/T9
Stourbridge, Eng, UK 24/D2
Stourport-on-Severn, Eng, UK 24/D2
Strakonice, Czh. 33/K2
Stralsund, Ger. 26/G1
Strand, SAfr. 80/L11
Strängnäs, Swe. 42/C4
Stratford, On, Can. 94/D3
Stratford-upon-Avon, Eng, UK 25/E2
Straubing, Ger. 33/K2
Strausberg, Ger. 27/G2
Streamwood, Il, US 99/P15
Streator, Il, US 93/K2
Stretford, Eng, UK 23/F5
Strømmen, Nor. 20/D4
Strömsund, Swe. 20/E3
Stroud, Eng, UK 24/D3
Struga, FYROM 40/E5
Strumica, FYROM 41/F5
Strzegom, Pol. 27/J3
Strzelce Opolskie, Pol. 44/A2
Stuart, Fl, US 97/H5
Stupino, Rus. 44/F1
Sturgis, Mi, US 94/C3
Stuttgart, Ger. 33/H2
Subang, Indo. 66/C5
Subotica, Yugo. 40/D2
Suceava, Rom. 41/H2
Sucre (cap.), Bol. 106/F7
Sudan (ctry.) 77/L5
Sudbury, On, Can. 94/D2
Sudbury, Eng, UK 25/G2
Sueca, Sp. 35/E3
Suez (gulf), Egypt 50/C4
Suez (canal), Egypt 77/M1
Suffolk, Va, US 97/J2
Sugar Land, Tx, US 96/E4
Suhāj, Egypt 50/B5
Suhl, Ger. 33/J1
Suifenhe, China 55/L3
Suihua, China 55/K2
Suining, China 60/E2
Suisun City, Ca, US 99/K10
Suizhou, China 61/G2
Sūjāngarh, India 62/B2
Sukabumi, Indo. 66/C5
Sukagawa, Japan 57/G2
Sukhinichi, Rus. 44/E1
Sukhothai, Thai. 65/B2
Sukkur, Pak. 62/A2
Sukumo, Japan 56/C4
Sulawesi (Celebes) (isl.), Indo. 67/E4
Sulechów, Pol. 27/H2
Sulejówek, Pol. 27/L2
Sullana, Peru 106/B4
Sulmona, It. 40/A4
Sulphur, La, US 93/J5
Sulphur Springs, Tx, US 93/J4
Sultānpur, India 62/D2
Suluova, Turk. 44/E4
Sulzbach, Ger. 31/G5
Sulzbach-Rosenberg, Ger. 33/J2
Sumatra (isl.), Indo. 66/B4
Sumbawa Besar, Indo. 67/E5
Sumbawanga, Tanz. 82/F2
Sumenep, Indo. 66/D5
Summerside, PE, Can. 95/J2
Summerville, SC, US 97/H3
Sumoto, Japan 56/D3
Šumperk, Czh. 33/M2
Sumqayıt, Azer. 45/J4
Sumter, SC, US 97/H3
Sumy, Ukr. 44/E2
Sun City, Az, US 92/D4
Sunbury, Pa, US 94/E3
Sunbury, Austl. 73/F5
Sunbury-on-Thames, Eng, UK 25/F4
Sunch'ŏn, SKor. 58/D5
Sundargarh, India 62/D3
Sundarnagar, India 53/L2
Sunderland, Eng, UK 23/G2
Sundern, Ger. 29/F6
Sundsvall, Swe. 42/C3
Sungai Petani, Malay. 66/B2
Sungaipenuh, Indo. 66/B4
Sungurlu, Turk. 44/E4
Sunningdale, Eng, UK 25/F4
Sunnyvale, Ca, US 99/K12
Sunset Beach, Hi, US 88/V12
Sunyani, Gha. 79/E5
Superior, Wi, US 91/K4
Superior (lake), Can.,US 94/C2
Suphan Buri, Thai. 65/C3
Sūq ash Shuyūkh, Iraq 51/F4
Suqian, China 59/D4
Şūr, Leb. 49/D3
Surabaya, Indo. 66/D5
Surakarta, Indo. 66/D5
Surallah, Phil. 67/F2
Surat, India 62/B3
Surat Thani, Thai. 65/B4
Suratgarh, India 62/B2
Surdulica, Yugo. 40/F4
Surendranagar, India 62/B3
Surgut, Rus. 46/H3
Sūri, India 62/E3
Surigao, Phil. 67/G2
Surin, Thai. 65/C3
Suriname (ctry.), Sur. 107/G3
Surrey, BC, Can. 90/C3
Surt, Libya 76/J1
Sürüç, Turk. 50/D2
Sūsah, Tun. 38/B5
Susaki, Japan 56/C4
Suşehri, Turk. 44/F4
Susono, Japan 57/F3
Susurluk, Turk. 50/B2
Sutton Coldfield, Eng, UK 25/E1
Sutton in Ashfield, Eng, UK 23/G5
Suva (cap.), Fiji 69/Y18
Suwa, Japan 57/F2
Suwałki, Pol. 27/M1
Şuwaylih, Jor. 49/D3
Suwŏn, SKor. 58/G7
Suzhou, China 59/D4
Suzhou, China 59/L8
Suzu, Japan 57/E2
Suzuka, Japan 56/E3
Svalbard (isls.), Nor. 46/C2
Svedala, Swe. 27/G1
Svendborg, Den. 26/F1
Sverdlovsk (Yekaterinburg), Rus. 43/P4
Sverdlovsk Oblast, Rus. 46/G4
Svetlogorsk, Bela. 44/D1
Svetlograd, Rus. 45/G3
Svetlyy, Rus. 45/M2
Svetozarevo, Yugo. 40/E4
Svilajnac, Yugo. 40/E3
Svilengrad, Bul. 41/H5
Svishtov, Bul. 41/G4
Svitavy, Czh. 33/M2
Svobodnyy, Rus. 55/K1
Swadlincote, Eng, UK 23/G6
Swakopmund, Namb. 82/B5
Swansea, Wal, UK 24/C3
Swarzędz, Pol. 27/J2
Swaziland (ctry.) 81/E2
Sweden (ctry.) 20/E3
Sweetwater, Tx, US 93/G4
Świdnica, Pol. 27/J3
Świdnik, Pol. 27/M3
Świdwin, Pol. 27/H2
Świebodzice, Pol. 27/J3
Świebozin, Pol. 27/H2
Świecie, Pol. 27/K2
Swift Current, Sk, Can. 90/G3
Swindon, Eng, UK 25/E3
Świnoujście, Pol. 27/H2
Swinton, Eng, UK 23/G5
Switzerland (ctry.) 36/D4
Swords, Ire. 22/B5
Sydney, NS, Can. 95/J2
Sydney, Austl. 72/H8
Syeverodonets'k, Ukr. 44/F2
Syke, Ger. 29/F3
Syktyvkar, Rus. 43/L3
Sylacauga, Al, US 97/G3
Sylhet, Bang. 60/A3
Sylvania, Oh, US 94/D3
Syria (ctry.) 50/D3
Syriam, Myan. 63/G4
Syzran', Rus. 45/J1
Szamotuły, Pol. 27/J2
Szarvas, Hun. 40/E2
Százhalombatta, Hun. 40/D2
Szczecinek, Pol. 27/J2
Szczytno, Pol. 27/L2
Szeged, Hun. 40/E2
Székesfehérvár, Hun. 40/D2
Szekszárd, Hun. 40/D2
Szentendre, Hun. 27/K5
Szentes, Hun. 40/E2
Szolnok, Hun. 40/E2
Szombathely, Hun. 40/C2

T

T'aipei (cap.), Tai. 61/J3
T'bilisi (cap.), Geo. 45/H4
Ta Khmau, Camb. 65/D4
Tabernes de Valldigna, Sp. 35/E3
Tábor, Czh. 33/L2
Tabora, Tanz. 82/F2
Tabrīz, Iran 51/F2
Tabuk, Phil. 61/J5
Tabūk, SAr. 50/D4
Ţaburbah, Tun. 38/A4
Tacámbaro de Codallos, Mex. 101/E5
Tacheng, China 46/J5
Tachikawa, Japan 57/F3
Tacloban, Phil. 68/B3
Tacna, Peru 106/D7
Tacoma, Wa, US 99/B3
Tacoronte, Canl. 35/X16
Tacuarembó, Uru. 109/E3
Tādepallegūdem, India 62/D4
Tadley, Eng, UK 25/E4
Tadmur, Syria 50/D3
Tadotsu, Japan 56/C3
Tādpatri, India 62/C5
T'aebaek, SKor. 58/E4
Taech'ŏn, SKor. 58/D4
Taegu, SKor. 56/A3
Taejŏn, SKor. 58/D4
Tafí Viejo, Arg. 109/C2
Taganrog, Rus. 44/F3
Tagawa, Japan 56/B4
Tagbilaran, Phil. 67/F2
Taguasco, Cuba 103/G1
Tagudin, Phil. 61/J5
Tagum, Phil. 67/G2
Tagus (riv.), Port.,Sp. 34/B3
Tahiti (isl.), FrPol. 67/F5
Tahlequah, Ok, US 93/J4
Tahoe (lake), Ca, US 88/C4
Tahoua, Niger 79/G3
Tai'an, China 59/D3
T'aichung, Tai. 61/J3
T'ainan, Tai. 61/J4
Taiping, Malay. 66/B3
Taisha, Japan 56/C3
T'aitung, Tai. 61/J4
Taiwan (ctry.) 61/J3
Taiyuan, China 59/C3
Taizhou, China 59/D4
Ta'izz, Yem. 52/D6
Tajikistan (ctry.) 46/H6
Tajima, Japan 57/F2
Tajimi, Japan 57/E3
Tajrīsh, Iran 51/G3
Tak, Thai. 65/B2
Takahagi, Japan 57/G2
Takahashi, Japan 56/C3
Takahata, Japan 57/G1
Takamatsu, Japan 56/D3
Takanabe, Japan 56/B4
Takaoka, Japan 57/E2
Takapuna, NZ 71/R10
Takasaki, Japan 57/F2
Takatsuki, Japan 56/D3
Takayama, Japan 57/E2
Takefu, Japan 56/E3
Takehara, Japan 56/C3
Taketa, Japan 56/B4
Takikawa, Japan 55/N3
Takoradi, Gha. 79/E5
Tala, Mex. 100/E4
Talā, Egypt 49/B4
Talara, Peru 106/B4
Talas, Turk. 50/C2
Talavera de la Reina, Sp. 34/C3
Talawakele, SrL. 62/D6
Talca, Chile 109/B4
Talcahuano, Chile 109/B4
Tālcher, India 62/E3
Taldyqorghan, Kaz. 46/H5
Talence, Fr. 32/C4
Talgar, Kaz. 46/H5
Ţalkhā, Egypt 49/B4
Tall 'Afar, Iraq 50/E2
Talladega, Al, US 97/G3
Tallahassee (cap.), Fl, US 97/G4
Tallinn (cap.), Est. 42/E4
Taloda, India 62/B3
Tāloqān, Afg. 53/J1
Talwāra, India 53/L2
Tam Ky, Viet. 65/E3
Tamale, Gha. 79/E4
Taman, Indo. 66/D5
Tamanrasset, Alg. 76/G3
Tamaqua, Pa, US 94/F3
Tamazula de Gordiano, Mex. 100/E5
Tamazunchale, Mex. 102/B1
Tambacounda, Sen. 78/B3
Tambov, Rus. 45/G1
Ţāmiyah, Egypt 49/B5
Tammisaari (Ekenäs), Fin. 42/D4
Tampa, Fl, US 97/H5
Tampere, Fin. 42/D3
Tampico, Mex. 102/B1
Tamra, Isr. 49/G6
Tamworth, Austl. 73/D1
Tamworth, Eng, UK 25/E1
Tamyang, SKor. 58/D5
Tan An, Viet. 65/D4
Tan-Tan, Mor. 76/C2
Tanabe, Japan 56/D4
Tanabi, Braz. 108/B2
Tanagura, Japan 57/G2
Tanambe, Madg. 81/J7
Tandā, India 62/D2
Tānda, India 62/C2
Tandag, Phil. 67/G2

Tandi – Uhers

Tandil, Arg. 109/E4
Tando Ādam, Pak. 62/A2
Tando Allāhyār, Pak. 53/J3
Tando Muhammad Khān, Pak. 62/A2
Tanga, Tanz. 82/G2
Tanganyika (lake), Afr. 82/E2
Tangará da Serra, Braz. 106/G6
Tanger (Tangier), Mor. 34/C5
Tangshan, China 59/J7
Tanjungbalai, Indo. 66/A3
Tanjungkarang-Telukbetung, Indo. 66/C5
Tanjungpandan, Indo. 66/C4
Tanjungpinang, Indo. 66/B3
Tanjungpura, Indo. 66/A3
Tānk, Pak. 53/K2
Ţanţā, Egypt 49/B4
Tantoyuca, Mex. 102/B1
Tanuku, India 62/D4
Tanzania (ctry.) 82/F2
Taolañaro, Madg. 81/H9
Taourirt, Mor. 76/E1
T'aoyüan, Tai. 61/J3
Tapachula, Mex. 102/C3
Tapolca, Hun. 40/C2
Taquara, Braz. 108/B4
Taquari, Braz. 108/B4
Taquaritinga, Braz. 108/B2
Tara, Rus. 46/H4
Ţarābulus, Leb. 49/D2
Tarakan, Indo. 67/E3
Taranto, It. 40/C5
Tarapoto, Peru 106/C5
Tarawa (cap.), Kiri. 68/G4
Tarbes, Fr. 32/D5
Tarboro, NC, US 97/J3
Taree, Austl. 73/E1
Tarhūnah, Libya 76/H1
Tarifa, Sp. 34/C4
Tarija, Bol. 106/F8
Tarin (Torino), It. 33/G4
Tarkwa, Gha. 79/E5
Tarma, Peru 106/C6
Tarnobrzeg, Pol. 27/L3
Tarnów, Pol. 27/L3
Taroudannt, Mor. 76/D1
Tarpon Springs, Fl, US 97/H4
Tarragona, Sp. 35/F2
Tarsus, Turk. 49/D1
Tartagal, Arg. 109/D1
Tartu, Est. 42/E4
Ţarţūs, Syria 49/D2
Tarumizu, Japan 56/B5
Tashkent (cap.), Uzb. 46/G5
Tasikmalaya, Indo. 66/C5
Tasman (sea) 68/E8
Tasmania, Austl. 73/C3
Tata, Hun. 40/D2
Tatabánya, Hun. 27/K5
Tatarsk, Rus. 46/H4
Tatāwīn, Tun. 76/H1
Tateyama, Japan 57/F3
Tatsuno, Japan 57/E3
Tatvan, Turk. 50/E2
Tauá, Braz. 107/K5
Taubaté, Braz. 108/H8
Taufkirchen, Ger. 37/H1
Taungdwingyi, Myan. 60/B4
Taunggyi, Myan. 65/B1
Taunsa, Pak. 53/K2
Taunton, Ma, US 95/G3
Taunton, Eng, UK 24/C4
Taunusstein, Ger. 31/H3
Taupo, NZ 71/S10
Tauragė, Lith. 27/M1
Tauranga, NZ 71/S10
Taverny, Fr. 30/B5
Tavşanlı, Turk. 50/B2
Tawau, Malay. 67/E3
Tawzar, Tun. 76/G1
Taxco, Mex. 101/K8
Tay Ninh, Viet. 65/D4
Taylor, Mi, US 99/F7
Taylorville, Il, US 93/K3
Tayshet, Rus. 47/K4
Taytay, Phil. 67/E1
Taza, Mor. 76/E1
Tchaourou, Ben. 79/F4
Tczew, Pol. 27/K1
Teapa, Mex. 102/C2
Tébessa, Alg. 76/G1
Tebingtinggi, Indo. 66/A3
Tecamachalco, Mex. 101/M8
Tecate, Mex. 92/C4
Tecomán, Mex. 100/E5
Tecpan de Galeana, Mex. 101/E5
Tecuala, Mex. 100/D4
Tecuci, Rom. 41/H3
Tefé, Braz. 106/F4
Tegal, Indo. 66/C5
Tegelen, Neth. 28/D6
Tegucigalpa (cap.), Hon. 102/E3
Tehrān (cap.), Iran 51/G3
Tehuacán, Mex. 101/M8
Tehuantepec (gulf), Mex. 102/C3
Tejen, Trkm. 53/H1
Tejupilco de Hidalgo, Mex. 101/E5
Tekax de Álvaro Obregón, Mex. 102/D1
Tekeli, Kaz. 46/H5
Tekirdağ, Turk. 41/H5
Tekkali, India 62/D4
Tel Aviv-Yafo, Isr. 49/F7
Tela, Hon. 102/E3
T'elavi, Geo. 45/H4
Telde, Canl. 35/X16
Telêmaco Borba, Braz. 108/B3
Telford Dawley, Eng, UK 24/D1
Telgte, Ger. 29/E5
Telica, Nic. 102/E3
Tellicherry, India 62/C5
Telok Anson, Malay. 66/B3
Teloloapan, Mex. 101/K8
Telšiai, Lith. 42/D5
Tema, Gha. 79/E5
Tembilahan, Indo. 66/B4
Tembisa, SAfr. 80/Q13
Temerin, Yugo. 40/D3
Temirtaū, Kaz. 46/H4
Tempe, Az, US 92/E4
Temryuk, Rus. 44/F3
Temse, Belg. 28/B6
Temuco, Chile 109/B4
Tenancingo, Mex. 101/K8
Tendō, Japan 57/G1
Tenggarong, Indo. 67/E4
Tenkodogo, Burk. 79/E4
Tennessee (riv.), US 97/F3
Tennessee (state), US 97/G3
Tenosique de Pino Suárez, Mex. 102/D2
Tenryū, Japan 57/E3
Teófilo Otoni, Braz. 108/D1
Tepalcatepec, Mex. 100/E5
Tepeji del Río de Ocampo, Mex. 101/K7
Tepexpan, Mex. 101/R9
Tepic, Mex. 100/D4
Teplice, Czh. 27/G3
Tepotzotlán, Mex. 101/Q9
Tequila, Mex. 100/E4
Tequisquiapan, Mex. 101/K6
Teramo, It. 40/A4
Teresina, Braz. 107/K5
Teresópolis, Braz. 108/L7
Terlan (Terlano), It. 37/H4
Termas de Río Hondo, Arg. 109/D2
Termini Imerese, It. 38/C4
Termiz, Uzb. 53/J1
Termoli, It. 40/B4
Ternate, Indo. 67/G3
Terneuzen, Neth. 28/A6
Terni, It. 38/C1
Ternopil', Ukr. 44/C2
Terracina, It. 38/C2
Terrassa, Sp. 35/L6
Terrebonne, Qu, Can. 95/N6
Teruel, Sp. 35/E2
Teslić, Bosn. 40/C3
Tessaoua, Niger 79/G3
Tessenie (Teseney), Erit. 52/C5
Tete, Moz. 82/F4
Tétouan, Mor. 34/C5
Tetovo, FYROM 40/E4
Tettnang, Ger. 37/F2
Teverya, Isr. 49/D3
Tewantin-Noosa, Austl. 72/D4
Texarkana, Tx, US 93/J4
Texas (state), US 96/C4
Texas City, Tx, US 93/J5
Texcoco, Mex. 101/R9
Texmelucan, Mex. 101/L7
Teykovo, Rus. 42/J4
Teziutlán, Mex. 101/M7
Tezontepec de Aldama, Mex. 101/K6
Tezpur, India 60/B3
Tezu, India 60/C3
Thai Binh, Viet. 65/D1
Thai Nguyen, Viet. 65/D1
Thailand (ctry.) 65/C3
Thailand (gulf) 65/C4
Thal, Pak. 53/K2
Thalwil, Swi. 37/E3
Thames, NZ 71/S10
Thames (riv.), Eng, UK 25/G3
Thāna, India 62/B4
Thanh Hoa, Viet. 65/D2
Thanjavur, India 62/C5
Tharād, India 62/B3
Thatcham, Eng, UK 25/E4
Thaton, Myan. 65/B2
The Dalles, Or, US 90/C4
The Woodlands, Tx, US 93/J5
Thebes (ruin), Egypt 52/B3
Theodore Roosevelt National Park, US 91/G4
Thessaloníki, Gre. 40/F5
Thetford, Eng, UK 25/G2
Thetford Mines, Qu, Can. 95/G2
Thibodaux, La, US 93/K5
Thiers, Fr. 32/E4
Thiès, Sen. 78/A3
Thika, Kenya 82/G1
Thimphu (cap.), Bhu. 62/E2
Thionville, Fr. 31/F5
Thívai, Gre. 39/H3
Tholen, Neth. 28/B5
Thomaston, Ga, US 97/G3
Thomasville, Ga, US 97/H4
Thomasville, NC, US 97/H3
Thonon-les-Bains, Fr. 36/C5
Thornaby-on-Tees, Eng, UK 23/G2
Thorne, Eng, UK 23/H4
Thornton Cleveleys, Eng, UK 23/E4
Thorold, On, Can. 95/U9
Thoubāl, India 60/B3
Thu Dau Mot, Viet. 65/D4
Thun, Swi. 36/D4
Thunder Bay, On, Can. 91/L3
Tianguá, Braz. 107/K4
Tianjin, China 59/H7
Tianmen, China 61/G2
Tianshui, China 54/F5
Tiaret, Alg. 76/F1
Ticul, Mex. 102/D1
Tidjikdja, Mrta. 78/C2
Tiel, Neth. 28/C5
Tieling, China 58/B1
Tielt, Belg. 30/C2
Tienen, Belg. 31/D2
Tierp, Swe. 42/C3
Tierra Blanca, Mex. 101/N8
Tiffin, Oh, US 94/D3
Tifton, Ga, US 97/H4
Tighina (Bendery), Mol. 41/J2
Tigris (riv.), Iraq 51/F4
Tijuana, Mex. 92/C4
Tīkamgarh, India 62/C3
Tikhoretsk, Rus. 44/G3
Tikhvin, Rus. 42/G4
Tilburg, Neth. 28/C5
Ţīmā, Egypt 50/B5
Timaru, NZ 71/R11
Timashevsk, Rus. 44/F3
Timbaúba, Braz. 107/L5
Timbó, Braz. 108/B3
Timimoun, Alg. 76/F2
Timişoara, Rom. 40/E3
Timmins, On, Can. 94/D1
Timon, Braz. 107/K5
Timor (isl.), Indo. 68/B5
Timóteo, Braz. 108/D1
Timrå, Swe. 42/C3
Tindivanam, India 62/C5
Tindouf, Alg. 76/D2
Tineo, Sp. 34/B1
Tingo María, Peru 106/C5
Tinley Park, Il, US 99/Q16
Tinrhir, Mor. 76/D1
Tiptūr, India 62/C5
Tiranë (cap.), Alb. 40/D5
Tiraspol, Mol. 41/J2
Tirat Karmel, Isr. 49/F6
Tire, Turk. 50/A2
Tîrgovişte, Rom. 41/G3
Tîrgu Jiu, Rom. 41/F3
Tîrgu Mureş, Rom. 41/G2
Tîrgu Neamţ, Rom. 41/H2
Tîrgu Secuiesc, Rom. 41/H2
Tîrnăveni, Rom. 41/G2
Tiruchchirāppalli, India 62/C5
Tiruchendūr, India 62/C6
Tiruchengodu, India 62/C5
Tirunelveli, India 62/C6
Tirupati, India 62/C5
Tiruppattūr, India 62/C5
Tiruppūr, India 62/C5
Tiruvannāmalai, India 62/C5
Titicaca (lake), Peru 106/E7
Titlagarh, India 62/D3
Titov Veles, FYROM 40/E5
Titusville, Fl, US 97/H4
Tivaouane, Sen. 78/A3
Tiverton, Eng, UK 24/C5
Tixtla de Guerrero, Mex. 102/B2
Tizayuca, Mex. 101/L7
Tizimín, Mex. 102/D1
Tiznit, Mor. 76/D2
Tlalnepantla, Mex. 101/Q9
Tlapa de Comonfort, Mex. 102/B2
Tlapacoyan, Mex. 101/M7
Tlaquepaque, Mex. 100/E4
Tlaquiltenango, Mex. 101/K8
Tlaxcala, Mex. 101/L7
Tlemcen, Alg. 76/E1
Toamasina, Madg. 81/J7
Toba, Japan 57/E3
Tobias Barreto, Braz. 107/L6
Tocantins (riv.), Braz. 107/J4
Tochigi, Japan 57/F2
Tochio, Japan 57/F2
Tocopilla, Chile 109/B1
Tocumen, Pan. 103/G4
Toda Bhīm, India 62/C2
Togo (ctry.) 79/F4
Tōkai, Japan 57/E3
Tōkamachi, Japan 57/F2
Tokat, Turk. 44/F4
Tokoroa, NZ 71/S10
Tokorozawa, Japan 57/F3
Tokushima, Japan 56/D3
Tokuyama, Japan 56/B3
Tōkyō (cap.), Japan 57/F3
Tola, Nic. 102/E4
Toledo, Braz. 109/F1
Toledo, Sp. 34/C3
Toliara, Madg. 81/G8
Tolosa, Sp. 34/D1
Tolú, Col. 103/H4
Toluca, Mex. 101/Q10
Tol'yatti, Rus. 45/J1
Tomakomai, Japan 55/N3
Tomar, Port. 34/A3
Tomaszów Lubelski, Pol. 27/M3
Tomaszów Mazowiecki, Pol. 27/L3
Tombouctou, Mali 78/E2
Tomelloso, Sp. 34/D3
Tomsk, Rus. 46/J4
Tonalá, Mex. 102/C2
Tonawanda, NY, US 95/V9
Tonbridge, Eng, UK 25/G4
Tondano, Indo. 67/F3
Tonga (ctry.) 69/H7
Tongaat, SAfr. 81/E3
Tongchuan, China 59/B4
Tongduch'on, SKor. 58/G6
Tongeren, Belg. 31/E2
Tonghae, SKor. 58/E4
Tonghua, China 58/C2
Tongliao, China 59/E2
Tongling, China 61/H2
Tongren, China 61/F3
Tönisvorst, Ger. 28/D6
Tonk, India 62/C2
Tonkin (gulf), Asia 65/D1
Tonoshō, Japan 56/D3
Tønsberg, Nor. 20/D4
Tooele, Ut, US 92/D2
Toowoomba, Austl. 72/C4
Topeka (cap.), Ks, US 93/J3
Topliţa, Rom. 41/G2
Topol'čany, Slvk. 27/K4
Torbalı, Turk. 50/A2
Torbat-e Ḩeydarīyeh, Iran 51/J3
Torghay, Kaz. 46/G4
Torhout, Belg. 30/C1
Torino (Turin), It. 33/G4
Tornio, Fin. 20/H2
Törökszentmiklós, Hun. 40/E2
Toronto (cap.), On, Can. 95/U8
Toropets, Rus. 42/F4
Tororo, Ugan. 77/M7
Torquay, Eng, UK 24/C6
Torrance, Ca, US 92/C4
Torre del Greco, It. 40/B5
Torre-Pacheco, Sp. 35/E4
Torrejón de Ardoz, Sp. 35/N9
Torrelavega, Sp. 34/C1
Torremaggiore, It. 40/B5
Torremolinos, Sp. 34/C4
Torrente, Sp. 35/E3
Torreón, Mex. 96/C5
Tôrres, Braz. 108/B4
Torres Novas, Port. 34/A3
Torres Vedras, Port. 34/A3
Torrevieja, Sp. 35/E4
Tortona, It. 33/H4
Tortosa, Sp. 35/F2
Toruń, Pol. 27/K2
Torzhok, Rus. 42/G4
Tosa, Japan 56/C4
Tosashimizu, Japan 56/C4
Tosno, Rus. 42/F4
Tosu, Japan 56/B4
Tosya, Turk. 44/E4
Totana, Sp. 34/E4
Totness, Sur. 107/G2
Tottori, Japan 56/D3
T'oufen, Tai. 61/J3
Tougan, Burk. 78/E3
Touggourt, Alg. 76/G1
Toul, Fr. 31/E6
Toulon, Fr. 32/F5
Toulouse, Fr. 32/D5
Toungoo, Myan. 65/B2
Tourcoing, Fr. 30/C2
Tourlaville, Fr. 32/C2
Tournai, Belg. 30/C2
Tours, Fr. 32/D3
Towada, Japan 57/G2
Townsville, Austl. 72/B2
Toyama, Japan 57/E2
Toyohashi, Japan 57/E3
Toyokawa, Japan 57/E3
Toyo'oka, Japan 56/D3
Toyoshina, Japan 57/E2
Toyota, Japan 57/E3
Tra Vinh, Viet. 65/D4
Trabzon, Turk. 44/F4
Tracy, Ca, US 99/M11
Tralee, Ire. 21/A10
Tramandaí, Braz. 108/B4
Tramin (Termeno), It. 37/H5
Tranås, Swe. 20/E4
Trang, Thai. 65/B5
Trani, It. 40/C5
Trapani, It. 38/C3
Trappes, Fr. 30/B6
Traralgon, Austl. 73/C3
Traun, Aus. 33/L2
Traunreut, Ger. 40/A2
Traunstein, Ger. 33/K3
Travnik, Bosn. 40/C3
Trbovlje, Slov. 40/B2
Třebíč, Czh. 33/L2
Trebinje, Bosn. 40/D4
Treinta y Tres, Uru. 109/F3
Trelew, Arg. 109/C5
Trelleborg, Swe. 26/G1
Trenčín, Slvk. 27/K4
Trenque Lauquen, Arg. 109/D4
Trento, It. 37/H5
Trenton, On, Can. 94/E2
Trenton (cap.), NJ, US 94/F3
Trenton, Mi, US 99/F7
Tres Arroyos, Arg. 109/D4
Três Corações, Braz. 108/H6
Três Lagoas, Braz. 108/B2
Três Marias, Braz. 108/C1
Três Pontas, Braz. 108/H6
Três Rios, Braz. 108/K7
Tres Valles, Mex. 102/B2
Treviglio, It. 33/H4
Treviso, It. 33/K4
Trichūr, India 62/C5
Trier, Ger. 31/F4
Trieste, It. 40/A3
Triggiano, It. 40/C5
Tríkala, Gre. 39/G3
Trincomalee, SrL. 62/D6
Trindade, Braz. 107/J7
Třinec, Czh. 27/K4
Trinidad, Bol. 106/F6
Trinidad, Uru. 109/E3
Trinidad and Tobago (ctry.), Trin. 104/F5
Triolet, Mrts. 81/T15
Tripoli (cap.), Libya 76/H1
Trípolis, Gre. 39/H4
Tripunittura, India 62/C6
Trivandrum, India 62/C6
Trnava, Slvk. 40/C1
Trois-Rivières, Qu, Can. 95/F2
Troisdorf, Ger. 31/G2
Troitsk, Rus. 43/P5
Trollhättan, Swe. 20/E4
Tromsø, Nor. 20/F1
Trondheim, Nor. 20/D3
Tropic of Capricorn 72/A3
Trowbridge, Eng, UK 24/D4
Troy, NY, US 94/F3
Troy, Oh, US 97/G1
Troy, Al, US 97/G4
Troy, Mi, US 99/F6
Troyan, Bul. 41/G4
Troyes, Fr. 32/F2
Trstenik, Yugo. 40/E4
Trujillo, Ven. 106/D2
Trujillo, Peru 106/C5
Trujillo, Hon. 102/E3
Truro, Eng, UK 24/A6
Truth or Consequences, NM, US 96/B3
Trutnov, Czh. 27/H3
Trzcianka, Pol. 27/J2
Tsabong, Bots. 80/C2
Tsakane, SAfr. 80/Q13
Tsetserleg, Mong. 54/E2
Tsévié, Togo 79/F5
Tshikapa, D.R. Congo 82/D2
Tsiroanomandidy, Madg. 81/H7
Ts'khinvali, Geo. 45/G4
Tsu, Japan 56/E3
Tsubame, Japan 57/F2
Tsubata, Japan 57/E2
Tsuchiura, Japan 57/G2
Tsukumi, Japan 56/B4
Tsuru, Japan 57/F3
Tsuruga, Japan 56/E3
Tsurugi, Japan 56/E2
Tsuyama, Japan 56/D3
Tuamotu (arch.), FrPol. 69/L6
Tuao, Phil. 61/J5
Tuapse, Rus. 44/F3
Tuba, Phil. 61/J5
Tuban, Indo. 66/D5
Tubarão, Braz. 108/B4
Tubbergen, Neth. 28/D4
Tübingen, Ger. 37/F1
Tubize, Belg. 31/D2
Tubou, Fiji 68/H6
Ţubruq (Tobruk), Libya 77/K1
Tucson, Az, US 92/E4
Tucupita, Ven. 106/F2
Tucuruí, Braz. 107/J4
Tudela, Sp. 34/E1
Ţūkh, Egypt 49/B4
Tukums, Lat. 42/D4
Tukwila, Wa, US 99/C3
Tula, Mex. 101/K6
Tula, Rus. 44/F1
Tulancingo, Mex. 101/L6
Tulare, Ca, US 92/C3
Tulcán, Ecu. 106/C3
Tulcea, Rom. 41/J3
Ţūlkarm, WBnk. 49/G7
Tullahoma, Tn, US 97/G3
Tulle, Fr. 32/D4
Tulsa, Ok, US 93/J3
Tultitlán, Mex. 101/Q9
Tuluá, Col. 106/C3
Tulun, Rus. 47/L4
Tumaco, Col. 106/C3
Tumbes, Peru 106/B4
Tumen, China 55/K3
Tumkūr, India 62/C5
Tumwater, Wa, US 99/B4
Tunceli, Turk. 50/D2
Tūnis (cap.), Tun. 38/B4
Tunisia (ctry.) 76/H1
Tunja, Col. 106/D2
Tunuyán, Arg. 109/C3
Tupã, Braz. 108/B2
Tupaciguara, Braz. 108/B1
Tupelo, Ms, US 97/F3
Tupiza, Bol. 106/E8
Tura, India 62/F2
Turbaco, Col. 103/H4
Turbat, Pak. 53/H3
Turbo, Col. 103/G4
Turčiansky Svätý Martin, Slvk. 27/K4
Turda, Rom. 41/F2
Turek, Pol. 27/K2
Tŭrgovishte, Bul. 41/H4
Turgutlu, Turk. 44/C5
Turhal, Turk. 44/F4
Turkey (ctry.) 50/C2
Türkistan, Kaz. 46/G5
Türkmenbashi (Krasnowodsk), Trkm. 51/H2
Turkmenistan (ctry.) 46/F6
Türkoğlu, Turk. 50/D2
Turks and Caicos (isls.), UK 104/C2
Turlock, Ca, US 92/B3
Turnhout, Belg. 28/B6
Turnu Măgurele, Rom. 41/G4
Turpan, China 54/B3
Tuscaloosa, Al, US 97/G3
Tuskegee, Al, US 97/G3
Tutayev, Rus. 42/H4
Tuticorin, India 62/C6
Tuttlingen, Ger. 37/E2
Tuusula, Fin. 42/E3
Tuvalu (ctry.) 68/G5
Tuxpan, Mex. 100/D4
Tuxpan, Mex. 100/E5
Tuxpan de Rodríguez Cano, Mex. 102/B1
Tuxtla Gutiérrez, Mex. 102/C2
Túy, Sp. 34/A1
Tuy Hoa, Viet. 65/E3
Tuyen Quang, Viet. 65/D1
Tuymazy, Rus. 43/M5
Tuzla, Bosn. 40/D3
Tver', Rus. 42/G4
Tweed Heads, Austl. 73/E1
Twello, Neth. 28/D4
Twin Falls, Id, US 92/D2
Two Rivers, Wi, US 91/M4
Tychy, Pol. 27/K3
Tyldesley, Eng, UK 23/F4
Tyler, Tx, US 93/J4
Tynemouth, Eng, UK 23/G1
Tyrnyauz, Rus. 45/G4
Tyumen', Rus. 43/Q4

U

Ub, Yugo. 40/E3
Ubá, Braz. 108/D2
Übach-Palenberg, Ger. 31/F2
Ubatã, Braz. 107/L6
Ubatuba, Braz. 108/H8
Ube, Japan 56/B4
Úbeda, Sp. 34/D3
Uberaba, Braz. 108/C1
Uberlândia, Braz. 108/B1
Überlingen, Ger. 37/F2
Ubon Ratchathani, Thai. 65/D3
Ubrique, Sp. 34/C4
Ucayali (riv.), Peru 106/D5
Uccle, Belg. 31/D2
Uchaly, Rus. 43/N5
Udagamandalam, India 62/C5
Udaipur, India 62/B3
Uddevalla, Swe. 20/D4
Uden, Neth. 28/C5
Udgīr, India 62/C4
Udhampur, India 53/L2
Udine, It. 40/A2
Udipi, India 62/B5
Udon Thani, Thai. 65/C2
Ueda, Japan 57/F2
Uelzen, Ger. 29/H3
Ueno, Japan 56/E3
Uenohara, Japan 57/F3
Uetersen, Ger. 29/G1
Uetze, Ger. 29/H4
Ufa, Rus. 43/M5
Uganda (ctry.) 77/M7
Uglegorsk, Rus. 55/N2
Uglich, Rus. 42/H4
Uherské Hradiště, Czh. 27/J4

ge, Ang. 82/C2
öngbu, SKor. 58/G6
söng, SKor. 56/A2
tenhage, SAfr. 80/D4
thoorn, Neth. 28/B4
jain, India 62/C3
ung Pandang, Io. 67/E5
hta, Rus. 43/M3
kiah, Ca, US 92/B3
kmergė, Lith. 42/E5
kraine (ctry.) 44/D2
aanbaatar (cap.), ong. 54/F2
aangom, Mong. 54/C2
an-Ude, Rus. 54/F1
anhot, China 55/J2
lchin, SKor. 56/A2
lhāsnagar, India 62/B4
liastay, Mong. 54/D2
Ilm, Ger. 37/F1
Ilsan, SKor. 56/A3
l'yanovka, Rus. 43/T7
l'yanovsk, Rus. 45/J1
Jmán, Mex. 102/D1
man', Ukr. 44/D2
markot, India 62/D4
meå, Swe. 42/D3
mm Durmān, Sudan 52/B5
mm el Fahm, Isr. 49/G6
Jmtata, SAfr. 80/E3
muarama, Braz. 109/F1
naí, Braz. 107/J7
necha, Rus. 44/E1
ngava (bay), Qu, Can. 87/K3
Jngheni, Mol. 41/H2
Jnião da Vitória, Braz. 108/B3
nião dos Palmares, Braz. 107/L5
nion, SC, US 97/H3
nion City, Tn, US 97/F2
Jnion City, Ca, US 99/K11
Jnión de Reyes, Cuba 103/F1
Jniontown, Pa, US 94/E4
nited Arab Emirates (ctry.) 52/F4
Jnited Kingdom (ctry.) 18/C3
Jnited States (ctry.) 88/
Jniversity Place, Wa, US 99/B3
Jnjha, India 62/B3
Jnna, Ger. 29/E5
Jnnão, India 62/D2
Jnterschleissheim, Ger. 37/H1
Jnye, Turk. 44/F4
Jozu, Japan 57/E2
Jpata, Ven. 106/F2
Jpington, SAfr. 80/C3
Jpleta, India 62/B3
Jpper (pen.), Mi, US 89/J2
Upper Hutt, NZ 71/S11
Upplands-Väsby, Swe. 20/F4
Uppsala, Swe. 42/C4
Ural (mts.), Rus. 46/F3
Urawa, Japan 57/F3
Uray, Rus. 46/G3
Urbana, Oh, US 97/H1
Urfa, Turk. 50/D2
Urganch, Uzb. 46/G5
Uriangato, Mex. 101/E4
Urla, Turk. 44/C5
Urmston, Eng, UK 23/F5
Uroševac, Yugo. 40/E4
Uruaçu, Braz. 107/J6
Uruapan, Mex. 100/E5
Uruguaiana, Braz. 109/E2
Uruguay (riv.), SAm. 109/E2
Uruguay (ctry.) 109/E3
Ürümqi, China 54/B3
Uryupinsk, Rus. 45/G2
Urziceni, Rom. 41/H3
Usa, Japan 56/B4
Uşak, Turk. 50/B2
Ushibuka, Japan 56/B4
Ushtobe, Kaz. 46/H5
Ushuaia, Arg. 109/C7
Usibelli, Ak, US 85/J3
Usilampatti, India 62/C6
Uslar, Ger. 29/G5
Usman', Rus. 44/F1
Usol'ye-Sibirskoye, Rus. 54/E1
Uson, Phil. 67/F1
Ussuriysk, Rus. 55/L3
Ust'-Ilimsk, Rus. 47/L4
Ust'-Kut, Rus. 47/L4
Uster, Swi. 37/E3
Ústí nad Labem, Czh. 33/L1
Ustka, Pol. 27/J1
Usuki, Japan 56/B4
Usulután, ESal. 102/D3
Utah (state), US 92/E3
Utraulā, India 62/D2
Utrecht, Neth. 28/C4
Utrera, Sp. 34/C4
Utsunomiya, Japan 57/F2
Utuado, PR 104/E3
Uvalde, Tx, US 93/H5
Uvarovo, Rus. 45/G2
Uwajima, Japan 56/C4
Uxmal (ruin), Mex. 102/D1
Uzbekistan (ctry.) 46/G5
Uzhhorod, Ukr. 27/M4
Užice, Yugo. 40/D4
Uzlovaya, Rus. 44/F1
Uzunköprü, Turk. 41/H5

V

Vaasa (Vasa), Fin. 42/D3
Vác, Hun. 27/K5
Vacaria, Braz. 108/B4
Vacaville, Ca, US 99/L10
Vadodara (Baroda), India 62/B3
Vadsø, Nor. 42/F1
Vaduz (cap.), Lcht. 37/F3
Vaijāpur, India 53/K5
Vakfıkebir, Turk. 44/F4
Val-d'Or, Qu, Can. 94/E1
Valdepeñas, Sp. 34/D3
Valdivia, Chile 109/B4
Valdosta, Ga, US 97/H4
Valença, Braz. 107/L6
Valença, Braz. 108/K7
Valence, Fr. 32/F4
Valencia, Ven. 106/E1
Valencia, Sp. 35/E3
Valenciennes, Fr. 30/C3
Valenza, It. 33/H4
Valera, Ven. 106/D2
Valga, Est. 42/E4
Valinhos, Braz. 108/F7
Valjevo, Yugo. 40/D3
Valkenburg, Neth. 31/E2
Valkenswaard, Neth. 28/C6
Vall de Uxó, Sp. 35/E3
Valladolid, Mex. 102/D1
Valladolid, Sp. 34/C2
Valle de Bravo, Mex. 102/A2
Valle de La Pascua, Ven. 106/E2
Valle de Santiago, Mex. 101/E4
Valle Hermoso, Mex. 101/F3
Valledupar, Col. 103/H4
Vallejo, Ca, US 99/K10
Vallenar, Chile 109/B2
Valletta (cap.), Malta 38/M7
Valley East, On, Can. 94/D2
Valls, Sp. 35/F2
Valmiera, Lat. 42/E4
Vālpārai, India 62/C5
Valparaíso, Chile 109/B3
Valparaiso, In, US 94/C3
Valsād, India 62/B3
Valuyki, Rus. 44/F2
Vammala, Fin. 20/G3
Van, Turk. 51/E2
Van Wert, Oh, US 94/C3
Vanadzor, Arm. 45/H4
Vancouver, Wa, US 90/C4
Vancouver, BC, Can. 90/C3
Vancouver (isl.), BC, Can. 90/B3
Vanderbijlpark, SAfr. 80/P13
Vandœuvre-lès-Nancy, Fr. 31/F6
Vänersborg, Swe. 20/E4
Vangaindrano, Madg. 81/H8
Vanimo, PNG 67/K4
Vanino, Rus. 55/N2
Vannes, Fr. 32/B3
Vantaa, Fin. 42/E3
Vanuatu (ctry.) 68/F6
Varadero, Cuba 103/F1
Varāmīn, Iran 51/G3
Vārānasi, India 62/D2
Varaždin, Cro. 40/C2
Varberg, Swe. 20/E4
Varel, Ger. 29/F2
Varennes, Qu, Can. 95/P6
Vareš, Bosn. 40/D3
Varese, It. 33/H4
Vargem Grande do Sul, Braz. 108/G6
Varginha, Braz. 108/H6
Varkaus, Fin. 42/E3
Varna, Bul. 41/H4
Värnamo, Swe. 20/E4
Várpalota, Hun. 40/D2
Várzea da Palma, Braz. 108/C1
Várzea Grande, Braz. 107/G7
Vaslui, Rom. 41/H2
Vassouras, Braz. 108/K7
Västerås, Swe. 42/C4
Västervik, Swe. 42/C4
Vasto, It. 40/B4
Vasyl'kiv, Ukr. 44/D2
Vaterstetten, Ger. 33/J2
Vatican City (ctry.) 38/C2
Vatican City (cap.), VatC. 38/C2
Vatra Dornei, Rom. 41/G2
Vaudreuil-Dorion, Qu, Can. 95/M7
Vaughan, On, Can. 95/T8
Vaulx-en-Velin, Fr. 36/A6
Vavatenina, Madg. 81/J7
Vavuniya, SrL. 62/D6
Vawkavysk, Bela. 27/N2
Växjö, Swe. 20/E4
Vázea Paulista, Braz. 108/G8
Vechta, Ger. 29/F3
Vecsés, Hun. 27/K5
Veendam, Neth. 28/D2
Veenendaal, Neth. 28/C4
Veghel, Neth. 28/C5
Vejle, Den. 26/E1
Velbert, Ger. 28/E6
Veldhoven, Neth. 28/C6
Vélez-Málaga, Sp. 34/C4
Velika Gorica, Cro. 40/C3
Velika Plana, Yugo. 40/E3
Velikiy Ustyug, Rus. 43/K3
Velikiye Luki, Rus. 42/F4
Veliko Tŭrnovo, Bul. 41/G4
Velletri, It. 38/C2
Vellinge, Swe. 26/G1
Vellmar, Ger. 29/G6
Vellore, India 62/C5
Vel'sk, Rus. 42/J3
Venado Tuerto, Arg. 109/D3
Venâncio Aires, Braz. 108/A4
Venaria, It. 33/G4
Vence, Fr. 33/G5
Vendôme, Fr. 32/D3
Vendrell, Sp. 35/F2
Venezia (Venice), It. 33/K4
Venezuela (ctry.), Ven. 106/E2
Venice, Fl, US 97/H5
Venice (Venezia), It. 33/K4
Vénissieux, Fr. 32/F4
Venkatagiri, India 62/C5
Venlo, Neth. 28/D6
Venray, Neth. 28/C5
Ventspils, Lat. 42/D4
Ventura (San Buenaventura), Ca, US 92/C4
Vera, Arg. 109/D2
Veracruz, Mex. 101/N7
Verāval, India 62/B3
Verbania, It. 37/E6
Vercelli, It. 33/H4
Verde (cape), Sen. 76/B5
Verden, Ger. 29/G3
Verdun, Qu, Can. 95/N7
Verdun, Fr. 31/E5
Vereeniging, SAfr. 80/P13
Vereshchagino, Rus. 43/M4
Verl, Ger. 29/F5
Vermillion, SD, US 93/H2
Vermont (state), US 95/F2
Vernier, Swi. 36/C5
Vernon, BC, Can. 90/D3
Vernon, Tx, US 93/H4
Vernon, Fr. 30/A5
Vernon Hills, Il, US 99/Q15
Vero Beach, Fl, US 97/H5
Véroia, Gre. 40/F5
Verona, It. 33/J4
Verrières-le-Buisson, Fr. 30/B6
Versailles, Fr. 30/B6
Versmold, Ger. 29/F4
Vertientes, Cuba 103/G1
Vertou, Fr. 32/C3
Verviers, Belg. 31/E2
Verwoerdburg, SAfr. 80/Q12
Verzasca (Gerra), Swi. 37/E5
Vesoul, Fr. 36/C2
Vesuvio (Vesuvius) (vol.), It. 38/D2
Veszprém, Hun. 40/C2
Vetlanda, Swe. 20/E4
Vevey, Swi. 36/C5
Vezirköprü, Turk. 44/E4
Viacha, Bol. 106/E7
Viana, Braz. 107/K4
Viana do Castelo, Port. 34/A2
Vianen, Neth. 28/C5
Viareggio, It. 33/J5
Vibo Valentia, It. 38/E3
Viborg, Den. 20/D4
Vic, Sp. 35/G2
Vicenza, It. 33/J4
Vichuga, Rus. 42/J4
Vichy, Fr. 32/E3
Vicksburg, Ms, US 93/K4
Viçosa, Braz. 108/D2
Victor Rosales, Mex. 100/E4
Victoria, Arg. 109/D3
Victoria, Austl. 73/B2
Victoria, Chile 109/B4
Victoria (cap.), BC, Can. 90/C3
Victoria (isl.), NW,Nun., Can. 86/E1
Victoria (lake), Afr. 77/M8
Victoria, China 61/G4
Victoria (falls), Zim. 82/E4
Victoria de las Tunas, Cuba 103/G1
Victoriaville, Qu, Can. 95/G2
Victorville, Ca, US 92/C4
Vidalia, Ga, US 97/H3
Videira, Braz. 108/B3
Vidin, Bul. 41/F4
Vidisha, India 62/C3
Vidnoye, Rus. 43/W9
Vidor, Tx, US 93/J5
Viedma, Arg. 109/D5
Vienna, WV, US 97/H2
Vienna (cap.), Aus. 40/C2
Vienne, Fr. 32/F4
Vientiane (cap.), Laos 65/C2
Viersen, Ger. 28/D6
Vierzon, Fr. 32/E3
Viet Tri, Viet. 65/D1
Vietnam (ctry.) 65/D2
Vigan, Phil. 61/J5
Vigevano, It. 33/H4
Vigia, Braz. 107/J4
Vigneux-sur-Seine, Fr. 30/B6
Vignola, It. 33/J4
Vigo, Sp. 34/A1
Vihāri, Pak. 53/K2
Vijayawada, India 62/D4
Vila de Sena, Moz. 82/G4
Vila do Conde, Port. 34/A2
Vila Franca de Xira, Port. 35/P10
Vila Nova de Gaia, Port. 34/A2
Vila Real, Port. 34/B2
Vila Velha Argolas, Braz. 108/D2
Viladecans, Sp. 35/K7
Vilafranca del Penedès, Sp. 35/K7
Vilanova i la Geltrù, Sp. 35/K7
Vilhena, Braz. 106/F6
Viljandi, Est. 42/E4
Villa Ángela, Arg. 109/D2
Villa Carlos Paz, Arg. 109/D3
Villa de Costa Rica, Mex. 100/D3
Villa Dolores, Arg. 109/C3
Villa Flores, Mex. 102/C2
Villa Gesell, Arg. 109/E4
Villa María, Arg. 109/D3
Villa Nueva, Guat. 102/D3
Villa Nueva, Nic. 102/E3
Villa Park, Il, US 99/Q16
Villa Regina, Arg. 109/C4
Villa Rosario, Col. 103/H5
Villa Sandino, Nic. 103/E3
Villablino, Sp. 34/B1
Villach, Aus. 40/A2
Villagarcía, Sp. 34/A1
Villaguay, Arg. 109/E3
Villahermosa, Mex. 102/C2
Villajoyosa, Sp. 35/E3
Villalba, Sp. 34/B1
Villanueva, Col. 103/H4
Villanueva de Arosa, Sp. 34/A1
Villanueva de la Serena, Sp. 34/C3
Villarreal de los Infantes, Sp. 35/E3
Villarrica, Par. 109/E2
Villarrica, Chile 109/B4
Villarrobledo, Sp. 34/D3
Villavicencio, Col. 106/D3
Villaviciosa, Sp. 34/C1
Villaviciosa de Odón, Sp. 35/N9
Villazón, Bol. 106/E8
Ville Platte, La, US 93/J5
Villefranche-sur-Saône, Fr. 36/A6
Villejuif, Fr. 30/B6
Villena, Sp. 35/E3
Villeneuve-d'Ascq, Fr. 30/C2
Villeneuve-Saint-Georges, Fr. 30/B6
Villeneuve-sur-Lot, Fr. 32/D4
Villeparisis, Fr. 30/B6
Villers-lès-Nancy, Fr. 31/F6
Villeurbanne, Fr. 36/A6
Villingen-Schwenningen, Ger. 37/E1
Vilnius (cap.), Lith. 27/N1
Vilshofen, Ger. 33/K2
Vilvoorde, Belg. 31/D2
Vimmerby, Swe. 20/E4
Viña del Mar, Chile 109/B3
Vinaroz, Sp. 35/F2
Vincennes, In, US 97/G2
Vineland, NJ, US 94/F4
Vinh, Viet. 65/D2
Vinh Long, Viet. 65/D4
Vinh Yen, Viet. 65/D1
Vinhedo, Braz. 108/G8
Vinica, FYROM 40/F5
Vinkovci, Cro. 40/D3
Vinnytsya, Ukr. 44/D2
Vintar, Phil. 61/J5
Viranşehir, Turk. 50/D2
Virār, India 62/B4
Virgin (isls.), UK,US 104/E3
Virginia, SAfr. 80/D3
Virginia (state), US 97/J2
Virginia Beach, Va, US 97/K2
Virovitica, Cro. 40/C3
Virudunagar, India 62/C6
Viry-Châtillon, Fr. 30/B6
Visākhapatnam, India 62/D4
Visalia, Ca, US 92/C3
Visby, Swe. 42/C4
Visconde do Rio Branco, Braz. 108/D2
Visé, Belg. 31/E2
Višegrad, Bosn. 40/D4
Viseu, Port. 34/B2
Vişeu de Sus, Rom. 41/G2
Visnagar, India 62/B3
Visoko, Bosn. 40/D4
Vista, Ca, US 92/C4
Viterbo, It. 38/C1
Vitória, Braz. 108/D2
Vitoria, Sp. 34/D1
Vitória da Conquista, Braz. 107/K6
Vitória de Santo Antão, Braz. 107/L5
Vitré, Fr. 32/C2
Vitrolles, Fr. 32/F5
Vitry-le-François, Fr. 31/D6
Vitry-sur-Seine, Fr. 30/B6
Vitsyebsk, Bela. 42/F5
Vittoria, It. 38/D4
Vittorio Veneto, It. 33/K4
Viveiro, Sp. 34/B1
Vizianagaram, India 62/D4
Vlaardingen, Neth. 28/B5
Vladikavkaz, Rus. 45/H4
Vladimir, Rus. 42/J4
Vladivostok, Rus. 55/L3
Vlagtwedde, Neth. 29/E2
Vlasenica, Bosn. 40/D3
Vlijmen, Neth. 28/C5
Vlissingen, Neth. 28/A6
Vlotho, Ger. 29/F4
Voerde, Ger. 28/D5
Voghera, It. 33/H4
Vohipeno, Madg. 81/H8
Voiron, Fr. 32/F4
Vöklingen, Ger. 31/F5
Volendam, Neth. 28/C3
Volgodonsk, Rus. 45/G3
Stalingrad (Volgograd), Rus. 45/H2
Volkhov, Rus. 42/G4
Volodymyr-Volyns'kyy, Ukr. 27/N3
Vologda, Rus. 42/H4
Vólos, Gre. 39/H3
Vol'sk, Rus. 45/H1
Volta (riv.), Gha. 76/F6
Volta (lake), Gha. 76/E6
Volta Redonda, Braz. 108/J7
Volzhsk, Rus. 43/L5
Volzhskiy, Rus. 45/H2
Voorburg, Neth. 28/B4
Voorschoten, Neth. 28/B4
Voorst, Neth. 28/D4
Vorkuta, Rus. 43/P2
Voronezh, Rus. 44/F2
Võru, Est. 42/E4
Voskresensk, Rus. 44/F1
Votkinsk, Rus. 43/M4
Votorantim, Braz. 108/C2
Votuporanga, Braz. 108/B2
Voúla, Gre. 39/N9
Voyeykov Ice Shelf, Ant. 83/J
Voznesens'k, Ukr. 41/K2
Vranov nad Teplou, Slvk. 27/L4
Vratsa, Bul. 41/F4
Vrbas, Yugo. 40/D3
Vreden, Ger. 28/D4
Vredenburg-Saldanha, SAfr. 80/K10
Vriezenveen, Neth. 28/D4
Vrindāban, India 62/C2
Vršac, Yugo. 40/E3
Vsetín, Czh. 27/J4
Vsevolozhsk, Rus. 43/T6
Vught, Neth. 28/C5
Vukovar, Cro. 40/D3
Vulcan, Rom. 41/F3
Vung Tau, Viet. 65/D4
Vunisea, Fiji 68/G6
Vyāra, India 62/B3
Vyatskiye Polyany, Rus. 43/L4
Vyazemskiy, Rus. 55/L2
Vyaz'ma, Rus. 42/G5
Vyborg, Rus. 42/F3
Vyksa, Rus. 45/G1
Vynohradiv, Ukr. 27/M4
Vyshniy Volochek, Rus. 42/G4
Vyškov, Czh. 33/M2

W

Wa, Gha. 79/E4
Waalre, Neth. 28/C6
Waalwijk, Neth. 28/C5
Wabash, In, US 94/C3
Waco, Tx, US 93/H5
Wad Medanī, Sudan 52/B6
Waddinxveen, Neth. 28/B4
Wädenswil, Swi. 37/E3
Wadern, Ger. 31/F4
Wadgassen, Ger. 31/F5
Wādī As Sīr, Jor. 49/D4
Wadowice, Pol. 27/K4
Wafangdian, China 58/A3
Wageningen, Neth. 28/C5
Wagga Wagga, Austl. 73/C2
Wągrowiec, Pol. 27/J2
Wāh, Pak. 53/K2
Wahiawa, Hi, US 88/V12
Wai, India 62/B4
Waikiki, Hi, US 88/W13
Wailuku, Hi, US 88/T10
Waipahu, Hi, US 88/V13
Waipio, Hi, US 88/U10
Wajima, Japan 57/E2
Wakayama, Japan 56/D3
Wakefield, Eng, UK 23/G4
Wakema, Myan. 60/B5
Waki, Japan 56/D3
Wakkanai, Japan 55/N2
Wałbrzych, Pol. 27/J3
Walcourt, Belg. 31/D3
Wałcz, Pol. 27/J2
Waldbröl, Ger. 31/G2
Waldkirch, Ger. 36/D1
Waldshut-Tiengen, Ger. 37/E2
Wales, UK 24/B3
Walla Walla, Wa, US 90/D4
Wallasey, Eng, UK 23/E5
Wallenhorst, Ger. 29/F4
Wallis and Futuna (dpcy.), Fr. 68/G6
Wallsend, Eng, UK 23/G2
Walnut Canyon Nat'l Mon., Az, US 92/E4
Walnut Creek, Ca, US 99/K11
Walsall, Eng, UK 24/E1
Walsrode, Ger. 29/G3
Waltham Abbey, Eng, UK 25/G3
Walton-on-Thames, Eng, UK 25/F4
Waltrop, Ger. 29/E5
Wanganui, NZ 71/S10
Wangaratta, Austl. 73/C3
Wangen, Ger. 37/F2
Wanxian, China 61/F2
Wapakoneta, Oh, US 94/C3
Warangal, India 62/C4
Warburg, Ger. 29/G6
Ward Cove, Ak, US 85/M4
Wardha, India 62/C3
Ware, Eng, UK 25/F3
Waregem, Belg. 30/C2
Waren, Ger. 26/G2
Warendorf, Ger. 29/E5
Warin Chamrap, Thai. 65/D3
Warmbad, SAfr. 80/E2
Warminster, Eng, UK 24/D4
Warner Robins, Ga, US 97/H3
Warren, Pa, US 94/E3
Warren, Oh, US 94/D3
Warren, Mi, US 99/F6
Warrensburg, Mo, US 93/J3
Warrenville, Il, US 99/P16
Warri, Nga. 79/G5
Warrington, Fl, US 97/G4
Warrington, Eng, UK 23/F5
Warrnambool, Austl. 73/B3
Warsaw, In, US 94/C3
Warsaw (cap.), Pol. 27/L2
Warstein, Ger. 29/F6
Warwick, RI, US 95/G3
Warwick, Eng, UK 25/E2
Wasco, Ca, US 92/C4
Washington, Pa, US 94/D3
Washington, NC, US 97/J3
Washington, Il, US 93/K2
Washington (cap.), DC, US 94/E4
Washington (state), US 90/C4
Washington, Eng, UK 23/G2
Washington (mt.), NH, US 95/G2
Washington Court House (Washington), Oh, US 97/H2
Waspán, Nic. 103/F3
Wassenaar, Neth. 28/B4
Watampone, Indo. 67/F4
Watari, Japan 57/G1
Waterbury, Ct, US 94/F3
Waterford, Mi, US 99/F6
Waterford, Ire. 21/B10
Waterloo, On, Can. 94/D3
Waterloo, Belg. 31/D2
Watermael-Boitsfort, Belg. 31/D2
Watertown, SD, US 91/J4
Watertown, NY, US 94/F3
Watertown, Wi, US 93/K2
Waterville, Me, US 95/G2
Watford, Eng, UK 25/F3
Wath-upon-Dearne, Eng, UK 23/G4
Watsonville, Ca, US 92/B3
Wattignies, Fr. 30/C2
Wattrelos, Fr. 30/C2
Waukegan, Il, US 99/Q15
Waukesha, Wi, US 99/P13
Wauwatosa, Wi, US 99/P13
Wavre, Belg. 31/D2
Wāw, Sudan 77/L6
Waxahachie, Tx, US 93/H4
Waycross, Ga, US 97/H4
Wayne, Mi, US 99/F7
Waynesboro, Pa, US 94/E4
Waynesboro, Va, US 97/J2
Weatherford, Tx, US 96/D3
Webster City, IA, US 93/J2
Wedel, Ger. 29/G1
Wedemark, Ger. 29/G3
Weert, Neth. 28/C6

Weesp – Żywie

Weesp, Neth.	28/C4
Wegberg, Ger.	28/D6
Weiden, Ger.	33/K2
Weifang, China	59/D3
Weihai, China	58/B4
Weilheim, Ger.	37/H2
Weimar, Ger.	26/F3
Weinan, China	59/B4
Weingarten, Ger.	37/F2
Weinheim, Ger.	26/E4
Weirton, WV, US	94/D3
Weissenburg im Bayern, Ger.	33/J2
Weissenfels, Ger.	26/F3
Weisswasser, Ger.	27/H3
Wejherowo, Pol.	27/K1
Weligama, SrL.	62/D6
Welkom, SAfr.	80/D2
Welland, On, Can.	95/U10
Wellingborough, Eng, UK	25/F2
Wellington, SAfr.	80/L10
Wellington (cap.), NZ	71/R11
Wels, Aus.	40/B1
Welshnafen (Nova Levante), It.	37/H5
Wenatchee, Wa, US	90/C4
Wenchi, Gha.	79/E5
Wenden, Ger.	31/G2
Wendeng, China	58/B4
Wenzhou, China	61/J3
Werdau, Ger.	33/K1
Werdohl, Ger.	29/E6
Werkendam, Neth.	28/B5
Werl, Ger.	29/E5
Wermelskirchen, Ger.	29/E6
Werne an der Lippe, Ger.	29/E5
Wernigerode, Ger.	29/H5
Wertheim, Ger.	33/H2
Wervik, Belg.	30/C2
Wesel, Ger.	28/D5
Weslaco, Tx, US	96/D5
West Allis, Wi, US	99/P13
West Bank	49/G7
West Bank (ctry.)	49/D3
West Bank	50/C3
West Bend, Wi, US	93/K2
West Bridgford, Eng, UK	23/G6
West Bromwich, Eng, UK	24/E1
West Chicago, Il, US	99/P16
West Columbia, SC, US	97/H3
West Fargo, ND, US	91/J4
West Helena, Ar, US	93/K4
West Ice Shelf, Ant.	83/F
West Indies (isls.)	103/F2
West Jordan, Ut, US	92/E2
West Lincoln, Ne, US	93/H2
West Memphis, Ar, US	93/K4
West Monroe, La, US	93/J4
West Palm Beach, Fl, US	97/H5
West Pensacola, Fl, US	97/G4
West Sacramento, Ca, US	99/L9
West Seneca, NY, US	95/V10
West Valley City, Ut, US	92/E2
West Vancouver, BC, Can.	90/C3
West Virginia (state), US	94/D4
Westerlo, Belg.	28/B6
Western Ghats (mts.), India	62/B4
Western Sahara	76/C3
Westerstede, Ger.	29/E2
Westerville, Oh, US	97/H1
Westervoort, Neth.	28/C5
Westhoughton, Eng, UK	23/F4
Westland, Mi, US	99/F7
Westminster, Md, US	94/E4
Westmont, Il, US	99/P16
Westmount, Qu, Can.	95/N7
Weston-Super-Mare, Eng, UK	24/D4
Westonaria, SAfr.	80/P13
Wete, Tanz.	82/G2
Wetter, Ger.	29/E6
Wetteren, Belg.	28/A6
Wettingen, Swi.	37/E3
Wetzikon, Swi.	37/E3
Wetzlar, Ger.	33/H1
Wevelgem, Belg.	30/C2
Wewak, PNG	68/D5
Weymouth, Eng, UK	24/D5

Whangarei, NZ	71/R10
Wharton, Tx, US	93/H5
Wheaton, Il, US	99/P16
Wheeling, WV, US	94/D3
Wheeling, Il, US	99/U15
Whickham, Eng, UK	23/G2
Whitby, On, Can.	95/V8
Whitefield, Eng, UK	23/F4
Whitehaven, Eng, UK	22/E2
Whitehorse (cap.), Yk, Can.	85/L3
Whitetail, NM, US	100/D1
Whitley Bay, Eng, UK	23/G1
Whitstable, Eng, UK	25/H4
Whyalla, Austl.	68/C4
Wichita, Ks, US	93/H3
Wichita Falls, Tx, US	93/H4
Widnes, Eng, UK	23/F5
Wiehl, Ger.	31/G2
Wieliczka, Pol.	27/L4
Wieluń, Pol.	27/K3
Wiener Neustadt, Aus.	40/C2
Wierden, Neth.	28/D4
Wiesbaden, Ger.	31/H3
Wigan, Eng, UK	23/F4
Wigston, Eng, UK	25/E1
Wijchen, Neth.	28/C5
Wijk bij Duurstede, Neth.	28/C5
Wil, Swi.	37/F3
Wilhelmshaven, Ger.	29/F1
Wilkes-Barre, Pa, US	94/F3
Willebroek, Belg.	28/B6
Willemstad, NAnt.	106/E1
Williamsburg, Va, US	97/J2
Williamsport, Pa, US	94/E3
Willich, Ger.	28/D6
Willmar, Mn, US	91/K4
Wilmette, Il, US	99/Q15
Wilmington, NC, US	97/J3
Wilmington, De, US	94/F4
Wilmington Island, Ga, US	97/H4
Wilmslow, Eng, UK	23/F5
Wilnsdorf, Ger.	31/H2
Wilson, NC, US	97/J3
Wimborne Minster, Eng, UK	24/E5
Winchester, Ky, US	97/G2
Winchester, Va, US	97/J2
Winchester, Eng, UK	25/E4
Windhoek (cap.), Namb.	82/C5
Windsor, Nf, Can.	95/L1
Windsor, Eng, UK	25/F4
Windsor, On, Can.	99/F7
Windward Passage (chan.), Cuba,Haiti	103/H2
Winfield, Ks, US	93/H3
Winneba, Gha.	79/E5
Winnetka, Il, US	99/Q15
Winnipeg (cap.), Mb, Can.	91/J3
Winnipeg (lake), Can.	91/J3
Winnipegosis (lake), Mb, Can.	91/H2
Winschoten, Neth.	28/E2
Winsford, Eng, UK	23/F5
Winston-Salem, NC, US	97/H2
Winter Haven, Fl, US	97/H4
Winter Park, Fl, US	97/H4
Winterswijk, Neth.	28/D5
Winterthur, Swi.	37/E3
Wipperfürth, Ger.	29/E6
Wisbech, Eng, UK	25/G1
Wisch, Neth.	28/D5
Wisconsin (state), US	91/L4
Wismar, Ger.	26/F2
Witbank, SAfr.	80/Q12
Witham, Eng, UK	25/G3
Witney, Eng, UK	25/E3
Witten, Ger.	29/E6
Wittenberg, Ger.	26/G3
Wittenberge, Ger.	26/F2
Wittlich, Ger.	31/F4
Wittmund, Ger.	29/E1
Witzenhausen, Ger.	29/G6
Włocławek, Pol.	27/K2
Wodonga, Austl.	73/C3
Wodzisław Śląski, Pol.	27/K4
Woerden, Neth.	28/B4
Woking, Eng, UK	25/F4
Wokingham, Eng, UK	25/F4
Wolfen, Ger.	26/G3
Wolfenbüttel, Ger.	29/H4
Wolfsburg, Ger.	29/H4
Wolgast, Ger.	27/G1
Wollongong, Austl.	73/D2
Wołomin, Pol.	27/L2
Woluwé-Saint-Lambert, Belg.	31/D2

Wolvega, Neth.	28/D3
Wolverhampton, Eng, UK	24/D1
Wombwell, Eng, UK	23/G4
Wŏnju, SKor.	56/A2
Wŏnsan, NKor.	58/D3
Wood Dale, Il, US	99/P16
Woodburn, Or, US	90/C4
Woodhaven, Mi, US	99/F7
Woodinville, Wa, US	99/C2
Woodland, Ca, US	99/L9
Woodridge, Il, US	99/P16
Woodstock, Il, US	99/N15
Wooster, Oh, US	94/D3
Worcester, Ma, US	95/G3
Worcester, Eng, UK	24/D2
Worcester, SAfr.	80/L10
Workington, Eng, UK	22/E2
Worksop, Eng, UK	23/G5
Worms, Ger.	33/H2
Worth, Il, US	99/Q16
Wörth am Rhein, Ger.	31/H5
Worthing, Eng, UK	25/F5
Wrexham, Wal, UK	23/F5
Wrocław, Pol.	27/J3
Września, Pol.	27/J2
Wuhan, China	61/G2
Wuhai, China	59/B4
Wuhu, China	61/H2
Wülfrath, Ger.	28/E6
Wum, Camr.	79/H5
Wūn, India	62/C3
Wunstorf, Ger.	29/G4
Wuppertal, Ger.	29/E6
Würselen, Ger.	31/F2
Würzburg, Ger.	33/H2
Wuustwezel, Belg.	28/B6
Wuwei, China	54/E4
Wuxi, China	59/L8
Wuxue, China	61/G2
Wuzhou, China	61/F4
Wyandotte, Mi, US	99/F7
Wyoming, Mi, US	94/C3
Wyoming (state), US	90/G4
Wyszków, Pol.	27/L2

Xa Binh Long, Viet.	65/D4
Xaçmaz, Azer.	45/J4
Xai-Xai, Moz.	81/G2
Xankändı, Azer.	45/H5
Xanten, Ger.	28/D5
Xánthi, Gre.	41/G5
Xanxerê, Braz.	108/A3
Xenia, Oh, US	97/H2
Xiamen, China	61/H3
Xi'an, China	59/B4
Xiangfan, China	61/G1
Xiangtan, China	61/G3
Xianning, China	61/G2
Xiantao, China	61/G2
Xianyang, China	59/B4
Xiaogan, China	61/G2
Xiaoshan, China	59/L9
Xichang, China	60/E3
Xicotepec, Mex.	101/M6
Xifeng, China	54/F4
Xigazê, China	62/E2
Xingcheng, China	59/E2
Xinghua, China	59/D3
Xingtai, China	59/C3
Xingyi, China	60/E3
Xining, China	54/E4
Xinji, China	59/C3
Xintai, China	59/D4
Xinxiang, China	59/C4
Xinyang, China	61/G1
Xinyi, China	61/F4
Xinyu, China	61/G3
Xinzhou, China	59/C3
Xique-Xique, Braz.	107/K6
Xuchang, China	59/C4

Ya'an, China	60/D2
Yabuki, Japan	57/G2
Yacuiba, Bol.	106/F8
Yādgīr, India	62/C4
Yagoua, Camr.	76/J5
Yahyalı, Turk.	50/C2
Yaizu, Japan	57/F3
Yakacık, Turk.	49/E1
Yakeshi, China	55/J2
Yakima, Wa, US	90/C4
Yako, Burk.	79/E4
Yakutsk, Rus.	47/N3
Yala, Thai.	65/C5
Yalova, Turk.	41/J5
Yalta, Ukr.	44/E3
Yalvaç, Turk.	50/B2
Yamaga, Japan	56/B4
Yamagata, Japan	57/G1
Yamaguchi, Japan	56/B3
Yamatotakada, Japan	56/D3

Yambol, Bul.	41/H4
Yamoto, Japan	57/G1
Yamoussoukro (cap.), C.d'Iv.	78/D5
Yamunānagar, India	53/L2
Yanagawa, Japan	56/B4
Yanai, Japan	56/C4
Yan'an, China	59/B3
Yanaul, Rus.	43/M4
Yancheng, China	59/E4
Yandoon, Myan.	60/B5
Yangjiang, China	61/F4
Yangmei, Tai.	61/J3
Yangon (cap.), Myan.	65/B2
Yangquan, China	59/C3
Yangtze (Chang) (riv.), China	55/J5
Yangzhou, China	61/H1
Yanji, China	55/K3
Yantai, China	59/E3
Yao, Japan	56/D3
Yaoundé (cap.), Camr.	76/H7
Yara, Cuba	103/G1
Yaransk, Rus.	43/K4
Yarımca, Turk.	41/J5
Yaroslavl', Rus.	42/H4
Yartsevo, Rus.	46/K3
Yarumal, Col.	106/C2
Yasny, Rus.	45/L2
Yasugi, Japan	56/C3
Yāsūj, Iran	51/G4
Yatabe, Japan	57/G2
Yateley, Eng, UK	25/F4
Yatsuo, Japan	57/E2
Yatsushiro, Japan	56/B4
Yauco, PR	104/E3
Yavne, Isr.	49/F8
Yawatahama, Japan	56/C4
Yazd, Iran	51/H4
Yazoo City, Ms, US	93/K4
Yecla, Sp.	35/E3
Yefremov, Rus.	44/F1
Yehud, Isr.	49/F7
Yejmiadzin, Arm.	45/H4
Yelabuga, Rus.	43/M5
Yelan', Rus.	45/G2
Yelets, Rus.	44/F1
Yellow (Huang) (riv.), China	54/G4
Yellowknife (cap.), NW, Can.	86/D2
Yellowstone (lake), Wy, US	90/F4
Yellowstone (riv.), Mt,Wy, US	91/G4
Yellowstone National Park, US	92/E1
Yen Bai, Viet.	65/D1
Yenakiyeve, Ukr.	44/F2
Yenangyaung, Myan.	60/B4
Yendi, Gha.	79/E4
Yenişehir, Turk.	41/J5
Yeniseysk, Rus.	46/K4
Yeovil, Eng, UK	24/D5
Yerevan (cap.), Arm.	45/H4
Yerköy, Turk.	44/E5
Yermak, Kaz.	46/H4
Yerres, Fr.	30/B6
Yeşilkent, Turk.	49/E1
Yessentuki, Rus.	45/G3
Yevla, India	62/B3
Yevlax, Azer.	45/H4
Yevpatoriya, Ukr.	44/E3
Yeysk, Rus.	44/F3
Yiannitsá, Gre.	40/F5
Yibin, China	60/E2
Yichang, China	61/F2
Yichun, China	61/G3
Yıldızeli, Turk.	44/F5
Yima, China	59/B4
Yinchuan, China	54/F4
Yingcheng, China	61/G2
Yingkou, China	58/B2
Yingtan, China	61/H2
Yining, China	46/H3
Yixing, China	59/K8
Yiyang, China	61/G2
Yizheng, China	61/H1
Ylöjärvi, Fin.	42/D3
Yŏch'ŏn, SKor.	58/D5
Yogyakarta, Indo.	66/D5
Yōkaichi, Japan	56/E3
Yokkaichi, Japan	56/E3
Yokohama, Japan	57/F3
Yokosuka, Japan	57/F3
Yonezawa, Japan	57/G2
Yong'an, China	61/H3
Yŏngch'ŏn, SKor.	56/A3
Yŏngdŏk, SKor.	56/A2
Yŏngju, SKor.	56/A2
Yongzhou, China	61/F3
Yonkers, NY, US	94/F3
Yopal, Col.	106/D2
York, Pa, US	94/E4
York, Eng, UK	23/W8
York, NE, US	93/H2
Yorkton, Sk, Can.	91/H3
Yoro, Hon.	102/E3
Yosemite National Park, Ca, US	92/C3

Yoshida, Japan	56/C4
Yoshkar-Ola, Rus.	43/L4
Yŏsu, SKor.	58/D5
Youngstown, Oh, US	94/D3
Yozgat, Turk.	44/E5
Ypsilanti, Mi, US	99/E7
Ystad, Swe.	27/G1
Yuba City, Ca, US	92/B3
Yūbari, Japan	55/N3
Yucatan (pen.), Mex.	101/H5
Yucatan Channel (chan.), NAm.	102/E1
Yuci, China	59/C3
Yueyang, China	61/G2
Yugoslavia (ctry.)	40/E3
Yūki, Japan	57/F2
Yukon (riv.), Can.,US	85/G3
Yukon Territory (terr.), Can.	86/D2
Yüksekova, Turk.	51/F2
Yukuhashi, Japan	56/B4
Yulin, China	65/E2
Yulin, China	65/E1
Yumbo, Col.	106/C3
Yumen, China	54/D4
Yurga, Rus.	46/J4
Yurimaguas, Peru	106/C5
Yur'yevets, Rus.	42/J4
Yuscarán, Hon.	102/E3
Yuzhno-Sakhalinsk, Rus.	55/N2
Yverdon, Swi.	36/C4

Zaandam, Neth.	26/C2
Zaanstad, Neth.	28/B4
Ząbki, Pol.	27/L2
Ząbkowice Śląskie, Pol.	27/J3
Zābreh, Czh.	33/M2
Zabrze, Pol.	27/K3
Zacapa, Guat.	102/D3
Zacapu, Mex.	101/E5
Zacatecas, Mex.	100/E4
Zacatecoluca, ESal.	102/D3
Zacatelco, Mex.	101/L8
Zacatepec, Mex.	101/K8
Zacatlán, Mex.	101/M7
Zachary, La, US	93/K5
Zadar, Cro.	40/B3
Zafra, Sp.	34/B3
Żagań, Pol.	27/H3
Zaghwān, Tun.	38/B4
Zagreb (cap.), Cro.	40/B3
Zāhedān, Iran	53/H3
Zahirābād, India	62/C4
Zahlah, Leb.	49/D3
Zākhū, Iraq	51/E2
Zakopane, Pol.	27/K4
Zalaegerszeg, Hun.	40/C2
Zalău, Rom.	27/M5
Zambia (ctry.)	82/E3
Zamboanga, Phil.	67/F2
Zambrów, Pol.	27/M2
Zamora, Ecu.	106/C4
Zamora, Sp.	34/C2
Zamora de Hidalgo, Mex.	100/E5
Zamość, Pol.	27/M3
Zandvoort, Neth.	28/B4
Zanjān, Iran	51/G2
Zanzibar, Tanz.	82/G2
Zaoyang, China	61/G1
Zaozhuang, China	59/D4
Zapala, Arg.	109/B4
Zapolyarnyy, Rus.	42/F1
Zapopan, Mex.	100/E4
Zaporizhzhya, Ukr.	44/E3
Zara, Turk.	44/F5
Zaragoza (Saragossa), Sp.	35/E2
Zárate, Arg.	109/E3
Zarauz, Sp.	34/D1
Zaraza, Ven.	106/E2
Zaria, Nga.	79/G4
Zărnești, Rom.	41/G3
Żary, Pol.	27/H3
Žatec, Czh.	33/K1
Zaventem, Belg.	31/D2
Zavitinsk, Rus.	55/K1
Zawiercie, Pol.	27/K3
Žd'ár nad Sázavou, Czh.	33/L2
Zduńska Wola, Pol.	27/K3
Zedelgem, Belg.	30/C1
Zefat, Isr.	49/D3
Zeist, Neth.	28/C4
Zeitz, Ger.	26/G3
Zele, Belg.	28/B6
Zelenodol'sk, Rus.	43/L5
Zelenogorsk, Rus.	43/S6
Zelenograd, Rus.	43/W8
Zelenokumsk, Rus.	45/G3
Zemst, Belg.	28/B7
Zenica, Bosn.	40/D3
Zentsūji, Japan	56/C3

Zepče, Bosn.	40/D3
Zernograd, Rus.	44/G3
Zevenaar, Neth.	28/D5
Zevenbergen, Neth.	28/B5
Zeya, Rus.	55/K1
Zghartā, Leb.	49/D2
Zgierz, Pol.	27/K3
Zgorzelec, Pol.	27/H3
Zhambyl, Kaz.	46/H5
Zhanatas, Kaz.	46/G5
Zhangaözen, Kaz.	45/K4
Zhangaqazaly, Kaz.	46/G5
Zhangjiakou, China	59/C3
Zhangshu, China	54/E4
Zhangye, China	54/E4
Zhangzhou, China	61/G4
Zhanjiang, China	55/K2
Zhaodong, China	55/K2
Zhaoqing, China	61/G4
Zhaotong, China	60/D3
Zhayyq (Ural) (riv.), Kaz.	46/F3
Zheleznodorozhnyy, Rus.	43/L3
Zheleznogorsk, Rus.	44/F1
Zheleznogorsk-Ilimskiy, Rus.	47/L4
Zhengzhou, China	59/C4
Zhenjiang, China	61/H1
Zhetiqara, Kaz.	45/M1
Zhezqazghan, Kaz.	46/G5
Zhicheng, China	61/F2
Zhigulevsk, Rus.	45/J1
Zhlobin, Bela.	44/D1
Zhmerynka, Ukr.	44/D2
Zhob, Pak.	53/J2
Zhodino, Bela.	42/F5
Zhongshan, China	61/G4
Zhoukou, China	59/C4
Zhouzhou, China	59/C4
Zhovtneve, Ukr.	41/L2
Zhucheng, China	59/D4
Zhuhai, China	61/G4
Zhukovka, Rus.	44/E1
Zhukovskiy, Rus.	43/X9
Zhumadian, China	59/C4
Zhuzhou, China	61/G3
Zhytomyr, Ukr.	44/D2
Zibo, China	59/D3
Zielona Góra, Pol.	27/H3
Ziftá, Egypt	49/B4
Zigong, China	60/E2
Ziguinchor, Sen.	78/A3
Zihuatanejo, Mex.	101/E5
Zile, Turk.	44/E4
Žilina, Slvk.	27/K4
Zima, Rus.	54/E1
Zimbabwe (ctry.)	82/E4
Zimnicea, Rom.	41/G4
Zinder, Niger	79/H3
Zion, Il, US	99/Q15
Zion National Park, Ut, US	92/D3
Zitácuaro, Mex.	101/E5
Zittau, Ger.	27/H3
Zixing, China	61/G3
Ziyyon, Isr.	49/G8
Zlatoust, Rus.	43/N5
Zlín, Czh.	27/J4
Złotoryja, Pol.	27/H3
Złotów, Pol.	27/J2
Znam'yanka, Ukr.	44/D2
Znojmo, Czh.	33/M2
Zoersel, Belg.	28/B6
Zoetermeer, Neth.	28/B4
Zográfos, Gre.	39/N9
Zolotonosha, Ukr.	44/E2
Zomba, Malw.	82/G4
Zonguldak, Turk.	41/K5
Zonhoven, Belg.	28/C7
Zottegem, Belg.	30/C2
Zouérat, Mrta.	76/C3
Zrenjanin, Yugo.	37/E3
Zug, Swi.	37/E3
Zugdidi, Geo.	45/G4
Zuidhorn, Neth.	28/D2
Zülpich, Ger.	31/F2
Zumpango de Ocampo, Mex.	101/K7
Zumpango del Río, Mex.	102/B2
Zunyi, China	61/E3
Zürich, Swi.	37/E3
Zutphen, Neth.	28/D4
Zuwārah, Libya	76/H1
Zuyevka, Rus.	43/L4
Zvishavane, Zim.	82/F6
Zvolen, Slvk.	27/K4
Zvornik, Bosn.	40/D3
Zweibrücken, Ger.	31/G5
Zwevelgem, Belg.	30/C2
Zwickau, Ger.	33/K1
Zwijndrecht, Neth.	28/B5
Zwijndrecht, Belg.	31/D1
Zwolle, Neth.	28/D3
Żyrardów, Pol.	27/K2
Zyryan, Kaz.	54/A2
Żywiec, Pol.	27/K4